The LightWave 3D Book

Tips, Techniques and Ready-to-Use Objects

From the Pages of LightWave Pro Magazine

SAN FRANCISCO

Acknowledgments

We would like to thank the following people and organizations:

Michael Meshew/Graphic Detail, Inc. (1-800-265-4041) for putting the CD-ROM together.

NewTek, Inc. for allowing the use of images and objects on the CD that were also included in the LightWave CD-ROM package.

The writers and staff of LIGHTWAVEPRO, The Journal for LightWave 3D Animators.

Special thanks to Tim Jenison, Allen Hastings, Stuart Ferguson, Arnie Cachelin, Fori Oruwora, Brad Peebler, Jason Linhart, Brian Thomas and the rest of the folks that help make LightWave 3D one of the coolest programs available.

Project staff for the first edition: John Gross, *Editor*; Tom Patrick, *Executive Editor*; Tarita Whittingham, *Production Director*; Rosemary Picado, *Copy Editor*; Michael Meshew, *CD-ROM Production*; Leah Yujuico, *Production Assistant*.

Cover illustration by Bryan J. Blevins
LightWave 3D logo on cover courtesy of NewTek, Inc.

ISBN: 0-87930-455-3

Published by Miller Freeman Books
600 Harrison St.
San Francisco, CA 94107
E-mail: mfbooks@mfi.com
Web: www.books.mfi.com

Printed in the USA
97 98 99 00 5 4 3 2 1

CONTENTS

Lighting the Scene—Cinematography, Lens Flares, and Space

Refining the Surface—Surfacing and Textures

Animating & More—MetaNURBS, Bones, Morphing, and Refraction

Using the Program—Algorithms, Platforms, and Networks

Handy Tips

Foreword to the First Edition

In my office at home I have a shelf system that has a slanted magazine rack built in. On that rack sit 28 issues of LIGHTWAVEPRO—every issue from October 1993 on. I'm probably one of the few people that has a copy of every issue. As a matter of fact, I have a couple of copies of every issue (and no, I won't sell them). When I look back at all of these magazines, I'm amazed at how fast the time has passed. The first issue of LIGHTWAVEPRO (October 1993) was released at just about the same time that LightWave 3.0 was released. Bones and Displacement maps were some of the new exciting features at the time, but now they have become a common tool in every LightWave animator's tool kit.

About eleven issues later (August 1994), LightWave 3.5 was released. Once again, there were some great new features added, plus you could get it unbundled from the Video Toaster. I just re-read my August 1994 Editor's Message and had to laugh out loud when I read the part about the "next great version" of LightWave (4.0) slated to be shipping by the end of the year—1994, that is. OK, it was a bit later than that (about a year), but it did finally ship and right now, LightWave 4.0 is used for high-quality animations in a number of different industries. But LightWave's not stopping there. I've been lucky enough to be "in" on upcoming LightWave versions and I'm pretty excited about what's coming down the line for LightWave 3D and Modeler. I think you will be too!

So, what do you have here in your hands? This book and CD compiles 100 of the best articles from the very first issue on. The tutorials and articles here can apply to pretty much all versions of LightWave (I assume you're not still using 1.0) and will remain a valuable reference tool for future versions as well. Even though the time has gone extremely fast since LIGHTWAVEPRO was first launched, I realize that what I said in my very first editor's message back in October 1993 still applies to me today: I'm a LightWave junkie! I was then and I am now, and I have a feeling I will be for quite a long time. One of the unique qualities of the LightWave community is in the sharing of LightWave tips and tricks that takes place among its members. I'm often amazed at how much of this goes on in different forms: tapes, magazines, Internet newsgroups and mailing lists and of course, LIGHTWAVEPRO. This tradition has grown up with LightWave. For as long as I can, I intend to make sure that the tradition continues.—*John Gross, Editor*

A Note About the Second Edition

Since the first edition of this book was published, LightWave has been revised and is available on more platforms. The book also has been revised to include articles using newer versions of LightWave, including version 5.5. You'll read tutorials and features published in *LightWave Pro* magazine through its final issue at the end of 1996, as well as a review of version of 5.0 of LightWave on the PC platform from *Interactivity* and another review of LightWave for Power Macintosh from *3D Design*. To make topics easier to find than in the first edition, the contents are organized by subject, rather than by date of publication, and there's a handy index. As in the first edition, the articles are reprinted just as they appeared in the original pages of *LightWave Pro*.

LightWave 3D in Review

by Mark Giambruno

LightWave originally began as the modeling program for the famous Video Toaster product, an add-on for the Amiga designed to do production-quality videographics and editing. Eventually, LightWave was ported to other systems including SGI, several flavors of NT, and Windows 95.

LightWave's capabilities are among the best known to the general populace due to its use on the television shows Babylon 5, SeaQuest, and others. This speaks well for LightWave's image quality and suitability as a production tool. It's also popular with interactive media designers doing high-res 3D environments.

User Interface

Good news and bad news regarding the interface. It appears to be nearly a straight port, so if you're moving from the Amiga to Windows NT, LightWave will probably feel like an old friend. That's the good news. The bad news for everyone else is that the interface is depressingly gray and un-Windows-like, popping up large, view-obscuring panels crammed with text and buttons.

LightWave consists of two separate applications, although they can be run at the same time. Layout is the name of the scene composition, animation, and rendering module, but it's often referred to as LightWave. The Modeler is the second app and now features a pipeline to Layout for transferring mesh back and forth. (In previous versions, the two apps weren't connected, forcing you to work in one or the other.)

Both applications support OpenGL, which allows you to view models and scenes in realtime shaded mode. Hardware acceleration is recommended. Despite the preview capability that OpenGL provides, the workflow still isn't comparable to having modeling and rendering functions in a single integrated package, because you have to save your models to the hard drive and then import them into Layout. The product has no online help and no undo in Layout.

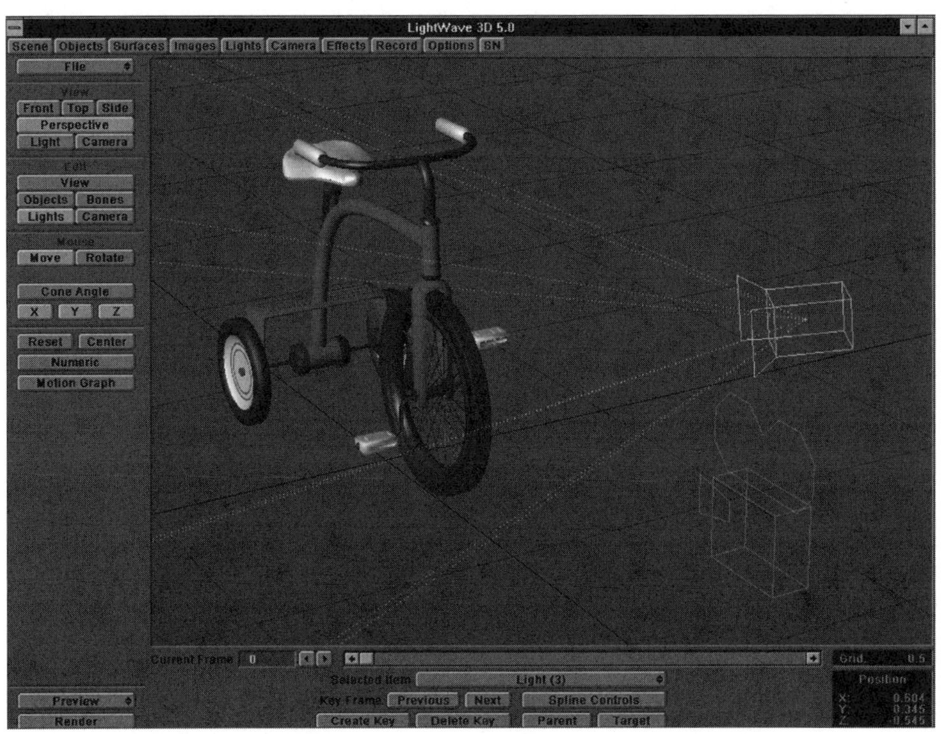

LightWave consists of two separate application programs. Layout (shown here) is where a scene is put together with objects from the Modeler and where lighting, animation, and rendering are performed.

On the plus side, Layout's viewport is larger than most and frequently used controls are only one or two clicks away. When using numeric entry, hitting Enter automatically advances you to the next parameter.

LightWave's Modeler application is feature-laden and sports some unusual mesh resolution enhancement and smoothing capabilities. Oddly, any view adjustments you make (pan, zoom, and so on) affect all four of the windows in Modeler, which increases refresh times and messes up views you might need. Unlike Layout, this application features a user-configurable 15-level undo.

Docs & Tutorials

The system comes with two healthy square-bound manuals. The Reference Manual is a screen-by-screen and button-by-button guide to every item in the user interface, explaining what does what and how to

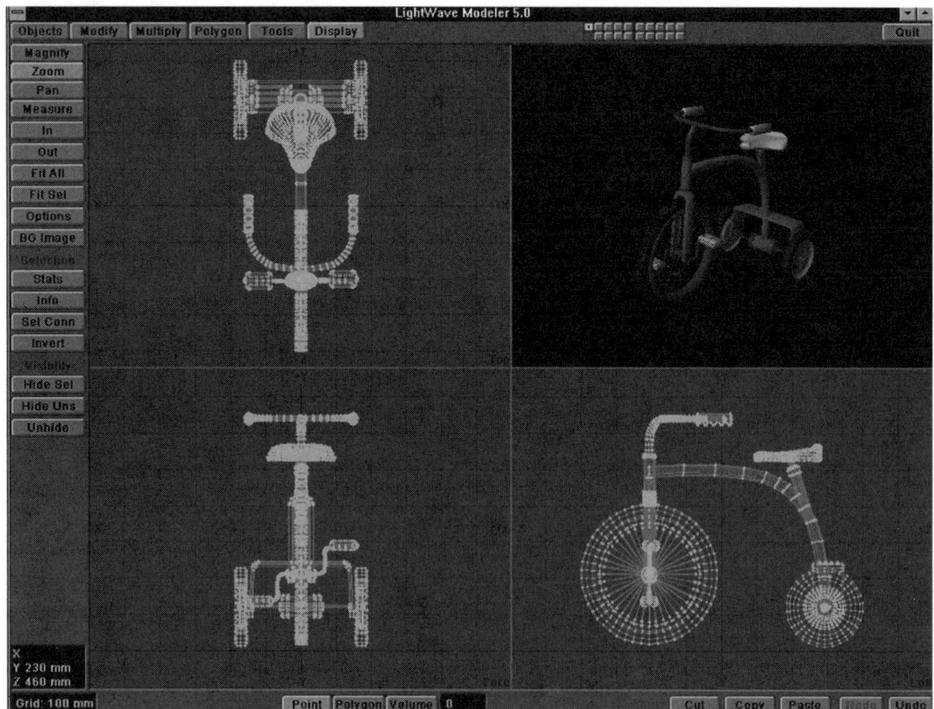

LightWave's Modeler features a very impressive tool called Metaform that allows the user to turn jagged, low-res mesh into smoothly blended objects.

use each function. The second manual is the User Guide, which is about two-thirds task-oriented information and one-third tutorials. The manual offers a lot of tips as well as procedure information to help develop strategies for both modeling and animation.

Both manuals have an index, and they're dramatically improved over earlier documentation. Unfortunately, the User Guide is poorly organized. For example, if you look up fog under the "F" section, it isn't there. You have to look under "C," then "creating," then "a fog effect." I've never seen an index that alphabetized using the words "a" and "the" before.

The tutorials are pretty good and hit the major points, including animation, modeling (basic and advanced), lighting, and mapping, but there were some errors that could be frustrating to new users.

Modeling

LightWave has unique and powerful modeling features, including Vertice Magnet (to pull points like a patch modeler), Vortex (acts something like Photoshop's Twirl filter on a 3D object), Pole (inflates and deflates objects), and the usual complement of deform tools.

Models can be shown or hidden among 10 layers, any of which can be moved into the foreground for editing or background for reference. While this scheme keeps the workspace uncluttered, it isn't as flexible or easy to use as some other programs' layering schemes or hide-and-freeze options that use multiple selection criteria.

The program features both 2D/3D trims and 3D Boolean operations, and the Smooth Shift feature allows you to extrude faces — great for constructing smoothly attached fins or wings to an existing shape, or to turn a flat edge into a smoothly rounded one.

One of LightWave's most impressive features is the ability to subdivide a polygonal object in three ways: faceted, smooth, or Metaform. Metaform takes great advantage of this ability and lets you create rather clunky looking low-res objects (or groups of objects joined together). You can pump up the resolution to smooth out the jagginess and blend the forms together.

MetaNURBS is a new feature that allows you to convert four-sided polygons into NURBS splines. Splines can be modified with the main tools, but you must freeze and reconvert the object into polygons before importing it into Layout.

In addition, LightWave has unusual and welcome utilities for locating and correcting non-planar polygons, which often show up as missing faces at render time. You can also hide portions of an object to make vertice-level editing easier.

Mapping & Materials

In keeping with LightWave's modular, separate modeler orientation, the processes of assigning and modifying materials are split between the two applications. Polygon surfaces are assigned materials in the Modeler, but modifications of a material are made in Layout. Even more awkward, while maps and attributes are applied in Layout, they must be saved with the Object file instead of the Scene file. Fortunately, there's a Save All Objects command in Layout in case you forget which of the ones you've altered. For mapping, LightWave has the standard complement of coordinate systems (planar, cylindrical, and spherical) plus cubic mapping.

LightWave features a lot of material options and interesting procedural textures. For example, in addition to the usual wood and marble shaders, LightWave has noise, underwater, crust, veins, crumple, and more. These can be used in a variety of ways to produce surface textures from crumpled steel to cauliflower.

Another unique feature is clip mapping, which works like a high-contrast opacity map to make sections of an object transparent, but allows shadow-mapped lights to "see" only the visible portions. Usually, a shadow-mapped light ignores opacity information, casting a shadow as if the object were completely opaque.

Texture Velocity allows a texture to animate on its own without setting keyframes, while Texture Falloff fades the map out at a given distance from the center, letting the underlying material show through. Other options include Sharp Terminator for planetoid lighting effects, glows, and adjustable edge transparency.

Lighting

LightWave has a standard light suite (point, spot, distant), all of which are shadow-casting and have easy-to-orient objects representing them in a scene. You can also choose a Light View that lets you see the scene from the perspective of a selected light.

Of course, no discussion of LightWave's illumination options would be complete without mentioning lens flares, which were pioneered in this product. Unlike some other programs, lens flares are easy to create in LightWave, can be produced by any light in a scene, and feature options like fringes, halos, and anamorphic streaks.

Cameras & Animation

The camera options in LightWave are among the most complete to be found in any 3D package. In addition to FOV (field of view) and focal length settings, the program has a video safe frame that shows what portions of an animation will be lost if played back on a television. You also have an option to set the film type, which adjusts settings to allow easier perspective matching to live footage.

You'll probably want to change the default setting for animation, which doesn't save changes unless you specifically generate a keyframe, even if you move an object on a given frame number. Imagine spending 10 minutes positioning objects only to have them snap back to their starting places when you preview — with no undo.

LightWave lacks a hierarchical timeline interface. You have to deal with the keyframe position of one object at a time, which makes it harder to interrelate their various motions. While the program does provide editable spline paths, they're limited to TCB control and aren't as easy to manipulate as a graphical Bezier control.

Particularly powerful is LightWave's ability to add bones to an object, allowing you to deform the surface mesh easily by manipulating the bone it is attached to. This is an excellent way to produce such effects as muscles flexing or a chest breathing without resorting to pulling points and making morph targets. New to version 5.0 is the Metamation feature, which allows you to animate low-res versions of objects and then have Metaform-type mesh resolution enhancement performed frame by frame at render time.

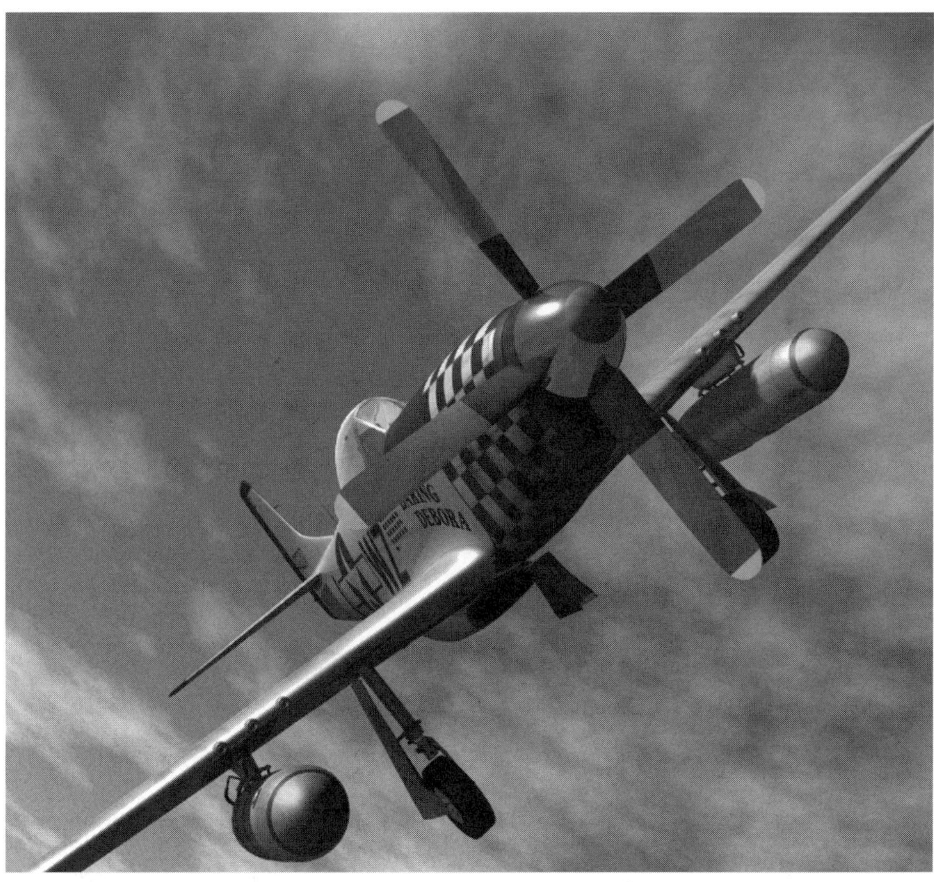

LightWave's standout features include fine shader libraries, excellent raytrace rendering, and video post effects. It supports distributed rendering across multiple platforms (with a few caveats).

Other features include the animation of light and camera parameters, morphs, fog, and object dissolves with keyframed envelopes that contain the varied settings. Dissolves make an object disappear over time or distance, so you can make it seem to fade into a foggy or underwater environment on cue (which can be difficult if you're only relying on atmospheric settings).

Rendering

The speed and quality of LightWave's renderer is well regarded throughout the industry and really does produce gorgeous results. Beyond that, there are options for depth of field (so that close-up or distant objects will be realistically out of focus) as well as several flavors of motion blur.

LightWave's high-end post-production capabilities allow compositing and effects to be done as part of the rendering process. The program supports image processing plug-ins, but unlike many other products, they have to be written specifically for LightWave.

LightWave always renders from the Camera viewport, regardless of the current viewport settings. While this is convenient for most situations, sometimes you may want an orthogonal render for custom mapping purposes. Fortunately, the Preview function allows you to render a quick wireframe version of the animation from any view.

LightWave allows up to 1,000 CPUs to be part of a ScreamerNet distributed rendering process, although mixed-platform rendering may be a problem due to differences in shaders or plug-ins.

Conclusions

LightWave is hindered by its outdated user interface design and reliance on separate Modeling and Layout modules. Experienced users who are accustomed to an integrated modeling/rendering environment will probably find the product frustrating in that respect. The animation capabilities are impeded by the

NEWTEK LIGHTWAVE 5.0

Pros

Powerful and unique modeling tools, high-quality shaders, and excellent rendering in a moderately priced package.

Cons

Clunky, dated interface, no undo function in Layout, animation controls lack a hierarchical timeline.

The Bottom Line

If you can live with the interface and its restrictions, LightWave Pro can turn out top-quality work suitable for any application.

absence of a full-featured proper timeline.

On the plus side, powerful modeling features, impressive shaders, and drop-dead beautiful renders are your reward for putting up with the unusual work-flow scheme. And don't forget all those lens flare options.

Overall, LightWave packs some very impressive features into a well-under $15,000 production-quality package. Users with a need to create broadcast or high-end multimedia environments and character animation — and who don't mind the idiosyncrasies — should seriously consider it.

Mark Giambruno recently formed CyberDog Studios with long-time coworkers and former Mechadeus employees Laura Hainke and Drew Vinciguerra. They plan to focus on the development of high-quality online gaming products.

NEWTEK LIGHTWAVE 5.0

Description

Production-quality polygonal modeling and animation system.

System Requirements

486 or faster PC (Pentium recommended). Windows 95 or Windows NT. 16MB RAM (Win95), 32MB RAM (WinNT). 10MB on hard disk. 24-bit color. CD-ROM drive.

Key Features

Crossplatform package available for Win95, WinNT, SGI, DEC Alpha, MIPS, Amiga. (PPC version has been announced.) Modeling Types: polygon, spline, MetaNURBS. Deforms: shear, twist, taper, bend, vertice magnet, vortex, pole. 2D/3D trims and Booleans. Metaform MetaBalls and MetaFormPlus allows low-res mesh to be increased in resolution and smoothed. Model pipeline between Modeler and Layout modules. Shader Channels: color, luminosity, diffuse, specular, glossiness, reflectivity, transparency. Expanded range of procedural textures, which can be auto-animated. Lights: point, spot, distant, all shadow-casting. Advanced lens flare options. Editable motion graphs and paths. Advanced camera controls and options. Bones deformation. IK with constraints. Nearly all attributes can be animated by keyframe or envelope. Rendering: wire-frame, quickshade (flat), raytrace. Alpha Channel support. Media: CD-ROM.

File Support

3D Import/Export: DXF. 2D Import: IFF, TGA, PCT. 2D Export: IFF, RAW, TGA, ALS, BMP, CIN, JPG, PIC, PXR, QRT, 6RN, RGB, SUN, TIF, VTI, ILA, XWD, YUD.

Suggested Retail Price

$1,495 (upgrades: $295 Amiga, $495 Win95 and WinNT).

Contact

NewTek, 1200 SW Executive Dr., Topeka, KS 66615; vox 800.862.7737, 913.228.8000; fax 913.228.8001; Web http://www. newtek.com.

A Preview of LightWave 3D 5.5

Here is a preview of LightWave 3D version 5.5; this information is provided by NewTek, Inc.

Explosive ideas that test the boundaries of 3D animation deserve a program that can realize them in exciting new ways. Creating worlds that no one's ever seen. Creatures that have never walked the Earth. Special effects, games, web sites—all creations that exist only in your mind. Until now.

LightWave 3D gives you an easy way to create the most sophisticated 3D animation imaginable, with formidable capabilities from an incredibly powerful, professional animation system. Its intuitive, complete, easy-to-use layout and modeling system delivers the ultimate in creative control, not to mention flexibility—the likes of which you've never seen. And unparalleled features for modeling, surfacing, lighting and animating are right at your fingertips.

LightWave 3D's depth of features hits the big time and prime time…in no time.

For the past six years, the NewTek team has collaborated with some of Hollywood's hottest creative talents to develop an advanced 3D animation system. LightWave 3D packs a wallop of a punch.

Raytracing, motion blur, MetaMation, inverse kinematics (IK), Bones, field rendering, lens flares, compositing—they're all here. LightWave 3D's OpenGL and Quickdraw 3D support mean you can see your creations in real time.

What's more, working with Hollywood studios, like Will Vinton and Digital Domain, NewTek improved LightWave 3D's anti-aliasing quality by 300 percent over earlier versions. NewTek also improved the accuracy of IK, and increased speed by 500 percent. Its robust plug-in architecture means you can choose feature options that match the way you work. And its exceptional image quality and throughput make LightWave 3D an ideal choice for special effects in television, film, commercial work, web page development, graphic arts, video games and education.

With all of this, plus an excellent return on investment, it's no wonder you can find LightWave 3D in more Hollywood animation suites than any other 3D program.

You can get all of LightWave 3D's great features and exceptional performance for an affordable price. LightWave 3D costs up to 75 percent less than comparable programs.

Breaking boundaries

It's no use having a great program if you can't run it. So LightWave 3D is available for all of the most popular platforms: Windows 95, Windows NT, Power Macintosh, DEC Alpha, Silicon Graphics Inc. and Sun Microsystems.

Support you can always draw on

It would be hard to rival the kind of support LightWave 3D offers. *3D Design* magazine said, "The endless number of tutorials available on the web, video training tapes, seminars, courses, and other training materials are absolutely amazing."

Throw in over 40,000 loyal artists who share what they know, and you can see why designers can't wait to get their hands on LightWave 3D. After all, by giving many 3D designers their start, and moving them from the garage to their own special effects companies, LightWave 3D has changed people's lives.

LightWave 3D 5.5

Naturally, LightWave 3D 5.5 includes all the great features found in earlier versions. But we've added a powerful list of new features and functions that make LightWave 3D even more attractive—and fun.

LightWave 3D 5.5's user interface maintains all the intuitive features and ease-of-use we've always had, but packages that with standard features of other computing interfaces you already know. What's more, you'll see higher resolution, greater color depth, coded button coloring for fast identification and even more creative options in how you approach your work.

Non-modal panels

Who says you can't do two things at once? With LightWave 3D 5.5, you can keep your panels (aka dialog boxes) open, move them to new screen positions, change values on a panel and view the result all without closing the box. Think of it as productive interactivity.

New OpenGL

With our new OpenGL, real-time texture viewing and user-selectable background color are a reality. Not only can you place textures interactively, you'll also get an even better view of your model or scene. In addition, the new RenderGL support takes added advantage of OpenGL hardware to accelerate the rendering process.

Multi-threaded rendering

Our multi-threaded rendering means that users on multiprocessor systems can leverage the additional power that comes from their system's extra CPUs. Since multiprocessor machines are also the wave of the future, LightWave 3D is staying at the leading edge of the technology you'll be using tomorrow.

Morph Gizmo

This great new feature is a quantum leap for character animation in general, and lip-sync in particular. With Morph Gizmo, you can visually morph an object between several targets—for example, a series of facial expressions or phonemes. Dialogue and facial expressions are meshed by dragging sliders (an expression or mouth position, for instance) into place and watching the combination occur in real time. It's extremely effective and efficient and so advanced, it's hard to believe it's so easy to use.

Direct 3D support

With Direct 3D support, Intel system users can now choose their API, use low-cost Direct 3D accelerator cards and use either OpenGL or Direct 3D to create real-time shaded environments. The choice is yours.

And that's not all...

As if all those features weren't enough, LightWave 3D has other new tools that make it more powerful, more versatile, and more fun than ever. A new volumetric lighting engine lets you create ultra-realistic lighting effects. Hyper-Animation Language lets you create your own scripts for controlling virtually every LightWave 3D feature. And if you want to attach an audio file for timing purposes, the new audio scrubbing feature is just the ticket.

There are also two new modeling tools—Dragnet and Smooth Scale—designed to help you work with organic models. Both are especially great for MetaNURBS objects. Try the new extender plug-in and see how easily it gives you added control over the objects you create with MetaNURBS.

Want more? You got it. We've added a motion capture data conversion plug-in for compatibility with Acclaim and Wavefront formats. If you do character animation, you'll quickly appreciate the bone hierarchy creation you get from Skeleton Maker. You'll also appreciate the new color wheel option for great color control. On top of all that, the enhanced plug-in architecture and a host of other new features mean there's almost no end to what you can create in LightWave 3D.

Check out some of the projects where you can see LightWave 3D in action:

- Babylon 5
- Blue M&Ms
- Blossom
- Courage Under Fire
- Dark Skies
- Deadly Tide
- GoldenEye (James Bond)
- Hercules: The Legendary Journeys
- Nixon
- Sliders
- Star Trek Voyager, Deep Space Nine and Next Generation
- The Titanic (television series)
- Xena: Warrior Princess
- The X-Files
- Unsolved Mysteries

High-speed meta modeling... for mind-boggling creations

LightWave 3D's unique MetaNURBS is an elegant and easy way to model objects by transforming polygonal models to NURBS surfaces in real time. MetaNURBS delivers incredible detail and flexibility, so you can smooth organic objects even though the model is actually based on polygonal geometry. (Too bad competitors still find MetaNURBS' secret as difficult to solve as an X-Files mystery.) And with LightWave 3D, you can switch seamlessly between polygonal modeling and the organic power of NURBS for the best of both worlds. Pretty cool stuff.

Interactive 3D workspace... when there's no time to lose

Who wants to wait to see what they've created? Not you. Which is why LightWave 3D supports OpenGL and QuickDraw 3D. Now you can see objects, surfaces, composition and lighting in real time. It's what you've been waiting for.

Inverse Kinematics... no missing links here

IK accounts for all those linkages between say, a finger and the shoulder of the arm it's attached to. Move an M&M around the table and LightWave 3D's IK automatically adjusts for the movement of all the linkages in-between without endless tinkering to create a realistic motion. It's fast. Efficient. Simple.

Raytracing...right on the beam

No 3D program is complete without raytracing and LightWave 3D's is hard to beat. Thanks to its realistic reflection and refraction, great shadowing capabilities and more, LightWave 3D is professionally recognized as one of the highest quality rendering engines in the business.

When it comes to Bones, we flex our muscles

LightWave 3D uses Bones to control any object's behavior, giving it natural-looking "life" and realism. Bones also relates beautifully to LightWave 3D's IK capabilities for believable, true-to-life animation. Turn on muscle flexing and joint compensation for ultra-realistic behavior.

Lens effects and flares with flair

With LightWave 3D, you get an almost inexhaustible list of lens and illumination effects, including point, spot, shadowing and lens flares, a technique we perfected. If you want depth-of-field, motion blur, field rendering and more, LightWave 3D is your program.

Plug-in architecture... building on your 3D foundation

With its extremely robust plug-in architecture, LightWave 3D is a magnet for third-party developer special effects programs and tools. So if you're looking for add-on features like collision detection, 3D painting, particle systems, image filters or just about anything else, you can choose from an impressive list of available plug-ins to create exactly what you need.

Laying it on thick

Another great LightWave 3D feature is infinite layered surfaces, which provides algorithmic textures plus image mapping. The result is a versatile tool for stacking image upon image as deep (or high) as you like. Create clothes with wrinkles, creases and ripples or make waves with layers and crests. You can also set variable levels of transparency. It's as real as it gets.

With our Boolean tool, things take shape fast

The Boolean principle is simple. Add. Subtract. Intersect. We use it to let you take simple primitives, like spheres or cubes, and create complex shapes quickly and effortlessly.

Spline modeling... a versatile tool of the trade

Our spline modeling tool lets you create any shape you can dream up in incredible detail and endlessly modify your creations. So there's nothing you can't create.

A new standard... a cel shader that's built right in

Say you have a 3D creation and now you'd like it to look like a hand-drawn 2D object. Or maybe you want to merge conventional 2D with 3D animation. No problem. The cel shader calculates shading and operates much faster than hand drawing because the computer draws the interim frames. Unlike other programs, LightWave 3D's cel shader comes standard with the package. And not only is the cel shader worth the cost of the package all by itself ... we expect it to revolutionize the industry.

If you design in 3D, LightWave 3D is for you

There isn't a 3D designer on the planet who can't use LightWave 3D. With its high-end rendering and modeling capabilities, plus power and quality to satisfy the most accomplished, demanding expert, it's easy enough for even beginning 3D designers to get astonishing, professional results.

LightWave 3D's interface thinks like you

Learning to use LightWave 3D is fast and easy. In fact, in about 20 minutes, you can become familiar enough with its intuitive interface and main features to be creative—and productive—right away.

The reason is simple. LightWave 3D's enhanced interface is designed to work the way animators think and work, with the same logic and the same ability to adapt to new ideas. And, LightWave 3D's interface is exactly the same across all platforms. So if you use LightWave 3D on more than one system—say, on a laptop at home or on the road and on a powerful workstation at the office—you don't have to change a single thing about the way you work.

One great program for every kind of animation

Unlike many animation programs, LightWave 3D is at home in any venue. Its front projection mapping allows you to seamlessly integrate 3D objects with 2D images for effects like photorealistic reflection, shadowing and refraction. For broadcast television, film and video design, LightWave 3D works seamlessly with animation and special effects. And for games, its ability to create efficient polygonal models quickly, smooth them out and move them around fast is hard to beat.

In the hot world of the Internet, LightWave 3D supports the VRML 2 standard, making it a rock-solid choice for sizzling web sites. VRML supports everything from texture and sound to hierarchical animation and morphing ... all directly from layout. To keep you ahead of the curve in this fast-changing world, we even provide the lastest VRML version with a free download from our web site.

In the graphic arts, where high-res output is in great demand, LightWave 3D delivers with up to 8000 lines of resolution. For visualization, such as weather mapping or 3D data displays, LightWave 3D allows you to chart any information with ease. And when it comes to education, LightWave 3D can make the most complex concepts simple and exciting.

For your earth-shattering ideas, get with the program

With all its power, sophistication and capabilities, LightWave 3D allows you to create anything you can dream up. And just like your creations, you've never seen anything like it. There's simply no other program that gives you so much professional performance, quality and flexibility for such an affordable price.

"LightWave 3D is a true filmmaker's tool. Anyone who knows filmmaking will feel comfortable with LightWave. It has a logical interface, and the output definitely has that film look."

Ron Thornton, Founder of Foundation Imaging,
Emmy Award-winning visual effects supervisor for *Babylon 5*

"LightWave 3D's interface is very easy to navigate around. With most 3D packages, you reach a peak in creativity due to their lack of effects and rendering quality limitations. With LightWave 3D, I don't think there's anything I can't create."

Michael Sherak,
Lead artist at Interplay Productions, Inc.

"LightWave 3D is the only software that we can depend on for 3D creatures. With its easy-to-use interface, it allows us to stay on budget, on schedule and make the creatures move and look great."

Everett Burrell, 3D supervisor,
Flat Earth Productions, Inc.,
Emmy Award-winning creature effects supervisor for *Babylon 5*

"LightWave will never leave my desktop. After dozens of national and international spots—with modeling and animation tools to meet the needs of the most demanding animator, extensive plug-in support to roll-your-own tools, and a phenomenal renderer that seamlessly integrates our 3D friends with live-action—LightWave 3D has proven to be the software we count on to produce characters of distinction."

Stephen Bailey,
Senior Animator/Technical Director, Will Vinton Studios.

LightWave 101

Course 1B: Basic Modeling Strategies

by Taylor Kurosaki

This installment of LightWave 101 will focus on modeling techniques which allow you to create seemingly complex objects simply and easily. Just because you don't have a tremendous amount of modeling experience, or aren't nicknamed "spline master" doesn't mean you can't model high-tech, cool-looking objects in LightWave.

The most important thing to have is the ability to visually break down any given object into its most basic components, and then have enough knowledge of Modeler to construct these basic shapes. Pieces which do not resemble any of Modeler's primitives can usually be created simply with any number of Modeler's tools. Finally, these basic pieces are assembled like "Legos" to create your final shape.

Note: To successfully complete your object it is essential to view your work in progress. I strongly suggest that you Export your object from Modeler into Layout and render tests from various angles. Subsequently your object(s) should then be saved from Layout, and as part of a default scene for your model. To make modifications, Import the object back into Modeler and edit the imported version. This method ensures that you are always working on the most recent version of the object. It also keeps surface values intact in Layout.

Sputnik: The Easy Way

A satellite is the perfect example of a model which can look fairly impressive without a great deal of frustration. For the purpose of this tutorial I will use the example of the satellite pictured in this issue and included on the *LWPRO* disk. The following examples are merely starting points to get you thinking in the right direction with regard to objects that you design. You might want to experiment by modeling a similar satellite-based on some of the principles mentioned within, and later apply these methods to other objects.

Two pieces of advice: 1) Never be afraid to experiment—there is no universally correct way to build LightWave objects. 2) Modeler is a production tool, not a conceptual tool. Paper and pencil are a much better way to figure out what it is you want to build. Sketch before turning on your computer.

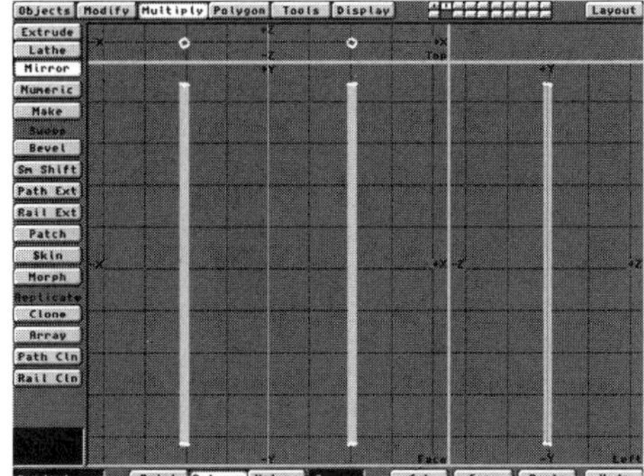
Figure 1

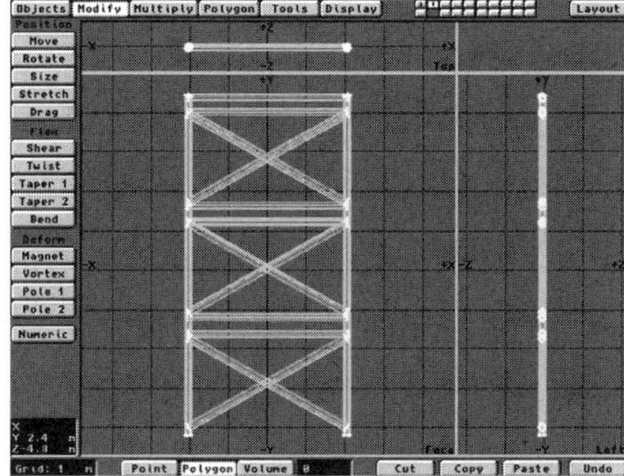
Figure 2

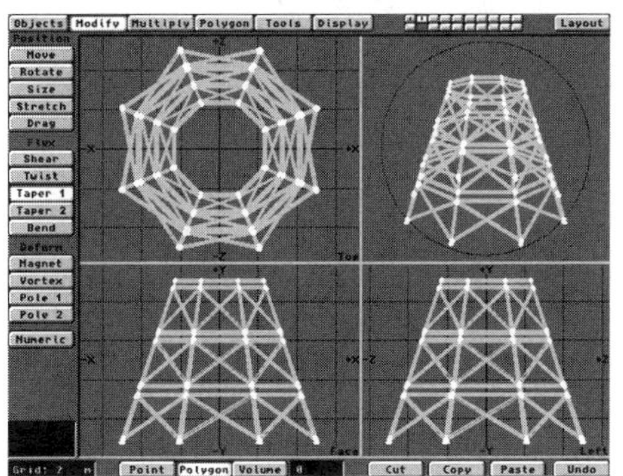
Figure 3

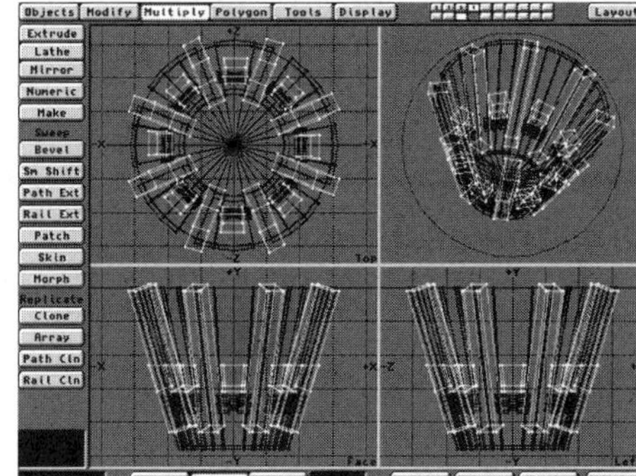
Figure 4

Primitives

Effective use of primitives is essential to successful modeling. The most obvious use of primitives in the satellite model are the upper and lower girder sections. These sections were built by creating a long, narrow Disc along the Y-axis for one of the support beams and Mirroring it across the Z-axis (Figure 1).

Next, another disc, with a slightly smaller diameter, is positioned horizontally between the two support beams. To create a diagonal crossbeam, **Copy** the horizontal disc and **Paste** it into another layer of Modeler.

Now **Rotate** (Modify menu) the copy by about 30 degrees on the Z-axis, and **Stretch** (Modify menu) as necessary to make the ends intersect with the support beams.

Mirror (Multiply menu) the copy on the Z-axis to create the opposite diagonal beam. **Copy** and **Paste** the diagonal and horizontal beams twice and five times, respectively, into various layers and **Move** (Modify menu) the copies along the Y-axis to complete the first girder section. (Figure 2)

Next, select and **Cut** the Polygons which make up one of the vertical support beams, so the original support beam and all of the cross beams are left. (one-eighth the final girder structure). Finally, **Clone** (under the Multiply menu) the girder section seven times around the Y-axis at an angle of 45 degrees to create the rest of the object.

Finally, use **Taper 1** (Modify menu) centered on the X and Z axis to obtain your final shape. (Figure 3)

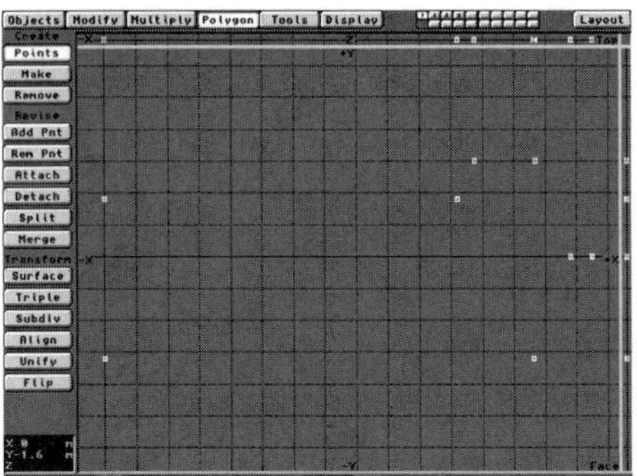

Figure 5

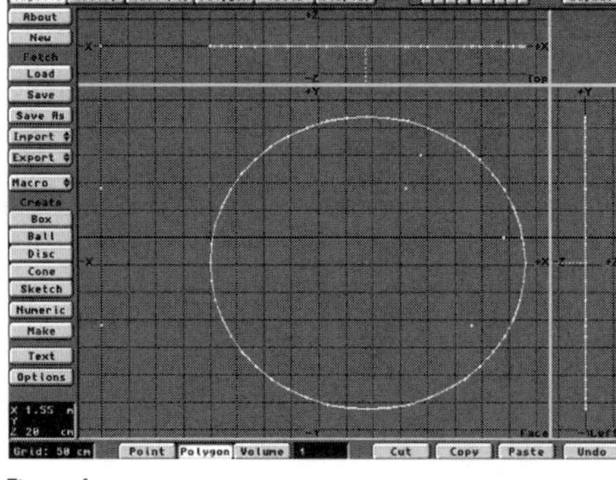

Figure 6

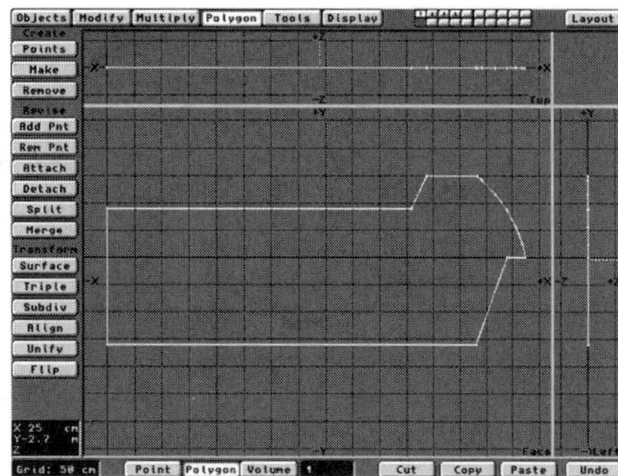

Figure 7

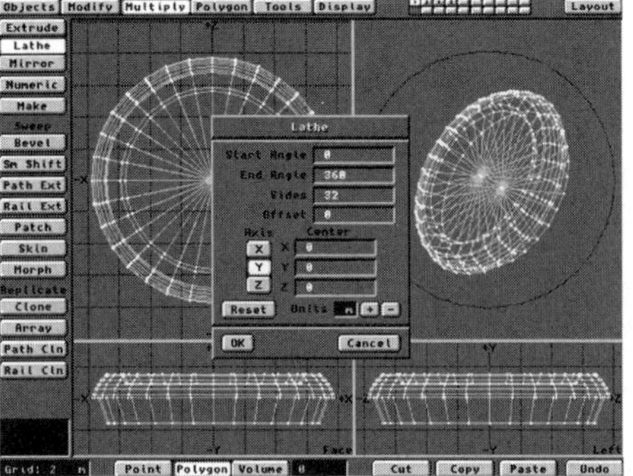

Figure 8

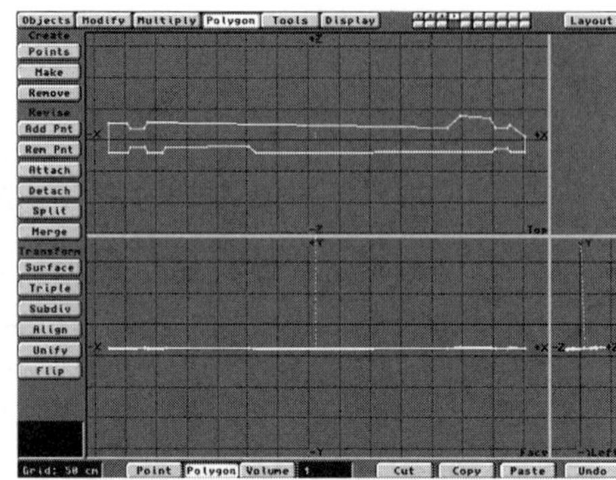

Figure 9

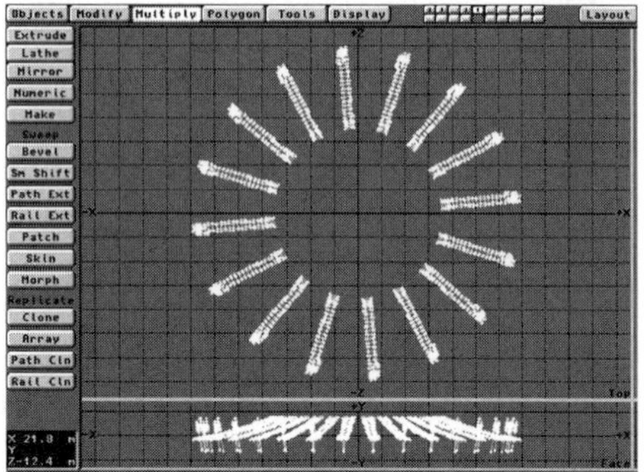

Figure 10

Other uses of primitives on the satellite are found in the lower, center section. This is where boxes are sized and positioned to intersect with the main body and cloned around the Y-axis to give the satellite some detail and dimension. (Foreground layer-Figure 4)

Sculpt and Lathe

The satellite's saucer section was easily created with a method I call "sculpt and lathe." In this instance, "sculpt" refers to the process of placing Points (Create **Points** under the Polygon menu) to sculpt the cross-section of the shape you want to build.(Figure 5)

In the case of the satellite, the outer ring of the saucer section is comprised, partially, of an arc. This shape is difficult to reproduce merely by placing points; it is much more effective to utilize primitives once again.

Select **Disc** (Objects menu) and draw out a Disc that intersects the two Points between which you want the arc. Once you **Make** (Enter) the Disc, select it (Figure 6) and **Remove** (k) the polygon which comprises it.

Now select and **Cut** (x) the points of the disc which do not fall between your original outer points. You are left with a perfect arc section for the satellite. To ensure a smooth arc, you must have an adequate number of points. Therefore before Making the Disc, select **Numeric** (n) and increase the number of sides to at least 32 or even 48.

Now that you have the outline for the saucer-section's shape, select the Points in order and **Make** them into a polygon (p) (Figure 7). To complete the shape, select the cross-section polygon and **Lathe** (Multiply menu) it around the Y-axis. (Figure 8)

Bevel, Julienne and Bend

The final components of the satellite are the reflector arms. The basic shape is made by creating points and making a polygon (Figure 9) in much the same way as the cross-section for the saucer piece.

To give the reflector thickness and an interesting edge shape you might want to **Bevel** (b) it with an inset of -140mm and a shift of -40mm (assuming your reflector is as big as mine). Keep in mind, however, to retain a top on the reflector and enclose your final object, **Copy** the original polygon and **Paste** the copy into another layer before performing the **Bevel** operation. Upon completion of the bevel, **Cut** the copy of the original polygon, **Paste** it into the same layer as the beveled polygon, and perform a **Merge** Points (Tools menu).

It's also a good idea to check the surface normals of all polygons and **Align** and **Flip** (Polygon menu) if needed so all surface normals are facing out.

To give the reflector arm a nice bend, perform the Julienne Macro (Objects menu) along the X-axis with anywhere from 10 to 20 divisions. Once it's been sliced, use the **Bend** tool (Modify menu) to arch the reflector arm slightly along the X-Axis. Enter the following parameters in the Bend Numeric requester:

Angle: 11 degrees
Direction:0 degrees
Center: 0,-0.45,.15m

All other parameters should be left at their default settings.

Finally, **Clone** the finished reflector fifteen times at a rotation of 22.5 degrees around the Y-Axis to produce the rest of the reflector arms.(Figure 10)

What Now?

The remainder of the satellite object was modeled using variations of the techniques described throughout this tutorial. Employ the strategies above to complete an object of your own, or try to construct a satellite similar to the example.

LWP

Taylor Kurosaki is a CGI Artist at Steven Spielberg's Amblin Imaging. While not writing LightWave 101 he works as a member of the visual effects team on NBC's seaQuest DSV. *Questions, comments, suggestions and ironing tips should be sent to his attention at 100 Universal City Plaza Bldg. 447, Universal City, CA 91608.*

Modeler Tips and Tricks

By John Gross

The following is a list of some of the best Modeler tips I know (tips specific to 3.0 are listed later).

- Using the right mouse button to add points will place and create points all at once. There's no need to click on Make or press the Return key!
- To use Modify tools such as bend, shear, twist, and taper on the opposite side of an object, choose Numeric and click on the opposite sense button. "+" will modify the "positive" side of the object, while "-" will modify the "negative" side.
- I've never seen it mentioned in the manual, but the black cross hairs in the middle of each Modeler View represent the object's center of rotation. If you want an object to rotate about its end, place the end at the black crosshairs.
- Find non-planar polygons by choosing Polygon Statistics (w) and pressing "+" to the right of "non-planar" at the bottom of the requester. After selecting all the non-planars, choose Triple (Shift-t) to turn them into polygons which by their very nature are planar.
- When you choose Cut, the object(s) cut are placed into a "hold area" in RAM. This can take some time; if you're sure you don't want to paste them anywhere, choose delete (z only, no on-screen button) instead. This clears selected items, but doesn't hold them in RAM. If you make a mistake, simply choose Undo and they will be put back.
- The keyboard command j (for jump) has no on-screen button equivalent. Its purpose is to "jump" any selected point(s) to the location of the cursor.
- Points and polygons may be selected with the static wireframe preview. Hold down Alt to rotate the view in-between selecting points/polygons.
- Once you let up on the mouse while selecting points, you will be in a "deselect" mode unless you hold down Shift and start selecting again. You don't need to hold down Shift continuously, only when you first press the mouse button again. As long as you keep the mouse button held down, you can let up on Shift and still be in "Select" (until you let up on the mouse again).
- Use the right mouse button to be in "lasso" selection mode. This allows you to draw areas around points, polygons, and volumes you wish to select. The same rules apply for select/deselect as with the left mouse button.
- What do you do if you have a large number of points in an object that have to be moved so they all reside in one plane (for example, a sphere with a flat side, or the side of a house that was handmade)? Simply choose the points, select Stretch, then Numeric, and enter a Factor of 0 for the axis you wish to be "flat." Then, for that same axis, use a Center value equal to the axis location where you want the points to appear.
- Use the Solid Wireframe Preview to see if you have any polygons that are flipped the wrong way.
- If you have complicated objects and you need to select a large number of polygons, use Volume Select; this way you will not have to wait for all of the polygons to become "selected" before modifying them.
- Find it hard to select those crosshairs to move windows around? If you have no preview in the preview window, you can click and drag anywhere in there to move the window crosshairs around.
- Pressing Help will display the keyboard shortcuts.

Modeler 3.0 Only

- Choosing Automatic Polygons in the Object Options panel will automatically create tripled polygons for any non-planar area when lathing and extruding splines.
- The Curve Division options in the Options panel will determine the amount of detail when creating PostScript fonts.
- When importing and exporting objects to and from Modeler and Layout, always clear out the old object and do a fresh import if you have made any changes in the other program that you wish to keep.
- The Sketch tool can make both curves and polygons. Use the Numeric option to decide which you want created.
- Magnet tools use bounding boxes. Use the left mouse button to draw out a bounding area in two views, then use the right mouse button to move the magnet.
- Using the new Offset value in the Numeric Lathe requester allows you to lathe while moving along an axis. Objects such as springs are now a snap to create. To see just how easy it is, try lathing a 1/2-meter-wide flat disk created off-center with a Start angle of 0, an End Angle of 1440, 64 Sides and an Offset of 5 meters.
- Clicking on an activated button will deactivate it.
- Try using negative Inset and Shift values when beveling skinny fonts. This prevents the edges from sticking through each other.
- You can import images into Modeler in order to trace around them. You must first load them into LightWave. Choosing Automatic Size will size the image to whatever object is located in the layer. If you wish to use the video aspect ratio for the background image, type in a size in multiples of 1.33(width) x 1(height).
- Don't forget about the new "fit" options! Pressing "a" fits the view to the object in all three views (same as always). Shift-a fits the view to the selected points or polygons in all three views, and Control-a fits the view only in the window where the cursor is located (very handy).
- The measuring stick in the display panel is extremely convenient. After you let go of the mouse button, the measurements will stay in the coordinates display until the mouse is moved.
- If you need to move a bunch of points to the same axis plane, simply use the Set Val button in the Tools menu.
- Use the new keyboard commands for Move (t), Rotate (y), Size (H) and Stretch (h) to access these commands quickly.
- The keyboard commands for rotating 90 degrees right (r) or 90 degrees left (e) are useful when you have designed an object in the wrong view. The object will always rotate about the cursor when you choose these commands.
- Pressing the space bar will cycle through the different selection modes.
- Layers with items in them will display a small dot in the foreground layer button.
- Holding down Alt while clicking on Save will save any objects in their respective layers. This saved item can only be loaded back into Modeler—you cannot load it back into LightWave.
- What exactly does the Max Smoothing Angle value in the Subdivide/Smooth requester represent? Think of the surface normals projecting out from two adjacent polygons. The angle between these two surface normals is the smoothing angle (if it helps to picture the angle better, imagine the normals projecting through the polygons until they intersect). Using 89.5 degrees as a default Max Smoothing Angle value means that any polygons up to 89.5 degrees will be smoothed across. If you Smooth Subdivide a box with a Max angle greater than 90 degrees, you will start getting what looks like a bale of hay.

LightWave 101
Methods of Modeling, Part 1

by Taylor Kurosaki

There is one very important concept one must learn early on with regard to LightWave Modeler: For the most part, Modeler is not a conceptual tool, it is an execution tool. You will be much more effective if you first decide precisely what it is you want to model before running the program. If you are replicating a physical object, look all around it and visually break it down into its basic components. If you are modeling from a drawing or photograph, try sketching it from different perspectives to grasp its whole shape. Once you have done this, you must next decide on a modeling approach.

Primitives-based modeling utilizes the basic shapes of boxes, discs, cones and balls. These shapes can then be used as they are, or modified with any combination of Modeler's tools. The following tutorial illustrates the process of building a model entirely from primitives.

Primitives Tutorial:
Lamp Table

In order to build a convincing table lamp, we need a table to set it on, so let's begin there:

Enter Modeler, and set the grid size to 200mm (use the < and > keys to zoom in or out). Select **Disc** under the **Objects** menu. Click on the **Numeric** button (n) and enter the values in Figure 1. Select **OK** and hit the Enter key to make the Disc.

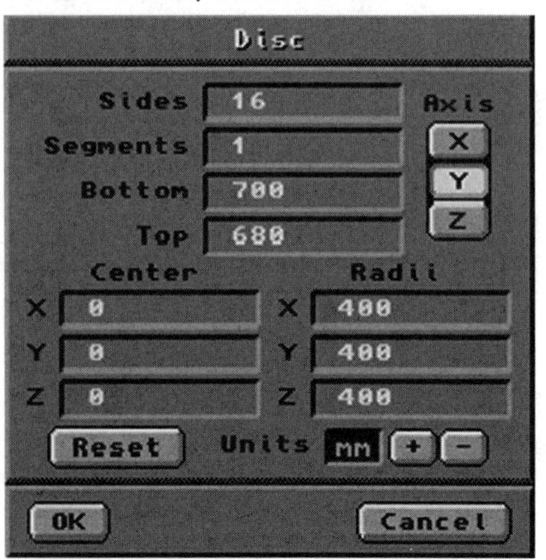

Figure 1

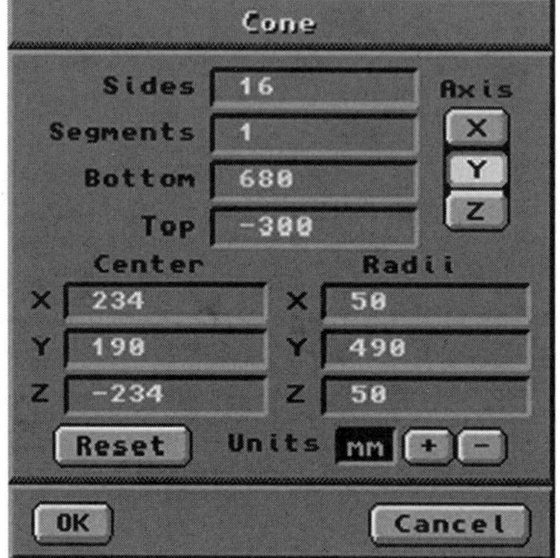

Figure 2

The table body will be made from the box primitive. Press the 2 key to enter the second layer in Modeler. Select Box from the Objects menu. From the Numeric requester, enter these values: Low: -250, 350, -250, High: 250, 680, 250 Segments: 1, 1, 1. Click OK and hit Enter to make the box.

The Cone tool will be used to make the table legs. Press 3 to make that layer active. Select **Cone**, open the **Numeric** requester and enter the values in Figure 2. Notice how the top value is less than the bottom value. This inverts the orientation of the cone such that it tapers from top to bottom. Click **OK** and hit enter to make the first table leg.

To construct the remaining three legs, select **Clone** from within the **Multiply** menu. Set the Number of clones to 3, with a Rotation of 90 degrees along the Y Axis. Click **OK** to clone the leg.

The table will look more conventional if the legs don't taper so much that they end at a sharp point (unless you would like holes in your floor). They have been constructed extra-long to begin with so we can go back and cut off the tips. The best operation for this purpose is a **Boolean** Subtract (**Tools** menu). A Boolean operation works by affecting the contents of the foreground layer with the contents of the background layer. More specifically, a Boolean Subtract works by cutting from the foreground layer any geometry that overlaps with geometry in the background layer. Additionally, Boolean is a Constructive Solid Geometry (CSG) operation. It adds polygons to any affected areas in the foreground layer, making the object appear solid where it was cut.

Press 4 to enter that layer. Press Alt-3 to put the table legs in the background layer. Select **Box** from the **Objects** menu. Draw out a box such that its top face has a Y value of 0, its bottom extends below the bottom of the table legs, and its sides extend beyond the table legs, as shown in Figure 3. Make the box by hitting the enter key.

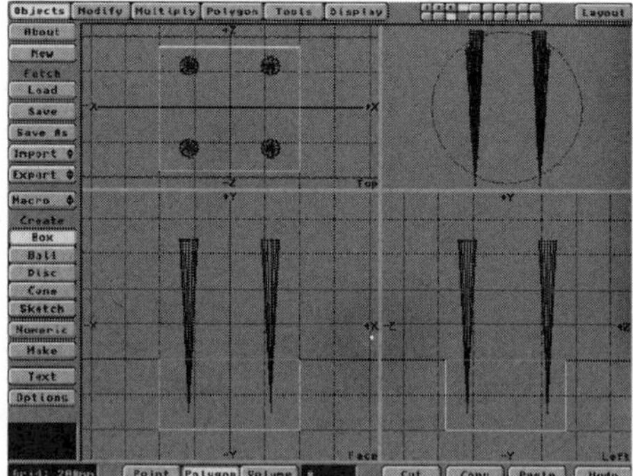

Figure 3

We have just created the template from which we will perform the Boolean operation on the table legs. Click the (‘) key to swap the foreground and background layers. Now select **Boolean** (**Tools**) and then Subtract from Boolean requester. As stated earlier, and true to its CSG designation, the Boolean operation automatically added polygons to the bottom of the table legs after cutting off the ends.

Finally, two false drawer handles are made simply by using the Ball primitive. **Cut** the Boolean template from layer 4. Select **Ball** from within the **Objects** menu, press n to bring up the numeric requester, and enter these values:

Ball Type:	Globe
Sides:	16
Segments:	8

Center:	0,570,-265
Radii:	15,15,15
Units:	mm

Click **OK**, and hit Enter to make the ball. Select **Copy** (c) to copy the ball. Next, press (t) (for **Move**), and move the ball -120mm along the Y axis. You may wish to hold the Ctrl key while moving the ball to constrain the movement to the Y axis only. Finally press the (v) key to Paste the copy you made of the ball to its original spot.

To save the table as one object, hold the shift key while hitting the 1, 2 and 3 keys to bring all four layers to the foreground (make sure layer 4 is also active). Hit (s) to save all four layers as "LampTable."

Another major modeling technique is freehand modeling. This approach gets its name from the process of creating polygons comprised of hand-placed points. These freehand polygons, or primitives, are then affected primarily by the Extrude, Lathe, and Mirror tools of the Multiply menu, creating the desired shapes.

Freehand Tutorial:

Lamp

Several freehand modeling techniques can be illustrated by the modeling of a lamp. The look we are trying to achieve is similar to a spiraling wrought iron design, with a pleated lampshade. We will begin by building the main body of the lamp:

Click on the **New** button under the **Objects** menu, or press (n). Go to the **Polygon** menu and select **Points.** Use the left mouse button to lineup the cursor, and the right mouse button or the enter key to place the points. To create the outline of the lamp, place points in the Face view at these XY coordinates: 0, 1225; 15, 1225; 15, 1205; 70, 1205; 70, 1195; 60, 1195; 20, 1180; 20, 735; 50, 735; 190, 710; 190, 700, 0, 700mm. [*Editor's note*: To quickly enter these points, use the Enter Points macro.]

De-select all points and reselect them in clockwise order. Once the points are selected, hit (p) to make a polygon containing them. This polygon represents the radius of the lamp.

Click the **Polygon** selection mode button at the bottom of the screen and select the newly made polygon. Go to the **Multiply** menu and select **Lathe**. Open the **Numeric** requester. Change the rotation of the Lathe to the **Y** axis. Otherwise, use the default settings.

Click **OK**, and press enter to lathe the lamp as shown in Figure 4.

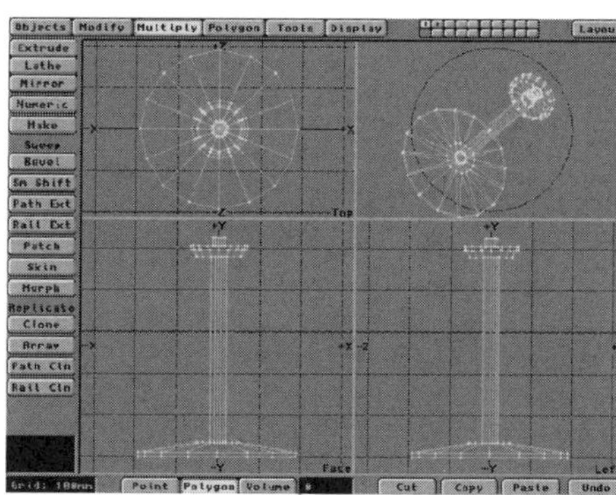

Figure 4

Next to build is the spiral section of the lamp. Whereas the main body of the lamp combined placing points with the **Lathe** feature, this piece of the lamp will utilize primitives, combined with lathing.

Press 2 to make the second Modeler layer active. Select **Disc** from the **Objects** menu. Open the **Numeric** requester and enter these values:

Sides:	16
Segments:	1
Bottom:	700
Top:	700
Axis:	Y
Center:	0,700,-40
Radii:	10,0,10
Units:	mm

Click **OK** and hit enter to make the disc.

Now select **Clone** from the **Multiply** menu. Enter 2 as the number of clones, with a rotation of 120 degrees along the Y axis. Click on **OK** to clone. The resulting three discs represent a cross-section of the spiral section of the lamp.

Select **Lathe** from the **Multiply** menu. From within the **Numeric** requester, change the lathe axis to **Y**, and enter an Offset of 500mm. The offset will cause the discs to spiral upward 500mm to the end of the lathe. Click **OK** and hit enter to lathe the three discs. Your object should look like Figure 5.

Now to build the supports for the lampshade. Press 3 to enter the third layer. Select **Disc** from the **Objects** menu and enter these values in the Numeric requester:

Sides:	16
Segments:	1
Bottom:	1.2
Top:	1.4
Axis:	Y
Center:	0.06,1.3,0
Radii:	0.002,0,0.002
Units:	m

Click **OK** and hit enter to make the disc.

Select **Mirror** from the **Multiply** menu. Center the cursor along the Y axis and mirror across the Y Plane, or select Y Plane with a position of 0 from within the **Numeric** requester. Hit the enter key to mirror the support.

Finally, to complete the lamp, we must build a lampshade. Move to the fourth layer in Modeler and make a Disc with these values:

Sides:	64
Segments:	1
Bottom:	1.1
Top:	1.4
Axis:	Y
Center:	0,1.25,0
Radii:	0.07,0.15,0.07
Units:	m

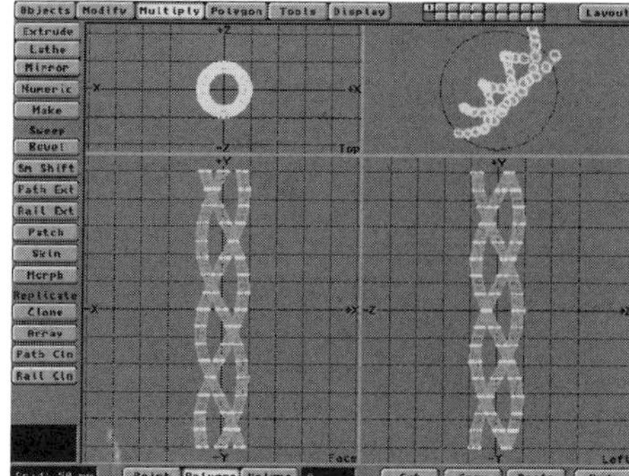

Figure 5

From the Top view, select every other pair of points along the Y axis, beginning with the pair at either 3, 6, 9 or 12 o'clock. Hit the (h) key to select **Stretch** from the **Modify** menu. From the **Numeric** requester, enter stretch Factors of 0.885 for the X and Z axes. Click **OK** to stretch the points inward.

Now we want to give the lampshade the correct shape. De-select all points. Click **Taper 1** from within

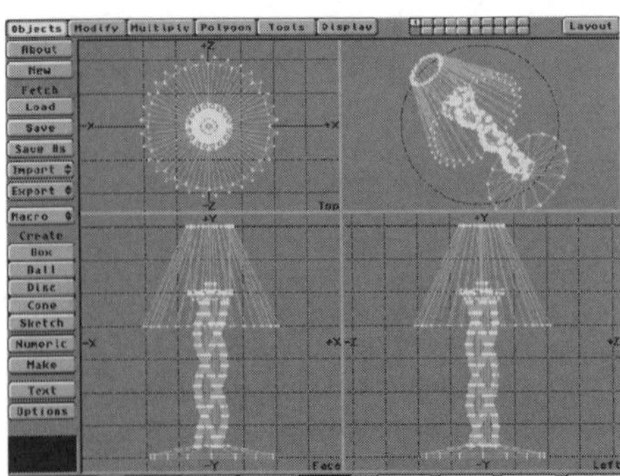

Figure 6

the **Modify** menu. Adjust the **Numeric** settings so they match these:

Axis:	Y
Range:	Automatic
Sense:	-
Factor:	3
Center:	0,0,0

Click on the **Apply** button to taper the lampshade.

To complete the lampshade, click the **Polygon** selection button, and hit (w) to open the Polygon Statistics window. From this window, select the two polygons with greater than four vertices. These are the polygons at the top and bottom of our lampshade. Press (x) to **Cut** them. Finally, hit (c) to **Copy** all the polygons of the lampshade, (f) to **Flip** the originals, and (v) to **Paste** the copies back down. Under the **Tools** menu, select **Merge** Points (m) to merge duplicate points. Your lampshade is now double-sided.

The lamp is now complete, save for a cord and light bulb (I'll leave those to you). Make all four of the lamp's layers active, and save the lamp as one object. Your lamp should match the one in Figure 6.

LWP

Taylor Kurosaki is a visual effects artist at Amblin Imaging. He can be reached at 100 Universal City Plaza, Bldg. 447, Universal City, CA 91608, or through John Gross on-line.

Metaform Magic

Designing from Scratch

by Ken Stranahan

You're at your wit's end. There's one week remaining to finish the project and you still don't have the model built. In all probability, the spline modeling you have to do will be as easy as crocheting a car cover, and in the end it may not even fit the car.

Let's face it—every time you get a more powerful tool on your computer your life gets more complex. Splines are great because you can model anything, and it will only take three or four weeks. That is, if you're a good modeler. But come on now, I have a life and I like having my weekends free. Have no fear, there is a new tool called Metaform. For me, it has virtually replaced spline modeling, and the great thing is that is makes modeling work much easier.

With Metaform you can start with incredibly simple objects. In fact, the first time I used Metaform I made my pre-metaform objects too complex. Also, it's not important to get the object's shape right the first time—you can adjust the shape in no time until it's perfect. This makes it a great tool for designing objects from scratch, and once you have the basic form worked out you can make dozens of variations in a matter of minutes.

So, let's discuss how to use Metaform. I think of it as being very similar to sculpting. You rough out a basic shape and then smooth it out. What Metaform does is subdivide an object and smooth out the polygons in between, just like sanding down the corners of a block of wood. The amount of smoothing is determined by the angle and distance between adjoining polygons. It sounds a lot more complicated than it really is, so instead of discussing the details of this tool, let's just jump right in and build an object — a car. It's easier than you may think. This pictorial guide will take you through all of the steps.

1. Think of a car in its most simple form. It's a box with two wheel wells cut out and a box on top for the windows and roof. Even easier, make a profile of the car. To do this, enter Modeler and make a flat box (use the Numeric tool) with multiple segments for the wheel wells and roof. Enter 3 for the Y, 6 for the X and 0 for the Z. Figure 1 shows a sample segmented plane.
2. Now it's possible to select the polygons that are in the wheel wells and in front and behind the roof and cut them out. Take the polygons for the windows and

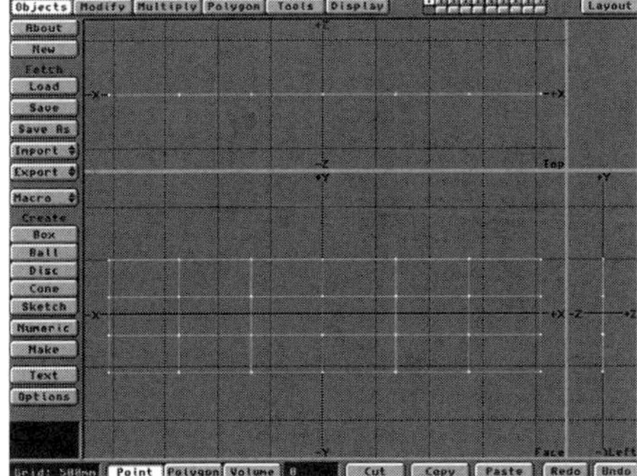

Figure 1: A simple segmented plane is where we begin.

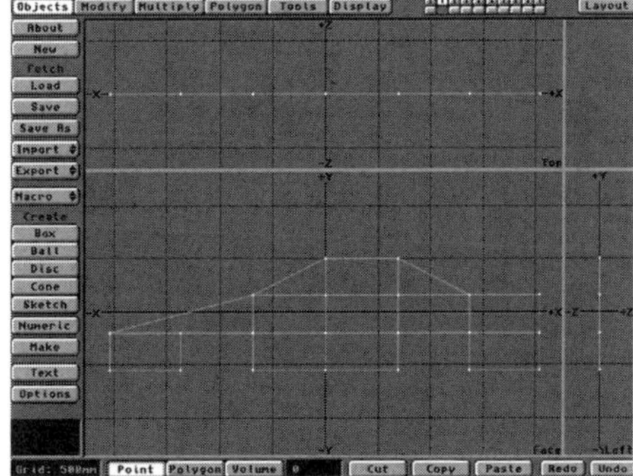

Figure 2: Points and polygons are deleted to form the basic profile shape of a car.

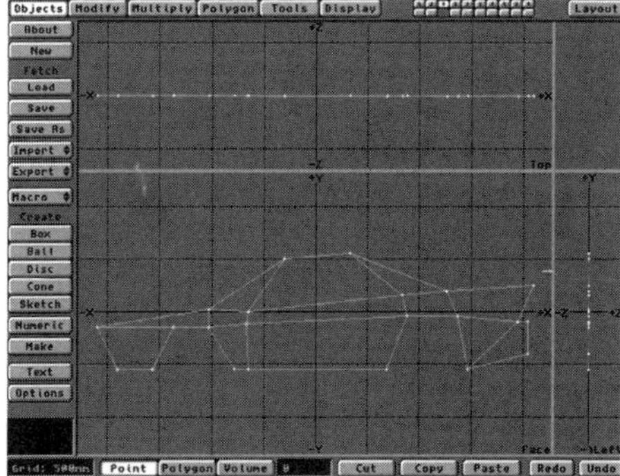

Figure 3: Our template after dragging some points and splitting a polygon.

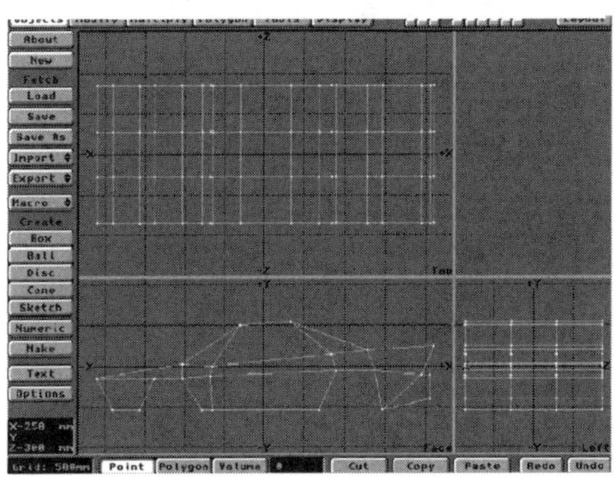

Figure 4: The extruded and centered primitive car shape.

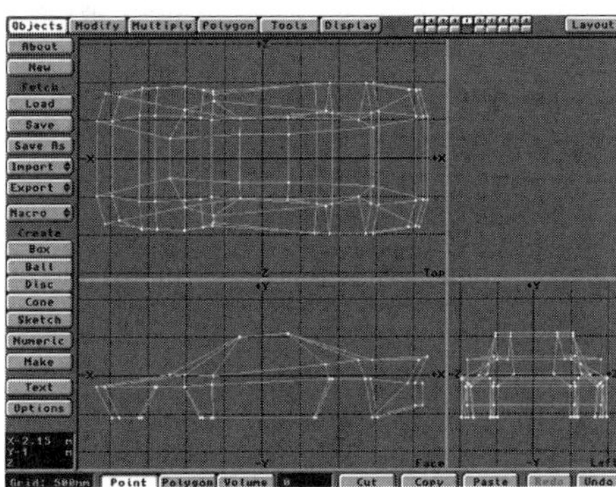

Figure 5: After moving, stretching and tapering our primitive car, we are starting to get a more recognizable shape.

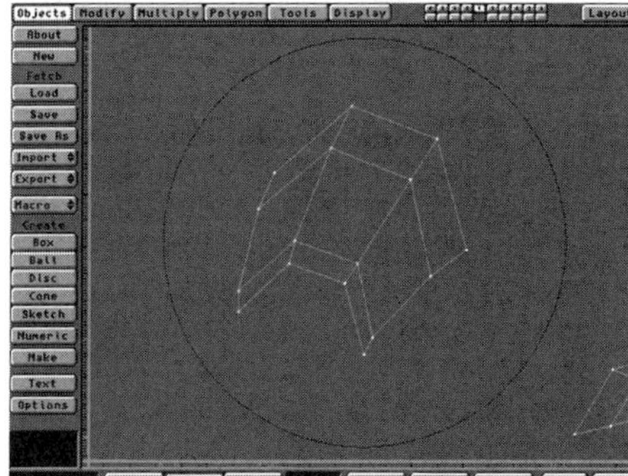

Figure 6: The static view of the wheel well section of the primitive car.

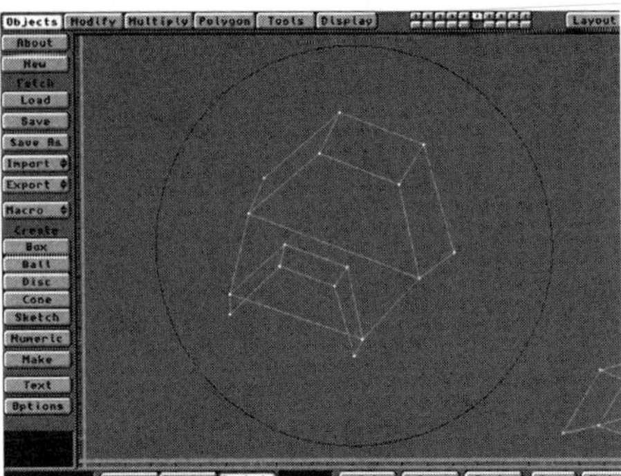

Figure 7: The inner points are selected on each side to create the inner wheel well side.

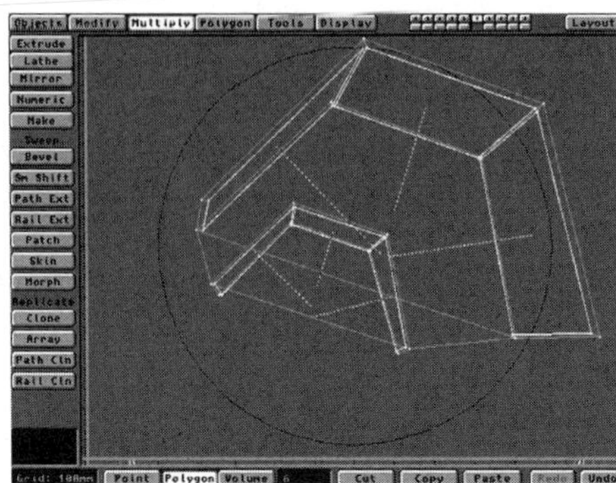

Figure 8: The sides of the wheel well are beveled slightly to create additional geometry.

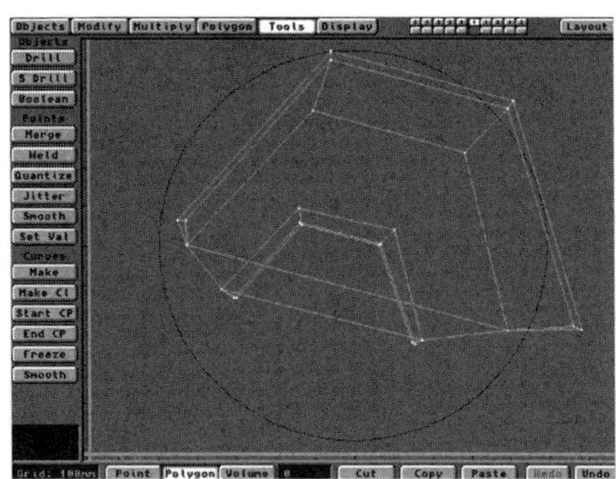

Figure 9: The sides after the points of the back polygons have been welded.

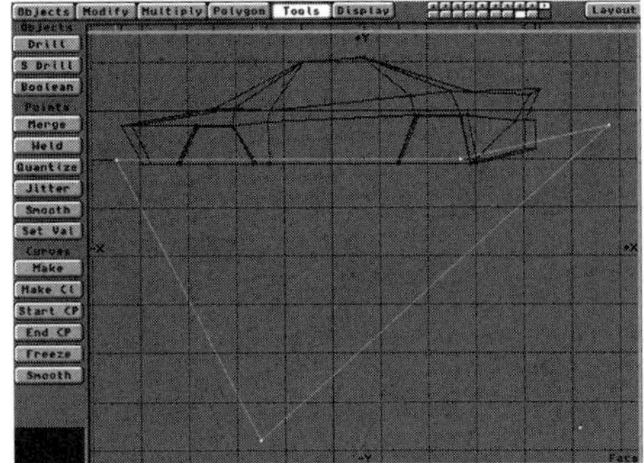

Figure 10: A solid box is created in order to stencil in a row of polygons at the bottom of the car.

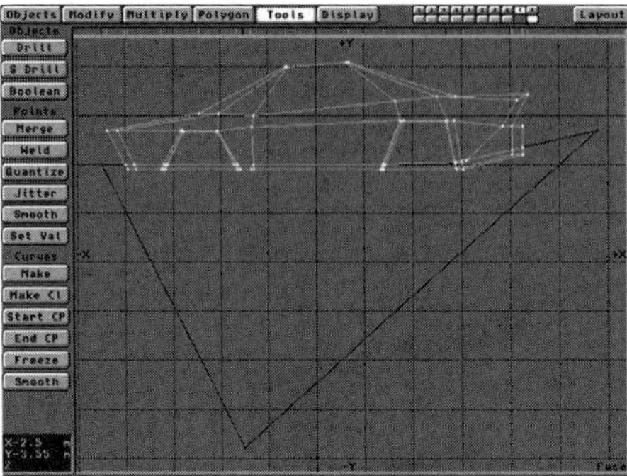

Figure 11: The newly added row of polygons at the bottom of the car.

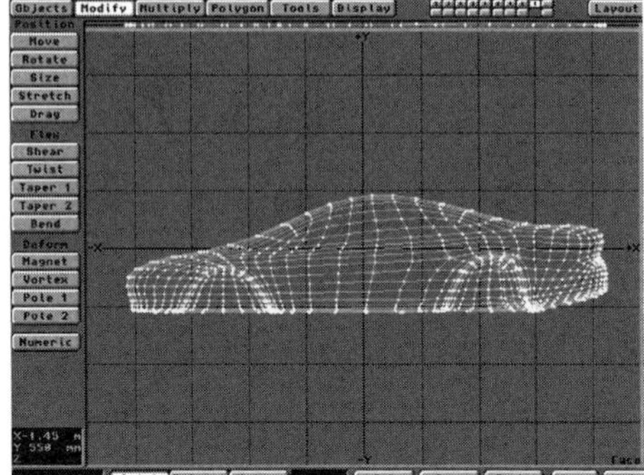

Figure 12: The final metaformed version of our car.

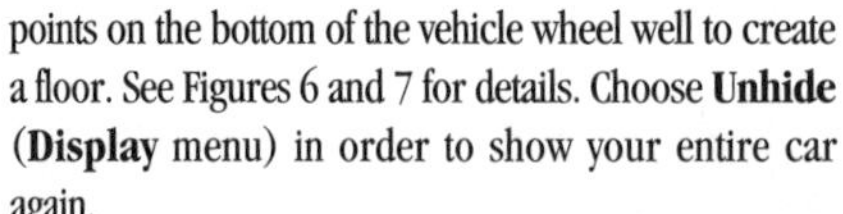

make them slant inward. Deleting the extra corner points so they become triangles should do the trick. Figure 2 shows the plane after sections are cut.

3. Now that we have the basic sections, it's possible to adjust the points to make more of a car shape. The **Drag** tool (**Modify** menu) is perfect for moving the points around. It is a good idea at this time to split the polygons at the rear bumper and add a point to the bottom one in order to give more definition to the bumper. After adding the point, it is necessary to split the bottom polygon because Metaform will only work with three- or four-point polygons. Use the **Split** command in the **Polygon** menu to get your vehicle template to look like the one in Figure 3.
4. Once the basic profile is finished it can be extruded to form the body. Do this with three segments so the body can have more shape (Figure 4). After extruding, the object can be shaped by stretching the points in the middle out toward the sides to give the sides some bevel. The roof and window points can also be stretched in to round them out, and the whole body can be tapered slightly toward the front. Then the row of points at the window line can be adjusted to give more curve to the windows (Figure 5).
5. Finally, polygons can be made to fill the middle of the wheel wells out. Select the "wheel well" section, then select **Hide Uns** (**Display** menu) to hide the rest of the object.

   Next, select the wheel well points that are "one section" in on the wells. Create a polygon inside each well and make sure that they face outward. Connect the points on the bottom of the vehicle wheel well to create a floor. See Figures 6 and 7 for details. Choose **Unhide** (**Display** menu) in order to show your entire car again.
6. By now the object is looking pretty good. OK, it actually looks like a box. But just a few more steps and it will look great.

   If you try Metaforming it now (by pressing **Metaform** under the Subdivide menu, or D) you will notice that the wheel wells and bottom of the car will curve in. This is because when the car is metaformed, the closer the points, the tighter the curve, and the points are pretty spread out at this time.
7. There are two tricks I use to take care of this. The first is to add polygons to the wheel wells so the edges stay flush with the body. For this, once again, select the wheel wells and single them out by using the **Hide Uns** tool.

   First, select the three polygons that make up the sides of the wheel well that would surround the top, front and back of a tire. Then **Bevel** (**Multiply** menu or b) the polygons slightly (Figure 8).

   Since it is really only necessary to have extra polygons on the outside edge of the vehicle, you can remove the polygons on the inside by welding the points (**Tools** menu) from the beveled polygons to the original polygons (Figure 9).

   At this point, you will need to cut out unneeded polygons by using the Polygon Statistics requester (w) to select any two-point polygons and delete them.
8. The second thing that can be done to add flatness to the bottom of the car is to stencil in a row of polygons that are close to the bottom of the car. To do this, simply build an extruded box in a background layer that cuts across the bottom of the object and use the Stencil (**S Drill — Tools** menu) tool. Then remove any extra points that may occur at the corners of the box. This is a quick way to add extra sections to a simple object. See Figures 10 and 11 for more detail.

That's it. You can now Metaform your object.

If you have problems Metaforming the car, it may be because you have to clean up your object. Metaform doesn't like sloppy object building and you will get render errors if you aren't careful. So merge your points, look for two-point polygons and fix the holes in your objects before attempting any Metaforming.

Metaforming this vehicle will provide a basic car shape. From here you can stencil in windows, add wheels and surface the object.

Remember that once you have the basic pre-Metaform object, the points can be modified to create any kind of car. Adding an air scoop is as easy as beveling in a polygon on the side of the car. A rear wing, or spoiler, can be added by beveling two of the rear polygons up and connecting them across the top by making polygons across and then removing any unneeded polygons inside the wing.

LWP

Ken Stranahan is an animator with Area 51.

Customizing Modeler
Using the Custom Pop-up Menus

by John Gross

Though LightWave 3D 4.0's manuals are a great deal better than previous incarnations, there are still a few small oversights. One perhaps not-so-small oversight was the omission of a section for Modeler's User Guide about configuring its custom command pop-up.

If you know how to configure the macro list in Modeler 3.5, you will still need to learn a few new things, as the process has changed a bit for 4.0. There's a bit more power, but things can be confusing the first time through.

You'll have to excuse the following text if it starts sounding too "manual-speak," but I thought I would leave it more or less in the original form intended for inclusion in the manual. I will jump in where necessary with additional information.

The Custom Command List requester allows you to create custom commands and define lists.

Using the Custom Command Pop-up Menu

Selecting the **Custom** pop-up menu in the **Objects** panel allows you to choose commands from a list. They appear in the following manner:

(1) Modeler's built-in commands of **Configure List** and **Configure Keys.**

(2) User-defined commands (based upon added plug-ins).

(3) Modeler's built-in **ARexx/Rexx Script** command.

(4) Individual plug-in commands added through the use of **Add Plugin** (alphabetized by the actual name of the function, as opposed to any user-defined name for the function).

Depending on the command chosen from the **Custom** pop-up list, an operation will occur or a requester will be presented for you to supply values in order to perform a function.

Adding Plug-in Functions to Modeler

Selecting the **Add Plugin** command from the **Objects** panel's **Custom** pop-up menu allows you to select a third-party plug-in file. A plug-in file can contain many functions or commands. For example, adding the supplied CENTER.P plug-in adds seven commands: BoundingBox, Center, Center1D, CenterScale, CenterStretch, PointCenter and Symmetrize.

Note: When you first add a plug-in, the names of the functions that appear in the **Custom** pop-up will default to the name of the function as listed in the actual plug-in file. You can change these names by editing Modeler's config file, known as Mod-config (Amiga) or LWM.cfg (PC). If you use Add Plugin to try to add a plug-in that is already loaded, you will not receive any additional entries in the **Custom** pop-up menu.

Important: When you exit Modeler, any plug-ins added by the **Add Plugin** command will be saved to the configuration file and be available the next time you start the program. They are alphabetized in order of the actual plug-in function name as defined in the plug-in file, rather than by the user-defined name that appears in the **Custom** pop-up menu. If you do not edit the names of the plug-in file functions in Modeler's configuration file, these two names will be the same.

When you first run Modeler, no plug-ins have been configured. You will need to add the plug-ins (files that end in ".P") that are located in the Plugins/Modeler directory. After loading all of the Modeler plug-ins, you should have a number of entries to both **Custom** pop-ups in the **Objects** and **Tools** panels. Before doing anything else, you may want to quit out of Modeler to save the config file, so your plug-ins will be remembered the next time you start.

Tip: Before adding any plug-ins, you may want to change the PluginDirectory line in Modeler's config file to point to the path where the Modeler plug-ins are located. After you make the change, the **Add Plugin** requester will automatically point to that location. If you installed LightWave to the default NewTek directory (PC), this line would be changed to read:

PluginDirectory D:\NewTek\Plugins\Modeler

Creating and Configuring Custom Command Lists

Selecting the built-in Configure List command from the Custom pop-up menu in the Objects panel presents a panel allowing you to create and save custom commands. This panel will appear when you access the Custom pop-up menus.

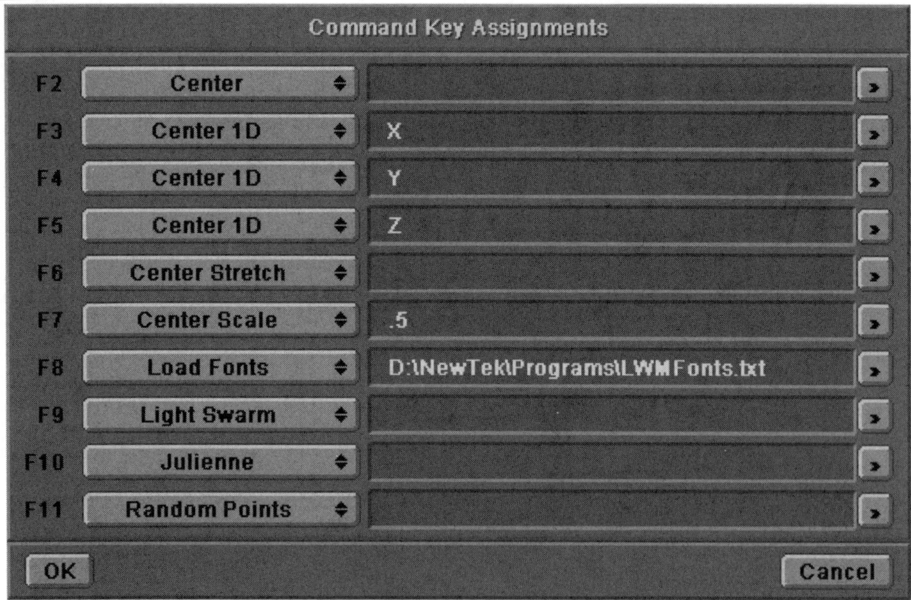

The Configure Keys requester lets you set up keyboard shortcuts for your favorite commands.

Custom commands are generally based upon functions that allow some type of user input as an argument. For example, the CenterScale function allows you to run it with an argument that is simply a number defining the scale value. If you enter no argument, it defaults to 2.0, which doubles the size of the object(s) in the foreground layer. If you use an argument, the function will not expect any input from you (as it normally does) but instead will scale the object according to your argument value.

Creating/Changing/Deleting a Custom Command

To make a custom command, you must first have some plug-in commands loaded. If you followed the steps above for adding plug-ins, you are ready.

If you select **Configure List** and look at the Custom **Command** List panel that appears, you will notice that any added plug-in commands are listed in the Command pop-up menu. Some of these commands support a user-defined argument such as CenterScale. The Load Fonts command will accept, as an argument, the name of a text file containing the complete paths of font files to load when the Load Fonts command is selected. If no file name is given, the Load Fonts command looks for a file named LWMFonts.txt and will load the font files listed in there.

Any gray input field to the left of a button with a right arrow on it is an argument field. There are two of these fields in the **Custom Command** List panel and 10 of them in the **Configure Key Assignments** panel. You can select the right arrow buttons to find and select a text file containing arguments for the selected command. If the argument is an alphanumeric value rather than a file name (such as the CenterScale argument), you can simply input it in the **Argument** field.

The **List Entry** pop-up menu contains any user-defined commands and reads (None) if none have been established.

Let's say that you wanted to create a custom command that loads three font files that you use for a particular client. The steps you would use are the following:

(1) Create and save (ASCII/text format) a text file that states, one per line, the complete path name of the three font files you would like to load. If the fonts were located in a directory called Client in a larger PSFonts directory, the text file would look something like this:
D:\PSFonts\Client\Fontname1
D:\PSFonts\Client\Fontname2
D:\PSFonts\Client\Fontname3

(2) Select **Configure List** from the Custom pop-up menu (Objects) and select the **Load Fonts** command in the **Command** pop-up menu.

(3) Select the right arrow button to the right of the **Argument** field below the **Command** pop-up menu and use the requester to find and select the name of your text file containing the font names.

(4) Enter a name for your custom command (e.g., "Load Client Fonts") in the **Name** field above the **Command** pop-up menu.

(5) Click on the **Create** button to create the custom command. The List Entry pop-up menu will now contain this entry.

If you later wish to change the name of this custom command or the argument file, select it in the **List Entry** pop-up, make any changes to the **Name** or the **Argument** fields, and then hit the **Change** button.

If you would like to remove a custom command from the list, simply select it in the **List Entry** pop-up and press the **Delete** button. Note that this only removes a custom command, not a command added by the configuration file or **Add Plugin**.

Important: After changing or deleting a custom command, make sure to save your list if you want the changes to be permanent (see next section).

Tip 1: Read the documents provided with a plug-in file to learn which functions allow for user-defined arguments.

Tip 2: Using custom commands, you could build many different versions of the same command. For example, you may have different font files used for different working situations, each of which could be accessed by creating custom commands that use the Load Fonts command with different arguments.

Tip 3: List Entry commands appear alphabetized in order by the name you define. In addition, they appear in the Custom pop-up menu before any added plug-ins. To provide some order to the Custom pop-up menu, you may want to create some List Entries such as "----------" to start the list and "z----------" to end the list. Make sure to assign benign commands (such as Rexx Script) to these entries so any data will not be changed by accidentally selecting them.

Saving/Loading/Clearing Custom Command Lists

Once you have constructed a list of user-defined

custom commands, you can save the list by selecting the **Save** button near the top of the Custom Command List panel. You will be presented with a requester with which you can choose a directory and file name for the saved list.

Selecting **Load** will allow you to load a previously saved list, replacing the currently loaded list. Selecting **Clear** will clear any list currently loaded, leaving the **List Entry** pop-up set to (None).

Note: The last loaded list will be written to Modeler's configuration file and will be loaded automatically the next time you start Modeler.

Tip: You may have different command lists for different working environments or clients. Each may contain specific user-defined commands pertaining to a certain client/project.

Defining a Startup Command

The pop-up menu to the right of the **Startup Command** label allows you to choose a command from the list of added plug-ins that will be run every time you start Modeler. A commonly used Startup Command is the Load Fonts command. Below the Startup Command pop-up, there is an argument field that can be used for any argument(s) for the Startup Command. In the case of the Load Fonts command, you would want to select the name of the text file containing the font paths to be loaded.

Tip: If no file name is given as an argument for Load Fonts, it will look for a file named LWMFonts.txt and will load the font files listed in there by default. If no such file exists, no fonts will be loaded. LWMFonts.txt needs to be located in Modeler's working directory (the location from which you start Modeler).

Note: The selected Startup Command will be remembered the next time you start Modeler.

Configuring Function Key Commands

Selecting **Configure Keys** presents the Command Key Assignments panel. From here you can attach commands to your keyboard's function keys. On the Amiga, you can use F1 through F10. On non-Amiga platforms, you can use F2 through F11 (F1 is reserved for Help key shortcuts).

Selecting an added command from any one of the 10 pop-up menus will assign it the appropriate function key. To the right of each pop-up menu is an argument field to input any user-defined argument (e.g., a text file or an alphanumeric value). To assign three commands that will center any items in the current layer along the X, Y or Z axes, perform the following tasks:

(1) Choose the Center 1D command from the pop-up menu corresponding to the function key you would like to assign this function to.

(2) Enter X in the argument field to the right of the chosen pop-up menu.

(3) Repeat the process twice more for two more function keys, entering Y and Z, respectively, for the two argument fields.

(4) Select OK to return to the main Modeler screen. Choose one of the newly added function keys. Object(s) in the foreground layers will be centered along the appropriate axis.

Tip: If the Center 1D command is used without an argument, a requester will ask you to choose which axis to center the object upon.

Note: Any changes to the Command Key Assignments will be saved when you exit Modeler and will be ready for the next time you begin a modeling session.

That's about it. You should now have a pretty good feel for configuring your own lists using Modeler's Configure List command. You may notice some little downfalls in this whole custom list thing. For example, I believe that only the functions appearing in the **List Entry** pop-up menu should appear in the Custom pop-up menu. With the current version, all of your custom commands are listed (alphabetized by user-supplied name in List Entry), followed by a list of all of the functions (alphabetized by function name in plug-in file). I feel that, by default, all of the added plug-in commands should be listed in the List Entry by their default names (and in the **Command** pop-up menu of the **Custom Command List** requester). This way, you, as the user, could define the order of all of the functions by simply renaming the List Entry to alphabetize them.

LWP

John Gross is the director of special projects for Amblin Imaging and the editor of LIGHTWAVEPRO.

Metaform Basics

A First Look at a New Way of Modeling

by John Gross

Along with all the new features in LightWave 3.5 comes one of the best new tools for modeling I have seen in some time. Hidden at the bottom of the Subdivide requester (Polygon menu) is a little button labeled Metaform. Metaform is a unique new way of subdividing polygons that allows you to create objects out of rough primitives and easily smooth them into gently (or sharply) curved objects.

This first *LWPRO* look at Metaform will start with the basics. Expect subsequent articles to explore Metaform in more detail.

Quit Talking. Start Doing

Enough talk about what Metaform can do. Let's put it to work.

To begin, enter Modeler and create a box using the default settings in the **Numeric** requester (n) (**Objects** menu). Make sure to select **Make** (Return/Enter) in order to actually create the box (Figure 1).

Copy the box and Paste it into the next two layers so we will have reference objects for later.

Go to the Polygon menu and select **Subdiv** (D) to access the Subdivide requester. Faceted and Smooth operate similar to earlier versions (with the added bonus of working on quadrangles as well as triangles).

Select **Metaform** and press **OK**. Notice what happened. A 'smoother' version of the object was formed inside the bounds of the original. You can select one of the other layers as a background to see how the object was formed.

Perform another **Metaform** operation. The box has subdivided once again into a smoother version (Figure 3).

That's it! You just created a ball from a box. Admittedly, this is a poor choice for using Metaform, as you could have simply used the **Ball** button to create one (without a few non-planar polygons to boot), but this should demonstrate what this tool is designed to do.

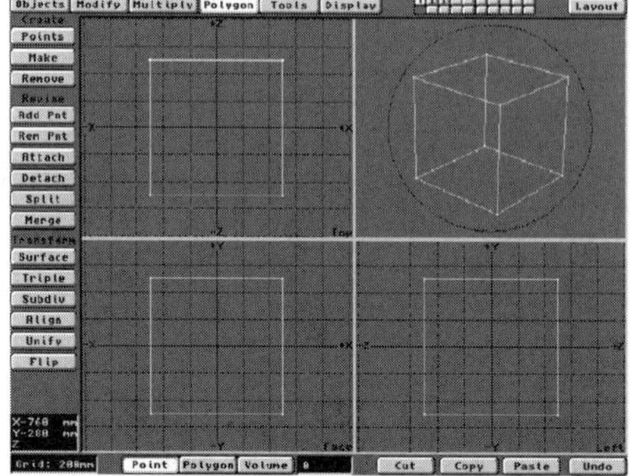

Figure 1: The default box before any Metaforming.

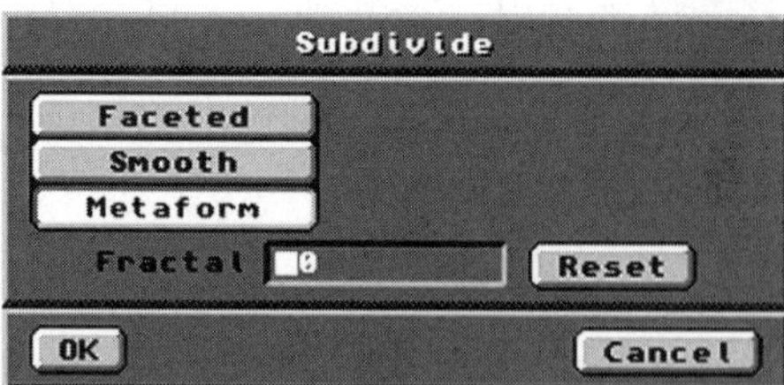

Figure 2: The Subdivide requester

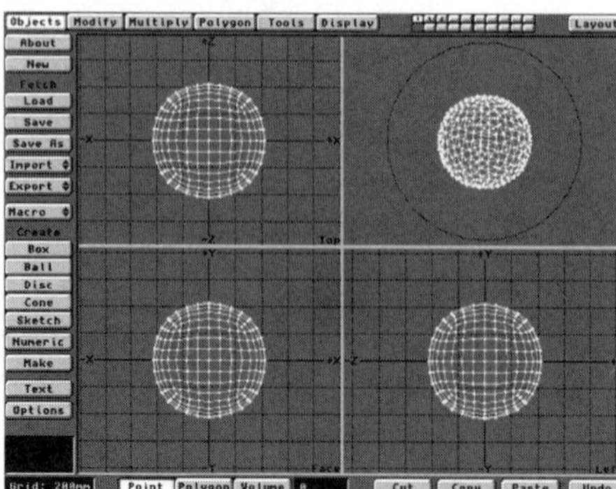

Figure 3: Two Metaforms on the box object pushed it into a sphere.

You've Got the Edge

The real power of Metaform unfolds when you start designing your objects with it in mind. Go to an empty layer to build a new box. Incidentally, the Next Empty Layer macro (nextempty.lwm) is quite useful here. If you are using the default macro keyboard commands you can use the **F6** key as the shortcut. [Editor's note: see Macro Basics in *LWPRO* issue No. 2, December 1993 for info on configuring the macro shortcuts].

As before, create a new box using the **Numeric** requester, but enter three Segments for X, Y and Z (Figure 4). This will create a box that has nine polygons to a side.

Copy and **Paste** this box into several other layers so we can return to the unaltered versions.

Select **Metaform** from the Subdivide requester (D) to get a smoothed version with rounded corners. Notice that the majority of the cube is still flat.

Perform another Metaform operation and notice that the corners and edges smooth out even more while maintaining the same basic cube shape (Figure 5).

Go to one of the other layers with the original segmented box and select all of the points in the middle left segment (Face view) using the right mouse lasso tool (Figure 6).

Select **Move** from the **Modify** menu (t) and move the selected points -220mm on the X axis. Holding the Control key down while you move will constrain movements to the axis you move along first.

Deselect these points and select the points composing the middle right segment. Move these points 220mm on the X axis so they are pushed in the opposite direction.

Repeat this process for all 'inner' segments of points, moving the points 220mm in the appropriate direction. You will have to go to another view in order to get all of the points moved properly. When you have moved all of your points, the object should look like the one pictured in Figure 6.

Use Metaform to round out the corners of this cube. If you compare these corners to the previous example, you'll find that there is a much smaller radius on the edges of this cube (Figure 7). This occurs because the segments were moved out towards the edges. Remember this when you want to control the amount of curve an edge has.

Something a Little More Complicated

Let's try something a bit more complex. If you read the review of LightWave 3.5 in the September issue of

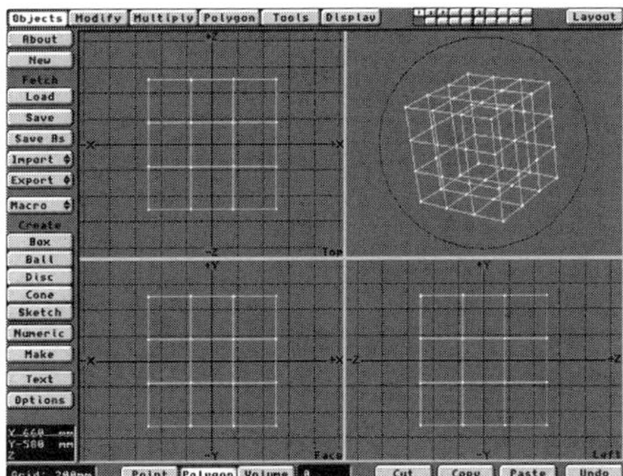

Figure 4: A three-segmented box prior to Metaforming.

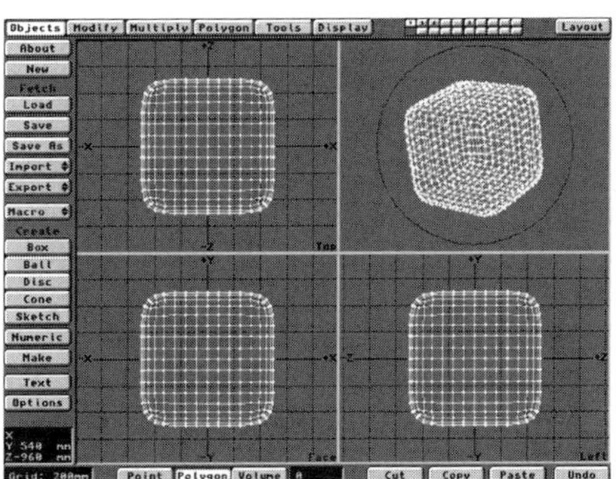

Figure 5: Two Metaform operations on the segmented box forming a rounded edges cube.

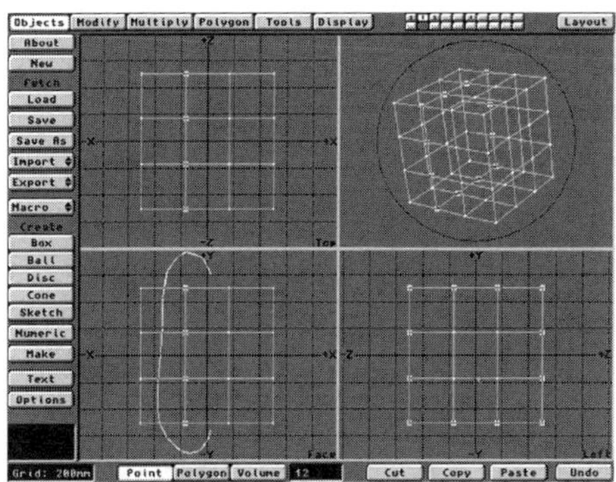

Figure 6: The segmented box after segments have been pushed towards the edge.

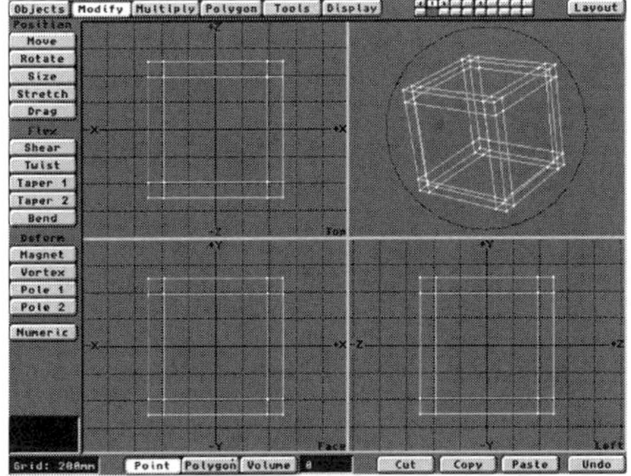

Figure 7: Pushing the segments towards the edges of the cube yields a tighter curved edge.

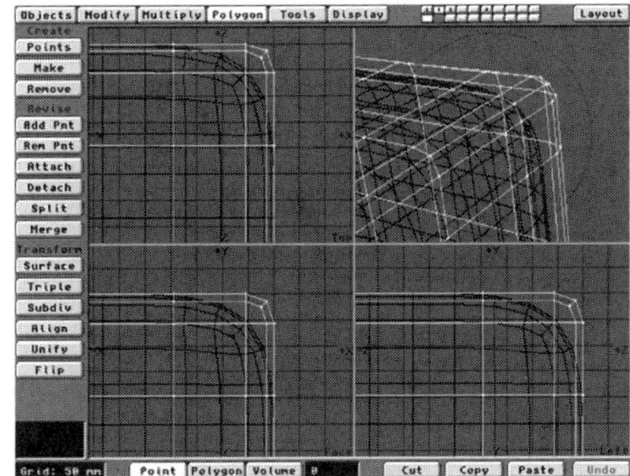

Figure 8: The results of our Boolean operation.

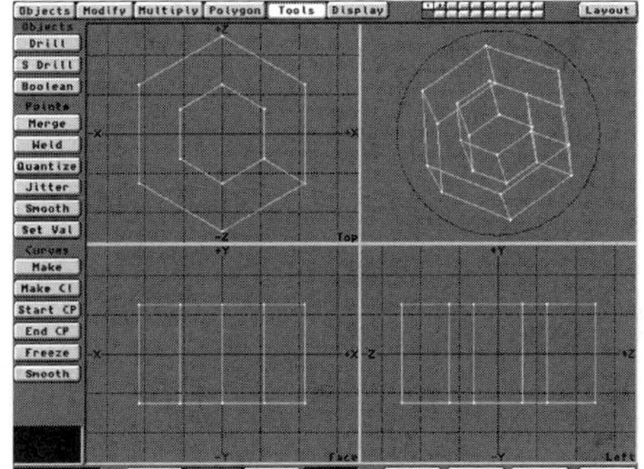

Figure 9: The disc with all quadrangles

VTU, you saw a chainlink-type object that had been Metaformed. I'll show you how fast a complicated object like this can be created.

Clear the Modeler screen by selecting **New** from the **Objects** menu. Select **Disc** and **Numeric** (n). Enter six Sides, -250 for Bottom and 250 for Top. Select the Y axis and make sure your units are set to mm. Leave all other values at their defaults. Select **OK** to close the requester, and **Make** (Return/Enter) to create the disc.

To make this easier to work on, **Rotate** the disc 30 degrees about the Y axis (from the center). The constrain key (Control) will constrain rotations to 15 degree increments if you use it.

Copy and Paste the disc into the next empty layer. In this new layer, select the **Stretch** tool from the **Modify** menu (h) and bring up the **Numeric** requester (n).

Enter Factors of 0.5, 2, and 0.5 for X, Y and Z. leave the rest at the defaults. Select **OK** to perform the Stretch operation. You now have the perfect beginnings of a successful Boolean operation.

Swap layers (') so the large, flatter disc is in the foreground while the taller disc is in the background layer.

Select **Boolean** from the Tools menu (B) and perform a **Subtract**. This will yield a disc with a hole cut through the middle (Figure 8).

Since subdivide options require three- or four-sided polygons, we must convert the top and bottom faces of our disc into quadrangles. Select the top and bottom polygons. A quick way to select them is to enter the Polygon Statistics requester (w) and select the two polygons that contain more than four vertices.

Metaform is a unique new way of subdividing polygons that allows you to create objects out of rough primitives and easily smooth them into gently curved objects.

Choose **Hide Uns** (=) from the **Display** menu to hide all of the other polygons. Deselect the bottom polygon and choose **Hide Uns** again leaving just the top polygon.

While this polygon is still selected, Choose the Point select button at the bottom of the interface and select the two points that are in the upper right quadrant of the Top view (not the two points lying on the Z axis) and then select **Split** from the **Polygon** menu. This will split the one big polygon into one large and one four-sided polygon.

Deselect these two points and select the next two in a counter clockwise manner. In addition, choose the Polygon select button to make sure that these two are within the new polygon that is selected. Select **Split** again.

Follow this procedure for the remaining sections, checking that you always have the proper starting polygon, until you have divided the original large polygon into six four-sided polygons.

Choose **Unhide** (\) to show all polygons and then select just the bottom, multi-point polygon and **Hide Uns** (=) all the rest to reveal just the bottom.

Repeat the process of splitting this polygon into quadrangles as outlined above. When finished, make sure all of your polygons are facing in the proper direction and Unhide everything (Figure 9).

Copy and **Paste** this object into the next empty layer. Select the first layer as a background layer to be used as a template.

Now we are going to take the object in the second layer, turn it sideways and attach it to the copy in the other layer. To turn it sideways, place your cursor in the Left view at the 0,0,0 location and press the 'r' key to rotate the object 90 degrees.

Now we need to move this object in the +X direction. If you select the four most positive X points of the original object and perform a point info (i) on them, you will discover that all of these points are located at 433.0127mm on the X axis (assuming you have followed all my directions correctly so far). Therefore, we know that we need to move the entire rotated

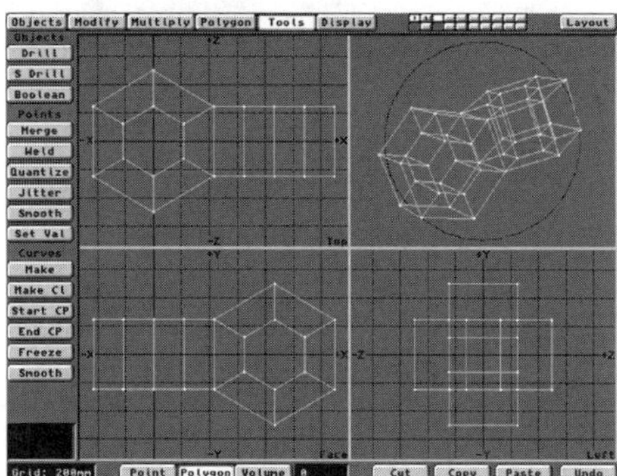

Figure 10: The primitive chainlink is shown above as part of Metaform's display.

object twice that distance to get the opposite ended points to match up.

Select **Move** (t) and the Numeric requester and enter 866.0254 for the X axis (make sure units are set to mm) and press **OK**. We're almost there!

Copy or **Cut** this object and **Paste** it into the first layer with the other disc. Select **Merge** from the **Tools** menu (m) and perform an automatic merge to get rid of all of the duplicated points. If you select the shared points between the two discs, you should get four points selected.

Lasso select the two shared polygons in the middle of the two discs and **Cut** them out. You should now be left with a primitive chainlink which takes much less time to actually build than reading about it (Figure 10).

Metaform this object a couple of times to get a unique shape that would have been extremely difficult to model with splines.

Render Away

Try rendering this link out to see how the object looks. You'll notice that Metaform does a great job of creating smooth, nice rendering curves. Make sure to check for non-planars (w) before saving and rendering Metaformed objects.

LWP

John Gross is the editor of LWPRO.

Modeler 3D Booleans Beginning to Advanced

By Grant Boucher

With enough new features to rank Modeler 3.0 as among the best on any platform, Stuart Ferguson, Modeler's chief architect, has provided powerful solutions to the most challenging modeling demands while maintaining the effortless and intuitive nature of the LightWave/Modeler environment. Paramount amongst these new features are the oft-demanded, but ill-understood, boolean operators.

This article will first take you through a simple tutorial and discussion of booleans, and then take you into uncharted territory with some real-world examples of their power and usefulness to the LightWave professional animator.

Boolean Background

Until now, most modeling in LightWave revolved around painstakingly crafting your own objects, point by point, polygon by polygon. This works very well for traditional subjects such as aircraft and automobiles, but how does one build a hole? How about a lot of them? Or Swiss cheese?

Similarly, combining two objects so that they weld into a seamless unit requires coplanar points so that polygons on both objects can be matched and merged (or welded). This is fine for small jobs, but how about joining a hierarchically created human hand, fingers, and joints?

The answer to these everyday modeling dilemmas is, of course, booleans. Booleans take their name from mathematics, but we'll leave the techno-speak right there. These tools in Modeler give us the ability to join objects together; drill holes through them; subtract one shape from the inside of another; and cut sections out of, or just punch holes through any object we want. Fortunately for us, Modeler makes it all so easy

For all of the accompanying examples, and all boolean operations, a basic rule must be followed. The object to be drilled, cut, sliced, or otherwise modified must be within your foreground (white or highlighted) layer, while the object to do the drilling, cutting, or slicing must be located in the background (black or darkened) layer. Refer to the accompanying illustrations for examples.

All of the examples use the apple that comes with LightWave in the Food subdirectory as the source object to be acted upon.

Note that the boolean functions are located in the Tools section of Modeler in the Objects subsection. While the three subsets of functions are separately named Drill (or Template Drill), S Drill (or Solid Drill), and Boolean (or CSG Boolean), they are all collectively referred to as the Boolean Operators sections of Modeler.

Template Drill

The four Template Drill functions require the background (or template) object to be a 2D polygon. These are the quickest and simplest of the boolean operations.

Template Drill/Core

In Layer 1, load the apple object from the Food subdirectory. Autosize the display (the "a" hotkey) and go to Layer 2. Select Layer 1 as the background (for now only). Using the Objects/Disc tool, create a flat disk (i.e., no Z depth) in the Face window and place it so that it lies over the apple object somewhere. See Figure 1 for a suggested configuration. Note that it does not matter where along the Z axis the disk resides as long as it "intersects" the apple from the Face view.

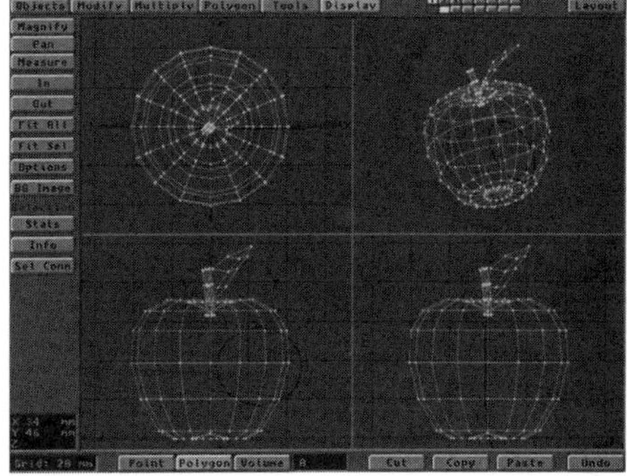

Figure 1

Also note that you might want to change your display to a Solid Moving one for the rest of these tutorials. Now, begin by selecting Layer 1 as your foreground and Layer 2 as a background. Select the Template Drill tool, then the Core button, the Z axis button, and finally, OK.

What should be left behind are whatever apple polygons fit within the boundaries of the disc object you created in the background, much like cutting out the core of an apple and throwing away the rest. Note that new points and polygons were created so that the core perfectly fits the shape we gave it. Also notice that only the outer skin of the apple remains; no internal polygons were created to give the core the illusion of solidity. We'll do that later.

Template Drill/Tunnel

If you haven't changed anything since performing the Core operation, a simple Undo will get us back to the solid apple again for our next tutorial. Otherwise, load a new apple object into another layer or cut out the left over core and reload the apple into Layer 1.

We're going to use the same background or template, object (i.e., the disc) as we did last time, so again select the apple as the foreground object and the disc as the background object. This time, select Template Drill, Tunnel, Z axis, OK and notice the effect.

We have essentially performed the reverse of Core, as we throw away any polygons that fit within the background or template object's shape and keep the rest. Again, the apple is a shell of its former self as no internal surfaces are created in this process.

Template Drill/Stencil

It is important to note that the LightWave 3.0 manual went to press before the Emboss feature was renamed to Stencil. Otherwise, all of the manual entries are correct; just cross out Emboss and replace it with Stencil if it becomes confusing.

One Undo or reset of your layers later and we can perform a Template Drill/Stencil on our apple, right? Not so fast. Notice that the requester has some surfacing options. Change the Default surface name to Apple Bite, click on the Rename (or Create) button; then hit Return or click the OK button, making sure that the Z axis is still chosen.

You will see that your polygons are split along the lines of your template object but nothing has been removed. Select the Polygons button at the bottom of the screen and press the W hotkey. Change the Surface Name to Apple Bite and press the + button next to With Surface. Select OK and you will see all of the polygons that were within the template object's shape are now highlighted, as they have been assigned the surface name Apple Bite.

This operation is the same as Core plus Tunnel, but both pieces of the drilled apple are left behind, with the inner piece polygons given the new surface name you selected. You can now cut the selected polygons and move them to another layer if you want to.

Template Drill/Slice

Getting back to our default apple over disc layers configuration, perform a Template Drill/Slice operation and you will see the same results as in Template Drill/Stencil. This time, however, all polygons retain their starting surface names. Neither the inner, nor the outer polygons will be renamed to anything new.

Solid Drill

All of the operations detailed above under Template Drill required the use of a 2D drill bit to punch a hole straight through our apple, along a selected axis with no option for more complex 3D kinds of operations. In general, Solid Drill performs the exact same operations as Template Drill, but our background, or template, object can be any 3D shape. In short, use Template Drill when you are drilling straight through an object, and Solid Drill when the drill changes direction or shape as it passes through.

To demonstrate the Solid Drill functions, we'll need to create a 3D object in our background layer. I chose a cone so that the object changes in more than one axis (see Figure 2). If the object was, for example, a cylinder the effect would be the same as a Template Drill (i.e., straight through). With a cone object, the

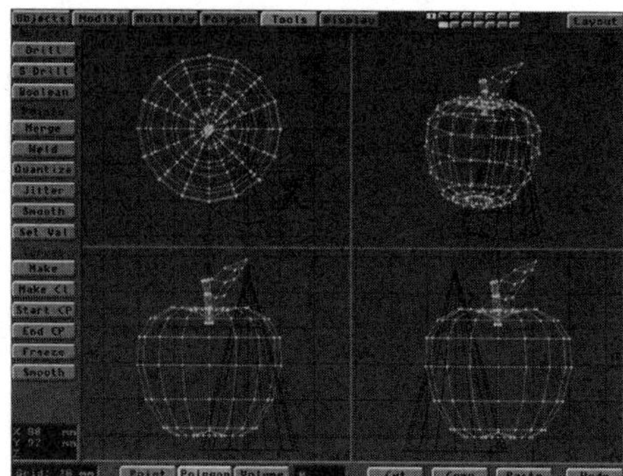

Figure 2

effect varies throughout the apple. Note that Solid Drill requires that your objects be solid (i.e., no holes in it) and intersect each other. After you get comfortable with the Solid Drill tools, try the same operations on an object with a hole in it and see if you can see what is going wrong.

Solid Drill/Core

Instead of leaving the insides of a punched hole in our apple like with Template Drill/Core, when you Solid Drill/Core a solid like a cone into an apple, the apple polygons that fit entirely within the volume of the cone are left behind.

Solid Drill/Tunnel

Just as Template Drill/Tunnel performs the reverse of Template Drill/Core, Solid Drill/Tunnel has the opposite effect of Solid Drill/Core. Now, any apple polygons that are outside the volume of the background cone object are left behind, while anything within the cone's volume is discarded.

Solid Drill/Stencil

When we Solid Drill/Stencil a cone into an apple we are left with both the polygons within the boundaries of the cone template and outside the boundaries. But they have been separated where the two objects intersected and the inner polygons have been given a new surface name we selected within the Solid Drill/Stencil requester.

Solid Drill/Slice

The result of performing a Solid Drill/Slice of our cone into our apple is identical to performing a Solid Drill/ Stencil above; however, all polygons retain their original surface names, both those inside and outside of the cone object template.

Boolean(CSG Boolean)

We have now arrived at the real heart of the boolean operator's section of Modeler. The CSG stands for Constructive Solid Geometry, which is the branch of 3D mathematics upon which these new Modeler functions are based.

These functions are similar to our previous Template and Solid Drill operations, but are different in that they can modify two solid objects in many ways; the result is always another solid object, not a polygonal shell. In other words, when you punch a hole, inside surfaces are left behind.

For this series of tutorials, we can use the Toroid Macro to create a torus (or donut-shaped object) for our background layer. I used the default settings for a torus and then used the Modify/Size and Modify/Move commands until I got a torus of the exact size and position I was looking for (see Figure 3).

CSG Boolean/Union

Causing the torus to Boolean/Union with the apple creates an entirely new object, which is shaped like an apple that bulges out in the middle like a torus. All interior polygons that existed within both objects are removed, and all of the remaining polygons retain their original surface names.

Notice that Modeler has created new points at the places where the two objects intersect in space and

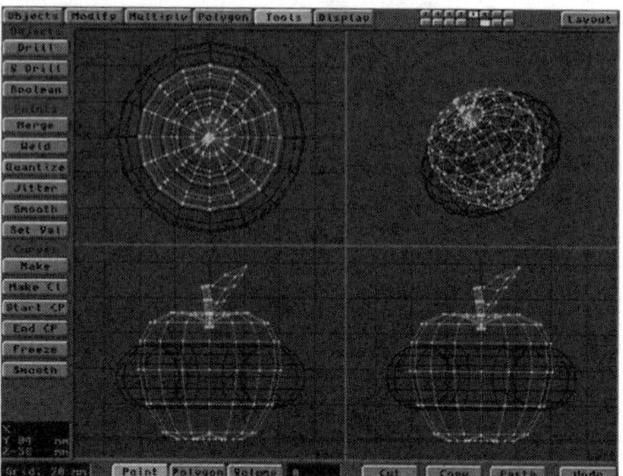

Figure 3

created new polygons to go along with them. The new object is therefore one complete solid unit and the joints can now be Phong smoothed across (if the Smoothing Angle setting permits) in LightWave's surfaces requester.

CSG Boolean/Intersect

CSG Boolean/Intersect is the opposite effect of CSG Boolean/Union in a mathematical sense. Instead of removing whatever points and polygons the two objects did not have in common, CSG Boolean/Intersect, removes everything that the two objects *do* have in common, leaving only the interior portions of the two objects behind.

This means that the portions of the torus that intersect, or overlap, with the apple will be retained.

CSG Boolean/Subtract

By far the most popular boolean function (and the one that is the default choice), the CSG Boolean/Subtract has powerful modeling possibilities. As can be seen by performing a CSG Boolean/Subtract on the apple with the torus, any object can be used to carve out a chunk from another object. In addition, any basic solid form or primitive can be drilled or sliced by other solids or primitives quickly creating extremely complex shapes that might be impossible or at least very expensive and time consuming to create using any other modeling method.

CSG Boolean/Add

Appearing to perform the same function as union, doing a CSG Boolean/Add on an apple with a torus will leave you with both the results of a CSG Boolean/Union and CSG Boolean/Subtract in the same layer. The points and subdivided polygons that mark the intersection of these two objects will be present, of course. This is the CSG Boolean version of the Template Drill and Solid Drill Stencil commands.

Important Notes

While the examples here involve relatively few polygons and are quick and easy to perform, you will undoubtedly be trying these techniques on much more complicated objects, especially if you follow along with the advanced examples below. In that case, if time is becoming critical, the LightWave manual recommends selecting only the polygons in your foreground layer (the object to be affected) that will obviously be involved in any boolean operation. This will allow Modeler to perform its calculations only on the polygons it needs, thus providing significant savings on time.

As soon as you feel comfortable with these operations, read the discussion on pages 51-52 of the LightWave manual on how boolean operations can be affected by the direction of your object's polygons. A thorough essay that should be read until completely understood, it will solve many of your advanced boolean problems and may even give you some new ideas.

Booleans-Advanced Examples

The tutorials above help in understanding the basics of Modeler's boolean tools, but the following examples and ideas should aid professional and amateur LightWave animators alike in developing their boolean IQ.

Window with a View

One of the growing uses for computer graphics imaging applications like LightWave remains architectural walk-throughs and elevations. One way of completing your building and home models is to construct them board by board, nail by nail, digitally recreating the underlying skeleton of the building to be rendered. Since most buildings constructed today were designed on a computer, and LightWave contains built-in routines for importing most of today's most common 3D dataset/model formats (i.e., Autocad DXF, Wavefront, and 3D Studio), this often turns out to be the easiest route to take for preexisting designs. But, what if the building is old, or in any case, you do not have access to 3D digital data regarding its design and construction? It seems ridiculously time-consuming to build every 2x4, especially when your client will never see it. However, those 2x4s set the positions of doors, windows, skylights, staircase openings between floors, recessed closets, and many other "holes" in your superstructure. It is much easier and faster to build the rough shape of your house, with large, flat unbroken walls and then punch out the doors, windows with boolean operators like Template Drill (for depthless items like windows panes) or Boolean/Subtract (if the depth of a doorway is required).

Let's do an example. In Layer 1, create a box using the Numeric default settings. Copy that box to Layer 2 and leave it there for now. Return to Layer 1 and select the topmost face. Use the Polygon/Triple tool, reselect the top polygons and then use the Polygon/Subdivide-Faceted tool to turn the top of the house into eight triangular polygons. Select the points directly in the center of the top polygons as seen in the Face View and move them up the Y axis until you have what appears to be a very crude house (hold down the CTRL key as you move then up to constrain the Move tool to Y only). You might also want to select the bottom most points of the box and raise them up to Y=0 just to make things look more natural. When finished, your object should look something like Figure 4.

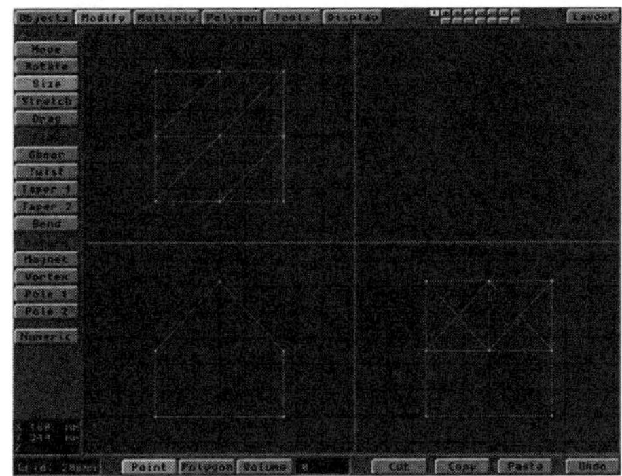

Figure 4

Now, if we were to start punching holes in this simple house, we would have a lot of windows and doors with no depth, or tunnel-like holes running through what appeared to be a solid chunk of house. In order to give our boolean windows and doors depth, we need to have both inner and outer walls in our home. Copy the house in Layer 1 and paste it into Layer 3. Select Layer 3 as your foreground object and Layer 1 as your background object and use the Modify/Size-Numeric command to shrink the foreground layer house to about 95 percent of its original size (use 0,0,0, as the center). Select the Polygon/Flip command so that our new interior faces points inward and cut and paste the contents of Layer 3 into Layer 1. See Figure 5 for a reference.

We now have a house with an inside and an outside, but no way out or in! Return to Layer 2 and Modify Move, Size, or Stretch the box into the shape and position of a door, using Layer 1 as the background layer as a reference. However, make the door thicker than the wall just to make sure our hole punches all the way through.

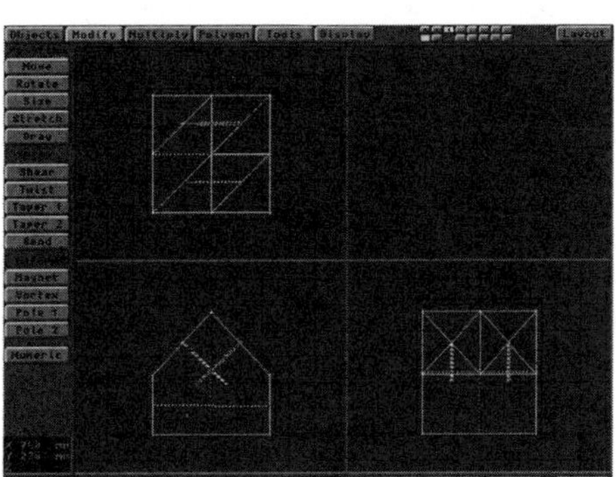

Figure 5

Now ready to cut our doorway out of the house, select Layer 1 (the house) as the foreground and Layer 2 (the door) as the background; use the Boolean/Subtract command and notice the result. You should be able to see completely though the doorway and into the house when you render a test or use a solid moving display to view your object in Modeler.

By changing the shape and position of the door in the background layer, we can create windows, side doors, and skylights. It's up to you to experiment with something a bit more substantial.

Text Cuts

Here's a classy use of booleans. You should already be familiar with Modeler's powerful Postscript Text creation tool, so let's take it a few steps further.

Select the Olnova Font with the Buffered Corners option and enter a mythical company name like "Sun Kissed" for our test. After a moment, use the default Multiply Extrude settings to extrude our new flat 3D logo in the Z direction. Proceed to an open layer and create a Tessellation Level 3 sphere, with the Ball-Numeric Requester, that is larger than the logo; position it so that it overlaps the extruded logo as seen in Figure 6. Make sure the logo is in your background layer as a guide. You may have to stretch the depth of the Logo to get the desired effect.

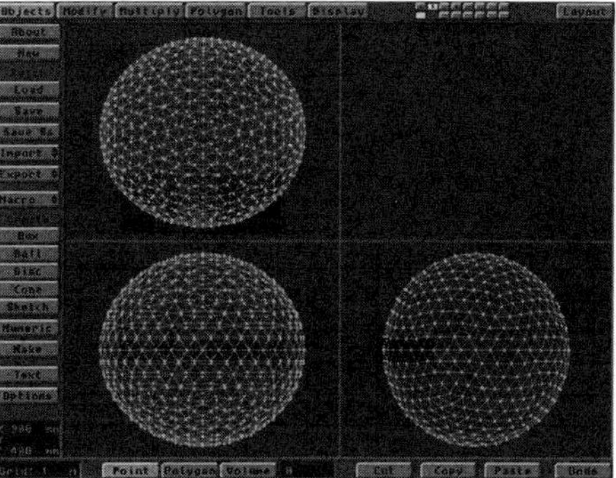

Figure 6

Select the Boolean/Subtract tool and wait until the operation completes. Export the new object to LightWave where we can load the OrangePeel surface from the Surfaces requester. You might need to change the Phong Smoothing Angle to 44.5 degrees to get the right effect.

The concept applies to beveled fonts cutting holes in wood objects like router bits as well as creating footprints in modeled sand or concrete.

Swiss Cheese and Asteroids

It should be easy to see how to make a wedge of Swiss cheese using Boolean/Subtract with some spheres in the background layer and a triangular wedge in the foreground. But here's a shortcut for your next space scene.

The new LightWave manual includes an excellent example of how to make an asteroid by repeated use of the Subdivide - Smooth and Jitter tools in the Modeler. However, this can leave your asteroid looking more like a wad of crumpled paper than a true deep space menace. What we need are some craters. I found a really easy way to make detailed asteroid craters is to put one copy of your asteroid object in the foreground layer and then a smaller version in the background layer. Position so the two objects intersect only partially and perform a Boolean/Subtract. Do this a half dozen times if your asteroid is small with large craters, and maybe twenty times or more if you want a lot of small craters on one large asteroid.

Apply a rough bump and diffuse map to get a rocky look (I overuse an 8-bit version of the Rock texture found in Leo Martin's ProTextures I) and your favorite spaceship to complete the scene.

Bad Apples and Fly-Throughs

Here's an interesting example of combining a few of Modeler's new features to create very simply and nearly impossible modeling/animating tasks. Load your apple object into the Layout and create some keyframes where your camera travels from outside the apple to inside, makes a few turns within, and then comes out the other side. Don't worry about rotation, just position. Once you have it the way you'd like, open the Motion Graph for the camera and turn Align to Path on and enter 10 or 15 for the Look Ahead (frames) value. While there, you might want to look at the velocity graph and adjust the Tension of any kinks or knots in your motion path. You can slide the Tension values with the mouse while holding down the "t" key on your keyboard for an interactive Tension control setting. Test your fly-through of the apple with

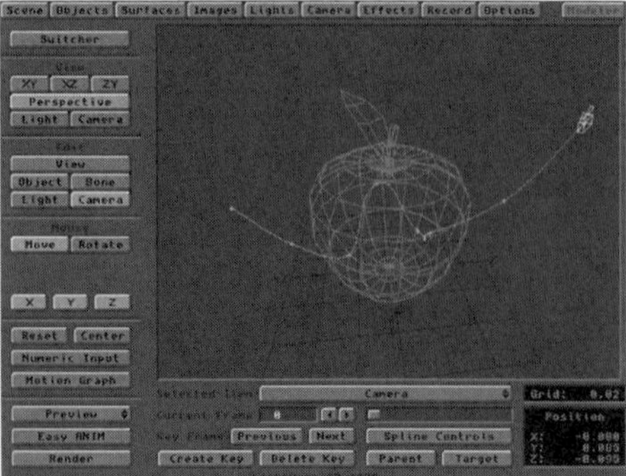

Figure 7

LightWave's wireframe preview features until you get it just right. See Figure 7 for an example.

Now, return to the Motion Graph settings and save the motion settings to a file called AppleFlythrough or something similar. Proceed to Modeler and import the apple into Layer 1 and create a small disc about the origin in Layer 2. Make sure the disc is in the XY plane and is centered at 0,0,0 (Figure 8). Select the apple as your background layer and proceed to the Multiply menu

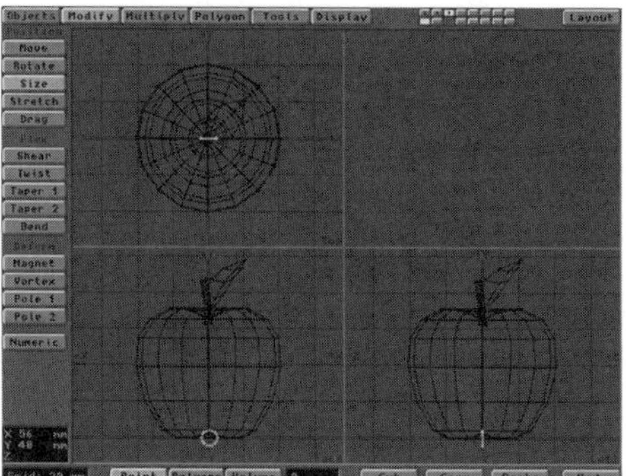

Figure 8

and click on the Path Extrude tool. Select the AppleFlythrough motion in the requester and select OK in the Motion path Extrude requester without making any changes since we want to use our entire motion file.

The path our camera makes through the apple is the basis for our 3D tube. Select the apple as your foreground layer and the Motion Path Tube object as your background layer and activate Boolean/Subtract in the Tools menu. In a few seconds, you will be left with the apple with a hole running through it that perfectly matches the camera path in Layout. Export the new apple object to replace the one left in Layout then check for yourself by returning to LightWave's layout.

Now, select the Camera view and render a wireframe preview. Before rendering any final tests though, rename the Default surface in LightWave's surfaces requester to Apple Insides and turn Smoothing on.

Note that this technique works just as well for flying- through asteroids and for building roller coasters from one tie, two rails, and a path that looks fun. Similarly, you can honeycomb the interior of an object by repeatedly subtracting a path or paths in the same fashion as above. If you wish to save this apple object, make sure to use a different name so as not to overwrite the original.

Grant Boucher is currently CGI Art Director for Nick Jr., Nickelodeon Studios, Florida

Useful Boolean Tips

- Boolean and drilling tools always work with two layers. The "cutter" is in the background layer and the "cuttee" is in the foreground layer.
- Drill (Template Drill) and S Drill (Solid Drill) work exactly the same except that S Drill uses solid objects while Drill can use a cutter that is a single plane. If you have a Drill panel open that allows you to select an axis for the drilling function, you are dealing with Template Drill which can use a single plane as its cutter.
- When using Template Drill, it doesn't matter where on the "cutting axis" the cutter is placed. It does not have to be intersecting the object to be cut.
- Use the ' key to swap foreground and background layers to make switching between objects easier.
- When using boolean operations on complicated objects, you can speed up the process by only selecting the polygons on the "cuttee" that will be affected by the boolean operation. Modeler will take into account only these polygons while computing the operation. If you do not select any polygons, Modeler will take into account *all* polygons and the operation will be slower.
- After performing a boolean function, merging points in the boolean area may result in "puckers" in the rendered object. One of the ways around this is to not merge points or try using a smaller Max Smoothing Angle for the surface in LightWave.
- If a boolean operation isn't working quite right, make sure the objects have been cleaned up. There should be no single or two point polygons; no doubled polygons; and no non-planar polygons.

-JG

Understanding Modeler Macros

by Mojo

In the April issue of *LightWavePRO*, I reviewed PowerMacros from CineGraphics and explained how wonderful it is to have complicated work done automatically.

However, I completely forgot to mention that macros come with the Toaster at no extra charge. These little utilities are tremendous time-savers and often perform tasks that would otherwise be impossible.

Unfortunately, these macros are not well documented, and it's been up to the user to decipher how to make them work. This overview should make your macro quest more successful.

Cachelin's World

Most of the macros to be described were written by NewTek's Arnie Cachelin, a mathematical expert. He has lent his expertise to help decrypt some of their more complex functions for this article.

For those who have never used Toaster macros before, the December '93 issue of *LWPRO* contains Cachelin's reference section for macros, offering a description of the basic functions of each one. This month's report offers a deeper look into the functions of a few of these.

Getting Started

All macros are run from the Macro pop-up menu found under Modeler's Object menu. To execute one, simply click on the macro button and select one as you would a normal Amiga menu item. If you don't see any listed, select the **<< Configure List >>** option. This calls up the macro list editor. Load the file **Modeler Macro List**, and you should have a directory ready to go. Not every macro is automatically listed, but you may add new ones with the handy **Add Macro** macro, which should now be part of your default list. Once you've completed a list, save it from the <<Configure List>> panel with a new name, and it will be loaded whenever you boot Modeler.

To avoid going to the macro button, assign your favorite macros to the function keys. Simply select **<< Configure Keys >>** from the macro list and click the arrow button to the far right of a function key slot. Simply click the macro you wish to assign to that key, and your shortcut is complete. All that's needed is to hit that function key to run the corresponding macro; further saving of the macro list is not necessary.

Logo World

There's a lot of money to be made with flying logos, and the people who work hard at it also manage to produce some pretty neat stuff. Of course, these top-notch flying logos can be difficult and time-consuming to construct, so several macros were created to help shave a few hours off that pesky work.

Logotron works as a replacement for Modeler's standard **Text** creation button. Simply start the macro, type in your text and choose a style. **Flat** produces simple 2D lettering; **Block** creates extruded text; **Chisel** adds a nice bevel to your lettering; and **Round** uses multiple bevels to add a rounded edge. Logotron also allows you to specify the depth of the extrusion and the edge width of the bevel. It even names front and side surfaces. Great-looking text is now only one easy step away.

Text offers the same features as Logotron, but permits up to four lengthy lines of text to be created (remember that you can continue typing past the inset box). It offers basic word-processing features such as left, right and centered justification of text. The **Center** button stretches the width of each line to justify right and left, while the **Scale** option sizes each line equally on the X and Y axis to avoid distortion, producing lines of varying height. The **% leading** option lets you dictate how much space to put between the lines. Thanks to this macro, your days of cutting and pasting text to create 3D messages are over.

Curve Text can really be a timesaver. It lets you create 3D text in the same styles as Text and Logotron, but also bends text around any axis (Figure 1). The **Radius** option lets you specify how tight a circle your text should be wrapped around—the more letters used, the larger the radius should be.

The **Spacing** parameter determines the gap between characters and can be a big help when wrapping a short logo around a large circle. It may also be necessary to increase this if a high-edge width is used for your bevel.

Figure 1A: Curved text around the Z axis. This option is the least problematic.

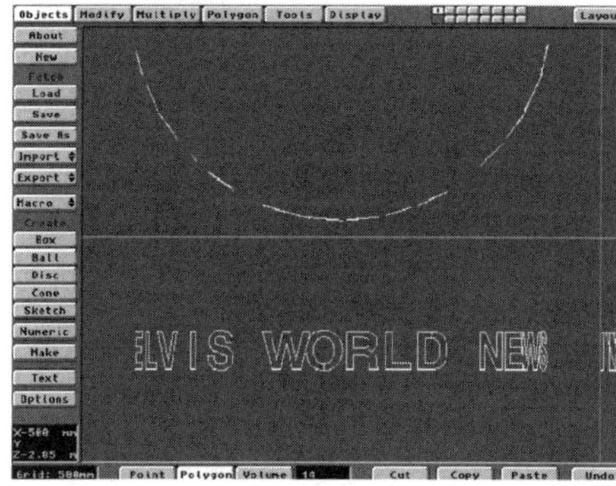

Figure 1B: Curved text around the Y axis. I had to make sure the radius was wide enough to remove the bothersome mirror images created by this option.

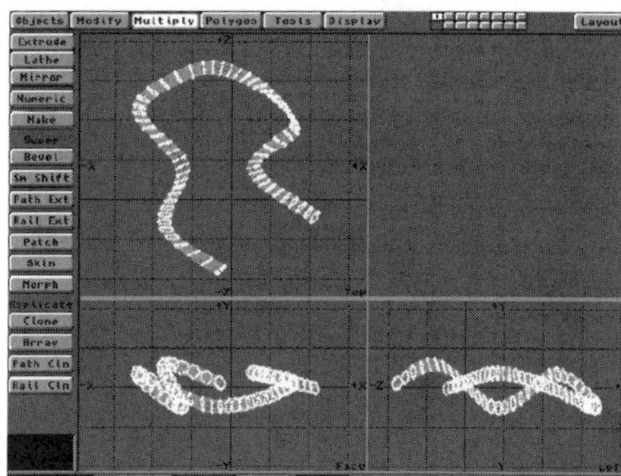

Figure 1C: Curved text around the X axis. Completely useless? You decide!

When wrapping text around the Y axis, try to keep the bend to a semicircle. Unfortunately, this option creates a copy of your text and mirrors it. If the text bends more than a half circle, characters may overlap and deleting them can be difficult. Hopefully, this can be fixed in a future version.

There may be hundreds of Postscript fonts at your fingertips, but do you find yourself always using the same dozen or so? The macro **LoadFonts** can help you avoid the tedious task of calling them up again and again. Load the macro itself into a text editor and follow its instructions on how to edit the list. While typing in your favorite fonts, they can be subsequently loaded into Modeler by simply running this macro.

Although these little ARexx wonders are a great aid in logo creation, they have a few quirks that you should keep in mind. The macros don't keep the changes made to numeric variables (such as radii and edge width), so you may want to jot down those numbers on a piece of paper when experimenting. And although the Text and Logotron macros remember text, Curve Text does not.

When creating text, remember that the **Flat** option makes the front and back faces of text with no edges unless the **Extrude Depth** is set to zero. All the depth options also have an odd habit of creating the extrusions in two segments, which almost doubles the number of polygons in the text. There's not much you can do about this, since deleting one of the segments also removes back faces. However, text rendering is usually easy on processor time, so don't worry too much about it—the benefits of these tools far outweigh their meager drawbacks.

Particle World

Single-point polygons (like the ones used to make starfields) are generally referred to as particles. Many advanced effects, such as explosions and underwater debris, can be achieved by using conglomerations of them, but working with several of the effects can be a frustrating experience. Thankfully, there are several macros that ease the process.

Of all 3D tasks, modeling is probably the most time-consuming and laborious.

Random Surface Points covers an object's surface with points and places this distribution in the next available layer. You'll end up with a scattering of points in the shape of the source object (Figure 2). By turning these points into single-point polygons (use the macro **Points to Polys**), this particle object could be used as an element in an explosion scene with the Space Fighter. Imagine exploding sparks that begin in the shape of the object being destroyed. (Watch for future issues of *LWPRO* for more details on creating explosions).

The Random Surface Points macro can also help you when modeling. LightWave author Allen Hastings recently wanted to cover a 3D landscape with trees, but found it difficult to place them precisely on top of such a non-linear surface. Using this macro, points were automatically scattered over the surface of the landscape. These points, now residing in a separate background layer, were used as a basis for the macro **Particle Clone**, which uses background points as a placement reference when cloning a desired foreground object. The cloned object's origins are located at the individual point locations when this macro is completed.

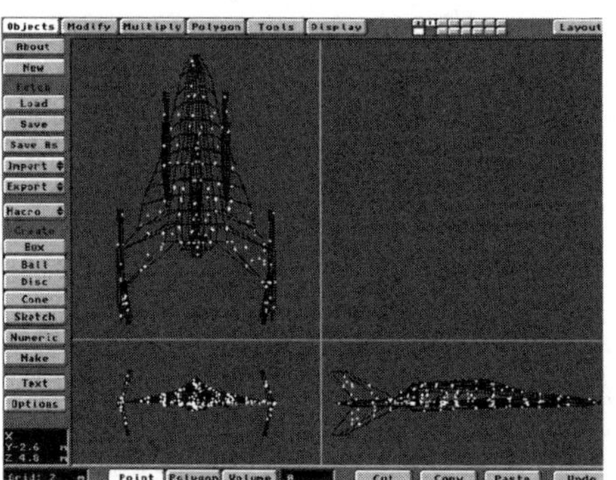

Figure 2: Here's an example of how Random Surface Points created a series of particles in the shape of the famous SpaceFighter object (seen in background layer).

Point Distribution creates filled scatterings of particles in spherical or cubic shapes (adjustable along X, Y and Z axes). Although many options are available to tailor your shape, only the **Falloff Towards Center** or **Edges** make any noticeable difference. I experimented with a wide range of variables and was unable to produce anything dramatically different from the macro's default settings. However, it is still quite useful for producing star fields, sparks, snow, rain and other particle-related objects.

In addition, particle distributions can be modified to produce bizarre animations. Here's a good example: Run the macro **Plane of Points**. This creates a 2D wall of points (lower the default number from 50 to 25 to save time). Now execute **Points to Polys** to transform the points into single-point polygons. (This is very important. Otherwise, points created by these macros will not be visible.) Save this object. Now run **Wrap to Sphere**. This transforms all the points in the plane into a spherical shape (you should later try **Spherize**, which stretches the 2D plane into a flat circle). **Save** this object as a morph target for the plane and **Load** it and the plane into **Layout**. Try executing a 30-frame morph with these objects and enjoy the results.

Remember that all of Modeler's tools work with single-point polygons as well as normal faces. This means that particles can be bent, stretched, swirled, magnetized and sliced into whatever shapes you like.

Modeler World

Of all 3D tasks, modeling is probably the most time-consuming and laborious. Fortunately, there are now a few macros available to do some of this work for us.

Halve reduces an object's size by half and allows it to retain its position in Modeler. Without this macro, an object offset from 0,0,0 would be shifted towards the center when sized. Halve prevents this without making it necessary to numerically enter the object's coordinates into the sizing requester.

Spline Cage is a useful tool for anyone having difficulty with spline patching. Perhaps the most difficult step in this task involves linking spline curves in a proper sequence. This macro, by default, produces a multifaceted, curve-based cylinder ready to be patched (Figure 3). By starting with this basic cage, it is quite easy to drag the points into new shapes. While it still may take some time to produce your desired results, you will avoid the problem of winding up with splines that cannot be patched. *[Editor's note: For more information on patching, see "Spline Patching Pitfalls" in this issue.]*

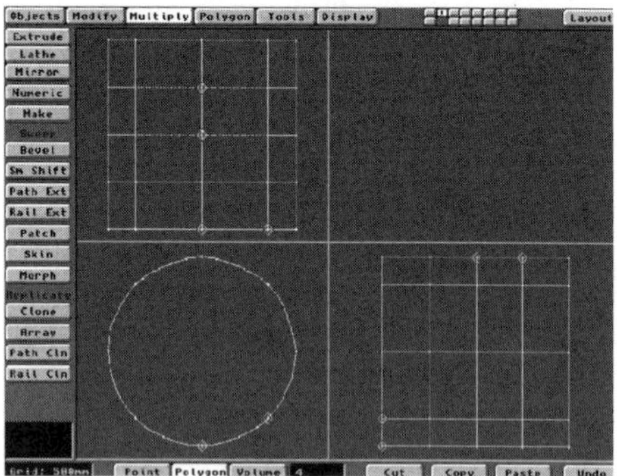

Figure 3: Creating even this simple set of splines for patching would produce a headache. Think of all the money you'll save on aspirin with the Spline Cage macro.

Router is a beveling tool that performs complex, multibevel operations in a single, user-definable step. You have control over the number of bevels, their depth and edge width (Figure 4).

Not for the faint of heart, the default settings of **Parametric Curve** automatically makes a spring as either a spline curve, polygon, solid tube or cloning path. However, to make a custom shape, you need the mathematical definition of a curve in parametric form (meaning equations for X, Y and Z). A solid understanding of trigonometry and precalculus is a necessity. If you feel up to it, the book *Calculus and Analytic Geometry*, published by Addison Wesley, may help. (The motion-path generator **Make Motion** uses a similar set of variables).

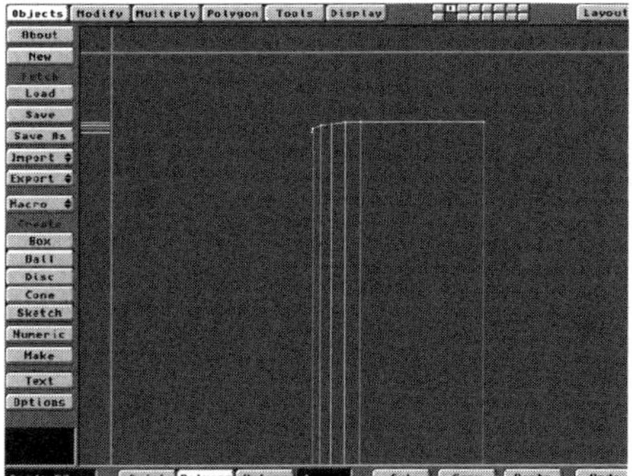

Figure 4A: A box with the front polygon selected was subjected to the rigor of the Router macro. The Round option gave us what is seen. This feature would be handy for making transparent objects since edge transparency works best with a rounded object.

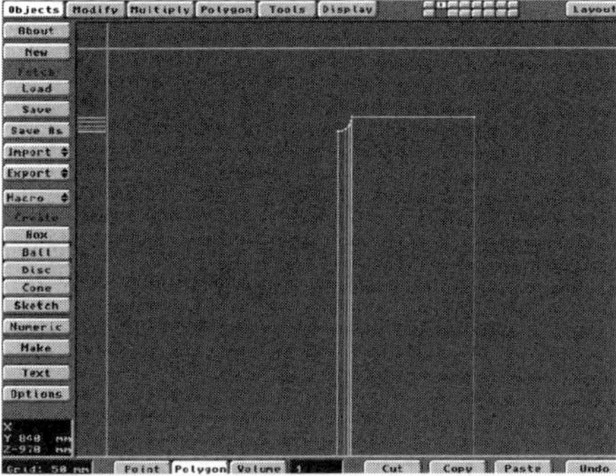

Figure 4B: The Hollow option produces a semi-reversed rounded edge.

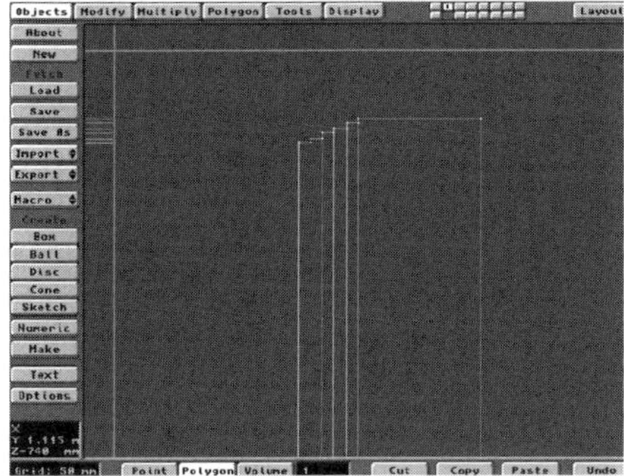

Figure 4C: Want to make a staircase the easy way? Try Router's Stairstep option.

Weird Tubes lives up to its name. Along any axis you choose, or at random, this macro builds plumbing consisting of tubes, boxes and balls. Although it was created to facilitate building small details in machinery, I can see this macro being used to create funky-looking structures or to spice up a Tim Burtonesque scene. In addition, various surfaces are assigned to help detail your bizarre creation.

Layout World

As stated earlier, although run from Modeler, some of these macros can help you build great scene files by eliminating bothersome, hard work in Layout.

Ever try to create an animation of a roller-coaster ride? Getting your camera to hug the tracks is no simple task. **Path to Motion**, however, makes it relatively easy by converting any spline-based Modeler curve into a motion file.

After creating the object you want the camera to truck along (tracks, a wormhole tube, etc.), select a single row of points along its surface and make a curve out of them in a separate layer. Run **Path to Motion** and input the number of frames you want the movement to use. **Skip Last Point** is an option you'll probably want to use; otherwise the camera hesitates when it reaches the end of the path. **Skip First Point** actually eliminates the first part of the move, which may or may not be useful. A motion file will be saved in the RAM disk to load into your camera's motion channel.

Remember to select the **Align to Path** (Motion Graph) option for the camera to point in the direction it's moving. If you'd like to rotate the camera independently of its movement, parent the camera to a null object, assign the motion path to the null and rotate the camera however you wish.

Keep in mind that the velocity along the path is linked to the space between points.

Keep in mind that the velocity along the path is linked to the space between points. The camera (or whatever object the path is assigned to) moves faster between more distant points. This would work well in the case of a roller coaster since the curved areas naturally contain more points than the straightaways. If you want a constant velocity, drag the points in your curve to evenly space them and perhaps even add a few points if you need to maintain the integrity of the curve.

It would be easier to approach the project from the other side. Start with your curve, save it as a motion path, than use the curve as a basis for a path extrude to make your object. Also remember that since the Sketch tool can be used to create curves, this macro allows for the freehand creation of motion paths.

On *Babylon 5* and *seaQuest DSV*, animators very often need to attach multiple light sources to objects, usually to serve as lens flares to simulate light beams, engine exhaust and running lights. The results are wonderful, but in the past, it meant a lot of time was spent carefully positioning lights on top of precise locations around the objects in Layout. Now with the macro **LightSwarm**, scene files are automatically created that do this.

The macro works by creating a scene in which lights are assigned to the positions dictated by points in Modeler. Begin by selecting the points on an object (or creating new ones) in the positions where you want lights to exist. After running LightSwarm, you are asked for a scene name and then given a requester to define parameters for two sets of lights for each point. This is beneficial in cases where you want a lens flare to have different qualities (such as color) than the actual light source. The second light-option name is defaulted to _OG, for *Outer Glow*, for cases in which two lens flares are needed in the same location to produce the desired effect. If you only want one light for each point, simply cancel the second set of options by deselecting the **Outer Glow Light** checkbox.

Now enter Layout and load the scene file containing the LightSwarm information. If you already have a scene in progress, make sure to choose the **Load From Scene** (Objects) option so the existing scene isn't cleared out.

The LightSwarm scene is created with all of the generated lights parented to a Null object, so their locations can remain relative to the Modeler choices. The idea is to parent the Null object to the main object, and then your lights will be in place.

Unfortunately, the macro errs by not telling LightWave the proper place to find the Null. You can get around this by creating a Null object in (or moving one into) the Toaster/3D directory. If a Null is located here, there won't be a problem with LightWave being unable to find it when you load your LightSwarm scene.

End of the World

I must stress how important it is to have pen and paper handy when experimenting with these macros. After a macro has been executed in most cases, it returns to the default settings. There's nothing worse than creating an object or scene with perfect macro settings, only to find them missing the next time. Hopefully, future releases of Toaster software will contain updated macros that remedy this.

The macros I haven't covered are either self-explanatory or too complex for the confines of this article. With experimentation, you should have most of these babies doing your bidding for you in no time at all —leaving you free to watch more episodes of *The Simpsons*.

LWP

Mojo expends more energy writing his biographies than he does his articles. He hopes to one day compile enough bios to fill a book and enough good articles to fill a few pages in a magazine. For the sake of his editors and future writing assignments, however, he may have to adjust this work ethic. His 3D work can be seen weekly on the syndicated television series Babylon 5.

Modeler Mysteries

Secrets of the Lost Tools

by Tom Williamson

Boy oh boy, those LightWave objects! We've all created plenty of scenes with them, but we're getting pretty tired of the living room scenes (complete with Beethoven, of course), and who *hasn't* used that damn Porsche? Most of you have probably moved on to object creation to bring your scenes to life. Some of you have even become modeling masters. The majority of animators just want to do animation, but they still need to get to know LightWave Modeler a little better. So let's get acquainted with some of the more enigmatic functions in our favorite modeling program.

Bend

O.K., I know this isn't a mysterious tool. But I seem to get a lot of questions on its use. Bend isn't very complex—it's just a little awkward at first. Knowing where to click when a bend is necessary seems to cause most of the confusion. I think of it this way: If I were going to reach into my computer screen and physically wrench on my model, I would grab the end I wanted, right where I wanted the bend, and pull one way or another.

Just pretend your model is stuck in space and that you're reaching in with a pair of pliers to grab the part you want to bend by left-clicking and dragging. Where you click has a major effect on how an object bends. This is difficult to explain and best left to experimentation. Remember, though, that the bend always occurs along the axis you are "sighting along." For instance, making a long, segmented tube along the Z-axis (which would appear as a disc in the Face view) and placing your cursor and bending from this view will result in your segmented tube bending as a pipe would along the Z-axis. Normally, you will be bending an object along its "length" axis, but certain interesting effects can be achieved by using Bend in the other axes.

If you need to bend the object in only one direction—with a semi-circular font logo, for example—hold down the Ctrl key (or the middle mouse button on a three-button mouse). This will limit the bend to the first axis you start moving in and bend angles of 15 degrees.

You've probably already noticed that, by default, the opposite side of the object is stationary, which is normal (and necessary in most instances). If you think you're grabbing the model in the right place but it's bending on the opposite side, you need to adjust your "sense." Just hit the Numeric button or the (n) key and click the (+) or (-) button next to Sense. This button controls which end of the object gets manipulated. When it is set to (+), the most "positive" side of the object (based on the positive and negative sides of the axis of bend) is affected; when it is set to (-), the "negative" side is affected.

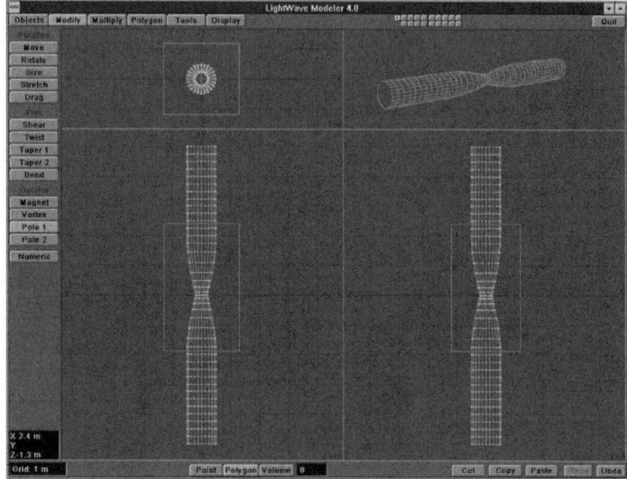

Figure 1: Using the Pole tool to create a venturi-like shape.

Magnet

Here's a wonderful feature that lets you push and pull on objects by using your pointer as a "magnet." To use Magnet, simply drag out a bounding box with the left mouse button (to determine the limits of the tool), and then use the right mouse button to enable the "magnet." The real trick is getting the box the right size and in the right position. When you start to drag the mouse, you'll notice the lines in the other views extend off the frame. This informs you that the area of influence extends forever along the axis you are sighting along. This can be adjusted (if you need it to be) by clicking in another view with the left mouse button and dragging the edges of the box where you need them.

You can also drag the whole box by left-clicking and dragging from the (+) in the center of the box. Remember that since the box represents a spherical area of influence, points near the outer edges (especially the corners) will not be affected. The (+) also serves an extremely important function—it determines where Magnet's greatest influence will be. Where you click when you start deforming the object also affects the way it works. Try to click close to the (+) for the most predictable results, but by all means experiment.

Pole

This is the tool I get the most questions about. It seems that the concept behind Pole is lost on most people, but in reality, it isn't all that complicated. Think of it as a Size tool with bounding box limits. The bounding box in this function works just like the one for magnetism (see above). After you've set up your bounding box, left-click and drag to scale the points within the box. As with Magnet's box, the greatest influence is at the center. (It falls off toward the outer edges.) With the exception of the bounding box, Pole works exactly like the Size tool. If you need to make a venturi-like shape in a pipe, for example, just build a cylinder with multiple segments, set up the bounding box where you need the constriction (with the (+) in the center of the cylinder), right-click and drag to the left. The middle of the pipe will shrink into a shapely hourglass figure (Figure 1)! Pole2 works in a similar way. This tool works like Stretch with a bounding box, allowing you to size differently on different axes.

Patch

Here's another cryptic tool, powerful but confusing. The basics behind it are that if you connect

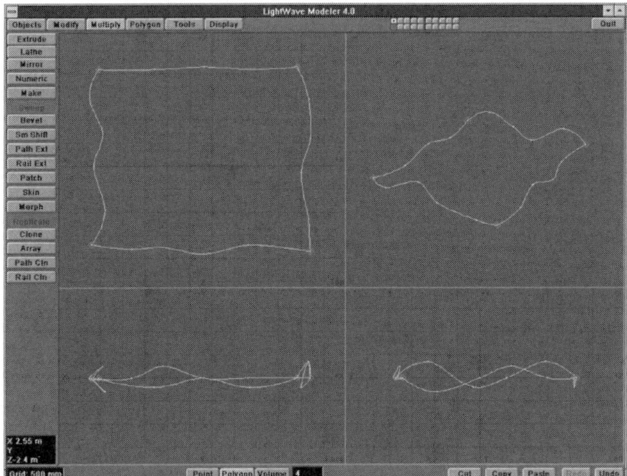

Figure 2: Four selected curves ready for patching.

enough curves together in just the right way, you can "patch" in between them. By patch, I mean you can create a polygon mesh that will approximate the curves to produce a solid form. To do this you have to have either three or four curves connected together (sharing points), which you can accomplish easily with the Weld tool. Since this isn't a tutorial I won't go into much detail, but let's make a Triscuit cracker from hell:

- Using Sketch, draw four curves (Figure 2) and connect them together by welding the points on the ends.

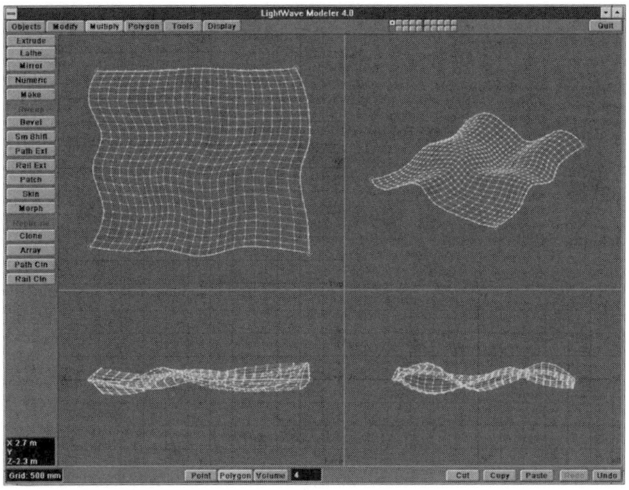

Figure 3: The four curves patched. (Make sure to check for non-planars when patching.)

- After selecting the curves one at a time, click the Patch (Shift-f) button. You'll be presented with a requester. The numeric fields are for the number of polygons you want your patch to consist of. The other buttons are for how you want the tool to approximate the curve: by Knots (more polygons at the bends) or by Length (equally spaced polygons). For now, use the default settings and hit OK.

The curves should now be patched. Depending on how crazy you went when you made your curves you should have a delicious looking 10 x 10 mesh cracker that pretty closely follows the shape of your curves (Figure 3). Mmm, yummy! Now try the tool again with an even smoother 20 x 20 mesh. With the Length buttons selected, you should get a more symmetrical mesh. You will most likely want to triple your polygons when you're finished, as this tool is notorious for generating non-planar polygons. You can use different Perpendicular and Parallel segments in your patches. These are always in relation to the last curve selected. Try changing the two values to see what happens.

Patch also works with three curves. The real trick here is the order in which you select your curves. The point that connects the first two curves you select becomes the radial point of the polygons. As with four-sided curves, the perpendicular and parallel segments are determined by the last curve selected. For three-sided curves, you should always patch "toward the corner." For more information on curves, see the "Curves" section.

Smooth Shift

This operation is very simple and very cool, but a lot of people have no clue as to what it does. Say you need a sphere with a raised ring around the center, like an orange wearing a belt (I don't know, it just popped into my head). All you need to do is select the polygons you want to be the "belt" and hit the Sm Shift (Ctrl–f) button. After entering the Offset (the thickness of the belt), hit OK, and there's your fashion plate Sunkist. What the tool does is take the polygons you have selected and move them the distance you specify along their normals (those little lines that tell you which way the polygon is facing). It also creates polygons to fill in the gap. A more practical example would be hair on a head. Just select the polygons you want to be the hair (after a Slice operation maybe, to create a separate surface?) and then offset the thickness you want the hair. I would recommend metaforming (under Subdivide) the resulting hair as well, just to make it a little nicer. Your humanoid never looked better, and he's not only the president, he's also a client.

Morph

When you have two polygons with the same point count, you can use Skin to put polygons between them. But what if you need intermediate sections? Morph to the rescue! This tool is also very simple: just select two polygons with the same point count, hit the Morph button, and set the number of segments. The result is a series of transitional segments that change from one shape to the next. I tried to come up with a real-world example, but I couldn't. In fact, I don't recall ever using this tool. But now you know what it does. *[Editor's note: I once made a chopstick using Morph. It allowed me to go from a rounded end to a squared-off end.—JG]*

Vortex

Vortex also works with your buddy, the bounding box. It acts like a tornado, twisting more at the center than at the edges (falling off completely at the edges of the bounding box, of course). Just left-click and drag out your box, and then right-click and drag to twist. The area where you click becomes the center of the vortex. This tool is great for creating swirling galaxies out of single-point polygons.

Array

Array does exactly what its name implies: it creates arrays of selected polygons. What's an array? Think of it as a grid with three dimensions. It works a bit like the Clone tool, allowing you to create multiple copies of your selected polygons, grouped together on as many axes as you specify. With one operation of this tool you can create a cube made up of tiny spheres that number 20 on the X-axis and 100 on the Y- and Z-axes. (It's possible to form an array with the Clone tool, but it would take multiple applications. Before the days of multiple Undo this was a pain.) Array also figures out your offset for you, spacing your multiplied polygons edge to edge. (The offset can be entered manually as well.) Keep in mind that the offset is calculated by the center of the polygons, not edge to edge.

Curves

Spline curves serve a number of purposes, and there are many ways to build them. The Sketch tool is a freehand curve creator. Just sketch out the shape you need and hit Make (Return). Your curve is approximated from your sketched line. You can also sketch with the right mouse button; when you let go, the curve is created automatically. If you need the ends connected, just drag points to the same place and use Weld (Ctrl–v). Once you get the curve in the right shape you can freeze it into a polygon. Just select it and hit the Freeze (Ctrl–d) button in the Tools menu. (Conversely, you could select the Numeric button (n) after drawing out your curve and select Polygon.) If you freeze an open curve, the ends will be connected for you.

The little "diamond" on one end of the curve is its start point. You can flip a curve like you flip a polygon,

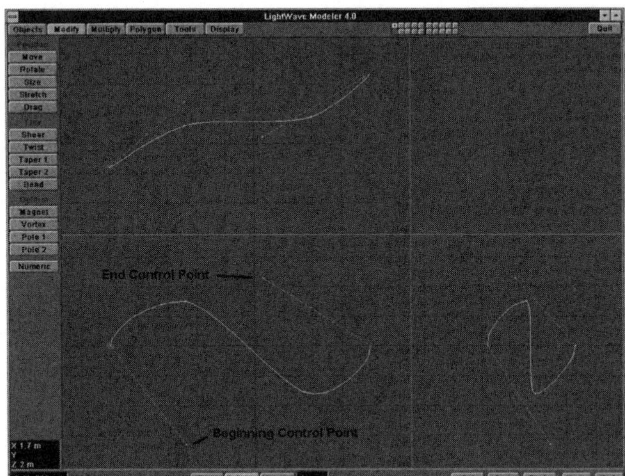

Figure 4: This curve has both a starting control point and an ending control point activated. Notice that the actual curve starts in from the control points.

and the start point hops from one end to the other. The start point will be important when you are patching.

You can move the start- and endpoints in a curve "down the line" (in the case of a start-point) or "up the line" (in the case of an endpoint) by selecting Start CP (Ctrl–b) or End CP (Ctrl–n). This is useful when you need the startpoints or endpoints of a curve to maintain a smooth curve, since the first and last points of a curve always "terminate" the curve. When you create start or end control points, you will see dotted lines connecting the new startpoint or endpoint of a curve to the "control" points (see Figure 4). The control points aren't actually parts of the curve but rather allow you to modify or control the end of your curve. Drag the control points around and watch the results.

You can also create a curve by selecting a series of points and clicking Make (Return) under the Tools menu or pressing (Ctrl–p). For a closed curve, one with connected ends, hit Make Cl (Ctrl–o). Using Make Cl automatically produces a smooth closed curve by using points in the curve as the start and end control points.

LWP

Tom Williamson is the effects supervisor for Santa Maria-based Computer Café. He's about 5'8", drinks a lot of Coke and is gonna be a dad in February 1996.

Fur and Hair
The LightWave Solution

by Gonzalo Garramuno

Although 3D computer graphics can reproduce reality with great accuracy, there are still some things that present a great challenge to the animator. Animals and human beings, for example, are one of the most difficult things to re-create on the computer because they require a great amount of detail. Since viewers are familiar with both people and animals, they expect to see wrinkles and individual hairs when close enough. For years, computer artists struggled to create realistic fur and hair through bump maps and textures, with little success. But, if you have seen some of the new television commercials, like the ones featuring a group of polar bears, you might have noticed that this problem seems to have been solved.

However, you might not be aware that LightWave can represent hair and fur in a way very similar way to that seen in those commercials. As a matter of fact, it has had that option since version 1.0, although, as you will see, it could not easily be implemented until version 3.0.

Enter Particles

Since its conception, LightWave has been able to draw particles (one-point polygons) and particle lines (two-point polygons). The latter are the ones we will be talking about here. If you think about it, fur and hair could easily be represented by a group of lines (hundreds or thousands) coming out from the surface (skin) of your object. But how can you put a line that conforms to the shape of your skin? By using booleans. However, the process needs to be repeated for hundreds or even thousands of lines, which makes the task impossible to do manually.

Since version 3.0, LightWave's Modeler has added the option of macros, which are ARexx programs that can tell Modeler to perform the same actions that you could do by clicking, only much faster and with any number of repetitions. Therefore, in order to have Modeler create fur and hair, what we need to do is write a macro. We do not need to start from scratch, as we may find some other macro that performs some similar action to what we are looking for. Go into Modeler, draw a ball in the center of the screen and choose the Random Surface Points macro. (This is accomplished by going into the Objects menu, clicking on the Macro button and keeping the left mouse button pressed while going up or down until you find it.) After you execute it, just press OK and see what happens. The macro performs a boolean function on your object and the result is a group of points that are laying exactly on the surface of your object. When I first tried the macro, I thought it was pretty useless and that it should be modified to do something more useful. I quickly realized that it could be changed pretty easily to allow the creation of hair. What we need to do is copy and size those resulting points, and then make a polygon with the new points and the old ones to get the lines that are coming out from the surface of the object. The macro included here does exactly that, and it is basically a modified version of the Random Surface Macro (whose file is named prick.lwm) included with LightWave.

Typing the Macro

In order to type in the macro, you need to be able to use an ASCII text editor. The Amiga computer has two text editors in its operative system (ED and Memacs). Refer to your manuals for information on them and the operative system. You can also use a commercial text editor like Cygnus ED or The Edge! or any word processor that allows you to save the documents as plain ASCII text.

You might want to load the Random Surface Points macro first and add the modifications instead of typing everything from start. If so, look for the file named "prick.lwm" in the "Arexx_Examples/lwm" of your Toaster directory.

After typing everything, save the file under a new name (like "Hair.lwm") in that same directory. Then go into Modeler, and use the "Add Macro" to add this new macro to your list. After that, you are ready to use it. If you get an error message while running it, return to your text editor and check the line where the error appeared. You probably mistyped something there or before.

Using the Macro

The usage of the macro is fairly simple.

Copy all the polygons that you want to have hair on top of into an empty layer. Then run the macro. The macro will pop up a requester with a number of options:

- Maximum number of points refers to the maximum number of hairs that you might end up with. To create a realistic effect, you should try to set this value pretty high (2000-15,000 is a good range) but keep your memory capacity in mind.
- Create Lines allows you to create the hairs. If not selected, the macro will act just like the old Random Surface Points macro.
- Number of Segments refers to the number of segments per hair. If more than one, it will allow your hairs to bend more smoothly if you use any tool on them.
- Line Size is the length of your hair. It works by using a scaling percentage. Values between 1.05 and 1.3 are usually OK. Values smaller than 1 will make your hairs go into your object. If using more than one segment, the sizing value will be performed for every segment each time.
- Center works in conjunction with Line Size and allows you to set the center where the sizing is going to occur. By default, it will find the center of your object by averaging the position of its boundary points. Therefore, the default values are usually OK.
- Line Angle allows the hairs to bend in one direction. Just set the maximum angle of bending.
- Rotation Center works in conjunction with Line Angle and allows you to set the center where the rotation is going to be performed. By default, it will find the center of your object by averaging the position of its boundary points. Therefore, the default values are usually OK.
- Rotation Axis works in conjunction with Line Angle and allows you to set the axis on which the bending is going to occur.
- Jitter Amount and Jitter Type allow you to add some random variation to the hairs. The amounts are unit numbers that you can select. The defaults values are 1/10 of your current object's size, which is usually OK.
- Put Results on Original Layer copies the hair on top of the polygons. Otherwise, they will remain in another layer.

If the results of the macro are not to your liking, simply click on Undo and try again with other values. If you get bad results with several sets of very different values, you may have mistyped a line in the macro.

Just go over the listing again and check the lines very carefully. Changing the names of variables or operations, or even placing periods where they shouldn't be, can render a macro useless.

After the macro finishes, you will probably need to do some work yourself, like erase some hairs that might intersect with an ear, or use the different Modeler tools to "comb" your hair.

When you go into Layout, if you have LightWave 3.5 you might want to try different settings for the Particle/Line Size. To do that, go in the Objects menu, select the hair object (or the one that has the hair on it) and change its value.

I should mention that it seems that LightWave seems to use a different algorithm (or a bug?) for shading particles, which makes the hair stand out a little, even if it shares the same surface as the "head."

Using shadow maps or raytraced shadows can help to avoid this problem a little.

LWP

Gonzalo Garramuno is a 21-year-old animator trying to make a living in Argentina. Since the salaries for animators are extremely low in his country, he has been forced to work as an editor, video operator and CG operator, and as a teacher to younger animators. He can be reached by e-mail at ggarramuno@houseware.satlink.net or by surface mail at Rosario 414, 3rd Floor, Buenos Aires, Argentina.

Macro Basics

By John Gross

Macros is one of the best new features in the 3.0 release of Modeler. Since it has an impressive ARexx command set, there are functions Modeler can perform only by using macros. This article will walk you through the basics of getting Macros to work on your machine.

Setting Up

Macros are simply ARexx programs that can be executed from Modeler. In order for macros to function properly, you must have ARexx running on your computer. To check if you have ARexx installed, just open a shell and type "rexxmast" (no quotes). If ARexx is running, you will get a message stating "REXX server already active." To make sure ARexx is running every time you start your machine, you can either add the command "Rexxmast" to your S:startup-sequence or your S:user-startup sequence. Conversely, you can place the RexxMast icon located in the System drawer into your WBStartup drawer.

Configuring a Macro List

Modeler 3.0 comes preconfigured with a macro list already set up for you. What do you do if you want to add macros and make them available all of the time?

When you enter Modeler and click and hold on the Macro button, you are presented with a pop-up menu with <<CONFIGURE LIST>>, <<CONFIGURE KEYS>>, and <<DIRECT COMMAND>> listed at the top of the pop-up with macros listed below. First, let's talk about configuring your macro list.

The default macro list is called ModelerMacroList and is found in the Toaster/3D directory. Due to some last-minute macro add-ons, this list does not include all of the macros that come with 3.0. One of the omitted macros is called Julienne; its function is to slice up an object along one axis to make bending, boning, and displacement mapping easier. Let's add this macro to show how configuration works.

Click on the Macro button and select <<CONFIGURE LIST>>. The Macro Script List window will appear, ready to accept input (see Figure 1).

At the top of the requester is the name of the current macro list, as well as buttons for loading, saving, and clearing the list. The List Entry pop-up menu allows you to choose any macro that is currently loaded. Below the pop-up is the name as found in the Macro pop-up menu, and below that is the actual path and name of the ARexx file script that executes the command.

Below the ARexx command are buttons for changing, creating and deleting an entry. Finally, at the bottom of the requester is a space for a start-up macro. This can be any macro that you would like executed each time you first enter Modeler.

To add a macro, you must first click on the >> button located to the right of the Command field. This presents a requester where you can choose the ARexx script you wish to add to your macro list.

This requester should default to the place where macros are stored (by default, they are located in the Toaster/Arexx_Examples/LWM drawer). This can be changed simply by editing the MacrosDirectory line in the Mod-Config file found in the 3D drawer.

Once you have found the correct directory, simply select the file called julienne.lwm and click OK. The Command line should now read: Arexx_Examples/LWM/julienne.lwm.

The next step is to enter the name as you want it to appear when you access the macro through the Macro pop-up menu. Place the cursor in the Name field and erase whatever is there. Type in Julienne and then click on the Create button. If you decide later that you want to use a different name, make sure you select the julienne.lwm command and then type in a new name and click on the Change button. (Of course, pressing Delete will remove the selected entry from the list.)

Your new macro will now appear in the Macro pop-up menu. However, if you wish it to remain there, click on the Save button to save it as part of your macro list.

Different macro lists for different modeling projects can be saved and loaded at any time.

Macro Keyboard Shortcuts

If you would like the ease of pulling up macros at the touch of a key, you can assign a different macro to each of the 10 function keys.

Just do this: In the Macro pop-up menu, select <<CONFIGURE KEYS>>. This allows you to choose your macros.

Notice the familiar >> button to the right of each line. Simply click on this and choose the macro you wish to assign to each key. When you're finished, click OK and your macros will be immediately assigned to your function keys.

Figure 1

When you exit Modeler, these shortcuts will be written to the MOD-Config file, so they will always be available.

Direct Command

Finally, we come to the last command choice in the Macro pop-up menu: <<DIRECT COMMAND>>. This choice allows you to select any ARexx command directly through a requester, as opposed to selecting it from the pop-up. Since I have my list configured to show all my choices are available, I usually do not use this option.

A Final Word

Don't be afraid to edit some of the ARexx macros. For instance, you may not like the directories which some macros are programmed to save to, or you may want a certain font to be loaded with the LoadFonts script. Either way, feel free to edit files so they work for you. Just make sure to work on a copy of the original in case you get all mixed up.

LWP

John Gross is the Editor of LightWavePRO.

Riding the Rails

A Rail Extrude Tutorial

by Arnie Boedecker

I have found that the best way to begin to use and understand Modeler is to master a few functions at a time. Some functions will be used on nearly every project, while others will rarely be touched. (Anyone out there a big Quantize user?) Obviously, the tools used largely depend on the project at hand.

A number of months ago, I stumbled across a project in which I needed to construct a glass table with a detailed metal bottom (see color pages). I knew that in order to build such an object, I would have to dive into some previously unused tools. What I found was Rail Extrude.

Rail Extrude, in my opinion, is a tool that hasn't received the coverage it deserves. I've found it to be extremely useful in creating wrought iron gates and similar detailed objects.

Operation: Glass Table

To construct the glass table object, only a handful of tools are needed, including Lathe, Mirror, Clone and, of course, Rail Extrude.

The first step is to create the glass tabletop. For mine, I wanted the circular glass slab to have slightly curved sides, for a more elegant, less boxy feel.

- In the Face view, plot a few points to make up a curve (or better yet, use the side of a disk), and move them out some distance on the X-axis.

I moved mine about 45 cm, which provided an accurate measurement from the center of the table out to its edge.

- Create two points on the Y-axis that line up with the top and bottom points of the curve.
- Select the points in a clockwise fashion and create a polygon (p) to lathe into the tabletop (Figure 1).
- Using the Lathe tool (Multiply), lathe the polygon around the Y-axis, using Numeric to set the number of sides to 100 to ensure a very smooth table edge.
- Select all of the top flat polygons and use the polygon Merge function (Polygon menu or Z), so that the top consists of one polygon rather than 100. Then do the same for the bottom polygons.
- Select the top and bottom polygons, and use the **Surface** button (**Polygon** menu or q) to label their surface as Glasstop.T&B. Label the side polygons Glasstop.Sides.

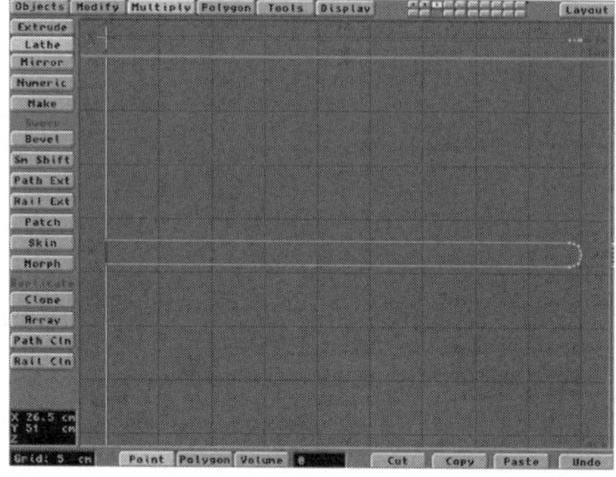

Figure 1

- Move the entire object up so it is not sitting on the 0 Y-axis. I moved mine approximately 35 cm.
- Save the object as TableTop.

I used different surface names so that I would be able to give the sides a smooth surface while keeping the top and bottom flat. Had I tried to smooth the GlassTop without assigning different surfaces, the sides would have smoothed into the top and bottom polygons, resulting in a very unnatural look.

The next step is to create the detailed table bottom. This starts off with the top support upon which the table top will rest.

- In the Face view, make a flat 2.4 cm disc with 16 sides (Objects/Disc/Numeric) and move it out a shorter distance than the edge of the table on the X axis (I used 32.5 cm). Next, lathe the disc around the Y-axis with 100 sides to complete the support.

Next, it's time to create the curved metal legs.

- In a new layer, with the support ring just created in a background layer, draw out a curve using the Sketch tool (Objects) in the side view. My curve had a slight S-shape to it, as needed for the table's design. The curve should be drawn from the edge of the support ring to the "ground" (0 on Y). Hit return to make the curve.

In the Face view, I shifted the top few points to the left to give the curve a desired path of the table leg. Also, I had to be certain that the top point of the table leg curve intersected the top support in the background layer. Once created, there would not be a gap in between the legs and the top support. This curve will serve as our "rail" in our Rail Extrude operation (Figure 2).

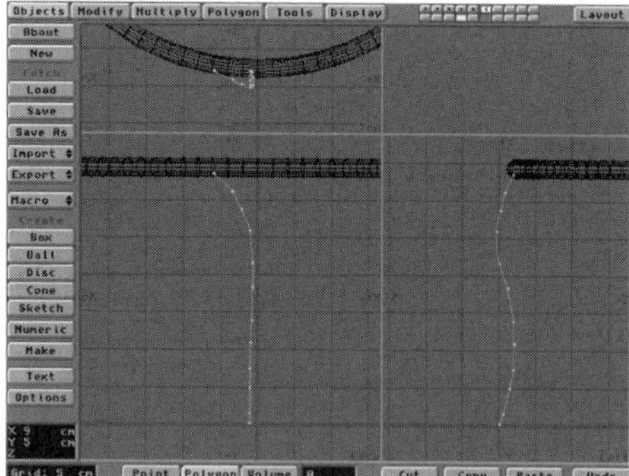

Figure 2

Riding the Rail

- In a new layer, with the "rail" in a background layer, create a 1-cm disc to use for the table leg. After moving the disc to the top of the curve, rotate it in all three views until it is perpendicular to the start of the curve (Figure 3).
- Select **Rail Ext** (**Multiply** menu) and choose **Uniform Knots** set at 20, and **Oriented**.

When attempting your rail extrusion, if it seems to be heading in every direction and completely out of the

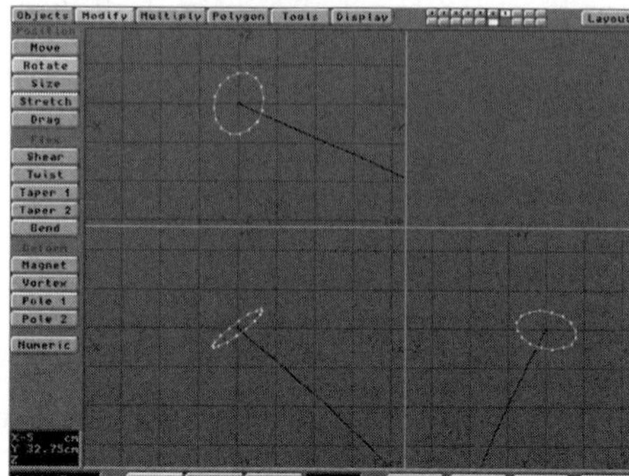

Figure 3

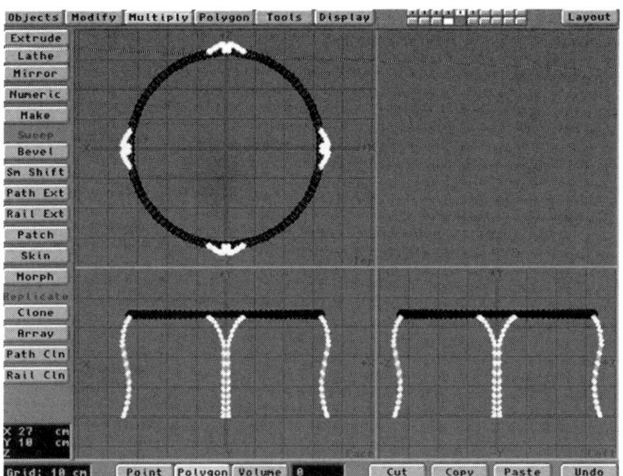

Figure 4

rails path, chances are the curve was drawn backward. To correct this, simply click **Undo** to erase the incorrect rail extrusion, move to the layer with the "rail" in it, and press (f) to flip the direction of the curve. Then return to the layer with the leg disc in it, make sure the "rail" is in the background, and try again.

If, once the disc extrudes correctly, you are dissatisfied with its shape, click **Undo** again to get rid of it, move a few points of your rail until it is more the shape you are trying for, and then try the rail extrude again. It took me a few attempts before I was satisfied with my table leg extrusion, so don't be afraid to shift a point here or there.

The extrusion just completed is only half of the complete table leg.

- To complete the leg, mirror (Multiply) the object just created on the Y-axis in the Face view.

The mirrored objects should just barely touch each other, giving the impression that they are connected somehow. This completes one of the four table legs. Now the table leg needs to be cloned three more times around the table.

- Hit the Clone button (Multiply) to bring up the Clone requester. Enter three for the number of clones and 90 degrees for the rotation on the Y-axis. All other settings should be left at the default. Click OK, and the leg will be cloned three times at equal spacing around the table (Figure 4).

Thanks For Your Support

The next step is to create the connecting leg supports. Since these supports have a perfectly smooth arc to them, the best way to create them would be to use the same lathing method used for the top support.

- In a separate layer, make a flat 1.1 cm disc in the Face view and move it out about 32.5 cm on the X-axis. Again, lathe this disc on the Y-axis with 100 sides.
- In the top view, with the table legs in the background, move the entire ring that was just created until it intersects two of the table legs correctly (Figure 5). The ring can be moved or rotated from the front most edge 90 degrees to align it in place. Move the ring down and align it from all three views to get it to intersect two of the legs. For those with LightWave 3.5, this becomes an easier task while using the visibility tools (Display menu).
- Once you are certain the intersection is correct, cut away all of the unnecessary polygons (highlighted in Figure 5), until you're left with one-fourth of the original ring arching between two table legs.
- As before, clone this piece three times around the Y-axis, with a 90 degree rotation value, to complete the leg support, connecting all four legs.

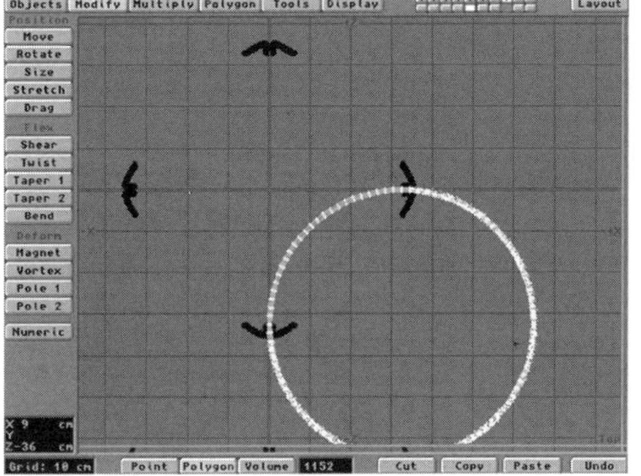

Figure 5

Add Elegance

The final step in creating the table bottom is to make the S-like details between each table leg, which gives the table its elegant appeal. This could be done simply with rail extrusion, as well.

- In a new layer, draw out an S-shape using the Sketch tool in the Face view, and hit the return key to make the curve.

I adjusted the curve's points as needed to make sure the curve was as smooth as possible. I also made sure the curve touched the top support, so the S-details would be connected to the rest of the table.

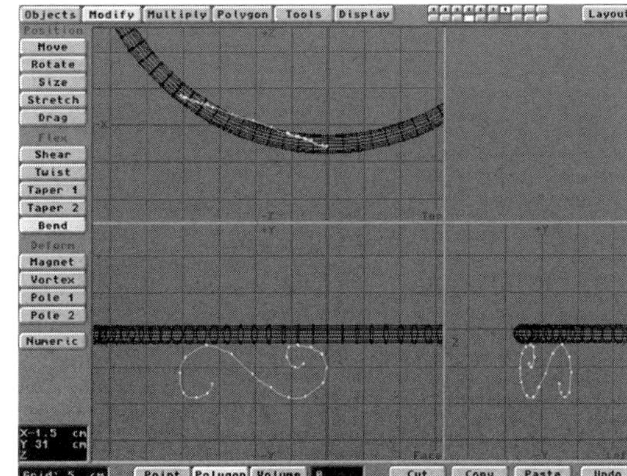

Figure 6

- Using Rotate (Modify), rotate the curve somewhat in the top view, so that the curve follows the arch of the top support, to which it would be connected. Make sure that one end of it is aligned with 0 on the X axis (Figure 6).
- Once satisfied with the curve's position and shape, move to another layer and create a flat 7 mm disc in the face view. Again, with the S-detail curve in the background, move and rotate the 7 mm disc in all three views until it sits perpendicular to the start of the S-detail curve. It may be necessary to flip the direction of the curve, as mentioned earlier.
- Once the disc is in place, use the rail extrude function to create the S-detail.

To create rounded-looking ends, I beveled the polygons on each end of the S-detail.

- Next, as with the table legs, mirror the S-detail, so that the edges just touch each other.
- To create the other detail, clone the S-detail objects, just as before, with the number of clones being three, with a 90-degree rotation around the Y-axis.

With the S-detail objects in the foreground and the table legs in the background, you can see that they are on top of each other. To correct for this, we simply rotate the S-detail objects 45 degrees around the Y-axis. It is better to use the numeric input requester in this case, so that there is no mistake of things being off-center.

- Now that all of the table bottom pieces are created, it's just a matter of cutting and pasting the legs, the top support, the leg supports, and the S-detail objects into a single layer. Merge points (Tools) and assign the surface name Tablemetal to the whole object, then save it as TableBottom.

Final Touch

You can now load your objects into Layout, surface them and render away.

I gave a metal surface to Tablemetal, and turned smoothing on. I gave Glasstop.T&B a glossy glass surface, and left smoothing off. Tabletop.Sides also received a glossy glass surface, but smoothing was turned on. I also gave it a bluish surface color and turned on **Color Filter**, to give the sides a tinted look.

This project was beneficial in that it helped me become more acquainted with the rail extrude function and the Clone requester. I realize that I am constantly finding new uses for previously avoided tools.

Learning to use the many tools in Modeler, even those rarely used, can provide a new outlook on what can or cannot be modeled, and with new tools like Metaform, it seems as though anything is possible.

LWP

Arnie Boedecker is president of Imagi•Nation Enterprises in Illinois. He can be reached at 603-D WatersEdge Drive, McHenry, IL 60050, (815) 385-8198.

From the Net

As the Screw Turns

by Dan Ablan

I see Jenny, and Johnny, and Timmy, and— oh sorry, *Romper Room* flashback. This is "From the Net," back in the '90s. You know, it's odd how right our parents were as we were growing up. Time really does go by fast, and the older we get, the faster it seems to slip on by. My Dad always told me to enjoy myself now: "Care free," he said. At the time, it didn't seem like it. Now, of course, I know he was right.

While I was growing up, my Dad sold screws. Honest! He did. His company distributes fasteners, such as nuts, bolts, and screws. I often worked in the warehouse for extra money during my summer breaks, and planned to go work for the company after college. Well, things change, and instead of counting and selling screws, I'm building them in 3D!

It's ironic that so many people have been discussing how to build a screw over the Internet lately. A few people e-mailed me with the question, and of course, it hit close to home. So, enough reminiscing, let's build a screw!

Lathe Me Baby!

The first thing you should do is figure out what type of screw you want to build. I decided on a standard hex head type 18-8. The next step is to build the thread for the screw. Granted, you can reverse the order of these things, but the thread is a good area to start.

• From the Objects menu in Modeler, create a box with the following settings.

	Low	High	Segments
X	40 mm	60 mm	1
Y	0	1 mm	1
Z	0	0	1

• Click OK and hit return to make the box. Nothing special here, but it should look like Figure 1.

• Next, select the Lathe tool from the Multiply menu, and from the numeric requester, enter the following settings:

Start Angle	0.0
End Angle	6600.0
Sides	800
Offset	200 mm
Axis	Y
Center	0, 10 mm, 0

• Click OK, and press return to perform the Lathe. Your threads are magically created. If only manufacturing real screws were this easy! You should have something like Figure 2.

• At this point, save the object. You may want to use it later for other objects you may need, such as a bedspring.

• Now, go to a new layer, and place the threaded portion you just created in a background layer. Select the Disc tool, and press (n) to call up the numeric requester. Enter the following values:

Sides		40
Segments		1
Bottom		0 m
Top		210 mm
Axis		Y
Center	X	0 m
	Y	105 mm
	Z	0 m
Radii	X	53.25 mm
	Y	105 mm
	Z	53.25 mm

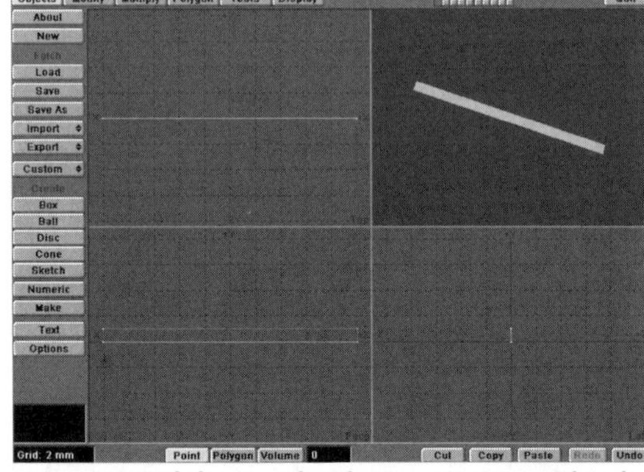

Figure 1: A simple box is made to begin creating a screw thread.

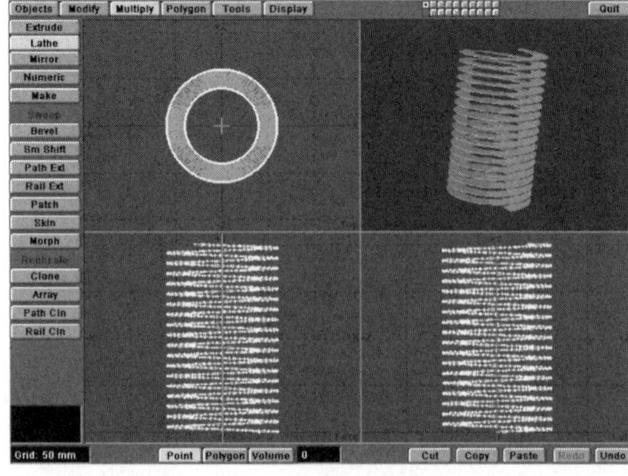

Figure 2: The Lathe tool is used to create the threads of the screw.

• Click OK, and press return or enter to make the disc. Make sure the threaded object is in the background layer, as in Figure 3.

Get It Together

Now that you have the threads and the center of the screw created, you need to bring them together to form the screw.

• Press Shift (b) to call up the Boolean Operations requester. Select the Union operation, and click OK. In a moment, you should have something like the object in Figure 4.

• If you get a "Polygon Partitioning Error," simply move the disc slightly off center. I got this error a few times, and added (like it told me) a small offset to the object and tried it again.

• Now, save your object.

• From here, select just the top polygon of the disc. This should equal only one polygon. Press (b) on the keyboard to call up the Bevel requester. Enter a Inset value of 10 mm and a Shift value of 10 mm. Click OK to bevel the top of the screw. Select the top polygons that include the newly beveled area, and give them a different surface name, so you can vary the smoothing. You should have an object that looks something like the one in Figure 5.

The Base

Now that the screw is starting to take shape, it needs some sort of base that allows it to be screwed in, right? In a new layer, select the Disc tool from the Objects panel, and enter the following values:

Sides		6
Segments		1
Bottom		-50 mm
Top		0 m
Axis		Y
Center	X	0 m
	Y	-25 mm
	Z	0 m
Radii	X	85 mm
	Y	25 mm
	Z	85 mm

• Click OK, and press Enter or Return to create the base of the screw. Actually, I think we are making more of a bolt than a screw, but the same principles will apply to for creating a wood screw, for example. Just as a side note, you could taper the top end of this bolt, and create less of a base to make the wood screw.

The last thing you need to do to create the base of the screw is bevel the edges slightly.

• Select the top and bottom polygons of the base, and press the (b) key to call up the Bevel requester. Enter an Inset and Shift value of 3 mm. This will take away the hard edge of the object, and create a more realistic shape. Your base should look like Figure 6.

The Finale

Once the base is complete to your liking, join it to the rest of the screw by either a cut and paste, or a Boolean Union operation. In the color pages, you can see the final bolt surfaced with default LightWave silver, however, it's been dulled using fractal noise, and less reflection.

These techniques are pretty basic. You may find a new way to create a screw or bolt, and if it works better for you than this method, by all means, go for it. Additionally, try altering the values mentioned here for different sized screws and you can also use the Modify tools, such as Taper.

LWP

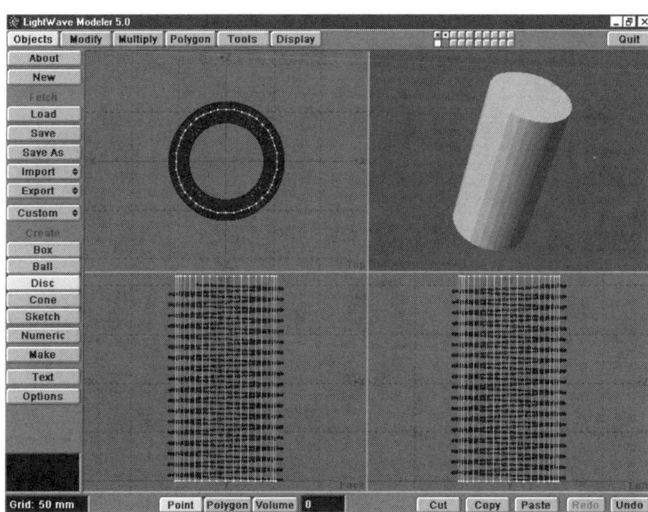

Figure 3: The lathed threaded part of the screw is in a background layer, ready to be joined with the center of the screw.

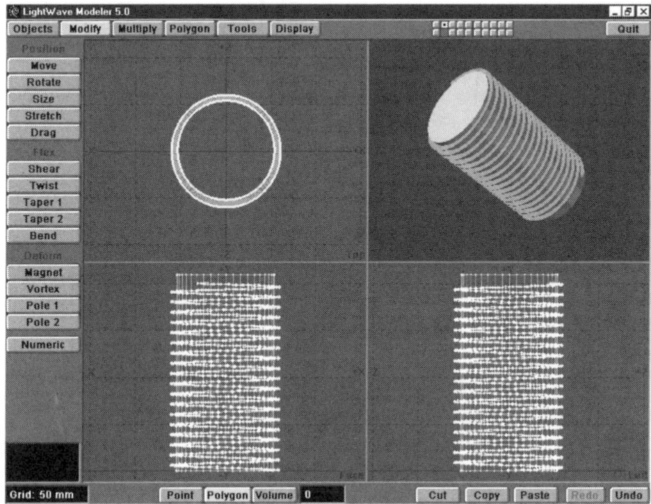

Figure 4: The object is joined with a disc using the Boolean Union operation.

Dan Ablan is an animator at AGA Digital Studios in Chicago and the author of The LightWave Power Guide, *published by New Riders Publishing. Reach him by e-mail at dma@mcs.net.*

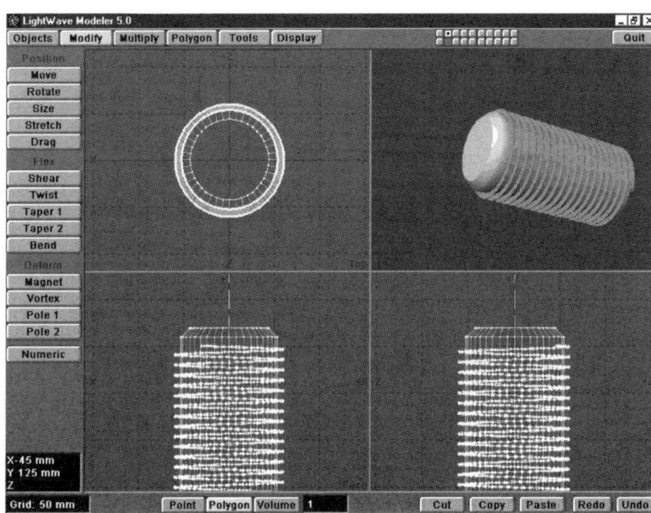

Figure 5: The head of the screw is bevelled.

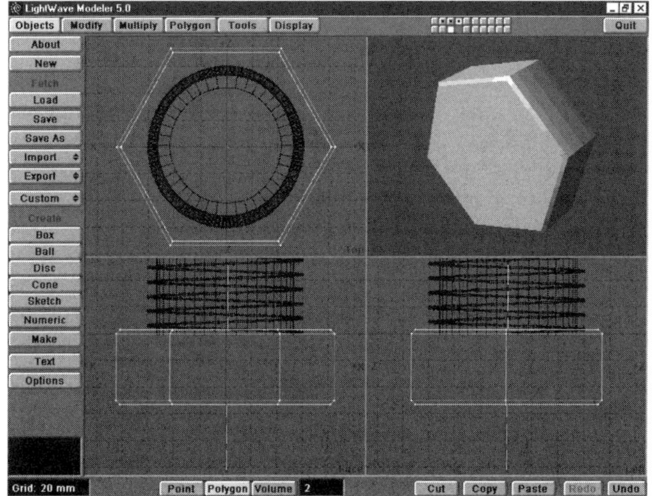

Figure 6: Once the base is created, the top and bottom portions are bevelled.

LightWave 101

Course 1A—Object Cleanup

by Taylor Kurosaki

Welcome to LightWave 101, where new animators with minimal experience will become more productive in LightWave. The more effective command of LightWave and Modeler's tools, the more time spent bringing your ideas to life and not wasting time merely navigating through the software.

With that in mind, the first step toward completing any animation is having an object or objects to animate. As important as modeling is, it's also essential to model sound objects and learn how to fix potential problems in models you create, as well as those you might acquire from other sources.

Figure 1: The Merge Points requester (m) allows you to merge points using a number a number of different formulas.

Improperly modeled objects, or objects which create rendering errors will detract from any animations you produce. The following techniques deal with the most common modeling problems and offer possible solutions. Most of the problems described won't necessarily be evident until the object is actually rendered. Importing from Layout to Modeler and exporting from Modeler back to Layout will be required to fix the actual iteration of the object from your given scene.

Remember to save your fixed object from Layout once it has been exported from Modeler. This is an important step to remember, as it ensures that you are always working with the same version of your object in both Layout and Modeler.

Merge Points

The first operation you should perform on an object you suspect has problems is **Merge Points**. From within the **Tools** menu, Merge Points can remedy one and two-point polygons (see below), as well as alert you to multiple polygons sharing the same space. (see Double Polygons below)

Merge points can also eliminate polygons with more than two points where multiple vertices share the same space. These polygons can render the same as one or two-point polygons but don't appear as such under the **Polygon Statistics** window. Performing a Merge Points exposes these problematic polygons for what they really are so you can remedy them.

When you select **Merge (m)**, a requester with three options will appear: **Automatic**, **Fractional** and **Absolute** (Figure 1). In almost all cases, you will want to use Automatic as this merges only those points that share the same space. If you have two points that you know need merging but Automatic will not merge them, Absolute will merge points that are located within a user defined distance from each other.

Also make sure that you only merge points located in the same layer. You cannot merge points if they are in two different layers.

One-Point Polygons

One-point polygons render as dots or particles. Unless your model is a star field, plankton field or a cloud of particles, one-point polygons are probably a mistake. To search for one-point polygons, type the **w** key while the **Select Polygon** button (lower left screen) is selected to bring up the Polygon Statistics window. This window details the number of one, two, three, four, and greater than four vertex polygons in the current modeler layer. The statistics window also allows one to select polygons based on the number of vertices or surface names. Selecting the **+** key will select the chosen polygons, while selecting the **-** key will deselect them if they are selected.

Once the undesirable one-point polygons are selected, you can select **Cut** to remove them from your object. If the point that made up the one-point polygon is also a part of another polygon, it will be maintained while the polygon is removed. If the point is not associated with any other polygons, it will be deleted along with its polygon.

Two-Point Polygons

Two-point polygons are similar to single point polygons in their problematic ways. Instead of dots protruding from your model, symptoms of unwanted two-point polygons are lines cutting through or laying on top of the object. The solution is the same as it is for single-point polygons.

Select all polygons with two vertices from within the Polygon Statistics window, then cut the polygon to remove it from the object. As with single-point polygons, if the points are needed by other polygons, they will be retained, otherwise they will be deleted along with the polygons.

Note: If your object intentionally contains one-point or two-point polygons, (i.e., the star field example above)LightWave version 3.5 now allows you to determine the rendered size of the **Particle/Line** within the **Objects** panel. Selecting **Small** renders particles the size of one pixel and lines one pixel thick, **Medium** renders 3x3 pixels, while **Large** renders particles 5x5 pixels in size and lines five pixels thick. Selecting **Automatic** Particle/Line Size renders a one pixel particle/line in Super Low Resolution and Low Resolution, three pixels in Medium Resolution, and five pixels in High Resolution and Print Resolution.

Flipped Polygons

Flipped polygons are a common modeling problem. A polygon with its surface normal facing the wrong way appears invisible when rendered. Think of a single-sided polygon as a two-way mirror; from the rear you can see through it, while from the front it reflects the surface values given back to the camera. The surface normal of a polygon in Modeler is the side that you will see when it is rendered.

To compound the problem of a flipped polygon, as you see through the back of the polygon nearest the camera, you will probably see through the back sides of the polygons of the far side of the object. The net effect is seeing through the object to whatever is behind it. To fix a flipped polygon, either select it and hit the **Flip** button (**Polygon** menu) or the **f** key. You can also select the **Align** button and all polygons in the current layer will become aligned in the same direction. If you use Align, you need to check your polygons afterwards as they may all be facing inwards and you will need to perform a Flip on all polygons.

Note: For Align to work properly, you should perform a **Merge** points operation first.

Double Polygons

Double polygons are typically two polygons sharing the same set of points in the same space. Even if these two polygons use the same surface, rendering errors can still result. The polygons are essentially competing with each other for visibility, because their surface normals are facing the same way. In this case, hitting the **Unify** (**Polygon** menu) button will remove the extra polygon. If you have determined that there are, in fact, two (or more) polygons sharing the same space, yet Unify has no effect, chances are these polygons are using separate sets of points. In this case, perform a **Merge** points and then Unify. If merging points doesn't work, it is probably a situation where the two polygons in question are not directly on top of one another. If this is indeed what is happening, zoom in on the problem area and manually remove or cut the undesired polygon(s).

Non-planar Polygons

Non-planar polygons are those which consist of four or more points which are not located in the same plane. Due to their bent nature, these polygons cannot be rendered properly. From some angles, non-planar polygons might render fine, while from other angles they aren't even visible. When an object containing non-planar polygons is animated, the non-planars may flicker as the object moves in space. The best solution for non-planar polygons is to turn the four or more vertex polygons into triangular polygons.

Triangular, or three-vertex polygons, cannot, by their nature, be non-planar. Under the **Polygon Statistics** window (**w**), select the **+** button to the left of **Non-planar**, and then hit the **Triple** button from within the Polygon menu.

To be absolutely thorough in weeding out non-planar polygons, you must change the **Flatness Limit** to 0 percent in the **Data Options** window (**o**) within the **Objects** menu before selecting Non-planars and tripling them. Alternately, you may choose to Triple every polygon in your object, although this makes it more memory intensive and increase rendering times as well.

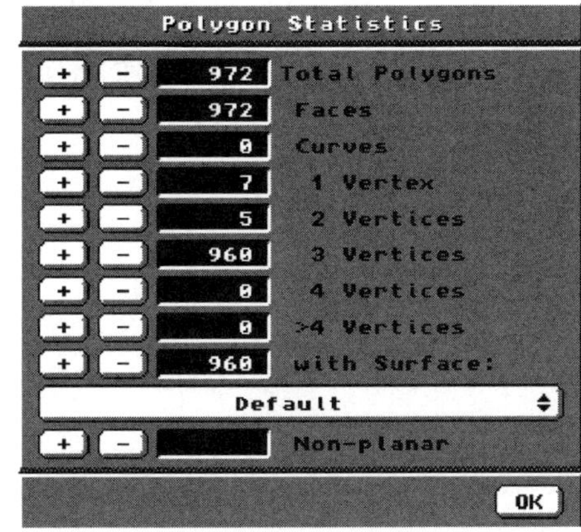

Figure 2: The Polygon Statistics requester contains information about all of the polygons in the current layer.

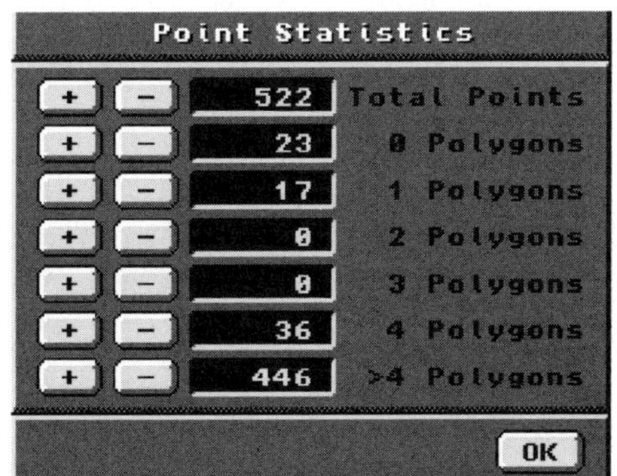

Figure 3: The Point Statistics requester gives you valuable point stats. You should not have any points continuing zero or one polygon unless you are specifically making them.

Points with no Polygons

Periodically you may find an object which contains points with no polygons. Although individual points don't render, and therefore don't cause rendering errors, it's still a good idea to eliminate of these extraneous points, keeping your object clean and simple in the event you want to go back and modify it later.

To find these rogue points, click on the **Point** selection button, press **w** to bring up the **Point Statistics** window, select all points which are associated with 0 Polygons, and Cut.

Last Resort: Double Side

If you encounter the types of problems described under non-planar or flipped polygons, yet none of the solutions seem to work, or if the object you are working with looks to have seams or holes in it, and you can't figure out how to fix it, there is one final potential solution. Copy all the polygons of your object, or at least all of the potentially problematic polygons, Flip the originally selected polygons, Paste the copied polygons back down, and **Merge** points.

You have given each polygon a duplicate with an opposite facing surface of the same name. This definitely fixes flipped polygons, and it may help with some cases of non-planar. Alternately, you can select **Double Sided** under the **Surfaces** panel in Layout.

Obviously, it would be preferable to actually fix the problems in your object, as opposed to merely covering them up. However, some objects can seem extremely complicated, especially if you aren't the original modeler. If you can't fix it, at least make it appear well done.

Hopefully these scenarios will be helpful when you invariably experience problems rendering objects. Ideally, when it comes to your own LightWave models, you will use these methods to fix problems as you are building. This is the least painful way to work, and if you're conscientious and thorough, problems can be avoided by the time you are working in Layout.

Next month, we will discuss different strategies and approaches to modeling. The use of simple shapes to construct more complex objects will be covered, including the use of primitives, lathing, cloning and subdividing.

LWP

Taylor Kurosaki is the former Digital Systems coordinator for Amblin Imaging and seaQuest DSV. *He now devotes all of his time to animating so he can miss all those boring meetings and turn Pearl Jam up while he works.*

Curve Selection Order and Matching Polygon Edges

If you do have to "dead-end" a curve into the side of another, as we did in "LightWave 101" on page 6, carefully choosing the proper number of perpendicular and parallel segments after selecting your curves in the proper order can give you smooth edges between adjoining patch areas.

- Figure 1 shows the Z curve in the thumb area of the splint as it would appear if it was not extended along the length of the splint. Select the curves in the order shown to patch the curves and select **Patch** (Ctrl–f).
- The Patch requester's Perpendicular and Parallel segment values are determined by the last curve selected (number 4 in this case). Enter 5 for **Perpendicular** and 10 for **Parallel.** In order to make sure that the segments are produced in relation to the knots (or points) along the curves, see that **Knots** is selected for both segments.

Figure 3 shows the first patch section created. Notice that there are five rows of polygon segments perpendicular to the last curve selected and 10 rows parallel to the last curve.

- Deselect all curves and then patch the area to the right of the last patch section by selecting the appropriate curves in the same order. (It doesn't matter if you accidentally select some faces along with your curves—they are ignored in the patch operation.)
- Deselect all curves and patch the large adjoining area below the two sections, using 10 for both **Perpendicular** and **Parallel** values. Figure 4 shows all three patch sections.
- Perform an **Automatic Merge Points** operation (m) to eliminate all of the duplicate points along the shared edges and eliminate "seams" in the rendered image.

One problem that you may encounter while performing a patch operation of this type is acquiring sections in your object with dissimilar curves. In the case of this splint, not running the thumb curve down the length of the splint created polygons like those in Figure 4. The problem is that we have lost the continuous defined shape by dead-ending the thumb curve. You can, however, run the curve down the length of the splint as outlined in the article and still follow the above procedures to make free-flowing shapes. Just because a curve is in an object doesn't mean that you have to use it to patch—it can be there just to help define the surrounding curves. Figure 5 shows the results of patching this way. Notice the smoother-flowing polygons.

What have we learned from this? If possible, try to continue your curves throughout an object to define the overall shape, and patch the proper ones to generate as even a patch area as possible across the surface. If you do have to dead-end a curve, here's a good way to get around it.

—John Gross

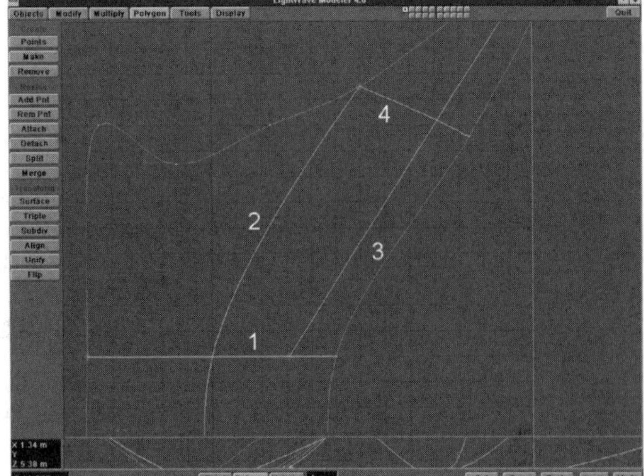

Figure 1: The four curves chosen in the proper order.

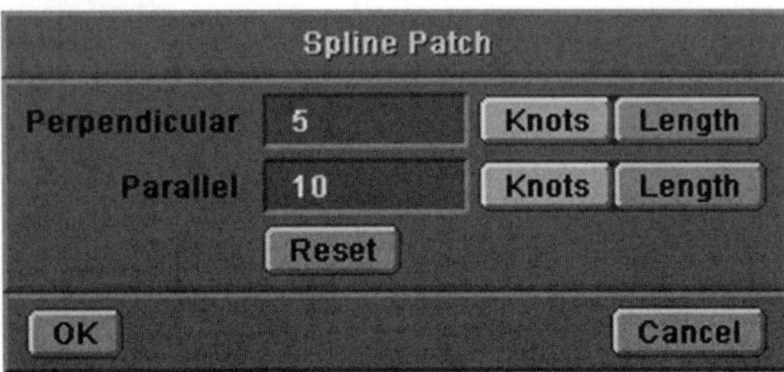

Figure 2: The Patch requester.

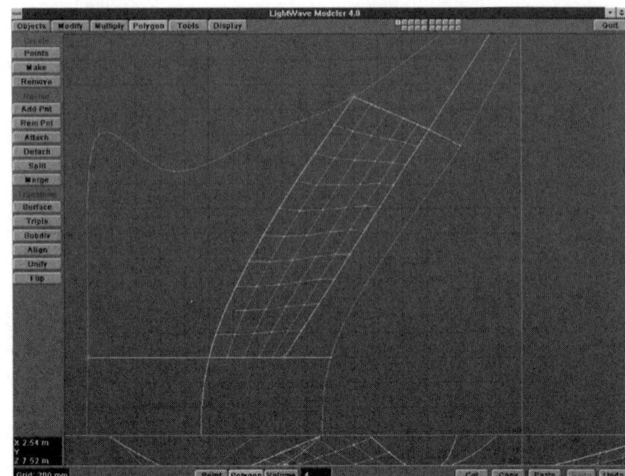
Figure 3: Perpendicular and Parallel polygon segments relative to the last curve selected.

10 Tips for Cleaner Objects

by Tom Williamson

Modeling is one of the hardest things in computer graphics to do correctly. With LightWave Modeler's easy-to-learn interface and powerful tools, a reasonably trained chimp could bash out objects. But it takes experience to recognize what needs (or doesn't need) to be built. It doesn't take much to get so caught up in an object that instead of spending time figuring out if you can build it, you never stop to think if you *should* build it. What I have compiled here are some tips for creating cleaner objects. By "cleaner" I mean more logical, better-thought-out objects that are not only more efficient but a lot more fun to work with.

Watch Your Polygon Count

There seems to be a serious misconception that the more polygons there are in an object, the better it is. Well, that simply isn't true. You can take a cube and subdivide until your face turns a lovely shade of red (with a little fractal noise thrown in). When you're done, it'll still be a cube. A cube with an impressive polygon count, yes, but still a cube. Now, I realize that's an extremely oversimplified example, but I believe I've made my point. Probably the most important step to modeling is preparation. Before you can build anything you must first determine what it is you really need. Will you be getting really close to this object? If so, more detail is necessary. If not, perhaps a simple flat plane with an image map and clip map will do. As you can see, there's quite a range, and where your model falls in this range depends greatly on the project.

Pre-visualization, storyboards and production sketches are very important to the modeling process. If you don't plan ahead you'll probably end up in Modeler again. The detail of your object depends on how it will be seen and the inherent complexity of the piece you're creating. Take, for instance, an airplane. If your animation has an airplane flying through the background of the scene, a simple object will do. Perhaps a count of 300 polygons. If your animation has the plane flying past the camera, you should probably boost the quality up to 3,000 polygons, maybe. If your animation has the plane fly toward the camera as we swoop in to count the rivets holding on the canopy, you better go for that big daddy-mac plane you've always wanted to build with 30,000 polygons! Then there's the topic of overdetailing small parts of an otherwise simple object. If your plane fuselage has only 200 polygons, why have a 1,200-polygon Pitot tube (a device used to measure the total pressure of a fluid stream)?

Figure 1: A typical smoothing problem...

I call this polygon balancing: keeping the detail logical throughout the model. Of course, there are times when an unbalanced model is desirable. Say your animation starts by flying out of the Pitot tube to reveal the plane, which then flies off into the sunset. If that's the case, then by all means detail that tube! In fact, you should do the surrounding area, too. But the tailgear? If it's not necessary, don't do it! As my good friend David Ebner likes to say, "Work is work." Here's my loose rule of thumb: determine what you need and add 20 percent. This works in all aspects of life and will keep you from going back into Modeler in the 11th hour instead of just hitting "F10" (render scene). Every so often you will have to go back and add detail to an object because a shot was added or the camera angle changed. But overall, this rule works. (It doesn't work in marriage, however, so make the number 40 percent. Those who didn't order their spouse fries because they said "I'll just have some of yours" can vouch for this.)

Hierarchies That Make Sense (The Art of the Null)

Another purpose of clean objects is to make animating a simpler task. A clean object is easier to see and work with, while a complex object can turn into a black blob very quickly. A group of objects in a hierarchy can get very messy if some thought doesn't go into keeping it clean. The order in which the objects are parented is also important. Try to think ahead when it comes time to build your scene. Let's use the

Figure 2: ...and a way around it!

example of a robotic arm. If your arm is going to be used in several shots, it would benefit you to make what I call a "master" scene. A master scene is made up of only one set of objects in a hierarchy. Once you've created it, you can use Load From Scene in the objects panel to bring the objects into the new shot. The first thing I usually do when creating a master scene is add a null object and name it after the object I'm going to put together. In this case we'll call it "ArmNull". Then all the objects are loaded in (in order) and parented to each other. The order in which you load the objects in can make a big difference in how easy it is going to be to animate your scene later. I try to import objects in the order of their parenting, which allows me to slide up and down in a logical order. For instance, if we load our arm base object first, then our fingers, then our elbow, then our upper arm and then our wrist, the object will be totally "out of order" when parented. When I'm animating, if I want the arm to reach up, I'll adjust the upper arm first, then the elbow, then the wrist, and so on. If the objects were loaded in this haphazard way, I'll be constantly shuffling through the list looking for the right object. If they were loaded in order, all I have to do is pop up the list and slide down one (or up one) to the next joint. The null is sort of an insurance policy. It allows for gross repositioning, regardless of what keyframes have been set with the objects.

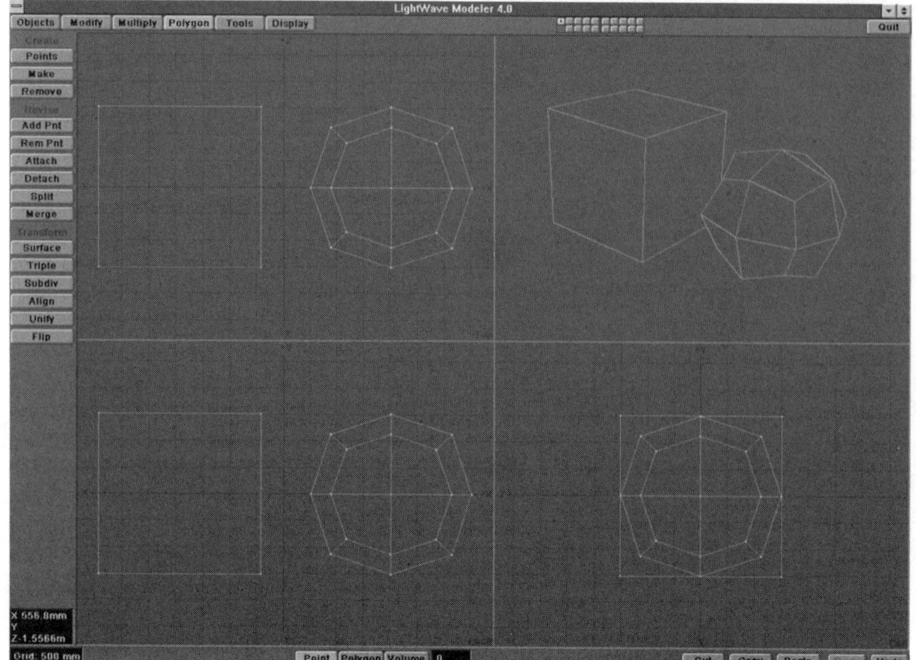

Figure 3: The results of one metaforming operation on a plain cube.

Build to Scale

Most of the time I try to build objects to scale, which makes it much easier to set up the scenes later. Not only do the objects load in ready to parent, but they also load in scale with previously built objects. With a car, for example, if you build the tires at 2.6 times the scale you built the body in, it's going to be difficult to get all these objects scaled and parented later.

There are several tools for keeping track of the size of objects in Modeler. First, the grid. The grid can be set to metric (default) or feet and inches—quite handy if you're using existing blueprints or plots. Another tool to remember is the old numeric button (n). If you're going to build a 10-foot globe, use the numeric button to make your ball exactly 10 feet. There's also the Measure tool (Display). This works like a virtual tape measure (oh no, I used the "v" word!). Just click and drag. The distance will read out in the coordinates box.

Round Those Corners

Another rendering pitfall is sharp corners. Take, for instance, a lamp base. The quick way of making the base is to pop down some points, make a polygon and lathe it. If you'll just pause for one moment and consider how it will be rendered, you'll get better results. Just go back and add a few more points to the sharp corners of the polygons and drag them into a rounded corner. It doesn't have to be a lot—maybe just a three-point curve—but the results are dramatic (or at least as dramatic as a lamp base gets). This process gets a little more complicated when it comes to extrusions and other solid objects. For a lot of objects, a simple bevel will do the trick; just use what amounts to a 45-degree angle (or equal shift and offset). This creates a very crude rounded shape, but can make a difference. The macro "shape text" (Amiga 3.5) or Polygons Edge Shaper (PC) is also very handy. It can round corners with little effort.

Hard or Smooth?

Here's a little tip: adjacent polygons that don't share points will not get smoothed. Some of you may have stumbled across this situation accidentally, when it wasn't to your liking. It can work to your advantage. A good example of this is a beveled font. Most of the time, adjusting the smoothing angle will solve the problem illustrated in Figure 1. If you don't want to mess with that or if you have a fairly complex font object, you can go for the sure-fire fix. Just go back to Modeler and select the polygons that make up the

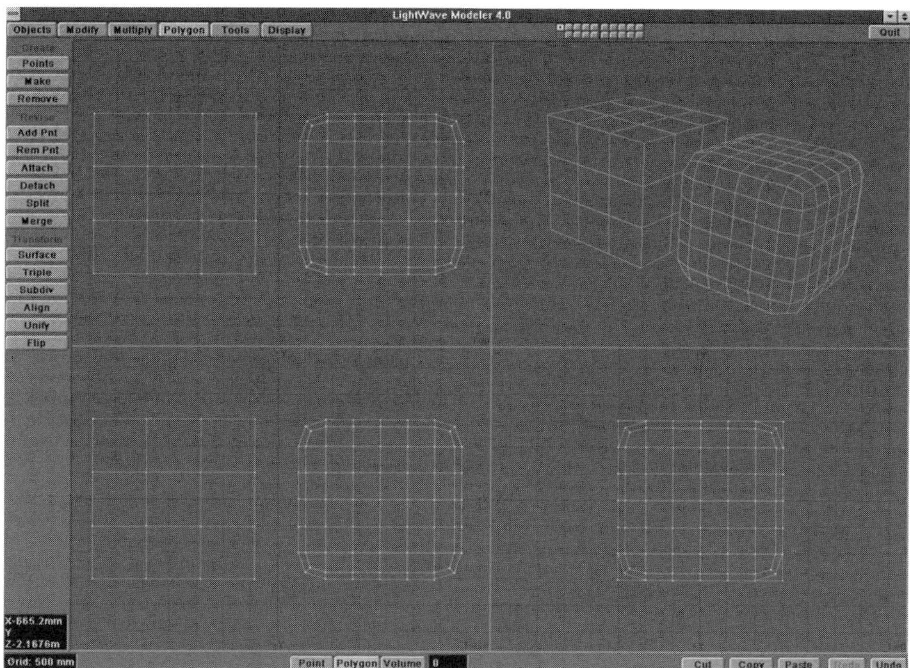

Figure 4: Multiple segments provide better, cleaner results.

bevel (you did save them as a separate surface, didn't you?). Now hit Cut and Paste. Looks the same, huh? Well, the difference is that the polygons of the bevel no longer share points with the front or sides. When rendered in Layout, the edges between the bevel and the front will be sharp, but the sides and the bevel will be smooth (Figure 2).

Non-Planar Polygons

Nothing will boggle your brain more than an unexplained rendering error. If this should happen to you, don't panic, but do check for non-planar polygons. Identifying these little boogers is easy:

- Go into Modeler (if you aren't already there).
- Load your object.
- Click on the Polygon select button.
- Hit the (w) key (Polygon statistics).
- Find the non-planar field (at the bottom).
- Click on the (+) next to the field.
- Stare in amazement!

All of the non-planar polygons should now be selected. If there are no selected polygons, your model is probably correct. Of course, this means something else is wrong, and you're back to square one. If you had a few polygons light up, then you've found the culprits. Now we must get rid of them. The simplest way to correct the problem is to triple the polygons. The logic here is that a triangle can simply never be anything but a plane. If you're feeling adventurous, you can go in and drag some points around. Or use the Set Val (Ctrl v) tool to flatten those suckers out, but this will probably give you more pain than pleasure. Usually about the time you get one polygon flattened, the one next to it gets whacked out of shape.

Metaforming

Ah, Metaforming—what a cool feature! This is a very handy tool for smoothing objects, but it can be a little unpredictable. The best way to get the results you want is to prepare your object and experiment. For example, look at the results of Metaforming the cube in Figure 3 (straight cube) compared to the subdivided one in Figure 4 (a cube created with three segments in all directions). The difference is clear. Now look at the cube in Figure 5 (same cube in second example with points moved to corners). With just a little preparation, the results are far better. Try changing your object in a few ways. You'll probably get different results every time. I try to think of Metaforming as sort of a rock tumbler for computers. Give it a blocky object and it'll give you a gem. One last thing: Try not to go too crazy with this tool, since you can rack up the polygons very quickly.

Detail vs. Image Mapping

A classic trap with object creation is determining what will be object data and what will be image-mapped. Again, this must be determined by how the object will be seen. Is it going to streak past the camera, or does it just sort of sit there, waiting for something to happen? If your object is barely going to be seen, an image map (or bump map) may be all you need. If you're going to dwell on the object, you're probably going to need that detail in true relief. Take, for example, my magic wonder sphere in Figure 6 (sphere with object detail) compared to wonder sphere lite in Figure 7 (sphere with bump-mapped detail). If they're just sitting there, the choice is obvious. But what about Figure 8 (sphere flying past camera, motion-blurred)? Can you tell which one I used? (If you must know, it's the bump-mapped one!)

The Edge

Here's a short tip: never use a flat plane to represent a flat object. Well, almost never. Every so often I see an animation of something "flat," or an object made up of flat surfaces, like a cereal box. The person who modeled it simply made a box and opened the top flap. He or she even made sure to flip the polygons and assign a separate surface for the inside of the box. Maybe the animator even subdivided the box and animated it with Bones (being sure to triple those poly-

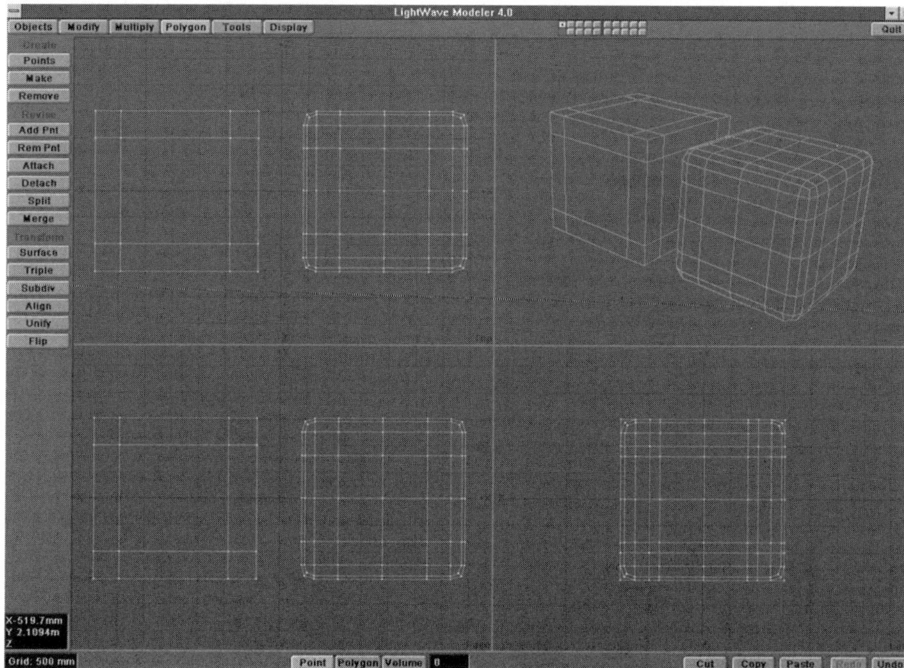

Figure 5: With a little preparation, the results are dramatic.

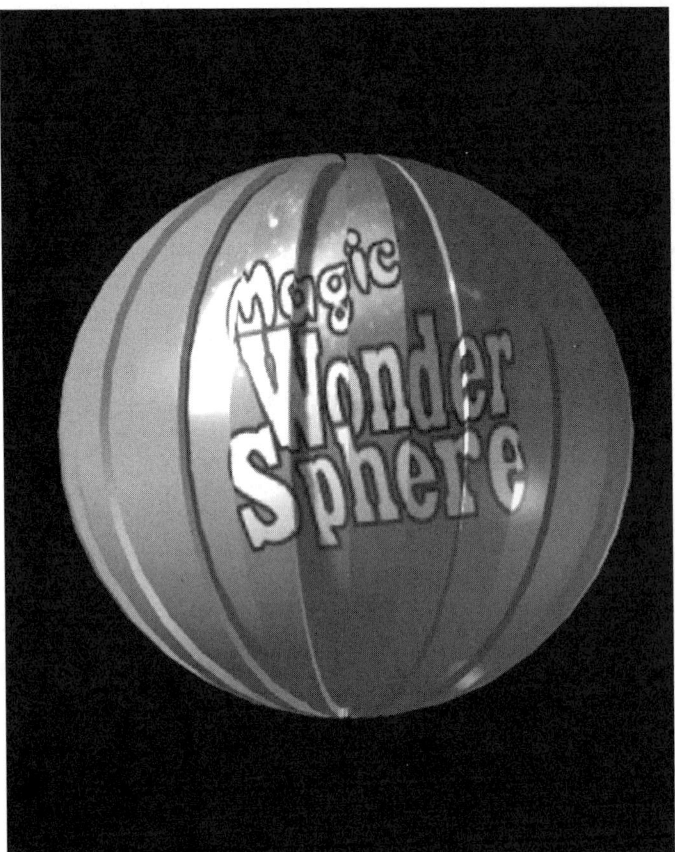

Figure 6: The Magic Wonder Sphere with object-based detail.

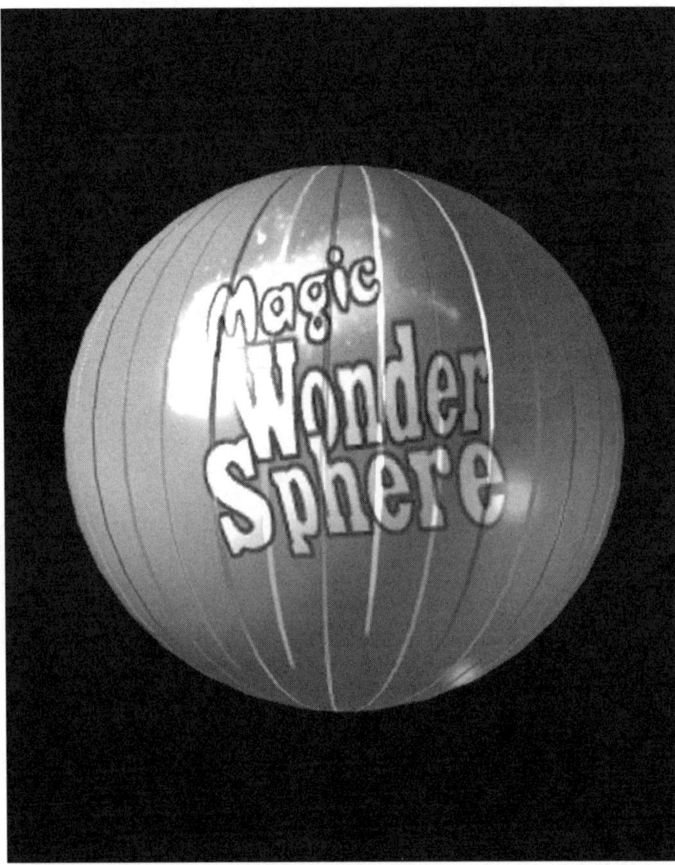

Figure 7: Wonder Sphere Lite with bump-mapped detail.

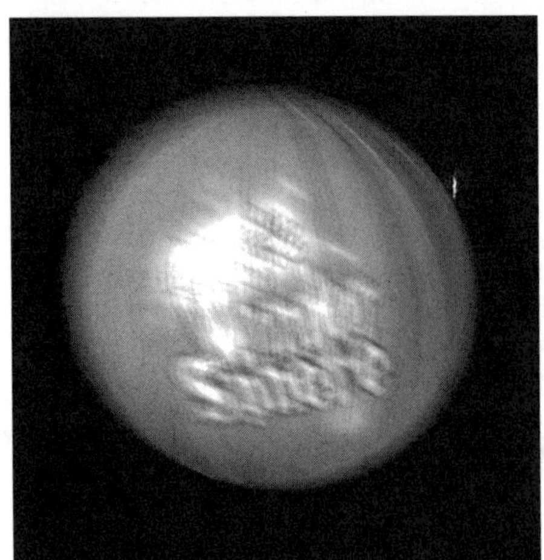

Figure 8: Which sphere is it?

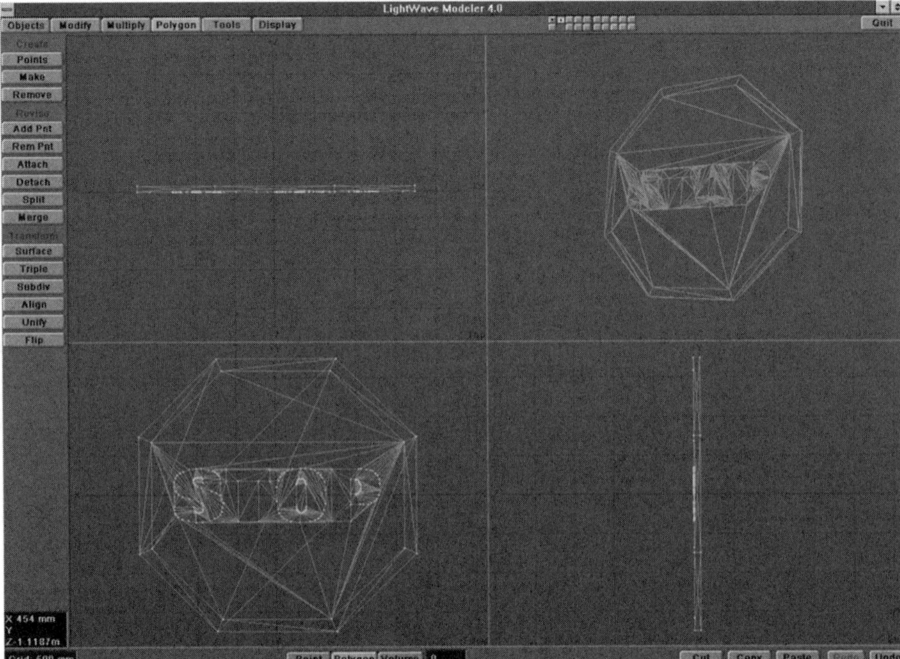

Figure 9: A triangled stop sign that's hard to look at.

gons). So what's my beef? That whirling box of Super Sugar Blamo Pops has no mass, no dimension. Take a good look at your cereal box tomorrow morning (you do start off with a balanced breakfast, don't you?). Even the thinnest cardboard has a noticeable edge, so why doesn't that object? Of course a piece of paper is pretty thin, and you can get away with a flat object. But very few other things are as thin as a piece of paper.

Cleanup

One of the last things you should do in Modeler is an overall cleanup. First, are there any one-or two-point polygons? You can check by clicking on Polygon select and hitting (w) (Polygon stats, again). The point count of all the polygons is given here. If there are any one- or two-point polygons, and you wanted them there, leave them alone. If not, hit the (+) button next to the appropriate field to select them, and then hit the (z) key (delete).

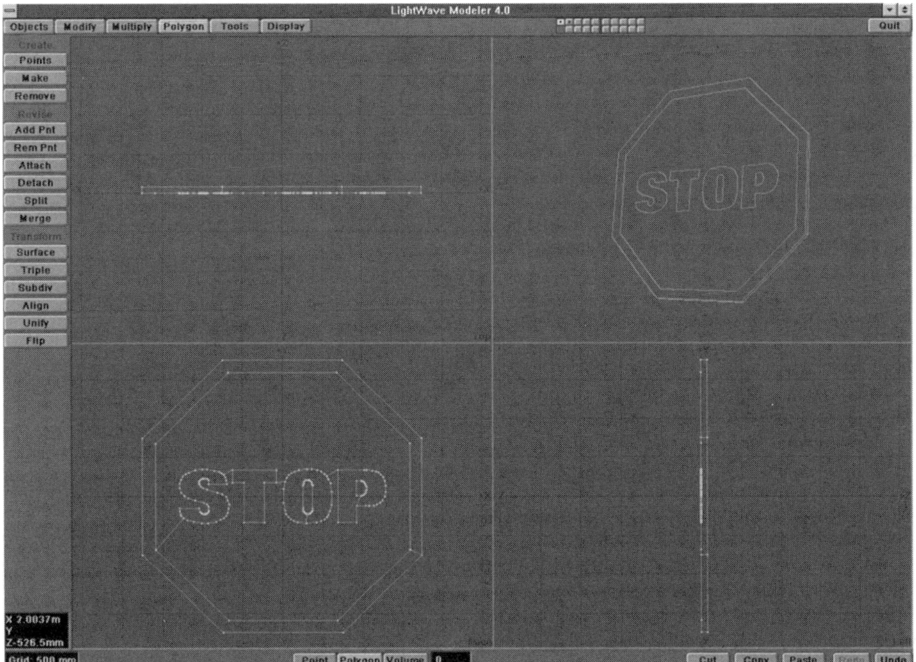

Figure 10: A cleaned-up stop sign is much better!

Next, check for any sneaky non-planar polygons that may have cropped up, and fix them (see above). Are there any groups of connected polygons on the same plane (for instance, the stop sign in Figure 9)? If there are, you can join them by selecting all of them and pressing Merge (Polygon menu) or (Shift + z). A cleaner object is easier to see and work with. Note the difference in the cleaned stop sign in Figure 10.

Now check your surfaces using the stats. All of your surfaces, and the number of polygons assigned to those surfaces, are in the pop-up list at the bottom of the Polygon Stats requester. To check the polygons, just select a surface and hit the (+) button. All the polygons having that surface are now selected.

Another annoying and invisible pain is duplicate points. A simple Merge Points operation (Tools menu) will fix this, and it's a good practice anyway. Note: If you used the sharp edge trick described earlier, you do *not* want to merge those points. Just cut them to an empty layer to keep them separate.

Duplicate and double-sided polygons are also not readily visible. Use Unify (Polygon menu) after merging points to fix these (unless you wanted some double-sided polygons, of course). If you are experiencing the problem of alternating flipped polygons (common in cross-program object exchange), use the Align button. This function should flip the renegade polygons so they face the same way as all the others, though sometimes they all end up the wrong way. If they do, just hit the (f) key (Flip polygon). Lastly, double-check the orientation, position and scale of your object, remembering that the world center (black crosshairs) will be your pivot point.

Well, that's 10. Of course, there are hundreds of little tricks that you will learn with experience. I've only begun to scratch the surface. Just keep some of these tips in mind next time you're staring bleary-eyed at that screen. You'll be building better objects in no time. Remember, a little preparation goes a long way, and will save you tons of time later. One last hint: try a little spray lacquer on your Super Sugar Blamo Pops. They'll stay crispier in milk longer!

LWP

Tom Williamson is an animator at Computer Cafe, in Santa Maria, Calif. He spends way too much time using computers and is wondering why these bios are written in third-person when everyone knows we write them ourselves.

Cut It Out!

Moving Clouds With Only One Image

by Dan Ablan

Can someone answer a question for me? Why is it that every client is always on a tight budget when it comes to animation? A budget that is not only short on money, but time. This tutorial is from a situation that came up a couple of months ago in one of those much too familiar animation projects. I was hired to put together a logo for a new business that was starting up in the area. The job was for a former Chicago weatherman who was also a pilot. He had the idea that the logo we were animating should give viewers the feeling that they were flying. And, of course, there's only about a day and a half to get it done. So, I came up with a few ideas, presented them to the client, and they weren't what he had envisioned. Later that same day, I met with him again, and showed him his logo flying out from behind some clouds. He liked that very much. Remember, he's a pilot. "But Dan," he asked, "what would it take to get these clouds moving? Can you get digitized clouds?" Well, the answer was "Yes, but not in one day." It would have taken too much time to locate the right cloud footage and have it digitized. Not to mention the realities of that limited budget thing. So, somehow, I came up with the idea of animating the clouds from one still image.

The Right Image

What I noticed while working on this project is that is very important to find the right set of clouds that won't be too difficult to pull apart. Luckily, I happened to have a CD of 100 royalty-free PhotoCD images of clouds. This is something that I was very thankful for. When I began animating full time, I began collecting anything I could, even if I didn't need it at the time. And I started a file containing items to scan, such as a beer bottle label, texture samples, and so on. When I came across the right CD sets, I picked up as many as I could. That way, when it was down to the wire, I wasn't spending my time looking for a decent image. When looking for an image, especially clouds, find one that has some definite separations in it. A cloud image that is too intricate will be a great pain to use for this tutorial.

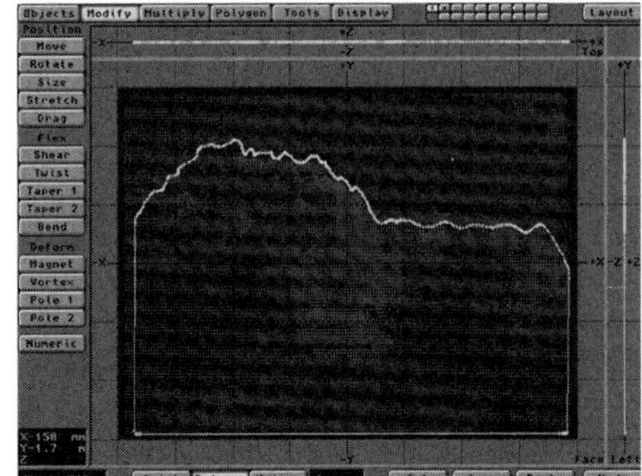

Figure 1: A polygon matching the shape of one portion of the original cloud image is constructed in Modeler.

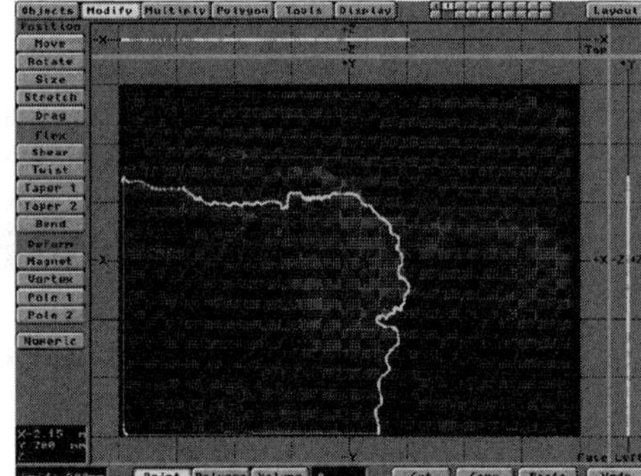

Figure 2: Another polygon is made matching the shape of a different area of clouds.

How It Works

All we're really doing here is taking one image (see Color Pages), cutting it up into two pieces, and painting the existing piece for a background. Once I selected the image, I loaded it into LightWave. Then, in Modeler, I used the display **BG Image** feature to see my clouds. Using the create point tool, I began setting points around the first cloud that I intended to move (Figure 1). I made the second cloud the same way (Figure 2). Next, I exported the first cloud object to LightWave and rendered it out fully white and luminous, and did the same for the second cloud object.

Once the rendering was finished, I went into ToasterPaint and called up the first cloud polygon image. Using the (j) key, I swapped screens and loaded the original full-color cloud image. Next, using the other layer as a template, I began cutting out the first cloud from the color image, to match the first polygon (Figure 3). The same process was performed on the second cloud (Figure 4). Using the white rendered polygon images as templates, I then guestimated where they would be when they started moving and where they'd end up. Based on that knowledge, I began painting out the clouds from the full-color image, which would be mapped onto the flat polygons (the ones that were just cut out). This was one of the most important parts of the project, because if I cut a section of clouds from a larger image and mapped it onto a polygon that moves over that original image, the same cloud would be revealed underneath. It was crucial that I change the final background image, or else the illusion wouldn't work. I did the same for the area of the second cloud.

Figure 3: Using the newly created polygon as a guide, the actual image is cut to match.

Soft Polygons

I was surprised that this idea was actually working at this point. But, given the peculiar size of the image and polygon, I had to mess with the sizing quite a bit to have the image cover all edges of the polygon. **Automatic Sizing** wasn't enough. The other major problem I encountered was that it was very obvious that there were polygons in the scene with cloud images mapped on them. Then, I remembered the good old transparency map trick. I went back into TPaint and loaded the first black and white cloud

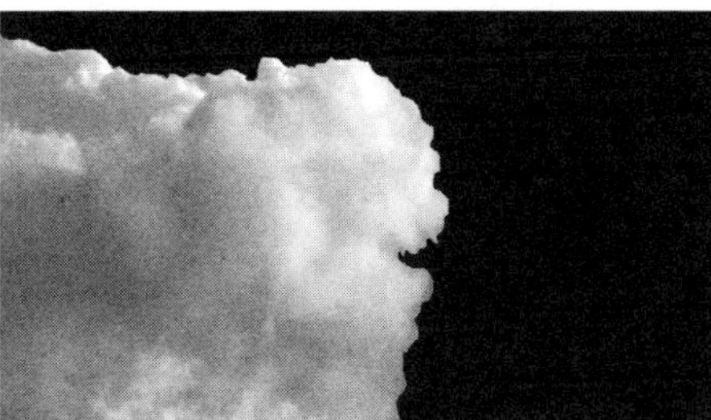

Figure 4: The same process is done for the other polygon.

Figure 5: A transparency map is made for each cloud polygon.

polygon image. I proceeded to fade off the edges all the way around the polygon (Figure 5). A transparency map reads the black and white values, and whichever part of the object has the lighter part of the image mapped onto it will be more transparent. When the color fades from black to white, the object fades from itself to transparent. To get this image to work, we will need to use **Negative Image** in the transparency panel. This way, the black and white values will be reversed, causing the image to fade away to white. This feature is really good for making those streaking wisps that you see flying behind a nice logo. You could also use a transparency map to make spaceship trails that fade off to nothing. Cut and save these as brushes.

I finished making the transparency maps and went back into LightWave. The transparency images were mapped using a planar image map on the Z axis, under the **Transparency texture** (T) button. I used the exact same size coordinates I had for the actual image map on each polygon.

Animation Speed

After a good bit of tweaking, it was difficult to see where the image-mapped polygons ended and the background cloud began. Because of the soft falloff on the edges, you couldn't see a seam unless you were looking for it. The animation still needed to be accurate, and look like real clouds moving. One step was taken care of by using a real image. The next step was to set the movement and timing right. The first cloud polygon was moved along the X axis from left to right and the second polygon was moved from right to left. Each moved just enough to be noticed, but didn't move fast. As a matter of fact, the amount they move across the screen is too minimal to show the difference with just a still image. The speed matched that of real clouds—at least, that's what the pilot told me.

As with any logo or object, it's a good idea to add some spline control to the movements. Even with the cloud polygons, I set a tension of 1 at the first and last keyframes. Now, all that was left was to put the logo in. The client liked that it traveled out from behind the clouds, so that idea was kept. Back in Modeler, I made a very simple polygon to use as a front projection image map on the clouds. This was placed behind the moving cloud polygons, with the final background image front projected onto it. Finally, the logo was animated up through and over the clouds to its resting position in front of them. Additional titles slid in from the left and painted brush strokes were revealed across the top of the logo. A transparency map texture was set to the Front Projection image map type so that there was no hard edge when the logo appeared (see Color Pages).

In the Beginning

When I was learning how to animate, I believed that in order for an animation to be decent, it had to be very intricate, with several trade secrets going into any project. What I soon learned is that some of the best-looking animations are the simplest. Some credit should be given to those who are purists, and build an object to exact scale, without any missing details. Then, there is the practical side, where clients get what they pay for and it looks good on tape. With a little work and some thought, you can come up with some terrific ideas.

LWP

Creating Cloud 9

1. Make a polygon the size of the part of the image to be animated.
2. Render it out fully luminous, so that you have a completely white surface.
3. Use ToasterPaint or a similar program to cut out the same areas of clouds for an image brush.
4. Use ToasterPaint or a similar program to soften/fade off the edges of the white rendered polygons.
5. When softening, use the range tool to fade from white to black, about 1/4-inch from the edges.
6. Remember that the ramped values from black to white will act as the "falloff" for the cloud polygons.
7. Cut out and save these fixed white images under a different name, for safety.
8. Place the black and white image as a transparency map, with the same size coordinates as the image maps.
9. Move the cloud polygons from left to right at a very smooth, slow pace.
10. Make one more polygon to match the top edge of the clouds for use as a front projection image map. This will allow you to "hide" a logo behind the background image of the clouds.

Dan Ablan is a LightWave animator for his Chicago-based company, AGA. Because his 8-track tape player recently broke, he can't listen to his favorite Bay City Rollers tapes, and luckily, has extra time to write for LIGHTWAVEPRO. *Dan can be reached via the Internet at dma@mcs.com.*

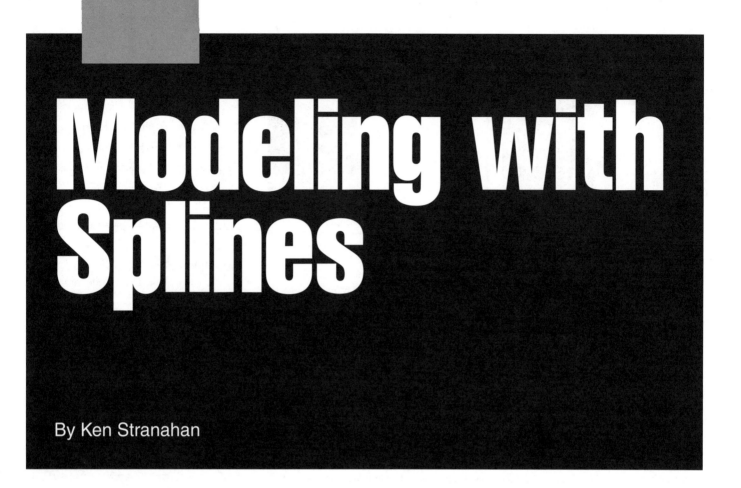

Modeling with Splines

By Ken Stranahan

Splines (or curves) are what I consider to be the most powerful tool in Modeler 3.0 and also one of the most confusing. Splines allow you to create complex, freeform objects—the kind of Curvilinear objects never before possible with regular polygonal-based modeling.

The basic concept is to make these things called splines or curves that define the surface of an object. You can link several of them together to form a Spline Cage. By selecting several connecting splines, the computer estimates the surface that would be formed between them and makes it into a polygon grid. This grid is called a spline patch. Put a bunch of these patches together and presto, you have an object. Okay, maybe it's not quite that easy, but I am going to show you how to use splines to start modeling complex shapes in no time.

Splines Away

Of the several methods to make a spline, the simplest is to use the sketch tool. This is as easy as selecting the sketch tool under the objects menu and then drawing in one of the three views and hitting Return. With sketch, the number of points comprising the curve is determined by the speed with which you draw it. If hitting Return gives you a normal polygon instead of a spline, check the numeric settings for the Sketch tool to make sure that Curve and not Polygon is selected.

Now, let's take a look at the spline. If you select the Drag tool from the Modify menu, you can drag any point in any of the directions to modify the curve. With the Drag tool, points do not have to be selected before moving them. Simply click and hold on to a point with the mouse button and drag it in any direction. Notice that the spline curve will follow the points fairly accurately.

If additional points are needed in a spline curve, select the spline and use the Add Points feature in the Polygon menu. Just click on the spline with the arrow where you would like the point to be added.

Another way to make a spline is by selecting a series of points and pressing the Make button under the Curves section in the Tools menu (CTRL-p). This spline will be drawn in the order that the points were selected. Pressing Make Cl or using the CTRL-o keyboard shortcut will give you a closed spline. A good trick to make points for spline curves is to take primitive shapes and remove the polygons leaving only the points which can then be hand selected. To do this press "k", for kill polygon, or click on Remove in the Polygon menu. Again, it's easy to manipulate the spline by adding or moving points.

You can further manipulate the spline by making control points at the ends. This allows you to control the angle at the end of the spline by moving the last point without having the control point as part of the object. It's easy to make a control point by selecting the spline and pressing CTRL-b (or selecting the Start CP button in the Tools menu) to make the beginning point a control point and CTRL-n (or selecting the End CP button in the Tools menu) for the end point. When the spline is selected, you will see a dotted line connecting the spline to its control point(s).The control point can be moved to change the bend of the curve without having to actually move the first or last point of the curve.

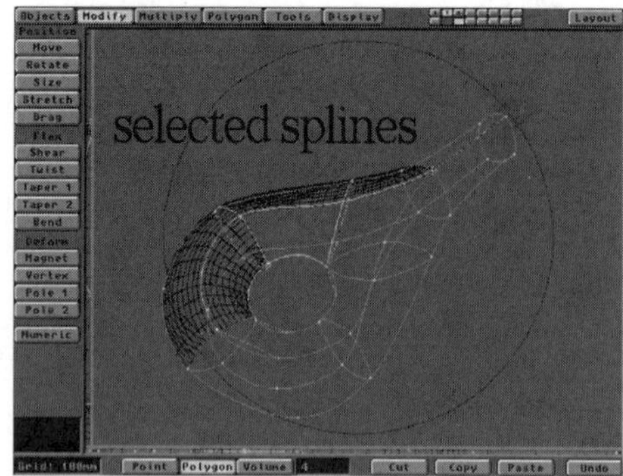

Figure 1

Patching the Splines

Now that you have learned to make a spline, you need to know how to put them together to make a cage. The best way is to build the splines by using the points in one curve for the crossing curves. I usually complete the building phase by making a few splines in the horizontal direction and then, using the points from the horizontal splines, connecting them in the vertical direction. To see the shape of the object more clearly when I'm making the splines, I use the static preview. This allows you to pick the points out from any angle, avoiding the tendency to pick the wrong points. It also allows you to rotate the object in three dimensions by holding the Alt button and dragging over the preview window. I find this one of the best ways to visualize the object in splines.

Sketching out the object is another way to build it. The splines can then be connected by selecting two points that are close to each other and using the Weld function in the Tools menu to merge the splines together.

Building a complicated spline cage isn't easy. Let's picture a closed spline in the X direction. This spline also has several closed splines connected to it in the Y direction. To make a patch, you must select three or four splines that are connected to each other by shared points that form square or triangular areas between them (see Figure 1). Select the Patch button in the Multiply menu or press CTRL-f to bring up the Patch requester. Here you can tell Modeler how many perpendicular and parallel segments (polygons) to create when patching a section. The perpendicular and parallel sections are always determined by the last curve chosen. The value entered for perpendicular segments will make that many "rows" of polygons perpendicular to the last curve chosen and, likewise, the value entered for parallel will make that many parallel sections of polygons to the last curve chosen. After selecting the number of segments, pressing OK will patch the section (see Figure 2).

Figure 2

One problem that can occur with closed splines is that it may be hard to determine which side of the spline the patch will be formed on. If you look at a spline when it is selected you will notice that it has a diamond around one of its ends; the diamond represents the beginning of the spline. Just like polygons, splines have directions. If the patch is not formed in the direction you wish, click Undo, and then change the direction of one of the splines by selecting it and pressing "f" (the diamond will move to the other end of the curve). Repatching it will often yield the desired results. Sometimes, however, flipping splines and repatching just won't yield the proper results. To avoid such a problem, connect several splines together to form one curve. Take a long spline and kill the polygons by pressing "k" or the Remove button in the Polygon menu; then, reconnect the points to make several smaller splines in its place. After many splines have been made end to end, the key is to select the small splines and smooth them together by selecting the Smooth button under the Curves section in the Tools menu (or pressing Ctrl-s). The result is long curve composed of separate sections that is still easy to patch because it has more sections to select from (see Figure 3). I recommend such a method to make long splines; it saves a lot of time by being able to select only the splines needed.

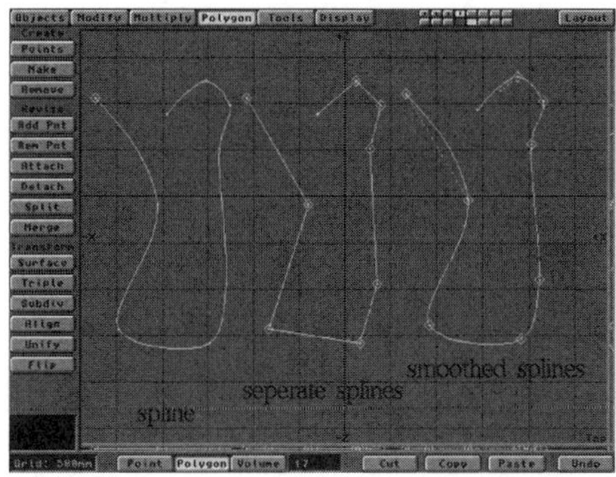

Figure 3

Closing that Cage

You now know how to patch a single section, so let's finish the whole cage. Making spline cages can get confusing enough, but when you start patching them,

Spline Tips and Tricks

By John Gross

- When dragging points with the Drag tool, dragging from a window where points are in line with each other will drag all of the points. To get around this, select the point(s) you wish to drag from one window, then drag them in the 'stacked' window. Only the selected points will be affected.
- When adding points to a curve using the Add Points tool, you will generally want to add the points in one window and then use Drag to move them into place from another window.
- Use the static preview to aid in selecting points and splines. The view can be rotated by holding down the Alt key.
- You can only patch splines that are connected to form a triangular area between three splines or a rectangular area between four splines.
- The last spline selected before patching will determine which way the perpendicular and parallel segments are created.
- When patching, it doesn't matter how long the splines are that you are using for the patch. What matters is that the area between them is bordered by splines that share points at the corners where they meet.
- Selecting Automatic Polygons in the Options panel (Objects menu) will create quadrangles where it can and triangles in areas that would result in the creation of non-planar polygons.
- It is wisest to try to make as many four-sided patches as possible and only use triangular patches where necessary to come to a point. For example, if you are patching a shovel, use quad patches all the way to the tip, and then have a tiny triangular patch right at the tip.
- When patching a triangular patch, make sure to select the spline farthest away from the "tip" last.
- For adjoining patch areas, try to use the same number of perpendicular and parallel segments. If you do not, you will have to stitch between these sections to get a smooth patch.
- When selecting curves, don't worry if you accidentally select faces as well. Any selected faces are ignored when patching.
- If you need to align polygons after patching, make sure to merge points first. Polygons that do not use shared points cannot align with each other.
- Use Background image (Display menu) to bring in an image loaded in LightWave to use as a template for drawing splines out.

-J.G.

selecting the splines becomes nearly impossible. This is where I use the perspective view the most.

After making a patch, you can deselect the splines and then select a few of the polygons . By pressing the right bracket key (]) or Select Connect from the Display menu, you can have Modeler select all of the faces that are connected to the ones you selected. At this time, you can check to see if the polygons are facing the right direction. If need be, they can be flipped and then cut and pasted into the background layer. To save time, I use the apostrophe (') key to swap the foreground and background layers. By cutting the faces that are made by patching and pasting them in a background layer, you will avoid selecting them while still having them as a reference for making your next patch.

When patching an object, you will want to keep in mind the amount of polygons that are being used because it is very easy to over do it. When making a patch, its recommended to adjust the number of perpendicular and parallel segments. You can also select how you want the patch to be formed. Patching by knots will adjust the spacing of the polygons where they are needed by looking at the number of points in the curve. Patching by length will space the faces evenly by looking at the length of the splines making up the closed area.

Clean up

After patching an object and rendering it in LightWave, you will find seams running across it. The reason for this is that even though neighboring patch points may be in the same position, they are created separately and the polygons do not actually connect.

There are several processes that I always do to finish an object. Press "m" to merge points (or select Merge from the Tools menu). Using automatic should clean up most of the seams. If you are still getting seams, you may have to stitch them together (see Sidebar). After merging points, I press "w" for statistics, making sure that the Polygons button at the bottom of the screen is selected. Next, I check for one and two vertices polygons. If any are present, there will be a number listing how many there are. They can be selected by pressing the plus sign (+) next to them and then cut. If any curves are present, they can also be cut and saved with the spline cage as a separate object.

From the same Statistics panel, I select non-planar at the bottom of the panel; non-planar polygons are basically those that are out of alignment with themselves and have surfacing problems. To relieve this, use the Triple command (Triple button in the Polygon menu or Shift-T) on the selected non-planars.

Finally, I check the point statistics (select Points at bottom of screen and then hit "w")for any points that are not connected to any polygons and cut them. I also use the Align and Unify tools under the polygon menu to check for flipped and extra polygons.

As you can see, spline curves are a great way to model objects. It may take a while but, once you get used to the way splines work, you can model just about any object with a little patience.

LWP

Ken Stranahan is an animator for Amblin Imaging where he is affectionately referred to as "Spline Boy." He is currently working on NBC's seaQuest, DSV.

How to Stitch a Patch

By Ken Stranahan

Sometimes the edge of patches just won't line up correctly. For example, you may have had to patch two neighboring areas with different segments which will not render correctly (see Figure 4). When this happens, there is something you can do to stitch the areas together. First, find the problem. I usually cut out the section that I want to work on and paste it into another layer. The polygons on both sides of the seam must be selected and then removed "k" leaving only the points. Any extra points that do not line up with the outer polygons should be cut. Next, form three polygons with the points around the seam (see Figure 5). After the polygons are selected, you can use the skin function to stitch across the problem area (to make it less confusing, choose the left and center polygons to stitch across first, then deselect and choose the center and right polygons to stitch across next). This will leave a few polygons you won't want. Choosing polygons that have more than three vertices from the Statistics panel will let you choose and cut the side polygons; the other unwanted ones can be chosen by hand. The remaining patch can be cut and pasted back to the original segment (see Fgure 6). Don't forget to clean up the object (merge points, unify and align polys) when you repaste the section. The process of stitching the polygons can also be done by hand, but this trick is significantly easier.

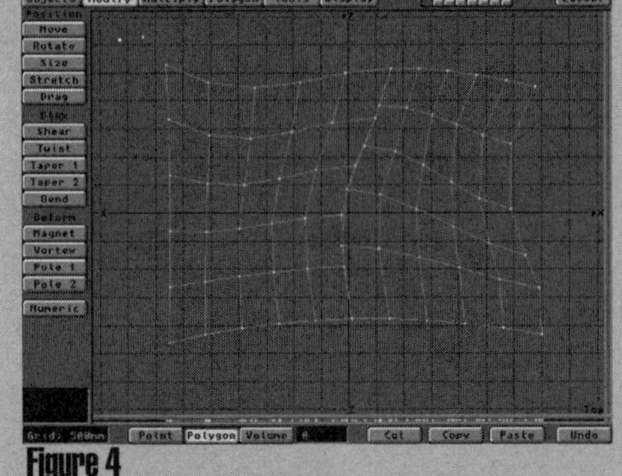

Figure 4

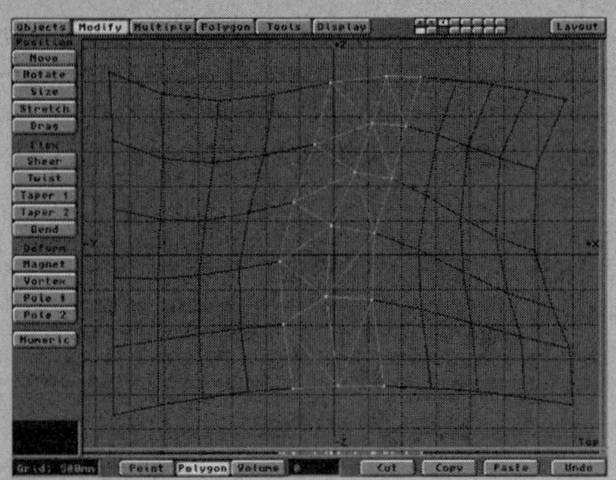

Figure 6

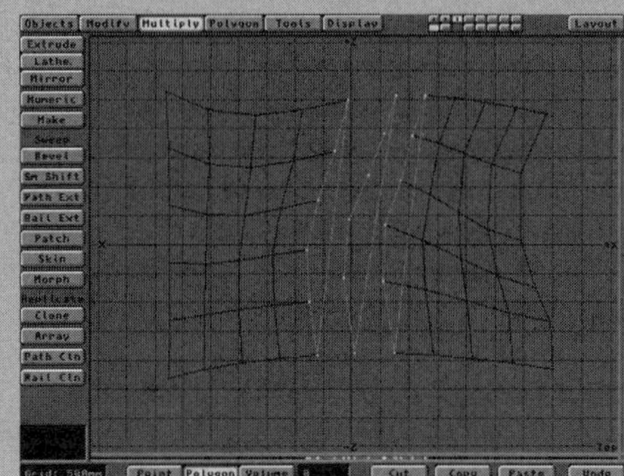

Figure 5

LightWave 101:

Basic of Splines, Part I

by Adam Chrystie

Enter the wonderful world of splines! Splines are useful for the creation of objects that have no apparent joints and objects whose shapes alter with no visible hard edges. In this month's lesson, we will be creating a simple mountain object.

The Rules of Spline Creation:

(1) A spline is made up of three or four curves that overlap to define a closed area.

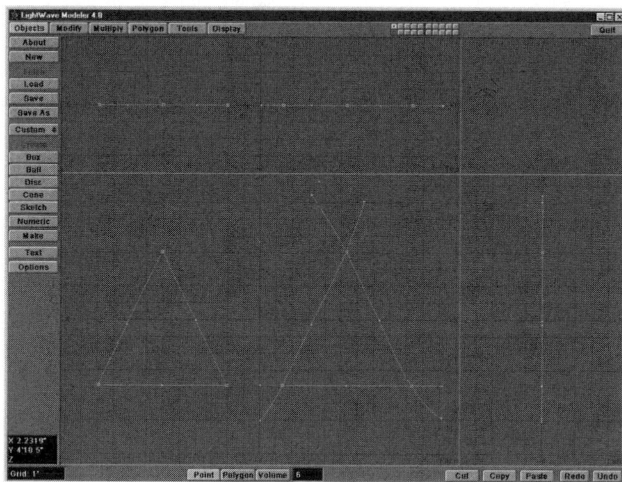

Figure 1

I try to avoid using more than four curves to define an area because the location of Modeler's patching is unpredictable. (You cannot select 10 curves and expect Modeler to patch all 10 sections. You must patch each section separately. Bummer! But have no fear. At SIGGRAPH, a NewTek employee I spoke with said the company was working on an autopatcher.) Always try to patch with four curves. If you patch with three curves, a visible crease may show along the shared axis of the patches. In the follow-up article, I will explore some methods for working around this drawback.

(2) The curves must be connected to each other somewhere along their lengths, which helps Modeler define the physical area where the patch will occur. These points must be fused together either by an Automatic or Absolute **Merge (Tools)** (m). You can also use the **Weld (Tools)** command (Ctrl–v in 4.0). The bottom line is that your curves must share actual points. The test is simple: Select a point where the curves appear to intersect. Now **Move (Modify)** (t) the point. If both curves alter their form, then the point is shared by both. If only one curve is affected by the point's movement, then the points were not shared. In this case, you would need to do a merge points or weld them together.

(3) When patching, you must be in **Polygon** Select Mode (bottom of Modeler screen) and you must select the curves that will define the patch.

(4) To patch the selected curves, hit the **Patch (Multiply)** (Ctrl–f) button and fill in the required numerical data. I'll discuss these fields a little later in this article.

Figure 1 shows two proper examples of splines that are about to be patched. The splines on the left have their points merged at the endpoints. The curves on the right overlap at points in between the endpoints. These examples illustrate how the patch area is created as a result of the locale of the overlapping points. I have selected the points where the curves are merged in order to make them more visible. Remember, when patching you must be in Polygon mode (at the bottom of Modeler's screen) and manually select the curves.

Shall We Spline Tonight?

Armed with this basic knowledge, let's make something before we move on to more advanced topics. So far, the splines in the images have been boring and flat. The main purpose of splines is to create nice, smooth 3D objects. So let's build a simple mountain-type shape. You could make one using three curves. I chose to slice my mountain into a few sections to give it a more controlled form.

- Make the front profile of the mountain in the front view by plotting points. Place the first point at Y = 0. The last point should also be at Y = 0. Use the **Create Points (Polygon)** tool to make the outline. Select the points from left to right or right to left and use **Make Curves (Tools)** (Ctrl–p). Now our object has guidelines for the X axis and the Y axis. Take a look at the figures for a rough idea of the shape. Try to mimic the curve that lies in the X–Y planes.
- Next, we need to define the base profile of the object. Again, we'll use **Create Points (Tools)** to make this outline. But first, click on the farthest lower left point of the mountain in the face view. LightWave will now have this point's location in memory. Why do we do this? To create the base profile, we will be working in the TOP view. Only the X and Z axes are in this view. By clicking on the lower left mountain point, we set Y to zero. Hence, when we work in the top view, all points that are created will position themselves at Y = 0. Proceed to create the base profile.
- Before you make this curve, deselect all the points you just created. Now go back and select the base points, beginning with the original point that was used to set Y = 0 and finishing with the point farthest to the right. Now you can turn these points into a curve by using **Make Curve** or (Ctrl–p). Both curves should share endpoints on their left and right sides. You should have something that looks like Figure 2.

We've created the base form and a vertical profile. Now we need to make some depth data for the mountain. We could use one curve to do this, but it would be a very boring object. Instead, we are going to use two curves, and we'll have to do multiple patches to complete the object.

- One curve should be built using the above steps between the left side and the middle of the object. The other curve should be between the middle and the right side of the object. The goal is to create two curves that join the top of the mountain to the

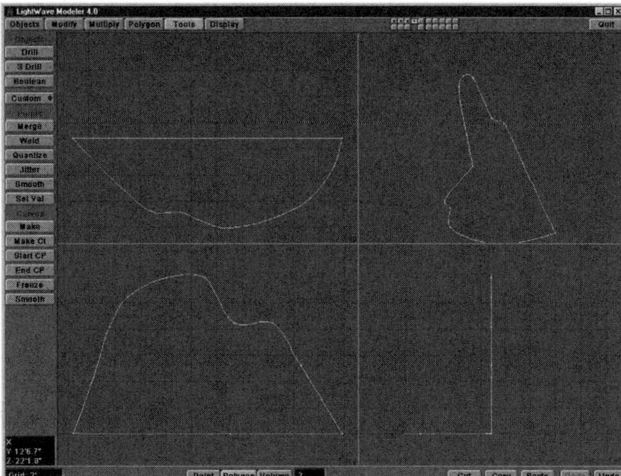

Figure 2

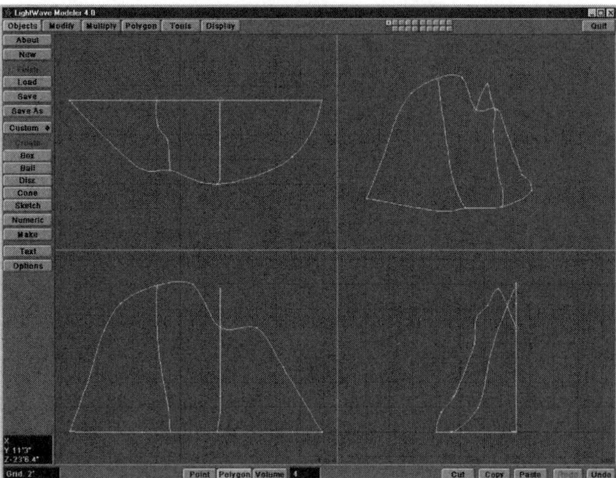

Figure 3

bottom of the mountain. Try to give the points some variation in their Z positions. The Z position of these curves will add ridges to the mountain. Remember to use the Top or Left views to set your Z position before you create the points. Use the Front or Left views to set the Y position for the points. Make sure that all points are aligned along their X axis. (Hint: They do not have to be perfectly aligned. We don't want the points to have too much variation between their X coordinates because you'd get a rather funky-looking patch. And if something looks funky in Modeler, it will look four times as funky when it's rendered.)

- Again, use **Create Points** to make the points and **Make Curve** to make the curve. Did you remember to highlight the points on the very top and extreme bottom of the mountain? If you forget to include them, the curves will not be sharing common points, and you'll have to deselect the points, reselect them in order (top to bottom or bottom to top) and then re-create them. You should have something that looks like Figure 3.

This is the way to go. You want to design your object so it can consist of many individual spline curves and sections of curves. In Part II, we'll apply this method in building a more complex object, a hand splint.

We're now ready to use the Patch (Multiply) (Ctrl–f) command. You must be in the Polygon Select mode to select the curves. The order of curve selection is important! The Patch operation makes the mesh's polygons converge in the direction perpendicular to the last curve selected. Say what? In other words, the Parallel and Perpendicular settings in the Patch requester are relative to the last curve selected. Let's take a look:

- Select the Base profile curve.
- Select the farthest left Depth Profile curve.
- Select the Shape Profile curve.
- Use the Patch command with settings at 10 for Parallel and Perpendicular. Also highlight Length for each.
- Click **OK**. Modeler should have made a patch on the left side of the mountain. If the patch was made on the right side, click on Undo. Then, push (f) for Flip Polygons and redo the above three steps.

If you've proceeded correctly, the result should not look good. Did you notice how the polygons tend to group together at the lower right section of the patch? Also, the mountain seems to have no real defining form at all. I get dizzy just looking at it. Here's the cure. We want the polygons to be grouped horizontally across the surface. Well, which curve is going to do this? That's right! The Vertical Depth curve that connects the base to the top of the mountain. You must make sure to select these vertical depth curves last. The order in which the other curves are selected is irrelevant. So undo that patch and select (in order) the Base curve, Profile curve and Vertical Depth curve.

Now, let's patch the middle section:

- Select the Top curve.
- Select the Bottom curve.
- Select the Left Vertical curve.
- Select the Right Vertical curve.
- Select Patch and use the same settings as before.

Now, we're going to patch the right side:

- Select the Top curve.
- Select the Bottom curve.
- Select the Right Vertical curve.
- Select Patch (Multiply) and use the same settings as before.
- If no new patch appeared, push Undo, and then hit (f) for Flip Polygons and try to patch it again.

When you're finished, you should have something that looks like Figure 4. If you received an error stating that the curves did not cross properly, go back and make sure that every curve is physically connected. Merge or weld points where necessary.

What About That Patch Requester?

One of the best features about splines is that you are able to have a large influence over the amount of polygons used during the creation of the object. This is what the Patch requester is all about. The requester's numeric fields are asking you how many divisions to use when building the object. We can make a patch with 100 parallel segments and 20 perpendicular segments if we wish. Remember that these data fields work in relation to the last curve selected. In our example, the last curves selected were always the vertical curves that attached the top and bottom of the mountain.

Let's give our object more vertical polygons:

- Undo the last patch.
- Select the curves in the proper order.
- Go to Patch and increase the perpendicular field. Now there should be more polygons traveling across the object's Y axis.

The Length option tells Modeler to make the subdivisions evenly spaced during the Patch operation.

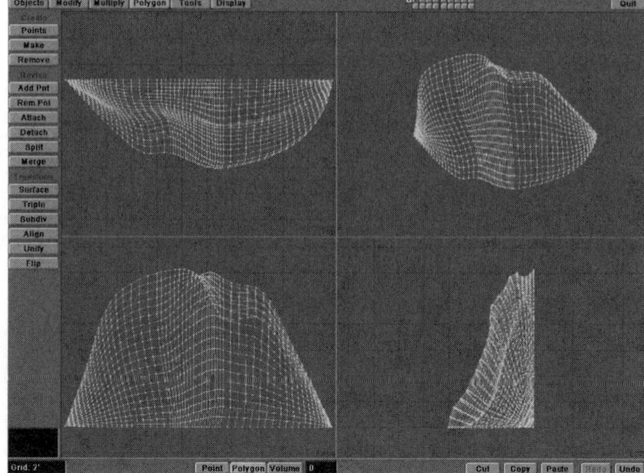

Figure 4

Selecting **Knots** tells Modeler to place more emphasis along the areas of the curves that were made with a higher density of points **(Knots)**, which, incidentally, usually occurs along bending areas. If you were patching around a curved 90-degree bend in a wall, using Knots would be a good choice.

Clean Up!

Let's undo that last test and repatch the mountain using a lower number of divisions. I used 20 subdivisions for each field and used Length for each field. Now that you've got your mountain shape, let's clean it up. If you wish, you can use the Mirror (Multiply) command to form the other side of the mountain. Be sure to merge points by pressing (m) after the mirror operation.

Modeler leaves the original curves in the object after patching is done. So let's get rid of them. Make sure nothing is selected prior to continuing.

- Enter Polygon Select mode.
- Push (w) to open the Polygon statistics requester. On the top of the menu you will see an area that says "Curves" and a number before it. This number tells us how many curves are in our object.
- Push the (+) symbol and Modeler will select these curves.
- Cut these curves and Paste them to another layer if you wish to save them for further use. Go back to the layer with your object.
- Push (w) again to enter the Polygon Statistics requester. On the bottom of the requester you should see a line of text that reads "Non-planar."
- Click on the little (+) sign. This will select all the non-planar polygons in our object.
- Now, use the Triple (Polygon) (t) command, which will convert the non-planars to triangular planar polygons. If a polygon is not planar, it can produce errors when rendered.

Onward! The polygon surface normals are probably pointing in opposite directions throughout various portions of the object. Why? If you used (f) to flip the curves during the patch phase this will also make the newly created polygons face the opposite direction. I had to use Flip once during the tutorial. Let's fix this!

Select some polygons in a horizontal fashion and you'll notice that some face inward and some face outward. Since we are modeling a mountain/mound shape, we want all the polygons to face outward. We do this in Polygon Select mode.

- Deselect all polygons by clicking in a gray area that is outside of the Modeler grid.
- Use the Align (Polygon) command. This will make all the polygons face one direction. The only problem is that we do not know in which direction they will face!
- So click on some polygons. If you see that they are facing inward, push (f) to flip the polygons outward.
- Save the object. (Note: I noticed in the pre-release Intel version that the Align command may not always function properly if a merge points operation is not performed first. This is usually not the case.)

Let's See It!

Load the object in Layout. I used the default surface and added a texture bump map. I then used the Crumple Bump Map texture with three scales and a size of 0.25 on all axes. Leave the amplitude at 50%. If your version doesn't have this texture, use Fractal Bumps with a higher amplitude setting and a texture size of 0.08 on all axes. You may leave Smoothing on or off. I like it off.

When this article originally appeared, Adam Chrystie was a cinema/video major at the University of California, Santa Cruz, sweating over the completion of his demo reel and looking forward to returning to the pro animation world. He loves music of many forms, biking, cultural festivals, studying languages and hanging out with friends while having nighttime beach bonfires.

LightWave 101:
Give Me a Hand!

by Adam Chrystie

In the October issue, we made a simple mountain using splines. This time we will be making a hand splint using splines and a bit of metaform. Please save your work often and use multiple file names. Never delete the spline cages once they are done—you can always improve this object once you have finished the tutorial.

The first step is to analyze our intended object. First, we must decide how we are going to model with our splines. Along which axis will we begin modeling: X, Y or Z? Another important decision is to determine how many key cross section splines you will need for the object. Key cross section splines are used to add detail and more pronounced curvatures in the object. I compare them to keyframes in the time line of our animations. As we build our object we will discover the need to create additional key cross sections.

Starting Out

The hand splint starts at the forearm and extends until the initial joints of the fingers. Another portion of the splint extends further to cradle the thumb. I know it's hard to visualize the object, so take a look at the screen shots to get an idea of what you're building. I had five key cross section splines that were modeled along the object's Z-axis. The initial curve consisted of three points. I decided to plot the curves first and then go back and move the points to make a more defined shape. See Figure 1 to get an idea of the shape I used for the beginning of the arm splint. Follow these steps to begin the splint:

- Create the curve in Figure 1.
- Select the **Copy** (c) button to store a copy of the curve in LightWave's memory.
- Go to layer 2 and use the **Paste** (v) button.
- Move the curve in layer 2 to the next key spline cross section (Figure 2).
- Continue to use this method of copying and pasting curves until you have something that looks like Figure 3. When you do, cut all the curves and paste them back into layer 1. *[Editor's note: A quick way to achieve this is to make all of the layers active and choose Cut, then Paste. All curves will be pasted into the first active layer.—JG]*

Now we need to make the other defining boundaries of our arm splint object. We must make curves for the right and left sides and the bottom of the object.

- Select all left points of the curves starting with the first curve and ending with the last curve. Do not skip a point. Select them in order! If you make a mistake, push the (/) key or click in a gray area on the bottom of the Modeler screen to clear all of the points.
- Push Ctrl–p or **Make** in the **Tools** panel to build a curve using these points.
- Do the same for all the right-hand points.
- Select all the center points of the curves in order and make a curve using these points.

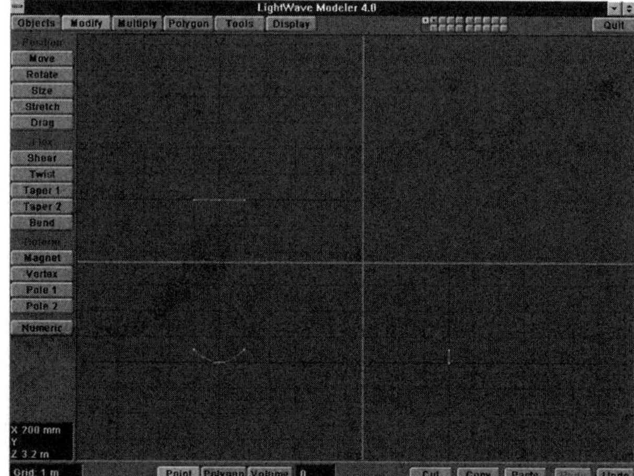

Figure 1

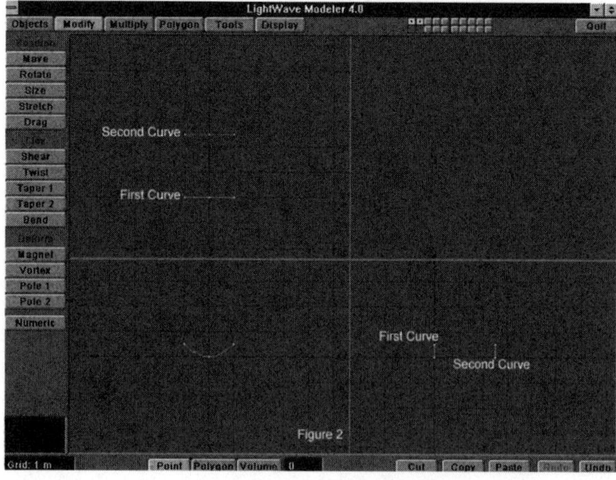

Figure 2

Adding Detail

Your screen should look similar to Figure 4. You might be noticing that this hardly looks like a hand splint! How are we going to define the hand area with only three points? By adding more points to the end of the splint object. More points will allow the mobility needed to shape the thumb region and the hand region. Let's get to it!

- Select the last curve.
- Select **Add Point** (**Polygon** panel) and add points to the end polygon. My splint had a total of six points. Try to add the points equidistant from each other (Figure 5).
- **Move** or **Drag** (**Modify** panel) each individual point so it mimics Figure 5.

Great! We're getting there! What would happen if you tried to patch the curves right now? Go on, try it. After patching, you'll notice that the splint looks like a smooth, curled piece of paper. It doesn't have the dramatic depressions that form a valley for the thumb to sit in. Overall, it is a very boring object. Let's take care of the thumb detail. We'll need to make a curve that will travel down the middle of the thumb. This curve will later be moved negatively along the Y-axis

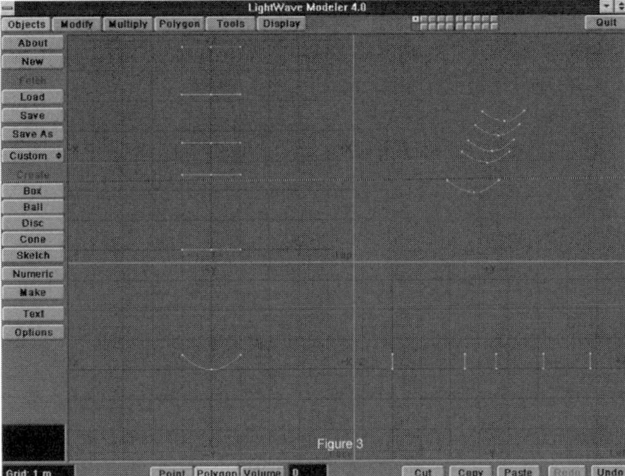

Figure 3

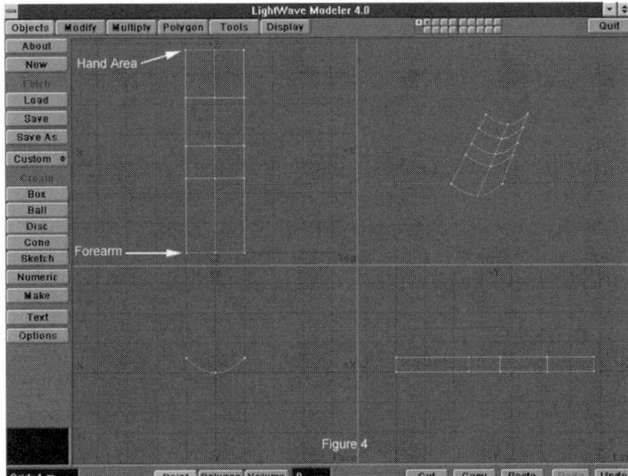

Figure 4

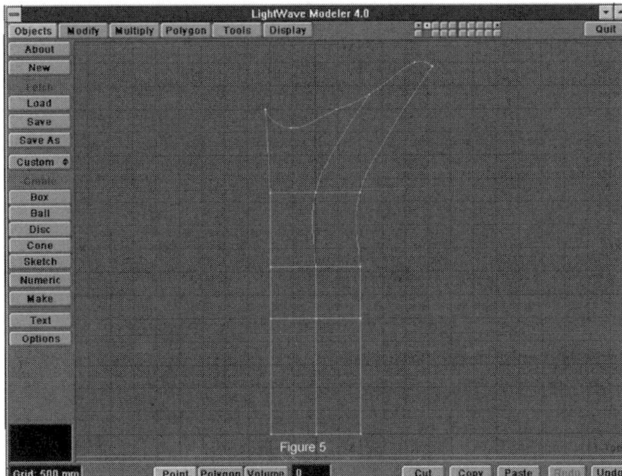

Figure 5

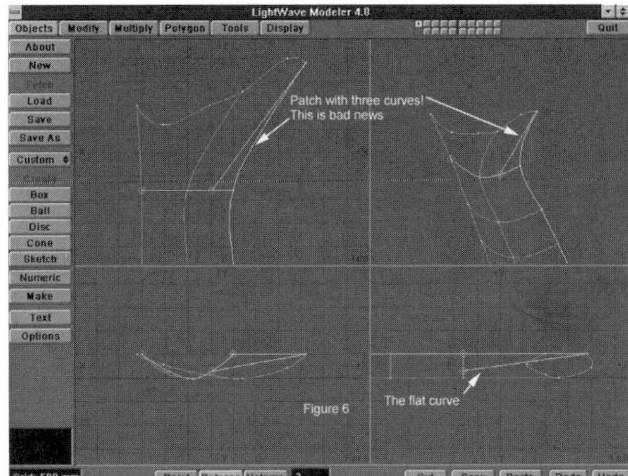

Figure 6

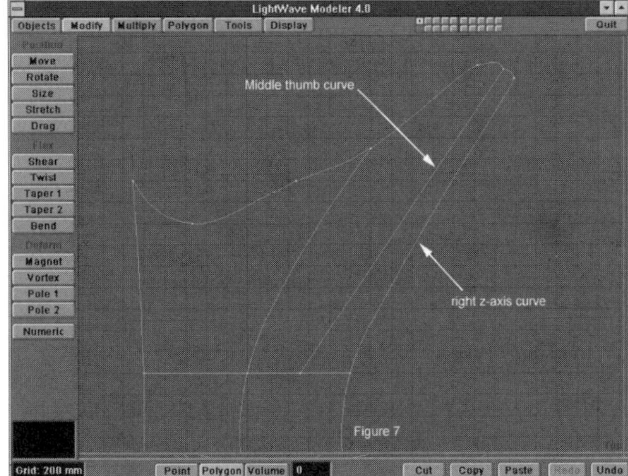

Figure 7

to create the needed depression in our object.

- Select the second-to-last cross-section curve.
- Use **Add Point** (**Polygon** panel) and add a new point between the center and right point of the curve.
- Select the point created in the above step and select the rightmost point of the last cross section curve. Make a curve out of these points (see Figure 6).

Problems and Solutions!

We've run into two problems with our model. Look in the Left view of Modeler. Notice that our new spline is a straight line. We will need to add another point somewhere along the curve. The other problem we have is that we've altered our model so there's a three-sided patch to the right of our "straight curve." See Figure 6 for details. Let's take the straight spline first:

- Switch to **Point** select mode (space bar) to make sure that no points are selected. Deselect any selected points.
- Switch to **Polygon** select mode and select the rightmost curve (the curve that runs down the entire Z-axis of the splint). If you selected a small curve, you've selected the wrong curve.
- Use Add Points (**Polygon** panel) to add a new point just below the point that was used for the creation of the previous straight spline.
- **Move** (**Modify**) the point above our new point so that it forms a smoother outline resembling a thumb. Don't worry if the curve isn't perfectly smooth. We will fix this later.

Your model should be similar to Figure 7. We have now added new points and rearranged the positions of our points while also retaining almost the original shape. We still have not converted the three-curved patch to a four-curved patch. Look at your monitor. You'll see that the curve in the middle of the thumb and the outer right-hand curve form two sides of a possible patch box. Check out the tip of the thumb and the second-to-last spline cross section. These two curves form the forward and rear sections of the patch to make a four-curved patch, which is what we want. We need to split the curve at the thumb's tip from the right-hand curve and to split the tip of the left side of the thumb from the last cross section. Here's how!

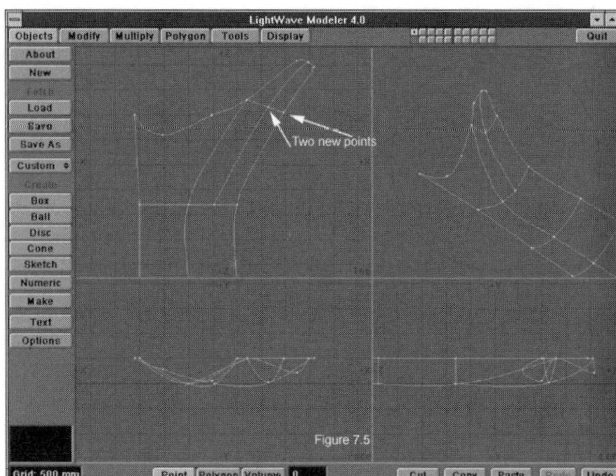

Figure 8

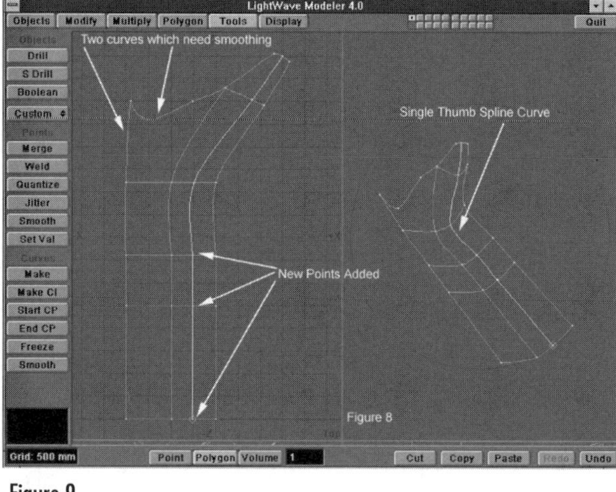

Figure 9

- Select the right Z-axis curve.
- Switch to **Point** select mode.
- Select the second-to-last point of the right-hand curve.
- Use the **Split** (**Polygon**) command to split the right-hand curve into two separate curves. This will form another small curve at the top of the thumb region.
- Switch to **Polygon** select mode. The two curves should be selected. Select the Right-hand curve and the new thumb tip curve if they are not already.
- Use **Smooth** curves (**Tools**) to make the two curves blend into each other. Be sure to use the smooth command that is in the **Curves** area of the Tools panel, not the **Points** area!

You need to perform the same steps to the left side of the thumb. The steps are exactly the same except that they are performed on the opposite side of the thumb.

Now it's time to fix the curve that will control the depth for the thumb region. Remember, this "straight curve" has only two points. After adding the middle point to the straight curve, we'll add another point to the right Z-axis curve. The new points will be used to create another cross section curve in the thumb region. (Later, you can alter the positions of these points to give the thumb more definition.) Look at Figure 8 and create a curve that is similar to mine or follow the steps outlined below:

- Change to **Point** select mode. Deselect any points.
- Change to **Polygon** select mode. (Remember, the space bar changes modes.)
- Select the middle thumb curve and right Z-axis curve.
- Use **Add Point** (**Polygon** panel) to create a new point on the middle thumb curve and right Z-axis curve. Look at Figure 8 for the point placements.
- Switch to **Point** select mode and deselect all points.
- Reselect the points of our soon-to-be curve in order from left to right or right to left.
- Make the curve (Ctrl–p).
- **Move** (**Modify**) the point's Y-axis positions. The middle point of the new cross section curve should be lower than the two outer points.

Take a look at the new detail that we've created in the thumb region. Notice how most of the patches neatly form quadrangles that have two points of a different patch in common. Almost all our splines neatly match each other in this fashion (or at least they should).

Can you find the area that does not conform to the above rule? Follow our thumb curve along the Z-axis. Somewhere the geometry should cease to form perfectly aligned quadrangle spline sections. If this is not corrected, heinous, model-threatening rendering errors will occur. Assume we use patch values of 5 for perpendicular subdivisions and 5 for parallel subdivisions without fixing the alignment error. You can see in Figure 8's wireframe preview window, that we already have two small patch regions that lie directly above one large patch region. The junction between these two curves is where the error will be produced.

Notice how the two smaller regions fit perfectly along the width of the larger patch section? As a result, after we patch the large section, we will have five polygons along the brim adjacent to the two smaller patch sections. But, after patching the two smaller sections we'll have a total of 10 polygons, which will be adjacent to the five polygons of the larger patch section. This really appears ugly on Modeler's screen, and believe me, it looks nasty when rendered in Layout. Since the points are shared, you'll get ghastly seams.

Well, because you're smart, you'll think to yourself: "What if I play with the subdivision settings to make the large patch section have 10 polygons? Won't that fix the problem?" Yes, it will, assuming that you select your curves in the correct order and create a number of faces in each small patch area that equals the number of faces along the adjoining edge of the large patch area. (See sidebar.)

There are two other solutions that will rectify the problem. A more advanced approach "stitches" the two dissimilar path sections together. (See Ken Stranahan's article in *LIGHTWAVEPRO* Volume 1, Issue 2, December 1993.) The second, easier method calls for extending the thumb curve down the entire Z-axis by adding new points to the preceding splines and then creating a new curve using these points. We will use this technique here. Finally, we will need to **Merge** (**Polygon** panel) the two Z-axis thumb splines together. After doing this you should have something that looks like Figure 9.

We're almost done using splines. Hang in there! There are a few modifications we should make before patching our model. Look at Figure 9. Can you find two curves that should be smoothed? Look at the left Z-axis curve and follow it down its length until you come to the last point. This point should also be the first point of our last cross section curve. Select both of these curves and use the **Smooth** curves (**Tools**) function on them.

Now we need to move some points around so our object has some curvatures along the Y direction. Basically, the perimeter points of the entire model should have larger Y values than the inner points. Check the points that were added to create the detail splines. Make sure these points are positioned correctly on the Y-axis. You might have to lower Y values of some inner points in the thumb region. The inner points should be positioned so they maintain the arch profile that we began our model with. Finally, look at the points defining the last cross-section curve in the model. The perimeter points of the thumb region initially should have Y values that match the other perimeter point's Y values. As we travel towards the left side of the cast, try to decrease the Y values gradually, forming a slight depression. The leftmost and rightmost points should have a Y value that is near the Y values of the other perimeter points.

Once you get things looking smooth, **Save** the curves as a separate object!

Patch Time

Yes, it is now time to use the lovely **Patch** (**Multiply** or Ctrl–f) command! Let's begin by analyzing the right-hand splines. To make life simple, I used

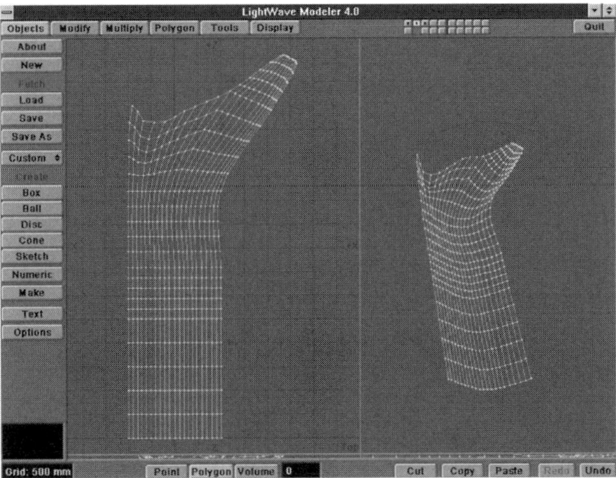

Figure 10

a value of 5 in each of the Patch requesters. I also set the Patch method to **Length**. All of these items are set after you select four connecting curves and issue the **Patch** command. I used values of 5 for two reasons: If we use equal patch values in conjunction with four-sided patch regions, then we do not need to concern ourselves with the order of curve selection since each patch is four-sided and equal in polygon resolution. (See October's introductory spline article, "LightWave 101.") Also, a polygon value of 5 gives us enough definition because there are many patch areas on the right side that do not span a great distance.

Do you notice a difference between the splines of the right side and the splines of the left side? There are more spline patch regions on the right side of the model than on the left side. So? Well, when you try to patch one of the left side regions, the resulting polygon mesh will not be permitted to follow the curve profiles accurately because the area is just too large to be well-defined by only five sets of polygons. Compare the patch regions of each side. How do their patch densities differ? Do they differ along the X-axis or along the Z-axis? In my opinion, they have contrasting X-axis values. The right side of the model's X-axis has two patch regions while the left side only has one patch region along the X-axis.

There are two simple solutions. We could add another long spline Z-axis spline to the left side, or we could alter the mesh's resolution when we issue the **Patch** (**Multiply**) command. I chose to increase the mesh's X polygon count by playing with the values of the Patch requester. Now is a good time to review the laws by which LightWave interacts with the parallel and perpendicular values in conjunction with curve selection order. Basically, I increased one field to 10 and kept the other at 5. Use the curve selection order that produces 10 polygons along the X-axis and five polygons along the Z-axis. Patch all the regions if you have not already.

Clean the Messy Mesh

Phew, are your hands tired! What I would give for an autopatcher plug-in! Let's clean up our messy mesh.

- Use the **Copy** button and **Paste** the mesh into layer 2.
- Make layer 2 active and make sure you're in **Polygon** select mode.
- Push (w) to bring up the polygon statistics screen and select all curves.
- Push (z) to erase the curves from the model.
- Use **Merge** points (**Tools** panel or m).
- Select **Align** (**Polygon**) to force all the polygon normals to point in the same direction. Make sure they are facing the way you want.

Oh So Shallow

The mesh has now been cleansed. Figure 10 displays my version of the object.

- **Copy** (c) and **Paste** (v) the mesh into layer 3.

A two-dimensional model is like dating a shallow person. We need to create some depth!

- **Extrude** (**Multiply**) the object slightly using one segment. I extruded the object so that you can see a noticeable depth when it's viewed in Modeler. Don't overdo it. Hey, how about some rounded edges?
- Click on the **Subdivide** (**Polygon** panel or Shift–d) button and select **Metaform** from the subpanel. I metaformed my object twice.
- The final step is to seek and destroy non-planar polygons by using **Polygon** Stats (w) and selecting the (+) button next to **Non-planar** polygons. Triple (t) these polygons.

Hey, it's time to save your object and render it out in Layout! While in Layout, you might have to boost the **Smoothing Angle** (**Surfaces** panel) to a higher value. I used 114 degrees.

Don't limit your splining experiments to this project. Alter these spline cages, patch them, and make morph targets for character animations. After metaforming, you might want to drill some holes in the object by using **Boolean** Subtract (Shift–b).

Have fun splining until we meet again.

LWP

Adam hopes that those who push for peace in the Middle East won't succumb to the forces of extremism, terrorism and political games. Peacemakers are the bravest of warriors, for they often face invisible enemies. Adam can be reached at adamchry@cats.ucsc.edu.

Spline Patching Pitfalls

by Greg Teegarden

Spline patching is probably the most significant feature to arrive in Modeler 3.0. Using Modeler's splines enable the user to create shapes and objects that were unobtainable with the previous release of LightWave. They have opened a new world of modeling options to CG artists, but with an unexpected side effect—plenty of headaches.

Spline patching is certainly not for the meek. To get those little noodles to behave can be a frustrating experience, even for experienced users. And to get a cage to patch properly requires a lot of patience and sometimes a little luck.

I, too, have experienced my fair share of spline frustration syndrome (SFS). SFS can be overcome, however, and 99 percent of all problems can usually be traced to a user error. I'm going to list the more common ones and a sure-fire method that results in a patch every time.

Creating the Spline Cage

For the following example, the head of a T-Rex that was built entirely with Modeler splines will be used. The project was originally a challenge given to me by Tony Stutterheim.

Since a background image can now be loaded into the Modeler layout screens, I took a physical model of the T-Rex over to a flatbed scanner, scanned a profile of its head and placed it into the background. This was used as a template or guide (Figure 1).

It was then just a process of laying down points along the outline of the image to obtain a rough representation of the head. One thing that's useful when building a spline cage is to think of the cage as a series of cross sections.

Once I had the profile splines of the T-Rex created, I started with the nose for my first cross section and then duplicated it back along the Z-Axis until I had what I assumed to be the correct number to start building the connecting splines or rails (Figure 2). I use the term rail to describe a spline that connects the various cross sections of an object, resulting in a patchable cage.

The creation of these rails is no small task, as where and how you lay them down determines how successful your patch looks in the end. As a general rule, I try to keep an even distance between rails unless I want more resolution on a particular part of the object, in which case a closer mesh is needed. Of course, some closeness between splines is inevitable. You can plan for those situations where you need splines towards the end of your cage, which I'll discuss later.

In order for the splines to patch properly, it is important to remember that the splines must share points. It is not necessary that these be end points.

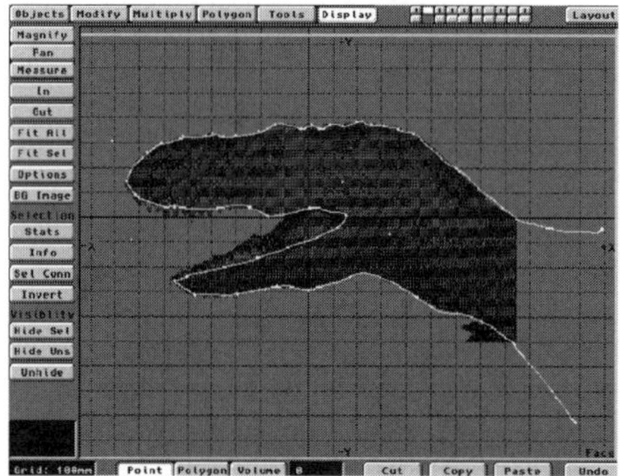

Figure 1: A scanned profile of a T-Rex is used as a template.

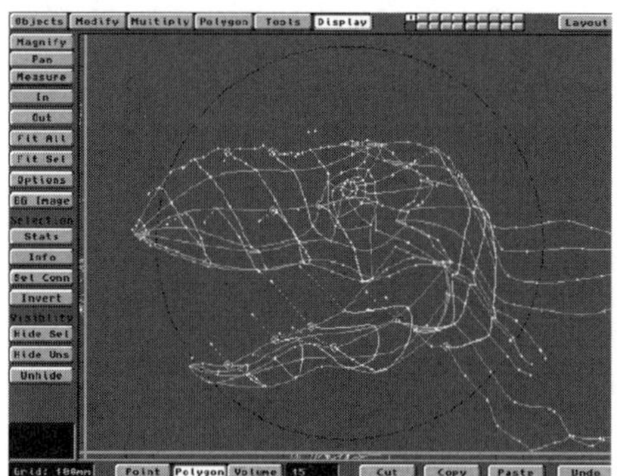

Figure 2: After completing profile splines, start building the connecting splines.

Mirroring the Spline Cage

It also helps to build only one side of an object assuming, of course, that it is symmetrical. After one side of the cage is built, it can simply be mirrored over the center line to get the other. But if you don't perform a few operations afterwards, you won't get a nice, smooth model.

In order to get a smooth model after mirroring your splines, the duplicated points must first be merged. Go to the **Tools** menu and select **Merge** from the Points section. Alternatively, you can use the keyboard shortcut **m**. Leave the setting on **Automatic**. This merges all points sharing the same space and fuses your splines together. If no points merge, you did not mirror the splines at the correct location.

Now the important part: press the **Smooth** button in the **Tools**/Curves section or use the **Ctrl-s** shortcut. This smooths your cross sections across one another so that when you build your patch, it won't show a seam where the two sides connect. Since only one side of the cage is going to be patched, the duplicate side can now be deleted, leaving behind points that appear to float in space. These are the control vertices of splines that make up the original half of the cage.

Deleting one side of a symmetrical cage is desirable because it's much easier to see what's going on if you don't have to look through unnecessary rails. Once the patching begins, the perspective window is used almost exclusively to select splines, with the **Display Options** set to the **Static** mode. Holding down the **Alt** key while moving the mouse allows rotation of the cage to any angle, making identification of the individual rails much easier and patching much faster.

Patching the Cage

After selecting three or four connecting splines (only that number works) and pressing the **Patch** button (**Multiply**/Sweep menu or **Ctrl-f**), you may notice that the default setting for a spline patch is a 10x10 mesh with **Knots** selected.

Personal experience has shown that this setting is not always ideal. I almost always use a 5x5 patch mesh with the **Length** buttons highlighted, as opposed to the Knots setting. The reason for this is twofold. First, a

10x10 patch mesh can quickly generate a huge mesh object as each patch contains 100 polygons. Secondly, the Knots setting is not always a good way to generate a patch, because it tends to make meshes bunch up towards the corners of your patch boundaries, which can create strange rendering errors at times. (Knots refers to the individual points in a spline, and if a number of points come together, you can get more polygons by these knots and fewer in the rest of the spline.)

Why would you want to patch by Knots? If a spline was rounding a corner, for instance, you would want more polygons around the corner to make it smoother. Patching by Length divides the spline and makes equal-sized polygons. See the comparison of Knots versus Length in Figure 3 for an example.

The most important aspect of patch modeling is that the less polygons used without sacrificing model detail, the better. Every now and then I see a patch model built by someone who brags that it has "over 50,000 polygons," as if that made it a better model. This is nonsense, unless the model warrants it. In most cases it doesn't, and all those polygons are just eating up valuable RAM and increasing rendering times.

Always use the most conservative numbers when building a patch mesh. It's not uncommon to use different values across the cage, but just make sure that where two patch meshes meet that they have the same number of polygons connecting to one another and sharing points; otherwise, it won't render correctly.

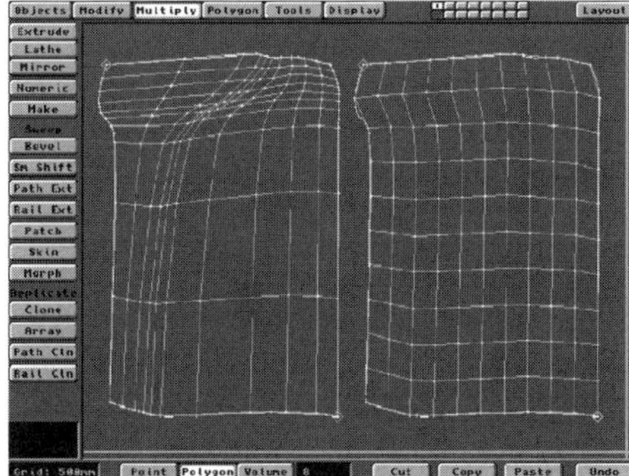

Figure 3: Compare the differences of patching by knots and lengths.

Stitching a Patch

So what happens when two patches bordering one another have different numbers of connecting polygons? This happens, and the best way to fix it is as follows: Select the polygons that touch one another; cut and paste them into a free layer; and hit the **k** (or select **Remove** from the **Polygon/Create** section) key to delete the polygons while leaving the points behind. Next, connect the points together for each corresponding side (the middle points are shared) and create normal polygons out of them. The result should be two polygons that share middle points.

It's now just a simple matter of **Skinning** (**Multiply** menu) them together. Afterwards, hit the **w** key to bring up your Polygon Statistics requester (make sure that the **Polygon** select button at the bottom of the screen is chosen first), select the **Non Planar** button at the bottom, which selects the two original polygons and then delete them.

If the original polygons happened to be planar, simply choose all the polygons that contain more than four vertices from the Statistics requester. These are the original polygons. All that remains now is a group that acts as a bridge to join two patches with different numbers of bordering polygons.

It's a good idea to **Align** (Polygon menu) these polygons before cutting and pasting them back into the original mesh. After bringing them back into the original mesh, make sure to merge the connecting points that are now doubled up. This technique worked well during the many times it was used during the creation of the T-Rex head. *[Editor's note: For another stitching technique, see "How to Stitch a Patch" on page 18 of* LWPRO *Issue 2.]*

Assuming all points are merged, the next biggest culprit could be duplicate splines sharing the same end points. Try using the Unify option in the Polygon panel.

Which Way Does that Patch Go?

Now for the fun part. Many people have had more than a little trouble trying to get a certain area of the cage to patch properly. Perhaps the mesh seemed to travel in the opposite direction or run the length of a single rail. Do not despair, as there is a way to avoid all these little annoyances

If a problem arises trying to get a certain area to patch, be sure all of your points are merged. Unmerged points always cause problems in one form or another.

Assuming all points are merged, the next biggest culprit could be duplicate splines sharing the same end points. Try using the Unify option in the Polygon panel to merge any duplicate splines.

Often what appears to be a properly constructed cage can have splines that aren't really connected to one another. To find this out, copy and paste each spline, one at a time, into another layer while studying to make sure that each one has a point where it should be. For example, I had a section of the T-Rex head that would not patch, and it was really bothering me. I finally copied each spline into another layer, and realized that one of them didn't have a common end point with another. I simply added a point to it in the proper place, brought in the other spline, selected the two points, welded them together and then pasted the new rails into the cage.

Sometimes after all that, there may be an area that just won't patch correctly, and here is where a little trick I learned almost always works. If all of the aforementioned potential problems have been checked and everything looks fine, try this. Assuming there are four boundary rails, with the one on top being north, the bottom south and the other two east and west, pick the west rail first, followed by the north, then south and, finally, east. This should result in a patch. Picking them in opposites also works occasionally.

Other times, the patch doesn't work no matter what order is chosen, as the mesh appears to patch backwards across the cage. This usually happens with three-rail cages. Immediately hit **Undo** then without deselecting your splines, hit the **f** (**Polygon/Flip**) key to flip the selected rails. This should correct the problem, resulting in a good, clean patch.

Backing into a Corner

As mentioned before, it is beneficial to have the higher densities of splines towards the ends of your cage. Keep in mind that almost all spline cages have areas where there can be a three-boundary patch, and this type doesn't render well. So here's the trick: Keep all your boundaries to four rails wherever possible,and have them run as close to the ends of the cage as they can be. Next, use a small, three-rail patch to close off the end. This should result in a clean-looking model that renders correctly.

A side note here on three-rail patches: Remember that the last spline picked determines the direction of the patch. Therefore, be sure to pick the spline opposite the end corner last so your patch continues to flow to the end of the cage, which, in turn, lines up with the rest of the cage's meshes.

LWP

Greg Teegarden is an animator for Amblin Imaging who has worked his way up the spline ladder to join the ranks of spline masters.

LightWave 101

Course 1D: Animating with Splines

by Taylor Kurosaki

To animate is to bring to life. However, creating life is often an incredibly painstaking process. Just imagine the work involved in hand painting thousands upon thousands of cells for an animated film. Now imagine a cartoon animator only having to paint every other frame of an animation. How about every fifth frame? Every tenth? Every hundredth? The labor and time saved would be enormous. Now apply this principle to computer animation. Imagine how tedious it would be to keyframe the camera, every object, and every light at every frame of your scene. Thankfully, this is not the case. The computer calculates the positions of the components of the scene based on their respective keyframes immediately preceding and following the current frame. In LightWave, interpolation, as this mechanism is called, comes to us in the form of splines. Certain characteristics attributed to keyframes affect the spline and determine how the object's position is interpolated. In layman's terms, animating with splines in LightWave is not unlike having your own overseas animation department:.

This installment of "LightWave 101" will cover the use of splines in LightWave animations. More specifically, effective use of the **Motion Graph** and **Spline Controls** will be illustrated, along with the **Align to Path** feature.

A few words of general advice: add keyframes as discriminantly and strategically as possible. Don't get me wrong, I'm not suggesting skimping on keyframes in any way. Rather, be wary of ending up with a messy animation full of unnecessary keyframes. This usually occurs when an animator tries to fix a problem in an animation by adding extra keyframes rather than first trying to adjust those which already exist. With very complex animations involving multiple, interacting objects, it may seem easier to "tweak" a motion by adding keyframes to counteract the negative effects of others rather than altering existing keyframes. This only serves to further complicate the animation when you invariably must go back to make later changes. Get enough of this and you may end up with a monitor lying in pieces on the sidewalk below. Don't be seduced by the dark side...fix it right the first time.

The Motion Graph

The Motion Graph window is an incredibly helpful feature that debuted with the 3.0 release of LightWave. It provides LightWave animators with a visual representation of their animations and allows interactive adjustment of an object's, camera's, light's, or bone's movement. The main area of the window contains a graph which plots movement along the three axes, heading, pitch and bank angles, object scale along any axis, and velocity. Values for the various channels are plotted vertically, while time is plotted horizontally. Through this interface, one can **Add, Delete, Drag, Shift** and **Scale** keyframes, and observe visually the results of changes made. While you can do all of this in the main Layout window, it is often easier to use the motion graph controls. Select the motion graph for an object, bone, light or camera by selecting the item in Layout and clicking on the **Motion Graph** button or by pressing the "m" key any time you have an item selected. Remember that dragging a keyframe with the left mouse button allows you to move the key up or down (except while in the Velocity channel) and dragging with the right mouse button allows you to move a keyframe right or left.

Spline Controls

One of the most useful purposes of the Motion Graph is the ability to visualize the effects of **Spline Controls** on a motion path. The Spline Controls available in LightWave are **Tension, Continuity, Bias** and **Linear**. Valid settings for the first three controls are -1 to 1, with 0 as the default. Linear causes an object to move directly from the previous keyframe directly to the selected keyframe without any spline deviation. When Linear is selected, it overrides all other spline controls from the keyframe on which it is selected to the keyframe immediately preceding it. It's important to note that spline controls are still valid to use at a keyframe with Linear selected since they can be useful in the path leading to the next keyframe.

Tension controls the velocity at which an object travels through a keyframe. A negative tension setting will cause an object to accelerate through the keyframe, while a positive tension setting will cause an object to slow as it passes through the keyframe, then accelerate gradually away from it. A tension setting of 1.0 will cause an item to come to a momentary stop at a keyframe. Figure 1 shows the effects of tension on the Velocity of an object. Frame 20 contains a tension of 1, while frame 40 has a tension of -1.

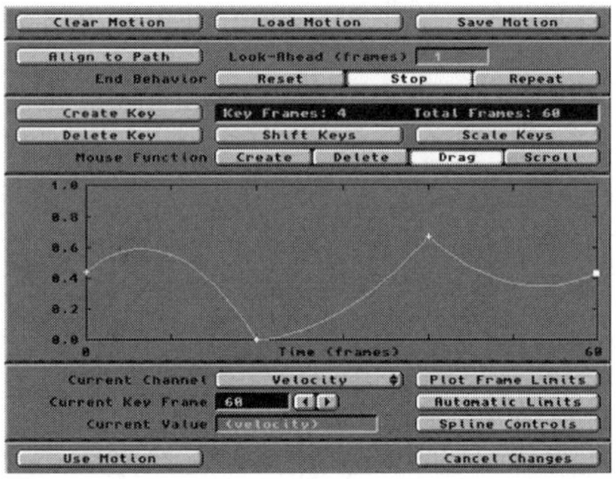

Figure 1

Continuity affects the smoothness at which the keyframe is incorporated into the spline path. With a continuity setting of 0, the spline curves fluidly through the keyframe. With continuity set to an extreme -1, the spline abruptly changes course directly at the keyframe, causing an object to alter its direction immediately as it reaches the keyframe. A continuity setting of +1 causes the spline to over-compensate before and after the keyframe and "stutter" at the keyframe. Positive continuity values are generally not common, unless continuity is used in combination with another spline control.

Bias allows one to offset the spline curvature before or after the keyframe. With a positive setting, the object will overshoot the keyframe, while a negative setting will result in a spline path which anticipates the keyframe.

All these Spline Controls can be altered directly in the Motion Graph using the keyboard. Hold the t, c, or b key and click and drag right or left to adjust the spline by eye, or enter the values numerically by clicking the **Spline Controls** button in the Motion Graph or from within Layout.

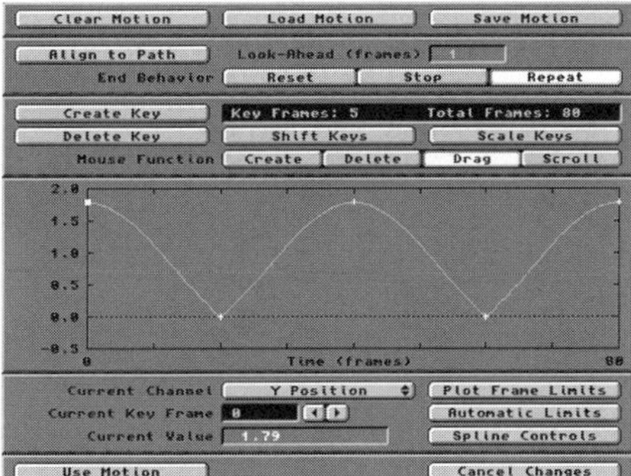

Figure 2

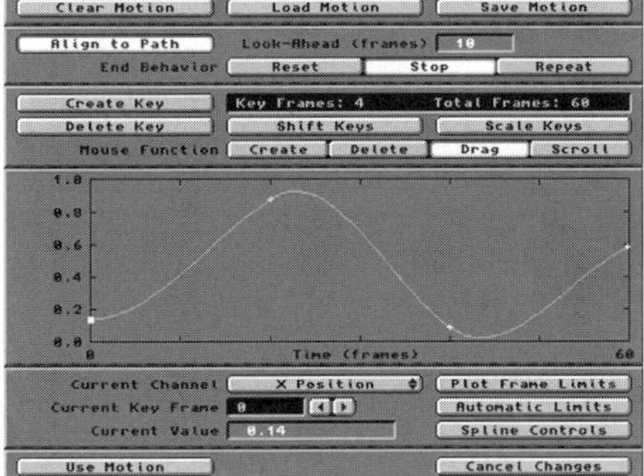

Figure 3

Follow the Bouncing Ball

Using Spline Controls is an excellent way to easily animate a bouncing ball. Figure 2 shows the spline path for the Y Position of a bouncing basketball. To reproduce the way the ball slows as it reaches its apex, surrendering to gravity, use a Tension setting of 1 for the keyframe at the top of the bounce (Frames 0, 40, 80; Figure 2). A tension setting of 1 literally causes the ball to stop briefly (for the duration of one frame, to be exact) before heading earthward. Conversely, to accentuate the force of the ball slamming solidly to the ground, use a continuity setting of -1 (Frames 20, 60; Figure 2). To keep the ball continually bouncing select an End Behavior of **Repeat** from the Motion Graph. In order to make a smooth loop, just make sure the first and last keyframes have identical values. Keep in mind, though, that a ball would not endlessly bounce unless someone were dribbling it, and upon each bounce, the ball would not rebound as high.

Driving School

Bias is a useful way to simulate an object with a lot of velocity and mass. Examples which come to mind are a speedboat or a race car. In these examples, the mass of the object, combined with its forward velocity, causes the object to overshoot the keyframe as it begins to turn. Use a bias setting of 1 to offset the curve in the spline path to after the keyframe. Figure 3 shows the X position of a race car as it drifts around corners, or slides on an icy road. Notice how the spline remains nearly straight until after the keyframes at frames 20 and 40. Whereas positive bias values would be used for a skidding race car, negative bias values would be used to simulate a perfectly in-control car. With a bias of -1, the curve in the spline path occurs before the keyframe as the car sets up and completes its turn before the keyframe (Figure 4). In conjunction with bias, **Align To Path** can be used to keep the car's heading aligned with its direction of travel. In the case of the skidding car, a **Look-Ahead** setting of five to 10 frames accentuates the sliding motion. For the in-control car, use a look-ahead value of 1 frame. Note: When using Align To Path, the object will reset its heading when it reaches the last keyframe, due to the fact that it has no more frames to look-ahead to. If you wish to use Align to Path and you experience this "last frame resetting," you may wish to extend the motion path past the last frame you will see in order to keep your object aligned.

Terminal Velocity

The **Velocity** channel is an especially useful component of the Motion Graph. It is an effective way to diagnose and smooth jerky animations in a number of ways. Assuming you are trying to produce an animation with a fairly constant velocity, the motion graph in Figure 5 would reveal some significant problems. Dragging the mouse while holding the right mouse button, the spline can be smoothed by spacing keys farther apart to lower the velocity or bringing keys closer together to raise the velocity. Alternately, tension can be used to raise or lower velocity values to smooth the spline. Figure 6 shows the path from Figure 5 smoothed out by adjusting tension and sliding keyframes. Ideally, however, inconsistent velocity values can be averted altogether by establishing a basic velocity by creating the first and last keyframes of your animation first. Keyframes in-between are then created subsequently to conform somewhat to the original two-keyframe spline. This is easy to do by going to the frame you wish and moving the item slightly from its original path. The resulting final velocity stays in the neighborhood of the previously set values.

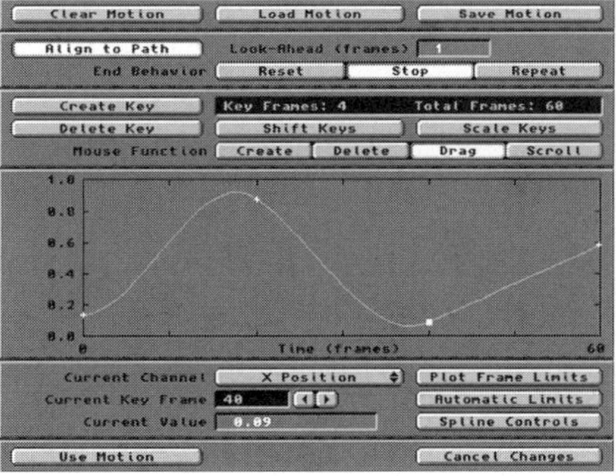

Figure 4

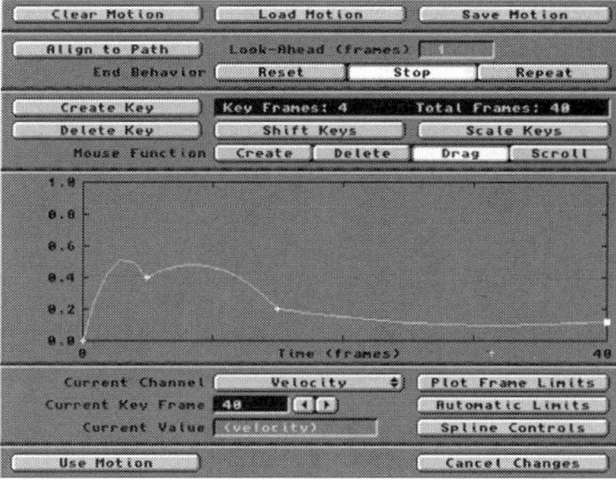

Figure 5

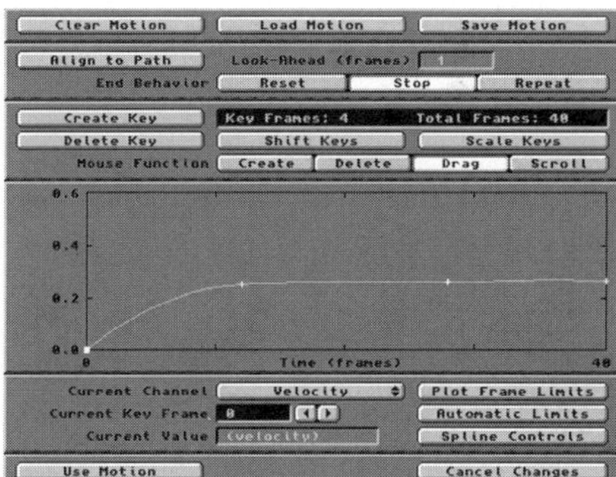

Figure 6

While these are very rudimentary examples of spline control use, the principles remain true as you tackle more complicated animations. Character animating, in particular, can be a very frustrating task. The Motion Graph becomes indispensable as it allows you to smooth out jerky motions visually and interactively. In general, however, spline controls enable you to create complex motions with minimal key-framing. Not only does this save time, but it keeps animations streamlined and simple. When you find yourself working on an animation containing several hundred keyframes, you gain a new level of appreciation for this fact. Truth be told, shattered CRT tubes are a pain to clean up.

Taylor Kurosaki is a visual effects artist at Amblin Imaging. Topic suggestions and comments should be sent to his attention at 100 Universal City Plaza, Bldg. 447, Universal City, CA 91608, or to John Gross on-line.

Tearing Through Canyons

By Wayne Cole

As 3D artists and animators we are constantly immersed in time and space. If you ask animators how they view a scene in its first inception, they usually admit that it is visualized as if they were in the scene in actual 3D space—not as a viewer apart from the scene seeing it on a movie screen, TV screen or printed page. That process starts when the translation from mind to form begins. We have to make sure things look good both spatially and temporally within the confines of a 4x3 or letter-box view frame. We have to ensure that our objects/actors appear to move naturally in virtual space (they are only electrons, after all). Even the dancing gas pumps and credit cards have to look "natural," and move with believable displacements for the amount of time we view them.

And there is the "other" space and time demanding an animator's attention: "How long is this gonna take to render?" and "Do I have enough [insert electronic media of choice] to store/archive these frames?" After all, you don't want to lose the frames of the animation—essentially your generation 0 master—until the program airs, the customer pays you, your production is done, your master survived the duplicating process, and all the duplicates are ready to ship.

We may spend a great deal of time and energy worrying about rendering time and media space, but because we are so saturated with 3D thinking, we often overlook 2D cheats that can save a bunch of time. Nir Hermoni's "Flying Through Canyons" article (*LIGHTWAVEPRO*, January 1995) reminded me of a similar project I did over a year ago. My approach, however, used 2D animation, combined with a feature of LightWave I have heard some people call a "quirk," in order to get around my inability to quickly model and paint a realistic "impressive landscape."

Stuck in 3D

The concept for the project was that a Remotely Piloted Vehicle (RPV) had to appear on screen in a form that suggested an engineering wireframe drawing. Then it had to materialize into its "finished form" in mid-flight through an impressive landscape. The RPV, by the way, was a small helicopter with a video camera mounted on for remote viewing/taping operations.

The RPV was going to be fairly easy to build since it was a mechanical object with many standard geometric shapes—things like cylinders, rectangular solids, and tubes with bends in them. Luckily, LightWave had just shipped with spline patches, so complex fuselage curves were easy to form. The landscape, at first, appeared to be another matter.

Stuck in my 3D mode, I thought about large spline patches, displacement maps...I probably played with at least four different ideas for generating this landscape. Meanwhile, the nervousness factor went up with each idea deemed impossible within the allotted time and budget. I was so entrenched in the 3D mindset that, for two days, I had the answer staring me right in the eyes and I didn't see it.

Rocket Science to the Rescue

One idea I tried used Scenery Animator to create a landscape DEM that I would convert to a LightWave object using Interchange. That part worked great. I had a wonderful spline patch of the Grand Canyon. All I had to do was to surface it to look like a real landscape in LightWave and then fly the RPV through it. I tried planar mapping expanded versions of Scenery Animator's map image of the landscape after snapping it from the Scenery Animator control screen. I tried building a convincing texture map in Brilliance. I tried selecting polygons in the mesh and applying different textures for water, sand and vegetation. All of which looked like what a dog leaves near hydrants.

Then it hit me. I remembered from back in my rocket scientist days that all those wonderful six-degree-of-freedom Link simulators for the space shuttle and other high-performance aircraft just gyrate around in front of a movie! At the same time, I remembered the little "quirk" in LightWave that, at the time I discovered it, I thought was a restriction instead of a useful feature.

The Immovable-Movable Background

If you load an image into a LightWave scene to use as a background image, the image is always dead-center in front of, and perfectly square in relation to, the camera view, no matter where you point the camera. So the solution to my landscape problem became quite simple: use a Scenery Animator sequence as a LightWave background image sequence, then wiggle the RPV around in front of this animated background to mimic appropriate flight attitudes, just like the simulators do.

One of the benefits of choosing this method is that the final LightWave animation rendered faster than it would have if a real 3D landscape had been used instead. All LightWave had to do was plonk an image from the background image sequence in the yon plane (see "Rendering Algorithms Part 1: The Theory of Z-buffers," *LIGHTWAVEPRO*, January 1995), then render a single object—the RPV.

While making the Canyon Clip I used Scenery Animator 4.0 to generate a landscape movie. This process will work with any other scenery generation tool, like Vista Pro or World Construction Set, as long as it results in the ability to save individual RGB images to be used for the background sequence. In Scenery Animator I chose to use a DEM for a real-life place rather than using a fractal-based imaginary landscape. I picked the Grand Canyon. (Well, the requirement *was* an impressive locale.)

- In Scenery Animator's Project menu, load a DEM file to define the landscape through which you wish to fly. Then, using the various buttons on the main screen, set up the attributes that Scenery Animator uses to "paint" the landscape (Figure 1).

You can control things like the minimum elevations

Figure 1: Scenery Animator Main Screen

at which snow and rock appear and the maximum elevation at which vegetation appears. There is a button to bring up a Sky Control panel, where you can define the cloud parameters for your particular scene. Water and tree characteristics are also definable. Finally, the direction and horizon angle for the sun must be entered.

Make a conscious and intelligent decision about light direction. Remember, you will want the lighting to favor the 3D object while creating enough landscape shadows to contribute to the feeling of depth. So avoid things like full backlighting unless you really want a silhouette scene. Above all, note the angle of the light in the landscape scene, because you need to be sure that the LightWave scene lighting will be consistent. If the landscape shadows go one way and the 3D object shadows go another, your final product will not look right.

- The next step in constructing a realistic-looking landscape involves defining colors to be used for water, rock soil, sky and vegetation. In Scenery Animator, you can control all these characteristics from the control panel that comes up when the Screen button on the main control panel is selected. You have full flexibility to make the colors as real or surreal as you want.

Exercise care in selecting colors in any RGB-based program, since your ultimate output will most likely become, at some point, composite video. Do not choose extremely saturated blues, greens, reds or whites unless you do not care about chroma crawl and exceeding "legal" NTSC color values. Even with careful color selection, it doesn't hurt to run the frames produced with your landscape generator through ADPro's (or another image-processing package's) Broadcast Limit filter just to be sure.

- Now that the landscape is characterized, set up the flight path of the camera through the landscape. In Scenery Animator, for example, the Map button on the main screen takes you to the camera control panel (Figure 2). The program offers a map of the landscape showing the camera location and its field of view within the area defined by the loaded DEM landscape. There are buttons to control your view of the map on this panel, as well as requesters where you enter the camera location, attitude and lens values. You also set the keyframes for camera motion and lens focal length. After you have defined the camera motion and are satisfied with it based on previews run from Scenery Animator's main screen, it's time to generate the movie in front of which your object will appear to fly.
- At this point, from Scenery Animator's Anim Mode menu, save the animation as IFF24 frames. These frames will form the image sequence for the LightWave animation background movie. Though the description sounds long, the entire process took me approximately two hours as a first-time user of Scenery Animator, and I suspect the time would be about the same to set up the same animation within other landscape generation packages.

Figure 2: Scenery Animator map screen

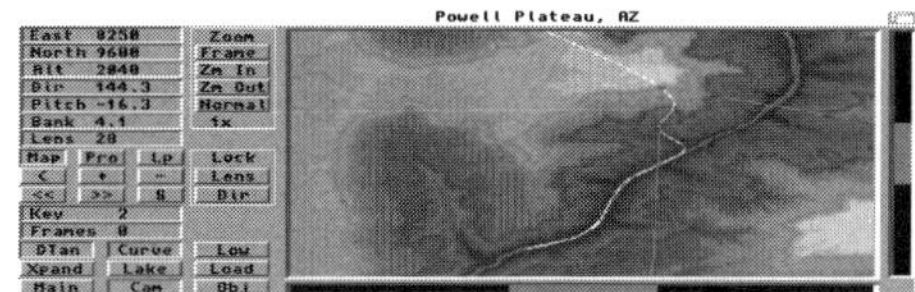

Figure 3: Layout showing a wireframe of frame 50 with background image.

Different packages have different standards for naming frames of an animation, and LightWave is no exception. Whatever landscape generator you use, you'll need to be sure that you label the frames it generates in LightWave-compatible form before loading them into LightWave. The landscape image names should look like "FlyThruxxx," where "xxx" is a three-digit number matching the LightWave animation frame in which you wish to have that specific landscape image used as a background. Note that all the images in the sequence should also be in the same directory.

The Flight Plan

Now comes the fun part (i.e., the LightWave part):

- Load the flying ship object that you've so painstakingly modeled (or so painlessly lifted from a commercial or public domain object set) into Layout.
- Click on the Load Sequence button (**Images** panel), and when the file requester comes up, select one of the images from the generated landscape fly-by. Be sure to delete the numeric portion of the image name, because Layout will automatically append the number of the frame it is currently rendering to the image name you enter in this requester when it looks for an image in the sequence to place in the background.
- To tell LightWave to do just that—use the sequence for a background—select the sequence in the **Effects** panel's **Background Image** pop-up requester. Now you are ready to begin setting up the motions of the object, light and camera.
- From the **Options** panel, select the **Show BG Image** button. As you advance and reverse the frames using the **Current Frame** slider, arrow buttons or requester, you will see a "pencil sketch" version of the background image (like that shown in Figure 3) change to the one that matches the frame currently designated in the frame requester.
- Use the **Move** and **Rotate** tools with your object selected to position it appropriately for the particular background image. You can even use a wireframe preview to check the motion of the object in front of a pencil-sketch version of your background movie.
- Another time-saving preview trick available in LightWave 3.5 and greater involves the ability to save and load wireframe previews. Use an empty scene with only the background image loaded and **Show BG Image** (**Options** panel) enabled. Select the **Preview** pop-up and make a **Bounding Box** preview of this scene—essentially, the pencil-sketch version of your movie. Now, from the **Preview** button pop-up, save your wireframe preview.
- Go to the **Options** panel again and enable the **Preview** button for the **Layout Background**. You'll find the Layout screen's Current Frame slider is much more responsive as you move from frame to frame. If, after looking at a preview with the object(s) in it, you don't like the object motion, simply reload the background-only preview, reposition your objects and make another preview. Then save the preview again if you have more objects to load and position.
- You can repeat this operation for each object in the scene. If the scene has many objects that require critical positioning with respect to the background, this method saves a lot of time in laying out the scene.

When positioning the object, remember that the scenery tilts and moves for the camera's apparent motion. So if your camera is set up like a chasing plane's view, be sure to have your object lead the camera through a motion. For example, if the background sequence does a sharp tilt to the left, it indicates the camera—er, chasing plane—is banking hard right. Assuming it is following the flying object, that object should have entered its hard right bank before the chase plane. It may even have started its roll-out by the time the chase plane starts its bank into the turn.

Light positioning is also important. In the turn above, the angle at which the light hits the object must change by the same degree of turn your background movie indicates the flight path took. You have the option of moving the light or parenting the camera to the object, keeping the light stationary and rotating the object through the turn. Remember, no matter how the camera moves, the background image will stay directly in front of it. So, to get the realism of the chase, move the camera toward and away, side to side and up and down in relation to the object.

If you made similar perturbations to the camera's position within the landscape generator animation, you now get the feel of real flight, with altitude, attitude and heading changes. And it looks like you are actually following the flying object rather than being rigidly—and unrealistically—attached to it. You don't even have to remember all the little zigs and zags you put into the landscape generator animation. Simply coordinate the LightWave camera motion and object motion to the major direction changes in the landscape animation.

Well, that's it! Just set the frame count for the animation and start the rendering. You'll be surprised how fast it goes with a background image sequence landscape instead of a real 3D landscape. See the color pages for an idea of what the result looks like.

The Cons

Are there drawbacks to this method? Of course. Your object can't cast shadows on the landscape. But by proper management of light direction and camera angles, those shadows, if they existed, would not be visible anyhow. Another potential disadvantage is that the object can't fly behind an element of the landscape. You can avoid this problem in a couple of ways. The easiest is to run an object that would believably be part of the landscape (a tree, for example) between the camera and the flying object every now and then. Another way, which is a topic for another time, would be to use the same image sequence as the **Foreground Image** sequence and a companion **FG Alpha Image** sequence to "manifest" those portions of the landscape behind which you want to fly into the foreground.

Close Enough for...

This method of using a 2D background movie to simulate flying through a 3D terrain may be eschewed by the 3D purist simply because it uses 2D animation. But the fact remains that this method can actually reduce both rendering time and the total time for completion of the project. It is also true that you can get a more realistic-looking landscape in a shorter period of time than if you try to create a spline patch landscape and then paint it. But the real advantage is that when you hear "And make it fly through a killer landscape," you know the landscape is actually going to be the easiest part.

The next time you have a difficult 3D problem, don't let any potential 2D solutions go unconsidered.

LWP

Wayne Cole is the proprietor of Infinity Heart Enterprises in Santa Barbara, Calif. He can be reached at (805) 964-9540, or via CompuServe at 76370,621.

Depth of Field

Improving Your Image Through Imperfection

by Ernie Wright

Anyone who is routinely forced to watch home videos knows that objects photographed with real cameras and lenses don't have to be in focus. This lens effect, called depth of field, is ordinarily absent from CGI, and although home movies might make us wish otherwise, the unnaturally perfect focus of objects at every distance from the computer camera is a sometimes undesirable CGI signature that limits the artistry and realism of our images.

LightWave's depth of field controls, at the bottom of the **Camera** panel (Figure 1), allow us to simulate the focal properties of lenses. But before we can use these controls effectively, we have to overcome a minor problem: Unlike real cameras, LightWave doesn't have a viewfinder. It's difficult to compose the image, deciding which elements will be in or out of focus, without doing some math.

Figure 1: Controls affecting depth of field are in the bottom half of the camera panel.

Near and Far

Figure 2 is a diagram of the geometry involved in doing depth of field calculations. The labels "near" and "far" refer to the limits of the range within which objects appear to be in focus. The question is, assuming you already have a perfect focus distance in mind, how do you figure out where near and far are?

There are three simple formulas that answer this question. Before using them, we need to know where to find the values we'll be plugging in, and, as you'll see, we need to be careful about the units we use.

Three of the values are on the Camera panel:

F Equivalent lens (focal length)
f Lens f-Stop
S Focal Distance

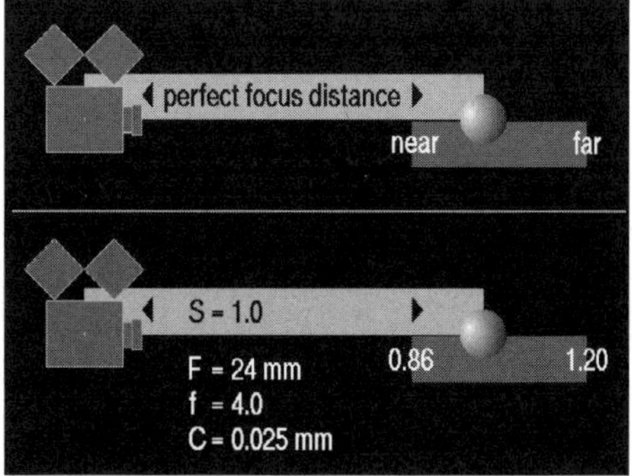

Figure 2: Objects within a range of distances from the camera appear to be in focus.

The focal length of a lens is the distance between the lens and the film plane. The Camera panel's **Equivalent Lens** readout is derived from the **Zoom Factor** and **Film Size** settings, so changing either of these will also change the focal length used to create depth of field.

Lens f-Stop sets the diameter of the lens aperture. In a real camera, the aperture is a circular window near the lens that can be widened or narrowed to control the amount of light that hits the film. The aperture diameter is usually expressed as a fraction of the focal length: an f-stop of f/4, which is the same as a setting of 4.0 in the Lens f-Stop control, indicates an aperture diameter that's 1/4 of the lens's focal length. (This can be a source of confusion; higher f-stop numbers correspond to smaller apertures because the number is the denominator in the fraction.) The aperture control on a real camera affects both the brightness and sharpness of the image, but LightWave uses the Lens f-Stop setting only in the context of depth of field, where it affects sharpness.

Focal Distance is just the distance from the camera to the point of perfect focus. This distance is measured along a line through the center of the lens and pointing in the same direction as the camera.

The fourth value we need is the diameter of the largest spot that still looks like a point on the image:

C circle of confusion diameter

This isn't a setting in LightWave. It's a number you'll use to define the fuzziness limit between in focus and out of focus (more on circles of confusion later).

Is your pencil sharpened? Let's begin. With **Zoom Factor** set to 3.2 and film size set to **35 mm motion picture** (the defaults), the focal length (Equivalent Lens) is 24 mm. The default Lens F-Stop is 4.0 and the default Focal Distance is 1.0 meter. For now, we'll use a fairly common value for circle of confusion diameter. So we have:

F = 24 mm
f = 4.0
S = 1.0 m
C = 0.025 mm

We then calculate H, the hyperfocal distance of the lens, or the distance at which "far" is infinity:

H = (F x F) / (f x C)
= 576 mm / 0.1 mm
= 5760 mm
= 5.76 meters

And now we're ready to find near and far:

near = (H x S) / (H + (S - F))
= (5.76 x 1.0) / (5.76 + (1.0 - 0.024))
= about 0.86 meters
far = (H x S) / (H - (S - F))
= (5.76 x 1.0) / (5.76 - (1.0 - 0.024))
= about 1.20 meters

Notice how units are handled here. H is calculated in millimeters, then converted to meters. When we need F again for near and far, we also convert that to meters (24 mm = 0.024 m). It's important to realize that even though it's convenient to think of LightWave's coordinate space as being measured in generic "units," the calculation we just performed requires that we think in meters. You might have a humanoid model that's five units tall, and you might think of the units as feet, but for purposes of depth of field calculation, the model is considered five meters tall. This is another good reason to make your models realistic sizes in metric units.

Focal Distance

So far we've pretended that you know what Focal Distance you'd like to use, but in fact you might not know. Let's assume now that you'd like a particular object to be in focus and you don't know how far away it is from the camera. The LightWave manual suggests you use the Layout grid to estimate the distance, but this advice is a little vague.

You can always use the Pythagorean theorem to calculate the exact distance (d), plugging in the position coordinates for the camera and the object:

dx = x2 - x1
dy = y2 - y1
dz = z2 - z1
d = square root of ((dx * dx) + (dy * dy) + (dz * dz))

If the object wasn't constructed near the origin in Modeler, you'll have to add the offset to the position reported by Layout before you do the distance calculation, because the coordinate location of objects in layout always refers to the origin of the object.

But what if you don't have the patience to find the square root of the sum of the squared differences of each coordinate? (Who does?)

Try this. Arrange the grid so that both the object and the camera are visible in the XZ View. Estimate dx, dy and dz by counting grid squares along X and along Z and then eyeballing dy in a different View, and write them down (or rearrange them in your head) in the following order: biggest, middle, smallest. A fair estimate of the camera to object distance is:

biggest + middle/4 + smallest/4

This shortcut (from Jack Ritter's paper in *Graphics Gems*, Academic Press, 1990) will at least prepare you to do test renders.

Circles of Confusion

For a better understanding of circles of confusion, take a look at Figure 3. When a point is at the Focal Distance, the light reflected (or emitted) from it focus-

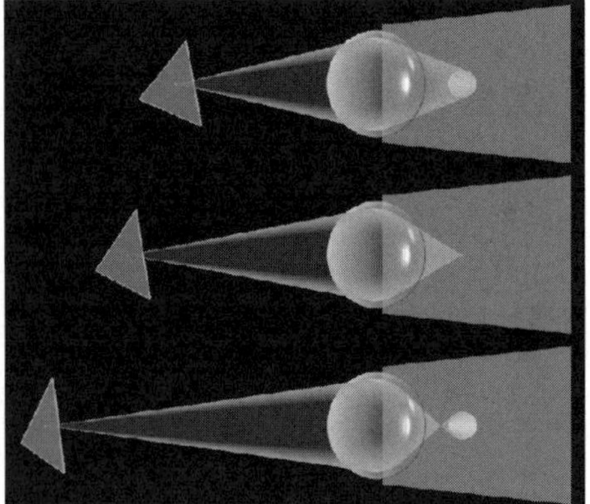

Figure 3: A point at the Focal Distance forms a perfectly sharp image. Moving it closer or further blurs its image into a circle.

es to a point on the image plane (the film). As the point is moved closer to or further from the lens, the image of the point becomes a circle, called a circle of confusion, whose diameter depends on how far from the Focal Distance the point has been moved.

Both the image medium (whatever it might be) and the human eye have limited spatial resolution — if a circle in an image is small enough, it might as well be a point. This is what is meant by a range in which things "appear to be" in focus. The circle of confusion diameter C that we used to calculate near and far is

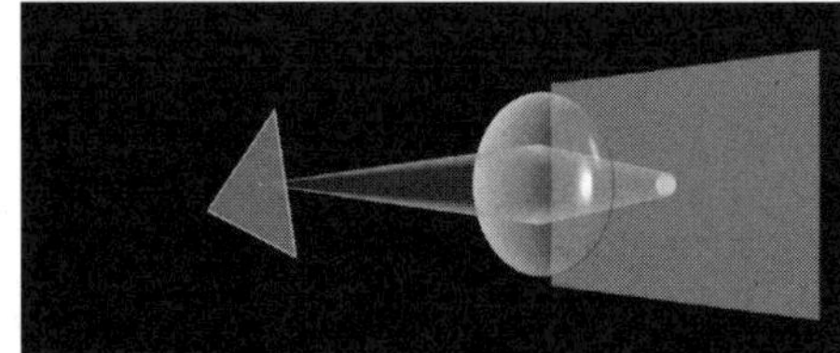

Figure 4: The effect of a smaller aperture (higher Lens f-Stop).

just the upper limit on the size of the circles. Over the limit, we say that objects are out of focus. Under it, they're in focus.

The actual value we choose to use for C is obviously somewhat subjective, but it's related to the resolution of the image medium. The value 0.025mm often used for 35mm motion picture film is about 1/1500 of the width of the image.

For LightWave rendering, you won't notice circles of confusion smaller than a pixel of course. A single pixel in a Medium-Res Overscan image is about 1/750 of the image width, or twice 1/1500, so with Film Type set to 35mm motion picture, you should probably use a value for C no smaller than 0.050mm. In general, let C be a fudge factor that makes the equations for near and far give you what you think are the right answers, based on what you've actually seen LightWave produce for various depth of field settings.

Antialiasing

You may have noticed that the depth of field controls aren't available when you first enter the **Camera** panel. This is because depth of field requires Antialiasing to be set at **Medium** or **High**. LightWave's depth of field simulation uses the same supersampling algorithm that's used to antialias images and create motion blur. It's important to realize that this puts (reasonable) limits on what you can do.

Figure 5 is an image of a 1-meter box rendered with Depth of Field. The camera is 2.5 meters away, and antialiasing is set to Medium. All of the Depth of Field settings were left at their defaults except Focal Distance, which was made a ridiculously small 0.05 meters. As you can see, the box is so far out of focus that it can no longer be rendered coherently. Keep this in mind when composing scenes that will use Depth of Field.

If you're comfortable with the math we've used so far, you can easily use the near and far formulas to tell you where "too near" and "too far" are. Increase the value of C so that it corresponds to a circle of confusion that's at the size limit of what LightWave appears

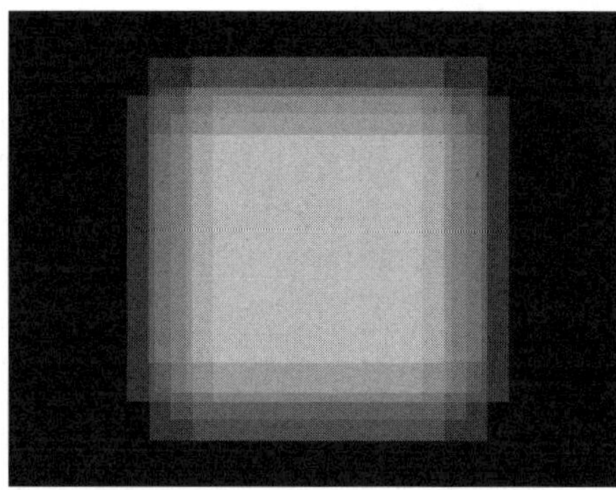

Figure 5: A box that's so out of focus it can't be rendered properly.

able to handle. A few test images with a 1-meter box will help you converge on the right numbers.

When to Use It

Depth of Field isn't something you're likely to use every day. As a practical matter, the Medium to High antialiasing it requires has a significant impact on rendering time, but more importantly, DOF is a powerful tool that you'll want to use sparingly, when a shallow depth of field (a small near-to-far distance) will enhance the composition of an image.

Shallow depth of field gives an intimate feeling to images containing small or nearby subjects because it doesn't allow the background to intrude on the viewer's attention. My wife uses a 50mm macro lens on her SLR to photograph Christmas ornaments (on the tree) from a few inches away. The only object in focus is the ornament itself. The surrounding elements—needles, small branches and a few lights—are blurred into a soft backdrop that halos the ornament and provides context without drawing attention away from the subject.

Changing focal distance is a way to gently push or pull the viewer's attention between the foreground and the background. You'll see this technique used fairly often in soap operas, where it complements the viewers' intimate relationships with the characters and, not incidentally, offers a little visual variety when the "action" is limited to two people in a room talking.

Shallow depth of field also enhances the 3D illusion. The naked eye doesn't ordinarily rely much on focal distance as a depth cue, but we easily recognize the effect in photographs. The sharply focused, high-contrast subject appears to float well in front of the more diffuse background. Just remember that this difference in focus seems most natural for subjects that are small or quite close to the camera.

LWP

For the past four years, Ernie Wright has been a programmer doing scientific visualization for several defense-related agencies (he won't say which ones). He also wrote the HAM routines for LightWave 3.5. He works from his home in Maryland while watching his 2-year-old daughter.

Depth of Field
Shortcuts to Reduce Rendering Time

by Arnie Boedecker

LightWave 3D is one of, if not the most, user-friendly 3D animation programs ever to hit the desktop computer. So many options can be activated by a simple click of the mouse. You want reflections? Click **Trace Reflections** (**Camera** panel). You want your object's surface to be smooth? Hit **Smoothing** (**Surfaces** panel). So if a depth of field effect was desired, wouldn't the best way to achieve that be to click the button labeled **Depth of Field** (**Camera** panel)? Not necessarily. Quite often, in my experience, clicking that simple Depth of Field button on my Amiga 4000/040 can double rendering times, which usually kills any chance of meeting the deadline. When you really want a certain effect, but that special effect happens to be a major render-hog, you sometimes have to find an alternative to the simple "click that button" technique.

Before jumping into my methods of battling LightWave's render-hog-monster, depth of field, I think it would be a good idea to briefly review what this function is (size up the opposition!). Depth of field is nothing more than the area in which things are in focus. So objects outside the depth of field tend to be out of focus. The further out from the depth of field an object is, the more out of focus it will be.

In my struggles, I've come across a couple of ways to fake depth of field, or at least cut some corners in rendering time when using that easy Depth of Field button. The method to use generally depends on what the particular animation shot involves. Is depth of field being used in a still or an animation? Is the camera in a stationary position or is it panning? Is the action in the background or the foreground? To show why these questions matter, let's take a look at some examples.

Don't Move!

The easiest method of faking depth of field is in a still frame. This may be common knowledge for most animators, but if you haven't discovered this little trick, it can add a very nice touch to your images. Rather than taking the extra setup time to measure the depth of field distances in layout and doing numerous test renders to preview the depth of field effect, simply follow these steps:

- Render out the frame without using depth of field.
- Save the image, and load it into ToasterPaint, or any other paint program.
- By using the Filled Polygon tool in Blur Mode, you can trace around the area or object you want to be out of focus, and manually blur those areas to give them the illusion of being outside the depth of field. This tends to force the viewer's attention to the area which is in focus, and gives the whole image a more realistic look.

In my example (Figure 1), I set up a simple bedroom scene, with a wooden chair fairly close to the camera. I rendered the frame, saved it, and loaded it into TPaint. Then, as described above, I used the Filled Polygon tool in Blur Mode to trace around the chair. I hit (a) for again several times until the chair was blurred to my satisfaction. As you can see from the final frame, this method successfully makes the chair appear to be out of focus, and directs your attention to the back of the room. Using this same technique, you can also shift the viewer's attention to a different part of the frame quite easily.

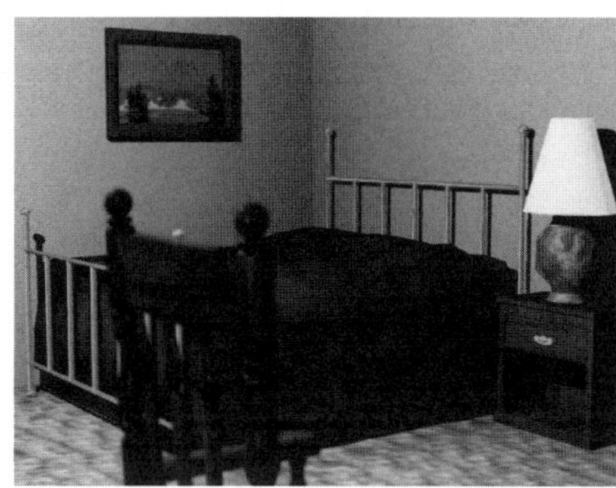

Figure 1

- In TPaint, load up the original rendered frame and blur the foreground elements. In my example, this includes only the chair. Save this frame as Part1.
- Reload the original rendered frame, this time blurring the background elements. In my example, this includes everything except the chair. Save this frame as Part2.
- Load Part1 into DV1 and Part2 into DV2. By using the fade effect from the Switcher, fade from DV1 to DV2.
- For standalone users, you won't have access to framebuffers DV1 and DV2, but you can still achieve this effect by using Part1 as a **Background Image** (**Effects** panel, and Part 2 as a **Foreground Image** (**Effects** panel). Then set an envelope for the foreground image from 0% to 100% over the number of frames that you want the fade to take place.

Using this procedure, it appears as though the camera focus is shifting from the background,and refocusing on the foreground. In my example, viewers would initially be looking at the back of the room, but as the fade takes place, their attention would focus on the chair.

Fixed Camera

OK, so still shots don't interest you. You want motion! What can you do in terms of depth of field? Well, for animations with a fixed camera, there is a possible solution. Many fixed-camera shots have some action coming onto or leaving the frame, with everything else remaining the same. In my second example (Figure 2), I have set up a fixed-camera shot of a street scene, with a car entering from the left and exiting to the right.

- First, I set up the entire scene, with all of the objects and lights in place.
- Then I rendered a single frame of the street, without the car in the camera's view, and saved this frame as STREETBKG.
- Next, I removed all of the objects in the scene,except for the car. I made sure to leave all of

Figure 2

the lights in the scene in their original positions. I saved this as a new scene, called STREETFGD.scn.

- I loaded the STREETBKG frame I previously rendered into TPaint, and blurred the area further down on the street to give it a depth of field look, as described in the first example. I then saved this frame over the original.
- With the STREETFGD.scn loaded into Layout, I loaded the STREETBKG frame as an image, and in the **Effects** panel, used it as a **Background Image**.
- I then continued to render the entire animation. Because of the constant lighting setup and camera position, it appears as though the car is actually on the street, and because the car is the only object in the scene, the frames rendered in only a few minutes each.

The only drawback is that the car cannot cast a shadow on the road, because the road isn't actually there—it's part of the background image. I got around this by building a fake shadow shape in Modeler and parenting the shadow object to the car. See Figure 2 for the results.

The Panning Camera

OK, so a fixed camera position just isn't going to cut it, either. You need action! As I mentioned before, the good ol' **Depth of Field** button often doubles my rendering time, so the following technique has saved many hours of rendering. But depending on the complexity of your scene, this method may or may not be a big timesaver.

Let's say you wanted to focus on some action in the foreground, and therefore have the action in the background be out of focus, all while the camera is panning. In my next example, I used the man and woman Humanoid object hierarchies. The man is in the foreground and is the focus of the shot. The woman is out of focus in the background, but also has some movements. Finally, the camera pans gently throughout the duration of the animation (Figure 3).

- I created the whole Humanoid scene as described above, and saved it as WHOLESCN.scn.
- I then removed the man object hierarchy from the foreground, and saved this new scene as BKGSCN.scn.
- Next, I reloaded the original WHOLESCN.scn, removed the woman object hierarchy in the background, and saved this new scene as FGDSCN.scn.

Figure 3

- I then rendered the entire BKGSCN.scn with just the woman and saved the frames to my hard drive. These frames rendered a little faster than the original scene would have, since the man object was removed.
- I then blurred each frame to give it the out-of-focus feel, to achieve the depth of field effect. This process can be extremely tedious, unless some sort of batch processing program, such as ProCONROL, is used. By selecting a sequence of frames, and then the operator to affect them (in this case, blur), the program does the tedious work of loading and saving each frame for you.
- Once the BKGSCN.scn was completely rendered and each frame was blurred, I loaded FGDSCN.scn into Layout. I then loaded the blurred background frames as an image sequence to be used as a **Background Image** (**Effects** panel). I proceeded to render that entire scene.

This provides the final result of the original scene, with the woman in the background, out of focus, and the man in the foreground. The total rendering time will be more than just the original scene without any depth of field effect, but significantly less than the original scene being rendered with LightWave's **Depth of Field** option active.

Now, what if you want the foreground elements to be blurry while the background is in focus? For instance, looking past something to focus on something else, all while the camera pans? I understand that with the alpha channel, the same technique I just used to blur the background in the Humanoid example could be used. But then I'd have to render the entire Foreground scene, and the entire alpha channel sequence, and then blur both of these sequences. Finally, I'd have to composite both of those image sequences with the background rendering. Personally, I haven't saved much time using this technique, with all of the confusion and extra necessary planning.

In my experience, the only easy way to achieve a focused background while the foreground is out of focus is by actually using that **Depth of Field** button. But there is a way to cut that rendering corner as well! For this example, I'm using a fireplace scene, with a couple on a couch enjoying the fire. I want the fireplace to be the focus of the shot, and therefore, I want the couple on the couch to be out of focus (Figure 4).

- First, I set up the whole scene, with the fireplace and all of the room objects in place, as well as the couple on the couch. With all the lights in place,and the camera motion set, I saved the scene as FPWHOLE.scn.
- Next, I removed the couch and the couple on it, and saved that scene as FPBKG.scn.
- Then I reloaded the original FPWHOLE.scn and removed all objects except the couple and the couch. Again, it's important that all of the lights remain in their exact positions, and that the camera motion remains the same. I saved this scene as FPFGD.scn.
- Then I rendered the entire FPBKG.scn. There will not be much savings in rendering time compared to the original scene, because the only difference is that I removed the couple and the couch. Keep in mind that if I used depth of field on the original scene, the render times would have doubled.
- When the FPBKG.scn was finished rendering, I then

Figure 4

loaded the FPFGD.scn into Layout. I set the appropriate depth of field to make the couple and the couch slightly out of focus, as if looking past them. I then loaded the background frames I just rendered as a background image sequence.

- I then rendered this scene. These frames will render quite rapidly, even though depth of field is being used, because the only objects in the whole scene are the couple and the couch.
- The final result is an animation the appears to have been a single complete scene with **Depth of Field** active. By breaking this scene into two separate ones for the foreground and the background, I was able to achieve a realistic depth of field effect without doubling my render times.

Again, the methods I just outlined are the ones I have developed along my rendering way. I'm sure that there are other techniques out there I have yet to discover, and mine may or may not save you time, depending on your particular scene. Hopefully, I have shed some light on how to cut some corners in rendering, and if you are not a big depth of field user, maybe these methods will spark an idea of how to cut some other corners from your rendering time. Just because LightWave offers an option at a click of a button, don't assume that's the only way to go.

LWP

Arnie Boedecker is owner of ImagiNation Enterprises, located north of Chicago, Ill. He is not worthy of an Internet address, but he can be reached at his place of business at (815) 385-8198, or on many of the LightWave bulletin boards. Arnie is co-founder of the Chicago LightWave Association, a poor cook, and desperately needs a haircut.

Anatomy of a Shot

The Seaming of "Cy's" Head

by Tom Williamson

This is the first article of what I hope will become a frequent feature of *LIGHTWAVEPRO*. The concept is to take a visual effect and explore every aspect of the shot in detail. For this first article I've chosen a shot that, at the outset, seemed like a piece of cake. But it rapidly became complex—very complex.

The Shot

The shot in question is from the motion picture *The Warrior of Waverly Street* from Trimark Pictures. It involves one of the main characters, the cybersuit (or "Cy" as he became known). During the "suit-up" sequence, Cy opens up his back to allow Spencer (played by Joe Mazzelo) to climb inside. After Spencer is locked into place, the suit closes up. For the shot of his head closing, a practical effects head was built to open and close. Unfortunately, the head didn't quite work right and the shells didn't close all the way (Figure 1). Computer Café to the rescue. We had already been contracted to "seam" the head closed with a CGI effect, but now it was also a salvage job. Once the footage was scanned the task at hand was clear, and seemingly simple.

Figure 1

The Plan

The original plan was to use Elastic Reality to warp the shells closed, then add the seam. This proved to be an extremely over-simplified idea. For one thing, the shot was unstable. Apparently the camera that was used had a little bit of a registration problem, and the shot was rocking pretty badly. The next problem was the suit wasn't locked down, and it also rocked back and forth the entire shot. Still another problem was smoke drifting through the background, eliminating any hope of using a still-frame. So now we had to come up with a way to isolate and steady the head for the addition of the seam (early match-move tests proved unfavorable) and then reintegrate the footage back into the scene. Here's what we came up with:

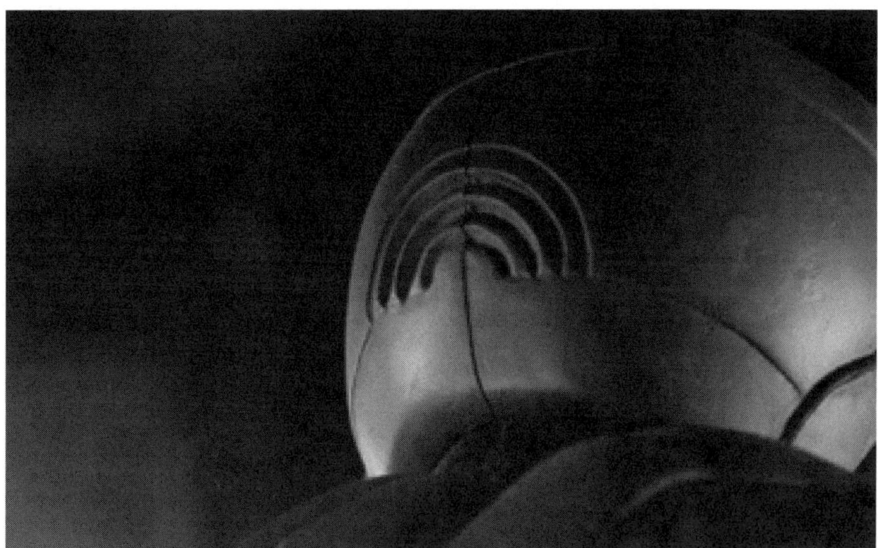

Figure 2

1. Warp the original sequence to correct the opened head.
2. Take the first frame after the head closed and

de-grain it.

3. Take that same frame and paint out the crack in the back of the head.
4. Animate the seaming effect on the de-grained frame and reveal the retouched one.
5. Composite the results into the original footage.

The Steps

The first step was warping the head closed. For this task we used Elastic Reality (Alpha version, of course). The shells were traced with spline shapes and tweened. For the effect to be unnoticeable the warp started when the head was about half closed. After setting up the shapes to close the head, the entire shot was rendered. Now we had a sequence that at least had the head closing all the way (Figure 2).

To create the de-grained frame, we used an averaging technique of taking 10 frames and merging them into one. We used Adobe Photoshop for this. The first step was to load all 10 frames as separate layers. Then the frames were carefully lined up (because of the "gate-rock") and the transparency was set for each layer to gradually add to the preceding layer. When all 10 layers had their transparency set, the frame looked normal, except for a noticeable lack of film grain. All the layers were flattened and the frame was saved. Then the seam (the crack in the back of the head) was painted out so that the helmet appeared smooth (Figure 3). That frame also was saved. By the way, it was about this time that Steven Worley was adding de-grain to the film grain plug-in he was developing for us. Unfortunately it wasn't ready when we did this shot, or the de-graining process could have been far more simple.

Once the footage was scanned the task at hand was clear, and seemingly simple.

The Mercury Effect

Now it was time for LightWave (again on the Alpha). The director wanted the seaming effect to appear as if a bead of mercury poured down over the seam, then "melded" into the head. For the mercury bead object a sketched curve was extruded and bent to the approximate curve of the back of Cy's head. Then each half was sheared with ease-in selected to approximate the curve of the vents on the back of Cy's head (Figure 4). Then there was a lot of point selecting and dragging to contour the bead object in and out of the vents. To help achieve this, the model was continually imported and exported to Layout until all the little adjustments were done.

Figure 3

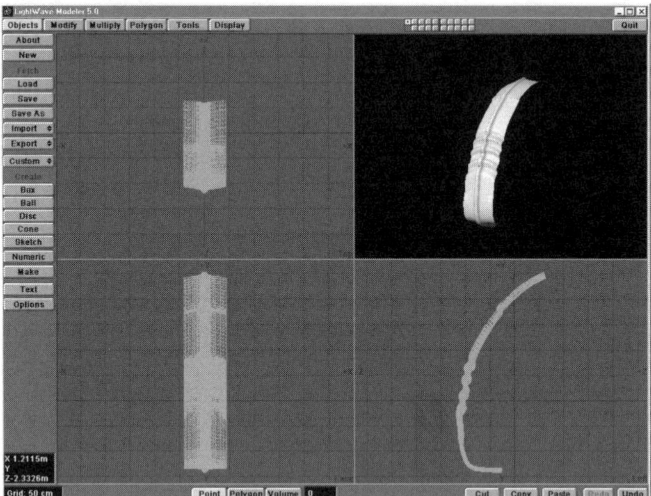

Figure 4

Final tweaking was made with a few bones (Figure 5). The surfacing of the bead was pretty straightforward, just chrome. A transparency and specularity map was applied to feather the edges (Figure 6) and a reflection map was created by crudely painting on one of the same frames (to keep the color consistent) and to have the suit reflect in the bead via a reflection map. A fractal bump displacement was sent through the bead object to give it a fluid feel and the bead was ready.

The film grain was matched by loading a plane object and front-projection mapping the original footage on it. Its surface was flagged to not receive film grain from the plug-in. Then a few test renders were made, adjusting the film grain plug-in until it was a perfect match. Then the test plane was cleared from the scene.

For the "melding" effect, a morph target of the bead object was made by flattening out the bead object and assigning a different surface name. The surfacing on the "meld" object was simple front projection of the "seamed" still of the head, and the same transparency map. After all that was set up, a sequence of the bead "melding" was rendered (Figure 7).

Next it was time to animate the flowing of the bead. This was achieved in Avid Matador Paint on an SGI Indigo2. A sequence of five frames of the de-grained still of the head was rendered in LightWave with artificial grain. Then the sequence of the bead meld was loaded into Matador and the bead was painted out progressively to appear as if it was flowing down the back of the head. The five frames were used in a looped sequence to avoid "grain-lock", the unwanted static look of a freeze frame. The bottom of the bead was hand painted (complete with a specular highlight) every frame of the flow. Now we had a sequence of frames with a bead of mercury flowing down the back of the head and melding to seal the helmet, just like the director wanted.

Then it was back to Elastic Reality. If the two sequences (the warp and the bead) were joined now there would be an obvious point where Cy freezes, because Cy rocks slightly back and forth the first part of the shot. The plan was to re-introduce the rocking into the bead sequence. To achieve this a spline shape was made of Cy's silhouette. That same shape was copied and offset just slightly. After the two shapes were joined, a motion curve was made of an oscillating sine wave. This made Cy rock back and forth. The rest of the frame was protected by a barrier curve encompassing the entire head. After several test renders with slight modifications to the motion curve, Cy was rocking again and the sequences could be joined.

The last hurdle was the smoke in the background. After the sequences were joined together, they were loaded back into Matador paint. A soft-edge, hold-out matte was created to mask Cy's head, and the background from the original footage was composited into every frame. At last the shot was done.

As you can see, what started out as a simple shot turned into a multi-platform, software hopping, rabbit-out-of-a-hat nightmare. It just goes to show you, *never assume the obvious*. I hope this article was as informative as this shot was painful. Look forward to more "Anatomy" articles in the future, and if you have a specific effect you'd like covered, drop me a line.

Tom Williamson is Vice President/Effects Supervisor for Computer Café Inc. He would like to get his hands on those GI-Joes that are collecting dust in your attic. He also needs a vacation. Reach him at: tomcatjr@concentric.net

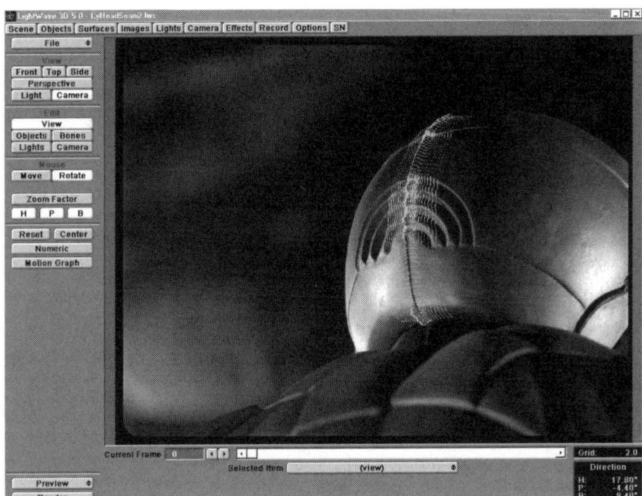

Figure 5

Figure 6

Front Projection Mapping

by Mojo

The 3D-animation market is booming right now. Every movie and TV show under the sun wants to get its hands on a computer and put you in front of it. Why? Because Hollywood's job is to fake reality as cheaply as possible, and 3D software has finally matured to the point where it excels at just that. Herding dinosaurs, exploding planets, talking cats and heroic mouthwashes have all been made possible by the 3D revolution, and the end is nowhere in sight.

However, in many of these cases, 3D is not used to completely replace reality, but enhance it or add to it—talking cats have to talk to someone, and big, bad monsters must threaten heroes. Many of you are probably familiar with LightWave's abilities to create these fanciful elements, but you may not be aware of the powerful tools it contains to help you merge the real with the unreal.

Figure 1: The background image in Modeler must be automatically sized to a TV screen-sized polygon to ensure proper alignment.

Figure 2: The U.N. building was traced with points and turned into a polygon. In this case, a square would have sufficed. If I wanted the ship to pass behind building tops, zooming in for better tracing would have been necessary.

Composite Shots

Compositing is the task of combining, or composing, several elements into one. Blue-screen shots are sometimes referred to as composite shots, or comps for short. In most cases, this calls for the seamless integration of special effects (mostly 3D elements) into live action that has already been filmed.

On the set, an actor may be filmed dodging and ducking the thin air, but later on, a special-effects person will need to add a hideous monster trying to do the hero in. This means the animator will need to work around the live action, matching the lighting, movements and pacing of the existing material. Any flaws in the work will probably be spotted by the audience, and the animator will never work in that town again.

Any flaws in the work will probably be spotted by the audience, and the animator will never work in that town again.

To make life easier on the effects people, these shots will normally be locked down. This means the camera will not move during the action, and the animator will not have to match the camera moves, perhaps the most difficult task of all (there are systems that digitally record camera moves and create motion files for 3D software, but this is expensive and most producers avoid the process).

At first this may seem limiting, but keep in mind that just about every composite seen on television (including *Babylon 5* and *seaQuest*) is locked off; I'll bet you didn't even notice.

LightWave's main compositing feature is called **Front Projection Mapping**, which allows you to combine 3D animation with scanned images or se-quences with a minimum of effort.

Do I Need a Projector?

No. The title of this feature is mainly there to help you understand what it does. Imagine projecting a movie on a screen while you're holding a flat piece of white cardboard over a small area of the screen. Forgetting about you for a moment, someone from the audience probably wouldn't be able to see that piece of cardboard, since it is also reflecting the projected image and is the same color as the screen. Even if you started moving the cardboard around, it would still remain invisible, since it will always be showing the same part of the image as the screen behind it would have.

This is exactly how Front Projection (FP) mapping works; instead of a movie screen, you have the background image, and instead of a piece of cardboard, you have polygons.

When you select the same image for an FP-mapped polygon as you have in the background, that polygon can be rendered invisible. Sound useless? Not when you start putting objects behind FP-mapped polygons.

When Did That Happen?

The accompanying image (color pages) of the LightWave Space Destroyer hovering behind the United Nations building was done with FP mapping. Sure, anyone could have put the ship on top of a background image, but putting it behind one of the buildings is what makes the shot believable. This is where FP mapping comes into play.

The first step was to create a polygon in the shape of the U.N. building. This is much easier than you may think, thanks to Modeler's ability to share background

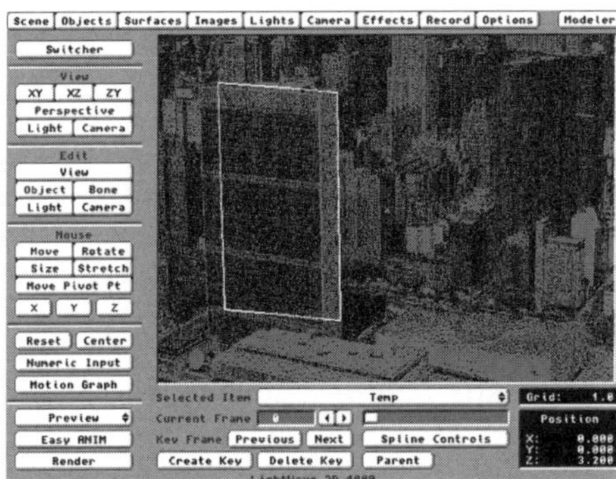

Figure 3: As long as you follow the magic cutout-making steps, your FP-mapping polygon should exactly match the locations you traced in Modeler. Make sure you don't move the camera in any way or your alignment will be off.

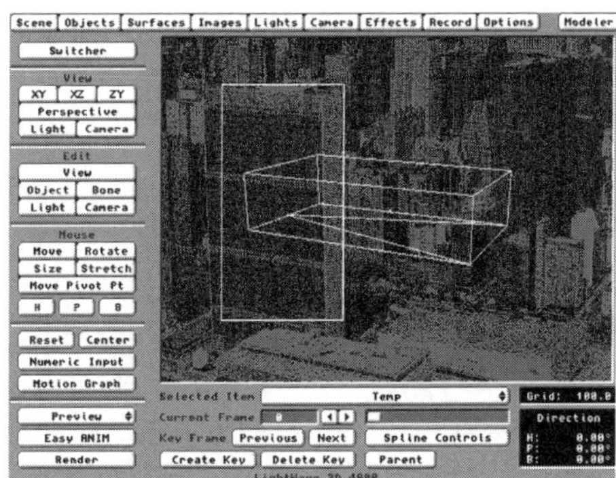

Figure 4: The spaceship is placed behind the cutout polygon. Special care was taken to rotate the ship so it would match the perspective of the original photograph.

Figure 5: The differences in tonal ranges within the shadow on the ship and the shadow on the ground show why this version has oversaturated ambient light.

images with layout. The **BG Image** button in Modeler (Display menu) lets you pick images that have been loaded into LightWave and display them in any of the three views. In most cases, you'll want to look at them down the Z axis. Once displayed, you can literally trace them with points and create polygons in the same shape as anything in the image.

To ensure your tracings line up with the BG image in Layout, you must create a video-sized polygon. The correct aspect ratio of a TV screen is 1:1.342, so numerically create a box with a radius of 1 on Y and 1.342 on X (the total height will be 2, with a width of 2.684). These numbers must be exact.

After you've made this polygon (it also helps to center it—try the Center macro), enter the BG Image menu again and choose **Automatic Size**. It stretches to the size of your new polygon (Figure 1). Now that your image is correctly sized, you can either discard your box or go to another layer and start making your cutout by tracing over the BG image (Figure 2). Zooming in and out for detail work will not effect your lineup. Believe it or not, whatever you make will now match up with the BG image in layout. Once you are finished with your cutout, save it.

Getting to It

Load the new cutout polygon into Layout and place the camera at 0,0,0. Make sure your polygon is at zero on X and Y and make the Z value the same as your camera's lens length (the default should be 3.2). Presto! Your cutout should now be placed directly over the appropriate areas of the BG image (Figure 3). Now you can put your object(s) behind this polygon, and they will seem to actually go behind that part of your background image (Figure 4).

Make sure your polygon's surface settings have a luminosity of 100 percent and a diffuse value of zero. This is important since your FP polygon can not disappear into the BG image if it has any diffuse value—it can catch light from your scene lights and become visible.

If you need to cast a shadow onto the FP polygon, then you must carefully play with lighting and diffuse/luminosity settings in order for the FP polygon to blend in but receive a shadow. Remember that 100 percent luminosity/0 percent diffuse can blend in perfectly, but can not receive a shadow. *[Editor's note: For more information on this subject, see* Compositing with Video *in this issue.]*

As you can see in the final rendering (color pages), the building appears to be casting a shadow upon the spaceship. This extra bit of realism was simple to achieve by placing a shadow-mapped spotlight at the correct angle in front of the FP polygon. Although this cutout is not visible because of its surface settings, it is still quite capable of casting shadows. All I had to do was make sure the spaceship object was close enough to the polygon to receive a shadow in the proper place.

Lights

Not everything in life is easy. FP mapping may seem to be an exception to this rule, and up to now it has been. However, the most important aspect of making a composite work is the lighting. Unless your 3D objects are lit to match the BG images, the effect will not look right.

Proper lighting is the key to 3D realism and is something that an animator must develop a feel for—magazine articles can't teach everything.

This scene took only minutes to set up, but hours to light. Proper lighting is the key to 3D realism and is something that an animator must develop a feel for—magazine articles can't teach everything. Fortunately, there are a few tips that may help you along the way.

The first step is to determine what direction the light is coming from. Shadows in the image will give you the best clues. If you look closely at the shadow the U.N. building is casting on the ground, you can see it's close to high noon.

I simply imagined my spotlight was in that scene and placed it at an angle that I thought would cast a similar shadow. Looking closely at which sides of the buildings are more brightly lit than the others also reveals where light is coming from.

Fill light will be the most difficult to simulate. On a sunny day, light is bounced off everything it touches. This bounce light is what fills in all the areas not in the path of the sun's light. Since LightWave does not simulate this automatically (nor do any other 3D programs I know of), the intrepid animator is left to come up with a way to do it on his or her own.

Fortunately, the image of New York I picked for my example seems to have been taken on a clear day (not altogether easy to obtain). This means higher contrast in the scene and darker shadows—lots of clues for me to determine my lighting. Conversely, cloudy days have soft lighting, virtually no discernible shadows, and are far more difficult to match. Avoid them if you can.

The New York scene required only the main spotlight on the ship and a correct level of ambient light to simulate natural bounce. Again, this was determined by the BG image itself. By looking inside the shadow the U.N. building is casting on the street below, I can see how much ambient light there was the day the photo was taken. After my initial render, I compared that with the area inside the shadow being cast on my spaceship and adjusted the ambient level accordingly (Figure 5 in the color pages).

Blue Moon

Another lighting factor is color. Quite often, live action may be photographed with colored filters over the lights or lenses. If compositing like this is being planned, colored lighting can actually make it easier to combine elements. If a large, blue light is cast inside a room to simulate evening, casting a similar shade of blue on your 3D objects instantly connects them to the scene. However, more subtle coloring can also push your scene over the threshold of realism.

Ever hear of color temperature? It's a technical way of determining how photographic film sees light. To oversimplify things, film sees sunlight as a bluish tone. Remember those Levi's 501 Blues commercials, where everything had a slightly blue tint to it? Or maybe you've just seen a low-budget movie where all the colors seemed washed out. This is no trick—this is actually how movie film sees sunlight. Special amber filters are put over the camera lens to correct this. Depending on the time of day and kind of filter, the camerapeople don't always manage to correct the image perfectly and a little blue still creeps in, but most of the time no one notices.

Look carefully at that image of New York. I didn't take it myself, so I don't know what the photographer did to correct the color temperature, but it looks to me like it's a tad on the blue side (assuming it prints the way my eyes see it). If that spaceship was really there that day, then the ship would also be given a hint of blue by the camera. It's a subtle detail, but by making my spotlight just a slight shade of blue (235, 235, 255), I helped mate the spaceship to the scene just a little bit better.

If the picture was taken towards the beginning or end of the day, a slight hint of orange to simulate sunrise or sunset might have been necessary. In any case, closely examine your background images for subtle color tints—it might wind up being that one, small detail that makes all the difference.

Finishing Touches

It will be difficult to tell how closely your LightWave elements match your backgrounds until you do a final render. If your backgrounds are from film (like this example), until your 3D objects are antialiased, they will probably appear far too crisp. In fact, I almost always turn off adaptive sampling and use the soft filter option to better match my element. So don't drive yourself crazy trying to match things until you've done a full render.

If you want to save time while in the testing stage, load your unantialiased images into ToasterPaint and carefully blur the LightWave elements only. This softens things up enough to give you a good idea of what a finished rendering looks like.

Although FP mapping is a powerful, new tool, making it work for you requires a solid understanding of the basics of 3D--modeling and lighting. Despite all the fancy features that now exist and have yet to come, animators who refine their skills with the "simple stuff" always come out ahead.

Author's note: More complex applications of FP mapping will be covered in the future—how far in the future will be determined by how many of you write in and ask for more.

LWP

Mojo works for Foundation Imaging as an animator and technical director on the syndicated television series Babylon 5.

Compositing with Video

by Greg Teegarden

Realism—we all strive for it in our animations, in one form or another. Whether it's realistic movement or careful attention to lighting, a perfectly constructed model or a flawlessly painted texture map, the goal of most computer-generated animation artists is to obtain a sense of reality that challenges the viewer to try and discern: Is it live, or is it Memorex? It is this mastery of tools that leads to the satisfaction of having done the best job possible to obtain your goal: the suspension of the viewer's disbelief.

Perhaps the easiest—yet, at the same time, the most difficult—method of achieving this goal is through image compositing. As mentioned in a previous article on this subject (*LWPRO* Vol. 1, Issue 3), image compositing will by default give a certain sense of realism, but it's a double-edged sword if it's not done correctly. If your computer-generated (CG) elements aren't married well into the environment, the very effect you are trying to achieve can be destroyed by the contradiction set in your scene.

Vanishing Points

In the May 1994 issue of *Video Toaster User*, the Toaster Gallery section contains a perfect example of the kind of contradiction I'm trying to describe. It's an image of a lighthouse composited over a mountain range during a sunset. From a lighting standpoint, it looks flawless. The model itself looks very good, and the overall mood of the scene worked nicely.

So what is wrong with it? Two things, in my opinion, give it away as a CG lighthouse. The first is the power of the light beam coming from the source—it is too bright and too opaque. That, however, is subjective and open for debate, as someone else may feel that it's not bright enough, or maybe the wrong color, etc.

The other mistake is not subjective: conflicting perspectives. We're looking up at the mountains, yet down at the lighthouse. Had we also been looking up at the lighthouse, it would have been a matter of tweaking with the light cone to produce a thoroughly convincing scene.

Effective Compositing

Look at the image on the cover of this newsletter. It shows the *seaQuest* Stinger craft resting on the edge of a

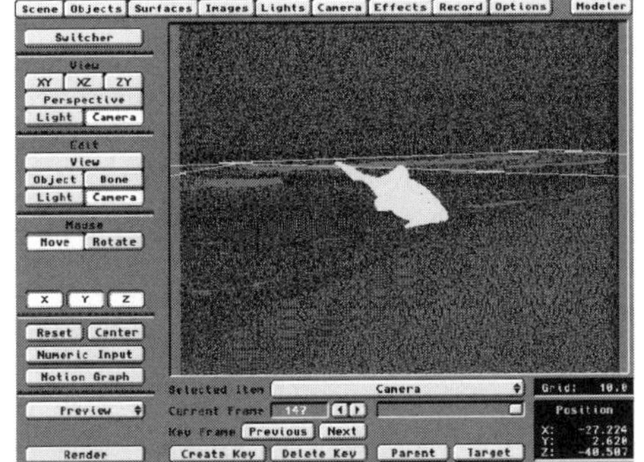

Figure 1: The ocean surface, Stinger and background image.ness.

Figure 2: This cone angle produces an unwanted brightness.

beach. The Stinger is, of course, LightWave CG, but the beach itself is video, and what marries the two together is careful attention to the details of effective image compositing.

The shot was accomplished by moving the Stinger through a large polygon that was front-projection mapped with the same ocean video sequence used for the background (Figure 1).

In all composite shots, it is important that the CG imagery or virtual camera have the same position and properties of the camera that actually acquired the image. It helps to be present when the background plate is shot, because at this time all the information needed to be recorded for use on your virtual CG camera must be taken. All essential measurements should be recorded, such as the distance from the camera to the object; position and rotation of camera in relation to the ground; camera lens used; distance between objects in shot, etc.

If you can't be there during the shoot, or if the image you're using as a plate was something scanned from a photograph, then use your best judgment to determine where the horizon lines fall.

The easiest way to determine whether your horizon lines are correct is to see if the bounding-box representation of your object falls to the same vanishing points as that of the background image. A vanishing point is the imaginary distant point where the edges of an object would meet if they were extended back into the image.

Matching vanishing points is crucial for determining the proper perspective for the CG element to match that of your background plate. The problem with the lighthouse image is that the vanishing points and horizon of the lighthouse did not match those of the mountain. The lighthouse's horizon line is fairly high, as we're looking down upon it, while the mountain's horizon is low. The way the image stands as rendered would suggest to the viewer that the lighthouse is at least a mile high, thus destroying an otherwise convincing illusion.

One of the reasons that this month's cover image works is because the two elements involved have matching perspectives.

Lighting and Shadows

Lighting is also important. The light falling on your CG element should be the same color and temperature as that of the background plate. Also consider reflected light when doing composition work, as it's very important to the selling of the image.

Shadows on the CG element should have the same values as those in the background plate. LightWave cannot change the intensity of the shadows that it casts on objects, so in order to lighten a shadow area, bounce light needs to be used to soften the contrast between light and dark areas created by shadows. In the Stinger image, the large fins on the back of the vehicle are casting shadows that contrast too much with the rest of the image. On the day that the background plate was shot, it was somewhat sunny with a fair amount of atmospheric haze. It was morning, so the sun was low in the sky and had a lot of yellow. Shadows cast by this type of lighting situation would be long and light, with very soft edges.

I recommend using shadow mapping to get soft-edged shadows. In this shot, however, I discovered that the cone angle of the spotlight was shining on the object used as the ground plane for the ocean, which, in turn, created an undesirable pool of brightness in the shot (Figure 2). I opted at this point to use a ray-traced distant light and relied on the Soft Filter option in the Camera panel to smooth the edges of the shadow. It was still a bit too defined, but looked better overall than the pools of light created by the spotlight.

By increasing the luminosity of the surface, the shadow cast onto it by the Stinger became lighter as the front projection-mapped background became lighter.

Creating visible shadows on your front-projected polygons can sometimes be a bit tricky. In order to allow your polygons to match the background, it's often necessary to add luminosity to the surface. If 100 percent luminosity is added to the surface, it will match the background without having to light the polygons.

The problem with using 100 percent luminosity is when it is applied, no shadows can be cast on a surface. Therefore, it is necessary to use lower (or no) luminosity settings while playing with the diffuse and lighting values for these polygons. If you can light the surface 100 percent, it will match the background plate seamlessly, but a mixture of diffuse and luminosity with some lighting will achieve the same goal.

The method used to lighten a shadow cast by the Stinger element onto the ocean surface polygon was to vary the settings of these two values. By increasing the luminosity of the surface, the shadow cast onto it by the Stinger became lighter as the front projection–mapped background became brighter. However, the polygons used to support the front-projection map then showed that map as brighter than the background image, creating an undesirable bright spot on the image.

I needed to lower the diffuse value of the ocean polygon to darken the front-projection map to match that of the background image. At the same time, I had to retain the luminosity setting of the shadow areas of the ocean surface, thus giving the appearance of a lighter shadow. I used values of 56 percent and 43 percent for luminosity and diffuse, respectively. This gave me a shadow that was visible, but not too highly contrasting. It also allowed the ocean object to seamlessly match the background.

I would like to see a LightWave feature with the ability to control shadow lightness through the Camera or Lights panel (as opposed to the method I just described, which is effective but rather tedious).

The Finished Animation

In the final animation, the Stinger vehicle is to enter the frame from the left, crash through the surf and come to rest partially on the beach. Since the vehicle is supposed to be in the water and interact with it, a number of different techniques were used to give the animation life.

Time was short, so I used Parallax's Matador—a high-end compositing package on the SGI platform—to do the final composite of the vehicle interacting with the waves. I used Matador to add wave splashes as the Stinger cuts through the water. LightWave could have been used to model the waves and bring them in with dissolve envelopes, but again, I did not have the time to make it look convincing.

Matador is the same package developed by Industrial Light and Magic that was used to composite the CG dinosaurs in *Jurassic Park*. Apart from the use of Matador, LightWave was needed to do the original composite frames, as Matador is a 2D program that only composites RGB images. Source files are still needed, and LightWave was more than adequate. Of course, it is desirable to have as complete a shot as possible before doing any 2D compositing in a third-party package, so it was necessary to use LightWave.

Since I was using an object surface for the craft to glide through, it was a little extra work to add a reflection of the Stinger to the water. The problem I discovered was twofold after I rendered the first frame. First, the reflected image was too bright, and second, it was too mirror-perfect with no breakup from the ripples of the choppy surf. The mirror reflection was easy to fix, as a fractal-bump texture provided enough distortion to break up the reflection as it would be on real water.

The brightness of the reflection was another matter entirely. After much experimentation, I found that if the surface was turned to black, with color highlights activated and a fog setting that gives a sense of atmosphere, the reflection of the Stinger took on the dark appearance that I wanted.

Some Final Notes

One final effect was to give the illusion of water running off the canopy of the Stinger as it hits the sand. That was again accomplished by the use of a fractal-bump map applied to the canopy, this time with a small velocity running on the Y axis. I might also add that even if I chose not to have the water stream down, the fractal bump map was required to indicate the presence of water droplets on the canopy itself. The fact that LightWave lets the user add a velocity to the map was an added bonus, and it worked out quite well.

Finally, you may be wondering why I chose to use a flat polygon as the ocean surface, as opposed to a mesh of polygons with a displacement map to simulate waves. I decided that the displacement map would give the appearance of ripples against the Stinger body, but it wouldn't match the waves in the ocean itself. Since the Stinger is cutting through the water, I decided to paint the disturbance to give the greatest sense of reality. If the Stinger was just bobbing in the ocean, displacement-mapped waves would have been ideal.

If you remember the basics of effective video compositing—matching perspectives, lighting and shadows—you'll be able to achieve some truly realistic results.

Greg Teegarden is an animator for Amblin Imaging and the resident composite artist. His work can be seen on seaQuest *and numerous commercials.*

Moving the Camera

by John F.K. Parenteau

I am, of course, prejudiced, but I feel the most important job on a production set is that of the cinematographer. Yes, many other positions such as director, actors and even production designers play an equally important role in bringing a script to life, but the camera person is the last bastion of truth before all the work of those other departments is recorded on film stock. It is the director of photography (another term for cinematographer) who designs, with the director, the method each shot is to be photographed, how it will be lit and in what method the camera will record it. And this brings us to the point of this month's column. I hear two complaints from young animators, and young camera people, for that matter: "Lighting seems so simple, but I can never make it look right" and "How do you move the camera?" The former we have dealt with and will continue to deal with in the future. The latter is a complex question that requires immediate attention.

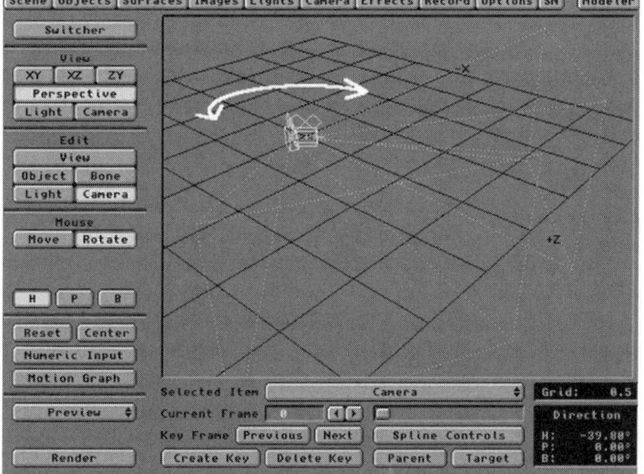

Figure 1

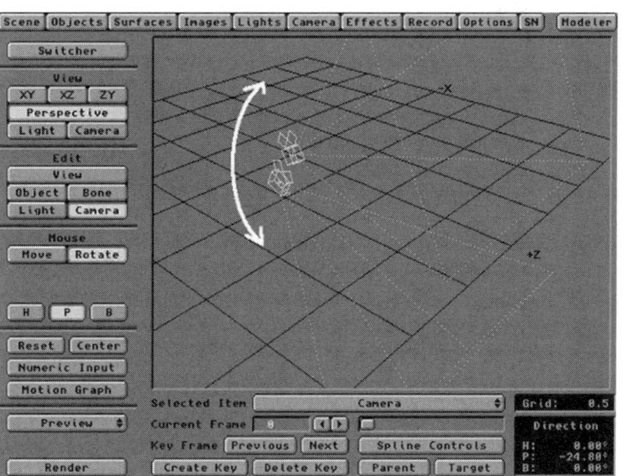

Figure 2

A Work of Art

Moving the camera is actually an art form. Watching some of the masters' greatest works, and how each shot seems to elicit the most appropriate response, makes you wonder if it was all planned. Believe me, it was. The best cinematographers pay as much attention to how the camera moves, or doesn't move, as they do to how it is lit. The process not only requires the knowledge of the rules of motion, but also an emotional understanding of what effect you are achieving by moving the frame.

Think of the camera as another actor. Just as an actor on screen chooses a method of approaching a performance, a good cameraperson makes a similar choice. An actor prepares for a scene by carefully studying the dialogue, and the situation in which the character has been placed. Picture the following scene from *The Shining*:

Jack Nicholson smashes a door with an ax as he chases his family through a deserted lodge. He is confused, angry and seemingly possessed as he hunts his wife and children. As the door smashes apart from the ax, Jack sticks his head through the door and exclaims, "Here's Johnny!"

Nicholson chose to deliver the line with a twisted smile rather than a more serious "I'm going to kill you" face. By contrasting his intent with a smile, the moment is even more disturbing. Choices such as these are made every day. The best actors make the best choices and thus achieve the most convincing performances. As a cameraperson, it is important to approach each shot with the same mindset. The camera is an actor as well, and as you choose how to reveal the scene through the lens, you are choosing what the audience will or won't see. Most horror films have a scene as follows:

Our hero (or heroine) has stupidly decided to go back in the house, even after he has found all his friends dead by mysterious methods. The camera starts in close-up, probably a handheld shot, as we move with our character through the hallways. The scene cuts to an over-the-shoulder shot (behind the actor, looking over a shoulder, called OTS), as we now follow the same character. Because of the strange, voyeuristic feel of the over-the-shoulder shot, we feel like something will come up behind him at any moment. Finally, as our OTS shot has become closer and closer, the character screams and turns to camera. We cut around to his point of view (the view from the actor's position, as if looking through his eyes) and see nothing. Cutting back to the OTS, the actor and we, the audience relax and he turns back to the hallway... and a demonic creature is waiting to pounce!

As you can imagine, the camera positions and movement had as much to do with creating a spooky mood as did the performance of our ridiculously stupid character. But this is an obvious example. Sometimes the most gross and obvious moves are the most simple to understand. Consider, however, the subtle pan, a short dolly move or even no motion at all. Each choice expresses its own emotion, and carries its own performance.

All the Right Moves

First, let's consider the basic moves possible with a camera, both in CGI and live action. The PAN is a pivoting motion left to right or right to left (Figure 1). The TILT is a pivoting motion up and down (Figure 2). A camera TRUCK or DOLLY is a physical movement of the camera in any direction on the X or Z axes (Figure 3). A BOOM is a physical movement of the camera in an up or down motion (Figure 4). These four basic motions comprise the simplistic forms of all camera movement. To understand how to manipulate these motions requires some understanding of basic framing.

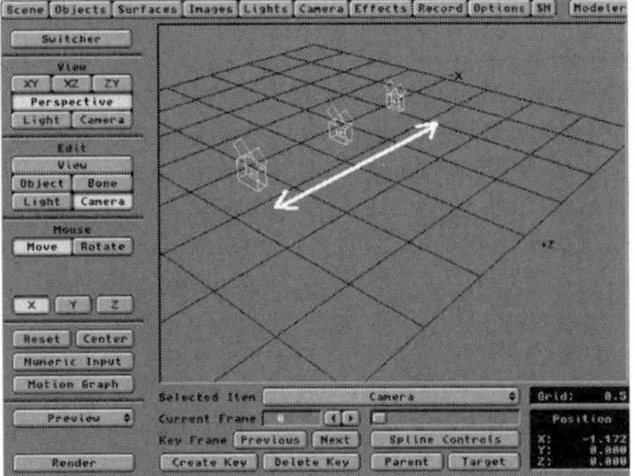

Figure 3

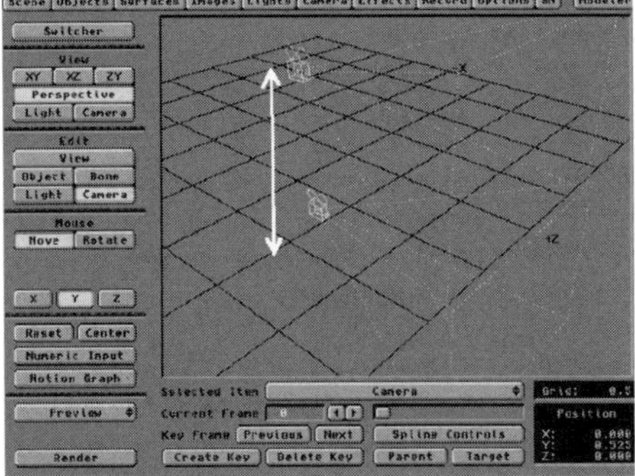

Figure 4

Figure 5

A Perfect Frame of Mind

When you photograph your friends or family with a still camera, whether you are conscious of it or not, you are considering the rules of framing. Though you may not realize or even understand these rules, natural skill can come into play. As you place your friend on the edge of a cliff overlooking a beautiful panorama, you automatically frame your friend to the side to see both the view and the person. To consciously understand why this is the most pleasing method of framing, it is important to understand the theory of thirds.

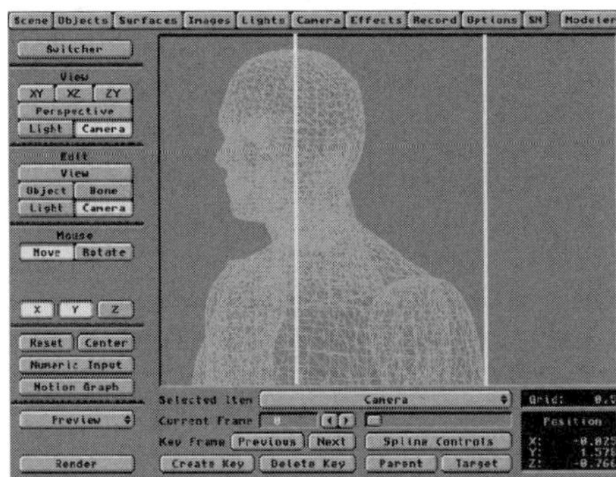

Figure 6

Consider the visible frame through the eyepiece, or on the LightWave layout screen. Break this frame into even thirds, vertically across the frame (Figure 5). Placing the object so that one of the borders between the thirds runs through the object creates the most desirable framing. If the object were placed in one of the side thirds, the frame would be unbalanced and would feel wrong. If the object were placed in the center, the frame would feel much more natural, but very uninteresting.

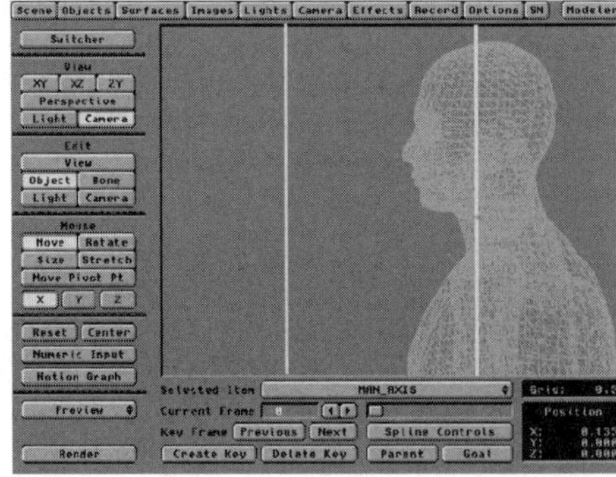

Figure 7

Extending this theory into the photography of people, it is important to consider "nose room." In a close-up of a person, looking off frame left, it is necessary to allow the subject room to look off. If the subject were framed center, or the nose was placed close to the left edge of the frame, the balance of the frame would be off, and the character would have no room to look (Figure 6). "Nose room" gives the character a place to look. Consequently, if the character is looking directly at camera, it is appropriate to frame him or her center. As the angle of the look moves further and further away from the camera, more room should be allowed as lead space. If our character is looking directly off screen, showing us a profile, we would tend to place him or her close to the edge of the frame (Figure 7). In addition to breaking the frame in thirds vertically, it is also important to consider horizontal separation. The same rules apply here, and must be considered as well.

As you transition, you're thinking from a still frame to motion, be aware of live and dead spaces in your shot. By limiting the action to a small area of the frame, the remaining areas may seem dead and useless. Try to utilize all areas in some way to prevent the audience from losing interest.

Remember that action does not have to take place from the sides or top and bottom only. Use the angles of the frame to break up these dead spaces. For example, a spaceship entering the frame from the left and exiting to the right may be appropriate in telling your story, but it may also be the most boring way to tell it. To add some excitement, have the ship enter from the top left corner and exit the bottom right. This utilizes all thirds of the frame and makes for a much more interesting angle.

With an understanding of the theory of thirds and the basic camera moves, it is now time to study more complex motions and the reasons why you might want to utilize them.

You're the Director

A crane shot in live action is a very popular move. Not only is it a great way to establish a scene, but it's also fun to ride. A crane is the combination of a boom and a tilt, with a little dolly often thrown in for good measure. Though it is a simple motion of dropping the camera from some height to the ground, there are many considerations. Though the boom may be dramatic, it will be relatively invisible unless some foreground elements are utilized.

Let's create a large monolithic building in an open field. The building is 1,000 feet high and a mile away from the camera. If we were to start up high and boom down to the ground we would see little or no effect. By placing a tree in the foreground and booming down past the branches, we can now see the effect of the crane. Add a few cars on the road approaching the building, or perhaps other, smaller buildings on the road approaching the camera. Now the parallax will be increased by adding additional objects at increasing distances from the camera. Remember, a crane is not effective unless you are craning past something.

Now our scene is of two cars chasing each other down the road. Our camera position is on the side of the road and the cars are approaching quickly. Utilizing a "Whip Pan" in this situation would be most effective.

As the first car approaches, the camera pans quickly with it until we see the car receding away from us. Suddenly the camera whips back down the road to catch the other car in hot pursuit, and again the camera pans with it as the car continues down the road. This shot actually uses a whip pan in two ways. First, as the car moves past the camera, it is necessary to pan quickly to keep the car in frame. As the first car moves away from us, we whip pan again, panning quickly back to the chasing car.

A more traditional method of shooting this scene might still convey the same information, but not in the same exciting fashion. If the camera were to just allow the cars to shoot through the frame without panning at all, the shot would be relying on the motion of the cars alone. The camera could also whip pan with the first car, then let the other car enter frame in pursuit. Again, the scene is exciting but not to the best of our ability. By whipping back to the chasing car, we are showing how close the two cars are to each other, and implying the speed at which they are traveling.

An age-old technique that has found its way back into mainstream use is the handheld shot, simply described as holding the camera in the hand rather than on any camera support system such as a tripod or dolly. Though it is a common technique used for point of view shots, shows such as *NYPD Blue* have recently began using handheld to create a "you are there" feel for the viewer. By removing the smooth look of a conventional camera head and dolly, the audience feels as if they are actually in the scene, viewing it in close-up. The handheld look should be used sparingly in most cases, as it can be distracting.

In a LightWave shot, however, this type of shot can help remove the fluidity associated with most CGI work. By nature of its definition, handheld removes the perfect framing or the exact steadiness found commonly in photography. By holding the camera on your shoulder, the frame tends to jump around and appear unsteady.

Though it is used to imply the view through someone's eyes, unless we are using some chemical assistance, the view through our eyes is usually much more steady. Yet, for some reason, it is this unsteadiness that we accept as our view on the world.

In the CGI world, utilizing handheld is somewhat difficult since the feel established by a live action camera is somewhat random. The best circumstances to make use of this technique is in a turbulent environment or, for example, near an explosion, essentially shaking the camera as if the shock wave hit. Sometimes it is much simpler to shake the camera, rather than shake the objects in the scene to imply a rough environment.

In live action, in an effort to maintain the versatility and mobility of handheld without the shakiness, the Steadicam was invented. A device that, with the camera mounted on top, counters the unsteady motions of handheld, has become quite popular. Many directors prefer to use Steadicam exclusively, thus removing the need for a dolly all together. In CGI, we cannot avoid achieving a Steadicam feel in all our shots. By nature, the computer camera is steady, unless we choose, by force, to make it otherwise. By adding a little bank to any CGI dolly shot, you will have successfully achieved a Steadicam feel without much effort.

Settle Down, Beavis!

Basic principles of camera movement can be applied to any situation with very desirable results. A common mistake among young camera people (especially CGI camera people), however, is moving the camera too much. It is important to simplify your shot to avoid doing too much. Though it may be cool to boom down, dolly back and tilt to reveal an object, it could be confusing and unnecessary to use such a complex move. It might be just as effective to simply tilt down to the object.

Though shots such as the whip pan example above are fun to create, these are specialized shots and should be used sparingly. Though it may be difficult to fathom, camera motion requires a certain emotional commitment. You aren't just panning and tilting the camera around. You, as the eyes through the camera, are revealing, or not revealing, information to the audience. What you choose to show, or choose not to show makes all the difference in the world. As mentioned earlier, the camera is also an actor. Try to perform your moves to help complement the scene and the other performers. Sometimes you might want to softly pan the camera across a shot to imply a quiet moment, or dolly quickly to a low angle of a creature to imply power. Every move the camera makes is important, and every frame should be considered.

Naturally Done

On a side note, I was recently watching *The Natural* and, as usual, marveling at Caleb Deschenel's simplistic approach to shooting a scene while still achieving a beautiful image. If you get a chance, rent this one; it's worth studying.

LWP

John F.K. Parenteau is a vice-president and general manager of Amblin Imaging, whose CGI work can be seen regularly on seaQuest DSV.

Complex Camera Moves

by John F.K. Parenteau

Last month we discussed many of the principles behind good camera motion, including some of the theories involved in various styles. If any piece of information is important to remember, keep in mind that camera motion is as much a character as the actors on the set. What you choose to show and not show makes all the difference in the world, as does how you show it.

Imagine a movie shot entirely from one wide angle. Though it has been done, it isn't an interesting way to use the medium. That's what plays are for. This month, let's take some specific examples of shots that are fairly difficult in live action, but are quite possible (I didn't say easy) in CGI. Though I describe a specific object, feel free to use anything available. It's the method used to shoot the object that's important in these exercises.

Quite frequently, the most complex moves for an animator involve a complex or violent motion of the object, camera or both. There are two methods to make this type of shot possible. Let's first address a shot with complex object motion and a relatively stationary camera. In this scene, we are looking up as a helicopter comes crashing down toward us. We will need to whip pan with the ship as it slides by the camera and, as the helicopter comes to a hard stop, we need to stop as well. The problems we will run into in this scenario are largely with the camera. As the ship starts in the distance, we have little or no camera motion. We will need to quickly ramp up motion to pan rapidly with our ship, then slow that motion down abruptly as the ship crashes. The trick is maintaining a consistent spline while still keeping up with the action. I always find it handy to rough out the move as best as possible early, including trying to manually track the camera. Start with a rough positioning for the move of the helicopter. Slide it up on the Y-axis a good distance, pitching it down toward the ground. Create a keyframe at frame 0. Now move the helicopter to the ground and create a keyframe at frame 150. (This is just an estimate of length at this point. Until we actually work out the entire move, it will be difficult to tell what frames are necessary to make it realistic.) Now, display frame 75, showing the middle position of the helicopter move. Place the camera beside the ship and create a keyframe at frame 75. Without changing the frame you are on, also create a keyframe at frame 0 for the camera. Now, move to frame 0 and tilt the camera up to the helicopter, creating a new keyframe for the camera at frame 0. Since we have roughly determined that our animation will end on frame 150, move to this frame and tilt the camera down to view the helicopter on the ground, creating a keyframe for the camera here. You may end up discarding most of the keyframes, but you need to start somewhere. Consider this your pencil sketch.

Of course, if you were to preview these motions, the effects would most likely be quite random and highly unacceptable. The camera will overshoot the ship in the beginning, leading it too much in its effort to reach the middle keyframe. As the helicopter drops by the camera, we will lag behind it a bit. This is what I mean by competing splines. Though the motions are simple, the actions and settings for each keyframe differ enough to change the individual characteristics of the motions as they relate to each other. Considering the drastic difference in the two motions in this example, with the helicopter dropping from the sky while the camera is just tilting to follow, it is quite obvious how the splines do not match up. But even the most subtle motions may not match either. Pay close attention to the previews to note differences in the motions. Sometimes it is even worth the time to create a wireframe preview for more specific information to view. Adjustments are not necessarily a mathematical process, but most likely a visual one. The significant issue to take into account is the condition of the spline of each object. Since neither the camera nor the ship is connected in any way, their splines are being affected independently by the keyframes that make them up. For this reason, it is important to create keyframes on the same frames for both camera and object. Even if slight differences in keyframe positions exist, the subtle effects these differences have on the motions will prevent a smooth comparison between the two motions.

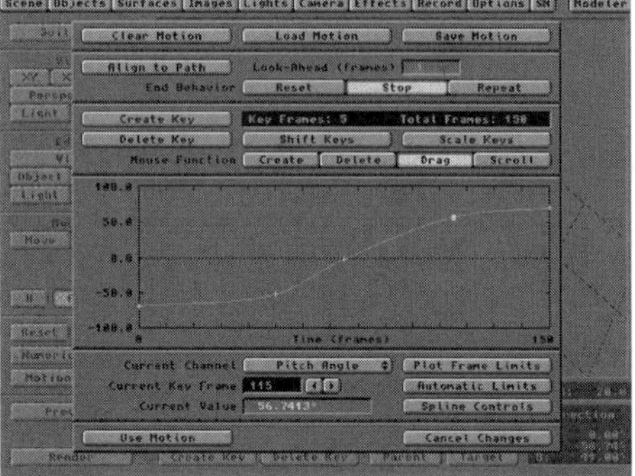

Figure 1

If you do create a preview, you'll notice that the camera moves much quicker than the ship, panning off then back on at the keyframe positions. No matter how hard you try, the splines will always react differently if the motions are even slightly different. In this case, the ship is dropping quickly through frame as well as rotating and pitching violently. The camera is only pitching, thus creating a much less complex spline curve. The next step we take is placing additional keyframes between our existing ones. I've estimated a keyframe position of 75 and 115. Though this is not exactly a precise split between the other keyframes, they are placed where the camera is farthest out of position. Pitch the camera back to frame the helicopter in center frame again at each of these keyframes. Make sure to create keyframes at these

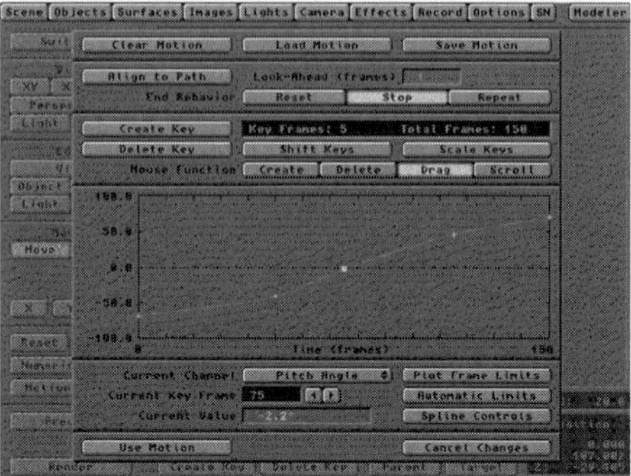

Figure 2

new positions for the helicopter as well. Now create a preview. Though the ship is in frame for most of the shot, it is no longer a smooth tilt. Examining the camera motion graph (Figure 1), we can see how the pitch spline is not an even progression. By evening this up, we can smooth out the unacceptable bumps in the tilt (Figure 2). Creating a new preview, the camera rushes through the tilt a bit more, actually tilting off the copter partially. This may or may not be a problem since perfection in a camera move isn't necessarily a desired effect. As an object moves quickly by camera, it is natural to lead the object rather than lag behind and miss the action. By inputting some bank in the keyframes for the camera (Figure 3), we can enhance the randomness of the shot.

Though this may be acceptable for this application, it may not be for others. It is important to be

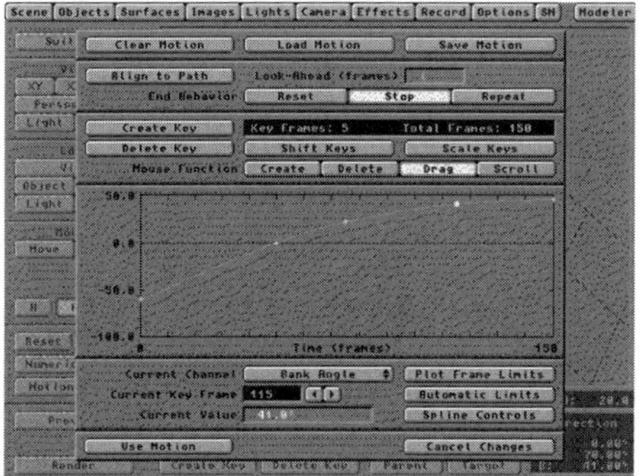

Figure 3

able to create a smooth move as necessary. The smoothest method of creating a tracking camera motion is by targeting the camera to the object. One of the newest projects here at Amblin Imaging is the new *Star Trek* series premiering in January, *Voyager*. We have been working out the move for the final jump-to-warp shot of the show. Not to give too much away, but the producers wanted to track a specific area on the ship as it came toward us, pivot on this area and then watch it jump to warp from behind. We had 11 seconds for the shot. That may seem like a long time, but to move a huge ship from offscreen, toward camera and by camera, then jump to warp, takes a long time. I actually attempted the simple method as described above with our helicopter, using individual splines for the camera and the ship, but found the complex pivot couldn't be ironed out. Instead, I created the motion for the *Voyager,* then saved the *Voyager* motion and applied it to a null object. By targeting the camera to the null, I would always track the object perfectly, since the null has the same exact motion. Why not track the ship itself?. The easiest reason is that I wanted the ship to enter the frame. By targeting the actual ship, I would never be able to pan the camera off at the start of the shot. I also wanted to track a specific piece of the ship's anatomy (not the bridge), and these areas did not happen to fall at the pivot point of the object. Needless to say, targeting the ship doesn't allow for any modification. By targeting a null with the same motion, I can modify various keyframes while still maintaining roughly the same motion. In the first keyframe I shifted the null object so the *Voyager* was offscreen. As the ship moved toward the camera, I shifted the null object on the X and Z axes to maintain a desirable camera view of the ship. I don't want to give too much away, but the shot would not have been possible without this function. Let's examine our helicopter scene with this new wrinkle.

Starting with our old scene, target the camera to the object. As you run through the anim now, the ship is always perfectly in frame, with its pivot point carefully placed in the center by LightWave. Though our move is a perfect pan now, it doesn't allow for much variation or adjustment. Now save the motion of the ship and apply it to a null object and re-target the camera to it. It is important to remove any rotational information from the null object. This will not affect the camera, but it will inhibit your adjustment of the object, since LightWave confuses axes when the rotation has been greatly affected. Move to each keyframe and use the numeric input to zero out the rotation. Also, remove the bank on the camera if you applied any in the previous exercise. (The pitch is disabled by the target function.) At first, nothing has changed, but the first frame needs adjustment. Drop the null object on the Y axis, pushing the ship to the top edge of frame rather than the center. Move to the second keyframe on the null object and enter your motion graph for the null. As you examine the Y axis, the spline between the first and second keyframe actually backs up, moving up to prepare its acceleration for the subsequent keyframes. By dragging the second keyframe down to prevent this, you will create a smooth tilt for the camera. Drag the second keyframe down just enough to create as straight a line between the first and second keyframes (Figure 4). Now use this motion and preview your animation. Note how the ship starts out of frame but enters smoothly as the camera catches up. At the end of the animation, I slipped the null back on the Z axis to center the ship. Viewing the motion graph once again, look at the Z axis and adjust the second-to-last frame to create a smooth transition between this and the last keyframe (Figure 5).

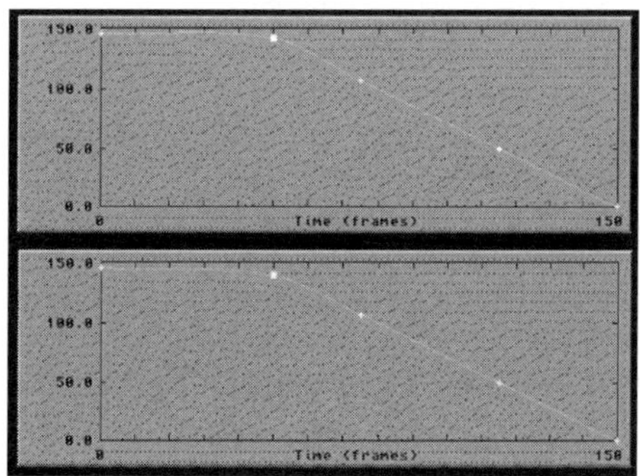

Figure 4

Though the examples above are good learning tools, keep in mind that each animation is drastically different. It is best to follow these basic rules for complex motions:

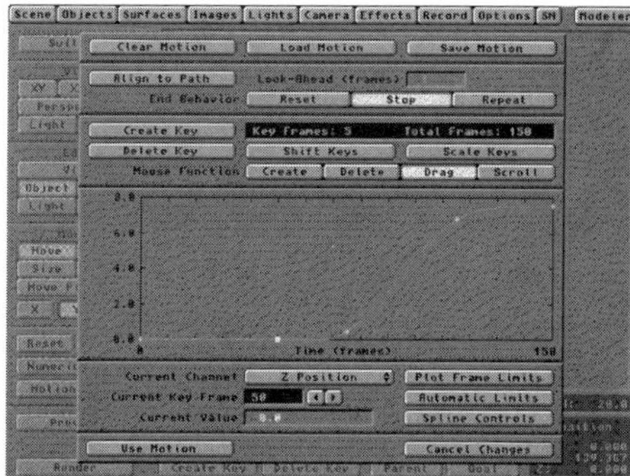

Figure 5

If both the camera and objects have motion, create keyframes for both in the same positions. For example, if you have animated your object and are now applying motion to the camera (though the camera motion doesn't require as many keyframes), put keyframes at the same frames as the object. This will help create similar spline attributes between keyframes for both. Use the motion graph religiously. Pay attention to overshoots on all axis. If the camera starts from a dead stop, holding for a second or two then moving, check the second keyframe to make sure none of the splines have backed up to start the move. This always produces an unwanted glitch in your motion (Figure 4).

Ignore the velocity graph for the camera if the camera is targeted to a null. Since several axes are ignored when the camera is targeted, the velocity graph is usually pretty scary. Pay closer attention to the null object velocity graph since it contains the master motion.

If the object is going to stay in frame during the entire animation, parent the null to the object rather than loading its motion. Since the null is parented to the object, the slight adjustments left and right and up and down to frame the object will require very little change in motion, and thus a simple spline. Imagine a null with the motion of an object loaded on it. Not only does the spline have to move from great distance to great distance, but it also has to make the new adjustments for proper framing. By parenting the null to the object, the null has no motion as it moves through space with the object. Thus, any minor framing adjustments you make create a spline with minimal change.

Try a few whip pans with both methods to see how they look. Remember that camera movement is not a science, but an art form. There is no right or wrong, only your perception of good or bad. Creativity is what most clients pay for, and that creativity is what gives you your own personal style.

LWP

John F.K. Parenteau is vice president and general manager of Amblin Imaging, whose CGI work can be seen regularly on seaQuest DSV.

Create Realistic Lighting

by John F.K. Parenteau

For quite a few columns now, I've focused on showing you how to re-create real-world lighting in LightWave. Though we have worked in general terms, the actual fact is that producing a realistic effect relies on much more than convincing lighting. A poorly modeled object or low-resolution textures can detract so much that even the best lighting will never look in the least genuine. At Amblin Imaging, the world of CGI effects is usually limited to the realm of the fantastic. Effects on *seaQuest*, though theoretically re-creating an environment we have all seen before, underwater, take a stylistic approach to this world. In truth, at the depth the submarines move, you would never see much more than the glow of lights within inky blackness. So authenticity is stretched for the sake of exposure and broadcast requirements. Yet, as we began work on the pilot of *Star Trek: Voyager*, we quickly came to realize that the stylistic would no longer apply. We were now dealing in a much more realistic world.

I know you're saying, "Realistic? It's in space, for crying out loud!" But space or not, *Star Trek* has existed for many years under conventions and practices people have become quite comfortable with. Though it may seem the wave of the future, and the most logical direction to take, CGI has been relatively non-existent in the *Trek* realm. Except for a few rare effects, this universe has existed solely in physical or dimensional models. Yet the future could not be held back, and Paramount (in very large part due to David Stipes, one of *Voyager's* effects supervisors and a LightWave fan) commissioned Amblin Imaging to create a computer-generated *Voyager* model to complement the new dimensional model. In the early plan, the CGI model was intended for extremely limited use, in cases where the motion-control rig was busy or specific shots when the *Voyager* was required to tumble or appear out of control (a motion-control nightmare). At the start of effects production, only two *Voyager* shots for the pilot were commissioned as CGI shots.

The Motion-Control Way

As many of you may already know, motion-control rigs have been utilized for years to produce effects shots ranging from the battles in *Star Wars* to *E.T.* riding across the moon. The basic process is quite simple, though limiting: The model is connected to a rod that supports it suspended in the air. The camera moves on a motorized, computer-controlled rig. By programming the camera to move past the ship, the illusion of the ship flying by camera is created. But there are inherent problems in this simple process.

First, since the camera is connected to a crane or boom arm, it cannot move around the object completely without seeing its own support system. The answer to this problem was to move the model in sync with the camera, allowing for additional, yet still limited, banking or other movement.

Second, to support the ship, a rod is connected somewhere on the ship. Though the mount can connect in several places on the model, it is nonetheless immovable during shooting. In addition, though the mount is painted to fade into the background, if the camera moves into a position in which the mount is in front of the model, the finished shot will show a hole in the model, in the shape of the rod, as it "punches" through the image. Thus, regardless of the mobility of camera and model, a motion-control rig can never truly move in a 360-degree path around its object.

Third, the models are commonly shot against black, with backgrounds matted in later. Most moderately detailed models must be in the four- to six-foot size range. Unless the motion-control rig is extremely large, and the background very wide, it is nearly impossible to make a model of this size appear tiny in frame. Shots of a ship receding in the distance are difficult, and when required, are often post-production tricks.

Fourth, since the rig is computer-controlled and highly accurate in its programmed move, it does not move at actual real-time speed. Averaging one frame per second, the camera moves slowly over the model, regardless of the speed of the final shot. If the ship were to pass over camera very fast, the camera would still move at one frame per second to photograph the shot, and compensate by moving a greater distance per frame. Motion blur, the smearing effect an object has on film as it speeds by camera, must be applied in post-production and lacks realism.

Of course, motion-control operators will point out that all the problems above can be worked out, and in truth, they are right. The corrections, however, take time and money. In the realm of CGI, these "problems" don't even enter the equation. Since the model exists in a 3D space within the computer, we can move it as far away as necessary, spin it, tilt it or fly around it. Motion blur is simply a button, and with the right amount of rendering power, just a few more minutes per frame. As we proceed into the first season of *Star Trek: Voyager*, these facts are becoming increasingly evident to the producers and the special effects staff. Though the model is still a major part of effects production, the world of CGI is slowly but surely becoming an important part of the show.

The CGI Way

No, it isn't that easy. No matter how much we all feel CGI is the answer, it is still a complex and difficult process at times. Several people (including David Jones, Bruce Hall, John Gross, Tony Stutterheim and Eric Barba) spent many weeks completely re-creating the physical model (what *Star Trek* calls its "real" model) in Modeler.

As a kid, I spent many an afternoon tearing apart perfectly good model kits to create my new and much more fantastic design. I remember how easy it was to grab a small piece from another model and place it on my ship to add relief. These small objects, called "nurnies" (a Ron Thorntonism), could have been the death of us on *Voyager*! Building a model from scratch can be much easier, since you can determine what detail and where to place it. In matching a dimensional model, the 100 frivolous bumps a model builder decides to throw on at the last minute can cause a CGI modeler to go mad! Our animators spent many days studying the model, photographing it and videotaping it, all with the sole thought of exactly matching an existing model. Though the model will continue to be improved and enhanced, the final product should match the original almost precisely. The best part of the CGI ship is that somewhere, hidden inside a room, is a small plaque with the names of the people who gave their all to make this *Voyager* come to life.

Modeling wasn't the only battle to be fought as we started up on *Voyager*. Texturing played an important role in creating a convincing model. Hours were spent creating bump maps, specular maps and diffuse maps in an attempt to give our CGI ship a realistic feel. After the long and painstaking process, the *Voyager* visual effects department told us it was all wrong! We quickly came to realize that we had textured our model to look as realistic as possible, when the dimensional model we were matching wasn't real at all. For example, careful consideration had been placed in making the textures clean and smooth, when in truth, the paint that had been applied to the dimensional model had left minute streaks over the surface—streaks we failed to match! Many issues arose that showed our staff the complexity of duplicating an existing model. On *seaQuest*, all the ships existed as CGI first. No practical model was ever created to match. Even the toymakers were required to contact us for designs since none had actually been done. The *Voyager* had been fabricated out of plastic components, carefully airbrushed and decaled with painstaking detail. It was important for our staff to approach the surfacing not from the standpoint of creating a realistic look, but rather a look that matched the dimensional model.

Lighting the Way

Practical lighting quickly became an issue as we placed CGI lens flares to match the fiberoptic lights designed within the dimensional model. Minute details became major issues. For example, the glowing panels on the front of the warp engines are created on the physical model by placing a small light inside a translucent shell. The small red light illuminates the panel, creating the soft glow through the milky white surface. On the CGI model, we aren't required to use a light to create the same effect. Instead, we simply apply luminosity to the outer panel. Though this seemed the easiest answer, it proved to be another detail overlooked. As I examined shots of the dimensional model provided by the *Voyager* crew, I noticed light kicking off the surface of these translucent panels. Though the panels appeared red from the light inside, the gleam of light off the outer surface was white. In truth, this is an unwanted effect of the actual model, but it was one that would make our CGI model stand out to the trained eye. By applying some diffuse value to the luminous panel, a similar effect was created. Many weeks of testing were required to achieve the look that the *Voyager* effects staff had become accustomed to in the past.

With dimensional model photography, the ship is shot with darkened windows, no warp engine glows and no practical lights. Each of these items are shot as separate passes and re-composited in the on-line bay to allow for the greatest control over each element. Though a similar process could be taken with the CGI model, Dan Curry, the visual effects producer, began requesting we provide a fully composited shot rather than individual passes. Careful consideration had to be taken to set values for windows, lights and glows to provide a properly balanced final image.

The final battle that continues to be fought is matching model photography lighting. David Stipes spent hours discussing with me the methods in which the dimensional model is lit. A key light is placed in an optimum position, usually to provide a shadow edge on the camera side of the ship. Light is bounced off a white card placed above the model. Other fill lights are placed on the side and bottom of the ship, with roughly the same value to provide an even fill across the shadowed areas of the model. Initial approaches to lighting the CGI *Voyager* appeared to be easy, but as we all know, nothing is actually easy!

Though the simple lighting setup worked well for the practical model, the CGI model was not flying a similar flight pattern. The reason for a CGI model, initially, was to provide moves unavailable to the motion-control rig. This often means that the basic lighting setup can no longer work to provide an acceptable look. Yet, since we are working in a computer, certain rules that apply in the real world are not even considerations for us. For the shot in the pilot that we call "The Wave Slap," when the *Voyager* is struck by a wave of energy (courtesy of Grant Boucher) and flung across the galaxy, we were faced with one of our most difficult lighting tasks. It was necessary to bring light from the back of the ship in increasing intensity, to accentuate the violence of the vessel being struck. Though it would seem simple to place lights behind the *Voyager*, if you recall the shot correctly, the ship was lifted back end first and tumbled forward. By simply placing lights behind the ship, the lighting may appear correct for the first few frames, but as the ship is raised, shielding itself from the lights, a huge shadow would be thrown across the saucer. In motion-control work, there would be little to do to solve this problem. In CGI, I simply applied keyframes to the lights, lifting them up to match the angle the ship had been tilted. This technique allowed the light to continue to reach over the edge and light the saucer. Just as the *Voyager* exits frame, the keylights are almost directly above the ship, rather than behind the wave.

It has never been said that motion-control photography is easier than CGI. The greatest complaints are that CGI cannot look as real. After several episodes of *Star Trek: Voyager*, the discussion on the Internet still rages as to which ships are CGI and which are models. Though it would be nice to be confused with reality instead, at least it's a step in the right direction.

By the way, for those of you who may be unsure which is which, there is a dead giveaway to the CGI *Voyager*. Whenever you see it from the rear, the LightWave *Voyager* will have lit windows in the very back end of the ship (below the shuttle bay). The real model doesn't have this, as there was no way to snake a light back there.

LWP

John F. K. Parenteau is one of the vice presidents of Amblin Imaging and CGI effects supervisor for seaQuest DSV.

LightWave-generated Voyager Footage (as of early-March)

Opening Sequence

Three of the six opening sequence shots use the LightWave-generated *Voyager*. The other three shots use the practical model. All of the background elements were generated by Santa Barbara Studios using Wavefront. The three LightWave-generated *Voyagers* are:

- The first shot of *Voyager* flying by sun
- The third shot of *Voyager* flying through space fog
- The last shot of *Voyager* flying by planet and jumping into warp

"Caretaker" (pilot)

- All Badlands and vortex footage
- All galactic wave footage
- Voyager getting hit by galactic wave
- Planets, stars and sun for all planet shots
- Blue anamorphic flare elements in transporter beam in/outs
- Alien fractal elements used in "Caretaker" beam-out effects
- Final jump-to-warp shot

"Parallax"

- All *Voyager*-at-warp shots (including stars and warp stars)

"Phage"

- Five shots of *Voyager* in asteroid lined with mirrors. The actual model was used in the foreground and LightWave-generated reflections of the CGI *Voyager*, alien ship and phaser beams were used for the backgrounds.

"Eye of the Needle"

- Micro wormhole shots seen on the *Voyager's* viewscreen

"Emanations"

- All shots of *Voyager* and ring planet/asteroids together.

General

- Many stock shots of *Voyager* flybys at warp and at impulse speeds

Digital Cinematography

by John F. K. Parenteau

So I'm sitting in a Henry bay writing this column. Just in case you aren't familiar with it (I wasn't sure myself what it was until recently), a Henry is an advanced paint box system, sort of a superhuman ToasterPaint. It's faster than a Harry (another paint box system) but much more expensive. Figure a rate card of $1,000 per hour, with a minimum of an hour for any work. We try to avoid using the Henry, but with some television effects schedules, a quick 2D system is invaluable. It's really an extremely mature DPaint in real-time. The best thing about it is the versatility of pulling mattes, rotoscoping, zooming in and out of a frame, or even bending and twisting the image. For you film buffs, the equivalent at motion-picture resolution is a Flame. Though they have quite a few different features, they are essentially the same type of box.

Well, back to the Henry bay. I'm hanging out here chatting with the Henry artist and asking for some fairly routine things: "Let's blow up this frame a bit, add some grain, etc." Simple requests, really. We're combining digital images with live action, pulling a matte for the character and rotoscoping some highlights.

It never really hits me until later how cavalier we've become in our modern image manipulation. I think back to the days of *Star Wars* and how complex it was to composite all the model passes for the battle sequences. Just look at that film on videotape now and you will be shocked at the horrible matte lines. [Editor's note: See July 1995 *VTU*'s "Last Word."] After looking at that and other examples, I've come to realize how important it is to be extremely aware of the spectrum of resolutions involved in digital cinematography. As a cameraman several years ago, I used to choose between 35mm, 16mm and even Super 8mm film without any thought other than the quality of the negative I was exposing. My greatest concerns were the speed of the stock, whether I was shooting daylight or tungsten, and what kind of grain structure I was looking for. As I move into the digital realm, I've come to realize how all these considerations are actually hacks of problems inherent in the system of exposing film. These same "problems" do not exist in a computer, though they must be carefully considered if we hope to match that "Film Look." In the world of CGI, and in particular our work with LightWave, we have, as a tool, an independent resolution renderer. Yet without the knowledge of what the various resolutions are, this function is of little use.

The basic settings (assuming the **Basic Resolution** is set at **Medium**), without activating the **Custom Resolution** button, are dependent on the frame aspect chosen. **D2 NTSC** (composite video) is 752x480, essentially the frame size you see on your home television. **D1 NTSC** (component video, also known as Abekas Aspect) is 720x486. D1 resolution is considered the highest resolution available on videotape. As a digital format, it doesn't suffer from signal loss in duplication. If you view D1-resolution images on a monitor (through TPaint, for example), they will be slightly mis-sized—squished, actually—on the horizontal. **Square Pixels**, a function used primarily for print work, is rarely utilized in video resolution. As the name suggests, this setting creates square pixels. (We'll get back to it later, as it applies to the film work we will discuss.) PAL settings (D1 and D2) are European standards and shouldn't be used for NTSC standard video. It is important to note that European video, known as PAL, is actually a higher resolution than our NTSC video.

Before we move on into the world of higher resolutions, let's discuss the **Camera** panel in LightWave. (I'll assume we all have the fortune of working with version 4.0. Those who don't, go to the back of the class.) In the black area below **Basic Resolution** and **Pixel Aspect** settings is some of the most important information for understanding resolutions.

Full Resolution describes the number of pixels (width x height) you are asking the software to render. The denser the pixels, the more detail in the image, and the larger it can be blown up before degrading begins. For example, take a video-resolution image into LightWave. Create a simple plane and map the image onto the plane. Place the plane so it just fills the frame and render it out. Notice that the image in Figure 1 looks just fine.

Figure 1: A full frame of video looks fine in full-frame format.

Figure 2: Pushing in on the video causes blurring and "pixelating."

Now move the camera toward the plane until only a small portion of the plane, and thus the image, is visible. Figure 2 shows the breakup of the image, called pixelating, as the information in the frame breaks down. Video resolution is barely high enough to withstand a full frame view. With some systems, like the Henry, a slight blow-up is possible. As you'll see later, the highest resolutions are required when rendering for projected film, for example, since the image will be viewed on a huge screen in a theater. It is actually a luxury to work at film resolution (anywhere from 1828x1332 or so and up). In Figure 3 I've shown a blow-up of a full-resolution film image. As you can see, the density of the pixels makes work such as rotoscop-

Figure 3: A film-resolution frame holds up much better when blown up.

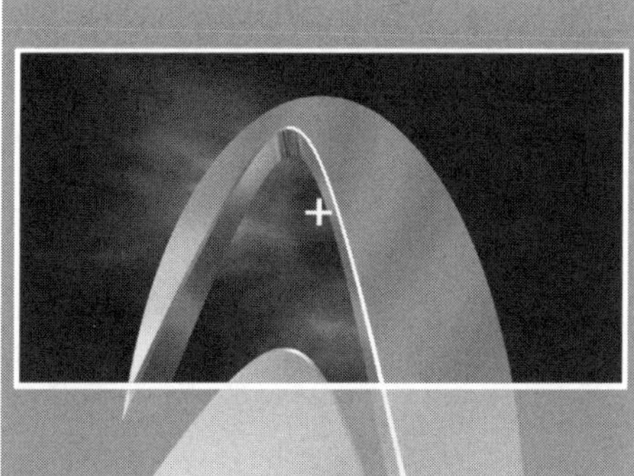
Figure 4: A sample framing with a 1.85 aspect matte.

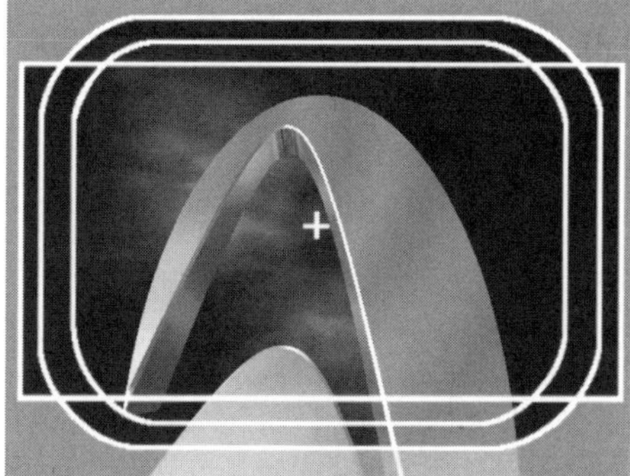
Figure 5: Using a combo matte (1.85 and 1.33 for television) allows for greater headroom.

ing in film resolution a breeze!

Just below **Full Resolution** is **Limited Region,** which we will pass over. This function is an effective tool for rendering only small portions of the frame while testing, but is not actually for final output (unless you wish to use it to crop a portion of a large image). Below Limited Region is **Pixel Aspect**. This can be the most confusing part of higher resolutions, so bear with me.

The pixel aspect is the ratio of the pixel width divided by its height, and describes the actual shape of the pixel. OK, keep that in the back of your mind and let me explain **Frame Aspect.** As you look at a television monitor, you might notice that it isn't actually square. A TV screen, and thus the image it displays, is really slightly wider than it is tall. If we go back to D2 resolution, you might remember it is 752x480, width by height. A pixel generated for television is not actually square, but slightly taller than wide. Even if a television screen was square, there would still be more pixels in the width than the height, to make up for the thinner video pixel. The Frame Aspect is the ratio of the height of the frame to the width of the frame. Allen Hastings, the creator of LightWave, gives LightWave animators the pixel aspects for D1 and D2 for both NTSC and PAL, so they don't have to figure them out. Just leave the basic resolution in Medium and toggle between D1 and D2. The Pixel Aspect changes slightly as the type of format is changed. The Frame Aspect is simply a function of the resolution width divided by the resolution height times the Pixel Aspect. Or, more accurately, the resolution width times the Pixel Aspect divided by the resolution height. It's all very confusing and not an issue for this article. [Editor's note: For more information, see Mark Thompson's "Aspect Ratios" article in this issue.]

What you really need to know is this: Pixels come in different shapes depending on the display device. Any method of viewing an image is considered a display device, from your home television to a projector in a movie theater. Video-resolution pixels, as mentioned before, are taller than they are wide. Film-resolution pixels are square for the most part, depending on some factors I will delve into later. As I mentioned earlier, a television screen is actually wider than it is tall. If you can picture most film resolutions as projected in a theater, these images are also wider than they are tall. This is the Frame Aspect. As we move into the realm of film resolutions, we must discuss the various Frame Aspects, or **Aspect Ratios**, available.

If you have purchased any laser discs in recent years, you might be aware of the availability of a "letterbox" version of many films. This is an effort on the part of laser disc manufacturers to retain the original style of the film, as seen in a theater. Motion picture film negative is exposed a single frame at a time, much like in a still camera, yet at a rate of 24 frames per second. If you were to examine a single frame of the print, you would notice that the frame is actually fairly square, yet when projected in a theater, the image is wider than it is tall. This is due to the Aspect Ratio the film was shot in. When camerapeople shoot a film, they use an etched piece of glass in the viewfinder to describe an area on the film negative (Figure 4). Even though this is the area chosen to be projected, the entire film is exposed and has an image on it. This choice is not arbitrary but rather a set of standards established years ago by cinematographers around the world.

Standard motion picture aspect ratio is considered 1:85, meaning the image is 1 inch tall and 1.85 inches wide. The etched lines in the glass the operator is looking through describe this area in a standardized position on the film. Once the film is exposed, it is processed as an entire frame, including the areas above and below the frame etchings. When the processed film is projected, the projectionist slides a metal mask between the film and the lens. This mask closely approximates the lines in the glass the operator uses to frame the image.

It's important to understand that when the film is exposed, the entire frame is exposed and the operator can see the entire frame size. The marks on the glass are just that: scratches on the glass. If, in the theater, you pulled the mask out from the projector, you would reveal the area not meant for viewing, often containing the boom microphone, crew people above the set, etc. Many films push the limit of the frame and accidentally reveal information they shouldn't. This is a rarity, since other factors are considered when framing the image, such as the eventuality that the final product will end up on television.

Commonly, 35mm theatrical film uses an aspect ratio of 1.85, as described above. Television shot on film is shot in a 1.33 aspect ratio, the frame being 1.33 percent wider than it is tall. Most motion pictures are destined for the video realm at one time or another (some quicker than others!), so camera operators use a Combo viewfinder, showing both the 1.85 and 1.33 aspect ratios (Figure 5). Anamorphic or Cinemascope film is shot using a special lens that squeezes the information onto the film. When examined manually—holding it up to a light, for example—the image will appear squeezed, with people and objects seeming tall and skinny (Figure 6). This **Aspect Ratio** of 2.35 (a whooping 2.35 percent wider than its height), provides a super-wide view for projection. A 70mm image, in most cases, starts on 35mm film, is shot in anamorphic 2.35, and optically blown up to 65mm film.

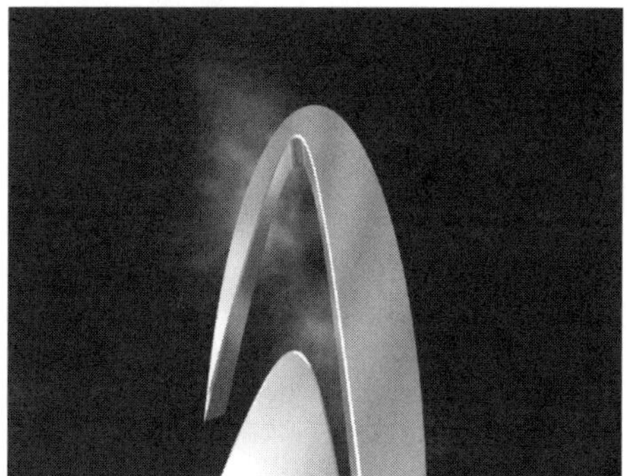
Figure 6: This anamorphic image looks "squeezed" before projection.

It's important to understand these facts as you translate into the digital arena. There are a couple issues inherent in the exposing of film stock that must be taken into consideration when composing your CGI image.

1) Remember that, as in live-action photography, you must provide information for the entire frame of film. As you compose an image—using a 1.85 aspect, for example—it is not acceptable to remove information from the areas above and below the 1.85 frame (e.g., using a mask.) If you remember the old Letterbox function in an earlier version of LightWave, a framestore was rendered out in an approximately 1.85 aspect, with black bars at the top and bottom. Though this looked

great on screen, it would never suffice for delivery to a film scanner. The science of masks on projectors is hardly that, but rather a close approximation of the standard established. The final product may actually go to television someday, and the 1:33 aspect is taller than 1:85.

2) Though no adjustments are required when rendering your image, it is important to understand the difference between flat and academy frames. Though the film negative can be exposed in any manner you desire (film is just a long strip of light-sensitive material; the frame is established in the camera), certain areas, by industry standard, are reserved for various uses. Thirty-five-millimeter film, as exposed in-camera, is considered Flat in that it is exposed in the center of the negative, relative to the left and right edges of the frame.

Finished 35mm film, called a Release Print, must allow space for the soundtrack on the right edge. Thus, the image is actually moved to the left to avoid this space. This adjustment is called Academy alignment. The process live-action film goes through from exposure on set until release print is long and arduous. Many versions are printed, sliced up, re-processed, optically affected and manipulated. Live action tends to remain in the Flat format until the final processes add sound to picture. When CGI records to film, none of these processes are likely to occur, unless the client intends to re-process your negative. If your CGI is to be cut right in with other finished negatives, requesting Academy from the facility that transfers your digital imagery to film would most likely be appropriate.

Now that you have a basic understanding of various frame aspects, let's break our concepts down to CGI language. Though the frame aspects of 1.85 and 1.33 are important to understand, the actual frame size is larger. Under the **Options** panel in LightWave, you will see a new button (as of 4.0) labeled **Show Field Chart.** This is a standardized chart that separates the vertical and horizontal frame into segments. Each direction is broken into 24 segments, reaching to the edge of the frame.

Go into Modeler (I've provided some of these objects on this month's *LIGHTWAVEPRO* disk, but it is handy, and simple, to construct them on your own) and create a box that is 1.85 meters wide and 1 inch high. Make sure the object is centered and load it into LightWave. In the **Camera** panel, set **Custom Resolution** to an Academy 2K resolution, 1828x1332, and the **Basic Resolution** to **Print**. It is important to reset the **Pixel Aspect** selector to **Custom** and input an **Aspect** of 1.0. With **Field Chart** on, move the box you just created toward the camera on the Z axis only, until the top and bottom edges rest halfway between the eighth and ninth hashmarks from center. Make sure your screen (if you're working on a PC) is large enough so you can see the dotted lines of the edge of frame. You have now established a 1.85 aspect ratio to frame your action (Figure 7). Hopefully, by the time this makes it to press, Allen Hastings will have added these custom safe areas for film into the program, but just in case, you now know how to make them yourself.

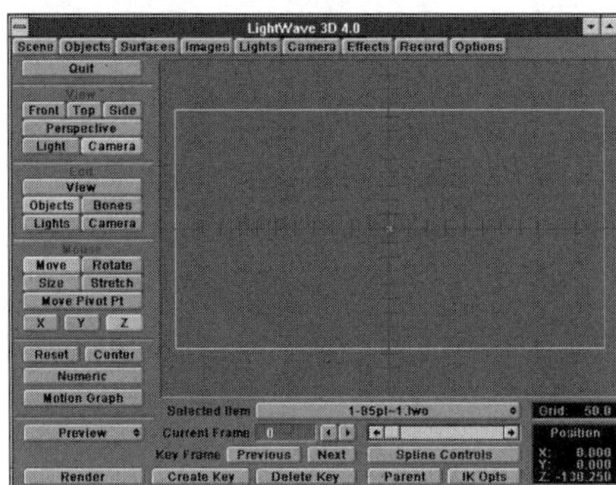

Figure 7: A 1.85 matte positioned in Layout.

Though you are framing for 1.85, there is a lot of area above and below the frame, and a bit left and right, not within your new motion safe area. Examine the Frame Aspect information field in the **Camera** panel. Notice that though we are framing for 1.85, our frame is actually 1.372. Go into Modeler and create a box 1.372 wide by 1. Bring that into LightWave and pull it forward on the Z axis. You'll notice that it fits exactly to the dotted lines left and right and top to bottom of frame. This is called Full Aperture, the entire exposed area of the film.

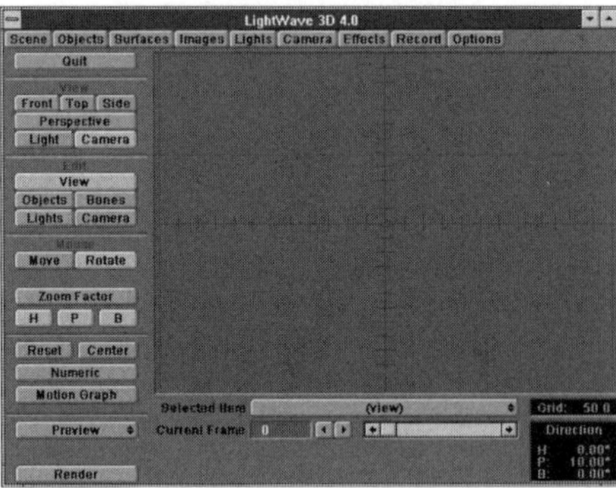

Figure 8: The 12-field chart now provided by LightWave assists in proper framing.

Figure 8 is a full-field chart that includes the fields and framing areas for 1.85, 1.75, 1.66 and full-aperture film. LightWave will always generate an image that fully fills the motion-picture frame. How you frame the images within that frame is up to you.

Anamorphic film squeezes an extremely wide image into the area with a frame aspect of 1.175. Earlier we discussed how pixel aspect was dependent on the display device. For most applications in motion-picture film, a standard square pixel with an aspect of 1 is used. Anamorphic, however, has a pixel aspect of 2, with pixels twice as wide as they are tall once they are expanded in projection. Standard 2K resolution for anamorphic, or Cinemascope (simply a brand name for anamorphic), is 1828x1556.

Input this resolution under **Custom Size**. If you leave the pixel aspect at 1, Layout will show a tall, thin frame. Set **Pixel Aspect** to 2 and look in Layout. Now the frame is much wider than it is tall—exactly 2.35 times as wide. When rendered, LightWave will compress the frame horizontally to fit within the film frame. On 35mm film, the 1.175 frame aspect is smaller than full-frame film, allowing room for the optical soundtrack. In actuality, 70mm film is 65mm film with an extra 5mm horizontally added for the magnetic soundtrack. Thus, an anamorphic image, blown up to 65mm film, fills the entire viewable area. In this case, it isn't important to provide information for the area above and below the frame since there is none! (A handy function of the resizable window in the NT and SGI versions of LightWave comes in handy at this point, and makes for a cool-looking interface. If you are working in Anamorphic resolution and your monitor is large enough, re-size your window lengthwise to the edges of the dotted lines. It not only looks cool, but it's fun to work in wide screen!)

Finally, I've listed common resolutions for various film formats. Most film work is done at 2K resolution. 4K is nice, but, of course, takes much longer to render. Remember, Flat means full-aperture film, and does not allow for the soundtrack on standard 35mm film. Anamorphic does not need to leave space for the soundtrack since it is added on later.

Flat	4K	4096x3112
	2K	2048x1556
Academy	4K	3656x2664
	2K	1828x1332
Anamorphic	4K	3656x3112
	2K	1828x1556

**Pixel aspect for Flat and Academy is 1, while Anamorphic pixel aspect is 2.*

Don't forget, since film resolution shows higher detail, it is important to build your CGI objects in a much higher resolution than you would for television. Otherwise, animation for a film finish is not much different from video resolution, regardless of what some so-called "professionals" think. With a bit more attention and care, any accomplished "video animator" can create just as accomplished film effects.

John F.K. Parenteau is a vice president and general manager of Amblin Imaging, and now, thanks to his editor, knows a bit more about the relation of video pixel and frame aspects to the world of film.

Demo Reels

by John F. K. Parenteau

Here at Amblin Imaging, the pattern is almost predictable. Every once in a while—usually on special occasions such as somebody's birthday—we gather and watch demo reels. There's a certain level of contradiction happening when we gather in the "Big Room" (our editing and screening room) for a round of reels from unsuspecting animators. Everybody is so eager to rip into the new tapes sent in, almost as if they want to find bad stuff. But, in truth, I think there is a sense of fear in the air as we have our laughfest, cheering, booing and throwing things at the screen. Most of us realize that, at one time, we were on the outside looking in, hoping somebody would take a liking to the images we sent in to Amblin. Many of our animators know that in the beginning their stuff wasn't all that great either. So, as we do our impersonations of Joel on *Mystery Science Theater 3000* to the demos, somewhere in the back in our minds, we are really looking for something not to make fun of, perhaps something positive among the sea of the unacceptable.

Actually, not everything is unacceptable. Quite a lot of work we receive has some considerable merit and is worthy of further consideration. The problem usually arises in the mode of presentation. Unless you have the opportunity to see a large number of demo reels, it is impossible to evaluate your tape with an objective eye.

Creating a demo reel isn't extremely tough. All of us see a type of demo reel as we sit in a theater or watch television at home every day. Think of your reel as a type of commercial or theatrical preview. Both are trying to sell something. Both are put together in an organized fashion to be entertaining and informative. Your work is much harder, however, since you cannot use dialogue to sell yourself. It is important to construct both an entertaining and brief example of the product. Let's examine some of the more general mistakes some animators make when constructing their reel.

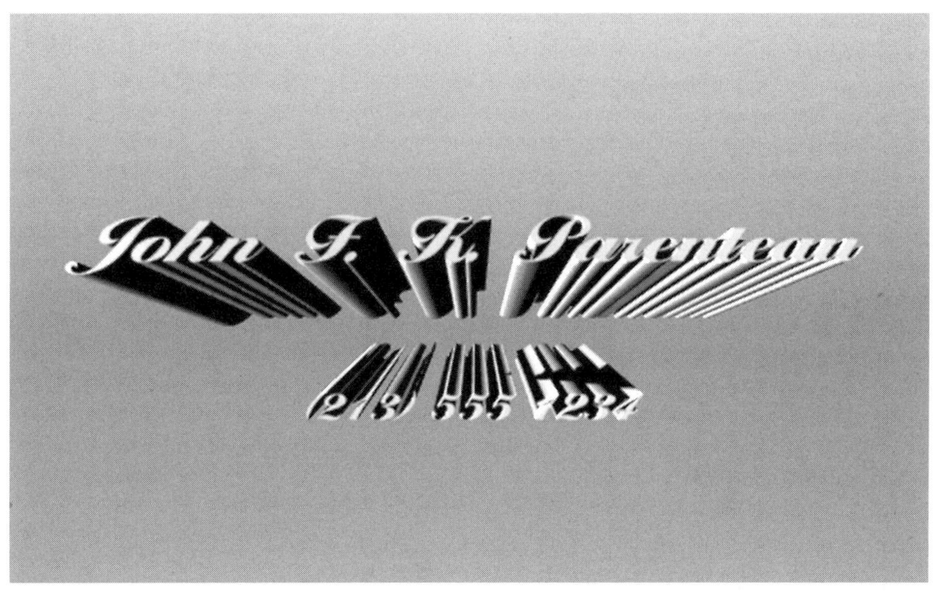

A good example of a bad example. This title card is difficult to look at and too confusing.

Length

There is a reason why most reels are about two to three minutes long: that is the average length of a song. The last thing you want is to have someone sit through a five- or 10- minute reel, no matter how great you feel about your work. Imagine *Jurassic Park* with no action—just a long series of shots of fantastic computer-generated dinosaurs. For about two minutes you would be impressed. "Look at that great work! Can you believe how realistic they look?!" But after a short time you'd be checking your watch and thinking about getting that free popcorn refill. No matter how interesting the work, you always want the audience yearning for more, especially when it is your reel. Yearning for more means they want to meet—and potentially hire—you! So keep the tape short and sweet. But remember, too short is just as bad. Try to have at least a one-minute reel, even if this requires you to create more animations.

Variation

Many animators have DPS' Personal Animation Recorder and use it to output their work. Many of those people have the horrible habit of looping animations and playing them over and over again. Not only is this far too repetitious, but that's what a rewind button is for! If viewers want to see the animation again, they can stop and rewind. The first impact is the most important. Make sure your animations have enough diversity so the viewer can see a few different moods you have created. Just as a cameraperson's reel has exteriors and interiors, day and night, it is crucial to show off all of your talents.

Music

And how about that two- to three-minute song? Never, ever use a song with lyrics. Words give the audience something else to think about, when you would rather have them thinking about your great work. We often find a soundtrack that has a good variation of highs and lows, fast segments and lulls. Try to avoid music that is too familiar. For example, many people like to use classical music. Though it is pleasant to hear, it doesn't carry the impact of a hard-hitting new piece, something unfamiliar to the viewer. Music carries a lot of weight with any visual, and more so with a demo reel. Pop in one of your favorite action moves at home and try to watch the best scene with no sound. Kind of loses something, doesn't it? Good music can raise the excitement level up high, and some of those little mistakes you had to leave in the reel can be easily overlooked. Movie themes seem to work best, if carefully chosen. Most music scores in motion pictures are hidden beneath dialogue and sound effects. If you choose the right piece, viewers will feel a sense of familiarity, but not enough to be distracting.

Title Card

I've always felt that the name card at the head of the reel should be as simple as possible. So many young animators try to create some fantastic animation just to display their name. In truth, the card at the beginning is usually ignored. It's the name at the end that is important. Assuming the viewer liked your work, it is from that card that they extract your phone number or address for further contact. Personally, I like a simple card: white letters on black, in a cool and tasteful font. Others may try something a bit more interesting, like a fade up or wipe on. The important point here is to avoid spending all your time animating your name card. Your effort is better spent making your animations in between the cards shine.

Laydown

No matter how great your work is, if you put it on a bad tape with glitches and hits in it, your prospective employer or client is going to quickly shut it off. If you are located in a city that supports any form of video production, it is possible to buy short VHS tapes (five-minute tapes, for example). Packages of 120-minute tapes can be costly, forcing you to recycle to save money, but recycling creates bad tape spots. Try using a tape only once to prevent this; five-minute tapes make it much less expensive. If you do not have access to an editing system or industrial dubbing rack, you may be forced to "hard record." Imagine you have two VCRs hooked up to each other. When you press play on the source and record on the recording deck, you have just performed a "hard record." On VHS, the first 15 seconds of the tape will have a rolling bar of color moving across the screen. It's important that your material doesn't start until well after this bar has passed and the image has stabilized. Make sure the head of your tape has at least 30 seconds of black to get past this glitch. In a perfect world, a professional facility would be making your dubs from a D1 master, but most people can't afford D1. Since you are working in a digital medium, try to lay off your work to the highest tape medium possible. Preferably, you have access, through a rental house somewhere nearby, to a Betacam deck. At least try to master on 3/4-inch. An investment in higher tape quality will pay off in cleaner-looking demos with a more professional appearance.

Labeling

It may seem trivial, but a proper label can make all the difference when a client goes to view a demo tape. One's first instinct is to view the tape that looks the most professional, and leave the unlabeled or handwritten 120-minute cassette for last. It all takes money, but you must invest to profit, and this is no exception. Any local printer can make up good-looking labels with your name and telephone number for a reasonable price. If you manage to buy short tapes, generic sleeves usually come with them.

That about covers the basics. Though most of the above sections outline the presentation side of demo reels, there is a much more fundamental reason why many of them fail. Ask yourself this question: What is my favorite CGI shot from TV or movies? Once you've selected something, examine the reason why you chose it. Most likely, the work is slick, with no errors, has smooth camera motion and is efficient in its purpose. These simple reasons should be the goal you strive for with all your work.

Is It Slick?

It's very easy to fall into the "slick is impossible on my budget" trap. But you must remember that slick doesn't mean expensive. Slick means doing the work as best as possible. For example, we often receive reels that show objects with low polygon counts or no textures. Though memory is an important exception to the rule, nobody is going to be impressed with a wild shot with primitive objects. If memory is a problem, use procedurals. Many *Babylon 5* textures rely heavily on Allen Hastings' built-in surfaces, and they look great! There is no excuse for lack of textures.

Modeling of your objects is, however, dependent on the RAM of your machine. Work carefully to take advantage of the memory you do have by building your model in the areas that are seen closely. Don't waste too much detail in modeling if the audience won't be close enough to care. That's where image maps can fill in.

Motion

Camera and object motion are often the most essential areas to focus on. Most potential employers quickly overlook shoddy modeling or texturing, but if the motion is bad, the errors pop out fast! Camera motion in particular is a crucial part of your talent and, regardless of what you feel your strengths are, it must be presented in a good light. Remember, you may not be able to see a tape glitch before it's too late, but with the preview function in LightWave, you can always see a camera error. Simple adjustments such as tension at the head and tail of the camera motion prevent abrupt stops and starts. Take the time to finesse the camera.

Object motion is equally important. Remember that you are telling a story with your shot. Don't use unnecessary motions just because they look cool. Try to be as economical as possible while still accomplishing the point of your shot. More often than not we see reels with wild camera and object motion that may look great to the animator's eye, but don't make any sense to the audience. Though you may think that a crazy 180-degree pan and zoom in is cool, it looks gratuitous and unnecessary to the people who want to hire you for their television show. Work on telling a story, whether it be a one-shot piece or a sequence, so employers feel confident you can produce the shot they need.

For the most part, what we look for in a reel is some sense of an accomplished talent. Nobody, even those of us at Amblin, ever started off with a reel that was perfect. That only comes with years of careful study and experience. So give yourself a break. Try to focus on a particular area that you feel your talents lie in, while allowing for some error in other areas. This doesn't mean blowing off textures if your strength is animation. What it means is simply being accomplished at those things you aren't great at. The textures or modeling may not knock anybody's socks off, but if there is a good sense of motion, your point has been made. An attention to detail is obvious, even if that detail isn't great.

Back in our "Big Room," we tend to make fun of everything. In a way, it's how we make our own shots better. Naturally, no matter how good a reel is, we still critique it. But deep down inside, we take note of the talent we can see on the screen, and log it away. When the time does arrive when we need a new animator, the jokes are forgotten and the quality reel stands out.

LWP

John F.K. Parenteau is a vice president and general manager at Amblin Imaging. His first demo reel wasn't so hot.

Style Is Everything

by John F. K. Parenteau

Style is everything. From the clothes they wear to the car they drive, people spend an enormous amount of time developing their style. It's a mistake, however, to assume that any style can be considered good or bad. Style is neither of these things, depending on who's judging it. The concept is extremely subjective. What one person may assume is a bad style (such as purple hair) may be stylish to another. It's all in how you look at it.

In this column I've spent quite awhile discussing the basics of lighting and camera design in LightWave. Once you've even partially mastered these areas, you'll have already begun developing your own style. In any form of photography or art, a style is developed early as a photographer or artist discovers the methods and techniques he or she likes to use to accomplish the job at hand. When I worked as a cameraperson for a living, I liked a particular type of diffusion (216), and I found a way to use it in almost any situation. I happened to enjoy the soft light that was created by this material. I quickly became known for this softlight approach.

Cinematographer Caleb Deschanel, one of my idols, is best known for such films as *Black Beauty*, *The Right Stuff* and *The Natural*. *The Natural* in particular captured my attention as the exact example of how I would like my work to look. The light is soft and motivated by a practical source, such as a window or lamp, yet uses a touch of fantasy to add sparkle to each scene. The film also uses camera and lighting design to help tell the story, a point you might remember me harping on numerous times. It is important to understand that style is not only subjective, but adjustable by the whims of the project at hand. All of the people below have a certain style that is considered their trademark, yet it's continually adapted to the conditions and environment at hand. Though adjusted, these cinematographers' styles are still evident in their work.

Let's take a couple of movies as specifics. It might be a good idea, at this point, to rent *The Natural* if you haven't seen it already. When Roy Hobbs, played by Robert Redford, is first called up to try out for the New York Knights, he meets his girlfriend (Glenn Close) in the barn at night. It is an intimate scene: they make love for the first time and promise to always be together. Since moonlight was the only source available, logically, in the environment, Caleb used a touch of fantasy to help out. The moonlight shone through the window, striking the hay at their feet. With the assistance of a light-colored sweater on Redford, the light was bounced from the floor, or his clothing, to underlight both characters in a soft glow. Nothing fancy—just a simple and elegant answer to a seemingly difficult situation. This is probably one of the best examples of a style. Caleb often makes use of practical lighting sources, whether they are actually existing (the sun) or fakes (the moon). In *The Right Stuff*, he used the flame of the rocket in contrast to the quiet of the desert to enhance the dangerous quality of the task Chuck Yeager had just undertaken: breaking the sound barrier.

It may sound cliché, but often the simplest approach is the best. An instructor of mine once recommended that once we illuminate the set, find one light to turn off. Cinematographers or animators frequently fail to carefully analyze the scene to establish the simplest answer to lighting and camera. Once you set the first light in the wrong place, the impulse of setting a second, third or fourth light becomes overbearing. From the first mistake, lighting becomes an effort to cover for previous errors, rather than creating a mood. You end up building a mood that isn't the one you wanted! The camera can be another nightmare, since a bad camera position for your master shot can produce impossible angle and coverage problems down the line. That's why storyboards were invented, and why they make sense, even in stick-figure mode. They help you understand the job at hand before it becomes the nightmare at hand.

Sane cinematographers never stay married to one style, but instead have the ability to modify their style to accomplish different tasks. In *The Right Stuff*, Caleb departed from the soft-light approach and used a much harsher look. Considering the difference in story lines, it only seems appropriate that *The Right Stuff*, a story about the early days of space flight, might take on a rougher feel. As Yeager is breaking the sound barrier for the first time, the sunlight is harsh in the cockpit, challenging him to go faster. Imagine if that was a super soft light spilling in the cockpit. The mood would be broken by this contradiction.

On the other hand, contradiction can play an important role in telling a story, if used in the correct instance. For *Empire of the Sun*, Allen Daviau used contrast to communicate the story. Not just contrast in light or dark, but in content as well. One of my favorite scenes is when the camp is under attack by the American forces. Young Jim runs to the top of the tower to watch a P51 Mustang (Cadillac of the sky) soar past him. As the plane approaches, the shot switches to slow motion, and the pilot seems to connect with young Jim. The contrast between a great air battle and this moment of connection between Jim and the pilot gives us a strange sense of insight into our character's life. The slow motion allows us to take a "timeout" from the battle, freezing the moment in time and in our memories.

It would be impossible for me to run through the many scenes and films that have affected me and my animations. I can only recommend that you seek out those styles you connect with and do your best to understand them. Any effort in that direction can only make you better. Be careful, however, to avoid mimicking. Remember that any lighting setup is not just a function of a person's style, but also a careful compromise between the look that is desired and the conditions and limitations of the set. You are trying to develop a style. Understanding the essence of your favorite cinematographer's thinking is the true goal, not matching exact setups.

Computer animation is, of course, a much different ballgame. Without the same diversity of tools available to a cinematographer, options are slightly limited. Yes, I mean only slightly. It's amazing how many looks can be created with only minor, and seemingly insignificant, adjustments to approach and design. Let's take a few examples of current, mainstream television effects to compare and contrast style, and to understand the limitations of each environment.

Ron Thornton, head of Foundation Imaging, has been directly responsible for the effects design of *Babylon 5* since its start. Ron has always had a keen sense of movement and drama— it's evident in every shot he touches. There's a certain power and elegance to the *Babylon 5* effects. Like Caleb and Allen, Ron has found ways to adapt his style to use, or perhaps avoid, some of the problems of his environment.

Ron works in a specific setting—namely, space—

that both limits and enhances his abilities to produce effects. For example, space, of course, hides nothing. There is no atmosphere or water to help hide some of the problems that might arise on a particular shot. This may seem trivial to you, the reader, but in truth it poses a particular challenge. Without the ability to fade in the distance, space has a way of destroying scale. Let's assume you have a very small ship in space. Try to place it so that it fills the left half of frame. Now take a very large ship, much larger than your small one, and place it on the left side of frame, pushing it back far enough to fit. How can anyone tell that they aren't the same size? They sure look the same!

Though the problem never goes away, there are ways to work around it. Take that same large ship and move it beside the camera. Place a slow and lumbering motion on the ship as it moves into frame. Now take the small ship and move it toward camera, keeping it relatively small, yet with a snappy, brisk motion, perhaps a barrel roll. The fact that the small ship appears small and moves with quick motions, while the large ship seems to plod along, will give the mind some information to apply scale. (By switching ships, you can create the same effect. That's part of the problem.) Ron utilizes the positives of space to disguise the negatives. Since space has no gravity, the ships must thrust and counterthrust to guide themselves through space. The elegance of the fightercraft as it whips around with its thrusters is a treat to see, and immediately removes any doubt that we aren't actually in space. So it is safe to assume, from an outsider's perspective, that a part of Ron's style is the elegance of his motions.

Just as Ron has his roadblocks and solutions, Tony Stutterheim and I face different challenges on *seaQuest*. Set underwater, *seaQuest* effects use fog to represent the depths of the ocean. This, of course, solves the problem of scale, as objects can fade into the distance. If we were to reproduce the ship test above in this environment, the large ship, since it had been pushed back so far, would be barely visible, while the small ship would appear much clearer. This situation, in turn, causes its own problems. If we were to actually re-create underwater conditions, the entire screen would simply be blue, and the effects would be extremely boring! We have found it necessary to "cheat" the fog way back to allow extra visibility in order to see anything underwater. Early in the first season, we attempted to truly re-create underwater, but quickly came to realize that the audience couldn't see anything! Though we are not faced with the clarity of space, we must solve the dilemma of lighting underwater. Fog tends to "milk" the image, reducing any color or contrast to a dull blue (in our case). Though this may seem to be a setback, we have developed a style of using practical lights and lens flares to self-illuminate the undersea colonies and ships. The underwater effect plays directly into my style, lending a soft feel to most lighting designs. I try to utilize as few lights as possible, which reduces overlighting and allows for contrast between the ship and the water—a most attractive look. I've always been a fan of slow, majestic camera motions. Working on *seaQuest* and *Star Trek: Voyager* has allowed me to bring this style to my animations. You can usually catch a shot I've animated or designed if its motion is in some way slow and majestic.

As you study the work on shows such as *seaQuest, Star Trek: Voyager* and *Babylon 5*—as well as the numerous feature, commercial and music video work you see on a day-to-day basis—take note of the things you like and don't like about the images you see. This is the first step in developing your own style. As you find techniques and looks you favor, you will begin incorporating these elements into your own work. But don't be a copycat! I've never known an artist that can look at another's work and admit it's perfect. In an effort to fix those imperfections we see, we find our own methods, and whether we like it or not, develop our own style.

LWP

John F. K. Parenteau is a vice president and effects supervisor for Amblin Imaging.

Movie Etiquette

How Not to Make Enemies on Set

by Tom Williamson

In the fast-paced world of moviemaking there are unwritten rules. Rules that need to be learned and heeded if you want to go anywhere in this business. With the growing success of LightWave 3D, there are more and more feature films and television shows are showcasing LightWave's tremendous power and flexibility. Facilities like Foundation Imaging and Amblin Imaging have opened the floodgates, and small graphics companies are springing up all over the place (mine included). When work began on our latest feature, several of Computer Café's employees joined me on set, most for the first time. As the evening wore on, I found myself answering a myriad of questions on terminology and etiquette, based on my 10 years in this business. I then decided to write this article.

Be Professional

This is the most important rule. When you consider the delicate balance of multiple departments, tons of equipment, actors, locations, personalities, technical problems and script revisions, it's amazing that movies get made at all! There is also a huge dollar amount connected to each single element that makes up a film crew. Filmmaking is incredibly expensive. Probably the one thing that makes it all work is specialization and professionalism. When a good crew is assembled, from the director to the craft services (the people who provide the snacks and drinks), it's amazing. The whole thing works like a well-oiled machine. That's why it's very important to stay professional. Your actions on set are a direct reflection of your company (and, in some cases, your field). I'm not saying you have to be a stuffed shirt, but when it's time to work put on your serious face. With over 100 people on the average film crew, you will meet an assortment of personalities, and this industry breeds eccentrics. But even that flamboyant, purple-haired makeup artist knows that when "final touches" (the call to make all last-minute adjustments to hair, makeup and wardrobe) is called, it's time to stop doing Ethel Merman impressions and get to work. Every person there is a highly skilled craftsman. They deserve your respect and courtesy.

Stay out of the Way

Depending on where you are shooting, things can get very cramped on set. When all the pieces come together for a shot there usually isn't much room left. There's the cameras, dollies, tracks, cables, lights, lightstands, c-stands, flags and a plethora of other equipment. Then there's the director, the first AD (assistant director), the second AD, the second second (another second AD, really!), the DP (director of photography), the camera operator (sometimes the DP), first AC (assistant camera), second AC and third AC. And don't forget the key grip, the grips (the people who handle all the equipment it takes to make a movie), electricians, the best boy (an electrician in training, traditionally nicknamed "Sparky"), sound, boom, hair, makeup, special effects, actors, stuntmen and a few dozen other people. When the shot's getting close, it's very important to stand clear. It's a fair bet that if someone's running in yelling "hot points ("I'm carrying something pointed"), watch your back," they're doing something more important than you at that particular moment. It really seems to come down to that: all the jobs are important, just not all at once. When there's lighting going on, the gaffer (the guy in charge of getting lights to the places the DP wants) rules the set. When there's an elaborate or dangerous special effect coming up, the FX guys rule the set. It's the same with most of the departments, and everyone else knows to get out of the way and stay quiet to let the department of the moment work. By the way, no matter who "rules" the set, the director is always top dog.

Keep Your Eyes and Ears Open

I would say that 90 percent of filmmaking is waiting. There is usually an incredible amount of "down time" to kill. When you're on a set, you'll notice a lot of people just standing around, including yourself. You'll also see a lot of walkmans, gameboys, books and other various ways of passing time. The busiest people are the camera crew and grips—they seem to always have something to do. Most people on set will be needed at one time or another, and the last thing you want to do is make everybody wait while they look for you. It's important to stay on top of what's going on. Most key people carry walkie-talkies (or just "walkies"), and by keeping your ears open you can keep pretty informed on what's happening. When you hear the words "picture's up," it means shooting is about to begin, and if you're needed, you had better be there. Other key phrases: "Rolling"—cameras are rolling (usually preceded by "roll sound"); "Cut"—cameras have stopped rolling, "Lock it up"—don't move; and "Fire in the hole!"—a loud sound is coming. And about a dozen other phrases get screamed and then echoed by the ADs and the PAs (production assistants). When you're on a sound stage it's important to listen for the bell, which will ring to signal a shot is about to happen. If you happen to be outside the stage, you'll see a "whoopee light" spinning around above the door. Don't go in! Even though most sound stages have very quiet double doors, you do not want to be the reason a shot was botched. If you just pay attention—as hard as it gets when you've been sitting for two hours—you'll stay out of trouble.

Show Some Respect

This shouldn't be too hard to follow. The thing to remember is that what you're doing is a privilege. If you're working on a movie set it's probably because you've worked your ass off and paid your dues. (Or you knew somebody—funny, eh?) The thing to remember is that everyone else there did, too. They wouldn't be there if they didn't want to be. It's very hard work, with long days and incredible deadlines. Most people on the set are there because they have a real love for the business, and they did what they had to do to get there. Treat everyone with respect, from the producer to "transpo" (the guys who drive the equipment around and shuttle people). When you're watching the crew in action you'll probably hear a lot of "Yes, sir" and "No, sir," and "please" and "thank you." These people are not kissing butt. They genuinely respect one another.

Stay Friendly

When people of different professions come together there is usually a lot of curiosity about the work other people do. I try to be as open and informative as I can. This really helps me when it comes time for me to rule the set. When I come running in yelling "Nobody move, I need a clean plate" (a shot with no actors in it, usually for rub-throughs or split-screens), everyone pretty much knows what I mean and gives me what I want. If you walk around brooding like the silent artist type, no one will want to talk to you. They will probably be grumbling under their breath when you're telling them what to do later. Being friendly also helps you make connections for future projects, and gives you someone to talk with to pass the time. It's the nice people you remember.

Know the Hierarchy

No one likes to have someone go over their head, and it's important to know the chain of command to avoid this. For our business, visual effects, there are several people we need to keep in communication with. The main person is usually the effects supervisor for the production. He or she is responsible for all the shops doing work on the film. Most questions and comments should be directed to the effects supervisor, who then can pass them to the proper person. If a dialog is opened by the effects supervisor and another department head for you, you may then communicate directly. Usually the effects supervisor is pretty busy and will make a point of introducing you to various department heads, allowing you to communicate freely. The last thing you want to do is go to the DP and say "It's way too bright" before you've been introduced. It's just not cool. Some effects supervisors like to keep a thumb on all involved shops; fortunately, they're the exception.

If you are going to talk about one of your shots with someone you don't know—the camera operator, for instance—be sure he or she is not busy and that you introduce yourself. If you have a specific problem, you should go to the department that can help. For lighting problems, talk with the DP or gaffer. If you need a "stinger" (an extension cord), talk with electric. If you need an "apple box" (a wooden all-purpose box, available in full, half, quarter and "pancake" sizes), talk to the grips. All creative decisions should be run by the effects supervisor or the director.

Usually, a film crew becomes very close very quickly. It's almost like a family. If you can, try to be there for the first couple of days while this "bonding" is happening, so you won't feel like such an outsider. If you only show up in the last week of production, or only for the shots for which you're needed, expect to feel like a red-headed stepchild. Do not confuse this with loitering. If you're not needed, you shouldn't be there, and you're probably not welcome. And you should always ask before bringing a visitor, especially on a bigger production. Secrecy is a very real and favored practice in this industry. Finally, try not to bug the director, who's got enough headaches. Try the second AD, then the first AD, before going to the head honcho.

This is by no means a complete list, but it covers the basics. Just using common sense will get you through almost any situation that should arise. If a problem should crop up, nip it in the bud. The quicker you smooth things over, the better. Keep these little tips in mind on your first few productions and you'll step on fewer toes. Remember, you're only as good as your last job.

LWP

Tom Williamson is the effects supervisor for Santa Maria, Calif.–based Computer Café. He's an avid fan of special effects, GI Joe and semprini. He also makes a mean chicken cordon bleu.

LightWave on the Big Screen

What to Remember When Rendering for Film

by Tom Williamson

The great majority of animators dream of sitting in a crowded theater, munching on popcorn and watching their own digital creations come to life on the silver screen. The reality of outputting your animations on 35 mm film is not as distant as it may seem. With the following information and a few dollars (perhaps quite a few, let's be realistic) you could be well on your way to filling that big white void with stunning computer-generated magic.

The Terminology

The first thing you have to know when you're going to output to film is a few of the terms from the motion picture industry. You need to sound like you know what you're talking about if you want people to take you seriously. We'll discuss only 35 mm film in this article, there are several film formats and each has it's own lingo, 35 mm is by far the most popular and accepted.

First off, let's discuss the playback differences of film and video. Normal film playback is at 24 fps (frames per second) as opposed to video's 30 fps. This in itself is enough to drive you nuts. For the proper playback of film on video the film must be "frame expanded" to 30 fps. This process is called 3-2 pulldown. In 3-2 pulldown every fourth frame is printed twice, hence the 3 and 2. If you do the math you'll see that by adding a frame after every fourth frame, the original 24 frames, they will add up to 30 (Are you completely confused yet? It gets worse!).

To mask the fact that every fourth frame is on screen twice (and tends to look jumpy when played back), a process of field integration is used. Every frame of video has two fields, alternating horizontal bands of image data that interlace. Each frame of video is 1/30th of a second, each field is 1/60th. This makes for smooth playback but sacrifices resolution. The 3-2 pulldown process can take the odd and even fields of two adjoining frames and create an "in-between" frame. This is done to the double printed frames and results in proper 24 fps to 30 fps playback that's very smooth. To see this process at work grab your copy of the THX wide-screen edition of *Star Wars* (you do have it, don't you?) and pop it in your VCR. If you have a steady still-frame you can frame advance through a scene and see the "in-between" frames at work (they'll be the flickering frames).

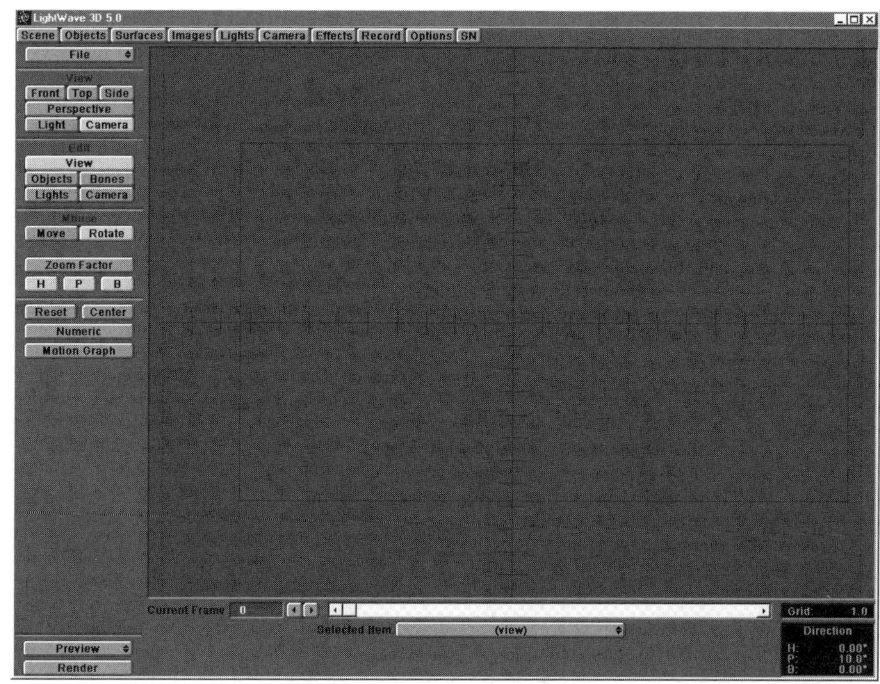

Figure 1: An academy crop. Note that the center is offset to the right to accommodate an optical sound strip.

Another mind-muncher is film measurement. Film is measured by feet plus frames. There are 16 frames per linear foot of film. If I have an image sequence that's 39 frames long it would be 2 feet plus 7 frames, which is usually displayed as <2+7>. Every piece of film has key numbers at the bottom of the strip. These number progressively count the feet. If you look at the film you will see a four digit number with a bullet "∑" every 16 frames. Frames with a bullet beneath them are foot markers. The next frames would be 1, 2 and so on to 15. Then the process starts over with the next foot marker. It should also be noted that there are four perforations ("perfs") per frame and there are tiny key numbers that relate to these. These numbers are rarely used and are best ignored.

Next is the issue of aperture. Normally film is shot at full aperture (the full frame is exposed) and projected at *academy* (cropped to a ratio of 1:85). This is very important to know when you're rendering to film. The academy crop also is off center to the right of the frame, which allows for the optical sound stripe. To get your framing right use this trick: Go to the camera panel and set your resolution to 2048 x 1556 (normal film res or "2K") and use square pixels. Now go back to Layout and turn on the field chart. Note the hash marks, we'll use them to set up our academy crop. Hold down the "l" key (to activate limited region) and pull in the left side 2 3/4 hash marks. Pull the top down and the bottom up 4 1/5, and pull the right half way to the first mark. This is the normal visible area of projected 35 mm film (Figure 1). If you leave this limited region on while you animate, and keep your composition in the box (keeping in mind what will be the new center of frame), you should see predictable results on the screen.

For render tests I always crop the frame so no one is surprised later when they aren't seeing the full image (besides, things just look cooler in letterbox, right?). It is, however, very important to render your final images at full aperture (filling the frame) because the academy crop is more of a guideline than a rigid standard and sometimes more or less of the frame is visible. Also, when the film is later transferred to video more of the top and bottom (and, unfortunately, less of the left and right) will be visible. For a more in depth look into aspect ratios and apertures see John Parenteau's article "Digital Cinematography" in the May 1995 issue of LIGHTWAVEPRO.

Rendering Tips

The real trick to getting computer animation to look good on film is to render it to look as if it was shot by a motion picture camera. This means intentionally adding all the little things that make film look like it does. Here's a few of those characteristics:

•**Motion Blur–** This is very important. With the exception of very high speed photography, motion blur is almost always present. To get your motion blur to look right first get the blur length to a realistic setting. This can be difficult to determine because in photography the length of the blur is determined not only by the speed at which an object is moving but also the camera's exposure (how long the film was exposed to light). It's best to experiment and get a length that looks esthetically pleasing but falls into the realm of reality. After you determine your length go back and determine what settings of anti-aliasing and dithering will be necessary to make the blur look realistic.

•**Film Grain–** This is a characteristic of film that is continually battled with by classic cinematographers. Seems strange that we would want to intentionally add it to our images, but it's very important to achieving a film look. To add realistic film grain I highly recommend picking up Steven Worley's Filmgrain plug-in (Figure 2) which will be available soon from NewTek. If nothing else turn on animated dither with 4x dither. Although some grain will naturally be introduced when you record out to film, it's worth it to render it into the image. The final look is more natural.

•**Light and Contrast–** To keep your images looking more cinematic try to limit the use of ambient light, and illuminate your scenes in pools of light. Also try to break up the light on your objects by using projected images and shadows. Keep in mind that the images on your computer and video will look different on film. The blacks will be richer and the whites will be brighter. On a video screen you can't have true black. This is because the screen is illuminated. Just look at the screen when the monitor's turned off. It's gray! On film the blacks are created by blocking the projector's light, resulting in true blacks (depending on the light level in the theater). The whites on film are just transparent plastic, so if the screen is kicking back a lot of light (and they usually do) you should have bright, clean whites.

•**Strobing–** This is the stuttering effect of viewing only 24 frames a second. Although you should not try to make your animations unpleasant to watch, this phenomenon is important. In the video world field rendering is used to get around strobing, but there are no fields on film. Luckily you don't really have to do anything to introduce strobing, it should occur naturally. Just fight the urge to field render and you should be okay.

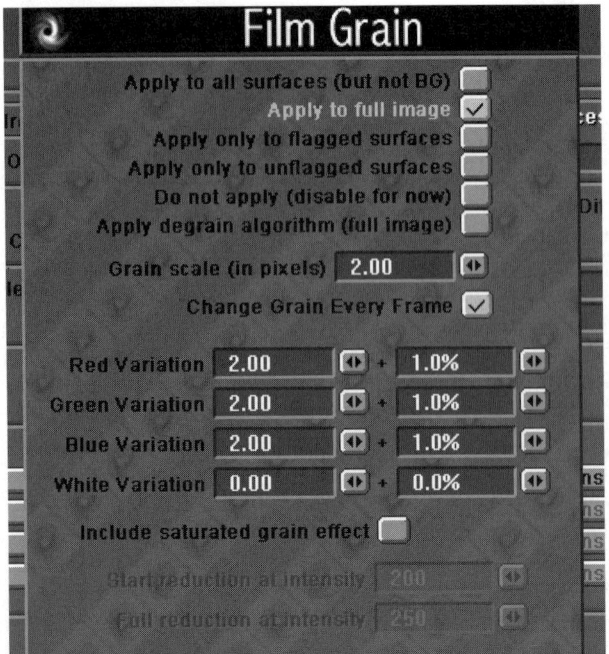

•**Composition–** When you're animating for film take advantage of the 1:85 aspect ratio. Watch a few movies with great cinematography to see how shots are composed. Use the frame to it's full effect. One technique is the rule of thirds. This is an age-old photographic method that makes for great composition. It's also very easy to do. Just divide your frame with imaginary lines into thirds, left to right and top to bottom. Where these lines intersect is where you frame your subject matter. Another thing to think about is how you "photograph" your scene. Try to keep your camera moves "realistic". In other words, don't do anything with LightWave's camera that couldn't be accomplished with a real camera. Think of the tools of a film crew, like cranes and dollies, and limit yourself to the capabilities of this equipment. Don't move too fast or whip around to much. Just think in real-world terms and ask yourself how a real cinematographer would shoot this scene.

Figure 2: The settings panel for Steve Worley's new Filmgrain plug-in, which will be available soon from NewTek.

Scanning

If your animation is going to be integrated into live action footage (35 mm) you will need to have the film scanned. Scanning is the technique of capturing the film frames as electronic images. There are several digital film services out there, so pick one based on reputation and cost. Usually the original camera negative is delivered to these facilities. It is then scanned and delivered to you on Exabyte tape (I'll discuss Exabyte tapes in the next section). When you order your scan they will probably ask if you want full or academy aperture and what resolution you want. Most often you'll need full aperture 2K images. These are 2048 x 1556 at most facilities, but check with the service before scanning begins. If you plan to move into the image (like a zoom) you may want to go to 4K, to prevent pixelation (where individual pixels become visible). Be sure to check the footage when it arrives for accuracy. Using a small strip of the original film (a "match clip"), check the framing and color. The process of scanning is still in it's infancy and subject to flaws.

Recording Out

The last thing to discuss is output, or recording out to film. This is where the money comes in. This is still a pretty expensive process. Most digital film service companies charge a setup fee, a per-frame charge and the lab costs. Expect to pay from hundreds to thousands for output of even a fairly short animation.

The technique for getting your frames on film varies depending on the platform your on. The easiest way is to use an SGI (whoa, hold on, I'll get to the Amiga). Most film recording services prefer SGI format frames (.rgb) delivered on Exabyte tape in the TAR format (Don't worry I'll go over each of these). The SGI format is the standard in high-end work, and LightWave has no problem rendering .rgb with the aid of HIIP.

Unfortunately it's not a very efficient format when it comes to storage. Most film output is at 2K, and a single frame in SGI format is over 9.5 MBs! If your going to do film work you better pick up a couple of 9 GB drives. If storage is a problem, I recommend converting the frames to IFF, they'll be smaller files and more manageable, just remember to convert them back before you output them. To send off your frames to the recording service just back them up on Exabyte and send them off. Exabyte is a tape backup medium that uses 8 mm video (actually data grade) tape. On the SGI it's as simple as connecting the Exabyte drive (they're

SCSI) and learning TAR, the tape archive format preferred by most services. Just put all the files in a directory and back it up. On other platforms it becomes a little more complex. You'll have to get your hands on a copy of TAR that runs on your system and get a tape handler. For NT you can use Hamilton C-Shell, which has all the UNIX commands. For the Amiga you can track down a copy of BTN Tape (better than nothing, get it?) and TAR.

All the backups discussed here require a lot of typing in shells. As far as I know there is no simple "point, click and ship" software available to do this. Neither the built in back-up in NT or SGI seems to be supported by the services out there. Some companies ~~do~~ allow you to send 4 mm back-ups or Syquests. And some allow you to send your images in formats other than SGI. But if you want to be compatible and spare yourself extra costs, stick with the SGI frames on Exabyte. It is also possible to output different resolutions, from D1 to 4K, but 2K is a happy medium and the most widely used.

Summary

Overall, the process of rendering to film is pretty simple. The information gathered here should be enough to get you started, But there's plenty more to learn. There is nothing quite like seeing your hard work on the big screen. Be it for a major motion picture or just part of you're college's film festival, there's nothing more rewarding. I hope all of you eventually get to experience this. Now, get back to animating!

Tom Williamson is vice president/effects supervisor for Computer Café Inc. in Santa Maria, Calif. He's happily domesticated with his wife Dianna, his son Austin, his two cats, Lance and Morgan, his dog, Rascal, and hundreds of action figures. Reach him on-line at: tomcat@terminus.com

Rules of Lighting

Benefiting From Contrast

by John F.K. Parenteau

The theory behind lighting is to produce an unnoticeable effect to compliment the given scene. Though that may sound like a dictionary definition, it is the ultimate goal of any cinematographer.

On set, the point of lighting is to illuminate the characters or environment in such a way that they appear to fit together as one cohesive unit. In CGI, this becomes even more crucial since a computer-generated model, by nature of being a model, tends to stick out.

In past articles, we have discussed the correct use of lighting and its appropriate positioning to give a natural effect to any scene. These basic rules of light placement (keylight, fill light, backlight and background light) will serve you as an animator many times. Beyond these simple examples, there is a whole realm of possibilities to consider when creating any new lighting design.

Following are a few rules:

Figure 1: With no fill our character looks foreboding, but disappears quickly into the background.

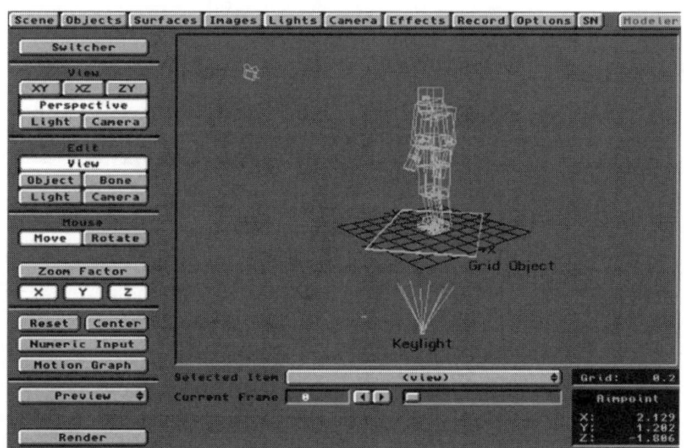

Screen shot (1): A simple setup can yield dramatic results (see above).

Rule No. 1: There are no Rules

In real-world lighting, the limitations of the physical environment are the only rules to adhere to, and many of these are flexible as well. The sole goal is to avoid any obvious, unattractive lighting, unless it's called for. Lighting is creating the mood—whatever it takes to create the mood are your only requirements.

In a CGI environment, the "no-rules" rule can be carried to its extreme. Since light sources are invisible in front of camera, a computer animator can even place "fixtures" in the shot. If there is anything more frustrating in real-world lighting, it is avoiding a fixture appearing in the frame, a problem we never have to worry about.

Rule No. 2: CGI is Unforgiving

In the everyday world, a characteristic of lighting called radiosity works wonders. As light strikes a surface, that light bounces off and strikes another surface and another, until it decays to darkness. Quite often, placing a white piece of cardboard under an actor's face is enough to reflect enough light for an exposure.

In our CGI world, radiosity doesn't exist by nature. Any given situation where light would tend to bounce, reflect, diffuse or soften as it bounces off other surfaces must be created manually. Though raytracing a light can give the most realistic shadow, it also offers the harshest shadow. Techniques of softening edges must be employed manually to help reduce this hard edge.

These types of situations occur regularly in CGI and it is the job of the animator to adjust appropriately.

Rule No. 3: Use Contrast

Contrast plays an important role in all lighting. In the days of black and white photography, a skilled cinematographer manipulated contrast alone. As a research project, rent the movies "Nosferatu" and "Citizen Kane". Both of these black and white films are excellent examples of how contrast can be just as effective in telling a story as the use of color.

A trick I used to play when shooting video was turning down the color on the monitor. If the shot looked good in black and white as well as color, I felt I had achieved an accomplished lighting setup.

Now rent the movies "Blade Runner" and "The Natural." Though both of these pictures were photographed in color, the cinematographers (both masters, Jordan Cronenweth and Caleb Deschenel) use a great deal of contrast in color, as well as light and dark to tell their story.

A flat, front-lit subject not only looks bad in CGI, but just looks bad.

Rule No. 4: Help Tell the Story

Every image, scene or sequence tells a story. Even a still is conveying meaning or purpose. Try to design your lighting and camera motion to complement your story. Remember that the camera you are using to photograph the scene, whether it be real or CGI, is an actor as much as the character in front of the lens. The cameraperson, is in full control of what the audience sees and doesn't see in the scene.

One of the most disconcerting things to see in demo reels we receive at Amblin Imaging is bad camera work. It is the most obvious detail to see, since even a bounding box preview will show errors.

If you are going for a mood, use the camera motion to help create it. The television show *NYPD Blue* is an excellent example of creating a mood for the audience. Considering the subject matter, the New York police force, the handheld feel they have established helps place the viewer in each scene, as if they were there.

In CGI, we have produced many a chase sequence where we used whip pans (panning drastically left or right to produce a blur in between) to help heighten the mood of the chase.

On the other hand, avoid gratuitous camera motion. If you are panning for no particular purpose, it probably isn't necessary. Keep in mind that, like the actors, the camera is garnishing a certain amount of attention as well. If you are whipping the camera around, banking and pitching for no reason, you are removing the audience from the scene.

Rule No. 5: If in Doubt, See Rule No. 1

Though rules two through four are valid and must be addressed, they are only suggestions of areas to take note. Any lighting design is dependent on the needs of the scene or shot. If you don't want contrast, don't have any contrast. Sometimes an evil character can be lit in a serene way to contradict the mood of the scene.

The preceding rules are only the tools of the trade and like any good tool, don't necessarily have to be used. Just be aware of them, and employ them when necessary. With these rules in mind, however, it is important to study ways to break up or diffuse light to create certain moods or effects. In the real world, a light source can be broken up in many ways. Various forms of diffusion, from high-tech "Tough Spun" to low-tech shower curtain, help to soften and mold

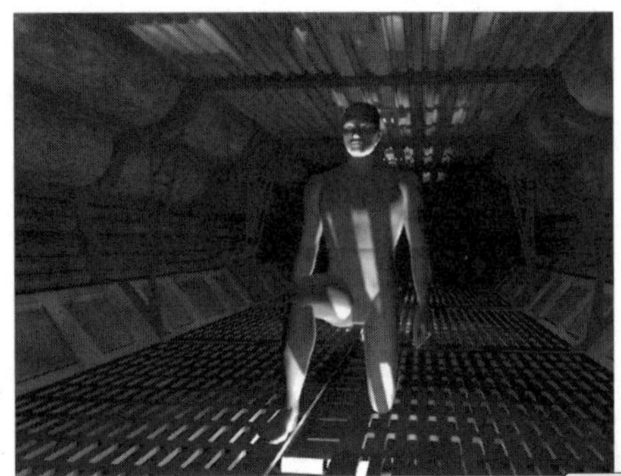

Figure 4: In a slightly more complex setting, we must take into account how light falls on our environment as well.

light before it reaches the character. In CGI, our methods are somewhat limited. By increasing or decreasing the cone size of a spotlight, we can increase or decrease the source and increase the soft edge of the light. Choosing between raytracing and shadow mapping assists in softening the edges of the shadow. There is little else we can do to directly influence the type of light created in LightWave.

But light is as much perception as it is reality, and careful consideration can create acceptable real-world effects.

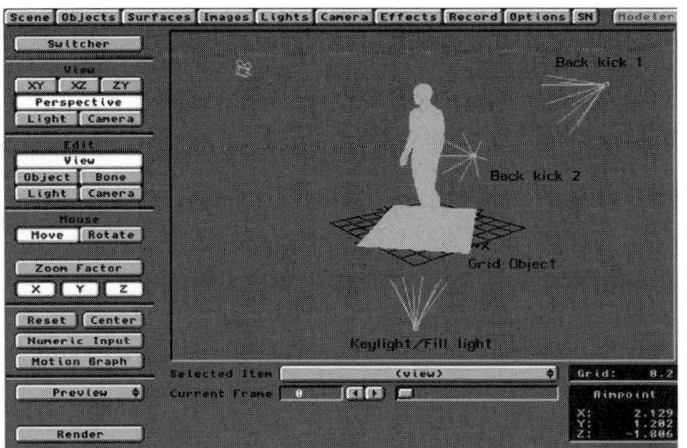

Figure 2: With the addition of a few lights, we should be able to separate our subject from the background.

Pass the Cookies, Please

In an effort to create an underlit mood, I modeled a grid in Modeler and placed it below my favorite subject, Humanoid from Crestline Software, and aimed a spotlight through it up onto Humanoid. Our grid, in real-world lighting, is known as a cukaloris. Any object used to break up light into a pattern is known as a cukaloris, or cuk (or cookie). It is important to note that the object creating the grid is a true 3D object. If a flat or single-sided object is used, errors may appear in your animation as the light strikes the surface at odd angles. If at all possible, extrude your cuk to avoid any rendering errors.

I've created a scene of the humanoid character against black. **Ambient Intensity** (Lights panel) is set at 0 percent (as it should be). Placing our grid cuk at our subject's feet, I positioned a spot light slightly in front of our character and below the cuk, making sure the light cone was wide enough to cover the width of the grid. At 150 percent **Intensity** and a **Falloff** of 18 percent, a soft decay of light should occur, while still allowing illumination at the head. You can see the result in Figure 1.

Though the light falls dramatically up the body, the shadows are much too harsh to appear realistic. In addition, the shadows are completely black. Though this may seem appropriate, it isn't realistic.

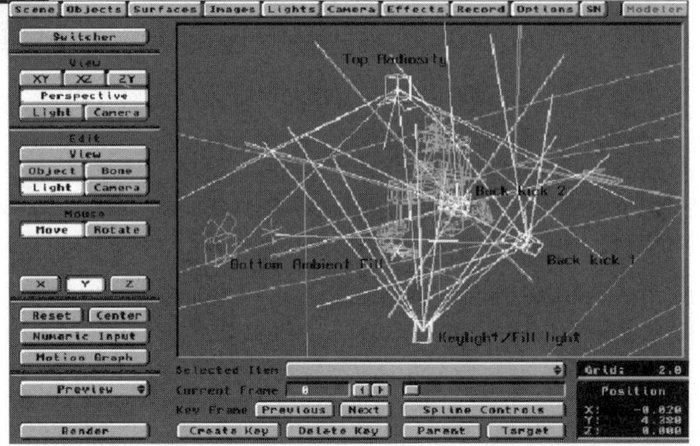

Screen shot (4): Modification of the light positions to avoid unwanted light spill is a must in the actual environment. Note how the back lights have been lowered to avoid overfilling the floor.

In past lessons we have created a fill light at or near camera position. In an effort to create a more appealing effect, I cloned the keylight, removing any shadow options and reducing the Intensity to 20 percent. Though in most cases the Falloff should be set to the same relative amount of the keylight, so that the visible Falloff ring is in the same positron for both lights, I have chosen to remove Falloff due to the low intensity of the light.

I have created a fill light effect that mimics light from the keylight spilling around the edges of the grid. If the fill light were placed

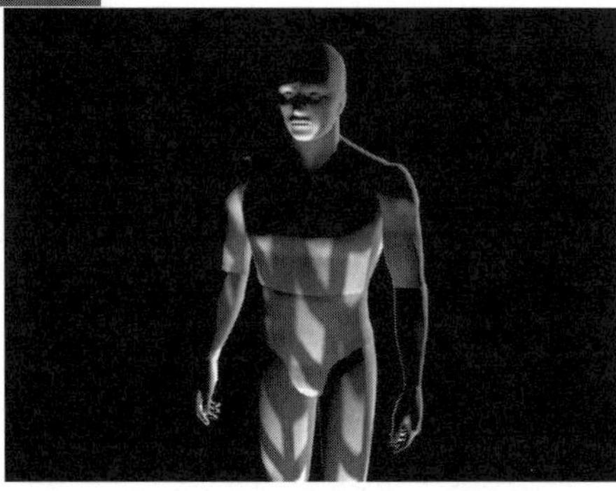

Figure 3: We have maintained the moody feel but no longer lose the shadows into the background.

beside our camera, its source would be invisible and questionable.

To correct the harsh shadow, I switched the keylight shadow option from **Raytrace** to **Shadow Map**, increasing the **Shadow Map Size** to 2048. Shadow mapping is a memory intensive process and your available RAM should be considered before using this setting. The larger your Shadow Map Size, the smoother the shadow edges created.

While these changes may be enough, I have taken our setup a step further (Figure 2). Considering our subject is standing on a grid, I placed a light behind and below Humanoid. This creates a back kicklight that helps pick our character out from the black background. In addition, another light was placed at shoulder height, behind and to the camera left of our man.

Though there is no motivation for this light, it assists the lower backlight in providing an added rim of highlight. Both of these lights were personal choices to add to the mood of the shot, and may or may not be necessary for your setup.

Now examine Figure 3 to see how the changes affected our character. Though it appears our subject is lit in an extreme manner, the added lights help the eye accept the drastic lighting without destroying the overall effect.

Into the "Real World"

It is one thing to produce a lighting example in a limbo environment. It is another to apply that same setup to an entire CGI setting.

Figure 3 exemplifies an appealing lighting setup for a moody feel. In Figure 4, I have placed our man in a hallway environment under the same lighting conditions. In an effort to maintain the same design, I have modeled the floor of the room with a grating similar to that used in Figures 1, 2 and 3.

Though the original lighting works well against black, certain limitations arise in our hallway. First, light streaming up from underneath can overexpose the ceiling. Using Falloff, we can reduce the amount of light overhead, yet removing it entirely will also reduce the amount of light reaching the face of our subject. Camera angles can be limited to assist with this, avoiding angles that favor the ceiling.

It is important to assign a source to our CGI light. In the real world, all light sources are visible whether we like it or not. In computer animation, we have the choice to make that fixture visible or invisible. In many cases, it is helpful to imply a light from off screen without showing its source. Yet to produce a truly believable feel, it is usually important to show a likely source, whether our light is originating from it or not.

Again, CGI can be much more flexible than a real set. For example, take the sources I have chosen in Figure 4. I have modeled simple light bars (tubes and a secondary outer tube with transparent edges for a glow effect) and placed them at intervals below the grating. Placing a string of flares in each tube gives a convincing effect of a light source.

If we were to use these point lights as the sole source of light, we would have omnidirectional light spilling all over our set. It is important to apply some Light Intensity to these lights to affect the close surroundings, but a high level of Falloff contains any unwanted light from flooding the set.

Our true light sources are spot lights with wide beams placed near the lightbars I have created. This enables us to use as little Falloff as possible while still controlling how our light falls.

If we were to put motion to this scene, it would be important to examine several frames as our man walks the hall to make sure there aren't too many dark areas.

When I teach lighting courses, I try to express the importance of creating a real-world effect in the scene. Rule number one applies well here. It isn't necessary to have our character lit every step of the way. It actually is more realistic to have him walk from light to dark then light again. With luck, the bars of light will crawl across our subject, creating a dramatic lighting effect.

The above examples create a situation found regularly in the real world as well as CGI. Contrast in lighting is an everyday occurrence that should not be avoided but rather embraced. In the future, we will examine other forms of cukaloris' and how to further affect LightWave lights for a more appealing feel.

In some ways, I have used techniques or perhaps models beyond what you may feel you are capable of, due not only to experience but also time, money or equipment. While advanced object design will only help "sell" your animation further, close scrutiny of the factors you are able to effect will do just as much to create a convincing image.

Make a constant effort to avoid the standard lighting design that computer animation has been known for. Regardless of the level of modeling or texturing, a great deal can be achieved by considering the four rules listed above.

LWP

John F.K. Parenteau is a vice president of Amblin Imaging. His work can be seen on seaQuest DSV, Weird Science, *and recently, the preview for the* Star Trek: Generations *movie.*

Sunshine on Your Shoulders

by John F. K. Parenteau

Re-creating accurate lighting in a computer-generated environment is no simple task. In the world around us, there are often so many functions of the light that eventually reach our eyes that it is almost impossible to count them.

Observe the simplest lighting possible and you cannot count on your fingers the number of surfaces that either reflect, refract, generate or absorb light. In *LWPRO* Issue 5, Greg Teegarden and I touched on some basics, such as faking radiosity and the simplest lighting setups that all animators should consider. Though both discussions were complete in their own, each is just a component of the consideration involved in creating a convincing light scheme.

Figure 1

Lighting is Difficult

While teaching cinematography to film students, one of the most difficult concepts was the complexity and consideration involved in lighting a set. In almost any situation, a light source is relatively easy to come by. It is the job of the cinematographer to make the lighting attractive. Interiors, though difficult in their own way, often provide their own answers. Almost every interior set has a window, lamp or fireplace —and if there isn't one, it's a simple task to convince a production designer to put one in.

Figure 2

Exteriors, however, are a different story. If a character moves about in an interior set, it is often from one area lighting to another. This means there are certain areas on a set that are naturally lit. An example might be a person in a night library setting. Each table has a lamp to allow for reading and you can always motivate, or justify your light from there. An exterior night is more difficult. We have all seen many movies where the key source of light is the moon. How often is the moon really bright enough to illuminate a whole city block? Yet, if you think about it, there are always street lamps to create gothic pools of light, or doorways lit with neon. A lighting source can always be found or created. The task is to use those sources to create an appealing image.

Call it a Day

The following is one of the most incorrect statements that can be made about lighting:

"Of course, day exteriors are the easiest!"

In both real photography and CGI, a convincing day exterior is the most difficult lighting set-up to produce. It's easy to place one light up high, rename it 'Sun' and call it a day, but this will hardly look attractive and never look realistic.

The problem is never too little light, but rather too much light, which makes everything in the shot all too visible. Especially with CGI, it may take considerably more work to surface and model objects if they will be seen in such a revealing quantity of light. To create successful daylight, we must understand two important concepts: Color Temperature and Contrast.

All light has a color temperature. As you might extrapolate from those two words, the temperature of the light helps determine the color of the light. Standard daylight, usually considered when the sun is directly overhead on a clear day, is 5400 degrees Kelvin. This is a nominal figure and can vary from 6000 to 4600 and beyond, depending on the position of the sun in the sky, the materials in the air (i.e. water particles, clouds, smoke, etc.), and the amount of atmosphere between the measuring device and the sun. The higher on the visible spectrum of light, the bluer light appears.

To compare, tungsten light (similar to most light bulbs) is approximately 3200 degrees Kelvin. Existing low on the spectrum, this light tends to appear orange or amber. A candle has a very low color temperature and thus is very warm whereas a welding torch is extremely blue/white and has a very high color temperature.

Comparing daylight at different times of the day can explain why many exterior shoots, especially fashion photography, are shot either early in the morning or late afternoon. When the sun is low on the horizon, the amount of atmosphere and atmospheric debris, is greatly increased. The light tends to be softened and warmed (lower color temperature) by the added diffusion. In contrast, midday sun appears whiter (higher color temperature) and thus harsher. In addition, when the sun is directly overhead, shadows are much darker. Late or early light (often referred to as "Magic Hour") comes from a much more pleasing side angle.

Contrasting Situations

Contrast in daylight conditions plays an important part in creating believability. Many photographers use varying amounts of contrast to create the special look they are known for. Nature photographer Ansel Adams used angles of sunlight to create fantastic shadows or slashes of sunlight. Fashion photographer Herb Ritts shoots largely in daylight with black and white film, using the contrast inherent in color as his palette. Both photographers have manipulated contrast to communicate on film. In CGI, contrast will help bring realism to your image.

In Figure 1, I have created a simple scene in which we are looking from inside a room through a window to an exterior. First, I suggest using a spotlight rather than a distant light to act as a sun so that there is more control over its direction and cone angle. The keylight is raytraced with **Trace Shadows** (Camera panel) turned on and the **Ambient Intensity** (Lights panel) is set to zero. I like to use a slightly warm light, thus mimicking magic hour, for my Sunlight. A color value of 255,224,160 gives a great late afternoon look. Experiment with your settings for best effect.

As in any CGI shot, compositing your computer generated image with a real video background immediately helps assist the shot's believability. In this case, I have used an ocean setting. Since there is no contrast in the background image, the sun must have been coming from directly behind the camera. In our setting, this will allow us to cheat our keylight to another location without it appearing too out of place. (If the sun in the background image was clearly on the left or right, casting shadows in a distinctive direction, we would be forced to mimic that direction with our light to maintain accuracy.) In this first setup, I have placed only a main keylight. Though the play of light into the room is appealing, the room appears far too contrasty.

Figure 3

Figure 4

Follow the Bouncing Light

All light has a tendency to bounce off of surfaces it strikes, thus creating an ambient light. With a small desk lamp in a night setting, the light from the lamp tends to fall off quickly due to lack of any great intensity. The sun, however, is very intense and will create a great deal of ambience.

In Figure 2, I have placed ambient 'source' lights in front of each window, disabling raytracing for these lights. This will mimic the ambience outside as sunlight bounces off the ground and sky, eventually bleeding into the room. The light cones are extremely wide (80 degrees) to give as nonspecific a source as possible. Light intensity is dependent on the amount of ambience you are seeking in the scene. In this case, I experimented and settled on a 35 percent intensity for both lights. Since ambient daylight tends to be a component of light bouncing off the sky and ground, it tends to be a cool, often bluish light.

In my CGI room, however, I have chosen to use the same color settings for my ambient lights as I did for my sunlight. This creates a much smoother transition between keylight and fill light. As you can see, this new light picks out the edges inside the room.

In Figure 3, I have deleted the ambience lights and increased the Ambient Intensity to 25 percent. The Ambient Intensity setting is highly unrealistic since it has no specific origination point. This means it strikes all surfaces from all sides. All surfaces are evenly filled from this non-specific light, and appear to have no edges. Rays of light, whether raytraced or not, all have a specific source. In Figure 2, ambience lights produce actual rays of light, striking the surfaces from one specific angle. Note the corners of the room. Dark areas (shadows) exist where the rays of light cannot reach. This creates definition of surfaces much more efficiently than an ambient intensity.

In Figure 4, I have added radiosity lights, estimating where the direct light would bounce off of surfaces onto other surfaces. Radiosity is a soft source that has fairly quick falloff. For this reason, I used settings of 17 percent intensity and 7.5 percent falloff. As mentioned in "Faking Radiosity," *LWPRO* Issue 5, these lights can be point lights placed just below the floor surface to avoid a hot spot. Radiosity from light striking side walls takes some testing. In this case, I placed radiosity lights just outside the windows to mimic light striking the window frame. This is a subtle effect and should not distract or compete with your main keylight. Do not raytrace these lights and make sure your floor surface is single sided, facing up. With the addition of well surfaced furniture and more realistic textures on the walls and floors, our scene will look downright real. This simple shot shows how basic consideration of how light falls can create a great looking image.

Another reason for using spots and points rather than distant lights is the ability to apply an **Intensity Falloff** (Lights panel). No matter how bright a light is, all light has a falloff value. Re-examine Figure 4 to see how falloff is best applied. Our keylight has a falloff limit well beyond our set. Though it has little effect on the amount of light striking visible surfaces, it does change the value of light over the distance it is throwing.

Composite This

Compositing into a realistic setting can be quite simple if you pay attention to a few basic rules. In my second setup (color pages), I am using the Humanoid object, sitting on a stool and placed in a live action tree environment. The tree image is a background image, and a plane has been placed under our subject with the same tree image **Front Projection** mapped on it (see image in the color pages).

Let's first place our keylight. If you note the shadows in the background and the shadow side on the trees, you can clearly see that the sun is low on the horizon on the left side of the frame. Careful analysis shows that the keylight should be set in a slightly backlight position, approximately 25-35 degrees off the ground, shooting light over the right shoulder of our subject. Though this accurately mimics the angle of the shadow in the background, the placement provides little if no light on our character's face. I have cheated the keylight around a bit to provide a little sunlight on the front side. If you now examine the shadows closely, our subject's shadow is not exactly matching. The cheat is acceptable, however, and hardly noticed. Due to the front projection mapped plane, I have chosen to use a Distant light source. Though I am unable to apply a falloff to this light, it will cover the plane evenly and thus allow the plane to match the background image better. The keylight will be the only light raytraced.

It took me a bit of analysis to establish the keylight color of 255,227,200. In examining the image, the sunlight appears extremely warm. This is actually not a component of the color temperature, but rather a function of the material on the ground. Dried up leaves and branches take on a deep brown color. As the slightly golden light of sunset strikes these surfaces, they reflect an amber hue. When choosing a light color, it is important to examine the entire frame. Note the light striking the leaves overhead. This light tends to be green due to the color of the leaves. In the distance, a white fence appears appropriately white. In noting all these variations, I came to the conclusion that the sunlight was still fairly high in color temperature. The value I have chosen is slightly yellow, which mimics a color temperature of around 4800 degrees Kelvin. Since I am using a front projection map on the plane below the character's feet, it is effected by the color of the light striking it. Using a slightly yellow light enables me to warm the character up a bit without discoloring the mapped plane under it. If you look closely, you can actually see the line where this warmer light is not matching the background image.

With our current lighting setup, we have established an extremely contrasty image inappropriate to the background map. For general fill light, matching sunlight bouncing off the sky in the distance, I have placed two point lights approximately two and a half meters from the front and the left of the shadowed side of our subject. These lights are the same color of the keylight placed just over the head of our character and have an intensity of 13 percent. A falloff of 1 percent should be applied to both lights.

To mimic the sunlight striking the ground around our subject, I have placed two point lights just below the ground plane. One is placed near the outstretched foot and another behind and to the right of our character. My plane is single sided, with the face pointing up, and neither light is raytraced. Using an Intensity of 35 percent and a Falloff of 13 percent gave the best results.

Finally, the efficiency of LightWave raytracing has provided a far too specific shadow in our scene. Adding some luminosity to our ground plane, while decreasing the diffuse (to prevent the plane from becoming brighter) will help dissipate the harshness of our shadow. A luminosity of 50 percent and diffuse of 75 percent in this case, best accomplishes this task.

Examining the final image of our new setup, the light striking our 3D element looks fairly appropriate. With better surfacing, however, the effect would be much more believable. Lighting for daylight is, as in any CGI environment, only as realistic as the CGI elements modeled, mapped and lit. Careful study of a background image, or careful planning for the look you wish to achieve will provide simple lighting answers for any setup. Just as in any real-world photography, attention to detail will pay the most dividends.

John F.K. Parenteau is a vice president of Amblin Imaging, where his experience as a cinematographer has helped add realism to the company's CGI effects.

Digital Cinematography

by John F.K. Parenteau

Since the first issues of *LWPRO*, I have written several articles adapting practical cinematography to terms identifiable in the computer. Though I hated to admit it, since it would require me to work on weekends, there was enough information and interest to easily form a monthly column on the subject. After some arm twisting and hard consideration (actually an impromptu conversation with John Gross), we have decided to make this a monthly column.

As the title above may suggest, I am now going to attempt to address quite a few different areas. Though I can be quite creative in choosing a subject, feel free to write in with any questions or comments, or just random praise. Specific problems make my job easier ... and I take compliments well.

Last month we discussed the five rules of lighting and how they can apply to our CGI world. It is important to understand that while there are many differences between a computer animated world of lighting and the real world, many lessons can be taken from a practical set and applied directly to the computer. For quite a few years before I discovered computer animation, I spent many days and nights trying to design lighting setups for various professional projects. You learn a lot just experimenting with different ways to light a scene, and I've tried to carry this experience into computer animation.

Any experimentation on your part can only assist you in understanding new "tricks" of lighting to give your animation an innovative look.

Figure 1: Our first look at the soft light effect. Note how the light gently wraps around the face.

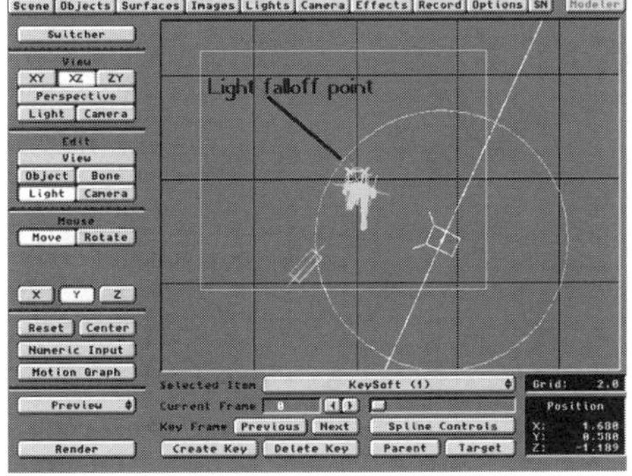

Figure 2: Our subject now resides in the tail end of the light falloff, a place where light is the softest.

The Real World

Though most of you may not have the time or motivation to work with an actual lighting package, everyday light can be just as effective. For example, take the lamp on your desk. Note how different the light looks as it falls raw onto the face of the desk as compared to the light that filters through your lampshade.

Now take a sheet of white paper and use it to bounce the raw light back onto another surface. The light through the lampshade appears much "softer" than the raw light, as does the "bounced" light off the paper. As discussed last month, fashion photographers shooting exterior locations often wait until the end of the day to shoot since the light is much "softer" at this time. This is due, in fact, to the greater amount of atmosphere between the subject and the sun. As the light from the sun races through the air, it strikes water molecules, dust particles and other atmospheric debris on its journey to the camera lens.

If we were to imagine the sunlight as it originates from its source as a single ray of light, this ray would essentially be broken up, bounced around and dispersed by all this debris before it reaches the film. By the time it exposes the emulsion, it has actually become five or 10 rays, much less powerful than the single original.

Though this is hardly a scientifically accurate example, it serves to exemplify how the term "soft light" comes to life.

On an interior set or stage, this atmospheric effect cannot be utilized, though there are ways to re-create it in a more controlled, and quite often more attractive manner. Though it has been known to have occured, it is quite rare these days to see an actual motion picture light that has no "diffusion" on it. Professional lighting has been through many evolutions throughout the years, many due to necessity and, most recently, many due to a change in approach.

In the black and white days of filmmaking, the film stocks were so insensitive to light, or "slow," that a large quantity of light was necessary just to achieve an exposure. Imagine in the days of the Buzby Burkley musical, when as many as 100 lights were used to illuminate a large stage, with each fixture reaching temperatures as high as 200 degrees. With no truly effective air conditioning (in truth, we still don't have effective air conditioning on today's stages), the conditions were hardly pleasant.

As film stocks became more sensitive, cinematographers were able to "soften" light by placing thin sheets of translucent substances in front of the lamps. Materials known as tough spun, grid cloth and others were created to help, yet many camerapeople used materials as simple as a shower curtain to diffuse their light. In the '70s, a return of the harsh light surfaced in an effort, many believe, to add a sense of raw realism to film. Though many great films were shot this way ("The Conversation" and "Butch Cassidy and the Sundance Kid," for example) it wasn't a very attractive form of photography.

Today, most cinematographers use a much softer look. Film stocks are increasingly fast and therefore a low level of light is necessary to expose a shot, using both an element of existing light rather than lighting a scene with motion picture lights as well as softening light in ways only possible with the newest filmstocks.

Soft Light in LightWave

I began this article with every intention of teaching you how to create a "soft light" look in LightWave. I honestly felt with a combination of raytracing or shadow mapping through a diffuse object, much like diffusion used on film sets, I might be able to achieve the desired look. Yet after several days of experimenting, I finally came to the understanding that finally, a real world scenario could not be achieved in similar fashion on the computer. Though this was disconcerting, I felt inspired by the challenge.

Once again, I returned to the basics I try to rely on. First, the theory of soft light. I imagined those rays of light bouncing off white sheets of paper or in a soft box, an effect I desired to re-create.

A softbox is the best looking form of soft light, in my opinion. A light is placed in a box of white show card. The box has one open end in it, which is covered with a translucent material like a shower curtain. The light from the fixtures bounces all around the box and finally strikes the material at the end, finally emerging as an extremely gentle light on the subject.

With the concept of how lighting is created in LightWave, this was just not possible. If the program had to compute that many rays as they split and bounced, I would still be waiting on my first frame to complete rendering. Instead, we must look closer at how we perceive this light, and attempt to simulate it.

Humanoid Again!?

Loading our favorite Humanoid figure (Crestline Software) and placing him on a stool, we now create our keylight. Placing this light on the right side of the camera, just above chest level of our subject, set the light to a 90-degree cone angle. While it is good practice to set the soft edge angle to the same setting as the cone angle (if you are looking for a soft edge light), this has little effect here since we are not seeing the edge of the light. (Soft edge angle does not effect the light in the center of the beam, only on its edge.) The key to a soft light is low intensity and quick falloff.

Therefore, I set the keylight to 100 percent **Intensity** and set the **Falloff** so it is just beyond our subject. Though raytracing is far more accurate at simulating how a shadow falls, there is little control over the softness of the shadow edge. In this case, we must resort to shadow mapping.

For people with less rendering power, shadow mapping is quite effective. It is important, however, to use as large a **Shadow Map Size** as your memory will allow. In this case, I have set the keylight Shadow Map Size at 1024K.

Though **Shadow Fuzziness** is said to increase the softness of the shadow edge, it has little effect on the primary subject. Thus, leaving this setting at one will suffice.

Lastly, a soft light practical source is generally large, rather than one small fixture. To help with the illusion, clone the keylight and move the clone to cast on the lower half of the body. This increases the apparent size of the source, yet since the cone angle is so large and crossover of light is great, it will still appear as one light.

Figure 1 shows the effect of this light on our Humanoid. The two major effects to take note of in this frame are intensity and falloff. A soft light can be very intense if necessary. What happens to this light after it leaves the lamp is another matter. A normal motion picture lamp, with a "clean lens" (meaning no diffusion utilized), can travel a large distance before falling off. In addition, this light is very harsh throughout most of its travel.

Figure 3: Though the added intensity creates a similar effect, the added brightness destroys our soft effect.

Figure 4: A visible source, called a "practical," always helps the illusion.

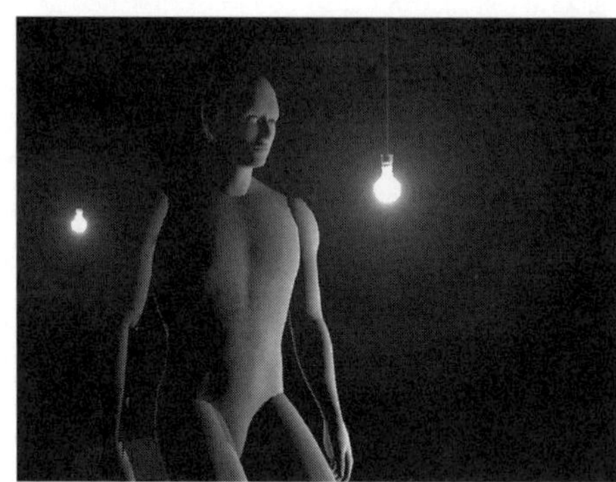

Figure 5: A touch of backlight helps separate our character.

A soft light, on the other hand, has lost a great deal of its ability to travel. In a way, the rays have been diluted and are much weaker. Though they still have a definitive source, and thus can be intense, they fall away quickly to darkness. By setting our falloff to a point just barely beyond our subject (Figure 2), we have created a similar effect.

In Figure 3, I have increased the intensity of the light to 200 percent, a factor of two over the previous setting. To compensate, I have multiplied our falloff by a factor of two so that our falloff ring is in the same position it was under lower intensity. As you can see, the light source is brighter, yet the effect is similar as it falls across the body. Note, however, how our "soft" effect is destroyed by the greater intensity.

Where's the Source?

As in any form of photography, a visible source of light always helps sell the effect. Recently, I purchased several Sylvania super soft lightbulbs and decided to model one for this example.

In a perfect world, it would be nice to use this light as the source for our effect, it isn't always feasible. On film sets, the practical light you may see in the scene is rarely used as the source of light. More likely, another lighting fixture is placed just off camera to achieve the angle actually desired. Quite often, a practical light will be placed just behind the subject yet the light miraculously reaches around to the face of the person. "Cheating" a light is a way of life for some of the best, and we will not shy away from our responsibilities here.

Dropping my light bulb from above frame, I have placed a point light inside. I have put a great deal of intensity on this light, since it is a light bulb, but I don't want this light to affect my subject. Thus, the Falloff has been set to 2,000 percent, enough to contain the light generated within the immediate surroundings of the bulb itself.

Renaming this light to Bulb.Glow, I have applied a bit of heavily dissolved lens flare to assist in the illusion. I have also placed another point light at the center of the bulb. This light has no intensity and half the flare size of the glow light, but is not dissolved. This helps give our lightbulb a center hot spot.

Figure 4 shows our final product. The addition of the visible source assists the eye, and thus the brain, in forming a logical conclusion for the light falling across our subject.

In Figure 5, I have added a little depth to our scene by placing another lightbulb in the distance from our camera. Using the same rules as our keylight, I have added a touch of backlight, helping "pick" our subject out from the blackness, by cloning one of the keylights and placing it below our second lightbulb. By increasing the intensity so that the falloff is just beyond our subject, we can create a subtle "rim" or outline quite effectively. It isn't necessary to use a shadow map on the backlight, since the edge is barely visible and does not need to be particularly soft.

The greatest challenge of lighting, both real world and CGI, is creating the illusion of the effect you wish to achieve. In this case, we have created a seemingly soft light without actually using any special techniques. As you examine other lighting setups, try to step back to see the whole picture, and learn other methods of "fooling the eye" to achieve new and interesting looks. As you learn to break down a lighting design, you will increase your skill at building an accomplished scene.

LWP

John F.K. Parenteau began his career as Director of Photography after receiving a degree in cinematography from the University of Southern California's School of Cinema/Television. Working on a variety of projects from television and theatrical to documentary, John has extensive experience with all photographic formats. John is currently Vice-President and General Manager of Amblin Imaging, working on such projects as seaQuest, Weird Science *and most recently, the theatrical trailer for* Star Trek: Generations.

LightWave and Live Action

by John F.K. Parenteau

As computer-generated graphics are used at an ever-increasing rate to augment live action, it becomes extremely important for us "CGI people" to understand how our craft relates directly to on-set cinematography. As we have reviewed in past issues, creating a real-world effect in CGI is usually a much more involved task than many realize. Programmers don't consciously try to make our work difficult; it isn't easy creating some effects in the computer without massive computing power. Even packages with longer histories of involvement in the entertainment industry don't always have a direct relationship from their workspace to the tools used on set.

Take, for example, a soft light effect. The theory to build a real soft box is to bounce light around a white box, then out one end covered with a heavy, yet translucent material. On set, most gaffers can produce a soft box in their sleep, knowing with confidence that this simple design has been used effectively for years. The laws of physics never enter a conscious level of thought.

To program a soft box light type in a program such as LightWave would require massive rendering power and would most likely be too time-intensive. Just the thought of the number of light rays splitting and bouncing around the inside of that box must give most programmers the shakes! Though it would be nice to have a button for everything a cinematographer uses on the set, it isn't really necessary, since most effects are possible with our current tools. As many of my fellow animators are fond of saying, "It'll just take a little messing around to make it work."

In future issues, we will examine how to make the tools at hand work in almost any application. But first, let's take a walk through LightWave and touch on some areas that have a direct relation to live action photography.

Scene Overview

In the film industry, a scene is usually described as a sequence of related shots. In LightWave, we use a scene to describe a single shot. The Scene Overview (Scene panel) feature allows you to examine the layout of your shot at any time. On set, a script supervisor, also known as "continuity," keeps track of each take and the actions that take place within it. If an actor raises a drinking glass with his right hand, the script supervisor is there to ensure that in each subsequent take and any "coverage" (other angles of the same action, such as close-ups), the actor uses the same hand.

Using LightWave's Scene Overview allows you to study each element, its keyframing, and any hierarchies that it is involved in. Suppose you are animating a complex hierarchical design, such as a robot, and the pieces loaded in the scene are not in order. Scene Overview will display the hierarchy in order for you.

Simply start with the shoulder, then highlight the upper arm in the Scene Overview. This selects that object in layout so that you don't have to search the object list for your arm. Compared to the rest of LightWave, Scene Overview is hardly a complex feature, but it is a handy one to have.

Light Types

As I mentioned at the start of this column, most 3D software packages lack the exact duplicate of equipment found on a live action set. This, however, is not a problem to us creative types, since we can create anything with the tools at hand, right? The functions of the three light types LightWave has to offer can simulate almost any form of practical lamp if used correctly.

A **Distant** light should be used in limited instances. Since this light is an overall light from a single source, it is best used to simulate sunlight for day exterior scenes, or space, where the keylight source is usually the sun. Remember, you cannot put falloff on a distant source, nor can an object move into or out of this light unless the light is blocked by another object (and raytraced).

As you may recall, I have an aversion to using ambient light. Though it does serve its purpose in limited situations, I feel it is better to imply ambient light from the source creating it.

For example, the sun emits light rays that strike our atmosphere, and eventually the ground. Though many rays reach the ground, many others are reflected and refracted by particles and debris in the air. This is what produces some of the ambient light visible to your eye. A good practice to help simulate this in 3D when making your sunlight is to apply raytracing settings to create realistic (yet often harsh) shadows. Once you have set this light, clone it, rename the new light as "Ambient" and remove the shadow options for this light. By setting the intensity to one-eighth or so of the sunlight intensity, a sense of ambient light is created from the actual source direction. In addition, radiosity for a day exterior can be simulated with a distant light pointing in the opposite direction of the main light. Keep the intensity low to avoid overfilling your object.

Spot Lights can function as most other forms of light. For example, one of these lights with **Spot Soft Edge Angle** set to zero simulates an open face or lensless lamp on set. Following is a list of practical motion picture lamps and a suggested setting for the corresponding LightWave light. These settings are intentionally vague. It is important to experiment with each to achieve the desired look. Avoid using these as plug and play values. Remember, each situation is different, and it is important to find your own look:

Lamp Type:	Open Face (no lens)
LW Light Type:	Spot Light
Color Temp:	White or slightly warm
Features:	Raytraced, no soft edge angle, low falloff, low cone angle

Lamp Type:	Fresnel lamp
LW Light Type:	Spot Light
Color Temp:	White or slightly warm
Features:	Raytraced, some soft edge angle medium falloff, med. cone angle

Lamp Type:	HMI (daylight lamp)
LW Light Type:	Spot Light
Color Temp:	Slightly blue
Features:	Raytraced, some soft edge angle, low falloff, medium cone angle

Lamp Type:	Soft Light
LW Light Type:	Spot Light
Color Temp:	Slightly warm
Features:	Raytraced, high soft edge angle, high falloff, wide cone angle

Lamp Type:	Arc lamp
LW Light Type:	Spot Light
Color Temp:	White
Features:	Raytraced, no soft edge angle, low falloff, wide cone angle, high intensity

What do all those lamp types mean? We've talked about soft lights before, but the others are as follows:

Open face—any motion picture lamp with no lens to focus the light being emitted, creating a harsher, non-softened light.

Fresnel lamp—any motion picture lamp using a fresnel lens to focus light emitted. A fresnel lens is a piece of glass with ridges that help direct and focus light (Figure 1). As the bulb behind the lens is moved forward and back, the lightbeam becomes tighter or wider.

HMI—daylight (5200 degrees Kelvin, nominal) balanced light.

Arc Lamp—daylight balanced light created by an electrical arc between two carbon rods.

As discussed above, many lights have sharp shadows while others have more diffuse shadows. Choosing between raytraced shadows and shadow mapping can help simulate both types. Though shadow mapping will create a fairly realistic soft-edged shadow, it requires a higher setting the closer you are to the shadow, and thus more memory.

Figure 1: Fresnel lenses.

Camera Panel

The camera panel contains the greatest collection of settings to help simulate live action photography. For those of you who are content producing full CGI shots, the following discussion may not apply (though it may be interesting).

From my standpoint, the truest form of an effect is one that is invisible to the viewer. Granted, many effects are readily noticeable, largely since many of them are monsters, spaceships or aliens. These stand out not because they are unbelievable, but rather because our subconscious mind, and often our conscious mind, knows that these things cannot exist. The best an effect of this type can hope for is to provide a momentary suspension of disbelief. *Jurassic Park*, for example, had CGI dinosaurs. Though these were perhaps the most realistic creatures ever created in the computer, they still stood out because we know that dinosaurs don't exist. This doesn't make them any less thrilling to watch, but the effect is visible. In a movie like *Forrest Gump*, however, many of the effects went unnoticed. I actually had several effects-savvy friends of mine ask if Gary Sinese was truly handicapped (and you tell me you didn't think Tom Hanks was actually playing ping pong). This is the purest form of special visual effect.

To create these effects, it is important to understand how many of the features of the camera panel apply to live action photography.

Basic Resolution settings are fairly straightforward. The lowest resolution usable in the professional world is **Medium Resolution**. With **Low** Antialiasing, the image generated is the equivalent of D1 video resolution, the highest-quality video available today. (It is important to remember when outputting to D1 to set the **Pixel Aspect Ratio** to D1 for proper image sizing.)

Film resolution varies depending on the output medium (e.g., 35mm, 65mm, VistaVision, etc.). Many facilities generate 1K files and size up to 2K for film recording. Though 1K is a fairly non-specific figure considering the number of image sizes this might suggest, the industry standard resolution when referring to this number is 1024x768. 2K usually implies 2048x1536. While scaling from 1K to 2K for scanning to film can be an acceptable solution to high rendering times, it is recommended that you render the highest resolution possible approaching your ultimate target resolution. 2K is suggested to maintain sufficient pixel density on the negative. Remember, use square pixels when rendering frames for film output.

When matching live action footage, it is important to match the CGI lens with the actual camera lens. Though LightWave uses a zoom factor setting, an Equivalent Lens display is provided. Below are a list of common 35mm motion picture film lens sizes and their equivalent zoom factor settings:

35mm film Lens	LightWave Zoom Factor
9mm	1.2
15mm	2
20mm	2.6
25mm	3.3
35mm	4.6
40mm	5.3
50mm	6.6
85mm	10.6
100mm	13.3
150mm	20

Accurate framing of the CGI camera is crucial for matching any live action. Though a Safe Areas function is provided under the Options panel, it is sometimes unclear to some as to the accuracy of these markings.

For video resolution, the entire layout screen is rendered as the visible image. Remember, however, that not all televisions can display the entire viewable area, called "TV Raster." Though it is fun to hope that all your animations will be viewed on the best televisions, you must take into account the lowest common denominator, including the 9-inch black and white television. Always frame your work slightly inside the frame of the layout screen to avoid cutting off any important information.

For motion picture work, there is no safe area function for the various aspect ratios. Turning on the "safe areas" display shows an example of television, or action, safe (the outer lines) and title safe (the inner lines). Television safe is the area of picture that is visible on most television sets. Actually, larger monitors will display an area greater than suggested by the larger box. The smaller box, title safe, is the suggested widest framing for any title information, such as a logo or credit. Note that you can only see the safe areas when viewing your scene through the **Camera** view.

By activating the **Letterbox** function (Camera panel), a set of dotted lines will appear on the layout screen to approximate 1:85 aspect for standard 35mm theatrical film (the LightWave letterbox function is actually a 2-to-1 ratio). This wide-screen aspect ratio is the standard projected size for 35mm film. The number actually means a unit of 1 in height by 1.85 units in width. By using a special lens on the production camera, the photographed imaged can be squeezed to a predetermined size, which, when projected through a similar lens that unsqueezes the image, creates the much larger 2:35 aspect ratio, describing a frame 1 unit in height by 2.35 units wide. This is what is commonly referred to as anamorphic or Cinemascope. Films that are shot on 35mm film but intended for release in 70mm are usually shot in anamorphic. The Letterbox function simulates the 1:85 aspect ratio, but remember to shut this function off before rendering your shot since this setting will draw black bars on the top and bottom of the frame.

When scanning to film, the entire frame of film is exposed. The wide-screen look is produced by sliding a matte behind the lens of the theatre projector, not by limiting the area exposed on the film frame. If this matte was removed, you would see additional information (probably the top of the set, a boom microphone, a crew member hanging out, etc.). It is important to provide the film scanning service with a full frame of information.

Motion picture film projected at 24 frames per second (fps) displays a single frame for 1/24 of a second, relying on persistence of vision to carry viewers to the next frame. Video, however, works in a slightly different way. Played at 30 fps, each video frame is displayed not once, but twice. A frame is comprised of two "alternate line" fields of information. For smoother video animations, you should use **Field Rendering**, with which you effectively get 60 images per second as opposed to 30. This will definitely give you a smoother, yet still video-looking, effect. If you are trying to avoid a video look, stay away from field rendering.

Depth of Field has been discussed many times in this newsletter, and I will save my analysis for a future column. It is important to note, however, that LightWave depth of field does not function in the exact way real-world depth of field does. Though LightWave is based on values found when using a real camera and lens, there is no correlation between the amount of light in your scene and the depth of field.

As described in most technical manuals, Depth of Field is a direct correlation between the amount of light reaching the film plane, the size of the aperture opening and the size of the lens. To break it down to basics: the smaller your aperture (and the larger your F-Stop), the greater the depth of field (more in focus); the wider your opening (smaller F-Stop), the less depth of field (less in focus). In addition, the longer the lens (greater the zoom factor), the less depth of field; the wider the lens, the greater the depth of field.

Many fashion photographers strive for as little depth of field as possible. To achieve this, they use extremely long lenses (e.g., 1000mm) and use as little light as possible, forcing them to open the aperture extremely wide (e.g., F1.3). The combination, as you might predict, creates a very small zone of focus, sometimes as little as a few inches, thus creating a softening effect that works well with more artistic photography. Make sure to experiment with your settings before final rendering to avoid any unnecessary surprises. Keep in mind that a wide aperture means a smaller F-Stop number and a decreased focus zone. A small aperture means a larger number and a larger area of focus. Also note that a background image is not affected by depth of field.

Many of the functions discussed above relate directly to compositing rather than pure CGI images. Though full computer-generated images will always play a huge role in the effects world, the exciting new frontier is in compositing with live action. You may not believe it, but you own an extremely professional and powerful compositing tool already: LightWave 3D.

At Amblin Imaging, we have begun immersing ourselves in some very involved composite shots over the recent months. Though we have experimented with many other software packages, we usually return to LightWave for most of our work. Like Amblin, it is in your best interest to stay as close to the cutting edge as possible with your abilities. Pick up books on motion picture production and buy the occasional *American Cinematographer* magazine. Though your interests may not be in photography, expanding your knowledge of the techniques will only enhance your ability to create.

LWP

After graduating from the University of Southern California's School of Cinema/Television, John F.K. Parenteau began his career as a cinematographer for motion pictures and television. Discovering computer graphics in 1991, he quickly found the versatility of visual design lacking on live action sets. Parenteau is currently vice president and general manager of Amblin Imaging, and one of the digital effects supervisors for seaQuest DSV.

See the Light

Faking Volumetric Lighting, Part I

by Alan Chan

Being the digital visionaries we are, we all remember, sometime in our past, seeing that one marvelous sunrise that was actually worth a thousand words. That wonderful, warm, glowing ball of plasma, under a slight staccato of clouds, brushing away the cold of the night, the rays of the sun shimmering in the golden air...

As you sit outside on your lawn, LightWave running on the laptop in your hand, you wonder what causes that magnificent display. Particles in the air, you conclude. The rays of the sun are reflected from particles in the air and into your eyes, making the rays appear brighter than the other areas. And as the clouds shift and move, they block out the rays of the sun from some particles and reveal others. It is this Brownian movement that creates the marvelous display of shimmering rays of light.

Hmmm—rays of the sun, huh? Shimmering rays of light. That's just what I need to spice up my flying logo, you think. But how do you go about doing it? Well, short of going out and shooting a frame of it as a background image, you could try a couple of different techniques.

Volumetric Schmolumetric

The 3D-ish techie animator's term for "rays of light" is Volumetric Lighting. Simply put, the presence of particles in the air (smoke, for instance) intersecting with the path of a lightbeam gives it the illusion of having volume, hence the term "volumetric." The more interesting side effect of this phenomenon is that if an object travels within this "volume" of light, it casts long visible shadows in the air. Imagine a volumetric light behind a logo, casting shimmering rays across your screen, and you can see why volumetric effects can sometimes be an effective element in your animation.

We cannot fake volumetric lighting with LightWave by brute force alone. It is theoretically possible to simply fill the scene with millions of half-transparent particles and let them pick up the light, but you'd probably run way out of memory, and your render times would go through the roof (and your neighbor's as well). So let's be smart. Let's only quantify the *edges* of any given volume, where the light meets the shadow. What am I talking about? We'll go through some tutorials, and hopefully the meaning of what I just said will become more apparent through some hands-on work.

The Tutorials

There are several ways of faking volumetric lighting, and in your eventual use of it you will be utilizing some, or all, of the following techniques, depending on light and camera positions, what happens in your animation and what you want to achieve. In rough order of complexity, they are:

(1) Visible lightbeams and oscillating lightbeams

(2) Shimmering logo shadows

(3) Objects with volumetric shadows

The key to good volumetric lighting is a firm grasp of the basic foundations of lighting and surface settings mimicking volumetric shadows, so this month we'll spend our time understanding the concepts and creating some lightbeams. Next month, after you've had some time to play with your ideas and everything's started to soak in, we'll tackle shimmering logos and volumetric shadows. As a primer, you may also want to re-read John Gross's article on creating realistic lightbeams, called "Spotlight On Reality," in the July 1994 issue of *LIGHTWAVEPRO.*

Let's begin.

(1) Visible Lightbeams/Oscillating Lightbeams

The first part, the visible lightbeam, is easily achieved. In fact, there is a lightbeam object included in the Objects drawer of your LightWave package, based on a concept courtesy of the honorable Mark Thompson, of Fusion Films fame. Revisiting this object provides the basic principles we need.

Load up the object (found in Objects/Tutorial/Lightbeam.obj), keyframe it so that its length is visible and test render a frame. Then examine the surface settings. Note the surface parameters on the lightbeam cone:

Surface Color	255,245,180
Luminosity	0%
Luminosity Texture Type:	Grid
Texture Falloff:	0,0,34.0
Texture Value:	85%
Line Thickness:	1.0
Additive	On
Diffuse Level	0%
Edge Transparency	Transparent
Edge Threshold	1.0
Smoothing	On
DoubleSided	On

All other values are at their default.

The two critical items on this list are the **Luminosity** texture and the **Edge Transparency.** The Luminosity texture here (Figure 1) is in fact a grid texture, but where's the grid? Notice that the line thickness of the grid is 1.0, which means that the grid lines

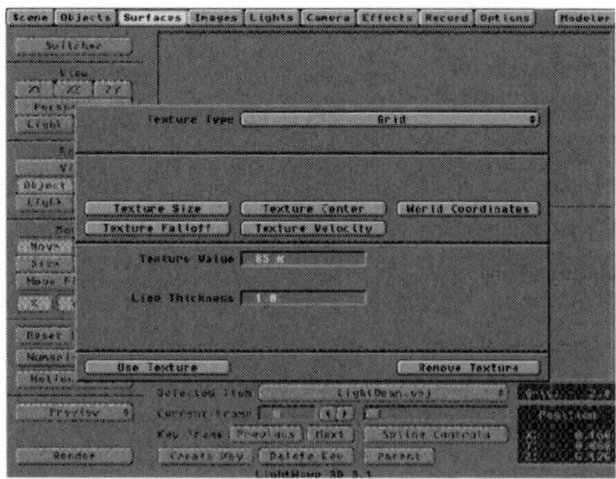

Figure 1: The Luminosity Grid Texture panel

are in fact so thick that they touch end to end and form a uniform surface. This crucial fact now allows us to add a **Texture Falloff** value to the texture, causing it to gradate slowly from 85% (from the **Texture Value** setting) to 0% (the setting on the main **Surfaces** panel) along the length of the light beam. Note that **Texture Falloff** values are noted in percentages over one unit (usually one meter in Layout), which means that a falloff value of 25, for instance, will cause a 100% luminous surface to gradate to the main surface panel setting for Luminosity (default: 0%) over four meters. Therefore, the settings described above designate a lightbeam that is 85% luminous at its source, slowly fading away to darkness in a little under three units. The **Additive** button then instructs LightWave to treat this surface not as a normal opaque surface, but as an additive function, where the computed surface

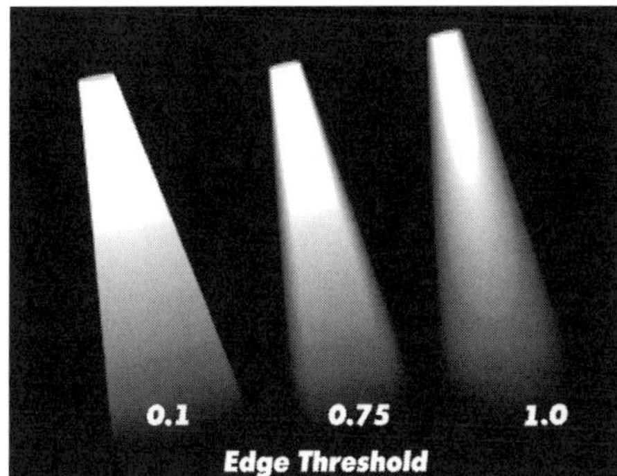

Figure 2: Lightbeams with differing edge threshold values

values are simply added to the RGB values behind the additive surface (like a lens flare).

Note that the **Edge Transparency** is set to **Transparent.** This makes the edges of the light cone transparent, giving it more of an ethereal quality. The sharpness of the transparency is varied by changing the **Edge Threshold** value. Figure 2 illustrates the effects of different edge threshold values. Note that values above 1.0 or below 0 do not make any additional effects.

Lightbeams 102

Now, with basic lighting behind us, let's try something a little harder. Like an oscillating lightbeam, the effect you'd get if you tried to shine a huge spotlight through a clump of trees. For this we'll need to go into our favorite paint program and make up a texture map such as the one in Figure 3. We'll save this as "Cookie.iff." (The term for a shape, or cutout pattern, used to make patterns with lights is a "cucaloris," or cookie for short.)

Now we'll replace the grid pattern with the cookie pattern, so that the alternating light and dark patches affect different parts of the lightbeam's luminosity. Make the texture move and you'll have shifting light-streaks, yes? Ah, but if it were only that easy. Sorry. First we have to map the texture along the length of the lightcone, for which we'll fall back on one of the earlier LightWave morph tricks (a variation of a Mojo-of-*Babylon 5* trick).

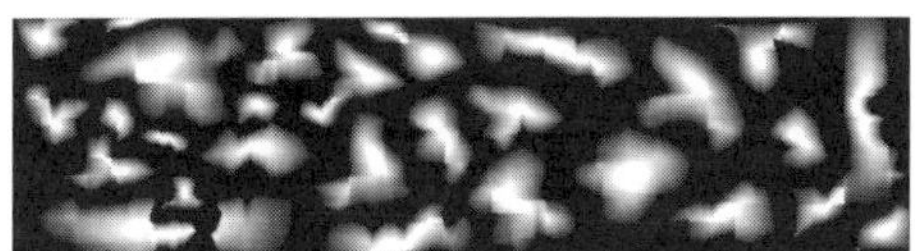
Figure 3: An IFF file used as a cutout pattern

- Begin by going into Modeler and, using the Disc tool, extruding a cylinder, making sure that the center of one of the ends of the cylinder is at 0,0,0. For this example, let's extrude a cylinder four meters in length. Select both disc polygons at either end of the cylinder (Figure 4) and cut them off, leaving just a hollow tube. Set the surface name of this object to "OscLightSurface" and save, then load it in Layout. (Amiga users can export it to Layout). Call this object "OscBeam.lwo."

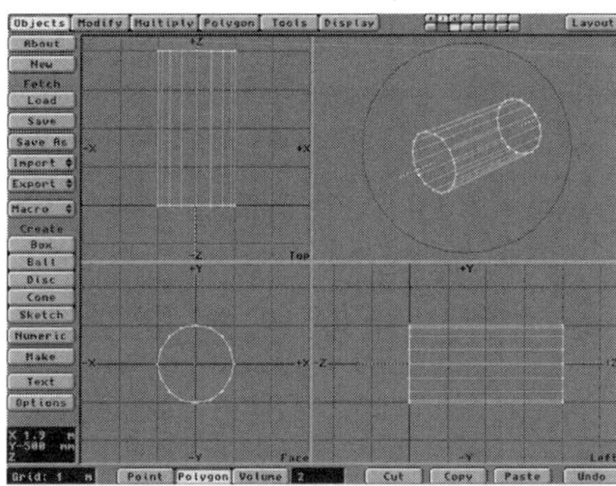
Figure 4: Preparing to cut off the ends of the lightbeam cylinder

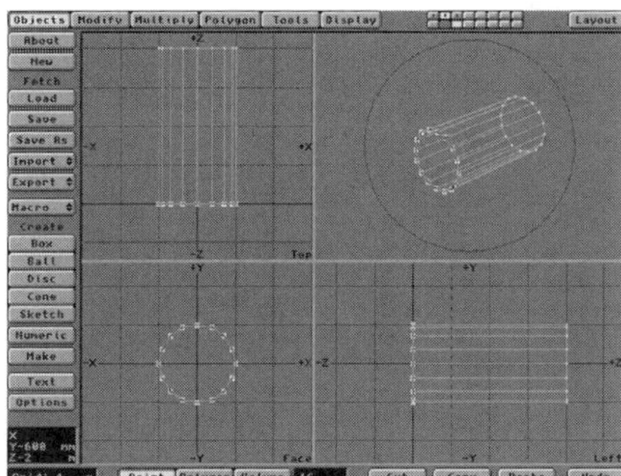
Figure 5: Selecting points on the zero plane

- Select all the points of the cylinder that sit on the zero Z plane (Figure 5) and hit (Shift+H) for the **Size** tool. Click on the **Numeric** button and enter the following values into the requester:

  Size Factor: 0

  Center XYZ: 0,0,0
- Hit OK. You will see that all the points you selected are now converged at the 0,0,0 point, and we have, once again, a cone representing a lightbeam. Do not use **Merge** Points on this object! Simply bring it to Layout as a new object, calling this one "OscBeamMorph.lwo."
- Returning to Layout, enter the following values for the surface "OscLightSurface":

Surface Color	255,245,180
Luminosity	0%
Luminosity Texture Type:	Grid
Texture Falloff:	0,0,25.0
Texture Value:	85%
Line Thickness:	1.0
Additive	On
Diffuse Level	0%
Transparency Texture Type:	Planar Image Map
Texture Image:	Cookie.iff
Texture Axis:	Z Axis
Automatic Sizing	On
Texture Center:	0,0,0
Texture Velocity:	0,0.02,0
Edge Transparency:	Transparent
Edge Threshold:	1.0
Smoothing	On
DoubleSided	On

- From the Objects menu, make the OscBeamMorph.lwo object 100% dissolved. Then select OscBeam.lwo as the current object, and enter these settings into the Metamorph section of the **Objects** menu:

Metamorph Target:	OscBeammorph.lwo
Metamorph Level:	100%

Figure 6: The completed oscillating lightbeam

Morph Surfaces: Off

- You will note that the OscBeam object has now turned into a cone. This is good. Set a keyframe and test render a frame (Figure 6).

What did we do? We texture-mapped the cookie luminosity map to create streaks down the length of the cylinder, then we morphed that cylinder into a cone so that the streaks would look as if they were originating from the point of the cone. Over time, the cookie texture slowly moves through the surface, causing the oscillating effect. Render a test anim and see for yourself.

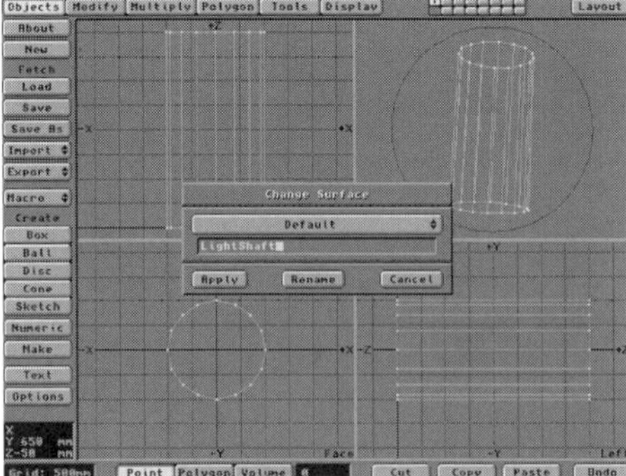

Figure 7: Creating a shaft of light in Modeler

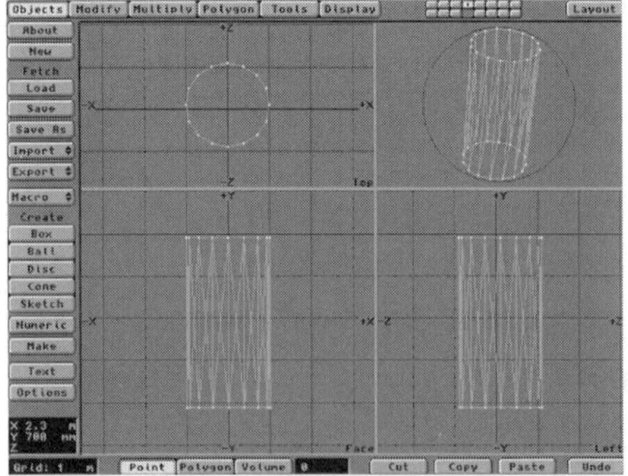

Figure 8 :The OscBeam object with tripled polygons

This sort of oscillating light source is best used in conjunction with other elements, such as tree objects or foliage. For instance, if you set up a tree scene, parent a light to the tip of the lightcone and move it, you'll have what looks like a lightbeam rifling through the trees. For further realism you could set a dissolve envelope on the lightbeam to cause it to be occasionally occulted by tree fauna.

As with anything of complexity, there are some limitations to this technique, but they are not impossible to work around. For instance, it can be very effective when this lightbeam is pointed toward the camera, but because of its falloff settings, the apparent intensity diminishes dramatically. To increase the intensity, you can either increase the Luminosity **Texture Value** of OscLightSurface (the maximum limit is 400% in 4.0), or, if that's still not enough, parent a second light cone to your first. The second option, of course, adds to your overall render times.

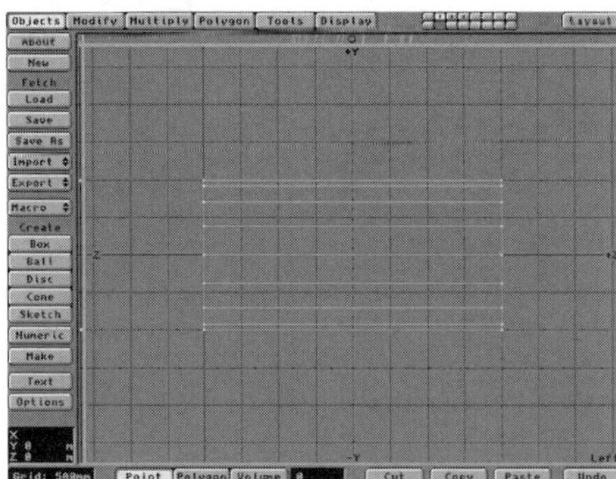

Figure 9a: The Shaft object before a 90-degree rotation

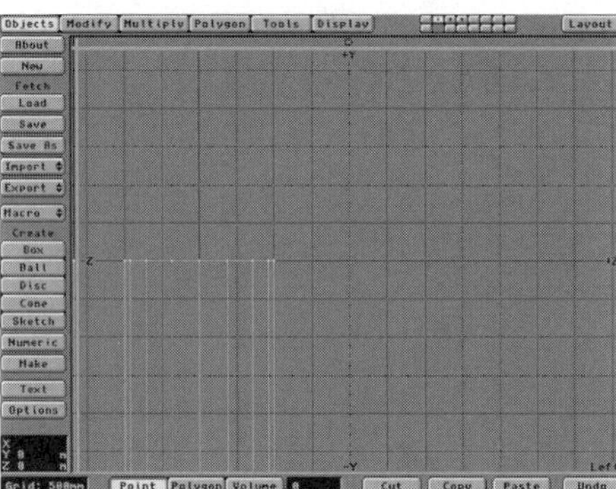

Figure 9b: The Shaft object after a 90-degree rotation

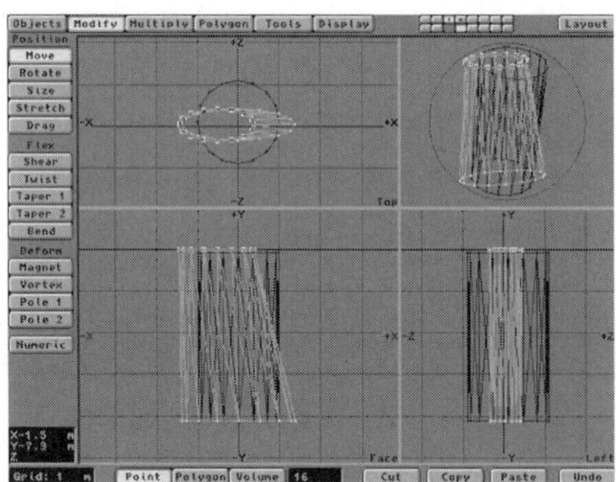

Figure 10: The morphed version of the shaft object

Getting the Shaft

Armed with this concept it is possible to extend it a step further, and construct another variation on volumetric lighting: the shaft of light that pierces a dark, dusty environment, say in a mining tunnel, or the abandoned house with the derelict roof letting in slivers of light. Instead of a cone, simply extrude the shape needed and use that instead.

- In Figure 7, I went back into Modeler and reloaded the OscBeam/lwo object. After changing the surface name to "LightShaft," I rotated the entire object by hitting (r) while the cursor was located at the crosshairs in the Left view (Figures 9a and 9b). This orients the lightbeam in the Y axis. Finally, I went to the Polygon menu and tripled the polygons (Figure 8). This object was then saved as "Shaft.lwo."
- Next, the points of the top and the bottom of the cylinder, respectively, were selected, and using the Stretch tool (**Modify** menu), I pulled and stretched the cylinder into an oval shape (Figure 10). This shape was then saved and loaded in Layout as "ShaftMorph.lwo."
- Again, I made the ShaftMorph.lwo object 100% dissolved, and made it the **Metamorph Target** for the Shaft object. The Shaft object should be set to 100% morphed without **Morph Surfaces** on.
- From the Surfaces menu, I applied the following surface settings to the "Lightshaft" surface:

Surface Color	255,245,180
Luminosity	0%
Luminosity Texture Type:	Grid
Texture Falloff:	0,0,25.0
Texture Value:	60%
Line Thickness:	1.0
Additive	On
Diffuse Level	0%
Transparency Texture Type:	Planar Image Map
Texture Image:	Cookie.iff
Texture Axis:	Y Axis
Automatic Sizing	
Texture Center:	0,0,0
Texture Velocity:	0,0,0
Edge Transparency	Transparent
Edge Threshold	1.0
Smoothing	On
DoubleSided	On

- Finally, I keyframed with the thin edge facing the camera and test rendered. For a more realistic look you may want to remove the cookie pattern, or add a slight Fractal Noise as a Surface Color texture. Add World Coordinates and a very slight Texture Velocity to simulate particles in the air, such as you would see swimming around in a bright shaft of light.

Combined with proper lighting, this technique can be quite convincing.

LWP

Alan Chan is volumetrically light in the head. Be nice and send him e-mail at alan.chan@oubbs.telecom.uoknor.edu, or call Vision Digital at (405) 447-7075.

Lords of Light

Faking Volumetric Lighting, Part II

by Alan Chan

In my many years of production work, I have never heard a more descriptive, tantalizing definition of what cinematographers are than Lords of Light. It is the director of photography (DP)'s job to tell the story with images. Painting with light is much more than setting a key, a fill and a rim light. It is a craft fine-tuned by a lifetime of experience.

We are all in the business of images, and the line between real and CG images is already a thin, blurry one. Just like a cinematographer, our computers give us the ability to paint with light. And just like a cinematographer, it will take us a lifetime to learn all the ins and outs.

LightWave animators are, perhaps, the digital equivalent of the cinematographer (and much more). As such, a good understanding of lighting theory is a big plus. (If you haven't given much thought to lighting in your animations yet, I suggest you start as soon as possible.) The tips and tutorials in parts I and II of this article work best in the hands of those who integrate them into a well-thought-out lighting scheme. In the end, it's all in the lighting.

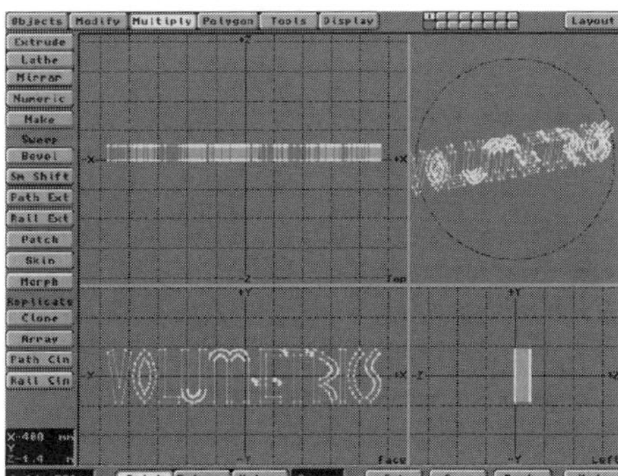

Figure 1: The logo to be extruded

Last month we looked at re-creating beam spotlights and using cut-out patterns to shape the beam. This month we'll push on further and examine some methods of faking volumetric shadows.

Volumetric Logo Shadows

Now that you've got the basics down through last month's article, the next little step must be to create the shimmering logo shadow. Whether you're going for the extra-realistic or the hyper-real artsy look, the basic construction is the same. The difference lies in the surfacing. Let's go through a quick session on building the object, then explore several different options and ways of surfacing. The trick to volumetric shadows is that you have to understand what each setting does, and how they interact with every other little setting to achieve the look you want, rather than just a standard, "click-on-Volumetric-setting-and-render" generic look. So pay attention.

Basic Construction

As I mentioned earlier, in faking volumetric shadows we are concerned with the edges of the given volume. Creating volumetric lighting for flying logos, is somewhat simple. Because most logos are essentially 2D in nature, we can use the outline of the logo itself to create the shadow shape.

Let's say, for instance, that you've scanned in or created, using the Text tool, the following 2D logo (Figure 1), and then extruded the logo to give it some depth.

- Make sure the front face of the logo is at Z = 0 (assuming, of course, that you're building it in the Z axis).
- Using the right mouse key, lasso-select all the polygons on the front face, and copy and paste them in a different layer (Figure 2). Extrude this in the -Z direction, away from the logo itself, a distance sufficient to your needs. (I usually extrude the object about 25 to 30 times the extruded length of the logo.) This will be our volumetric "shadow edge." Select the polygons at either end of the extrusion and cut them away, which again leaves a hollow object in the shape of the logo (Figure 3).

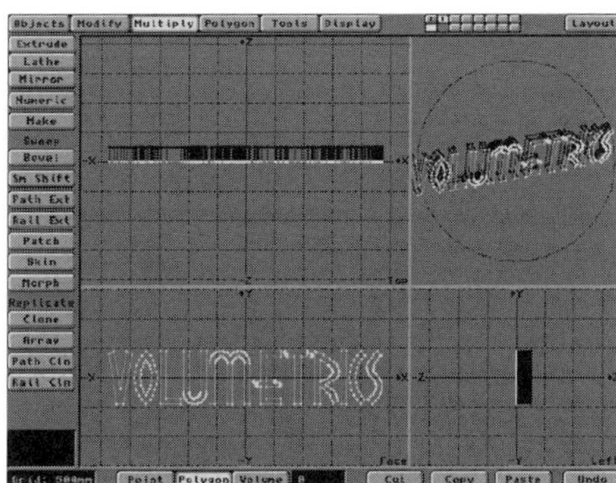

Figure 2: Copying the front face to a new layer

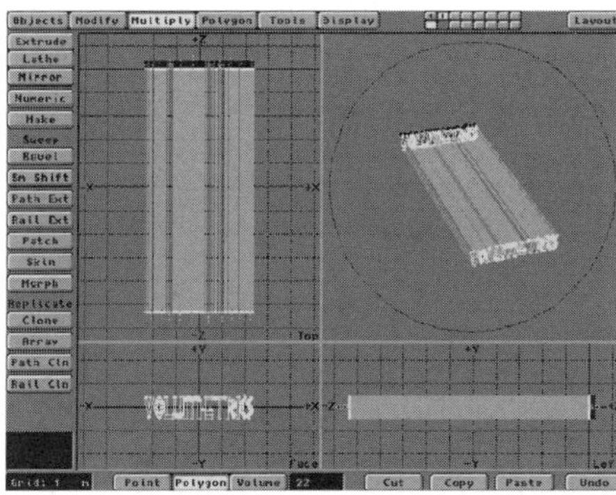

Figure 3: The extruded shadow edge

- One final thing: make sure the lightbeam polygons are facing inward. If they're not, select all the polygons and perform a Flip function (Polygon menu) on them. That way, when the lightbeam is rendered, only the edge furthest away from the camera point of view is rendered. Give the surface a name and export it to Layout. Make sure to parent the volumetric lightbeam object to your logo.

You now have a volumetric object ready to surface!

The Realistic Look

The realistic look presupposes a lightsource behind the object and a sort of hazy (read: foggy) day, so you might want to begin by adding a little fog to your scene if you have objects in the background as well. Figure 4 shows an example of a realistic volumetric lighting scene. For this scene, the surface settings for the lightbeam object are as follows:

Surface Color	9,10,20
Luminosity	100%
Diffuse Level	0%
Transparency	0%

Figure 4: An example of volumetric shadows

Transparency Texture	
Texture Type	Grid
Texture Falloff	0,0,10.0
Texture Value	75%
Line Thickness	1.0
Edge Transparency	Transparent
Edge Threshold	2.5
Smoothing	On
Double Sided	Off

In addition to the streaks of light, two flares named FlareStreaks and FlareGlow were parented to a null object to provide the "practical" light source:

FlareStreaks	
Flare Intensity	200%
Flare Dissolve	70%
Central Glow	On
Red Outer Glow	Off
Glow Behind Objects	On
Central Ring	Of
Random Streaks	On
Anamorphic Squeeze	On
FlareGlow	
Flare Intensity	300%
Flare Dissolve	0%
Central Glow	On
Red Outer Glow	Off
Glow Behind Objects	On
Central Ring	Off
Random Streaks	Off
Anamorphic Squeeze	On

(all other settings are left at their default values)

FlareStreaks is 70% dissolved to provide just a hint of lightstreaks, whereas FlareGlow is the primary flare in this combination. Using multiple flares gives precise control over certain parameters—in this case the slight random streaks effect, which would be too overbearing if we only had one flare control.

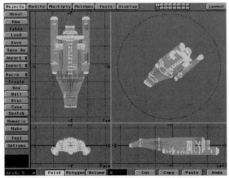

Figure 5: The spaceship object loaded into Modeler

Note that the volumetric surfaces for this scene work to the contrary of the additive process that we've been doing with the lightbeams tutorial. The surface color is very close to black, and in conjunction with the bright background flare, works almost like a subtractive process, darkening the shadow areas. (It's "deleting" light instead of adding it, which, if you think in terms of real volumetric shadows, is scientifically accurate.) Also, the transparency settings are flip-flopped. The transparency of the shadows actually begins at 75% near the logo and gets progressively more opaque the further away it gets, which is technically incorrect. However, for our camera angle this inaccuracy is unnoticeable and actually more aesthetically pleasing.

The Artsy Shadow

For our animated company logo we made a decision not to have the logo do any sort of fly-in. We opted instead for exaggerated lens flares and an art-nouveau type of volumetric shadow (see color pages). The surface settings are:

Surface Color	0,60,200
Surface Color Texture	
Texture Type	Fractal Noise
Texture Size	0.05,1.0,1.0
World Coordinates	On
Texture Color	229,197,45
Frequencies	3
Contrast	0.5
Luminosity	100%
Diffuse Level	0%
Transparency Texture	
Texture Type	Planar Image Map
Texture Image	Cookie.iff
Texture Axis	Z Axis
Automatic Sizing	
Texture Velocity	0.007,1.0,1.0
Edge Transparency	Transparent
Edge Threshold	0.15
Smoothing	On

Note that the transparency values here contain a very slight velocity setting to cause a slow movement of the texture across the shadow object. Also, with the surface color texture set to Fractal Noise and World Coordinates, a patchy-smoky look is added.

Objects in the Particle Stream

When I began writing this article I asked members of the LightWave mailing list on the Internet for specific examples of volumetric lighting. One of the requests I got was to achieve something similar to the final shot in the *Star Trek: Voyager* opening sequence, where the neighborhood sun flares up and floods all of space with volumetric light. (Yeah, well, we all know that don't happen in space, pardner.) The lighting effect for that sequence was generated by Santa Barbara Studios using another software package, but we can easily achieve this effect in LightWave using some of the concepts from last month's article.

- Begin by loading up your favorite spaceship object into Modeler. If you're like me and you built your craft with several different movable parts, you'll need to load the objects into Layout, use Save Transformed and load all the transformed objects into one layer so they are all in their relative positions (Figure 5). Remember, however, to reset your position, rotation and scale for your main parent object first, to ensure that your shadow edges can be easily matched up later.

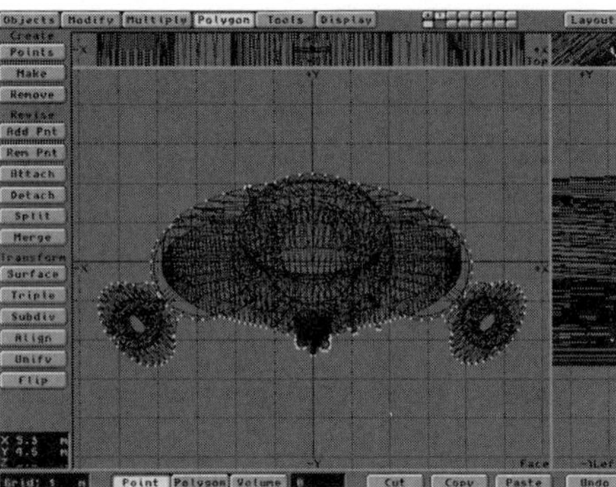

Figure 6: Points comprising the outer edge of the ship

Now, when you picture the shot in your mind, note that the shadow extends directly forward, from the bow of the ship. This makes it a little easier for us, since we can simply extend the shape of the ship to create our shadow edge. (OK, so the shadows are at a slight angle. Let's keep it simple for now.)

- Load your ship or your Save Transformed pieces into one layer in Modeler. The Z axis will be the one to extend our shadow edge in, so expand the XY view and select all the points that are on the outer edge of your ship object.
- Cut and paste them in a different layer, which will form the basis of our shadow edge object (Figure 6). If your object is too complex you may want to delete every other point, since your shadow edge object doesn't have to be as detailed as your ship, and depending on camera distance, doesn't have to be precise. For most cases, the camera has to be a fair distance away anyway so that you keep the volumetric effect in frame.
- For the next part we'll need to use some common sense. Upon examination of the points in the scene, we can see we've pulled off more points than are necessary: points that are duplicated in the Z axis, points representing "nurnies" (a Ron Thornton word for the little tubes and whatnot sticking out on spaceships) and such. By exercising a little common sense and consideration, we can decide which nurnie points can be deleted and where the shadow edge for our ship object should begin.

In this spaceship example, there are several basic areas and depths that we can determine after a study of the locations of the points: the body of the ship itself, the two side thruster units (nacelles) and the support arms connecting the thrusters to the ship's body. In Figure 7, note that the group of points in groups (1) and (4) are indicative of the main body, group (2) represents the support arms, and groups (3) and (5) are from the thrusters. To simplify the shadow edge, we'll need to collapse the points onto a single plane, which ideally should be the frontmost edge of that particular group.

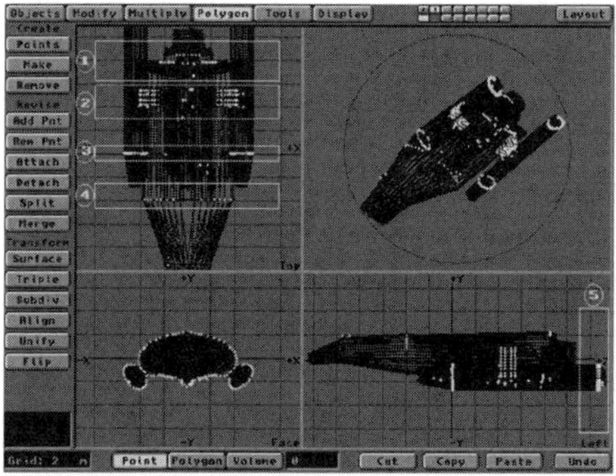

Figure 7: Point groups for the shadow edge

Collapsing Points

In looking at groups (3) and (5), we determine that the shadow edge should be at the front tip of the thruster, just before it begins to taper off.

- Selecting a random point from that tip, hit the (I) key. An Information panel pops up (Figure 8). Note the Z coordinate value for this point—in this example, it is 0.0302. Next, select all the points in groups (3) and (5) and hit (H) to Size. Click on the Numeric button and enter the following values in the requester:

  X Factor: 1
  Y Factor: 1
  Z Factor: 1
  X Center: 0
  Y Center: 0
  Z Center: 0.0302 (the value we retrieved from the Information panel)

- Hit OK, and all the selected points will collapse onto the front edge of the group. Do a Merge Points function (m) immediately, to eliminate any excess points. Repeat this procedure for group (2), then for groups (1) and (4). Note that the main body of the ship tapers off from the very rear of the ship, so the shadow edge begins almost from the rear (Figure 9).

Figure 8: Information giving us the value for the Z axis

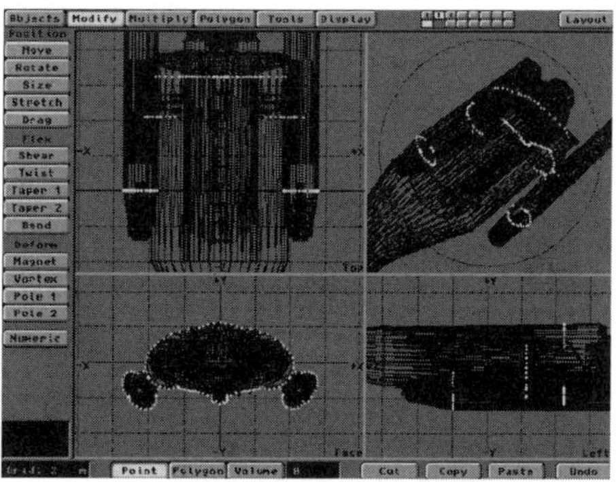

Figure 9: Point groups collapsed onto respective planes

Creating the Shadow Edge

Once we've cleaned up the points, we'll begin using them to make the shadow edge. Select the XY view again, and begin selecting points in order to create a polygon or polygons that encompass all your points (Figure 10). Because of the differing depths of our points, some of these polygons will be grossly non-planar and corrupt, but that's OK, as they are only the means to an end.

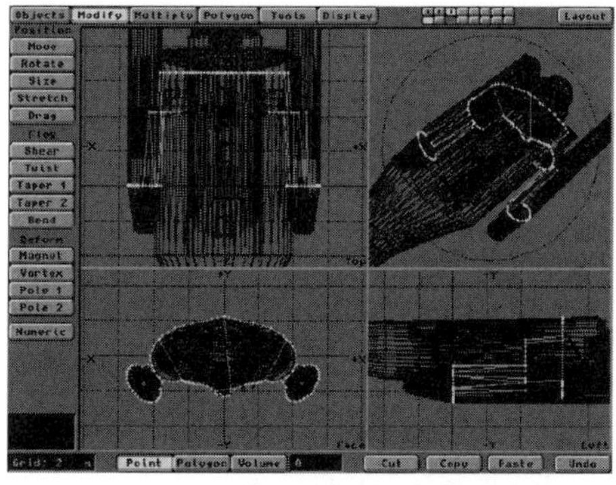

Figure 10: Points to polygons for the shadow edge

- Select the polygons at both ends of the shadow edge object and delete them, leaving your ship with a nice, hollow shadow edge. (Notice in Figure 11 that I'm a neat freak and had to collapse the far end of the shadow edge. This step isn't necessary.) Name the surface "Shipshadow" and Export your object to Layout.

In the Surfaces panel, select "Shipshadow" as the current surface and enter these surface settings:

Shipshadow surface

Surface Color	9,10,20
Luminosity	100%
Diffuse Level	0%
Transparency Texture	
Texture Type	Planar Image Map
Texture Image	Cookie.iff
Texture Axis	Z Axis
Automatic Sizing	
Texture Falloff	0,0,15.0
Texture Velocity	0.01,0.03,0
Edge Transparency	Transparent
Edge Threshold	0.7
Smoothing	On
Double Sided	On

- Save the shadow edge object again and parent it to your spaceship.

You now have a column of shadow edge extending from your ship. Using a dissolve envelope on the shadow column, we will be able to throw a volumetric shadow in time with our lens flares..

Building the Scene

To achieve believable CGI effects shots, you must be able to break any given scene down into its simplest elements. Our volumetric shadow works best only in certain circumstances, so we must accommodate its shortcomings and work around them.

In breaking down the sequence, I noted that I would need at least two lens flares to achieve the effect we are after. One of the flares must have Glow Behind Objects activated to provide the background flare behind the ship object. The other flare provides additional flare intensity and a central ring. Most importantly, with Glow Behind Objects turned off, the flare renders in front of the ship and shadow object, providing a flare "bleed" characteristic of lights in a fog.

Upon test rendering, however, I decided to give the flare a more prominent "hotspot" by simply adding one more flare.

The following flares were thus parented to a null and positioned behind the moon object (which, incidentally, is not to scale), and their values ramped up as the moon slides out of the way. Simultaneously, our dissolve envelope for the shadow edge is also ramped down from 100% dissolve to 0% dissolve so that the shadow edge is only visible at the time of the flare. After some test renders, these were the final values I settled on:

Light Name	SunGlowBehind
Light Color	255, 247, 214
Light Intensity	0.0%
Lens Flare Options	
Central Glow	On
Glow Behind Objects	On
(all other settings off)	
Flare Dissolve	0%
Flare Intensity Envelope Keyframes:	
Frame 0	70%, tension 0.86
Frame 54	140%, tension -0.21
Frame 67	300%, tension 0.96
Frame 77	290%, tension 0.27
Frame 150	70%, tension 1.0
Light Name	SunFlare
Light Color	255, 247, 214
Light Intensity	0.0%
Lens Flare Options	
Central Glow	On
Central Ring	On
(all other settings off)	
Flare Dissolve Envelope Keyframes:	

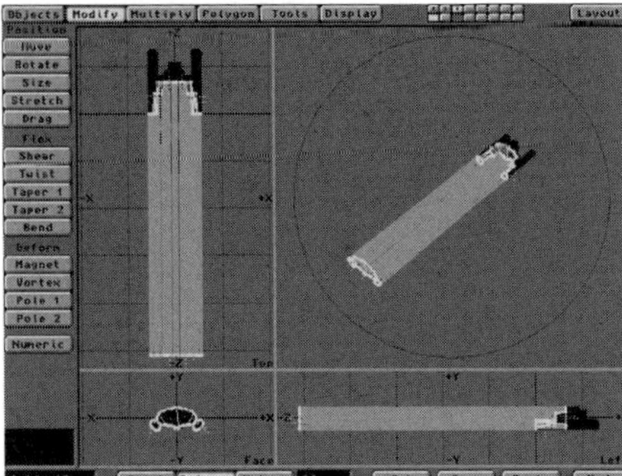

Figure 11: The extruded shadow edge

Frame 0	0%, tension 0.0
Frame 54	0%, tension 1.0
Frame 67	30%, tension 0.96
Frame 84	28%, tension 0.0
Frame 153	0%, tension 1.0
Flare Intensity Envelope Keyframes:	
Frame 0	0%, tension 0.33
Frame 54	10%, tension 0.75
Frame 67	300%, tension 0.96
Frame 80	290%, tension 0.27
Frame 153	70%, tension 1.0
Light Name	SunHotSpot
Light Color	255, 247, 214
Light Intensity	0.0%
Lens Flare Options	
Central Glow	On
Central Ring	On
(all other settings off)	
Flare Dissolve	0%
Flare Intensity Envelope Keyframes:	
Frame 0	0%, tension 0.45
Frame 54	2.5%, tension 0.86
Frame 67	105%, tension 0.96
Frame 82	105%, tension 0.27
Frame 153	35%, tension 1.0

Integrating The Background

One major drawback of this method is that the shadow edge works best against an empty space. If you try to add an object behind it, say a planet, the illusion of subtractive light is destroyed. (Try it and see.) A solution is to render the background elements separately and composite them into the scene, making sure to dissolve the background out at the peak of the flare. For our example, I simply attached a Dissolve Envelope to our background stars object and matched the dissolve to the flare. Figure 12 shows a rendered frame from the peak of the flare.

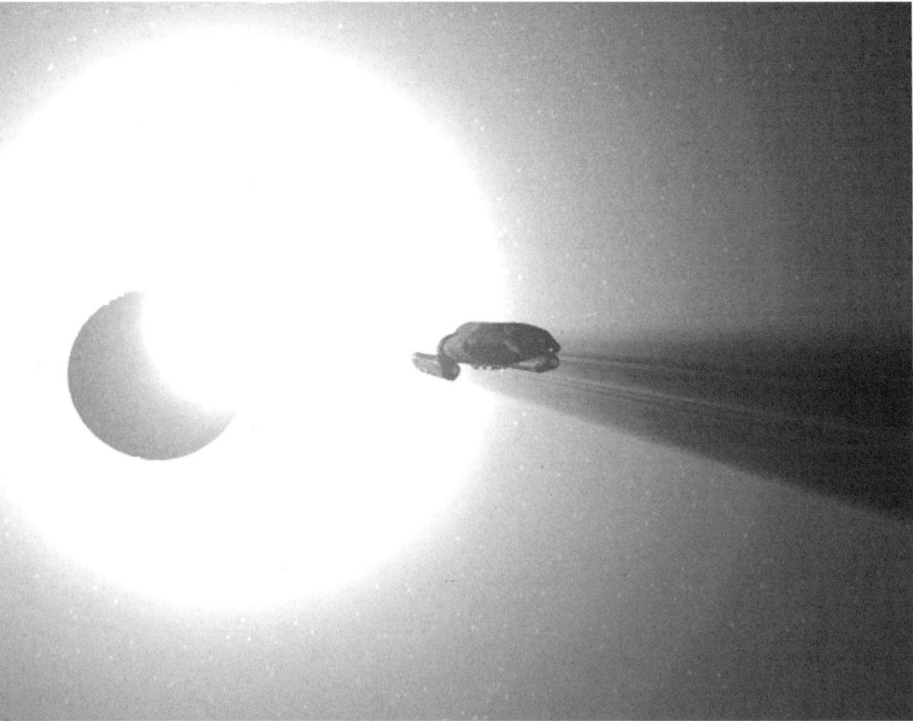

Figure 12: The results of the volumetric shadow edge

Trek On

Now that you're knee-deep in volumetric waters, take some time and try some more advanced tricks. Here are a few suggestions.

- Shadow Edges off of the axis: Estimate the angle and rotate your object in Modeler, taking care to note the exact amount of rotation on each axis. Copy your points and extrude. Export to Layout, surface, parent to object and enter negative rotation values for the shadow edge keyframe.
- Glow Behind Objects: Note that the Glow Behind Objects option renders the flare parallel to the visual plane—that is, if your flare is the same distance from the camera as another object, the flare will appear to cut through the object. You might wish to use this to your advantage. Remember that a Glow Behind Flare cannot be located between an opaque object and a transparent object. In this case, the transparent object will be rendered solid while in front of the glow behind.
- Custom Cookies: Aside from using a standard cutout pattern, consider using individual cookie patterns for different projects. Use a paint program to create gradients and slices to integrate into your shadow edges. You may one to consider animated patterns as well.

Every shot is different and every effect requires a new approach. Hopefully, these concepts will inspire you not just to re-create this effect, but to experiment and come up with your own examples of volumetric lighting. As we stand on the bleeding edge of the digital future and stare out at the glorious sunrise that started all this volumetric thought, just remember these words an ancient sage once said: it takes vision to create.

Alan Chan is having digital visions again. Be nice and e-mail him at alan.chan@oubbs.telecom.uoknor.edu, or call Vision Digital at (405) 447-707

Spotlight on Reality

by John Gross

You've seen spotlights in commercials and Movie of the Week intros, but how are they created?

Since LightWave light sources do not actually display 'beams' of light, one must build and surface any beam of light to be shown. The following step-by-step tutorial shows how to build and surface a beam of light that can be used in any animation.

The Model

- In Modeler, create a **Disc** using the **Numeric** requester (**Objects** panel) with the following values:

Sides	32
Bottom	0
Top	14
Center	0,0,7
Radii	4,4,7
Units	m

  All other values remain at their default.
- Select the two end polygons of the tube and cut them out. Change the surface name to *OuterBeam* (**q**) for all of the remaining polygons.
- Copy the tube into another layer. Select **Stretch** (**Modify** panel) and input 0.6 for the X and Y Factor values while using the **Numeric** requester Leave the other values at their defaults (make sure units is set to m) and press **OK**. Change the surface name to *InnerBeam* for all of these polygons.
- Select both layers as foreground layers. Choose **Taper 1** (Modify panel), then **Numeric** and select **Z** axis, - Sense and a factor of .05. Leave all other values at their default and make sure that the units is set to m. Click on the **Apply** button to taper the beam at the origin. The finished light beam should look like Figure 1.
- Save the two layers as a single object called *LightBeam* and load it into Layout.
- While in the **Objects** Panel, turn off all three shadow options: **Self Shadow**, **Cast Shadow** and **Receive Shadow** for the LightBeam object. You do not want a beam of light to cast or receive any shadows. Remember that these options apply only to the current scene and are not saved as part of the object.

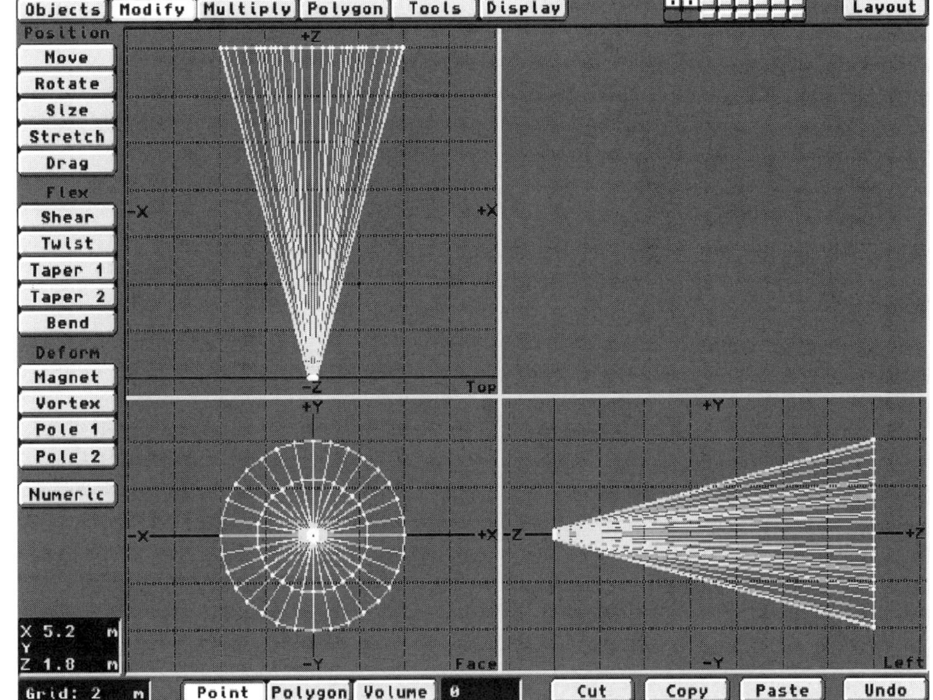

Figure 1

The Surfaces

Next, we will apply some surfacing to our light beam to give it a realistic look. One of the methods used to produce a convincing beam of light is to have the beam fade away at the wide end. We could use a **Transparency** texture falloff, but the problem there is that it will be a linear falloff. Beams of light do not fall off in a linear fashion. They are brighter at the light source, remain fairly bright for a distance and then fade off in an exponential manner. Often the end of the light beam will round off. For these reasons, I recommend that you do not use a transparency texture with a value entered for **Texture Falloff**, but rather an image to re-create the exponential falloff of a light beam.

Figure 2 shows a sample of an image (LightBeamFalloff.Brush) that works to ramp the transparency in a nonlinear fashion. It was created in ToasterPaint using the Range tools and then cropped in ImageFX to create a brush. The image is 224x480 in resolution. The white in the image will make the object completely transparent in those areas.

- Click on the Surfaces button to bring up the Surfaces Panel. You should have two surfaces for the LightBeam object, OuterBeam and InnerBeam. Select the following parameters for the two surfaces:

OuterBeam Surface

Surface Color	220,220,230
Surface Texture Map	
Texture Type	Fractal Noise
Texture Size	1.8,1.8,6.0
Texture Color	185,185,190
Frequencies	3
Contrast	1.0
World Coordinates	On
Luminosity	100%

Figure 2

Diffuse	0%
Transparency Map	
Texture Type	Planar Image Map
Texture Image	LightBeamFalloff.Brush
Texture Axis	Y
Texture Size	8.0,8.0,14.1
Transparent Edges	On
Smoothing	On
Double Sided	On

InnerBeam Surface

Surface Color	225,225,255
Surface Texture Map	
Texture Type	Fractal Noise
Texture Size	1.4,1.4,5.0
Texture Color	190,190,200
Frequencies	3
Contrast	1.0
World Coordinates	On
Luminosity	100%
Diffuse	0%
Transparency Map	
Texture Type	Planar Image Map
Texture Image	LightBeamFalloff.Brush
Texture Axis	Y
Texture Size	4.8,4.8,14.1
Transparent Edges	On
Smoothing	On

- Rotate the beam or change the camera position so you can get a good look at the beam and do a test render (don't forget to set key frames).

The beam looks pretty good, but we're not quite done. If you need to shine the light on anything, you'll need to have an actual light source to do it with.

- From the Lights Panel, add a new light and give it the following parameters:

Spotlight Parameters

Light Name	BeamSpotLight
Light Color	240,240,250
Light Intensity	100%
Light Type	Spot
Intensity Falloff	5%
Cone Angle	18%
Edge Angle	5%

- Return to the Layout window and parent the BeamSpotLight to the LightBeam object. The spot light will jump into position inside of the LightBeam object. If you rotate the LightBeam object, the actual light source should also be rotating simultaneously.

If you are using LightWave 3.1, you'll notice that using these parameters will give you a cone of light that fits right inside of the modeled beam (take a second and look through the spot light in the Light view mode).

- For LightWave 3.1 users, adding a lens flare increases the realistic look of your light beam. Simply select the **Lens Flare** button in the **Lights** Panel for the spot light before clicking on the **Lens Flare Options** button and enter the following parameters:

Lens Flare

Flare Intensity	20%
Fade Off Screen	On
Fade Behind Objects	On
Fade in Fog	On
Central Glow	On
All other options	Off

This is a good starting place for your light beam. You may need to stretch the beam to fit your needs. If you stretch or size the beam in LightWave, there is no need to change any surface values. You can even size it out from 0 to full size in a few frames (try 5-8) to 'turn it on.'

Problem Solving

You may need to change the colors of the beam surfaces and the fractal noise that they travel through depending on the environment your beam is in. (Incidentally, **World Coordinates** is chosen for the **Fractal Noise** so the beams appear to travel through air particles as they move.)

If you need to create a different size or shaped beam in Modeler, however, make sure to adjust your surface values to compensate for the new object.

If you intend on traveling close to the light beam, you will most likely want to model some type of light fixture to place at the bottom of the beam. If this is the case, it is convenient to parent the LightBeam object to the light fixture and simply rotate the fixture around to move the beam.

To save rendering time, remove the InnerBeam and use only the OuterBeam. The fewer the transparent objects, the faster LightWave can render.

Finally, if you notice that the end of your light beam has edges showing, try increasing the **Z Texture Size** slightly to make the image map a bit larger to compensate.

LWP

John Gross is a supervising animator for Amblin Imaging and Editor of LIGHTWAVEPRO. *He can be reached electronically at jgross@netcom.com. On CompuServe, contact him or at 71740,2357.*

Lens Flare Madness

by Mojo

For decades, if a director wanted cool lighting effects in a film, it took a team of rotoscope artists to accomplish it. The glow of a spaceship engine? Easy. Simply create photographic blowups of every frame in the sequence, have the roto guy rough out in pencil the glow for each frame, then airbrush the finished product on acetate and photograph it against a light table. Of course, the finished film has to be sent to the optical department to be re-composited into the original footage.

These days, we just press the "lens flare" button. The history of LightWave's lens flare effect dates back to 1992, when Ron Thornton felt it would be an important feature in the production of the original *Babylon 5* pilot. Although it certainly helped contribute to the expensive look of the effects, the early lens flares required a lot of tedious envelope setting and manipulation. With the release of version 3.5, the lens flare now has a multitude of features that make it easier to use than ever.

Up and Down

Back in the early years, lens flares were simple, additive effects layered over the entire image after it was rendered. If we wanted a lens flare to go behind an object, it was necessary to carefully examine the scene frame by frame to determine when the flare should be obscured. An envelope then had to be created that ramped the flare up and down over the appropriate frames.

Now you can press the "fade behind objects" button in the lens flare menu and it's completed for you. When this is active, LightWave will figure out what objects are between the camera and the lens flare and ramp them automatically. However, circumstances may arise when this is undesirable: a lens flare should show through the base of a lightbeam, or a transparent or gaseous object. In this case, by clicking off the "cast shadow" option, the lens flare will be instructed not to fade behind the desired object. If the object needs to cast shadows, you may need to resort to the old-fashioned method of hand-ramping a flare.

The biggest lens flare complaint has always been the need to manually adjust the size of flares that move to and from the camera. Thanks to the new "fade-in distance" feature, this tedious enveloping is now a thing of the past.

Figure 1: The damaged Narn cruiser from *Babylon 5*. Perfectionists may want to create envelopes to make each flare shimmer a little to add realism.

To use this feature, set up a flare as you would normally. Give it a size you feel would be appropriate based on the effect and the flare's current distance from the camera and then type that distance into the flare's "nominal distance" box. Don't worry if you're having trouble figuring out the distance. Just type in any number and adjust either it or the flare size until the distance is correct. Once the flare looks fine, you won't have to worry about it again: LightWave will increase and decrease the size to maintain your settings whenever the flare (or the object it's parented to) is moved closer to or further from the camera.

The "fade-in fog" button has a similar effect, but obviously only works when fog is turned on. Once the flare has reached the maximum distance of the fog, the flare will be completely ramped down. I find that dissolving the flare out with an envelope can help or even replace this effect when necessary. Again, using the example of the engine exhaust, the flare would appear to shrink inside the engine object if fade-in fog was utilized. This would look wrong, while dissolving the flare out as the object dissolves into the fog would appear more natural. I would recommend fade with distance and a simple dissolve envelope on the flare instead of using fade-in fog at all.

Putting On the Squeeze

"Anamorphic squeeze" and "anamorphic streaks" mimic the look of photographing a bright light source with a wide-screen movie lens. When a wide-screen movie is made, the lens scrunches up all the information and the resulting image on the film is actually stretched vertically. The projector is fitted with a sort of "anti-lens" that stretches the image horizontally to correct it and fill a wide screen. Since lens flares are actually created by the lens itself and not in the scene, they end up being round on the finished anamorphic film. It is the expanding of the image when it is projected that gives this flare its ovalic shape. The blue streaks are simply an odd characteristic created by the lens.

Given this information, if realism is important to your animations, the anamorphic options should only be used in letterbox mode (or when compositing lens flares into existing anamorphically shot footage). Sure, few movie watchers know the whys and wheres about anamorphic lens flares, but these effects are never seen on anything other than big-screen movies (TV shows never have them since they are not shot with anamorphic lenses). In addition, they should only be used to simulate lens flares from bright light sources, such as flashlights or aircraft lights, and not effects (like engine exhausts). Of course, this only applies when realism is a goal—there really are no laws when all you want to do is make stuff look cool.

Tricks of the Trade

Headlights, engine exhausts, laser beams, explosions—these are some of the more obvious lens flare applications used by just about everyone who owns LightWave. However, after using it almost every day for the last several years, some of us old timers have come up with a few neat lens flare tricks that we feel can now be passed down to the young folks.

Ever want to rotate a lens flare? On a few occasions I have needed to make those neat ethereal streaks spin around in a heavenly fashion. The only way to accomplish this is to put a lens flare on a polygon and physically rotate it. You'll need to ren-

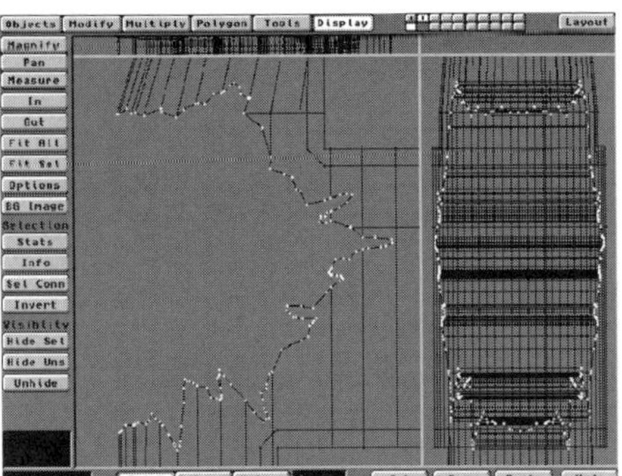

Figure 1A: Although not necessary, using point lights for lens flares helps you keep track of what's what, since point lights look like lens flares.

Figure 2: A spectacular image to be sure, yet somehow devoid of a certain something.

Figure 2A: Ah! Lens flares over the glowing panels do just the trick. What panache!

der a flare and save the RGB file to map onto a polygon. Make sure the flare is relatively small (maybe 60 percent) to keep the edges of the screen completely black, since you'll need to use this image as a transparency map as well. Unless the edges of the map are completely black, the edges of the polygon will be visible (use negative image for the transparency map). If the flare will get close to the camera or fill the screen, you will probably have to render the image as either high-resolution or print-resolution to avoid jagged edges in the flare streaks (for very pronounced streaks, make the light color zero and increase the size of the flare). This technique was used to create the Switcher's popular "flashbulb" effect, in which (you guessed it) a lens flare quickly spins into and out from the camera. This trick may also be desired to rotate the points of a star-filter lens flare.

When lens flares get big, it becomes much easier to see through them. This is a nuisance when trying to cover up a large area with a flare (such as an engine exhaust) and you always end up with an uncontrollably huge glow. How do you fix it? Double up your flares. Two flares in the same space can be controlled to create a strong center with a soft, manageable glow and not be too large.

One flare needs to be designated the hot spot (usually white) and the other serves as the outer glow (providing color). The hot spot should generally be about half the size of the outer glow and dissolved out as much as 50 percent. (The outer flare will add to the central one and bring up the apparent intensity—two 100 percent flares would create a flare with a 200 percent center and appear much too strong.) I usually turn off every flare effect except central glow—the deletion of especially the random streaks option creates a much softer, generally more pleasing effect. Also, remember that the incredibly useful Lightswarm macro allows for the creation of double flares, so use it to save time when creating multiple sets of flares with similar attributes.

An incredibly cool, although time-consuming, lens flare effect is the heat fissure. By lining up dozens of low-intensity flares in close proximity, you can simulate a hot, glowing tear, welding streak, lava flow and many others. The idea is to put so many flares next to each other that they lose their circular shape and blend into one another, appearing to become a straight (or curved) line of light. Figure 1 shows a scene from *Babylon 5* in which a damaged Narn cruiser has just been hit by an energy weapon. I wanted the metal to appear burning hot and knew the best way to do that was to line the damaged area with enough flares to simulate the effect. Since more than 100 flares were needed for the shot, the Lightswarm macro quickly became my best friend.

In Modeler, I isolated the points around the damaged polygon and copied them to another layer (Figure 1A). Using the drag points tool with the grid snap off, I positioned them to be more or less equidistant from one another. I then ran the Lightswarm macro and guessed at a lens flare setting. The key is to make the flares just large enough to cover the edge of the object.

The first rendering showed that the flare size was good, but individual circles were still apparent. This meant more flares. Back in Modeler, I added close to double the number of points I started with and ran another Lightswarm. This time the circles disappeared but the huge number of flares adding to each other created a center line that was too hot, so I had to re-run Lightswarm and give all the flares a 30 percent dissolve.

This procedure worked great. Then came the tough part—manually giving over 100 flares proper fade with distance parameters since Lightswarm doesn't incorporate new features yet. Also important was making sure that only a few flares had light intensities. A nice orange haze over the surface of the ship was important for realism, but only a few evenly spaced lights with falloff were necessary. Absent-mindedly leaving effects flares with 100 percent light intensities is a common mistake, so keep an eye out for it.

The entire effect took perhaps half a day to get right, yet the results are clearly worth it. Always test out your effects with just a few flares to get a ballpark idea of how many you'll need and what their settings will be. This will save you a lot of rendering time and mean fewer visits to Lightswarm.

Believe it or not, lens flares can create subtle effects as well. My favorite is to place a dissolved flare (about 40 percent with outer glow only) over a visible lightsource or window. Figure 2 shows several luminous slits in a futuristic building's hatchway. However, Figure 2A displays the same slits with several lens flares placed over them; the result is much prettier and effective. The look is quite similar to photographing a scene with a fog filter and takes the harshness off a flat, luminous polygon. Use this to add just a touch of class to any scene.

I hope this gives some food for thought to all you flare-crazy animators. Lens flares look great, yet are so easy to use that few people give any thought to when they should be used. Like any other special effect, restraint is the key. After your 10th shot of a flare-encrusted UFO, the novelty begins to wear off. Use flares to add a little zest to your scene—not to hide poor modeling. If your shot doesn't look good without lens flares, you need to brush up on some other skills before you hit that oh-so-tempting button.

LWP

Mojo has a thing for engine exhausts.

Simple Space Stuff Part I

by Mojo

I know what you're thinking. You're saying to yourself, "What?! A feature in *LWPRO* on how to do space scenes? You've gotta be kidding me! Space is easy..."

Easy, huh?

Yeah, right.

Easy to get wrong, that is.

It may sound pompous and arrogant, but in the two years that *Babylon 5* has been in production I have yet to see any Toaster-generated space scenes that match the richness of Foundation Imaging's.

While I've seen plenty of space backgrounds behind many flying logos, they just don't measure up.

And it's not just me – many people have asked me questions about how we do it; questions that I honestly thought everyone knew the answers to.

So, no more assumptions – the following behind-the-scenes tour of *Babylon 5* will presume that everyone reading this needs to be taught, from the ground up, how to put together a convincing LightWave scene in outer space.

Figure 1: Overly bright lighting with fill has often been the norm for science fiction. However, don't look for anything like this to actually appear on *Babylon 5*.

A Sky Full of Stars

The most important element of a space scene is the stars, which are those little pin pricks of light you see if you look up at the sky when it's dark.

Okay, I won't be that simplistic. However, I would suggest looking at the stars. You'll notice that there are a great deal of them (on a clear night, anyway). They also vary widely in intensity, as any number of them are closer, further, greater or smaller. This celestial variety must be copied within LightWave in order to be convincing. You'll need a large number of single-point polygons with varying surface names to accomplish this.

Two starfield objects are provided for you with LightWave—Stars is a random scattering of points with a single surface, making for a thin, flat starfield. ActualStars is a little better, since it contains realistic groupings of stars and several surface names that can be lightened or darkened for extra realism.

Each of these on their own wouldn't satisfy even Duck Dodgers, but combined properly they create a starfield that would make Captain Picard proud.

On *B5*, we use two sets of each, for a total of four star objects, all rotated at different angles. The ActualStars object has had several extra surfaces added, all of which were painstakingly adjusted to get the desired effect (seven to 10 surface names created in Modeler should be enough).

Star densities were set with intensities anywhere from 10 to 100 percent. This was done by tweaking the **Surface Color** channel, not **Luminosity**, so some groupings could be given a slightly blue or reddish tinge. One of the Stars objects has also been given a slight dissolve to offset the full visibility of the other.

To avoid making all the object settings every time we do a space scene, we have a scene called 'Local Space' that contains only our starfield and nebula (more on that later). This way, after the main elements of a scene have been choreographed (like spaceships), all the space objects and their settings can be called up by simply hitting **Load From Scene** under the objects menu. By selecting Local Space when requested, all our heavenly elements are put into place in no time.

With a little tinkering and just a few test renders, this formula should result in a starfield that looks as good or better than *B5*'s in less than half an hour. That's only 2.8 percent of the time it took to create the entire universe.

Motion in the Ocean

Since most of you will probably not be satisfied with rendering a bunch of still frames, here are a few tips that might be handy when animating in space:

1. Always use **Particle Blur**, found in the Motion Blur section of the camera menu. This will streak your single-point polygons as the camera pans past them. It will look funny in stills, but when in motion it prevents the stars from strobing and shimmering. The default setting of 50 percent for **Blur Length** should be fine for most scenes. Increase at your own risk.
2. Bring a power source. Electrical outlets are few and far between in our galaxy, and those who neglect this crucial element won't get very far. Battery supplies work well, but the new solar-powered cells on the market would be ideal when working in the direct sunlight of space.
3. Parent your starfields to a null object. Sometimes, to increase the feel of movement in a scene, we'll actually move the stars in an opposite direction from which a ship is traveling. Since we use four (and sometimes more) starfields, having them all attached to a null object can save minutes of tedious animating.

Hyperspace

At some point in their space career, every space cadet wants to copy the hyperspace effect from *Star Wars*, in which the viewer travels at such high velocity that the stars streak past like solid lines.

The idea is to have the camera move past many single-point polygons with a high degree of Particle Blur. This cannot be done with the normal starfield object, regardless of how fast you move, since all the polygons are located at the edges of this hollow object.

You'll need to make a solid block of particles using Modeler's **Point Distribution** macro. Try making several 1,000-point blocks, each with a different surface name and combining them into one (see reasons for various surface names above).

This particle object should most likely be far longer in the Z direction than X and Y, since you don't want to run out of stars as you travel down the center.

Load your starblock object into Layout and surface it appropriately. Upon your first render, you'll notice that the points conglomerate towards the center as the object recedes into the distance. This is easily fixed by adding fog to the scene or setting a distance dissolve for the object so only the desired number of stars can be seen at any given time.

As the stars approach the camera, they will slowly dissolve into view. By carefully balancing the Blur Length and the speed of the camera, you can easily mimic one of the more memorable scenes in science fiction film history.

Alternatively, for a more subtle effect, try loading several different starblock objects and move them past the camera at different speeds.

If you lower the Blur Length to a more manageable size, you can produce a statuesque zooming starfield, similar to the one seen on *Star Trek* or in *B5*'s opening title sequence.

The *B5* Blues

Perhaps the most prominent aspect of the *Babylon 5* galaxy is the striking blue nebula, prevalent in the majority of scenes. While it is certainly pretty to look at, unbeknownst to most people, it serves a practical purpose which has made it essential to our shots.

In most cases, any major solar system would contain one sun, meaning that the majority of light radiates from one direction. Therefore, objects in space would be rich in shadow since only half of it can be lit at any given time. Most space-oriented productions add a lot of unnatural fill light to lessen these shadows and make their objects more visible. Let's face it—it is very difficult to see a ship shadowed in black against the black background of space. The fill light is a necessary evil.

Or is it?

Besides looking so nice, the blue nebula on *B5* silhouettes the dark areas of ships in front of it, making their shape very clear to the viewer. This prevents an object from getting lost in a black background and therefore permits the celestial realism of high-contrast lighting without fill light. If it weren't for that nebula, *B5*'s special effects lighting wouldn't be very special (see accompanying images).

Although it is a simple object, many animators trying to emulate the look have been scratching their heads over the exact details of it's creation. (Luckily, I'm in a good mood right now so I'll spill the beans but, please, don't tell anyone else.)

Figure 2: More realistic, single source lighting adds a dramatic touch to this shot. However, the dark areas of the model become lost against the black background of space.

Figure 3: The blue nebula silhouettes these dark areas, allowing for the instant recognition of the object's shape despite dark lighting.

The nebula itself was painted 1500x400 pixels on a PC using a paint program with sophisticated airbrush and blurring tools (sorry, Toaster Paint!). It needed to be very wide so the camera could pan across a scene without the nebula disappearing.

It also had to be mapped onto a curved polygon to hide its flat nature. This allows the nebula to stay within the camera shot, even with a pan of up to 180 degrees.

The painted image is actually a blue and black color map and the nebula object is sized larger than the starfields; otherwise, the stars behind the nebula would be blocked out and the square edges of the object would be seen.

The nebula could have been painted in black and white and applied as a Transparency map to the object, solving some of these problems. Although this would also allow the color sliders to determine the color, Transparency takes considerably longer to render and so the color map path was chosen.

Different color nebulas are created by changing the actual image map; not the object. The nebula does not extend to the top and bottom of the screen as a purely stylistic choice. By not completely filling the screen, it prevents scenes from getting too blue, and allows us to tilt it on occasion for a different look (although the object can easily be stretched along the Y axis to fill more or less of the screen upon demand).

Of course, keeping the nebula to a minimum also reduces render times.

Nebulas Made Easy

Lazy animators who wish to create a nebula without even clicking a paint icon are in luck. A poor man's celestial phenomena is as easy as creating a simple sphere, sized slightly larger than LightWave's starfield objects.

Surface it with fractal noise of any color you like, with the noise size approximated at around 100,000.

A sphere is preferable to a flat plane, since it allows you to point the camera in any direction without losing the nebula. This produces nice results, although it will have none of the specific characteristics of the *B5* nebula, like shape or hot spots.

The noise nebula also takes far more time to render.

Go ahead, be daring! Paint something! Even Dpaint AGA has what it takes to produce something usable. It's not difficult because the nebula is a fairly abstract shape. Start with a few bright splotches and begin to smear and blur them with various sized brushes.

Nothing described in this article is very difficult to produce. Hopefully, a few gaps have been filled in for you or a few sparks have been ignited that will send you on your way to creating your own spectacular space scenes.

LWP

Mojo is a Libra and therefore believes that all fish are pink and red ants wear tuxedos.

Simple Space Stuff

Part II—Cool Tricks From *Babylon 5*

by Mojo

Last month, I began explaining how the *Babylon 5* universe was created. The mysteries behind majestic starfields and sweeping nebulas were finally revealed. This month, let's delve deeper into the secrets behind this LightWave-generated galaxy and see what else can be learned.

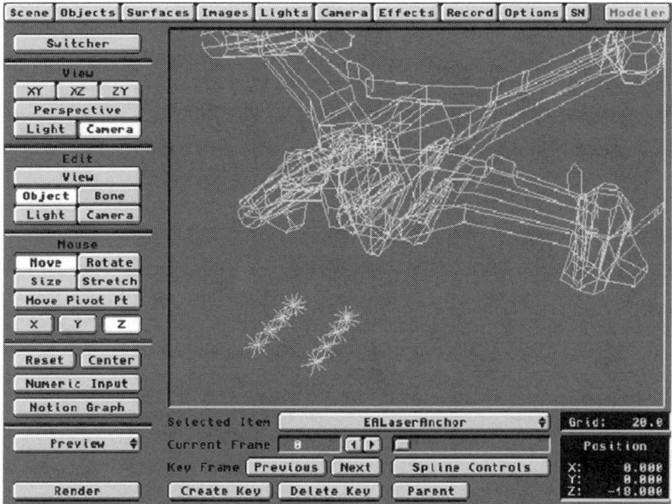

Figure 1: As this wireframe shows, the lens flares need to be positioned close to one another to avoid visible iterations.

The Jumpgate

One of the most prominent effects seen regularly on the show is the hyperspace generator; a man-made jumpgate that creates a vortex allowing instantaneous travel to other galaxies. Fans of the show have raved about these sequences, although it is deceptively simple to duplicate.

The generators themselves are four simple objects that look somewhat like rails lined with solar energy cells. A single generator object was made and cloned three times, with all the pieces arranged into a diamond-like shape (all of them are parented to a null object to make the assembly easy to move).

The gateway comes to life with a violent explosion of lens flares that track down the length of the rails. Four flares (one for each generator) with identical envelopes meet at the far end and combine into one big flare, which appears to 'phase in' the vortex itself.

The vortex is a very long tube with a spiraling fractal noise pattern and transparent edge. The fiery noise pattern is orange and moves inward when a craft is entering hyperspace, or blue and moving outward when someone is leaving (the color difference is actually a visual Doppler shift which occurs when objects approach the speed of light—real science.).

The tube is just a long, subdivided object tapered at one end to force the perspective of it extending into infinity (we never see it at an extreme angle). The tube is subdivided so it can be twisted into a morph target which allows the fractal noise to appear as if it were spiraling. If the tube were straight, the noise would simply move in a straight line. But, if the noise-laden tube is morphed into a twisted shape, the noise will follow these curves and travel in a spiral. Morphing is important, since the noise would not follow the contours of a twisted source object—textures always move in a straight line regardless of an object's shape. The object must be deformed after it is mapped.

A transparency map consisting of 95 percent black, fading to white only towards the end, is applied to the tube. This permits the tube to stay solid and feather off only at the edge.

The tube is sized to zero and dissolved out at the beginning of the sequence. When the four flares merge into one, the tube is dissolved in, sized up and moved out to the center of the generators. It is timed with the fading central flare to look as if it emerges from this point. Objects traveling down the tube are moved quickly and disappear with a lens flare when they reach the end. Since the tube is tapered, ships need to be sized down as they recede down the vortex in line with the forced perspective trick. It also makes them appear to be moving much faster.

Each one of these elements, separately, is very simple. But when tied together with the proper timing, a fantastic sequence is created. Keep this in mind when designing your own space scenes.

Not Laser Beams

Space battles are an important part of science fiction and laser beams are essential for space battles. The laser beams used in *B5*'s dogfight scenes went through several generations until we arrived at the satisfactory result we use now. [Note: In keeping with the show's strong footing in real physics and science, it should be mentioned that laser beams are not actually part of the *B5* universe. The combat fighters are equipped with highly charged plasma weapons, which would result in 'bolts' being fired (a laser would be a solid beam) and a natural luminescence (lasers are invisible in a vacuum).] Early in production, we used thin, luminescent objects as plasma bolts which worked well, but I wanted to improve the effect.

For the episode "Signs and Portents" (which featured the first all-out battle sequence of the first season).

During the making of "And the Sky Full of Stars," there was a brief scene in which a Starfury fired its weapons at a Minbari cruiser. The firing was an afterthought and I didn't feel like taking the time to load the plasma bolt objects, so I simply threw a few lens flares into the scene. The angle was almost directly behind the fighter, so I didn't think anyone would notice that the bolts were round and not elongated.

Much to my surprise and delight, the final rendering revealed that the scene's motion blur also blurred the lens flares. In addition, since the flares were moving so fast, they were very blurred, resulting in an oval-ic, elongated flare that looked much like a traditional, glowing, rotoscoped laser beam. When it came time for "Signs," I decided to experiment with this technique using lens flares as a permanent replacement for our plasma bolt objects.

Initial tests proved that at anything similar to a right angle (like a side view of a ship firing), the motion blur would stretch out the lens flares too much. This 'thinned out' the effect and the flare lost most of its concentration. Bolts would either have to fire slowly or high antialiasing (with more blur steps) would have to be used.

Neither option was attractive.

Instead, I tried tying several lens flares together in close proximity and this worked like a charm. They still blurred into a cohesive bolt, yet the extra flares filled in the 'thin' spaces created by motion blurring.

I created a scene with four flares for each bolt (the Starfury has two main guns), resulting in two rows of four flares each, all tied to a single null object. This null could then be permanently parented to the ship and moved along the Z axis (the Starfury's line of fire) to simulate bolts being fired (this hierarchy ensures that the bolts will always travel in the direction the ship is facing). The flares, of course, move along with the null (saving the headache of moving all of the flares individually).

Interactive lighting during these battle scenes is very important, so two of the lens flares that make up the bolts (one for each side) have their light intensity left on with a sharp falloff. This allows the plasma bolts to actually cast light onto surfaces they closely streak past. In addition, two lens flares (again, with light casting on and falloff) are attached to the end of the Starfury's guns. These flares are ramped up and down with each blast fired to simulate the blaze of the guns. They make the weapons seem much more powerful and the brief light cast upon the face of the ship as it fires is very dramatic.

For scenes in which plasma bolts are fired far from the camera, an image map of the blurred flares has been placed on a polygon (keyframing all the sets of bolts can be time consuming). This looks great from a distance, although to spice it up, a single, dissolved lens flare is placed on top of the polygon to give the beams a soft glow.

Creating these battles scenes is certainly a lot of work, but the results are worth it. This technique for creating plasma bolts (or, yes, even laser beams) may take a little time to master, but the brilliant glow of lens flares make this the only way I know of to achieve such classic results.

And the Sky Full of Clouds

Our first season featured an ambitious two-part saga, "A Voice in the Wilderness." This mini-movie featured more than one hundred new special effects shots, many of which took place in an atmosphere—something we had never tackled before.

One particular sequence had a shuttle blasting from below a planet's surface straight up into the sky. I had to create realistic looking clouds for this shot and knew that a flat polygon with a fractal noise transparency layer would be the answer.

However, as nice as this looks (the surface is included with LightWave), it wasn't quite good enough. The noise pattern was too regular and there were just too many clouds in the sky. If there was a way to have a second layer of fractal transparency, I knew the effect would work better. But LightWave only has one transparency channel ... right?

Additive Transparency

Using LightWave's **Additive** feature (Surfaces panel), there is a way to fake a second transparency channel.

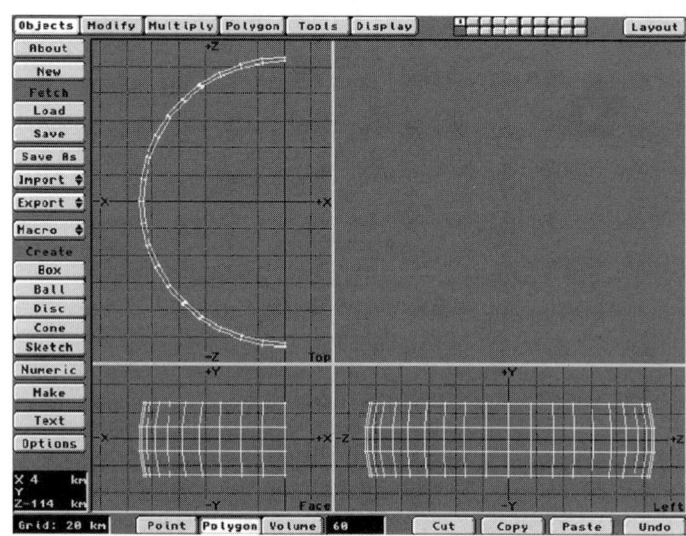

Figure 2: This image depicting the nebula object was mistakenly left out of Part I. See last month's *LWPRO* for details.

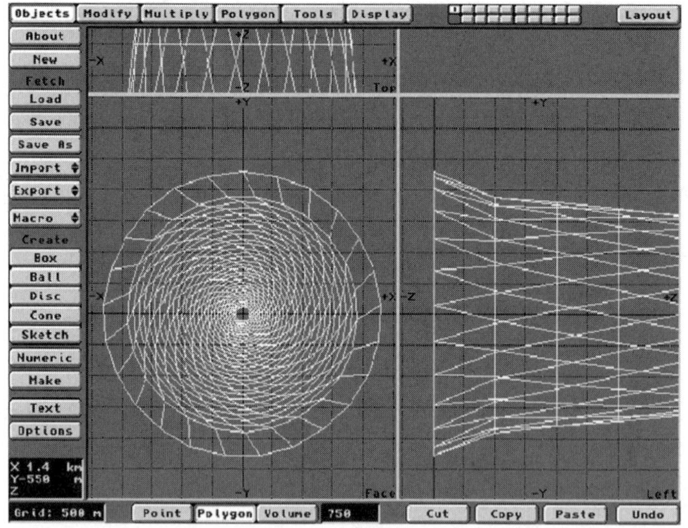

Figure 3: The morphed vortex object. Note that the polygons are triangular—tripling polygons meant to be deformed helps avoid rendering errors; three-sided polygons are more "flexible."

Surfaces that are additive allow parts of the scene that are behind them to be 'added' into the surface color of the surface. If a surface is 100,100,100 and the background is 100,100,100, the new surface color will be computed at 200,200,200. If an Additive surface has zero color, the background will be added completely in and the surface will appear transparent. By selecting **Additive** and by giving a surface 0 percent diffuse (so it appears black) and a luminosity map which ranges from 100 percent to zero, you will effectively be giving that object transparency from 100 percent to zero. This technique works best on objects that would normally not be effected by light within the scene, such as distant clouds, smoke, electricity and other luminescent phenomena. To help you understand this trick, I'll show you how to create a lightbeam object without using a transparency map.

Make a one meter long lightbeam object out of a cone, making sure the tip of it is at 0,0,0 in Modeler and the base of it is located at one meter on the +Z axis. You can also delete the base polygon so the beam is "open-ended."

Back in Layout, surface it with whatever color you like, but instead of transparency, go into the Luminosity channel. Select the Grid texture and make the **Line Thickness** one (this leaves no spaces between grid squares and creates a solid block of texture) and the **Texture Value** 100 percent. Make sure you give the texture a **Texture Falloff** on its Z axis of 100 percent and set the Luminosity value under the surfaces menu to zero. This will make the object 100 percent luminous at its tip, falling off to no luminosity after one meter (the cone's end). Also make sure to set the Diffuse level to 0 percent. Click **Additive**, make sure the object's edges are **Transparent** and render a test. If done correctly, you should have a perfect lightbeam object without ever having touched the transparency channel. If you have render errors at the tip of the cone (showing up as facets even though smoothing is turned on), make your cone out of a one meter long disc and taper the tip so it is very small.

Of course, the transparency channel is still free. If this lightbeam were a car headlight, you could run a moving fractal noise texture through it and simulate fog or other debris. If you were unsatisfied with the type of lightbeam and wanted to use a custom transparency map, you could create the object in the traditional way and use the luminosity channel to add extra transparency.

Despite our Hollywood status, all the folks working on **B5** are still just a bunch of regular guys who love 3D. All of the unique effects we create are simply a result of persistence and a little imagination. Despite all our expensive hardware, these are the elements that make our work special—elements that everyone reading this newsletter has in plentiful supply. There is no excuse why any of you cannot go forth and create your own spectacular 3D universes.

LWP

Dead in Space

Creating Flares and Explosions for a *B5* Ambush

by Mojo

One of the shots I'm most proud of this season on *Babylon 5* is from the episode "Revelations," in which a heavy Narn Cruiser is ambushed by a mysterious attacker. It exits hyperspace into an evil-looking sector of the galaxy and immediately has a hole punched through it from underneath by the enemy's powerful energy weapon.

The scene turned out to be one of my favorites and, much to my surprise, the producers liked it so much they decided to use it during the opening credits every week. Since this shot has such high visibility, I thought I'd share some of the details of its creation and prove that anybody with LightWave and a few hours to kill can make millions of people say "Wow!" every week.

Space, the First Frontier

One of the distinguishing characteristics of *Babylon 5*'s space scenes is their strong use of celestial phenomena, such as colorful nebulas and phosphorescent whirlpools. Not only do such backdrops look nice, but they allow us to light scenes darkly, with shadowed objects still visible in silhouette. In addition, they often provide visible sources for fill light and provide a refreshing break from the overused norm of black sky and white stars. When the script calls for a new area of space to be visited, we spend just as much time making the background look right as we do the action.

"Revelations" called for the Narn cruiser to visit enemy territory. These bad guys are evil and nasty, so I wanted to design an area of space that reflected this—a place that you could tell was dangerous simply by looking at it.

Since TV production has such a hectic schedule, there is never time to create every element from scratch. A while back, NASA sent us some striking images taken by the repaired Hubble space telescope, and we've incorporated these into the show when we can to provide a little touch of "real" science.

One of these images, of a fiery orange-red gas cloud, looked particularly hellish and seemed as if it had the right stuff to be the basis of "evil" space.

After spending a little time in Photoshop, I had the image cropped and processed to the point where it looked good. Some blurring was necessary to remove some of the low-resolution artifacting, but in this particular image, extreme sharpness wasn't necessary. What *was* important was making sure the image was NTSC-safe. Reds and oranges are video's worst offenders, so I brought the colors to well below the safe level; even when technically safe, reds can bleed a lot if they're too saturated. I also didn't want the colors to look too overstated, or else they would have detracted from the explosion—the focal point of the shot.

The image (1300x700) was mapped onto a curved polygon and placed behind everything else, even the stars (see the August '94 *LWPRO* for more information on nebulas). I had to be careful not to pan the camera too far, or else it would see the edge of the nebula. (The image didn't taper off at the sides and there was a limit to how far I could stretch it before it looked bad.)

Since this scene was described in the script as being at the rim of the galaxy, I added a subtle ring of stars across the middle of the screen, all with **Particle Size** set to Small. The object was also dissolved out 50 percent to avoid sharp flickering (very bright, small particles against a dark background would alias and shimmer like crazy).

Once I was happy with the setting for my shot, it was time to get into the thick of it and blow up a perfectly good ship.

Ouch! That Smarts!

The script had the cruiser getting hit and exploding in one blow, but I decided to break it down into two stages in order to build a little bit of emotional impact: the first hit would make it clear that the Narns didn't stand a chance and the second would finally destroy it (after we had begun to feel sorry for them).

I wanted that first hit to be really violent and look as if a hole was literally "punched" into the ship. As the beam hit the bottom of the cruiser, there was a momentary pause to suggest a power buildup before it burst through the top. I felt it should be as powerful and as devastating as possible when it finally broke through—like a bullet through a balsa wood factory.

After it was hit, I thought it should "sink" in front of the camera, implying that this one blow had really crippled the ship. Although the actual physics of this is wrong (in space a damaged ship would certainly not sink), I felt the depressing feeling viewers would get seeing this gutted ship fall past the camera far outweighed the incorrect mechanics of it.

Now I just had to figure out how to accomplish everything!

Figure 1: This is what it looked like in layout. Notice the hulking square explosion polygon. It's facing the camera and not orienterd in the direction of the ship.

Down and Dirty

The first step was to use Boolean functions and cut a nice chunk out of the Narn cruiser model. This new version of the ship was parented to the original and cross-dissolved with it while the lens flares of the initial explosion covered the area in question. (This is also why the far side of the ship was chosen to get hit.) Keep in mind that if you're going to try this, make sure you set the dissolve envelope splines to **Linear.** Otherwise, even in a one-frame transition, you'll see a shimmering between objects.

As the beam slices through the top, there are three basic elements that create the impact: lens flares, particles and a real explosion mapped onto a polygon.

Ah, lens flares...there are no less than 120 of those little suckers in this scene file. That's what was needed to create the "burning hole" effect of fire surrounding the area cut from the ship as it sinks past the camera. (The details of this particular effect were explained in the November '94 issue of *LWPRO.*) Of these, only a few were actually needed for the initial impact flare-up. They were ramped between 100 and 300 percent for a few frames to highlight the beginning of the blast, then brought down to a manageable level. (The damaged version of the Narn ship was dissolved in during this period.) These flares also had a matching light intensity envelope, so the orange light from the explosion would be cast on the ship's surface. A falloff was used to keep the light from scattering across the entire object, helping to convey the sense that this is a very large vessel.

Just as the first flares reach a crescendo, a massive outpour of sparks rises from the point of impact. Instead of using a spherical particle cloud, I created a plume of points that stretched vertically, once again helping to emphasize the upward force of the explosion. The object was made by stretching, tapering and using the magnet tool on a macro-generated point distribution of 600 particles. I then saved this object as a source and dragged conglomerations of particles toward the edges and upward, saving this as a morph target. An enveloped morph of this object over 30 or so frames would create the illusion of the sparks moving at various rates.

The particles are then sized to zero, parented to the ship and sized larger at a very quick pace in time with the explosion (along with the simultaneous morph). Several layers of sparks were added to create extra density and simply make it look more exciting.

The finishing touch was the real explosion on a polygon. As good as lens flares and sparks are, there's simply nothing quite like a good old-fashioned fireball. A commonly available CD-ROM called **Pyromania** features frame sequences of several explosions, one of which is a sort of nuclear-style blast heading upward. We don't normally use them on *B5* due to the limitations of polygon mapping, but in this case everything seemed just right to make use of them. In addition, because we don't use such explosions very often, they would create the extra impact I was looking for.

Creating this effect is just about as simple as it sounds. I put a flat polygon on top of the ship in the area I wanted the plume to come from and planar-mapped the image sequence of the explosion. I gave the sequence a frame offset of -12 so it would begin on frame 12 of the animation and made sure the polygon was dissolved out until then.

One thing to keep in mind when using polygon-mapped sequences is dimensionality. If you're not careful, the 2D element in your 3D world can be detected. This usually happens if you move at too extreme an angle to the polygon and its perspective begins to shift. As a result, the image on the polygon will start to "flatten" out, much the same way an image on a piece of paper does if you look at it at an angle. Whenever you use an image on a polygon in this fashion, make sure it faces the camera as squarely as possible at all times, even if it means rotating it during the course of your animation. A good rule of thumb might be to avoid using this trick when you have extreme panning camera moves. In this case, the move was subtle and the polygon was always directly facing the camera, providing the perfect opportunity for this technique.

The main problem with using explosion sequences like this are the polygon edges. When most of these explosions were filmed for the CD, the flames went off the edge of the screen. When mapped onto a polygon, this means that once your explosion reaches that point, it will simply vanish off a hard edge. This would be a dead giveaway of the trick and look pretty awful to boot. In this case, the gas cloud reaches fairly high before it gets to the edge of the frame, so I simply had to make sure the polygon was dissolved out before it got that far. This worked out well, since I really only wanted the fireball for the beginning of the explosion to highlight the impact. After that was accomplished, the lens flares and particles did a more than adequate job of completing the effect.

Finishing Touches

It's always the little things that make a good shot work well. One of my favorite elements in this case is the blue vortex that disappears behind the cruiser during the shot. The idea is that the ship is attacked just as it emerges from the hyperspace vortex, so I added it to the shot for several reasons.

First, I think it looks nice. As a rule, it's important to have more than one color in an image if you want any one color to stand out. In this case, it's the blue of the vortex that makes the reds and oranges of the nebula and explosion so vibrant—it gives your eye something else to reference.

There was also an emotional consideration.

I thought it would make the Narn's situation seem even more hopeless if you saw their only form of escape close behind them while being attacked.

It drives home the fact that they are all alone in a very bad neighborhood, and also presented an opportunity for some neat lighting. (If you look closely you can see the blue light from the vortex play across the back of the cruiser.)

In the end, a combination of several simple techniques makes this shot work extremely well. However, the most important element of this scene is its design. A lot of thought went into *why* to make things look a certain way and not just *how*. Consider this when creating your own scenes and you may find that a little attention to *why* may save you a lot of *how*.

LWP

Mojo has been in therapy, trying to resolve his emotional attachment to explosions. He is making progress and has recently conceded his Superior Elvis Fan complex to Colin Cunningham, who obviously needed something to turn to after working on Robocop: The Series.

Pyromania
Creating Realistic Explosions

by Mojo

Babylon 5 is a new science fiction television program that deals primarily with humanity's social progress in the future. Since it is science fiction, viewers expect to see aliens, spaceships, strange planets and, without question, the occasional space battle.

Unfortunately, the high cost of traditional model-based special effects has meant that fewer space battles have made it onto the airwaves recently. Thanks to computer graphics, this trend has been reversed and *Babylon 5* has proven that large scale space battles are once again indeed possible on a television budget.

Of all the elements needed to create intergalactic warfare, creating realistic explosions was unquestionably the most difficult. After much experimentation, I eventually developed an easy, fast-rendering, low-memory technique that produces surprisingly decent results.

Far Away, So Close

Distant explosions are simple. Just attach some expanding particles to a lens flare and voila, a little boom is created in the distance. Getting up close and personal is another matter. More detail is needed, specifically the flaming black-and-orange-organic-swirly thing we're so used to seeing blow up in the movies. Fractal Noise seems like the logical choice to somehow accomplish this, but the noise needs to travel outward from the center like a billowing cloud—not something this texture does on its own. A tip I learned on the *B5* pilot film provided the key to making this whole thing work.When given a velocity, Textures (such as Fractal Noise) will only move linearly—straight along the X, Y or Z axis. To get them to move in any other pattern requires you to morph the object it's applied to into a shape similar to the direction of desired movement (like the Saturn's rings tutorial in the latest Toaster manual). I knew a 3D ball probably wouldn't work, so I morphed a cone into a flat disk (Figures 1 and 2).

On this cone, a texture moving along the Y axis would move upwards from the base to the top point. If this point is dragged down to zero on the Y axis, the texture will still move along this path but now appear to travel from the outer edges of the "cone" to the center. If the texture is given a negative velocity, it will reverse course and seem to radiate from the center. Before you create this morph target in Modeler, you may want to delete the base polygon of the cone (highlighted in Figure 1); otherwise, this polygon will intersect with the ones dragged down and rendering errors will occur. Save the cone and its morph target and make sure you name each with different surfaces (I usually leave morph targets named default).

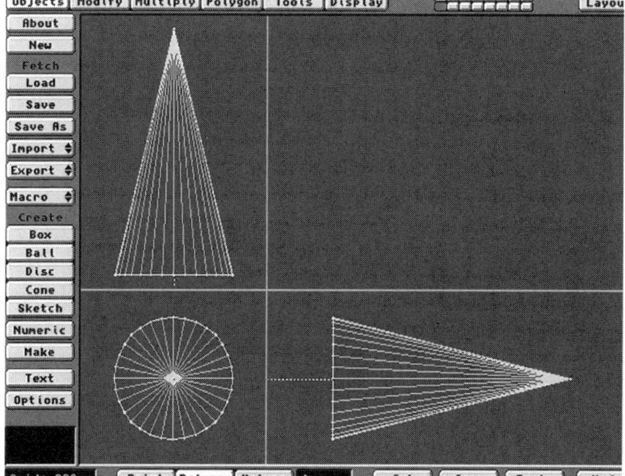

Figure 1: This is the source object. Delete the bottom polygon, apply a surface name and save it.

Layout

Once you've loaded both objects into Layout, leave the cone permanently morphed into the disk and dissolve the morph target completely out. Orient the disk so it is directly facing the camera. Since this is a flat effect, you want to be sure the disk is never at an angle or else its 2D nature will reveal itself.

Surface it with a yellow-orange color and add black Fractal Noise with a negative velocity along the Y axis (on a 1 meter disk, I suggest approximately .1 **Texture Size** values). Before going any further, try to render a simple 30 frame test of the morphed disk against a black background. Seeing it animated before you clutter it with the other explosion elements shows what it does and probably includes a few ideas for other uses of this object.

Since few fireballs have hard edges, you'll need to create a circular transparency map for the disk which gradually dissolves its edges. As good as they are, I found that ToasterPaint's transparency tools didn't quite provide me with the results I was looking for. Instead, I rendered a white lens flare in LightWave against a black background and saved the RGB file. The soft falloff of a lens flare lent itself to a perfect map for this purpose. Just make sure the flare is small (so it actually dissipates to black on screen) and turn on negative image when you **Planar Image Map** it (**Y** axis) onto the disk. Render a test frame to be sure it looks right.

Spark of Life

You'll definitely want to make some particle objects to simulate flying sparks. These are a must if you want a realistic explosion and are probably the easiest part of the entire assembly. Since we're aiming for a two-part explosion, you should create two separate particle balls, perhaps each with different characteristics. I used the **Point Distribution** macro to create a ball of single point polygons that could be sized from zero to a much larger size in Layout. Figure 3 shows a skewed particle spray I created for a second point ball. By expanding the sparks outward toward the camera, they appear to move much faster and add a nice contrast to the first ball, which expands evenly in all directions. It might also be a good idea to create several surfaces within the points so you can make multi-colored sparks. Save these objects out and you're ready to earn your virtual pyrotechnician's license.

Some Assembly Required

Now it's time to put everything together and actually make something. First, load and clone your disk first, since you'll need two of them for the multi-part explosion effect. It might even be a good idea to use two separate cones with different surface names so you can apply varied surface settings (like alternate colors or texture speeds). Size the first one to zero and create a key at frame 1 for it. Size it up to almost fill the screen at around frame 5, then have it scaled down to about half its size by frame 30. It should look as if it expands rapidly and slowly dies down. Make sure you also set a similar dissolve envelope for it, so the explosion object fades away as it scales down.

Place your first particle ball in the center of the disk and keyframe its size at zero. Expand it to at least three or four times the size of the screen and key that near frame 20 so it coincides with the first disk object. You probably want these to dissolve out slowly, maybe beginning a few frames into the animation. The surfaces should have at least 100 percent Luminosity and be bright in color. Also, make sure you turn on particle blur (Camera panel) or else you won't see any sparks. Increasing the **Blur Length** might not be a bad idea, either.

For all these envelopes, especially motions and dissolves, use the spline controls frequently. The fine-tuning they provide can make all the difference in realism. Start them off quickly with a **Tension** of -1 and ease them out slowly with a **Tension** of +1.

The second stage of the explosion should more or less be a repeat of the first part, although offset by five or 10 frames. If you want the second part to be more violent, use more particles for the second wave of sparks and size up the disk larger —perhaps have it scale down and fade out over a few extra frames. Everything should be over by frame 30 or 45. Also be certain to move the second disk slightly in front of or behind the first; if they occupy the same space you will get rendering errors.

Last but not least, place a lens flare right in the middle of the object and ramp it up and down appropriately. You may want to stagger its envelope, having it die down after the first part and flare up again with the surge of the second stage.

The Secret of Comedy and Explosions

Proper timing of all your elements is the key to this effect. All the individual pieces may look great, but unless they are orchestrated properly it just will not seem right. You probably won't get it right the first time, so be prepared for multiple test renderings. Fortunately, render times shouldn't be too long unless you add even more disks for increased density in the gas cloud (multiple levels of transparency are a real render hog). Constant tweaking of the dissolve and motion and flare envelopes will inevitably help you tailor the explosion to your liking.

Don't be afraid to also play with the surface settings to help you get the desired effect. Changing the Texture Velocities and Sizes can make a big difference. Nothing here is set in stone; like everything else in 3D, bold experimentation will reap the best rewards.

Mojo has realized that nobody out there really knows anything about him. Though he has written bio after bio, Mojo has yet to print any factual information. Is he afraid of something? Is his past so sordid and depraved that even the smallest detail would result in his immediate prosecution? Young readers should understand that a career in 3D animation does not automatically dictate a life of deviance and seclusion. As in the case of Mojo, this only happens if you are extremely lucky.

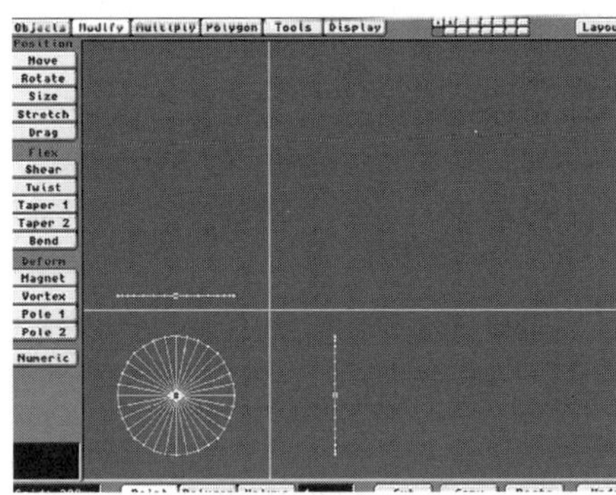

Figure 2: The top point of the cone is dragged down to create a flat disk. Give this the default surface setting and save it as your morph target. The animated texture will be forced to follow the contours of the disk.

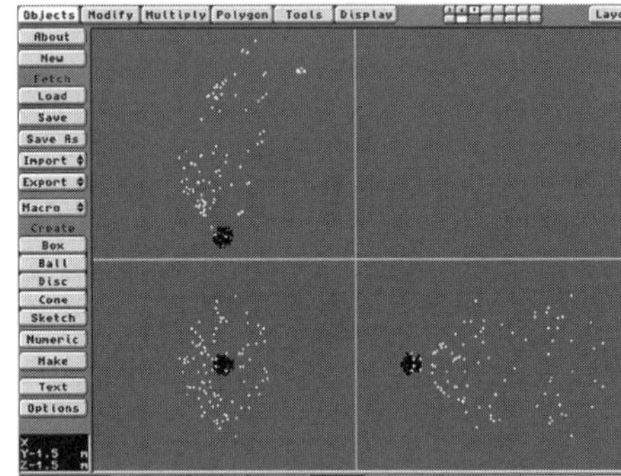

Figure 3: The background layer shows the original ball of particles. The foreground displays how they were stretched and tapered into a shape which will expand out into the camera.

Great Balls of Fire

Hellfire & Brimstone, LightWave-style

by Colin Cunningham

Jerry Lee sure had the right idea, pounding away on his piano and then burning it to the ground for an encore. While that cat could torch a stage without batting an eyelid, mastering flames on the CG front is tricky enough to stop even The Killer dead in his tracks. There are a billion different ways to create realistic fire and heat effects in LightWave, so I'll primarily cover a few techniques used to burn up the screen on *RoboCop: The Series*. They may not be suited for all situations, but hopefully they'll inspire all you virtual arsonists out there to create your very own completely non-lethal pyrotechnics.

In episode 17, "Heartbreakers," our metal hero must battle corruption at the highest level and recover the stolen prototype for a weapon called the Heartbreaker, a microwave-emitting gun that can cause instantaneous heart attacks in its victims. The climax of the show has RoboCop being blasted by the device, an effect I was asked to develop. Since the beam of the gun is invisible (it's just a large microwave oven), I was halfway done already. I began work on the main effect: making Robo's body armor glow red-hot as he is bombarded by the deadly rays. After piling through a dozen harebrained schemes, including actually torching Robo actor Richard Eden (a suggestion not appreciated by the producers), I finally settled on using my old friend the lens flare. Though this was met by dirty looks and verbal abuse from my FX buddies, I thought it would work just fine. There is a saying I'm sure you've all heard at one time or another, "When in doubt, use lens flares," and for this particular effect, that adage couldn't be more true. Though impressive, lens flares tend to be overused, especially the kind that make your eyes water, with lens reflections and random streaks firing out of every corner. While lens flare abuse should certainly be punishable by death (or, more fitting to this article, being torched), I found flares to be a key element in simulating fire FX. When used creatively, they can add subtle realism to most scenes.

Glowing Armor

My first few attempts at making a nice glow effect involved positioning some flares over Robo's body armor. Just as my co-workers suspected, the results looked like lens flares, each of them clearly visible. The flares also lacked the concentrated, uniform glow we desired; dissolving the glow 50 percent blended them together nicely, but the overall glow was too soft and not intense enough. The solution rested in the way the flares were spaced (Figure 1). Glow A consists of five flares arranged in a circular pattern; each flare is set at 100 percent glow with 0 percent dissolve. As you can see, each of the five flares is quite noticeable. Glow B, however, is made up of 13 flares arranged in a similar but tighter pattern. The flares range from 100 percent glow at the center to 40 percent glow and 20 percent dissolve at the outer edge of the circle. By adding more flares and placing them closer together, we allow the central glows to bleed together, forming a uniform and more intense glow. Using this cluster technique, it's possible to create complex shapes made entirely of lens flares.

There was more to the shot than I had first thought, however. Robo's armor had to gradually glow red-hot

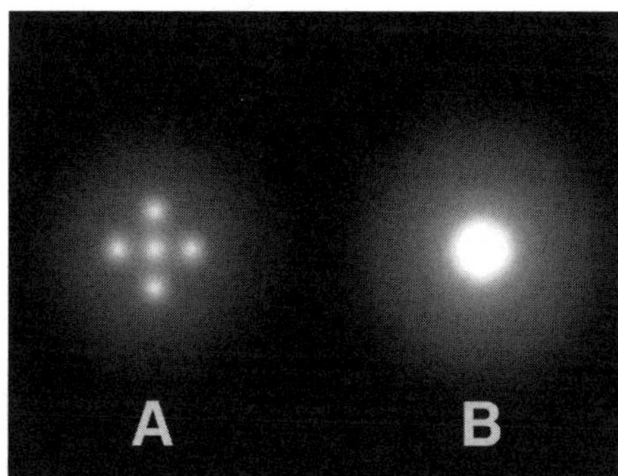

Figure 1: To avoid seeing individual flares (A), pack them tightly so their central glows "bleed" together (B).

as the camera tracked him stumbling backward into a wall. While it sounds like a difficult task, LightWave's new Background Layout Preview function simplified the process. I needed to lock the flare cluster to his chest as he stumbled around, so after generating a background preview from the footage of Robo, a null object was stuck to the center of his chest, traveling with him every step of the way. I simply made keys for the null every three frames or so, fewer when necessary. Once that was complete, I parented seven lens flares to the null (five for the body, two for the helmet) and arranged them in a tight cluster pattern (Figure 3). To conclude, I set up dissolve envelopes for the flares to make them fade in gradually. Aside from a few minor adjustments every few frames, the flares moved with the null and the glow looked as if it was locked to Robo's chest as he struggled. As far as coloring goes, try setting the flare color to R 255 G 154 B 0 and turn on Central Glow and Red Outer Glow in the Lens Flare menu (Random Streaks and Outer Ring should be turned off). The combination of the two colors adds a realistic, fiery look to the flare and works nicely (see the color pages for the results).

Heat Ripples and Hotspots

Before moving on to creating actual flames in LightWave, there are a few more things we need to know about lens flares. The one problem I ran into when using flares was that the screen became too washed out and bright as more flares were added. Figure 2 shows two different approaches. Glow A is one lens flare set at 125 percent glow. Although the central hotspot is the correct size, it's not intense enough, and the haze around the glow completely washes out that half of the screen; it looks more like a

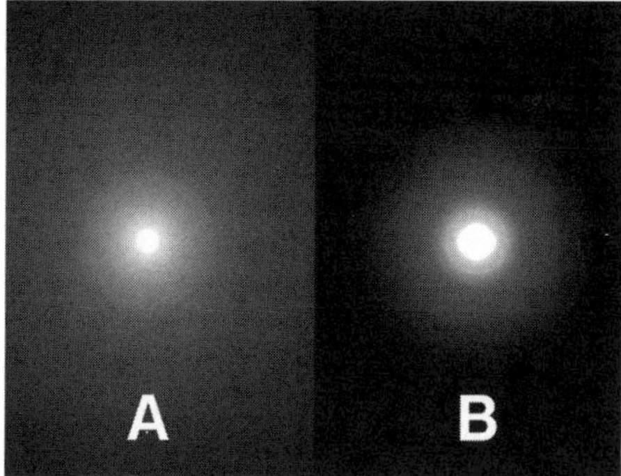

Figure 2: While single, large flares wash out the screen (A), many clustered flares produce a more intense glow without excess haze (B).

Figure 3: Parenting a lens flare cluster to a null object allows for more control when rotoscoping to background footage.

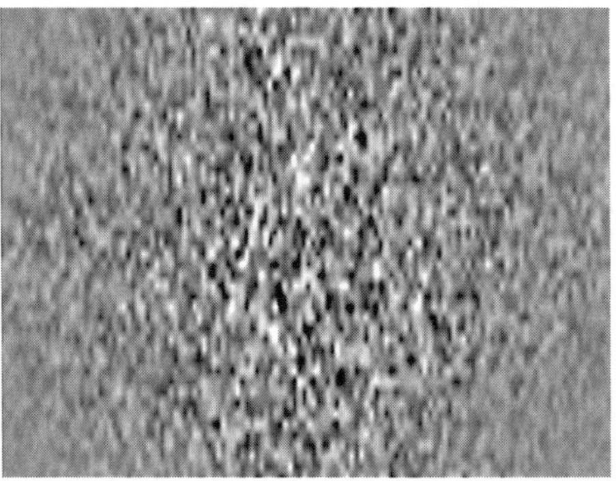

Figure 4: Use the default surface setting to better visualize your travelling bump map before using refraction.

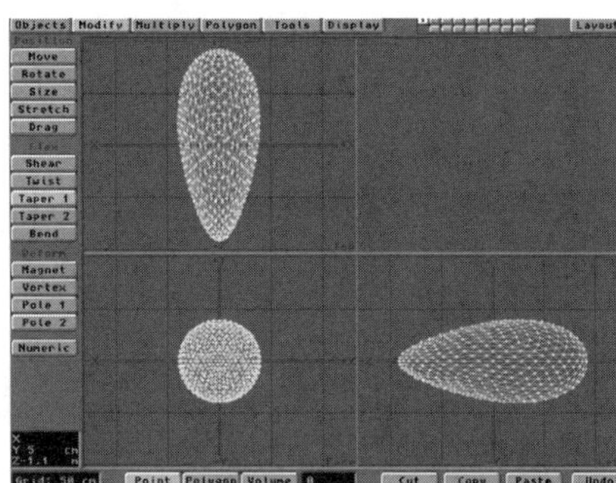

Figure 6: Taper the ball by a factor of 0.5 along the Z axis to get the general shape for the fireball.

light seen through fog. Glow B, however, is comprised of five tightly knit flares with 40 percent glow. This gives us an equally sized but more intense hotspot without the unnecessary haze that accompanies large lens flares. The desired effect is up to you, but hopefully you now have a better idea of how to manipulate lens flares and coax them into doing your bidding.

Although the flare method looked just fine, there still seemed to be something missing from the shot: Robo's armor didn't really look, well, hot enough. I thought nothing more of it and went to see *True Lies* with the rest of the department. We went for a few drinks after the show and talked about a few scenes that caught our fancy, particularly the ones with the Harrier jets. The heat signature they emitted really gave the impression that hot exhaust was blasting out of the jets. It was this element that could give my scene more realism; with this in mind, I awoke the next morning and got right to work adding heat ripples to RoboCop's glowing body.

The first stop was Modeler, where I built a box 2.692 meters wide by two meters high by 0 meters deep (see last month's article "Interactive Refraction" for more details). Name the surface of the box "Screen" by hitting "q" for Change Surface (Polygon menu) and save this object as "screen." Hit "q" again and rename the box surface "Screen.REF." Save this copy of the object as "Screen2" before exiting to layout.

Position the camera at 0,0,0 and make a keyframe for it by hitting return twice. Next, load in the "Screen" object and position it at X 0, Y 0, Z 3.2 before making a keyframe. The next step is simple enough: for my scene I loaded the background footage of Robo as an image sequence and planar-mapped it onto the screen along the Z axis (don't forget to hit automatic sizing). Set the luminosity to 100 percent and the diffuse value to 0 percent. Now comes the interesting bit. Load in the "Screen2" object and position it away from the first object at X 0, Y 0, Z 3.1 (remember to make a keyframe). Enter the Surfaces menu and set the "Screen.ref" surface as follows:

Color: Doesn't Matter
Specularity: 0%.
Transparency 100%
Refractive Index 1.25

Go into the BUMP MAP menu and set the values as follows:

Size X 0.021 Y 0.045 Z 0
Texture Falloff X 50 Y 30 Z 0
Texture Velocity X 0 Y 0.035 Z 0
Amplitude 325% Frequencies 1

Exit into the Camera menu and select Trace Refraction before rendering. Simply put, as the bumps move up the invisible refraction screen, they distort the image sequence on the screen behind just as heat ripples distort things behind them (Figure 4). A texture falloff was added because RoboCop happened to be standing center-frame and I wanted the heat signature to fade off gradually away from him. Because we had a Screamer at our disposal, I wasn't too concerned about rendering time (it turned out to be a couple of minutes per frame), but you may want to try faking refraction as mentioned in Dan Ablan's "Faking Refraction" (September 1994). I received better results using refraction, but not everyone can afford to wait an hour for a render.

Fireballs-a-Plenty

Now comes the part where we actually destroy things. At this point, Robo's armor is glowing more intensely by the second and it looks as if he'll be nothing more than a hunk of burnin' scrap if something isn't done fast. Just when things appear bleak, Robo reverses the polarity of the Heartbreaker beam, blasting a huge fireball across the room that incinerates

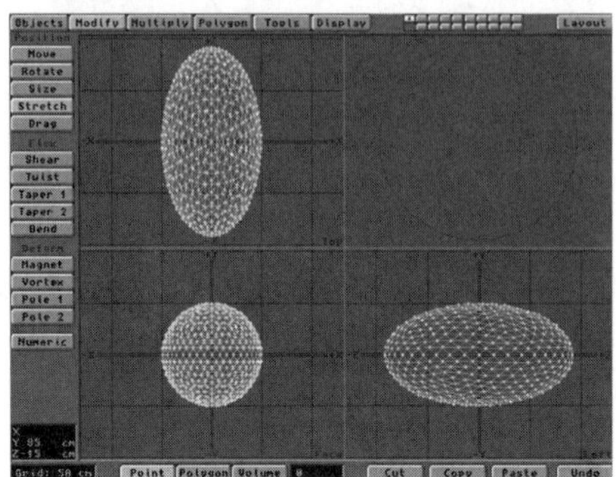

Figure 5: Stretch the ball by a factor of 1.84 along the Z axis

everything in its path, including the bad guy. Some real pyrotechnics were actually set off during filming, but the fireball itself was to be a LightWave effect. This was by far the easiest and most enjoyable part of the scene.

While in Modeler, select the Ball tool in the Objects menu and create a Level 3 Tesselation with the default radius (hit "n" to enter numeric values for tools). Once created, use the Stretch tool (Modify menu) to stretch the ball by a factor of 1.84 along the Z axis (Figure 5), again using "n" to enter numeric values. Next, use the Taper 1 tool (Modify menu) to taper the object by a factor of 0.5 along the Z axis; make sure the sense is set at "-". We've just created the general shape for our fireball (Figure 6). Hit "q" and name the surface "Fireball-OUT." Now select all the polygons in the object by holding down the right mouse button and lassoing the entire object; you can make sure all polygons are selected by hitting "" for Select All Connected. Copy and Paste the object in the same layer and while the polygons are still selected, Size the object (Modify menu) by a factor of 0.95. Keep the polygons highlighted and hit "q" to rename the smaller object "Fireball-IN." Although we now have two fireballs (one inside the other), save the layer as one object called "Fireball" before exiting to Layout.

Although the shape is definitely important, it's the surfacing of an object like this that can determine its success. That said, load the fireball object and enter the surfaces menu. I achieved a nice effect by surfacing as follows:

Fireball-OUT

COLOR 226 225 155
ADDITIVE On
LUMINOSITY 0% with GRID
Texture as follows:
FALLOFF X 0, Y 0, Z 85
VALUE 90%
LINE THICKNESS 2
DIFFUSE 0% with GRID
Texture as follows:
FALLOFF X 0, Y 0, Z 90
VALUE 100%
LINE THICKNESS 2
SPECULARITY 0%
TRANSPARENCY 4% with FRACTAL NOISE

Texture as follows:

SIZE X 0.07, Y 0.08, Z 0.6

VELOCITY X 0, Y 0, Z -0.3

VALUE 100%

FREQUENCIES 6

CONTRAST 2.0

EDGES Transparent

EDGE THRESHOLD 1.0

SMOOTHING On

DOUBLE SIDED On

Fireball-IN

Everything is identical to Fireball-OUT except the following:

COLOR 251 45 0

The GRID textures for LUMINOSITY and DIFFUSE have a value of 85% and 100%, respectively, and both have a TEXTURE FALLOFF of 62% on the Z axis.

The reason for the Grid textures was to make the Fireball gradually fade out toward the tail so the shape of the object isn't evident (the transparent edges helped as well). Though the Fireball looked pretty good on its own, I parented a small cluster of lens flares at the tip to give it a furniture-destroying glow (see the color pages). If all goes well, your fireball should look like a fireball, complete with traveling flames. Using this as a template of sorts, you can modify the shape or surfacing of the object to come up with some interesting effects of your own.

I'm sure that with some practice and plenty of experimenting, the fire department will come a knockin' in no time. As for me, Robo blew the bad guy to hell and I'm still trying to regrow my eyebrows.

Cluster lens flares together for a more uniform, intense glow. Use many small flares packed together instead of one large flare to avoid excess glow washing out the scene.

Create two 2.692m x 2m screens in Modeler, Screen1 and Screen2. Position Screen1 to fill the entire camera view and position Screen2 slightly closer to the camera. Map image sequence onto Screen1 and make Screen2 refractive with a bump map traveling up it.

Create a Level 3 tesselation and stretch and taper one end. Name the surface Fireball-OUT and select all polygons. Then copy, paste and shrink the object slightly. Finally, name the smaller object Fireball-IN and save the two as one object. Experiment and HAVE FUN!

LWP

Colin Cunningham is enrolled in the infamous classical animation program at Sheridan College in Canada. He is currently working on a 3D cartoon short that he calls "a cross between Evil Dead *and* Itchy & Scratchy. *Cunningham can be reached at (905) 338-8033 at any time, because Sheridan students don't sleep.*

The Complete Nebula Guide

by William Frawley

Although Mojo briefly but effectively discussed nebula creation in the August issue of *LWPRO*—and I do substantiate Foundation Imaging's hand-painting method as the most capable—I feel compelled to elaborate on a few aspects of the various techniques, with a focus on the subtleties of utilizing transparency-mapped nebulas.

While employing transparency-mapped textures increases rendering time, their use in this case allows nebulas to be localized in any region of the scene while keeping any objects behind visible. In other words, nebulas don't always have to conspicuously serve as a background for silhouetting objects in the stark lighting conditions of space, but may simply exist for their own merit, beauty itself.

But before we immerse ourselves in the details of this somewhat more involved technique, let's see how easy it is for LightWave's own procedural surfacing capabilities to create that simple, single-color background nebula.

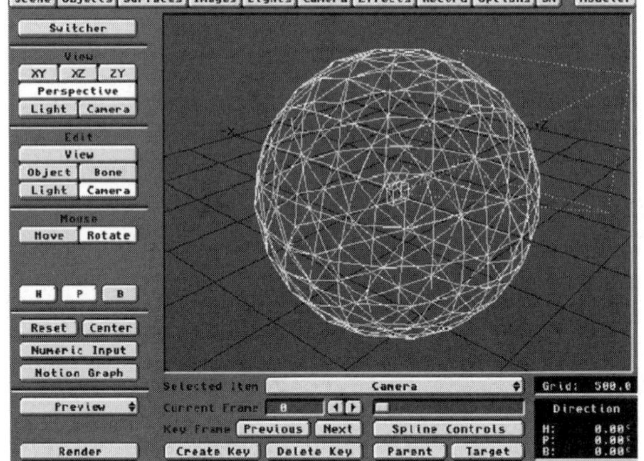

Figure 1

Procedural-Only Method

Using Fractal Noise luminosity and transparency procedural textures applied to the inside of a sphere, your entire scene contained within then becomes surrounded by patches of nebulas good enough for a subtle background effect. Add a spherical collection of single-point polygons (particles) for stars, and you're ready to roll.

Begin in Modeler by creating a two-level tessellated sphere with a radius of 1km for all axes (an even unit of 10 helps later when working with texture value percentages). You'll need to access the Ball tool's control panel by selecting **Ball** in the **Objects** menu, then **Numeric** (n) to manually alter the parameters.

Enter the above figures leaving everything else at default, then press Enter to accept the requester and Enter again to make the sphere. Press (a) to fit the entire globe within view.

Though more important in planet and moon creation, using Tessellation in this case, produces a smoother outline to the ball, especially when seen at close proximity.

At this point, the polygons making up the sphere all face outward, which is not what we want. They should face the opposite direction so that they will be seen from inside the sphere. To rectify this situation, use the **Flip** tool (f) in the **Polygon** menu, being sure that none (or all) of the polygons making up the sphere are selected to reverse the direction in which they face. Remember, if none are selected, they're all selected. Lastly, rename the surface (q) "Nebula" and **Export** this object to Layout, naming the object "Nebula.sphere."

Just Scratching the Surface

Back in Layout, move the Camera along the Z axis to either the origin (0,0,0) or as far back on the Z axis (negative direction) before it leaves the inside of the sphere just created (Figure 1). Use the **XZ** view to visually aid with the camera placement.

By placing the camera as close as possible to the inside wall of the sphere, the maximum amount of the nebula's real estate can be seen when feedback for adjusting the surface parameters is required. Make sure to create a keyframe (Enter key twice) at zero for both the camera and Nebula.sphere object.

In the **Surfaces** panel, select a color for the nebula. I chose a blue with RGB values of 70,0,170. Leaving the Luminosity value at 0 percent, press **T** beside it to access the Luminosity texture panel. Enter the following values, leaving all others at their default:

Texture Type	Fractal Noise
Texture Size	250,50,250
Texture Value	100 percent
Frequencies	6

In essence, the fractal noise generates a pattern of luminosity roughly 25 percent of the width and depth and five percent of the height of the object. Depending how bright you want the nebula, feel free to adjust the Texture Value to anything between 75 percent and 200 percent. Anything higher tends to wash out the detail of the fractal pattern. At this point, select **Use Texture**, turn on **Smoothing** and do a test render to check your results.

As you can see, the nebula fills the entire interior of the sphere, which is not exactly what we're shooting for. Large patches are necessary where the nebula is invisible or transparent. Leave the Transparency value at 0 percent and then create a transparency texture map with the following values:

Texture Type	Fractal Noise
Texture Size	500,500,500
Texture Value	200 percent
Frequencies	6

Your results should be more favorable this time, providing that large patches of nebula with relatively smaller patterns of detail are used. For a bit more variety, however, try varying the Transparency texture values for the size, especially increasing the X and Z values by a factor of three. Also, try rotating the nebula sphere using the Bank axis so it appears to be tilted diagonally.

Alternatively, you could set the Luminosity to a constant value of, say, 100 percent and use the Surface Color texture to modulate the color between black and whatever color you want the nebula to be. Using this method, you can move and rotate your camera any-

Figure 2

Figure 3

Figure 4

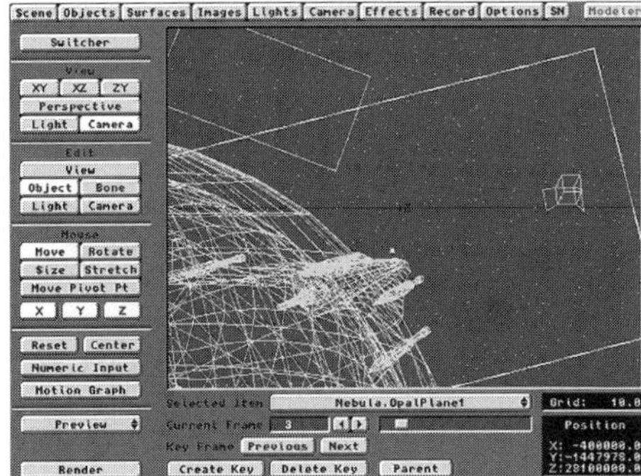

Figure 5

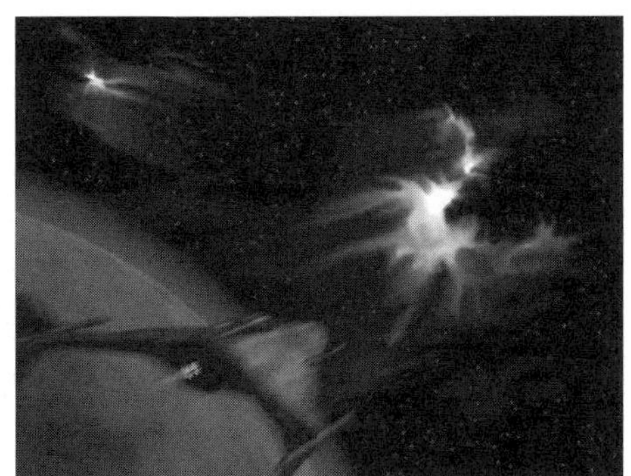

Figure 6

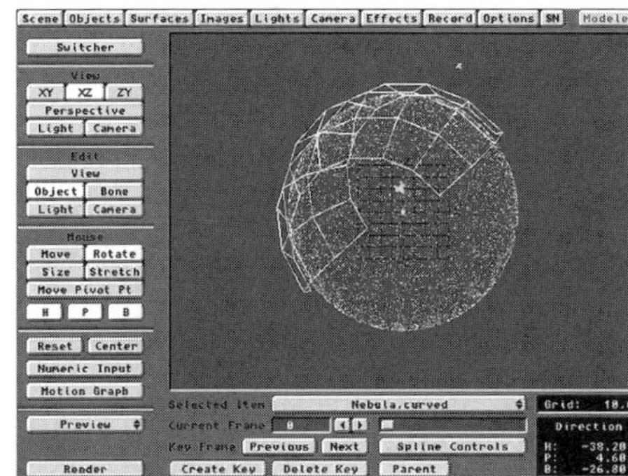

Figure 7

where and always have a general nebula pattern for background highlighting, with no painting skills required on your part. Add some stars and your foray into basic nebulas is complete (Figure 2).

Rolling Your Own Local Nebulas

For more dramatic color nebulas such as those seen on *Babylon 5*, we must go beyond LightWave's procedural surface texturing. However, with a slight deviation from the Foundation Imaging technique alluded to by Mojo, we can place the nebula anywhere within camera's view without worrying about the edges of the nebula image or what objects will or won't be seen behind it. In this case, we can even map the image onto a flat plane, but a transparency map is needed to do this.

To begin, paint a nebula with your favorite 24-bit or AGA paint software. I chose to use OpalPaint (Centaur), but you could also try ImageFX (GVP), Brilliance (Digital Creations), DPaint AGA (Electronic Arts) or, if you have it, PhotoShop (Adobe). Having a graphics tablet for this part helps tremendously. Once complete, save this image as a 24-bit IFF (Figure 3, see color pages). Now this image can be used as the basis for the transparency map.

Transparency Maps 101

Why do we need a transparency map in the first place? Well, with this method of mapping the full-color nebula image onto a plane object as a surface color texture, if there are any other objects in the scene behind this plane, they will not be visible because there haven't been any areas within this object's surface designated as transparent. Thus, applying an image map as opposed to a procedural texture allows exact control over which regions are or aren't transparent. And since we want the nebula to gradually become more transparent near its edges, it would seem that the actual nebula image itself inherently contains the required data, with only minor modifications necessary.

Recall that when applying images as any other texture map except surface color, only the luminance values (brightness) of the image are used, with white representing full intensity and black zero intensity for that particular texture type. Any values between the extremes are varying degrees of intensity. For our transparency map, simply convert the full-color nebula image into a grayscale negative so that any black in the original becomes white (transparent) and vice versa (Figure 4). This is easily done in any image processing program such as ADPro (Elastic Reality) or ImageFX. Even ToasterPaint will suffice.

When using these Color To Gray operators, be sure to adjust the relative weights of the RGB components in order to compensate or increase the opacity of certain portions of your nebula.

For example, after applying the Negative operator, if the Color To Gray default values for the Luma weighting favoring the green components are used for the transparency map, much of the blue in the nebula image will be too transparent and hence won't be visible.

Compensate for this with larger values (relative to the others) for the blue component. Notice that the blue areas are then darker in the grayscale transparency map. If, however, this results in areas of intense hotspots for other colors, use the Dynamic Range operator to reduce values for the upper limit.

Don't be concerned if this all sounds a little abstract at this time. Once you've rendered the nebula scene, you can return to this point and adjust the values for the transparency map accordingly. For now, save the grayscale image as "Nebula.trans."

Enter LightWave and load the color nebula image and its associated transparency map from the **Images** panel. Create a plane in Modeler with the aid of the **BG Image** (**Display** menu) feature to match the dimensions of the nebula image. Rename the surface (q) "Nebula.plane" and **Export** this object to Layout.

Back in Layout, enter the **Surfaces** panel and select the "Nebula.plane" surface for editing. Enter the Surface Color Texture panel (**T**) and apply the color nebula image as a Planar Image Map on the **Z Axis**. Select **Automatic Sizing** for a perfect fit.

Next, enter a Luminosity value of 300 percent and change the Diffuse Level to 0 percent, as we do not want the scene's lighting conditions to affect this surface. Proceed to enter a Transparency texture in the same manner as the Surface Color image map, but use the "Nebula.trans" image map instead.

Finally, position the nebula object anywhere in your scene as long as it faces the camera view (Figure 5). Add a few stars and render away (Figure 6). For added realism, it helps to increase the scale and distance so some of the stars (particles) will appear in front of the nebula. Also, because this object is self-luminous, you can turn off any lights to save some rendering time.

The Final Frontier

At this point, I call your attention to Figure 7. This is the technique Mojo described of mapping the nebula image onto a curved polygon object, which is sized marginally larger than the starfield. This then negates the need for a transparency map because every object lies in front of the nebula, even the stars. For this nebula object, I simply deleted a few top and bottom rows and some of the sides of a globe-type ball, then flipped the remaining polygons inward.

The image in the color pages shows the result of using the "outside stars" nebula as before, but with the sky-filling technique, different regions can be magnified for different projects, including reusable nebulas.

To Summarize the Various Techniques:

1. PROCEDURAL/Interior Sphere/Fractal Noise Transparency or Luminosity
2. PROCEDURAL & IMAGE MAP/Interior Curved Polygon or Flat Plane/Fractal Noise Color/Nebula Image Transparency Map
3. IMAGE MAP/Flat Plane/Color Nebula Image Map/Nebula Image Transparency Map
4. IMAGE MAP/Interior Curved Polygon/Color Nebula Image Map

Engage!

LightWave 101

Course 1C: Basic Surface Strategies

by Taylor Kurosaki

This installment of "LightWave 101" will begin to explore one of the most critical components of 3D: object surfacing. In terms of creating a photorealistic CGI environment, effective surfacing is crucial. For example, there is currently a completely computer-generated commercial for Levi's Jeans featuring a figurine pulling rubber balls out of a shoebox.

To be sure, the modeling involved was extremely straight-forward and simple, consisting only of basic variations of spheres, boxes and cylinders. The animation was fairly basic and the movements weren't exactly lifelike (nor did they necessarily have to be). Even the lighting was less than realistic with its hard-edged, ray-traced shadows and lack of natural reflective light.

That said, I am still constantly fascinated with this commercial. The surfacing work in this spot is so realistic that at times the distinction between computer generated and reality is blurred. It isn't even the texture maps themselves which are excellent; in fact, the only texture maps I can remember are the stripe and star on one of the rubber balls, and the wood texture on the figurine. What makes the surfacing so realistic, in this case, is the way in which light affects the objects, the way light would affect similar objects in reality. The rubber ball appears to "feel" rubber. The figurine looks to be made of stained and painted wood. The surfaces on these objects make them seem tangible.

The satellite object from last month's issue will again be used here as an example. Obviously, I want the satellite to look realistic, but more specifically, it should look like it's been in orbit for quite some time. It should appear metallic yet grungy, not unlike the "dirty" ships in the *Star Wars* movies. This can be accomplished easier than you may think.

The areas of the satellite we will surface are the Upper and Lower Girder sections, the Ring section and the Center structure. Let's begin by first selecting the Surface Color for these three sections. Keep in mind that this is merely a starting point, as the Diffuse percentage will greatly affect the appearance of the surface color.

Figure 1

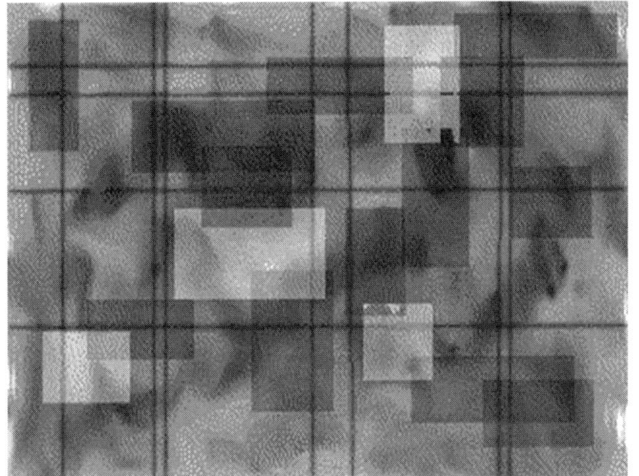

Figure 2

For the Ring section I have chosen the values of 200, 210, 225, which is a slightly bluish, light gray. To create contrast the Center section uses the darker values of 100, 110, 120. The Upper and Lower Girder sections use a dark gray of 60, 60, 60. The resulting surfaces appear in Figure 1.

Obtaining a dirty metal appearance involves primarily a combination of Specular and Diffuse image mapping. Before diving into the theory behind this surfacing technique, a few definitions are necessary: Diffuse is the amount of light returned from the object back to the camera. In the real world, an object which is 100 percent diffuse returns all light hitting it, while an object which is 0 percent diffuse absorbs all light reaching it (thus making it appear black). Although LightWave doesn't actually reproduce this phenomenon (it's called radiosity), it does simulate it by reducing the color values by the percentage of the diffusion. For example, an object with a Surface Color of 255,0,0 with a light of 100 percent intensity perpendicular to it and a Diffuse value of 100 percent will appear as pure red when rendered. Reduce the Diffuse level to 50 percent, and the rendered color is equivalent to 127,0,0. Lower the Diffuse to 0 percent and the object appears black (0,0,0).

Specularity refers to the amount of shine an object appears to have. A polished chrome surface would be extremely specular (100 percent), while dry clay would have no specularity whatsoever (0 percent). This tutorial will describe how to use a combination of Diffuse and Specular attributes to simulate a dirty, weathered, metallic surface.

Diffuse Mapping

To obtain a tiled, metal plate surface, a map similar to the one shown in Figure 2 works well. It can be painted in grayscale in any paint program by selecting rectangular areas and filling them in with varying shades of gray.

My preferred method of painting this type of map is to use Adobe Photoshop, beginning with a light-gray

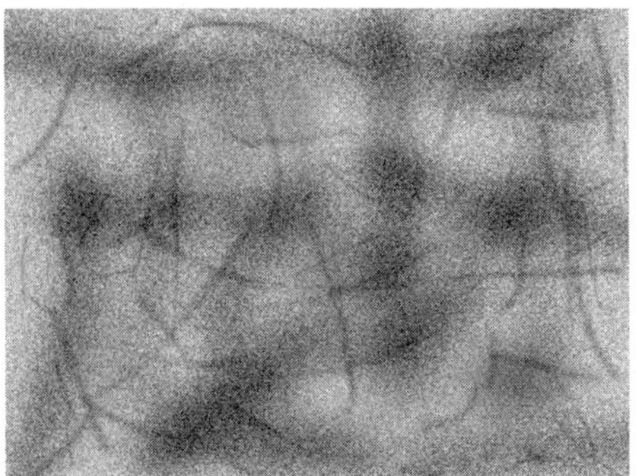

Figure 3

Figure 4

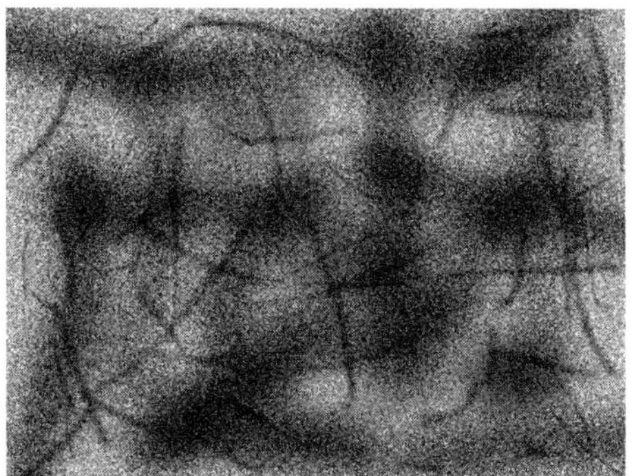

Figure 5

background. Independently select various rectangular areas, and adjust the contrast and brightness of the selected areas into differing regions of light and dark. Finally, perform a noise or blur operation on the whole image to grunge it up. The darker areas of the map will correspond to areas of less diffusion, while lighter areas appear more diffuse.

More specifically, totally white areas (255,255,255) translate to areas of 100 percent diffusion, completely black areas (0,0,0) result in areas of 0 percent diffusion, and medium gray areas (127,127,127) render with 50 percent diffusion. The end result is a light and dark pattern on the object which consists of several shades of the object's original Surface Color.

Due to this fact, Diffuse Maps (and other surface maps, except Surface Color) need only be grayscale images, as their color information is discarded in favor of the object's Surface Color. The image in Figure 2 was used as a diffuse map on both the Ring and Center sections of the satellite with the following settings:

Ring Section
Texture Type .... Cylindrical Image Map
Pixel Blending .... On
Texture Axis .... Y Axis
Texture Size 3.75, 16.0, 3.75
Antialiasing .... On
Width Wrap Amount 7.0

Center Section
Texture Type .... Cylindrical Image Map
Pixel Blending .... On
Texture Axis .... Y Axis
Texture Size 6.26, 8.0, 6.26
Antialiasing .... On

All other values should be left at their defaults.

For the satellite's Upper and Lower Girder sections, the map in Figure 3 was painted. This map was also created in Photoshop using the airbrush tool with noise added, although it can be created just as easily in any paint program. When applied as a Diffuse map, the darker areas appear as dirty areas on the surface, while the lighter areas appear clean, allowing the true surface color to show through more visibly. The following values were used here:

Upper and Lower Girder Sections
Texture Type .... Cylindrical Image Map
Pixel Blending .... On
Texture Axis .... Y Axis
Texture Size 10.55, 50.0, 10.55
Antialiasing .... On

Again, any values not listed were left at default.

Figure 4 shows the Ring, Center, and Upper Girder sections of the satellite with their Diffuse maps in place.

Specular Mapping

The satellite is now comprised of light and dark patterns through the use of Diffuse maps. On the Ring and Center sections, the Diffuse maps appear as weathered metal plating, giving the satellite a mechanical, assembled look. The Diffuse map on the Girder sections serves a different purpose—to look like dirty piping. The satellite is now shaded like it is comprised of metal, but it doesn't have the shiny properties of metal.

This is where the Specular Level setting is helpful. If the satellite was perfectly clean and polished, it would have a constant specularity across its surface (somewhere between five and 20 percent, for example). In our case, however, the Specular level would not be constant due to its tarnished state. Dirty areas would appear less specular than cleaner areas.

This is the perfect application for a Specular Image Map. In the case of the satellite's Girders, the shape of the Specular Map should be the same as the Diffuse Map, due to the fact that the dirty (less diffuse) areas should correspond to less shiny (less specular) areas.

Therefore, a variation of the Girder's Diffuse map will work well as its Specular map. In this case I darkened the Girder's Diffuse map, saved it, and applied it as a specular map (Figure 5).

Darkening will lower the overall specular level throughout the map. [Note: Surfaces that are too specular are always a sure giveaway of CGI. A little specular goes a long way, so keep your specular maps on the darkish side.]

I then applied the same specular map to the Ring section of the satellite. This map will add the highlights necessary to complete the metallic look for this object. See the color section for the completed satellite with these surfaces in place. The values used are listed below:

Upper and Lower Girder Sections
Texture Type .... Cylindrical Image Map
Pixel Blending .... On
Texture Axis .... Y-Axis
Texture Size 10.55, 50.0, 10.55
Antialiasing .... On

Ring Section
Texture Type .... Cylindrical Image Map
Pixel Blending .... On
Texture Axis .... Y-Axis
Texture Size 16.05, 103.75, 16.05
Antialiasing .... On
Width Wrap Amount 5 0.10

Other Maps

Another type of map which adds realism to your objects is a Bump Map. This type of map will cause bumps and ridges to appear in the surface of the object, depending on the shape of the image. With a Bump Map, the dark areas of the image appear to be inset from the surface, causing shading to "fall into" those areas. With the satellite object, use the diffuse map image and settings as a Bump Map on the Ring and Center sections. A Texture Amplitude anywhere from 100 percent to 200 percent should work well.

LWP

Taylor Kurosaki is an animator at Amblin Imaging. As usual, the majority of the techniques described above were systematically, though painlessly, taken directly from the brain of Eric Barba, among others. Thanks guys. Questions, comments and a comb should be sent to Taylor's attention at 100 Universal City Plaza, Bldg. 447, Universal City, CA 91608.

Real Textures

by Enrique Muñoz

Since the first version of our favorite 3D program, LightWave has had the ability to do procedural textures. With each revision, however, we've gotten a few more textures. In this article, I'll look at the most recent set of textures—specifically, Crust, Bump Array, Veins and Crumple.

This tutorial is not going to be the kind where you simply follow the directions and input some values. The point is to show alternatives to these new textures. I've learned through my own experience that just letting go and doing something, then going back and looking at what you did and understanding it, is the best way to learn how LightWave works.

Remember, these texture examples are just that: examples. These are the settings that I have found most useful, but getting the right surface setting with textures takes a lot of experimentation and testing.

Just One Plane

First we are going to need an object to place our texture on. Go into Modeler and select the Box tool. Make a 1.345-meter-by-1-meter plane in the Face view. Give this object any surface name you want and export it back to Layout. Move your camera up close to our object so that you can see the texture settings clearly (Figure 1). Using LightWave 4.0's Surface Sample spheres(s) is an alternative, but there are some problems involved. We will look at these problems in depth later in this article. If no surface setting is specified for a particular field, leave it at its default state. Before applying our values, let's think of what we can actually make.

Bump Array

This tool can be used to make textures with consecutive bumps for their all-around surface. Some good examples are golf balls, a skillet, the eyeballs of a fly and stained-glass dimples. Another thing that we can do with this texture is make snake skin. Huh? Well, think about it. What is real snake skin in its most basic form? A colored surface with dimples. Isn't this what Bump Array is for? Using this kind of thinking throughout this tutorial will help you understand the lessons and how to use these textures effectively. To get this surface, apply the following attributes:

Surface Color	0, 65, 80
Surface Color Texture	
Texture Type	Fractal Noise
Texture Size	0.1, 0.1, 0.1
Texture Color	198, 0, 0
Frequencies	4
Contrast	2.0
Diffuse Level	100%
Diffuse Texture	
Texture Type	Bump Array
Texture Value	50%
Radius	0.3
Spacing	0.1
Bump Strength	-0.5

Apply this to your favorite snake object, and voilà!

Crumply

When you think of Crumple, crumpled paper comes to mind. When you think of crumpled paper you start to think of something rough, like a rock. You can also use this texture on transparent objects, giving them a chipped-glass effect, especially if you have Trace Refraction turned on.

We could actually go to the opposite extreme and make sand! Just apply the following attributes:

Surface Color	180, 150, 100
Diffuse Level	80%
Diffuse Texture	
Texture Type	Fractal Noise
Texture Size	0.1, 0.1, 0.1
Texture Falloff	0.1, 0.1, 0.1
Texture Value	100%
Frequencies	2
Contrast	1.0
Specularity	15%
Color Highlights	On
Glossiness	Low
Bump Map Texture	
Texture Type	Crumple
Texture Size	0.5, 0.5, 0.5
Texture Falloff	0.5, 0.5, 0.5
Texture Amplitude	15%
Number of Scales	4
Small Power	0.75

One interesting thing about Crumple is that if the **Texture Amplitude** is set to a negative number, it will start looking like the Bump Array texture when you have the Spacing set to a smaller number than the Radius.

Veiny

What could we use the vein texture for, other than showing what the name implies? Things that come to mind are a flagstones-type texture (with a little work) and the hull of a spaceship (a la *Babylon 5*). If you're trying to re-create the hull of the *seaQuest*, here's your ticket to achieving it.

Our first example of using Veins to achieve a flagstones-type texture involves setting our Bump Strength to a negative number. We do this so the vein texture sticks in rather than out, which would cause the vein texture's "in-betweens" to look like little rock fragments. Next, change the **Coverage** and **Ledge Level** to a small number, so it appears as if it is the "cement" between the rock fragments.

To get the *seaQuest* texture, set your surfaces to a shade of dark blue and use Veins as your **Surface Color** texture, but with no **Bump Strength.** Next, use the texture in any of the other maps and use a center offset with a bump strength of -.5. This should give you something resembling a blue leopard (if there was one).

If you followed everything correctly or just want my specific settings, here they are:

Surface Color	0, 0, 60
Surface Color Texture	
Texture Type	Veins
Texture Size	0.1, 0.3, 0.1
Texture Color	55, 120, 205
Coverage	0.1
Ledge Level	0.1
Ledge Width	0.3
Bump Strength	0
Diffuse Level	90%
Specular Level	80%
Specular Texture	
Texture Type	Veins
Texture Size	0.3, 0.4, 0.2
Texture Center	1.0 (for all axes)
Texture Value	0%

Coverage	1.0
Ledge Level	001
Ledge Width	.175
Bump Strength	-0.75
Glossiness	Medium

Crusty

When I think of Crust I envision something organic (and sometimes gross). It doesn't always have to be used for just these purposes, though. Instead of having regular, patterned dots, like those you get with the Dots texture, you can now have randomly placed dots with variable sizes. By just putting the Ledge Level and

Figure 1: The simplicity of the Surface Test Scene

Ledge Width fields to zero, we get rid of the edges and are left with just the dots. If **Bump Strength** is set to a negative number, we can get some results that we would have never thought imaginable. The moon is only one example. We can create this effect by using the texture in any two maps, such as a Diffuse and Luminosity or a Surface Color and specularity map (with different size offsets and centers). Remember, these textures don't just add a value—they also shade your surface.

So what other tricks can you think of? Well, with a little experimentation, I've come up with a neat little tactic for forming condensation on the surface of the infamous Popcan included with LightWave. (You can actually use this trick with any type of object—a glass cup, champagne bottle, etc.)

- Go into Modeler and load the Popcan from your objects directory. Press the (q) key (or Surface under the Polygon menu). Name the new surface anything you want, and save it as a new object (WaterChill for this example).
- In Layout, load in both Popcans. Change the new Popcan's (WaterChill) pivot point to 0.062 on the Y-axis, because if it is sized from where the pivot point was, the Popcan will stretch from the bottom to the top. That's incorrect! It should size from the center to all its sides. Size it to a slightly larger margin. (For this example, change it to 1.03, 1.01, 1.03.)
- Go to the Surfaces panel and select your WaterChill surface. Apply the following attributes:

Surface Color	200, 200, 200
Diffuse Level	100%
Diffuse Texture	
Texture Type	Crust
Texture Size	0.01, 0.01, 0.01
Texture Value	100%
Coverage	0.3
Ledge Level	0.3
Ledge Width	0.4
Bump Strength	1.0
Specular Level	100%
Glossiness	Low
Reflectivity	20%
Transparency	100%
Refractive Index	1.33
Smoothing	On

Now just set your lighting, set up your layers of Refraction (see past issues of *LWPRO* for more information) and turn on Trace Reflection and Trace Refraction. Wait a couple of hours (seriously) and you'll have your own virtual pop can.

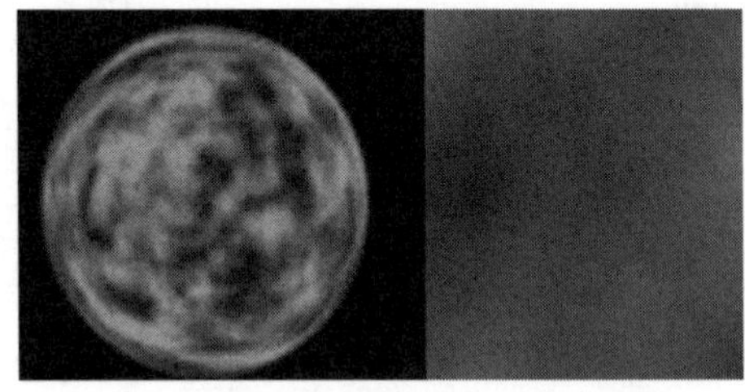

Figure 2: The difference between Surface Samples and actually rendering out the surface

Surface Samples Problems

The reason why I didn't want you to use LightWave's new Surface Samples was the many inconveniences associated with it. The first problem is that it (Surface Samples)doesn't take into account your global environment settings. What I mean is, it doesn't use the lighting you have set in your scene, or any fog settings or background images. Another problem is that it doesn't take into account what type of object this surface is going to be used on.

For a better understanding of the above sentence, do the following: load in the Gold Surface from your surfaces directory and render out our surface plane to your display buffer. What do you see? It should be a plane with darkness and brightness spots. Now render a Surface Sample by typing a lowercase (s). Do you see the difference between using Surface Samples and actually rendering out your real surface (Figure 2)? On your Surface Sample, you see a sphere with a completely different look. It has a surface that actually looks something like what a cow would have (a gold one, at least). Even though we have the exact same settings, we get different results. This happens because spherical reflection maps are computed upon different-shaped objects (in our case, a plane and a sphere). You will also get this problem when applying textures or images.

The moral of the story? Never commit to a surface without rendering out your object in its final environment with your surface settings.

LWP

Enrique Muñoz is a senior animator for Digital Imaging, based in Ontario, Calif.

LightWood in LightWave

by Dan Ablan

If you read *LWPRO* on a regular basis, it's safe to assume that you are well-versed on the capabilities of this great 3D program. It is probably also safe to say that you know how to import surfaces and textures into your animations from all types of sources. Imagine, though, that you are new at all of this, and only wanted to use the system and software you paid for. Why should you have to purchase extra textures if you just spent so much money on your system? On the other hand, what if you aren't new at all, but still have to meet a deadline, and there is no time to generate realistic textures? Well, here is a simple tutorial that works well for both new users and the experienced.

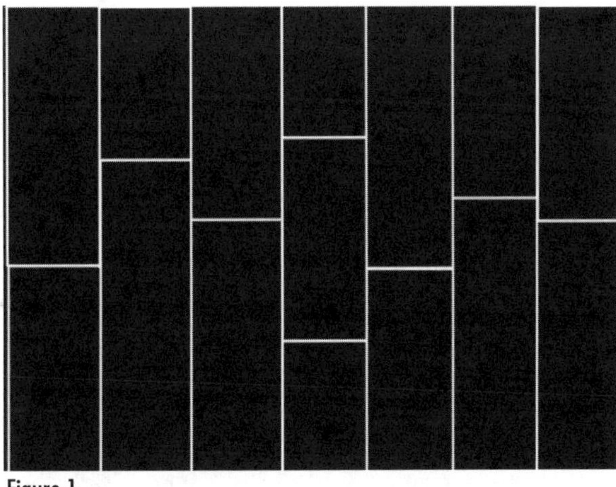

Figure 1

Figure 2

Two Steps

The credit for this idea should go to my good friend Arnie Boedecker, who created a fantastic living room floor with this technique. I took it one step further, using the final image as a background for a logo job. Perhaps you can use it for something else, maybe paneling a wall or a log cabin. All you need is ToasterPaint, LightWave, and a little time.

We're going to take that familiar lightwood surface and use it to make a random, wood-slat floor (Figure 1). Start by loading the **Get Small** project. If you're not running with a lot of RAM, close CG and LightWave if they're open. Enter TPaint. The first task is creating a black and white image that has two purposes. The first is to help line up our wood floor slats, and the second is for a bump map. Select an unfilled rectangle as your drawing tool, with the smallest circular or square brush. Draw out a long vertical rectangle, so you have a white outline on black. Continue drawing out vertical rectangles, but make their vertical positions vary. You can use the **Set Grid** feature of TPaint to help keep even width. Figure 1 shows what the final image bump map image should look like.

Remember, this will serve as an outline for your floor and where the wood slats will be, so play around with the randomness of the lines. Once you're happy with what you've done, **save** it as an RGB image, as LightWood_Bump. Now, with this image still loaded, hit the **J** key to jump to TPaint's other screen. Load the **lightwood** image from the **Wood** directory. This is the part that gets somewhat tedious, but it's worth the effort. Begin to cut different parts of the lightwood image and TXMap it down.

When you cut out a section of the lightwood image, or the whole screen, make sure you **Copy This Brush**, under the **Brushes** menu. This will hold what you've cut in a temporary buffer. Use the **J** key to jump back to your other screen with the black and white bump map image. Under **Options**, using the right mouse button, select **TXMap**. Choose a filled rectangle as your drawing tool and the smallest square as your brush (not the pixel brush). Go to any one of the black and white rectangles and TXMap your image into just one of the areas (Figure 2). Cut different areas of the lightwood image and shrink, flip, darken and lighten to create random pieces of wood. Don't be afraid to cut an area, stretch it out, and then cut it again. The more ways you manipulate the lightwood image, the more random it will be. **Save** this as LightWood_Tall. Hit the **J** key again to jump back to the original lightwood image. Cut out another area, copy the brush, and TXMap it into place. Darken or Lighten this one a bit. Continue this process, filling up each space on your bump map, until you have what looks like random pieces of wood, like a floor. Remember to be creative and flip your brush, stretch it, or crunch it to vary the texture. In addition to darkening and lightening, add a little color of white, or brown to a few of the areas for more randomness. Figure 3 shows the final wood image in TPaint. Each seam should match the black and white image you created earlier. Again, save the image.

Into LightWave

Once you've made your bump map and wood floor, close TPaint and enter LightWave. Here's a tip: You can quit and close TPaint all in one move. Hit the left shift and the tilde key all at once (Tilde is the key just left of the number 1 key). The first thing you need to do is make a one-sided polygon in the shape of a rectangle in Modeler.

Make sure your surface is facing the camera, name that surface something like WoodBKD, and

Export this as a new object, saving it as LightWoodBKD_obj. Go to your images panel and load the two Toaster Paint images you just created, LightWood_Tall and LightWood_Bump. To help save memory in LightWave, you may want to change the LightWood_Bump image to two colors.

Under the surface panel, select the WoodFloor surface, and click on the **T** button next to **texture color**. Use a planer image map, on the Z axis. Click automatic sizing and turn off antialiasing. Antialiasing is turned off in this panel, because we'll turn it on under the camera panel for rendering. If both antialiasings are turned on, the images can become blurry. Click on Use Texture. Set your **specularity** level at about 70 percent. **Glossiness** is High. The next thing to do is create the separation between the slats of wood. Since the slats of wood were placed down using our bump map as a template in paint, the seams will match up evenly with the bump map in LightWave.

Click the **T** button next to **Bump Map**. Also set planer image map, Z axis and automatic sizing. Set the amplitude to -55 percent. Click **use texture**. Move your camera view so the flat polygon (LightWoodBKD_obj) we just created is filling up the whole screen.

Figure 3

Figure 4

Now render the image to see how it looks. You may want to vary the amplitude for the bump map and adjust the specularity a bit. If you like what you see, **save all objects** and save the scene. Go a step further now by changing the light source. Make the distant light a spot and change the color to a soft amber or pale yellow. Doing this will warm up the image. Remember, LightWave defaults its light color at white. Look around—the light around you is never pure white. Angle down from the top left, so that not all of the area is hit by the light (Figure 4). Turn on Trace Shadows and render in Medium Resolution with low antialiasing.

It will take a little time to render, but you can then save the image and load it back into LightWave, using it as a **background image.**

This is a fairly simple technique, but very effective. You can use it as a background image, like I do, or repeat it for a flooring like my friend Arnie does. If you were going to use it as a floor, consider making it glossy, and set a reflection level of about 15%. Turn on **Trace Reflection** and you'll see some nice results. You might want to make the images (LightWood_Tall and LightWood_Bump) seamless, so you can repeat them over a large area.

By taking existing images already in your system and spending a small amount of time manipulating them, you can create truly realistic textures in LightWave. For example, although the ever-familiar Verde-Pompeii Marble image is nice, it's overused. I've seen it used time and time again in animations, CG pages, etc. But you can still use it... just take it one step further. If you were making a floor for a living room scene, and had absolutely no time to get any textures, and only had what your system came with, you could use the Verde marble image. Color that floor grey. Then, diffuse the Verde Pompeii image, as a planer image map — there you go, grey marble. You may even notice it looks a bit like carpet. Bring it into Art Department Professional and reduce the colors. Back in LightWave, use it as a bump map with diffusion, for some random bumps. Try coloring that LightWood image white, yellow, green or whatever with the same diffusion method. Or, use the bump map example on the Verde Pompeii image for a marble wall look.

Sometimes not having all the great texture packages and imaging programs is a good thing, because you're forced to use your imagination to make the most out of what you have. Possessing that ability is a great asset in any situation.

LWP

Dan Ablan is animator/owner of AGA in Chicago and animates with LightWave. Recent projects include work for Kraft and The Dial Corporation and trailers for Star Trek: Deep Space Nine. *Dan is also co-founder of the Chicago LightWave Association.*

He can be reached at (312) 239-7957 or by e-mail at dma@mcs.com.

LightWave 101: It Cleans!

by Paulo Felberg

I've seen a lot of people asking how to create good-looking, realistic wood surfaces, but no one is asking how to preserve them. Preserve them? Why, just save them on disk and that's it. But what about in the real world? There it's necessary to keep our floors well-cleaned and polished to maintain them. For that, we'll need a good wood cleaning and polishing product. Have you ever thought about using LightWave? Well, one client asked me to do just that. He wanted to create a 3D animation to show off his new wood cleaning product.

From looking at the color pages, you can see the effect is not a simple surface morph. The scene consists of the cleaning product package placed on a dark, dirty wood floor. A flannel cloth with the cleaning product rubs the floor, affecting only that part of the surface, cleaning and changing colors to a very shiny and reflective wood surface. This simple tutorial will show how easy it is to scrub away.

Building the Objects

I'm not going to get into the details of how the product package bottle was modeled and mapped. It's not essential for the cleaning effect. Anyway, if you wish, you can try modeling your own product package before continuing. For this tutorial, we will use very basic shapes. For an actual animation, you will most likely want to modify your objects to add more detail and realism.

Let's enter Modeler to make our floor object.

- Select Options (Display menu) and set Orientation to Logo (XY) and Unit System to Metric. All values will be entered in meters.
- Select Box in the Objects menu. Select Numeric (n) and enter the following values in the Box Numeric requester:

Low	High
X = -2	X = 2
Y = 0	Y = 0
Z = -2	Z = 2

- Leave the number of segments set to 1 for all axes.
- Press OK and then Make or return to make the box.
- Select the object polygon to see if it is facing up. If it's not, hit (f) to Flip (Polygon menu) it.

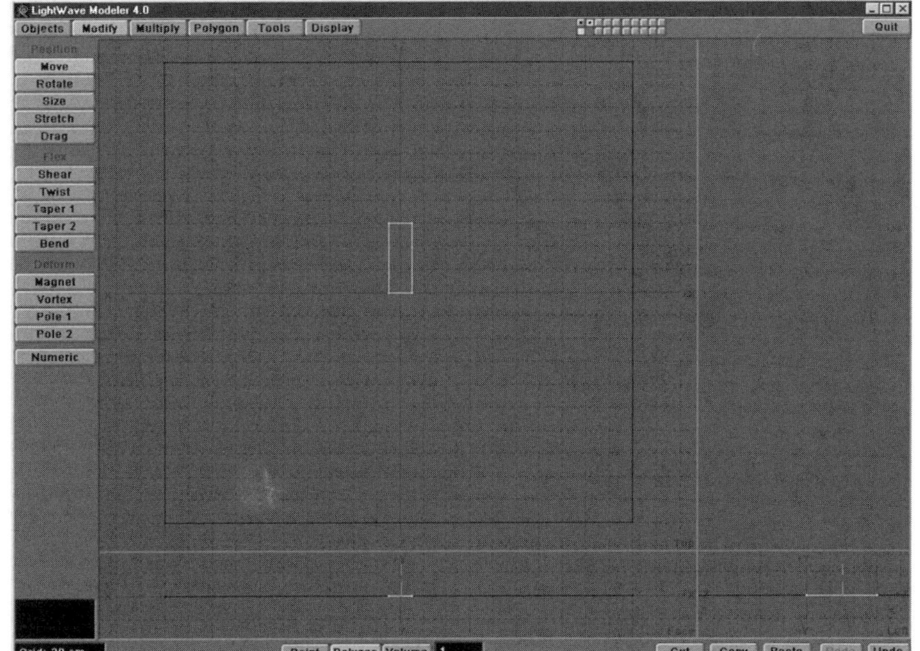

Figure 1

- To name the object surface, hit (q) for Surface (Polygon menu) and enter "DIRTY". Press return to change the surface name.
- Save the object as "DIRTY.lwo".

Now that we've built our dirty floor, we need a flannel cloth to clean it up. Let's make our flannel a simple flat box. While in Modeler, build it by using the Box tool again.

- Go to the next Layer by pressing 2.
- Again, enter the following values in the Box Numeric requester:

Low	High
X = -0.10	X = 0.10
Y = 0	Y = 0
Z = -0.15	Z = 0.15

- Leave the number of segments set to 1 for all axes, press OK, and then hit Make or return to make the box.
- Select the object polygon to see if it is facing up. If it isn't, flip it.
- Name the flannel surface by hitting (q) and entering "FLANNEL". Press return to change the surface name.
- Save the object as "FLANNEL.lwo".

The last object we need to model is the clean portion of the floor. Since the flannel cloth will clean only part of our dirty surface, we only need to model that part. Also, since our flannel cloth is the cleaning object, and in our scene it will be moving in the positive Z direction, we know our clean floor will have the same flannel X size. So, we'll model the clean floor from the "FLANNEL.lwo" object.

- While in the second Layer, hit (h) for Stretch, select Numeric and set Z value to 2.
- Select Move (Modify Menu) and select Numeric. Move the object to Z = 0.30. This will set the object's pivot point to be located on one side of the object. We want this because we will make our

clean floor grow from that side away as the cloth moves back and forth.

- Hit (q) for Surface, rename the object surface "CLEAN", apply it and Save the object as "CLEAN.lwo". Be careful not to overwrite the "FLANNEL.lwo" object.
- Press (ALT-1) to show the first Layer in the background, hit (a) to fit all views to the objects. If you did everything correctly, you should see something like Figure 1.

Surfacing

Before continuing this tutorial, consider creating your own wood texture. It would be better to have a seamless wood texture to avoid seams when rendering. If you have already performed Dan Ablan's "Lightwood in LightWave" tutorial in January 1995's *LWPRO*, you probably already have your favorite wood texture. But if you wish, you may use the Lightwood image from the wood directory. For this tutorial it will work just fine.

- Exit Modeler and enter LightWave Layout.
- Load the three objects modeled.
- Enter the Images panel and load your wood image texture or the Lightwood image from the Wood directory.
- Enter the Surfaces panel and set Current Surface to "DIRTY".
- Apply the Surface Color texture (T button) as a Planar Image Map using your wood texture or the Lightwood image. Select the Y Axis and World Coordinates. World Coordinates is essential to match the dirty and the clean surface sizes. It will avoid texture discrepancies while animating. If you are using the Lightwood image provided in LightWave, you must also set Texture Size to X = 3.0 to avoid a texture seam.
- Set Specular Level (Surfaces panel) to 20%, Glossiness at Medium and Smoothing on.
- To give the wood texture a dirty look, set Diffuse Level to 100% and apply a Fractal Noise Diffuse Texture (T button) with the following settings:

Texture Size	0.3, 0.1, 0.5
Texture Value	40%
Frequencies	3
Contrast	1

[For more information about Fractal Noise and dirty surfaces, take a look at Mojo's "Top 10 Uses for Fractal Noise" in May 1995's LWPRO.]

- Click on Use Texture.
- Select Save Surface (Surfaces panel) and save this surface as "DIRTY.srf".
- Save the object (Objects panel).

Let's set our clean surface:

- Back in the Surfaces panel, set Current Surface to "CLEAN".
- Select Load Surface to load the "DIRTY.srf" surface we just saved.
- Remove the Diffuse Level Fractal Noise texture applied (Shift-click on the T button).
- Set Reflectivity to 40%.

Adding a reflectivity level increases the clean polished wood look. So, any object placed near the clean area will be reflected in the "cleaned wood."

- If you are using LightWave 4.0, set Reflection Options to Ray Tracing+Backdrop.
- Save the object.

Our flannel surface is not essential for the effect to take place, but it would help with the overall scene look. It was modeled very simply, with hard angles and little detail. So, let's apply a simple bump map to give it some dirtiness and some irregular surfaces:

- Set Current Surface (Surfaces panel) to "FLANNEL".
- Set Surface Color (Surfaces panel) to 0, 130, 0, Diffuse Level to 100% and Specular Level to 0. Turn Smoothing on.
- Select Bump Map (Surfaces panel) and set Texture Type to Fractal Bumps. Set Texture Size to 0.03, 0.03, 0.05, Texture Amplitude to 200% and Frequencies to 3. Click on Use Texture.
- Save the object.

Let's Clean It Up

First, we must load another object into the scene to represent our product package. If you haven't modeled it yet, you can use any simple object to represent it. Just position it close to the clean area, so it's reflection will be seen. Its position will vary according to its size and shape. Just be sure to position it close to the clean area and with its base touching the floor.

- Select Add Null Object (Objects panel) and save it as "TARGET".
- Position the "TARGET" object at 0.1, 0.0, -0.7 and create a keyframe at frame 0.
- Target the Camera to the "TARGET" object.
- Set the Camera position to 0.6, 0.6, -1.5 and set a keyframe at 0 for the camera.

Let's position our "CLEAN.lwo" object a little bit higher than the dirty floor to avoid render errors.

- Move it to 0, 0.001, -1.0 and set keyframes at 0 and 60.
- Now, set the "CLEAN.lwo" object Z size to 0 and set a keyframe at 0.

As you'll notice, our animation will be quite short (two seconds). You may increase time as you wish.

The last object to set up is the "FLANNEL.lwo" object. As we did with the clean floor, we need to position the flannel cloth higher than both floor objects.

- Move the "FLANNEL.lwo" object to Y = 0.002 and set keyframes at 0 and 60.

Now, let's set the flannel movement.

- Move the "FLANNEL.lwo" object to Z = -0.85 and set a keyframe at 0.
- Move the "FLANNEL.lwo" object to Z = -0.25 and set a keyframe at 60.

Lighting

You don't need to add any special lighting for the effect to take place. But, you may try these settings to increase the dark, abandoned, realistic look.

- In the Lights panel, set Ambient Intensity to 0 and Light Color to 255, 255, 190.
- Set the Light Type to Spot, the Shadow Type to Shadow Map and set the Spot Soft Edge Angle to 30. Click Continue.
- Set the Light Target to the "TARGET" object and position it at 0.5, 1.5, -1.5. Create a keyframe at 0.

The Results

- In the Camera panel turn the Trace Reflections option on. This will enable the product object to reflect in the clean floor.
- Set Backdrop Color (Effects panel) to 0, 0, 0, so our floor will not reflect any colored sky.

You may adjust the other settings in the Camera Panel as you wish.

- Don't forget to change the Last Frame value (Scene panel) to 60.
- Save the scene as "CLEANING.lws".
- Since we made a short scene, you should try to render it all. But, if you don't have time to spare, just render frames 0, 30 and 60. With them, you'll have the beginning, middle and end of the animation, giving you an idea of how movement would work.

If you did it correctly, your images should look like what's displayed in the color pages.

The clean-floor effect.

One Step Further

You could try making your own floor surface, giving it more realism. Of course, you'll have a better look. Also, try adding some more texture and maybe some displacement mapping to your flannel cloth. Don't forget that it must be tripled and subdivided first.

Add more objects to the scene: a chair, a table. Make it real. You can also model your package and even the liquid itself, giving your scene a better look.

Of course, you're not obliged to work only with wood surfaces. You may use your favorite; just be sure it looks real. You can't clean rocks with a flannel cloth!

LWP

Paulo Felberg is a designer and animator based in Rio de Janeiro, Brazil. He can be reached at (55 021) 541-6962 or via the Internet at paulo.felberg@inside.com.

Top 10 Uses for Fractal Noise

by Mojo

When it comes to object surfacing in LightWave, fractal noise is your best friend. It is without a doubt the Pocket Fisherman of procedural textures. With a solid understanding of how the texture works and a little creativity, it can be used to make anything from cows to clouds. The following list includes just a few of its many uses; experimentation will yield many more. Readers are encouraged to send in their own Fractal Noise tricks for future publication and claim the glory they rightly deserve.

What It Is

Fractal noise is a procedural texture, which means the computer generates it mathematically. There is no actual artwork involved. Therefore, you can get as close as you want to any surface with this texture and never see any aliasing. Using the velocity channel, you can also animate the texture along any or all axes, giving it movement and life at whatever speed you desire.

The splotches this texture creates usually look best when sized to approximately one-tenth of the object size. (A default of one meter works well on a 10-meter surface.) If the texture is sized too large, you may see nothing. If too small, you'll get an overly fine pattern that shimmers like crazy.

Contrast determines how soft the splotch edges will be. A default of three creates a medium softness, while higher numbers bring the edge to a sharp line. The frequency values make either a more or less complex pattern. Low numbers create fewer and less-defined splotches (which may pulsate when animated). Higher settings provide sharper, more-defined patterns (and take slightly more time to render). The limit is 16.

OK, let's get cracking. Drum roll, please!

Top 10 Uses for Fractal Noise

10. Cows: The spots on the cow object provided with LightWave were produced using a high-contrast fractal noise pattern. Don't see much use for cow creation? The exact same technique (though with different colors) was used to form the pattern on the Vorlon ships in *Babylon 5*. A velocity along the Z axis provides the motion sometimes seen on the inside of the ship's petals. With a little bit of tweaking and perhaps a larger texture size, this same process makes a nice-looking camouflage texture, good for a tank, plane or anything else designed to kill and maim.

9. Dirt: Many people already use fractal noise to make a surface look dirty or smudged. This looks best when used with a low contrast and a color similar, yet darker, than the object's base color. It also helps to stretch out the noise in the direction it might naturally occur on a surface. The road object, for instance, might look best with dirt stretched along the Z axis.

A better way to create fractal dirt is to use it as a diffusion and/or specular texture. If an object already uses a color image map, this is a necessity; it also takes the guesswork out of deciding on a darker color for the noise. Simply make the diffusion value 100% for the surface and lower it for the texture value inside the fractal noise control panel (the lower the value, the darker the noise will appear). This will reduce the **Diffuse Level**, allowing less light to hit the object in the pattern of fractal noise and creating a more realistic-looking dirt.

By applying the same values in the **Specularity** channel, you can make the surface appear less shiny in the same dirty areas. This will greatly add to realism, especially when creating metal surfaces.

8. Brushed Aluminum: Speaking of metal, designing a good brushed-metal texture (made famous by the *Terminator 2* logo) is a snap with your old buddy fractal noise.

As explained earlier, apply the noise as a diffuse and specular map. The trick is to stretch the noise out along the X axis (assuming your logo is facing you) so far that the noise becomes a series of straight lines. Start with a size approximately 10 times larger on the X. If it is stretched too far, your lines may get too thin and alias like crazy. Also, take care to make your differences between surface and texture value small, again to avoid aliasing and to capture the subtle contrast in brushed metal.

Using the trick as a subtle bump map can make the surface look even better, though it greatly increases render time. Experiment!

7. Windows: Creating windows on buildings or spaceships is a snap. However, having a bunch of uniform, solid blocks of light never looks quite right. Looking at photos of real buildings at night reveals the caveat: there's stuff inside those windows. Whether it's people, drapes, furniture or plants, little things here and there break up the light coming from the window. By adding a fractal noise pattern in the luminosity channel of your windows, you can produce a good facsimile of this look. Follow the same rules for generating a channel of fractal diffusion and play with the size, contrast and texture value until it looks right.

6. Shadowing: Fractal noise can be applied to surfaces in less direct ways. In Hollywood, when a set is looking a little too flat, the light hitting it will often be broken up with something called a cookie, a piece of cardboard with random patterns cut into it. The cookie is placed a foot or two in front of the light, and presto! Lots of subtle shadows now cover the set. This same trick can be accomplished easily with LightWave and—you guessed it—fractal noise.

Make a simple, flat polygon and apply a clip map of noise to it. (Render it in front of the camera to make sure the size of the pattern is what you want.) Using a clip map literally cuts holes in your polygon. For this example, the holes are in the shape of fractal noise (contrast has no effect here). Place this polygon in front of a shadow-mapped light source and lots of subtle shadows will cover your LightWave set.

Moving this polygon toward and away from your light makes the shadows bigger or smaller, just like in real life. Adding a velocity to the noise shifts your shadows, perhaps creating the effect of leaves blowing in the wind outside. Make sure to turn on Double Sided for this polygon. If it faces the wrong way, you won't see anything!

5. Smoke: Begin by constructing a well-subdivided tube. This will be the smoke object, so place it in Layout wherever you want the effect to protrude from. Add a **Fractal Bump** displacement map to it, with a slow, upward velocity along the Y axis. This makes the tube bob and weave like billowing smoke. Use **Fractal Noise** in the **Transparency** texture channel, with a similar velocity along the Y axis. A low contrast is probably best, as is overall slow texture velocities, for duplicating the smooth, flowing feel of smoke.

Make sure **Edge Transparency** is set to **Transparent** to fade the edges of your tube and click off **Double Sided**. (There's no reason to see the inside polygons of your tube.) Unfortunately, the one channel of fractal transparency is simply too dense and regular to effectively mimic smoke. Wouldn't a second layer of transparency be useful?

By clicking on the **Additive** button near the top of the **Surfaces** panel, you can effectively use the **Surface Color** channel to help add transparency to the object. With **Additive** selected, the color of anything beyond the surface (including other objects, the background, and even the object itself) gets "added" to the color of the surface. If the color of the surface happens to be dark or black, it will appear transparent when the background is added (anything + zero = anything).

By modulating the surface colors, you can make more splotches of transparency. While you can adjust values in any of the "big three"—**Surface Color**, **Luminosity** or **Diffuse Levels**—I generally use the luminosity and diffuse values. This way, you don't have to worry about areas of the surface that aren't lit, as Luminosity will make the surface appear self-lit.

In Luminosity, add another layer of fractal noise, perhaps making the texture size a bit larger than the Transparency channel (making the pattern seem less regular). Changing the **Texture Velocity** also adds a bit more randomness. And be sure the Texture Value is zero and the Luminosity value is 100%, as in the transparency channel.

To get our dark areas, the **Diffuse Level** should be zero or very low. If you like, add a very subtle fractal noise pattern in this channel to further break up the color scheme of the smoke. Add Bones to the tube for more realism, and use them to expand and contract the smoke slowly, or make it sway with the wind.

4. Pyro: Explosions are a snap with fractal noise. However, if you want to know the nitty-gritty of how to make one, go back and dig up the July 1994 issue of *LIGHTWAVEPRO*. It's described there in full detail, so I refuse to waste any more paper on it here.

3. **Sparks**: As a companion to the non-existent explosion trick, the sparks that go with them can also be enhanced by fractal noise. Although they are created using only single-point polygons, these sparks are nonetheless still affected by all surfacing parameters, including textures and fractal noise.

Try adding noise in the transparency channel of your sparks. This creates a greater variety in luminosities among the particles and a velocity that will make them twinkle. Noise can also be used on all kinds of particle systems. Try adding it to a starfield for a more realistic spread of densities, or to underwater detritus to fake different sizes. Use noise in the color channel as well to add variety.

2. Trickling Water: Whenever you have an object (say, a dolphin) breaking the surface of water, try running a specular-only fractal noise pattern down the Y axis. From a reasonable distance, this creates the effect of water beads dripping down and can greatly enhance realism. Did I say dolphin? Sorry, I meant submarine. Everyone knows that computer-generating a dolphin would be too hard.

1. Clouds: Yes, LightWave's horizon colors may be gorgeous, but they simply look boring without some nice, white, fluffy clouds thrown in. And so easy to make! Just pick up the September 1994 issue of *LIGHTWAVEPRO* and see how it was done for an episode of *Babylon 5*. Oh, OK, stop crying, I'll tell you anyway...

Simply make a large, flat polygon to serve as your sky. Give it a white color and add fractal noise to the transparency channel. With the right settings, the holes the noise creates will look just like clouds! Try stretching the polygon out a bit on the Z axis if the pattern looks too regular.

In addition, chances are that using only one channel of transparency will create too many clouds in too regular a pattern. Remember how the smoke effect managed to use **Additive** combined with **Diffuse Level** and **Luminosity** to "cheat" another fractal transparency channel? Well, you can use the same trick here. Simply click on the **Additive** button and add fractal noise to the luminosity channel. As long as your Diffuse Level is 0%, it will act just like transparency. Just remember to make the **Luminosity** value 100% and the **Texture Value** zero. It would probably also be a good idea to make this texture size larger (maybe even double) to break up the pattern. By tweaking this second channel a little bit, you should be able to produce very realistic clouds.

Well, that's all, folks! I hope you've enjoyed our journey through the wondrous land of fractal noise. With a little imagination, I'm sure that even you can come up with thousands of applications for this wonder-texture.

LWP

Mojo works as an animator/technical director for Foundation Imaging.

Hair-Raising Effects

Creating a Photoshop-like Filter Image

by Bill Frawley

It's funny how ideas work their way up from the murky depths of the unconscious to the brain's frontal lobe. Shortly after experimenting with the grass object mentioned in Mark Thompson's "Displacement Mapping: What's It All About" article in the premiere issue of *LWPRO*, I recalled the technique of texture mapping an image sequence onto a rectangular grid of sphere objects, producing an interesting "movie screen of balls." Then the epiphany happened. Why not utilize this technique with LightWave's two-point polygons?

By color mapping an image or sequence of images onto a randomly scattered array of two-point polygons (lines) created in Modeler, a modulating effect is produced comparable to altering an image with an algorithmic filter in Photoshop. In other words, the original image takes on a stringy, hair-like texture. Furthermore, applying an animated Fractal Noise Displacement Map to the lines causes each filament to randomly undulate, giving life to the image like an oscillating bed of underwater kelp.

LightWave acting as image processor too? How much more can we ask of this venerable piece of software?

Building the Fibrous Image Screen

To begin this simple task, enter Modeler and select the **Polygon** menu to make a two-point particle (line). Do this by selecting **Points** under the Create section and while in the Top view, place a point at 0,0,0 and select **Make** (Return or Enter) to create the point. Do the same for the second point at 0,0,-300(mm). Now turn these two points into a line by clicking in a blank area and then selecting **Make** or simply hitting the p key to make the polygon.

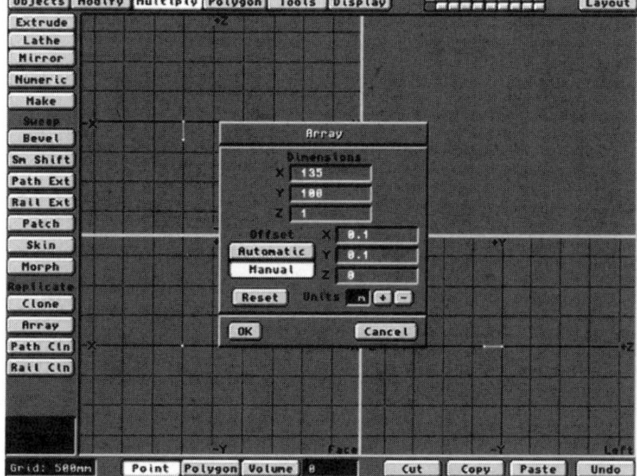

Figure 1: Use of the new Array tool to clone a two-point polygon (line) into a grid with dimensions matching the default video aspect.

Figure 2: After dragging out a Volume-Exclude bounding box around only the bottom points, the Jitter tool is used to randomly scatter them to create 'blades' that are oblique when viewing the XY plane.

In order to create a gridplane of these lines, access the **Array** tool in the **Multiply** menu. Since the field of lines should fill the entire Layout screen, dimensions suitable for this video mode need to be used; that is, an aspect ratio of 1.346:1 in the XY plane. With that in mind, enter 135 for the X and 100 for the Y dimension. So the entire collection of cloned lines doesn't become stacked on top of one another, select Manual offset and enter X and Y values of .1 (100mm) and a Z offset of 0, assuming that 'units' is set for meters (Figure 1). This will yield a nice, densely packed block of 13,500 lines, suitable for 'holding' our image without a large gap between each line. Press "a" to view the entire array and deselect the original line (/) so our next operation will be global and apply to all polygons.

Now we must randomly scatter all the points closest to us in the Face view into a natural looking, grass-like pattern in order to see some of the sides of the oblique lines from the Face view (Layout's default view). Otherwise, only points and no lines will be seen, which is boring for our purpose. Later, it will be discovered that by not jittering the back plane of points, a regular grid anchoring the fibers ensures less chaos in the final image. Therefore, to select only those points lying in the -Z plane, drag out the Top view so it fills the screen. Press "a" to fit all the polygons into the view. Choose **Volume-Exclude** (space bar) as the selection mode and while holding down the left mouse button, drag out a box so that only the lower row of points fit inside it. Remember, in Volume-Exclude selection mode, only those points or polygons (depending on what tool will be used next) lying within the box will be affected by the next operation. If you make a mistake, simply press the right mouse button and try again. Now for the jittering.

In the **Tools** menu, select the **Jitter** tool (J) and enter a radius of .1,.1,.03 for X, Y and Z respectively (Figure 2). [Editor's note: Modeler 3.5 has new Jitter options—use Gaussian. This will randomly scatter all the front points no further than the distance to their neighboring points (100mm) and vary the height of each line by plus or minus 30mm.]

Once complete, arrange the screen back into the 4-quad view. Press "a" again to fit the entire object within the view. Next, center the image filter object on the X and Y axes only. Use the **Center 1D** macro which should have been included with LightWave. It needs to be run once for each of the aforementioned axes. Change the surface name (q) to

"FilterPlane." Finally, Export this new object to Layout as "Filterplane".

Arranging the Elements in Layout

Re-enter Layout and change both the view (F6) and edit (C) mode to **Camera**. Obviously, the filter-plane doesn't quite fill the view, but it's not a problem. Simply move the camera slightly forward so that it does. In order to constrain the camera's axis movement to the Z direction only, deselect the X and Y buttons, then move the camera forward to approximately -16, or until the filterplane object completely fills the view. Set a keyframe for the camera at frame 0.

With the necessary elements in position, the next task is to load in the image that is to be mapped onto the filterplane object. Enter the Images menu and load an image of your choice. I chose the Video Toaster 4000 framestore that came with the Toaster, as it contains a variety of different elements to best demonstrate the desired effect. Surfacing the object comes next.

Surfacing the Filter Plane

Enter the Surfaces menu and make sure "FilterPlane" is the current surface selected. To confirm that this is the surface to be edited, the Polygon Usage should read 13,500. Now select the **T** button beside Surface Color to access the texture mapping control panel. **Planar Image Map** the Texture Image chosen earlier onto the **Z** axis and select **Automatic Sizing**. Choose **Use Texture** to accept your changes.

Set the Luminosity to 100 percent and change Diffusion to 0 percent. This allows the surface to remain visible regardless of the lighting conditions. At this point the surface texturing is complete. Press F' to do a test render.

To make the image a little more interesting, modify the waviness pattern of the 'blades' with a nice Fractal Bumps Displacement Map in the **Objects** panel. Enter the following Displacement Map parameters for the FilterPlane object:

Texture Type	**Fractal Bumps**
Texture Size:	2,2,.3
Texture Falloff:	0,0,300
Texture Center:	0,0,-.3
Texture Amplitude:	.4

This texture size results in fractal bump patterns roughly 15 percent of the objects' width and height and completely covering the depth (300mm) of the blades. The Texture Center represents the starting point of the displacement. In this case, -.3 corresponds to the front most or closest points of the blades to the camera. This is where the texturing begin; however, with the texture falloff on the Z axis set to 300 percent, the displacing of the blades totally diminishes in effect towards the back of the blades (Z=0). Finally, the amplitude controls how far the blades are bent laterally. In other words, this parameter controls the severity of how much the blades are pushed to their side. It is the optimization of this displacement map that ultimately determines how effective this technique becomes. The Layout screen should now look like Figure 3. Render the image now and compare it to your last one. The new image should be a great improvement. However, this journey wouldn't be complete if it ended here.

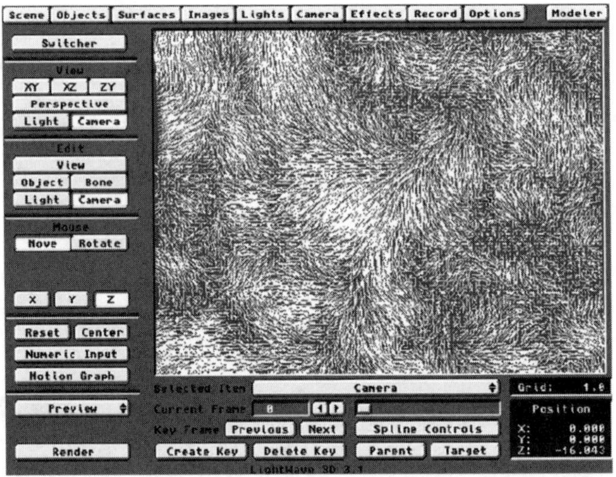

Figure 3: This is how the scene looks in Layout after the camera is positioned to fit the entire 'Filter Plane' into view. Note the effects of the Fractal Bump displacement map to the surface of the blades.

Some Additional Tips

The real power of this 'filtering' technique becomes apparent when an animated or moving displacement map, either fractal bumps or ripples is applied to a sequence of images that have been either created or digitized with a Personal Animation Recorder or VLAB Motion board. Once the sequence in LightWave has been processed with the hairy filter method, save the individual frames and use these frames as is or modulate the original images in any of the various ways described below. Done properly, a surrealistic animated effect similar to the garden sequence in Lawnmower Man can be achieved.

For some truly wild compositing effects, consider overlapping, but slightly offsetting two filter objects with two different images or sequences mapped onto their surfaces. By animating their respective displacement maps, the regions and strength of each image will constantly vary. This presents another cool dream sequence. Or you could take the conservative approach and achieve a more subtle filtering effect by compositing the hairy image with the original in your favorite image processor or as a background image in LightWave.

If you are fortunate enough to own ImageFX, try this nifty effect. Load the unaltered, original image into the main image buffer and the LightWave-processed hairy image into the Alpha buffer (convert to grayscale to save memory). Now use the "Distort" feature located in the Effects menu. Set up a batch process with a sequence of images using this effect and you'll be able to crank out those Peter-Gabriel-MTV-hallucinating-type music videos (if that's what you really want to do).

For those not restricted by time, try modeling the blade elements with multiple segments instead of just one. Then apply the Bend or Shear tools (instead of Jitter) to smaller regions of the plane for more realistic-looking bends in the individual filaments. Additionally, for greater color variations in the final rendering, place a simple plane polygon behind the filter plane. Either surface this simple plane with a solid color or map another image onto it. Then use a shadow-mapped spotlight to generate shadows falling on the back plane (see color pages). Remember, only a spotlight will produce shadows with particles (points or lines).

Lastly, try this same image map filtering technique on an array of spheres (or any geometric shape, for that matter). Currently, I'm in the process of exploring the possibilities of animating image-mapped, single-point particles.

Furthermore, with LightWave 3.5's ability to adjust the rendering size of single-point polygons or two-point lines, look for more realistic-looking trees, grass, starfields and crazy effects like the techniques presented here.

LWP

Prometheus' Laboratory

by Grant Boucher

Sooner or later, you are going to start playing with those little buttons marked **T** next to your surface settings. While many of you use LightWave without getting deep into either modeling or surfacing, I am sure you've watched an episode of *seaQuest* or *Babylon 5* and asked yourself, "How in the world did they do that with LightWave?" I've had a lot of fellow LightWave users ask whether I used other programs to achieve high-end effects like fire, lava, plasma, dissolving spaceships, dripping mud, etc. In general, the answer is no. Everything you see on any episode of *seaQuest* is duplicatable with LightWave.

Our beta version of LightWave has some minor (and major) improvements, but rarely are those required to achieve a given effect. Usually they just make our lives easier as animators or give us new shortcuts to replace effects achieved through previously more complicated means. LightWave has had the core tools for such things since its earliest versions, and it's a major reason for its abundant use in the broadcast special effects market these days.

In my article on the plasma effect in a previous issue of *LWPRO* (Frankenstein's Lab, Issue 5), I tried to give you some logical building blocks for working with LightWave so that you could recognize when the techniques used in that exercise (i.e. sequential image mapped transparency and shaping surfaces with morphing and scaling) could be useful for similar effects such as lightning and lasers.

This article is intended to be another in a series on what I like to call the 'Zen' of LightWave procedurals. I want to continue to give you an idea into the thought process behind high-end special effects, so that the next image I see from you (either on the air, in print, or on your demo reel) shows me something I haven't seen before.

Chaos and LightWave

By now, I am sure you've heard of the **Fractal Noise** procedural lurking beneath most surface and object settings of LightWave. In fact, I used Fractal Noise with displacement mapping to create a rippling flag in the premiere issue of *LWPRO*. We are going to use almost identical settings and techniques to create fire.

Fractal Noise is a mathematical function which generates random looking variations between two settings. For example, when Fractal Noise is used as a surface color, you select two colors to randomly vary between. To make a diseased apple, you might make the main color red, and the Fractal Noise texture color brown or green. The **Texture Size** determines how small or large the pattern of variation will be, while the **Contrast** setting determines how smoothly the two disparate colors blend together. Contrast values lower than 1.0 become softer and subtler, while Contrast values greater than 1.0 become sharper and more defined. Fractal Noise can be used in all types of LightWave surface mapping, as well as displacement mapping (as in the case of our flag) and clip mapping (i.e.: if you wanted sharp random holes to appear in an object).

Figure 1

For example, load the Texture Examples scene that came with your version of LightWave and render the first frame (Figure 1). I'm going to go through these individually with a short sentence on each to give you an idea of the power and versatility of LightWave's built-in procedurals (especially Fractal Noise).

Starting from the upper left, the Rippling Chrome cube is simply the **Ripples** texture applied as a bump map to a surface with an environment reflection.

The Marble Cube is an example of a whitish Marble texture applied to a blackish-grey cube, purely as a surface color texture.

The Color Gradient Cube uses the **Grid** texture under Surface color to create a purple line on a blue-colored cube. **Texture Falloff** in the Y direction causes the purple line to fade away the further it is from the **Texture Center** (in this case, the bottom of the cube). Once the Grid effect reaches 100 percent **Falloff**, the grid is gone completely and leaves only the native surface color behind.

The Cloud Cube uses Fractal Noise as a transparency map. The surface color of gray could be anything we wanted, as the fractal pattern only concerns the opacity, or transparency of the surface.

The Dotted Cube used the **Dots** procedural as a surface color map.

The Brushed Metal Cube uses Fractal Noise again, but this time as a bump map (**Fractal Bumps**). The surface of the object uses the Fractal Reflections image map that comes with LightWave as a reflection image. Notice that the Texture Size on the Fractal Noise bump map is much smaller in the Y direction than in the X and Z directions. This causes the fractal pattern to be stretched out across the faces of the cube, giving us the appearance of brushed metal.

The Wood Cube uses a sample of the **wood** procedural as a diffuse map.

The Rippling Gold Cube is identical to the Rippling Chrome Cube above, except that a surface color of gold has been applied to all reflections by turning the **Color Highlights** option on.

The Checkerboard Cube uses the **Checkerboard** texture as a transparency map. Notice how easy it is to put

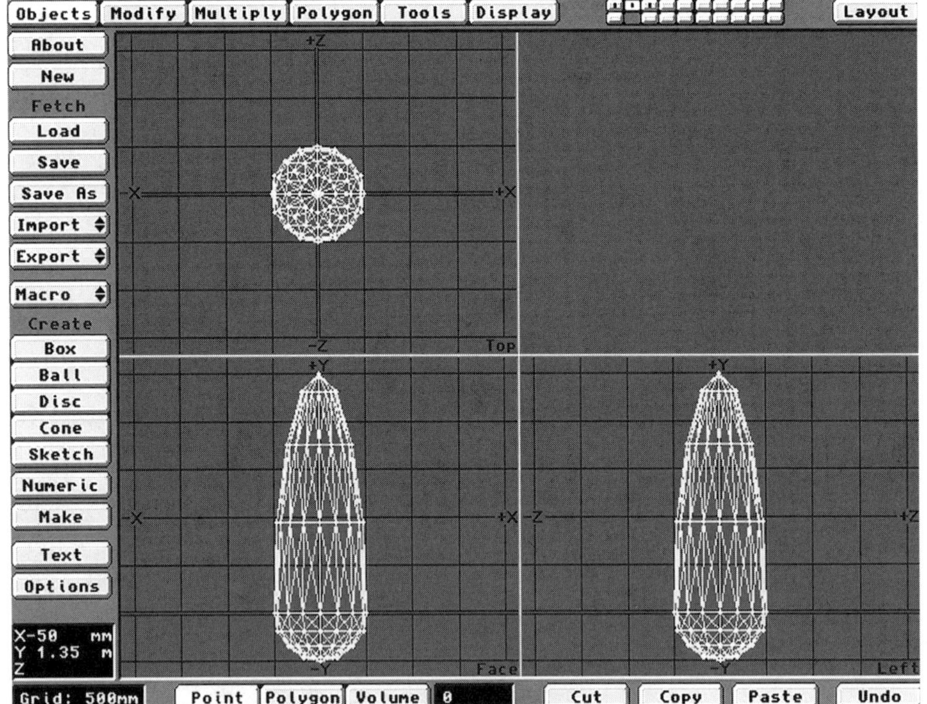

Figure 2

clean holes into objects without using the modeler and without increasing the number of polygons.

The Underwater Cube uses the **Underwater** texture as a surface texture with colors of white on blue to create that "bottom of the swimming pool" effect.

The Orange Peel Cube uses Fractal Noise as a bump map again, but this time with a small Texture Size to give a grainy feel to the surface. The orange surface color lets you know this is the surface of an orange, but the same settings can be used for sand and dirt effects.

Finally, the Grid Cube uses the **Grid** texture as a surface map to place grids on the cube.

Clouds and More

So what does all of this have to do with fire? Take another look at that Cloud Cube. If you applied that surface to a hemisphere you made in Modeler and placed your camera within it in the Layout, you could have a sky full of clouds. If you applied that surface to a Modeler cone and shrunk the texture size a little, you'd have a steam vent, aerosol spray, or torpedo trail. If you changed that same cone's surface color from white to black or gray, you'd have a smoke trail or volcanic plume. If you make that same object's surface color a fractal mixture of red and yellow (with shades of orange in between), you would get something that begins to look like fire.

Dissecting Mother Nature

So that is the essence of the fire texture, but like most good things, it's not going to be that easy. First, let's begin tackling fire by taking it apart, in LightWave terms.

Shape—A candle flame could be cylindrical, conical, or elliptical (i.e. egg-shaped). In either case, it is an easy task for Modeler. If we were going to place fire on a fireplace log, we might create an elongated cylinder or maybe a couple of flat polygons, or sheets of polygons might do the trick. Since we can't really make solid fire, we have to fake it a little.

In Modeler, select the **Ball** function in the Objects menu. Immediately select **Numeric** (**n**) and chose **OK** to accept the default settings. Press the **Return** key or select **Make** to create the sphere.

Next, select only the top four rows of points (i.e. any point with a Y value greater than zero) and proceed to the **Modify** menu. Select **Stretch** and the **Numeric** option to bring up the Stretch numeric requester. Stretch the selected points by a factor of five in the Y direction, leaving all other values at the default. After stretching, you should have an egg-shaped object that loosely resembles a candle flame (Figure 2).

The object will be much larger than a real candle flame, but I wanted to make the modeling easy as possible. You can scale the candle flame down in the layout according to your needs, without the need to adjust your texture sizes. I use this same fire object for large and small fires, so I am always scaling it up or down as needed. Save this object and enter Layout.

Color—There are many types of fire, with colors that range from bluish-white to yellowish-orange. Let's choose a more animated color scheme like red, orange and yellow. We'll choose a candle flame to be more specific. That will determine many of our other parameters.

Let's use a Fractal Noise pattern to range from red to yellow, and we'll make the Texture Size taller in the Y direction and narrower in the X and Z direction, since flames stretch upwards. Also, I have chosen to make the texture sizes small, which may resemble a bonfire more than a candle flame. You can easily adjust the Size values to meet your needs.

The following table gives the appropriate values to enter for surface color and texture:

Surface Color	255,0,0
Texture Type	Fractal Noise
Texture Size	0.1,0.3,0.1
Texture Center	0,0,0
World Coordinates	Off *
Texture Falloff	0,0,0
Texture Velocity	0,0.03,0.001*
Texture Color	255,255,0
Frequencies	3
Contrast	0.5

* Note that if you turn World Coordinates On, you can bank and pitch the candle flame and the flames will always travel upwards (i.e. in the +Y direction).

Luminosity—Flames do not receive shadows, nor do they shade according to the light sources around them. In LightWave terminology, that calls for 100 percent luminosity.

Transparency—You can see through parts of a flame, as well as the edges. Similarly, the flame fades away slowly as it travels away from the source until it disappears completely. It does not have any hard edges at all. To solve these many problems, we'll first use **Transparent Edges** to give our flame a soft-edged look. Many transparency-based effects work better with Transparent Edges turned on. For the holes, we'll turn to Fractal Noise again, but this time as a transparency map. With a falloff in the Y direction (starting from our texture center at the bottom of our flame Y=0), the flame will go from solid (0 percent transparency) at the bottom to invisible (100 percent transparency) at the top.

The following table gives transparency and texture values:

Transparency	100%
Texture Type	Fractal Noise
Texture Size	0.05,0.15,0.05
Texture Center	0,0,0
World Coordinates	Off (but see * note above)
Texture Falloff	85,40,85
Texture Velocity	0,0.03,0.001
Texture Value	0
Frequencies	3
Contrast	1.0

Movement—Flames travel upwards, so that calls for using LightWave's **Texture Velocity** functions. A +Y direction causes our fractal pattern to travel up and through our candle flame object. While not strictly necessary, a small amount of X and/or Z texture velocity will cause the fractal pattern to undulate slightly as it travels up the flame. This keeps our candle flame from looking too ordered and predictable.

Similarly, with LightWave's displacement mapping feature (Objects panel), our candle flame can waver to and fro and appear to have actual depth. The **Texture Velocity** settings for the **Fractal Bumps** displacement should be the same as those for our surface color and transparency map, but the **Texture Size** might be two or three times larger. Make sure you increase the number of polygons in your candle flame object to account for displacement mapping distortions. Otherwise your flame will crease sharply rather than flow smoothly. Also, start with a small **Texture Amplitude** such as .1.

Advanced Options

Diffusion & Double Sides—I selected **Double Sided** (Surfaces panel) to add additional layers of fire in our candle flame and to brighten up the color of the total object. A professional animator's trick when dealing with transparent objects that begin to disappear in scenes due to combination of transparency and transparent edges is to increase the Diffuse setting to greater than 100 percent. Since Diffuse is just a formula, you can bring up the amount of color applied to an object, before it is made transparent by going as high as 200 percentDiffuse (with LW 3.1). This tends to wash out your object, which can cause other problems but works great for our already 100 percent luminous, unshaded candle flame.

Additive —Many animators turn Additive on when using fire in their scenes. Additive causes the colors behind your Additive surface flame to be "added" to the color of the surface (up to 255,255,255). This can add a nice lightning effect for rocket engines and similar fire-like effects. Try it in a scene to see whether you like Additive on or not.

Glows—The Flame scene included on this month's *LWPRO* disk has three lens flares added to the candle flame to give a hot core and glowing edge to the candle flame. This gives the candle the appearance that it is actually generating light in your scene.

Flickering Light —For added realism, a point light has been placed at the center of the flame so that the flame lights the area around the candle. By ray-tracing shadows through the candle flame and perhaps adding a Light Intensity envelope, the light can appear to flicker, adding to the sense of realism in our scene.

Modifications and the Future of Fire

Some animators use the Marble texture as a luminosity or diffuse map to add yet another layer of random variation to their flames. Similarly, since flames come in many colors, from blue to white, you can expand on the ideas expressed in this article to develop any kind of flame or flame-like effect. Perhaps you can think of a reason to develop flames that reflect like gold or silver?

You might also want to take a look at Leo Martin's ProTextures Volume II. It has a great, seamless Fire image map which I've used extensively for fire and lava type effects.

With the rumor of more procedurals due for release with LightWave 4.0 and programs like Forge by Steve Worley's Apex Software available to LightWave animators, the possibilities for procedural animation techniques is expanding geometrically. If Fractal Noise can be used to create most of nature's wonders, imagine the possibilities with a hundred Fractal Noise-style procedures.

LWP

Grant Boucher is a supervising animator for Amblin Imaging and teaches seminars on LightWave uses when he has spare time (not too often). His main system hard drive at Amblin is named Prometheus.

The Surfacing Jungle

Tips and Techniques for Polishing Up Your Images

by David Ebner

A lot of 3D animators out there seem to have their strength in one area or another. Yet every aspect—lighting, modeling, surfacing and animation—is important. Any weakness in just one of these areas can bring the whole piece down. I've seen a lot of tutorials aimed at modeling and even more dealing with animation. This one is strictly designed for obtaining more desirable surfaces and offers suggestions and a look at some of the new possibilities offered by LightWave 5.0. We'll also examine a few new plug-ins that expand the LightWave's capabilities.

Approaching Your Surfaces

I like to work on surfaces under a fresh scene aside from that containing animation movement. Placing a couple of colorless lights under the general conditions and lighting ratios of which the subject will be placed, I start examining the model and surface breakdowns. By working in this surfacing scene, I can also make key frames, like a scratch pad, up close on certain surfaces and with differing orientations. Your objects should be surfaced so they can be successfully placed under different lighting conditions to affect the tone, illumination and mood while the object itself maintains balance.

A lot of people are finding that because they have surfaced their model during or after animating and lighting, they end up having to resurface or repaint maps for different shots. Your car shouldn't get a new paint job depending on the scene and neither should your surfacing. True, a little tweaking from scene to scene may be advantageous for experienced surfacers, but generally try surfacing models this way.

Image mapping

I see people still trying to map an entire surface of an object with a single image. Break that surface down into smaller, geographic regions. You can still use the same surface characteristics such as diffusion and specularity, but by breaking up the surface into regions of differing axes perpendicularly, and by using related images for these surfaces you'll greatly reduce the smearing and stretching of images along your object. In the example pictured, the body of this creature was divided into several surfaces based on whether or not I would map downwards (Y axis), sideways (X axis) or front on (Z axis). Once these regions were assigned with their appropriate surface names, reference images from the Modeler screen were captured (screen grabbed) and images were painted. Capturing the reference image along the same view that is being mapped enables you to perfectly line up the texture and details with the geometry and features.

With some time invested in making sure the edges of the image maps don't contrast in color or value against the neighboring images, you can achieve very precisely detailed surfaces making up what appears to be one uniform surface. Even with the introduction of 3D paint programs I still have not experienced the precise and predictable results as with the methods just described. You simply can not bypass the work it takes when it comes to achieving believable image mapping.

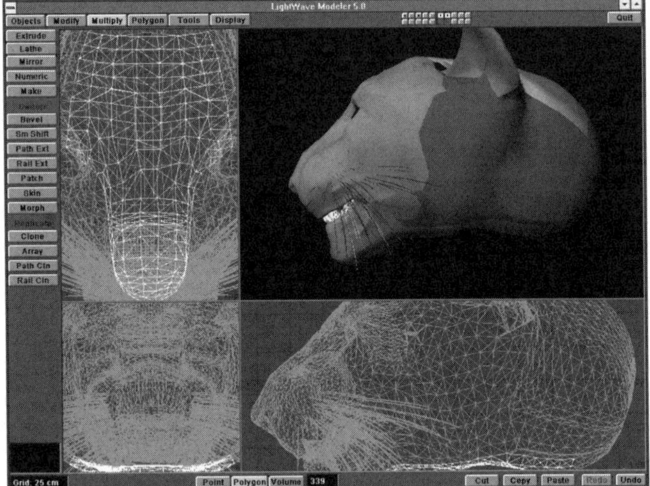

Figure 1: The panther's head was surfaced separately from the body.

Diffusion/Luminosity/Lighting

The source of light can be thought of as an umbrella under which many surfaces are present. The relationships of brightness between these surfaces are primarily defined by the diffusion and luminosity against other surfaces.

First, it is important to note that within the color values or color mapping there also is the definition of value or tone, meaning lightness and darkness. With three-dimensional shapes, it is usually desirable to have no shading introduced by the color map. The distinction of differing colors, therefore, is to allow the lighting given in the scene to properly shade the surface. Upon the introduction of light, the model takes on a new look as it is being rendered. The shading and addition of shadows give the model further form.

Upon default, the Diffuse Level is full strength allowing the full effect of the lighting given, while Luminosity is set to off at zero. To affect the tone of a surface beyond that of the color map, enter a new value or introduce a texture defining the diffusion. This diffusion surfacing control is independent of light levels creating specularity highlights or shadows.

The introduction of luminosity further intensifies the brightness of the whole surface. This illumination, however, is not derived from the source of light but is obtained evenly by its own value or applied in relation to an image or procedural map. This self-illumination reduces the effect of light shading and of shadows and may completely overcome them. Since luminosity is independent of light, surfaces which acquire their brightness from this control do not adapt well in different light. This control should be reserved for those surfaces truly generating their own light or for simulating certain lighting effects.

The exchanging of diffusion value into that of luminosity can be a quick way of shadow strength reduction. An example being a backdrop object in which you do not desire the shadow of a logo to be so dark. With some luminosity/diffusion balancing you can achieve this without lessening the light, though the shading effects also will be diminished. Before breaking the rules it is important to understand these relationships and characteristics

Additive Surfaces

This switch in the Surfaces panel is often overlooked and sometimes not taken advantage of due to the lack of understanding. When this mode is invoked the entire surface is treated differently and for an entirely new purpose. This tool gives you the ability to gently or intensely lighten anything behind these surfaces with defined shapes, procedures or images. A good example of its use is in cloud additions in which the dark tones always marry with the back drop. Also I accomplish light rays, subtle surface glimmers, artificial specular highlights and secondary reflections with it. Only values above 0, 0, 0 with this kind of surface have any effect as the tone also determines the strength. A transparency map therefore is not needed in most cases since the dark regions of the surface are transparent by default. The overall strength of this surface can be controlled with the diffusion or luminosity values, though usually I tend to use these surfaces as luminous as opposed to diffuse.

Reflection Mapping in Variable Lighting

If your model is going to be placed in different lighting setups you'll have to remember that a reflective surface will acquire some of its brilliance (if not all) from the reflectivity. This is particularly important to note if using an image to define the reflection as opposed to the environment. The image used must "know" or be modified for the lighting conditions. A sequence of images or surface morphing may be necessary to get realistic looking reflections while animating through changing light. Without compensating for conditions, reflections tend to be way too bright in darker lighting.

Multi-Mapping with 5.0

Beginning LightWave surfacers often keep forgetting that some of the algorithmic textures use the surface color or value in the main part of the surfaces panel with the effect. Veins for instance adds its effect to the color value. This concept is important to grasp because starting with 5.0 you can have multitudes of textures and maps and it is important to know how they are ordered and combined.

LightWave's image mapping capability has now expanded allowing you the ability to stack or blend image maps and procedural textures together in each of the texture areas. This is achieved with a new button labeled "Add New Texture" located alongside "Previous" and "Next" buttons for navigation. The maximum strength of a texture (whether image based or procedural) is controlled with a texture opacity field.

Alongside each image map you now have the option of adding an adjacent image defining the strength of the image map. The tonal values of an image applied as a texture alpha defines the strength (transparency) of the map. This way you can apply color, diffusion and other factors in just the areas you want. A good example of this can be related while surfacing a planet's atmosphere. Some colorful gases are desired within your already defined cloud work. Without building an additional set of geometry with more transparency calculations factored in, you can now lay in another image map with a high contrast alpha image map to achieve the desired effect. This way you avoid incurring painful rendering times and do not have to alter the original image map. If the new gases are too strong, simply lower their texture value.

Also with 5.0 you can further limit the extent of your image map by checking off the width tiling on the texture height and/or texture width. By doing so your image will only affect the area within the numeric sizes centered, of course, around the texture center. It is now possible to have a color map such as photo of cardboard for the whole box, and the use a second image sized down and re-centered for the label all in one surface.

Figure 2: It's a good practice to screen capture reference images from Modeler

Remember that, as soon as you have an image map used with 100 percent Opacity, no other textures previous to that one will show their effect (assuming that you are not using Texture Falloff) as the last 100 percent Opacity image map fully replaces any previous surface values. You can test this by trying to use multiple transparency maps, each with 100 percent Opacity. Only the last will show its effect, while "hiding" the others.

With three different limiters you have possibilities never before so easily achieved in combining several images for surfacing.

With procedural maps there already is an inherent definition of texture strength though you still have the overall texture opacity level which can be used to dissolve out a texture. Random bumps can be made even more irregular by combining two textures of different coverage, just as additional variances of underwater and veins can easily be obtained.

The ordering of textures is important to keep in mind. The last texture to be added can be thought of as the top layer of application or the final coat of paint. The transparency of this texture or areas of non application can be thought of as worn away paint revealing the next layer. The bottom of the stack is the surface color or value in the main part of the surfaces panel.

Though the combination of textures so far is limited to priority and strength weighted in a normal application, I am looking forward to one day maybe seeing some other methods such as additive and subtractive.

Surfacing Tools in Modeler

Also exciting is the surfacing tools offered directly in Modeler. You can now characterize your surface's color, diffusion level, specularity and glossiness, double-sided on/off, smoothness and smoothness angle all in Modeler. These are limited in that you can not apply texture maps; that is to say until you use the "Power Texture" plug-in. With this new plug-in which looks much like Fori's Power View for OpenGL viewing before OpenGL modeling and Layout views became a reality, you can now interactively apply texture to your surface, seeing the results as you position and scale your image.

Some More 5.0 Surfacing Additions

LightWave 5.0 is a major advancement, especially in the area of interactivity. This of course is exemplified with the dynamic OpenGL layout, modeling and previewing modes. Another rad tool with 5.0 is the image viewer accessible through the generic plug ins interface. This viewer not only displays images loaded but also a frame from an image sequence. Along side "Polygon Edges" in the Objects panel is "Cel Look Edges" which gives a color and weight definable outline that follows the contours of surfaces. This is very effective when balancing luminosity against your diffusion, achieving more of a two-dimensional rendering effect. Also try this with Allen Hasting's Cel-Look shader.

Pertaining to the overall quality of output, Anti-aliasing has been improved upon in different ways. There is now a numeric control over the anti-aliasing strength of image maps as well as the addition of new anti-aliasing rendering options which offer greater results.

New Plug-ins

It is very exciting seeing LightWave and third-party tools develop with more and more diversity and capability. I'm impressed with this growth and the fact that the ease of use and organization of the program and features have been maintained. One very exciting new add-on being offered now is the film grain plug-in by Steven Worley. Originally developed for and commissioned by our facility, Steve's grain plug-in is perfect for aiding in the integration of 3D into feature film work. Steve has achieved the realistic appearance and behavior of film grain and has programmed this with user-adjustable parameters for surface application, selected surface application or complete image application. He has also developed an algorithm for the removal of film grain from shot footage. His attention to detail goes to the level of grain strength tapering based upon the film print transparency to grain ratio of actual printed film.

Another impressive surface plug-in is included with version 5.0, the surface blur. With this plug-in you can now soften surfaces individually. At SIGGRAPH, I was able to take a look at some very impressive additions such as Particle Storm, a new and improved Mesh-Paint, Vertilectric, Wavefilter and WavenetPRO along with a peek at a few in development. These plug-ins are all excellent, adding additional tools and ease of use to LightWave.

LWP

David Ebner is an animator and president of Computer Cafe Inc. in Santa Maria, Calif., who enjoys good cinema and good food. Just like all of you. I hope.

Your Friend the Null

Fully Utilizing the Null Object

by Glen David Miller

You're probably wondering what an article on Null Objects is doing in the pages of *LWPRO*. In fact, though, it makes perfect sense. If I had to place a wager on the least used feature of LightWave, especially by beginners, I'd say it's the Null Object. Yet using nulls can help you avoid many near-disasters.

First of all, if you are keeping your LightWave program up to date (and you should be), from version 3.1 on, you will find an **Add Null Object** button above the current object pop-up menu.

At present, nulls save as part of the scene file, rather than as an object [Editor's note: To change the name of one of these nulls, select **Save Object**]. In 3.0 and all previous versions, a null object can be found in the objects directory as the only object not contained in a subdirectory, unless, of course, you've changed that fact yourself. In these versions, nulls are saved as objects.

What is a null object, anyway? In simple terms, a null object is an axis without the ability to render. It is the most basic object that LightWave understands. Through 3.1, the Null was displayed as a dot. In 3.5 (and 3.2 for you Raptor folks) the null took on the shape of a six-pointed axis marker.

So what good is a null?

Overcoming Gimbal Lock

First, there is axis, or gimbal lock. This problem is a side effect that occurs due to the way LightWave calculates rotations. If you were to position, for example, the spaceship object with the Pitch set to 90 degrees, you would notice that both the Heading and Bank move in the same direction. In essence, you have no heading control. Gimbals work the same way in the real world. If you are ever around one, give it a try. It seems impossible to overcome, and without a null object it would be. The normal way of getting around gimbal lock is to design your objects correctly in the first place. Spaceships and other vehicles should be built looking into the +Z axis. However, if you need to pitch too far, you can't avoid gimbal lock.

Figure 1

Here's how to beat it. After loading your object, take note of the pivot point. If you don't move your object, it should be located in the center of the screen. Then, using the method contained in your current software, load a null.

It should load in the same place as the pivot point of your object. The key is to parent the spaceship to the null, create a key at frame 0, then rotate the null 90 degrees in Pitch. Now you can reselect the spaceship and rotate around Heading Pitch or Bank. The gimbal is no longer locked.

The only other thing you need to remember is that when moving the spaceship, move it by means of the null. In other words, let the null control the movement of the spaceship, but let the spaceship itself control its rotations. Normally, you would want to keep the spaceship keyframed at 0 on X, Y and Z, but there may be times where offsetting the spaceship can produce desirable results. For instance, rotating a stationary null would produce a smooth, "orbit-like" motion for an offset spaceship.

When moving your objects throughout your scene, you may find it necessary to come up with a clever combination of rotations for your object and your parent null in order to give the movement the appropriate look.

Another Cool Moving Sheen

Moving sheens are often called for when performing logo work. Many sheens are achieved by moving an image map across a particular axis of an object. This is a good method, but what if you want a sheen to move around a logo? Again, the null makes this possible. Here's what you need to do.

After you have your logo (one with a bevel looks nice here), you will need to find a good image to reflect. An image with a lot of contrast, such as Figure 1, works best.

This image is loaded into LightWave (**Images** panel) and placed in the Reflection Image pop-up requester in the **Surfaces** panel. The rest of the surface of the logo should be set as follows:

Surface Color (Select your own, as the color will show through slightly)

Diffuse Level	25%
Specular Level	50%
Glossiness	Low
Reflectivity	75%
Soothing	On
Max Smoothing Angle	25°

All other values should remain at their defaults. Of course, depending upon your logo and your animation, you may need to change any of these values to obtain different looks.

Now, without moving the logo (and it should have been centered in Modeler), load a null object. Next, parent the logo to the null, then parent the camera to the null. You will now be able to move and rotate the camera to any position you wish. Remember to place a keyframe at frame 0 for both the logo and null object, as well as the camera.

For the rotating sheen to occur, we are going to have to rotate the logo, thus "moving" the reflection map around it, by rotating the null. Select the null object, click **Rotate**, and move your mouse around while holding down the left mouse button. It doesn't seem like much is happening except that your grid is moving around.

Look at the scene from one of the three orthographic views to see what is actually going on. Notice that even as the logo never seems to move (in relation to the camera), it is spinning around in space. Now, rotate the null so that the Heading and Bank have a setting of 360 degrees. Keep the pitch at 0 degrees. Create a keyframe for the null in this position at another frame. Let's use 150 for this example. After generating a wireframe preview, notice that the 150 frames loop cleanly. This gives you the ability to render only 150 frames, but you can output this sequence numerous times to film or tape for a longer animation.

If you only need a five-second, single-pass animation of your logo, you might place a Tension of 1 at keyframe 150 for the null object. This will slow the logo down to a stop at the end. After saving the scene, render it and you will see highlights moving around the surface of the logo. A positive setting for Heading and Bank will cause the sheen to move to the left and a negative setting will cause a move to the right. For this technique to work in its most basic form, the background needs to be set as a solid color, such as black. However, you are not restricted to using only a solid backdrop. You could build or paint a backdrop and load the image as a Background Image (**Effects** panel).

Null Offsets

A big area where null objects are helpful is when you need what I call "Offset Control." Offsets can, for one thing, make controlling multiple objects simple.

A great example of Offset Control exists in a computer-generated animation shown during this year's SIGGRAPH. In the animation, multiple rows of hammers move up and down in sync, banging their "heads" on metal anvils. Here is how to copy this technique using LightWave:

First, load the Hammer object from the Tools subdirectory. Notice that the pivot point of the hammer is toward the bottom end of the handle. That is a great position for the rotation that this hammer will take. Next, load a null object. [Editor's note: If you have version 3.5, you can easily add a null by selecting **Object** as the edit item and hitting the + key on the numeric keypad. Hitting the - key will ask to clear the selected item.] As in the spaceship example, it should load right on top of the hammer's pivot point if you have not moved the hammer. Make the null the parent of the hammer object. Then create a key at frame 0 for both objects.

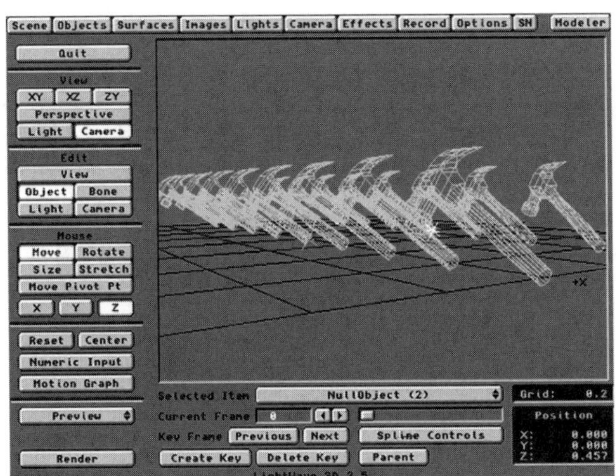

Figure 2

Set the hammer's heading for 180 degrees and rekey the hammer at frame 0. Next, enter the **Objects** menu and select the hammer as the current object. Click Clone Object and enter 8 into the field. After pressing return and exiting the Objects menu, you will see only one hammer. However, if you click on the Selected Item menu, you will see that eight hammers have been added. Select the second hammer. Then turn off Y and Z in the Move section and slide the second hammer along the X axis just to the left side of the original hammer. Create a keyframe for this hammer at frame 0 in this position.

Continue to move the next three hammers along the X axis to the left and create a keyframe at 0 for each. Then move the last four hammers along the X to the right and key those.

Once all of the hammers are separated, select the null and rotate the Pitch. Notice how the row of hammers moves in sync. There is also the added benefit of having to move only one object. Place the Null's pitch around -50 degrees and keyframe it at frame 0 and also at frame 50. Then pitch the Null down so that the heads of the hammers are flat against the "ground" (-90 degrees). Keyframe the null with this rotation at frame 20. With the null still selected, click on the **Motion Graph** button and select **Repeat** for the End Behavior. Click **Use Motion**.

Generate a wireframe preview to see the row of hammers move. Chances are that you will want to change your camera view a bit before generating the preview. At this point, save your scene as "RowOfHammers."

In the original SIGGRAPH animation, there were rows and rows of hammers. You, too, can have the rows and motions without a lot of effort. Make the Current Frame zero. Enter the **Objects** panel and select **Load from Scene**. Select the RowOfHammers scene in the requester and select OK. LightWave will ask you if you also want to load the lights from the scene. For this example, there is no need to do so.

In Layout, just like when the hammers were cloned, you should see only the original row of hammers. The new row is lined up with the original. Select NullObject (2) and, under Move, turn off both the **X** and **Y** axes. Move the second null back along the Z axis so that the second row of hammers is well behind the first row. Then keyframe the second null. Click the **Motion Graph** button (NullObject (2) selected) and, after entering the menu, select the Z Position as the Current Channel. Move the keyframe at 20 and 50 to the same Z Position value as frame 0.

Click Use Motion. Then make a wireframe preview. As you can see, there are two rows of hammers in sync (Figure 2). You can continue to add rows to your heart's content—or at least until you're out of RAM.

As you can see, using nulls can help you achieve many effects that otherwise would be difficult or impossible. There are a few more features I wish LightWave had that would benefit all the techniques discussed above. Some examples are the ability to cut, copy and paste sections of the motion graphs—to not only repeat the motion but repeat the motion a number of times and then stop; better still, to repeat a specific range of keyframes in the middle of a motion file a set number of times and then continue the file to the end. It would be really great if, to assist null offset animation, LightWave had the ability to morph one motion file to another. Even without these additions, however, the null can be a very helpful tool.

LWP

You Bonehead!
Part I: A Beginner's Look at Bones

by Dan Ablan

Ahh, yes. Bones. By now, most of us know what they can do. We know you can make inanimate objects come to life. We know that Bones can make solid objects bend and deform. But not many people use Bones on a regular basis, because they're either too tedious to set up, or when you do, weird things happen to your object. Well, believe it or not, they are not nearly as complicated as you may think.

If you've worked on any other 3D platform, you'll see that only a few, like LightWave, have Bones. Bones are an advanced form of free-form deformation that enable the animator to create fluid character animation. You can even make smooth-flowing curtains with just a few Bones. Bones will also allow you to simply deform an object, and in a sense, model in LightWave's Layout. It's good to think of LightWave's Bones as handles. You probably already know all of this, so let's move on.

I thought I'd put together a tutorial from a fun animation I did when I first got LightWave 3.0 and Bones. Arnie Boedecker and I have a series of Bone tutorials we're putting together for *LWPRO*, based on a big project just completed. There were quite a few tricks we picked up when doing those animations (like those flowing curtains I just mentioned), so keep your eyes on future issues of *LWPRO*.

The scene I'm talking about in this article is probably one of the most common animations people have tried using Bones, thanks to, you guessed it, the Listerine ads. Those sensational animations were produced by a company called PIXAR, but there is no reason you can't put together an animation like that at home using LightWave and Bones. Just so no one is misled, we'll call our product Blisterine.

Proper Construction

- The first thing to do is build your bottle. This type of object is pretty easy to build using **Lathe**, so I won't go into details. The way I built mine was by going to the store, buying a bottle of Listerine, and placing it on top of my computer. Then I built it. A more mathematical approach can be used by measuring. Plus, you can grab a frame of the bottle, then trace over the image in Modeler.
- For the label, I used Modeler's **S Drill**, **Stencil** feature (**Tools** menu) to stencil in the label area on the bottle. To create the label image, I found the ToasterFont that looked as much like the original label's fonts as possible. Then I made sure that the spacing was the same, and the size of each section of words. What the words read, however, is not at all what's on my bottle. I composed black letters on white in CG, then imported that frame to ToasterPaint and drew the border. I saved this as a full-size image, so that in the animation, when the bottle jumps forward and lands in front of the camera, you can clearly read the label. It takes up more RAM in LightWave, but it's well worth it when everything is sharp and clear in the final piece. For this tutorial, you can use the pop can supplied in the Toaster's objects directory to save time.

With Bones, anything you want to deform needs to be made up of many polygons. For instance, if you took a storm window off of your back door and tried to bend it, it wouldn't bend at all, or it would crack. But, if you took a screen off of that door and tried to bend it, it would bend very smoothly and easily, right? That's because the screen is made up of many segments. Think of your objects the same way.

In Modeler, to create many segments, use **Subdiv** (**Polygon** menu). You first need to **Triple** (**Polygon** panel) anything before you subdivide. [Editor's note: With Modeler version 3.5, you can subdivide three-sided *or* four-sided polygons.]

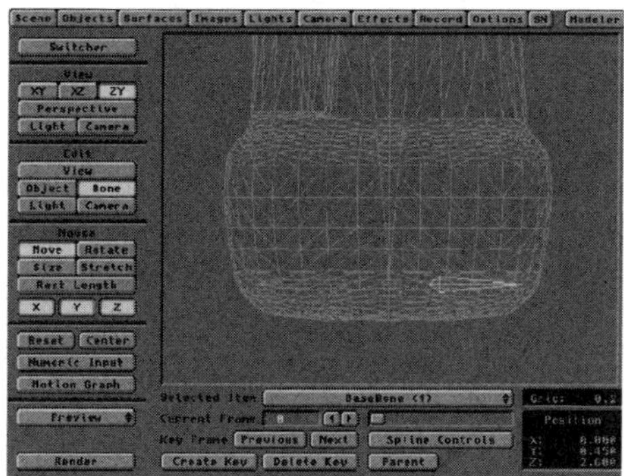

Figure 1: The first base Bone in place as an anchor.

You should also make sure to check for non-planar polygons (Polygon **Stats-Display** menu) and triple any that you find. If your whole object is composed of triangles, you will have no non-planars. This is best for objects that will be deformed in Layout.

- Once this is done, **Export** your bottle to Layout, saving it as bottle.sbdv or soemthing similar. Remember that Bones affect the points of an object, not the polygons, so when you start moving your Bones, don't be confused by the bounding box of your object staying in place.

The Setup

One thing to remember is that Bones are saved with the scene file, not the object. Bones have an unlimited influence on an object. If you don't limit the influence with the **Limited Range** setting in the **Object Skeleton** sub-panel, your entire object will be influenced. The more common way of taking care of the influence is by placing other Bones around the object.

On my Blisterine bottle, I've placed four Bones in the base, renaming them base Bones. Those base Bones don't move because they will act as anchors for the object. Because I'm going to move and rotate the other Bones, the anchors hold the bottle on the ground. The result is a bottle that bends and twists. If those base Bones weren't anchoring the bottle, the entire object would move.

Under the **Objects** panel in Layout, you'll see another button labeled **Object Skeleton**. This is where Bones are loaded, cleared and renamed for your scene. In order to place Bones to a specific object, that object must be selected before you go to the skeleton panel.

- Click **Add Bone**. Rename that Bone "basebone." Return to Layout. You'll see what looks like a squared necktie. That's your bone (Figure 1). This Bone has no effect on your object yet. Select **Continue** and return to the Layout window.
- The next thing to do is choose the object, select **Bone** and choose **Rest Length** from the mouse function control area in Layout. Do not confuse Rest Length with Size. The size will actually change the shape of the object, whereas the rest length determines the amount of influence the Bone has.

The larger the Bone rest length, the more influence it will have on your object. Since I'm placing this first Bone as an anchor, it's sized to half the length of the base of my object. When I add the next three Bones, they will be the same size as well. From this point, you can repeat the process, or if you are working with LightWave 3.5, the **Add Child Bone** feature in the skeleton panel can be used.

This function will clone the Bone and parent it to the currently selected Bone, so you don't have to reset the rest length. **Add Child Bone** is really helpful when putting bones in a snake- or rope-type object.

- Now, rotate the Bones you just added so that you have a base Bone in four places on the base of the bottle—north, south, east and west—and create a keyframe at zero for each. So far, these Bones still have no effect on your object. To make them have influence, press (**r**) to determine the rest position and direction. If you now move or rotate these Bones, they will affect the object. However, we don't want to move these. They're the anchors, remember?
- Go back into the Object Skeleton panel by pushing (**p**) on the keyboard while a Bone is selected. Add another Bone (not a child Bone). Rename it "bottombone." This Bone will be used to control the bottle's lower half. Change the Rest Length and rotate it 90 degrees vertically. Think of this Bone as a leg for our bottle.

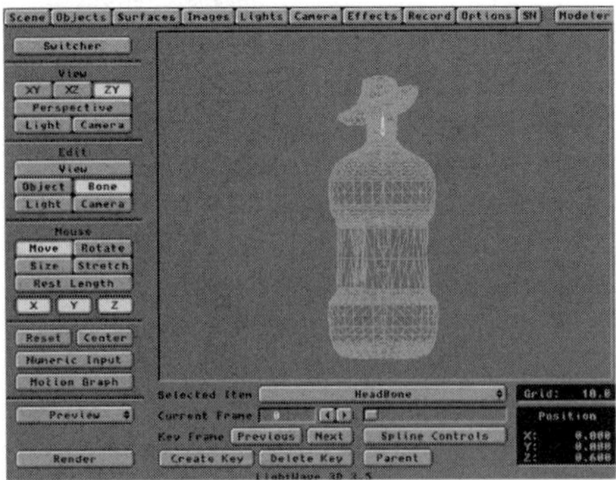

Figure 2: The neck Bone in place.

- Add another Bone and rename it "chestbone." Place this one in the top middle portion of the bottle. Finally, add only one more Bone, renaming it "neckbone," and change the rest length, then rotate it to fit it in the neck area (Figure 2). Once your Bones are in place, type (**r**) on the keyboard and create a keyframe for each bone.

If for some reason you set a Bone wrong, you can deactivate the Bone from the skeleton panel by de-selecting **Bone Active.**

- Now, save the scene. Get into the habit of saving the initial Bone setup. That way, if your bone movements get totally out of hand, you can reload the setup scene, and not have to deal with resetting all of those Bones.

Simple Surfacing

I've tried surfacing the Blisterine bottle a number of ways, and recently came across a way to save time by not using traced reflections. You'll definitely need to trace refraction for a glass bottle, though. By loading the Fractal Reflections image and using it as a **Reflection Image** with 10 or 15 percent **Reflectivity**, you'll achieve a nice abstract reflected look, and help your object appear more real. It's a great setting for getting clear plastic to look convincing.

Originally, I made both the bottle and liquid inside it. Each had different surface properties and different refraction indexes. To get true refraction, the light would need to go into the bottle at one setting, pass through another, and leave at yet another setting. Polygon count was high, so just for grins and giggles, I tried something else. I resurfaced the body of the bottle with a different name. I took the liquid out of the bottle and kept one refraction level for the whole thing. Then, I surfaced the body section the color of my liquid, with the neck portion of the bottle fully transparent (see below). In the final animation, the effect was barely noticeable, and saved time rendering because there were fewer polygons and less refraction to calculate. The downfall of this procedure is that the liquid in the neck area won't slosh around.

Bottle Surface Settings

Color	184, 122, 46
Diffusion	90%
Specularity	80
Glossiness	High
Reflectivity	10%
Reflected Image	Fractal Reflections
Transparency	60%
Color Filter	On
Edges	Normal
Smoothing	On
Refractive Index	1.3

Neck Surface Settings

Color	200, 200, 200
Diffusion	80%
Specularity	80%
Glossiness	High
Transparency	100%

The Motions

Now it's time to animate. One thing to learn is to be patient with your movements. Too often, animations are rushed to get a certain amount of movement accomplished within a certain time frame. Work to avoid that. With Bones, timing is everything. The best way to know how to move your character around is to study motions from everyday life. When creating a more cartoonlike character, the movements are exaggerated, so watch how traditional cell animations are drawn and animated.

From here, it's totally up to you how everything will work. For my bottle, I decided to make it look around, then lean back, lurch forward and flip in the air, landing in front of the camera. This became a little tricky, because the Bones bend the object, but keyframes needed to be set for the bottle as well. The chest Bone moves back, making the bottle lean, then it quickly swings forward, and at that point, the bottle starts to flip up in the air. Keyframes for the bottle needs to be set when it starts its jump, in mid-air, when it's upside down, and again when it lands. To add to the whole motion, consider stretching your object on the Y axis, when it lands, while moving the Bone forward quickly, then back, as if the bottle almost loses its balance when landing. The motions for this movement are on this issue's disk with a pop can object ready to animate.

What really helps sell the character, whether it's a bottle, can, glass, or even a square box, is proper keyframing of the motions. To take your animation one step further, consider adding hands, feet or weapons to your object. Since I'm from Chicago, I thought it appropriate that the Blisterine bottle was connected—you know, with the Mob.

Once you've set up the object's movements with Bones, save the scene. Then create the surrounding scene, and simply use the **Load From Scene** (objects panel) feature to import your Bone sequence. I've put my mobster in a scene, but made it black and white to fit the time period. By parenting a machine gun, among other objects, and keyframing that, the illusion is created that the bottle is holding the gun (see color pages).

Remember This

Bones are a very powerful tool. What I've learned in working with them over the past year and a half is patience. The latest project with bones went so well because the entire animation was storyboarded first. We knew what we wanted to accomplish, and when it came time to animate, everything fell into place.

By the way, there is a Ninja and Rambo Blisterine bottle animation in the works.

LWP

Dan Ablan is a LightWave animator for AGA in Chicago. He's done work for The Dial Corporation, Kraft Foods, NBC in South Bend, and others. He can be reached at (312) 239-7957 or via Internet at dma@mcs.com.

Beginner's Steps

- Think of Bones as handles to pull and push an object.
- Objects need to be tripled, and sometimes subdivided, to bend properly.
- Rest Length sets the amount of influence of the Bone.
- Sizing a Bone changes the size of the object, not the Bone.
- Use Add Child Bone (LightWave 3.5) to save time.
- Always save the scene once Bones are in place.
- Save scene with Bone movements under a different name.
- Be patient with the amount of movements.
- Stretch the object while moving Bones for added characteristics.

Taking That First Step

Actually Doing Something With Bones!

by Arnie Boedecker

Since the release of Toaster 3.0 (LightWave 3.5 for you standalone types), LightWave has taken a huge leap forward with the introduction of Bones. Following soon after were a bundle of informative articles on this new feature. In theory, the idea of Bones was great, until you actually sat down and moved one of 'em. Many users are still struggling to get any outstanding results in a reasonable amount of time.

Now, if you already know how to use Bones, and can get pretty nice results, I'm sad to say that this article has nothing to offer you. Go ahead, turn the page with disgust and mumble some derogatory comment like "Not another Bones article." For the rest of you, who want to actually do something specific with Bones but don't know exactly where to start, this article may help.

Just Do It!

OK, the first question is, "What do we want to do?" The most common thing that you see Bones being used for is to animate the inanimate. You know, give that piece of furniture a spring in its step, make that logo dance its little heart out, etc. So, to keep things within the Toaster arena, let's make a toaster come to life. We'll be using the ChromeToaster object that came with the Video Toaster. Now the question becomes, How should we bring it to life? To keep things simple, we'll put together a walk sequence for our little toastin' buddy. Let's get started.

Boneable Toast

The first step in using Bones to manipulate an object is to make sure that it is "Boneable." What I mean is, you must make sure that your object is constructed in such a way that Bones can distort it without destroying it. Generally, only a few things need to be done to accomplish this. You want to make sure that all of the polygons are tripled. This way, every polygon will have only three points, and cannot become non-planar when distorted, which would cause rendering errors. You also want to merge duplicate points so that the object doesn't "come apart at the seams" while being distorted. So let's make our Toastin' Buddy Boneable! (No snickering please.)

- Load Modeler.

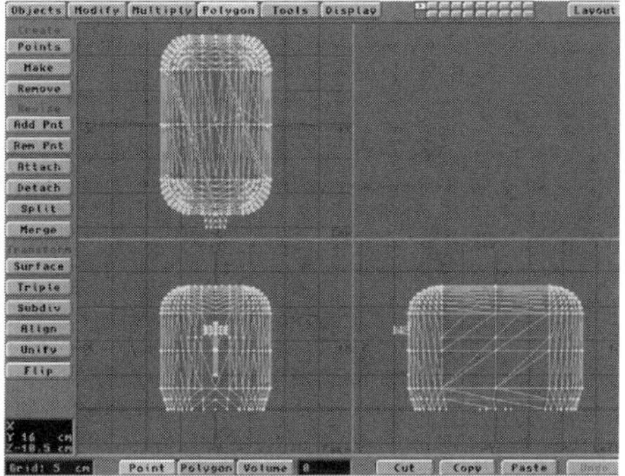

Figure 1: ChromeToaster after polygons are tripled and subdivided.

- Load the ChromeToaster Object (most likely found in the Objects/Kitchen directory) into layer 1.
- Hit the (a) key to fit the object into all three views.
- Triple the object's polygons using the Triple button in the Polygon panel (shift+T).
- To ensure that the object will distort smoothly, you might want to Subdivide the polygons once more (Subdiv in the Polygon panel or shift+D). Be sure to use Faceted Subdivide.
- Next, be sure to Merge Points (Merge in Tools panel or m:) using Automatic merging selection. If you Subdivided once, as I did, 26 points should have merged, and you should end up with 1,248 polygons (Figure 1).
- Save this object as Toaster.sub.

Any Skeletons in Your Toaster?

The next step is to create a skeleton for our toaster out of—what else—Bones! How you plan to manipulate the object determines how you set up your skeleton. I want to make our toaster "walk" forward with kind of an inchworm style, where the front end lifts and moves forward, and then the rear lifts and catches up. Let's do it!

- Quit Modeler.
- Load the object Toaster.sub into Layout.
- To achieve my "inchworm" effect, I'll need separate Bones in the front and rear. I'll also need some extra Bones in the front, which will allow for more fluid movement and help the toaster "dip down."
- Add the first Bone to the toaster by clicking on **Add Bone** in the **Object Skeleton** subpanel (**Objects**).
- Rename this Bone FrontFootBone.
- Give it a Rest Length of 0.1 and hit **Continue.**
- In Layout, select **Bone** as your current edit item and move the Bone to (-0.05, 0.025, -0.125).
- Create a keyframe at frame 0 and hit the (r) key to signify this as the Bone's rest position.
- With **Bone** still selected as your edit item, hit the (p) key to bring up the Bones subpanel, and click

Key	FRONT FOOT BONE(1)	TOP BONE(1)	REAR FOOT BONE(1)
0	-.05, .025, -.125	0, .125, 0	-.05, .025, .015
5	none	0, .125, 0	none
15	none	0, .075, .005	none
20	-.05, .025, -.125	0, .075, .005	none
25	-.05, .060, -.130	0, .095, 0	none
30	-.05, .025, -.175	0, .105, -.012	-.05, .025, .015
35	none	none	-.05, .060, .005
40	none	0, .105, -.012	-.05, .025, -.045
50	none	0, .075, .005	none
55	-.05, .025, -.175	0, .075, .005	none
60	-.05, .060, -.180	0, .095, 0	none
65	-.05, .025, -.215	0, .105, -.012	-.05, .025, -.045
70	none	none	-.05, .060, -.055
75	none	0, .105, -.012	-.05, .025, -.095
85	none	0, .075, .005	none
90	-.05, .025, -.215	0, .075, .005	none
95	-.05, .060, -.220	0, .095, 0	none
100	-.05, .025, -.265	0, .105, -.012	-.05, .025, -.095
105	none	none	-.05, .060, -.100
110	none	0, .105, -.012	-.05, .025, -.130

on **Add Child Bone.**

- Rename this new child Bone FrontFootBone as well. You should now have FrontFootBone (1) and (2). Hit **Continue.**
- Move FrontFootBone (2) to (0.1, 0, 0). Make a keyframe at frame 0 and hit (r) to designate its rest position. Both FrontFootBones will be controlled by FrontFootBone (1).
- Create two rear Bones in the same manner: Add a Bone, renaming it RearFootBone. Give it a Rest Length of 0.1 and move it to (-0.05, 0.025, 0.015). Create a keyframe at frame 0 and assign its rest position (r). Then add a child Bone, renaming it RearFootBone. Move RearFootBone (2) to (0.1, 0, 0). Create a keyframe at frame 0 and assign its rest position (r).
- Next, we want to add two more Bones up front, which will help the toaster "dip down," as mentioned earlier. In the Skeleton subpanel, add another Bone and rename it TopBone. Give it a Rest Length of 0.1 and hit **Continue.**
- In Layout, parent the TopBone to FrontFootBone (1).
- Move TopBone to (0, 0.125, 0). Create a key at frame 0, and assign its rest position (r).
- As before, add a child bone to TopBone. Rename the child TopBone as well. Move TopBone (2) to (0.1, 0, 0). Create a key at Frame 0, and assign its rest position (r).
- Save the scene as Toaster.Skeleton, or something similar. That's it! You've got a skeleton to manipulate your toaster (Figure 2).

Walk the Walk

OK, let's put this toaster into action! The movements forming the walk sequence will be as follows: The front end will dip slightly, as if to "push off." The front end will rise from the ground, move forward, and descend to the ground again. Then the rear will lift and move forward to meet the front again. Ready?

- Begin by creating a keyframe at frame 5 for TopBone (1), and give it a spline tension of 1. This will let the toaster rest for a few frames before going into motion.
- To sink the front end down slightly, move TopBone (1) down to (0, 0.075, 0.005) and set a key at frame 15. Make a key at frame 20 to give the dip a short pause.
- The toaster will now begin its first step. Create a key for FrontFootBone (1) at frame 20, with a tension of 1, and then move it to (-0.05, 0.06, -0.13) and keyframe it at frame 25. Move TopBone (1) to (0, 0.95, 0) and key it at frame 25, as well.
- The front end will descend to the ground, so move FrontFootBone (1) to (-0.05, 0.025, -0.175) and key it at frame 30. Move TopBone (1) to (0, 0.105, -0.012) and key it at frame 30 as well.
- At this point, the rear begins to rise, so create a key for RearFootBone (1) at frame 30, with a tension of 1. Then move RearFootBone (1) to (-0.05, 0.06, 0.005) and key it at frame 35.
- The rear will descend to the ground. Move RearFootBone (1) to (-0.05, 0.025, -0.045) and key it at frame 40.

Our toaster just took its first step! (Honey, get the camera!) To have our Toastin' Buddy continue walking, repeat the steps we followed for the first step, only continue to move the bones on the Z axis. You'll notice that the object itself never moves, as it only has one keyframe (so don't try a bounding box preview!). It's the bones distorting the object that actually make it move. Keyframes for the next couple of steps, as well as the ones just covered, are detailed below. From there, try and figure them out yourself.

Ready to Render

Once you're happy with the walk sequence, you're just about ready to render. The ChromeToaster's default surface has fractal bumps and reflects its surroundings (it's chrome). To render this out you might want to remove the BumpMap (rendering will be much faster) and you might want to make the toaster reflect an image like fractal reflections, rather than its surroundings. If you tried to test render the walk sequence using only the default black background with the current surfaces, the chrome would just be black. One other note: I found that the black slot on the front of the toaster flickered during a test animation, since the slot is just a polygon placed on the side of the toaster. To fix this problem, I used the Stencil tool (Stencil in the S Drill requester, Tools) to cut in my own slot. If you do this, be sure to triple the new polygons.

Finally, with the addition of a floor and Trace Shadows (Camera panel) on, the toaster comes to life as it struts its way across the screen.

What's Next

Anything you want! Once you get the feel for how bones work, you can make your objects do all kinds of things. Mess around and you'll have your toaster jumping through hoops at a circus in no time!

Arnie Boedecker has sold his spleen to be allowed on the Internet, and can be contacted at awb@ais.net. Or you can call him the old-fashioned way at (815) 385-8198. Arnie has no interests other than animation, and should therefore be considered potentially dangerous.

Animal Animation Tricks

Put a Horse Through Its Paces With Bones

by James M. Curtis

One of the hardest things to do in 3D is animate living things. This is especially true of animating animals that we are familiar with. This month's tutorial will take you through the steps to animate a horse using Bones. We will create a normal-paced, four-legged walk.

I will be using version 3.5 LightWave Modeler and Layout for this tutorial. The method was designed as a way to overcome 3.5's limitations, but its application is still useful for versions 4.0 and 5.0.

A Horse is a Horse

To complete this tutorial, you'll need a horse object. The one used here is from the public domain. I've had it for years, and can't recall where I got it. I have modified it substantially from its original form, adding more detail and correcting some anatomical and polygonal errors.

This tutorial is written based on my horse object. The parameters described here may need to be adjusted for any other horse. Variations on the following procedures can also be applied to other four-legged animals.

Preparing the Horse

One of the difficulties with LightWave 3D 3.5 (and to some extent 4.0) is how Bones work. As you put bones into an object, and proceed to bend (rotate) a bone, it tends to affect other parts of your object. Even turning on Limited Region (Objects-Bones Panel) and setting a smaller Influence range doesn't always cure the problem. The greatest distortion occurs at points directly across from, or behind, the bent bone. [Ed note: version 5.0 includes some great new features - Falloff Type, Muscle flexing and joint compensation - that allow for more intuitive bone displacement -jg]

There are ways to circumvent this. One is to make sure the limbs are all straight out to the sides, so that the influence of the bones being initially near other parts of the object is minimized. In my experience this helps, but it leaves an unnatural crease at the joints in the animal. So, how do we prevent this?

The method I've successfully used, involves splitting the object. Here's what to do:

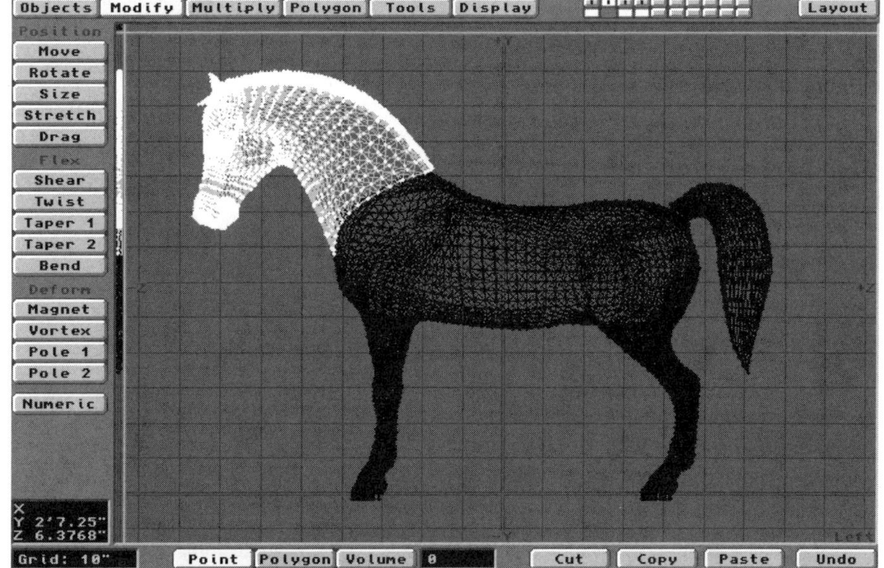

Figure 1: The head of the horse model Cut and Pasted in Modeler.

Figure 2: Tail is Cut and Pasted into a separate layer.

- Take the object and load it into Modeler.
- From the Left View, choose the Polygon Select button at the bottom of the screen.
- Use the Right Mouse button to Lasso all of the polygons of the head and neck.
- Cut these polygons and paste them onto Layer #2 (Figure 1).
- Now Lasso the polygons associated with the tail (or select the Tail surface if there is one).
- Cut these polygons and paste them in Layer #3 (Figure 2).
- Go to the Top View, select the Exclude button at the bottom of the screen.
- From the Top View, drag out the bounding box around the left half of the object (right side of the screen).
- Be sure you are dividing the object into equal halves (X=0). Cut the polygons.
- Paste these in Layer #4 (Figure 3).
- Layer #1 should now have only the right half body remaining (Figure 4).
- To Save the objects, choose one layer at a time, and select Export "New." Name them: Horse_RightSide.lwo, Horse_HeadNeck.lwo, Horse_Tail.lwo, and Horse_LeftSide.lwo.
- Return to layout.
- Add a Null object to the Scene, name it Horse_Axis.lwo.
- Parent all four of the horse objects to the Null object.
- Save the Scene as Horse_Setup.lws

You should now have the objects loaded and still in the shape of the complete animal.

Making the Bones

You may be wondering why we split apart the horse object into four separate pieces. Remember

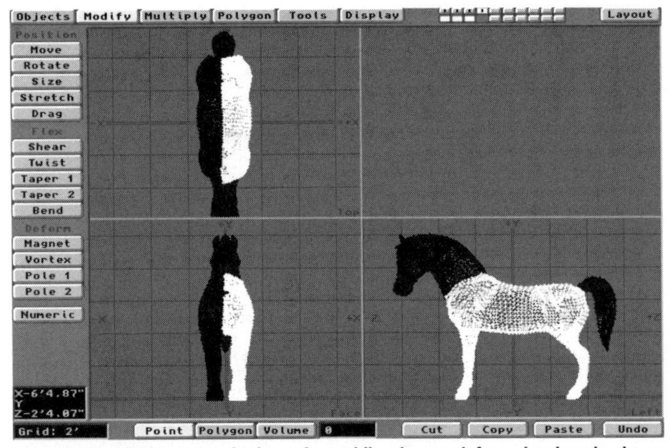

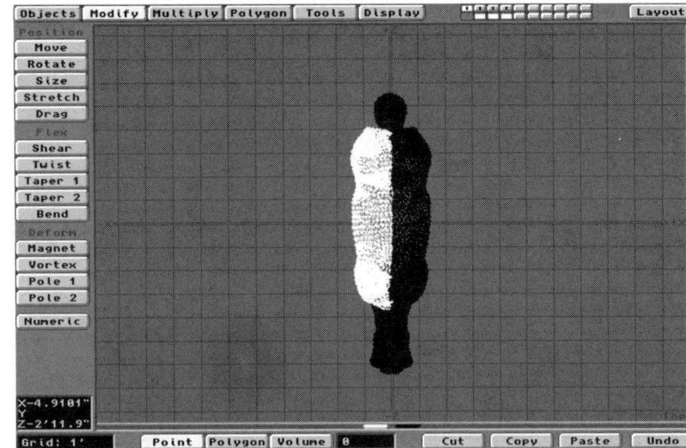

Figures 3-4: The horse is split down the middle, showing left- and right-side objects.

what I said about Bones tending to affect parts of an object that lay closest to the bone when bent? Well, by splitting the object into these parts we have eliminated the possibility of bone influence from bones that lay directly across from each other.

The first two sets of Bones will be used around the inner perimeter of the left and right halves of the body (at X= 0). They keep the seams together so they don't "flex apart" as the leg bones are bent. There are five support bones in each half, plus four bones in each leg area. In all cases, Limited Region is not selected. Please note that the first two groups do not have parenting.

Bone Rest Parameters for Horse_LeftSide.lwo body support group

L_MainSupport-Bone
Rest Position 0.0, 1.34, -0.88
Rest Direction 0.0, 3.6, .0
Rest Length 1.845

L_ChestBone
Rest Position -0.04, 2.44, -1.32
Rest Direction 0.0, 73.8, 0.0
Rest Length 1.085

L_BackBone1
Rest Position 0.0, 2.44, -0.77
Rest Direction 0.0, 20.2, 0.0
Rest Length 1.195

L_BackBone2
Rest Position 0.0, 0.0, 1.06
Rest Direction 0.0, 16.6, 0.0
Rest Length 1.01

L_RearSupport
Rest Position -0.06, -0.12, -1.02
Rest Direction 0.0, 115.0, 0.0
Rest Length 0.805

Bone Rest Parameters for Horse_RightSide.lwo body support group

R_MainSupport-Bone
Rest Position X=0.0, Y=1.34, Z=-0.88
Rest Direction H=0.0, P=3.6, B=0.0
Rest Length 1.845

R_ChestBone
Rest Position 0.04, 2.44, -1.32
Rest Direction 0.0, 73.8, 0.0
Rest Length 1.085

R_BackBone1
Rest Position 0.0, 2.44, -0.77
Rest Direction 0.0, 20.2, 0.0
Rest Length 1.195

R_BackBone2
Rest Position 0.0, 0.0, 1.06
Rest Direction 0.0, 16.6, 0.0
Rest Length 1.01

R_RearSupport
Rest Position 0.06, -0.12, -1.02
Rest Direction 0.0, 115.0, 0.0
Rest Length 0.805

The next two groups are positioned inside the front and back leg of Horse_LeftSide.lwo. They are used to bend the actual legs. These bones have Parenting.

For the front leg section:

L_ShoulderBone
Parent None
Rest Position -0.24, 1.94, -0.7
Rest Direction . 0.0, 90.0, 0.0
Rest Length 0.675

L_UpperLegBone
Parent L_ShoulderBone
Rest Position -0.08, -0.1, 0.53
Rest Direction 0.0, -8.8, 0.0
Rest Length 0.615

L_LowerLegBone
Parent L_UpperLegBone
Rest Position -0.0, -0.02, 0.605
Rest Direction 0.0, 11.2, 0.0
Rest Length 0.57

L_AnkleHoofBone
Parent L_LowerLegBone
Rest Position 0.0, -0.02, 0.565
Rest Direction 0.0, 23.8, 0.0
Rest Length 0.7

For the back leg section:

L_HindQuarterBone
Parent None
Rest Position 0.22, 0.00, Z=0.53
Rest Direction H=0.0, P=80.8, B=0.0
Rest Length 0.855

L_HindUpperLegBone
Parent L_HindQuarterBone
Rest Position 0.0, 0.0, 0.855
Rest Direction 0.0, -31.6, 0.0
Rest Length 0.855

L_HindLowerLegBone
Parent L_HindUpperLegBone
Rest Position 0.0, 0.0, 0.52
Rest Direction 0.0, -41.2, 0.0
Rest Length 0.58

L_HindAnkleFootBone
Parent L_HindLowerLegBone
Rest Position 0.0, -0.04, 0.58
Rest Direction 0.0, -20.4, 0.0
Rest Length 0.685

The next two groups are positioned inside the front and back leg of Horse_RightSide.lwo. They are used to bend the actual legs. These bones have Parenting.

For the front leg section:

R_ShoulderBone
Parent None
Rest Position -0.24, 1.94, -0.7

Rest Direction 0.0, 90.0, 0.0
Rest Length 0.675

R_UpperLegBone
Parent R_ShoulderBone
Rest Position 0.06, -0.1, 0.53
Rest Direction 0.0, -8.8, 0.0
Rest Length 0.625
R_LowerLegBone
Parent R_UpperLegBone
Rest Position -0.02, -0.02, 0.605
Rest Direction 0.0, 11.2, 0.0
Rest Length 0.57

R_AnkleHoofBone
Parent R_LowerLegBone
Rest Position 0.04, -0.02, 0.565
Rest Direction 0.0, 23.8, 0.0
Rest Length 0.7
For the back leg section:

R_HindQuarterBone
Parent None
Rest Position -0.22, 0.00, 0.53
Rest Direction 0.0, 80.8, 0.0
Rest Length 0.855

R_HindUpperLegBone
Parent R_HindQuarterBone
Rest Position -0.04, 0.0, 0.855
Rest Direction 0.0, -31.6, 0.0
Rest Length 0.855

R_HindLowerLegBone
Parent R_HindUpperLegBone
Rest Position 0.0, 0.0, 0.52
Rest Direction 0.0, -41.2, 0.0
Rest Length 0.58

R_HindAnkleFootBone
Parent R_HindLowerLegBone
Rest Position 0.0, -0.04, 0.58
Rest Direction 0.0, -20.4, 0.0
Rest Length 0.685

Now you should have all of the bones placed inside of both Horse_LeftSide.lwo and Horse_RightSide.lwo. Select each Bone in turn and hit "r" to set them. Now, as you rotate a leg bone, the opposite leg will not be affected. There should also be no distortions where we added the support bones. Check out Figure 5 to see how the skeletal structure of bones looks from the Side View.

Animating the Walk

We are now ready to rotate the bones and set up key frames for the walk. So how do we start? How do we create a walk that looks right? Simple. We use a reference. Thankfully, the material we need is as close as the nearest public library. The book "Animals in Motion", by Edward Muybridge, is my reference of choice. In fact, since the book breaks down the walk cycle into several visual steps, the images can serve as the walks' key frames. The angles for the Bone skeleton are based on one of these sequences.

For this walk, a complete cycle (or stride) will occur in 44 frames. This means that each bone will rotate into its' exact starting position every 44 frames (at 0,44,88,132, 176, etc.).

• Rotate the bones and create keys according to the list below.

Keys and Pitch Settings for Bone skeleton of Horse_LeftSide.lwo:

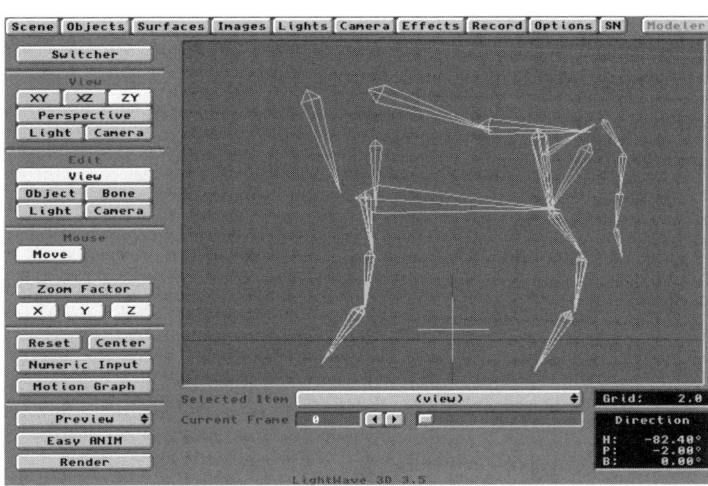

Figure 5: A Side View in Layout showing positioning of the Bones within the horse model.

L_UpperLegBone

0	-6.6
4	-16.4
8	-25.6
12	-30.2
16	-34.8
20	-14.4
24	29.4
28	36.0
32	27.2
36	12.0
40	3.4
44	-6.6

Motion Repeat

L_LowerLegBone

0	11.2
4	11.2
8	11.4
12	5.4
16	3.2
20	-25.6
24	-63.0
28	-50.6
32	-7.8
36	11.2
40	11.2
44	11.2

Motion Repeat

L_AnkleHoofBone

0	27.4
4	37.0
8	37.0
12	30.4
16	33.2
20	-19.4
24	-35.2
28	-23.0
32	-3.0
36	7.8
40	16.4
44	27.4

Motion Repeat

L_HindQuarterBone

0	66.6
4	63.6
8	74.0
12	81.8
16	88.0
20	97.0
24	91.6
28	85.8
32	85.6
36	86.0
40	84.4
44	66.6

Motion Repeat

L_HindUpperLegBone

0	-12.4
4	-27.6
8	-44.0
12	-34.4
16	-22.0
20	-16.8
24	-21.2
28	-25.4
32	-33.6
36	-36.2

40 -31.0
44 -12.4
Motion Repeat

L_HindLowerLegBone

0	21.2
4	39.6
8	49.0
12	85.4
16	60.0
20	38.6
24	47.6
28	50.6
32	47.0
36	29.4
40	11.8
44	21.2

Motion Repeat

L_HindAnkleHoofBone

0	26.8
4	-31.8
8	-26.6
12	-26.6
16	-23.4
20	-12.0
24	-16.6
28	-0.2
32	4.4
36	34.8
40	28.2
44	26.8

Motion Repeat

Keys and Pitch Settings for Bone skeleton of Horse_RightSide.lwo:

R_UpperLegBone

0	4.4
4	30.0
8	31.8
12	21.8
16	14.0
20	6.2
24	-2.6
28	-11.2
32	-19.0
36	-28.0
40	-11.8
44	4.4

Motion Repeat

R_LowerLegBone

0	-30.0
4	-55.0
8	-25.4
12	11.0
16	11.2
20	11.2
24	11.2
28	11.2
32	11.0
36	11.0
40	-12.8
44	-30.0

Motion Repeat

R_AnkleHoofBone

0	-44.2
4	-39.0
8	-24.4
12	0.6
16	5.0
20	17.0
24	25.2
28	29.0
32	29.0
36	35.2
40	-8.2
44	-44.2

Motion Repeat

R_HindQuarterBone

0	94.4
4	90.0
8	86.0
12	91.6
16	85.2
20	77.6
24	76.0
28	89.8
32	101.8
36	108.2
40	116.2
44	94.4

Motion Repeat

R_HindUpperLegBone

0	-20.6
4	-20.8
8	-24.6
12	-45.8
16	-35.8
20	-30.4
24	-35.4
28	-56.8
32	-62.4
36	-57.6
40	-53.8
44	-20.6

Motion Repeat

R_HindLowerLegBone

0	47.2
4	43.2
8	40.2
12	49.4
16	30.2
20	27.2
24	19.8
28	42.6
32	53.2
36	66.8
40	50.6
44	47.2

Motion Repeat

R_HindAnkleHoofBone

0	-10.0
4	3.0
8	-5.2
12	4.4
16	28.2
20	32.0
24	25.8
28	-48.4
32	-53.2
36	-34.2
40	-16.0
44	-10.0

Motion Repeat

Now do a Preview animation set to 44 frames. You should have a very convincing walk cycle. Note that at this point it merely walks in place. To make it walk forward, it will take a little bit of experimentation to find exactly the right position for the Horse_axis.lwo null. My horse object moves 2.15 meters for every complete stride.

You should create keys for the axis null every four frames. This allows you to fine tune the placement of the horse, and prevent "sliding" during the walk. For a look at a rendered frame of the horse walk scene check out the color section.

Options

There are a few things that can be added to make the animation more natural:

1) Put some bones into the head and neck to bob the head up, down, and to the side slightly as it walks. Put a larger bone at the base of the neck to keep it from being distorted as you bend and rotate the head.

2) Do the same thing with the tail.

3) The movement of both head and tail should be synchronized to the 44 frame loop of the walk.

Wrapping Up

There are many other motions you can achieve with the object. I have successfully animated a gallop and a rearing horse. In fact, I have used the rearing-up motion to animate two mythological Centaurs battling each other with swords and shields. This scene really took some planning to put together.

This wraps up this tutorial on walking a horse. I hope that you have gained some valuable tips, and the inspiration to try some motions out on your own.

LWP

Jim Curtis specializes in character modeling and animation. He can be reached at JMC Graphics by voice at (216) 354-6239.

Humanoid
Human Form and Motion

by John F.K. Parenteau

In 3D animation, one of the most difficult tasks to accomplish is the creation of a convincing human form. Every aspect, from modeling to animation, often requires the most sophisticated software to achieve anything that even remotely resembles the shape and motion of the human body. Until recently, I felt that only a high-end software package could simplify the process. Then I discovered Humanoid by Crestline Software Publishing.

First Impressions

My first experience with the Humanoid data set came late on a Sunday night as I sat down to create a set of computer-generated storyboards depicting a basketball game for a client. After creating my basic objects and setup, I began loading the Man data set for placement. I had never really looked at Humanoid before, and couldn't have told you where the manual was among the scattering of paperwork in my office. Yet within moments I was positioning my character in the scene. In the variety of poses that were required, I was certain I would run into problems with the objects as they were twisted and bent. To my surprise, the objects rendered perfectly. With such confidence, I began using Humanoid for a number of applications. Each time, I was pleased with the ease of manipulation and the quality of construction.

The Package

The objects, a data set of a standard man, a strong man, a woman and a child, are pre-grouped in provided scenes. Each data set is carefully designed to look and animate in as straightforward a fashion possible. Upon reading the manual, I discovered that the designer, Tim Wilson, has provided the user with an amazing collection of information to draw upon. Several sections deal with all important facets of animating Humanoid, including the proper movement of all joints as well as suggested settings for various poses. Excellent walk-and-run cycles are provided in separate scenes.

The novice animator will find that even without reading the manual—much less understanding it—the Humanoid figures are extremely easy to handle. Though the objects alone require approximately 6.5MB of hard-drive space, the scenes only consume an average of 2MB of RAM. The software should work well with even the simplest Toaster system.

Even the most-advanced LightWave user should be pleased with the possibilities of Humanoid. The manual outlines several approaches for creating more advanced animation, including using the morph targets provided. When constructing the models, Wilson maintained the morph integrity between all four data sets, allowing complete morphing between Man, Woman and Child. In addition, various head targets are included that, with careful planning, allow an animator to sync Humanoid's lips to dialogue.

Specifics

Let's examine some specifics, not only in animating Humanoid, but in all animations.

As in any creature animation, it is important to spend time studying actual motion. Before starting an animation, practice a little play-acting around your house or office. The Industrial Light and Magic animators, prior to beginning work on *Jurassic Park*, took acting lessons, each strutting around a small room pretending to be a T-Rex. You may feel silly, and probably do look silly, but it is important to put yourself in the role before beginning.

After careful study of how you would like your motion to look, it is much easier to see your motion as it is created on-screen. Little details are important: Knees are rarely locked straight, shoulders sway when walking, the heel lands before the toe, etc.

Examine the walk-and-run cycles provided. These are excellent examples of a complete motion. Though it is not necessary to stick precisely to the limits suggested in the manual, it is important to adhere to the suggested bend-axis for each limb.

Advanced Effects

Though Humanoid is designed for hierarchical animation, the use of bones should not be completely discarded. While experimenting with my data set, I found that the subtle use of bones could add some interesting effects to an animation.

Positioning a small bone in the front of the neck and sliding it down on the Y-axis creates a convincing simulation of swallowing. Placing a bone across the front of the chest object, sizing it slightly on the X-axis and moving it on the Y simulates breathing.

Be aware that bones do not affect the hierarchy connected to the boned object. For this reason, any use of bones must be subtle. For example, excessive

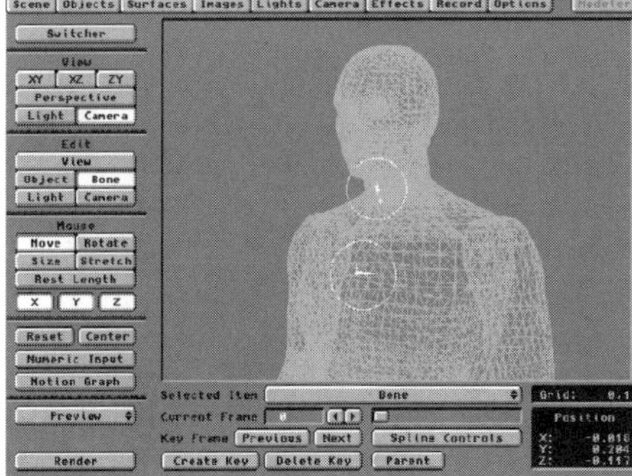

BonesApplied
This image shows two bones placed in the humanoid model to simulate swallowing in the throat and breathing in the chest.

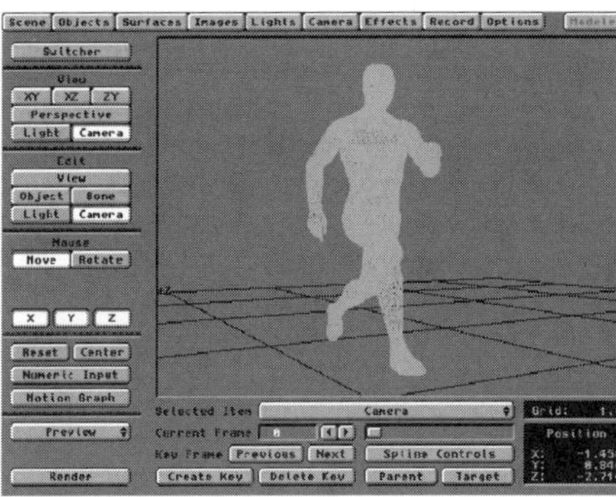

RunningMan
A frame from the Run Cycle.

stretching on the chest bone pulls the arm sockets away from the upper arms.

Use small rest lengths and limited motion to avoid any unplanned consequences. For the throat bone, use limited range to avoid dragging the back of the neck along with the front.

Morphing can help you achieve similar effects with greater ease. Take the chest object into Modeler and, with the magnet, drag the chest out and up slightly. Export this as a new object into your scene and apply a morph envelope to the original chest. Don't necessarily use 100 percent as your high morph percentage; vary the percentage, depending on the difficulty of breathing. A similar technique works with swallowing.

Be careful to limit the magnet size so as not to stretch any unwanted points. To produce a smooth shape, the magnet tool works best with a large quantity of polygons. It may be necessary to subdivide the object. This, of course, affects your morphing, as it also subdivides the number of points in the object. It is best to import the object, subdivide it and re-export it before modifying the shape. Save both the new source and new target in a separate file to avoid mixing with the original data.

This brings us back to our motion study. Applying such effects may seem simple, but realism requires a bit more attention to detail. Take our breathing example. As a person breathes, their chest expands and their stomach compresses. The greater the effort of breathing, the more this effect is heightened. Thus, it is important to apply a bone in the stomach that contracts a bit as the chest expands. Also, don't forget the importance of body language. If our character is breathing heavily, they are probably not standing straight, but rather are bending over, perhaps resting on the knees. These are circumstances where careful study plays an important role.

The one disadvantage of morphing is the danger of getting lost in morph targets. A LightWave animator must rely on envelopes to bring their character to life, and there is no simple graph similar to the motion graph to keep track. In functions as complex as syncing to speech, your object is morphing so many times in a short span of time, it is often impossible to keep up. As you plan your animation, it may be helpful to develop a timeline graph that keeps track of the morph process.

Problems

Since the objects are designed for hierarchical motion, seams do exist between each object—for instance, between the arm and the torso object. There are several ways to get around this, depending on your application.

If you are producing stills only, design your pose, then save each object out in its transformed version (**Save Transformed**, **Objects** panel). Loading these back into Modeler, you can save all the objects together, creating one object in the desired pose.

If you are animating Humanoid, avoid getting too close to seam areas. The body has a single surface name, which helps to blend the limbs together. Avoid bright colors; seams may become visible as the limbs cast shadows across the seamed area. It is helpful to Raytrace or Shadow Map the keylight when working with the data sets, since the separate objects allow light to seep between them, especially when an extreme backlight or sidelight is used.

Although the included walking and running scenes are good, both fail to incorporate one important point about motion. If you load the running scene, note that under the Scene Overview all key frames for each position are placed on the same frames. Though this allows for easy looping, it is not accurate. No two muscles in the human body respond to impulses from the brain at the same time. Thus, as a leg moves forward, the knee is slightly behind in its response.

Try to avoid creating a key for all object positions on the same frame. A few frame differences can help produce a much more convincing animation. Also, avoid looping motions, especially with regards to human or animal motion. Each step should be allowed the possibility of a slight difference that a repeated motion will not allow. Once you've created your animation, write down the key frames for each limb.

Develop another graph that continues the motion beyond the initial cycle. For example, if the upper leg is raised at frame 20 and then set down at frame 40, add 20 frames onto frame 40 to bring the leg back to its raised position. Add another 20 frames onto frame 60 (the second raised-leg keyframe) to place the leg back down, etc.

Summary

The Humanoid software proves to be an excellent source for accurate human form and motion for LightWave. A carefully written manual complements the quality objects provided.

With careful study, Humanoid provides the animator with endless possibilities. From basic poses to lip syncing, Tim Wilson and Crestline Software have produced a superior package for the LightWave professional.

LWP

John F.K.Parenteau is an animator for Amblin Imaging. His work can be seen on seaQuest *and numerous commercials.*

RATING: * * * *

Company Mentioned:
Crestline Software Publishing
P.O. Box 4691
Crestline, CA 92325
(909) 338-1786
Suggested List Price: $195

Replacement Animation

by Glen David Miller

Replacement animation? "Huh, what's that? I've never heard of that. What good is it?" Most people respond the same way when hearing this term for the first time.

Replacement animation is simply the replacing of one object for another or nearly similar object. To be a little more specific, an example of replacement animation would involve a scene showing a dripping area of water. This is a common sight after most rainstorms. First, the water flows to a low spot on the edge of a window frame. As the water collects, a small teardrop shape begins to form in the lowest area. Then, as the teardrop grows in size, its weight overcomes the surface tension. Suddenly, the teardrop separates from the main area of water and drips downward.

While it may be easy to imagine or even draw these four steps, in LightWave, it's not quite as easy. And without the replacement animation technique, it would be nearly impossible to accomplish.

While there are many more uses of replacement animation, our technique involves using four objects. The first is a flat plane with numerous faces that have been tripled. The second object is a form of the first object-plane. With the third object we will continue to finesse the drop shape until it reaches the point just prior to the break. The final two objects will complete the break. The first will resemble the first plane with a slight bump in the middle of the plane. We can reuse one of the above shapes for the plane. The second will be the teardrop shape that falls below us.

If at this point, the above explanation seems a bit much or even over your head, stick with me. I feel that one of the key rules every animator must follow is to study nature. While some might say, "The water drips," you and I both know that there are numerous specific steps that occur when a drop of water falls. An animator must know how to identify those steps and mentally or physically make a list of the useful steps he or she will need in order to complete the project. When, for example, Disney animators begin a sequence that involves wildlife, they study the specific creatures they will be drawing. Preplanning is a step too often overlooked by beginning animators. Get specific! You might even want to redraw the water drip sequence to become a little more familiar with what we'll be modeling, or even go make your own drip. Whatever the case, study, study, study.

On the technical side, in this article, we'll be covering spline modeling, metaforming, transforming polygons and points, and finally, we'll quickly cover some ideas behind our use of envelopes. Let's get started.

The Objects

We'll begin in Modeler. In the lower left-hand window, the front view, we need to create five points. As you can see in Figure 1, these points will make up the shape of our water plane and water drop. After entering the points, deselect all of them. Click, in order, the first and second points (again, see Figure 1) and then press Ctrl-p to make a spline. Re-select the second, third, fourth and fifth points and again enter Ctrl-p to make a spline. There is a specific difference in the two splines we have created (Figure 2). While the first is a straight line, the second is a curve. Remember, when spline modeling, two points that are connected become a straight spline-line. Three or more points form a spline-curve.

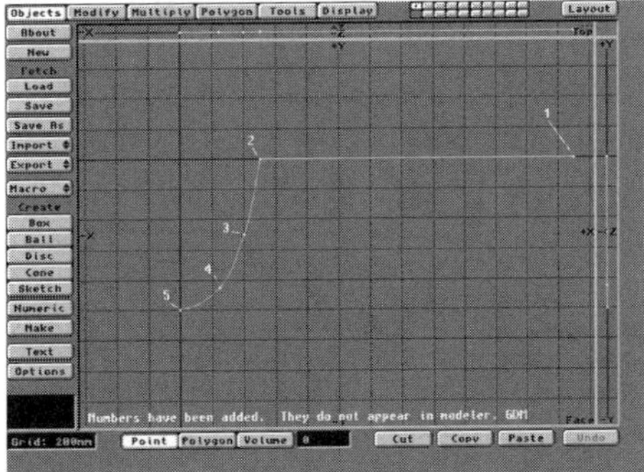

Figure 1

Make sure when creating two-point splines that you do not accidentally create two-point polygons. To illustrate the difference, go to a new layer and enter four points, then de-select them. Select two of the points and press Ctrl-p. Now, select the other two points and press (p).

They look pretty much the same, don't they? Under **Polygon** select mode, select both lines. The first difference to be noted is that the spline has a small "head" on one end. Also, when looking in the polygon stats window (w), you will see that there are two polygons, one face and one curve. Figure 3 shows all of the final possibilities you might run into. The first shape is our object with a spline-curve; the second shows multi two-point segments that have been smoothed (Ctrl-s) to form curved splines; the third shows all two-point splines; and finally, the last object shows two-point polygons or faces. The overall warning is this: a face won't patch and it won't smooth. A spline won't render. Remember to keep your p's and Ctrl-p's straight.

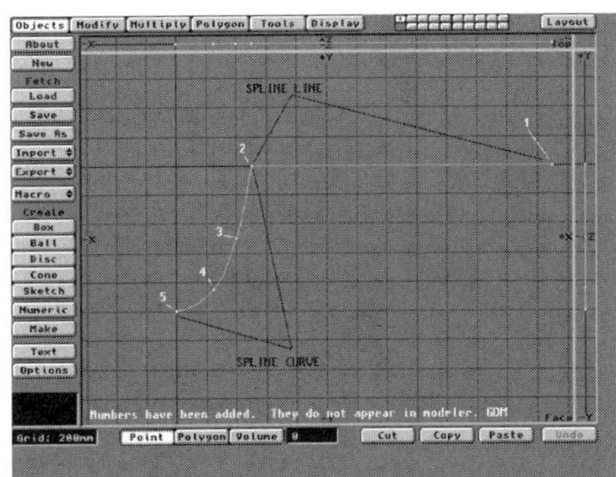

Figure 2

Go back to the original layer. Now that we have the basic cross-section of our object, go to the **Multiply** menu and select **Lathe**. Align your Lathe axis with the fifth point of our object running along Modeler's Y axis.

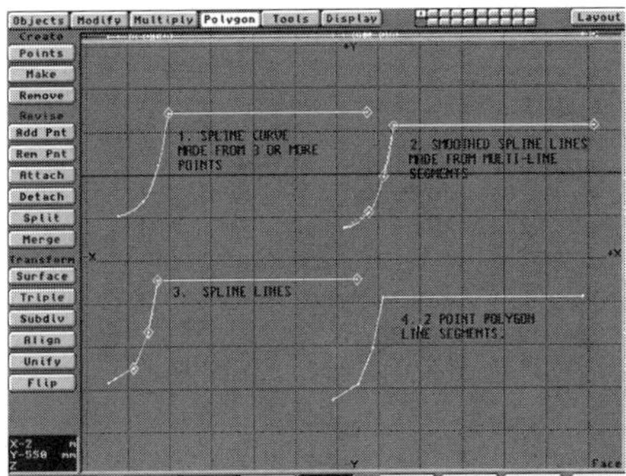

Figure 3

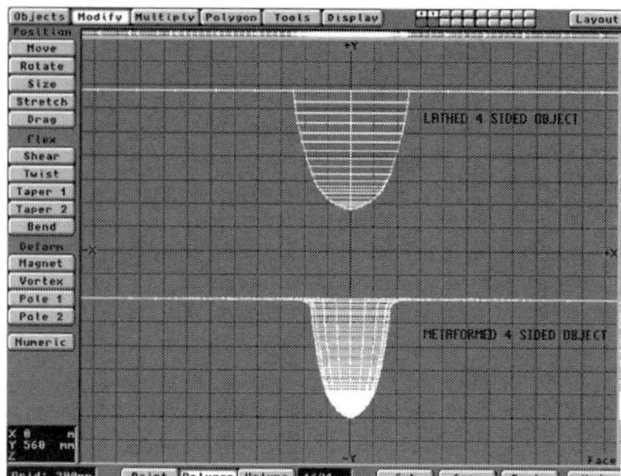

Figure 4

Select Numeric and enter 4 into the number of sections. Lathe the object. Our raindrop doesn't look too smooth, does it? Since the object is made up of quads, it is the perfect subject for Modeler's Metaform tool. Go to the **Polygon** Menu and select **Subdiv**. Under the subdivide menu that appears, select **Metaform**. After Metaform finishes working its magic, you'll see that the object is smoother. Metaform it again. See Figure 4 for the desired shape.

Save this object as "Drop 2." Copy the object and paste it into another layer. Place this copy in the background and re-select the original layer as the current foreground layer. Use the **Volume** select mode to choose only the polygons that make up the lower drop segment (Figure 5).

Your next step is to select the **Taper2** tool. Using

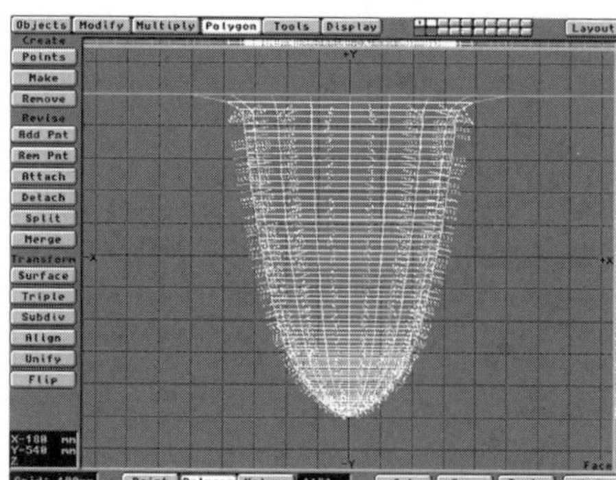

Figure 5

Numeric, select **+ Sense**, **Ease In**, **Y Axis**, and then finally, **Keep**. While holding the left mouse button, move your mouse (centered on the object in the Top view) and taper both sides of the drop of water. Save this object as "Drop 3."

Go to a new layer and place the drip layer (the layer you were just working in) in the background. In the front view, add points around the right-hand edge of the drip shape in the front view in the form of the side of a water drip. Make sure that your first and last points fall on the Y axis line of the original drip shape. Turn these points into a spline by pressing Ctrl-p. Next, lathe the shape around the Y. If you want, count the number of edges and match this second drip object to the first drip, but it isn't important. Save this object as "Water Drip."

Now go back to the second layer (the one we copied the first time) and choose Stretch. Place your pointer on the same level as the flat plane and stretch your object until the drip shape becomes almost a flat section of the plane. Save this object as "Drop 1."

The Animation

Enter Layout. Load all of your objects in the following order: Drop1, Drop2, Drop3, and finally, Water Drip. Here is where the fun comes in. If at any time you feel light(wave)-headed, slow down and reread this section.

Under the Objects panel, select your **Current Object** as "Drop1." Under **Metamorph Target**, select "Drop2." Next, change your Current Object to "Drop2." Place "Drop3" as the Metamorph Target of "Drop2." Also, set the **Object Dissolve** of "Drop2" to 100 percent. Next, change your Current Object to "Drop3." Here, the only step you must perform is to set "Drop3's" Object Dissolve setting to 100 percent.

Returning to "Drop1," the following settings need to be entered into the **Metamorph** Envelope (**E** button). Create keyframes as listed with the given values and bias settings:

Keyframe	**Value**	**Bias**
0	0%	0.0
30	100%	-1.00
36	100%	1.00
37	21%	-0.48
44	22%	0.0
47	23%	0.0
51	12%	0.0
59	9%	0.0
65	44%	0.0

Now move to "Drop2," and enter the following settings into the **Metamorph** Envelope:

Keyframe	**Value**	**Bias**
0	0%	0.0
20	0%	1.00
35	100%	0.0
36	0%	0.0

Since "Drop3" has no envelope, leave it blank.

Move to the "Water Drip" object and enter the following settings into the **Object Dissolve** envelope:

Keyframe	**Value**	**Bias**
0	100%	0.0
36	100%	1.00
37	0%	0.0

The only other step is to keyframe the "Water Drip" object at a slightly lowered position than the "drip" at frame 36. The objects should overlap. Then, place the "Water Drip" object much lower out of frame falling down the Y axis and keyframe the object somewhere around frame 60. Now, after saving the scene make a preview. You should see the drop of water form and then break off and fall.

You advanced animators might have noticed that the morph target envelopes overlap at times. This allows a smoother morph from object to object across a range of objects, rather than an A to B movement followed by a B to C movement.

LWP

Glen D. Miller is one of the newest animators to join the Amblin Imaging team. Striving to become a digital creature expert, he animates while listening to Jimmy Buffett, Tori Amos and Patty Loveless. He can be reached on CompuServe at 73223,3535.

Mighty Morphin' Morphing Tricks

by James G. Jones

What is morphing?

Well, this article doesn't have anything to do with 2D image morphing, the type made popular (perhaps too popular) by Michael Jackson's music video "Black and White." And, although morphing is "mighty" powerful, I'm certainly not talking about those annoying adolescents in multi-hued spandex who gallivant around the tube on Saturday morning.

This is about 3D morphing: the ability of LightWave to change the geometry of one object to match the shape of another.

Limitations

There are a few limiting factors. First and foremost is the requirement that the source object and the target object have the same number of points. Trying to morph an eight-point box to a 34,000-point Tyrannosaurus will not work.

Furthermore, with few exceptions, the target object should be modeled directly from the source object. In practical terms, this means you create a source object in Modeler, then bend, stretch, twist, move, resize, rotate, push, pull, dent, drag, kick, mangle and otherwise reshape your original object into its morph target. In some instances, you might have to resort to moving points around individually.

One very important thing to remember is to save the source object before getting out the hammer.

Another limitation is that as the points of the source object move to their new positions in the target object, they move in straight lines. However, there is a way around this that we'll get to in just a moment.

Digression on Theory

Many of us have a difficult time understanding just what is going on with source objects, target objects, metamorph levels and envelopes. If I had to describe the basic principle involved in a succinct manner (and I guess I do), I'd say that you should think of a morph target merely as data that the source object "looks" at to determine what shape to become. If you keep that thought in mind, I think everything else will be a bit more understandable.

How to Set Up a Morph

It's all about percentages, envelopes and who is targeting whom.

Say you have three objects: a bust of Bill Clinton, a mailbox and a back half of a horse. They were all modeled from the same object and have the same number of points.

This is obviously a hypothetical situation, so just pretend you're doing the following steps:

- Load the three objects into Layout. Set the mailbox and horse's butt to 100% **Object Dissolve** (**Objects** panel). You could just move them out of camera view, but I like to use Dissolve because it's right there in the objects panel.
- Set the **Metamorph Target** for Clinton to be the mailbox, and set the **Metamorph Level** to 100%.
- Set the **Metamorph Target** for the mailbox to be the horse's hiney, and set the **Metamorph Level** to 100%.

Now close the Objects panel. What do you see? Yes, that's right: Bill Clinton is a horse's ass. (I've always wanted to say that.)

But why? OK, here's what's happening: the mailbox is 100% morphed into the shape of the horse's behind. The bust of Clinton is 100% morphed into the shape of the mailbox. But since the mailbox is now shaped like the equine posterior, that is the shape to which William is morphed. Get it? If not, read the preceding paragraph again. Slowly.

This is called a "chain" of morph targets. In other words, object 1 is morphed to object 2. Object 2 is morphed to object 3. Object 3 is morphed to object 4. (Object n is morphed to object n+1, for you math heads.) This can go on for quite a spell—up to 16 times for any one source object, according to the manual. Rumor has it, though, that you can actually have far more than 16. I, for one, am not about to set up a 97-object chain of morphs just to find out the real maximum. If you have excess time on your hands, feel free. [Editor's note: For those of you without excess time, the limit is 40!]

To control the morphs over time, you use envelopes. For example, you'd set up an envelope for the Clinton bust object with a keyframe at frame 0 equal to 0%, and a keyframe at frame 15 equal to 100%.

Then you'd create an envelope for the mailbox that goes from 0% at frame 0 to 0% at frame 15 to 100% at frame 30.

The resulting animation would show Clinton's head at frame 0, changing to the mailbox at frame 15, changing to the horse's hindquarters at frame 30.

Morphing Real Objects

Enough theory...here's a slightly more complex (and less political) example that you might actually find useful.

How about morphing a flat plane to a sphere?

Having an animation where a flat plane changes to a sphere is one of those things that sounds easy to do at first, but turns out to be a bit tricky in reality. Here are a couple of approaches I've worked out: one solves a problem with the Wrap-To-Sphere macro in Modeler, is very simple and gives OK results. The other is a bit more complex but looks much better.

Method One

- In Modeler, use **Box** (**Objects** menu) to make a flat plane that is twice as wide as it is tall. For this example, 2 meters wide (along the X axis), 1 meter tall (along the Y axis), with no depth (along the Z axis). Be exact. Use **Numeric** (n) to enter the pre-

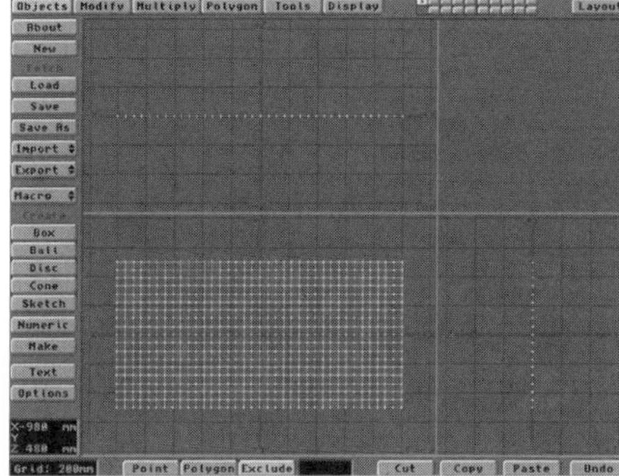

Figure 1: Make a flat plane in Modeler, 36x18 subdivisions.

cise values. Enter 36 subdivisions along the X axis and 18 subdivisions along the Y axis. You should end up with a flat plane that looks just like Figure 1. Use the Center macro to center the plane if you built it off-center.

- You will notice that the polygon's surface normals will be facing toward you (toward the negative Z axis). **Flip** them all (**Polygon** menu or f) so they are facing away from you (toward the positive Z axis). This will make sense in a moment, trust me.
- Save this object as "FlatPlane."
- Now go to the **Macro** button and choose "Wrap-To-Sphere." When the requester appears, click on the **All** button and set the inner radius to 0.5 meters. Click on **OK**.

You will now have a nice-looking sphere, and you will notice that the polygons are facing the way they should—outward.

- Save this object as "Sphere."
- Now load these two objects into Layout and set up a morph from the FlatPlane to the Sphere over a period of 30 frames. Don't forget to set the Target object (Sphere) to 100% dissolve. Make a wireframe preview and the first problem you'll notice is that the flat plane turns inside-out on its way to the sphere shape.

This is not good. However, you could always run it backward and do an animation of an imploding grapefruit.

By the way, I have no idea why this macro flips the points around like this. I just use macros, I don't understand them.

- To solve this problem, go back to Modeler and **Import** the FlatPlane.
- Use the **Rotate** tool (**Modify** menu or y) to turn it 180 degrees on the Y axis. Now the polygons will (surprise) be facing the right direction—toward the camera.
- Save it again and **Export** it back into Layout.

Well, the flat plane no longer turns inside out and the morph looks fairly good. However, look closely at the corners of the flat plane as it changes to the sphere. They fold back on themselves in a rather unpleasant manner. This is what prompted me to come up with...

Method Two

This approach uses the previous two objects and creates a third object, a cylinder, as an intermediary between the flat plane and the sphere.

- Load the FlatPlane object into Modeler.
- Click on the **Volume** button. It should say **Exclude**. If not, click on it again.
- Using the left mouse button, draw out a selection box in the Face view around the right half of the plane. The left edge of the selection box should be

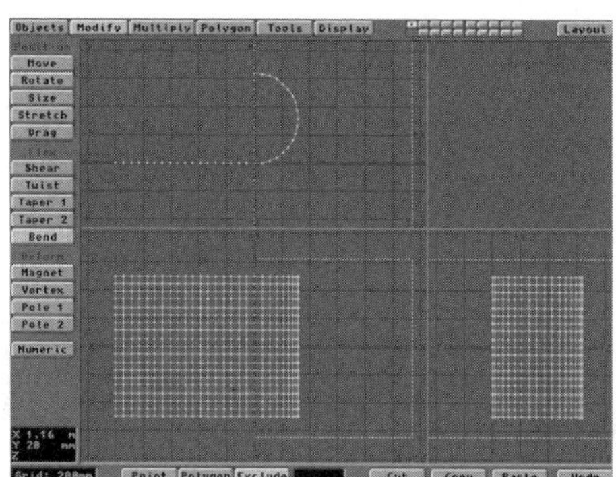

Figure 2: Use the Bend Tool to bend the right half of the plane back 180 degrees.

exactly at the center line (where X = 0). Now, when you go to bend this object, it will only affect the right half.

- Activate the **Bend** tool (**Modify** menu) and **Numeric**. In the requester, enter the following values:

Axis	X
Range	Automatic
Sense	positive (+)
Angle	180
Direction	90
Center	0, 0, 0

- Click on Apply.

You should see something like Figure 2. If the plane's end points do not bend back far enough where they are located at X=0, click **Undo**, select all of the middle points (where X=0) and use the **Set Val** tool (**Tools** menu) to set all of the middle points to X=0. Then you can repeat the above step. Sometimes, after centering an object, the middle points may be located at X=-0. Those points will not be affected in a volume that rests on them.

- Now turn off **Bend**, and move the volume selection box to surround the left half of the flat plane. This time, the right edge of the selection box should be at the center line. Choose **Bend** and **Numeric**, and use the same values as before, except change Sense to negative (-) and **Direction** to -90.
- Click on Apply.

You should have a cylinder. However, you'll notice that it's not centered.

- Use the Center macro to center the object at 0, 0, 0.
- Save this object as "Cylinder."

Setting Up the Morph

- Load all three objects—"FlatPlane," "Cylinder" and "Sphere"—into Layout.
- For Cylinder and Sphere, adjust the Object Dissolve to 100%.
- Set the **Metamorph Target** for Cylinder to Sphere, and the **Metamorph Target** for FlatPlane to Cylinder.
- Create a metamorph envelope (**E** button) for FlatPlane with keyframes at 0 and 30. Set the tension for keyframe 0 to -1 and the tension for keyframe 30 to +1.
- Make a similar Metamorph Envelope for Cylinder, but set the tension for keyframe 0 to +1 and the tension for keyframe 30 to -1.

Notice that the morph envelopes overlap. While the plane is morphing to the cylinder, the cylinder is morphing to the sphere.

- Make another wireframe preview and see what you think.

Because of the overlapping morph envelopes and the tension settings, the cylinder object is exerting more influence at the beginning of the morph, which makes for a more aesthetic change to a spherical shape. Note also that some of the points of the flat plane no longer travel in a straight line to their destination.

Some Morph Tips

- Any texture map that you have applied to the flat plane goes along for the ride when you morph it into the sphere.
- If you need to see the back of the sphere after the morph, do a one-frame dissolve to a sphere that has the points where the edges merged. Otherwise you'll see a seam.
- If you want to see the sphere morph down into a flat plane, simply set up your morphs so your plane object starts out 100% morphed and then goes down to 0%, or morph the sphere into the flat plane.

Morphing as Movement

Morphing is about movement. The points move. The polygons defined by those points move.

Why not use a morph to move a whole object?

Why would you want to, considering that LightWave allows you to move objects directly in Layout and set keyframes and all that?

Well, say your animation needed a mosquito. A rabid, hyperactive, directionally challenged mosquito, to be precise.

- Create a small (maybe 500 mm on each side) cube in Modeler.
- Move it (t) off to the lower righthand corner of the Face view.
- Save this object as "Box1."
- Move it again, this time over to the lower lefthand corner.
- Save as "Box2."

- Do the same for "Box3" and Box4," except move the box to the top left and top right areas of the Face view, respectively.
- Load all four boxes into Layout.
- Set **Object Dissolve** to 100% for Boxes 2, 3 and 4.
- Set the **Metamorph Target** for Box1 to Box2, Box2 to Box3, and Box3 to Box4.
- Make a wild, wacky metamorph envelope for Box1, Box2 and Box3 (Figure 3). Give each envelope a different total number of frames: something like 60, 52 and 46 frames, for example.
- Activate **Repeat** for each envelope.
- Make a wireframe preview that lasts for 300 frames.

Since the repeating morph envelopes overlap and are of different lengths, the motion of the box will not repeat for quite a number of frames, and you will get a sort of pseudo-random movement of the box as it flits about. Also note that the first envelope, for Box1, has more influence than the following envelopes. So too for Box2, and so on. Thus you might want to adjust the envelopes so that those earliest in the chain have a smaller range of values than the latter envelopes. For example, 40% to 60% for Box1, 20% to 80% for Box2, and 0% to 100% for Box3. This will tend to distribute the influence of the morph targets more evenly and the box will tend to hover around the center of mass of the four boxes.

Morphing Particles

Remember how I said there are exceptions to the rule about the target object having to be modeled directly from the source object? Here's an interesting one:

The effect is that of a cloud of several thousand stars drifting past the camera, *Star Trek*-like. Then the stars all change direction and race toward each other, congealing into the shape of a series of letters, or even a logo.

- First create some text in Modeler. Use the **Text** button **(Objects** menu or W).
- Load the Olnova Heavy font and type "HELLO." Click on **OK.**
- Center the text with the Center macro.
- Write down the size of the rectangular area occupied by the text plus a bit. For instance, if the maximum X value of the text is 1.64, write down 1.7 for the maximum X. If the maximum Y value is .39, write down .4 for the max Y. Approximations are fine.
- Go to an empty layer and put the text in a background layer.
- Choose the Point Spread (Point Distributions) macro and click on **Square** and **Constant.**

As a test to see if your size settings are OK, enter 100 for the Number of Points, and then enter the max X, max Y values that you wrote down into the first two Radius boxes below. Put a zero (0) in the third box.

- Make sure that Units is set to "m" for meters and click **OK.**

You should get 100 points arranged in a rough rectangular shape over the letters in the background. This macro actually creates single-point polygons, or particles, thus saving a step.

- If the size of the area covered by the particles is correct, delete the 100 particles, re-enter the Point Spread macro and do the same thing with 10,000 points.
- Go get a soda—this will take a while. It took about five minutes on my machine.
- When the Point Spread macro is done, you'll have exactly 10,000 particles.
- Click on the **Copy** (c) button.
- Rotate the particles 180 degrees around the Y axis.
- Click on the **Paste** (v) button.
- You now have 20,000 particles.
- Choose **Drill (Tools** menu).
- Click on the **Z** Axis and the Core button. Then click **OK.**

A couple of minutes later, you should see a reduced number of particles in the shape of the word "HELLO."

- Click on the **Polygon** button and then use **Stats (Display** menu or w) and write down how many particles remain. I had 10,983.
- Save this object as "Letters." This will be the target object. Considering the size of it, you might want to delete all the polygons before saving. LightWave only looks at the points of a target object; polygons are irrelevant and just use up additional space on disk. [Editor's note: For morphs using **Morph Surfaces,** you will need to leave your polygons on the target object.]
- Clear this layer (z).
- Use the Point Spread macro again, except set the Number of Points to the amount you just wrote down, and set the Radius boxes to 10, 10 and 10. Again, make sure your Units are set to meters. Click **OK.**
- Go have another soda, or go to the bathroom because of the last one.
- Save the resulting object as "PointCloud." Do not delete the polygons, as this is the source object.
- Return to Layout and load both objects.
- Set the Letters object to 100% **Object Dissolve.**
- Set the **Metamorph Target** for PointCloud to Letters.
- Make a metamorph envelope for PointCloud with a keyframe at 0 equal to 0% and a keyframe at 60 equal to 100%. Make the Tension equal to 1.0 for both keyframes, while you're at it.
- Set the camera position to 0, 0, -6.
- Make a wireframe preview from 1 to 60.

This is just a small sampling of the many uses for object morphing. Of course, with Bones, you can do many of the tasks once done with morphing much easier and with more control (though Bones have their own limitations). I didn't even touch on Surface Morphing, which would require a fairly involved article all by itself. One day you might find yourself scratching your head over a particularly difficult project, and who knows—maybe morphing an object here or an object there will provide part of the solution.

James G. Jones is an independent animator whose business, Nibbles & Bits, is located in Colorado, where the air is clear and the oxygen insufficient. He can be reached via e-mail at jgjones@usa.net.

Mighty Morphin' Television Antennas

by Alan Chan

The scene opens to a huge warehouse at night. The stiletto chirpings of crickets overwhelm the senses as CGIMan steps into the warehouse, hot on the pursuit of the field-rendered Video Wizard.

As CGIMan looks up, he sees a television set heading straight for his head! With speed-of-light reaction, he sidesteps the box of electronic doom, and it bounces off the floor harmlessly, antennas vibrating from the landing...

CUT TO REALITY

Whether you're animating the next CGI epic or just simple flying logos, there are times when you're faced with the challenges of a flexing object. Car and television antennas and the like vibrate when hit, slowly coming back to a standstill over a good number of cycles. So how can we simulate this phenomenon in LightWave? There is a quicker way than setting keyframes until your eyes hurt: morph targets.

To explain the idea, let's use the plot device in our most excellent script opener. We'll animate a falling television set.

The Theory

We will use multiple morph targets to realize this vibrating antenna (animating CGIMan is up to you). To this end, let's brush up on our morphing theories.

(1) At the absolute base level of a morph, LightWave takes a certain point from the source object and the same point (determined by the point order) from the target object, and calculates the morphed point based on the Metamorph Amount at that particular frame. For instance, if the first point in the source object is at 0, 0, 0 and the first point of the target object is at 6, 0, 0, a Morph Value of 50% will cause the morphed point to be at 3, 0, 0 (Figure 1). Repeat this procedure for the number of points you have in your object, and you will end up with a 50 percent morphed object. So you can probably see why objects with the wrong point order turn into a mess of points instead of materializing into the target object, and why you need to have objects with identical point counts.

(2) The source object is the one that is affected, not the target object. If you set a Metamorph Target and a Metamorph Amount for an object, you will see the changes in that object, not in the Morph Target. The target object serves only as a set of data that LightWave uses to reshape the source object.

(3) To use the Metamorph Target object as a morph target, LightWave requires that you load it into the scene file. Therefore, the standard operating procedure is to hide it so that it does not appear in the final rendered sequence as a separate object. That's why you would usually set the target object's Object Dissolve envelope

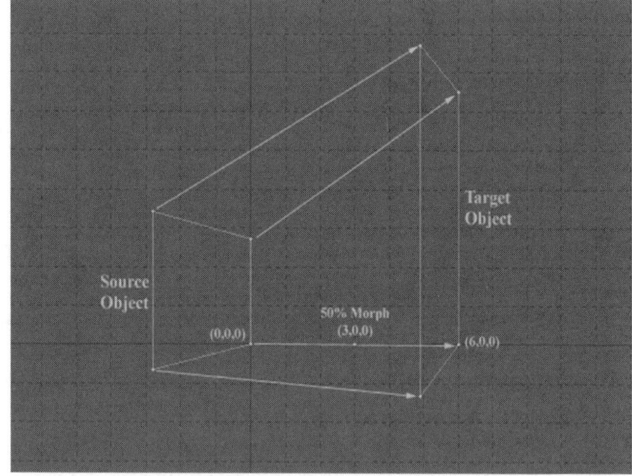

Figure 1: LightWave's linear morph.

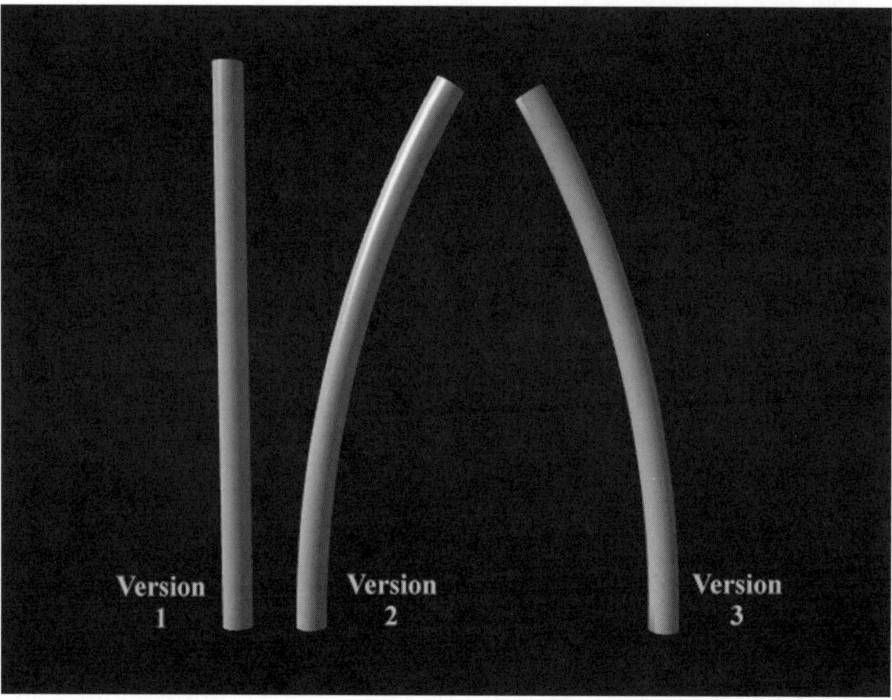

Figure 2: Objects we will use to simulate a vibrating antenna.

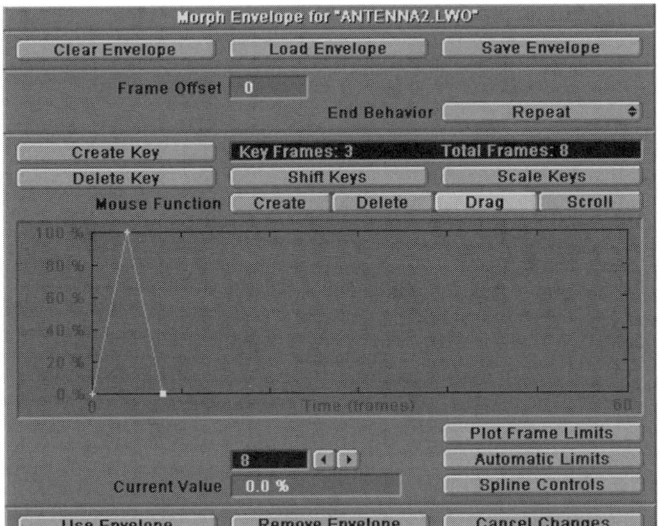

Figure 3: An envelope to generate a repeating vibration in the antenna.

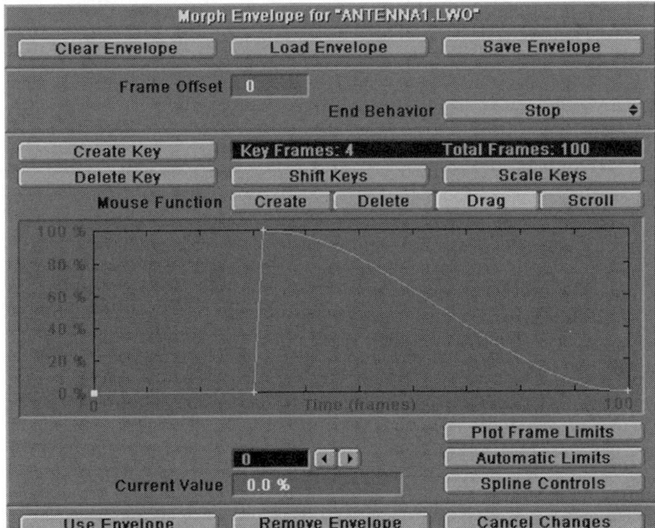

Figure 4: An envelope to control the amount of "bounce" in the antenna.

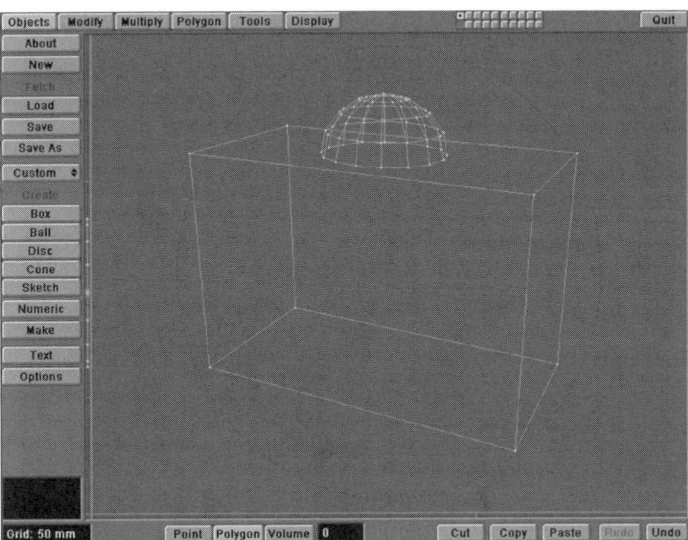

Figure 5: A wonderfully simple TV set object.

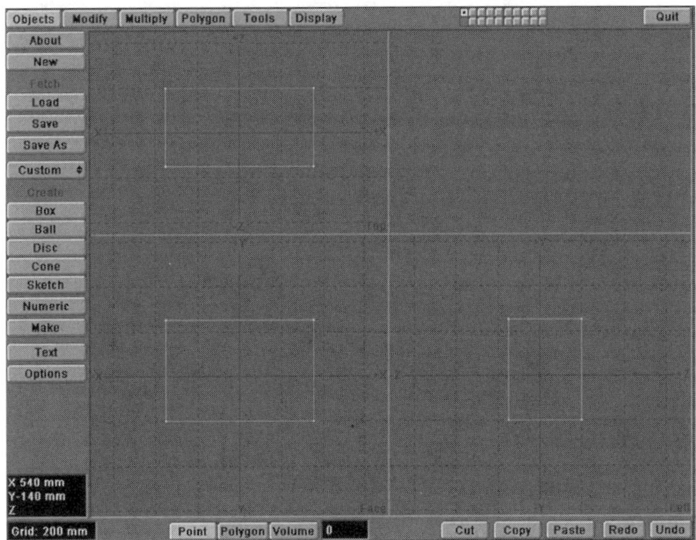

Figure 6: Dragging out a box shape for the TV set.

to 100%, or move the object out of camera view. (In addition to setting the Object Dissolve to 100%, I also parent my target object to the source object. Though it's a somewhat unnecessary step, in bounding box form, it allows me to use the dotted line bounding box to estimate the morphed position.)

(4) We can specify multiple morph targets for an object in the following way: After specifying a target object for the source object, assign a Metamorph Target to the target object itself. After the source object is morphed into the target object, the target object itself can then be morphed into a third object (Figure 2). With this "layered" morphing method, we can perform one morph after another to the same source object.

Irrelevant to this tutorial, but worthy of note: With the Morph Surfaces option, LightWave also allows for morphing surface values, but surface morphing can only be achieved from the source object to the first target object. There are no provisions for layered surface morphs.

The Execution

Having refreshed our thoughts on morph theories, it's time to take these concepts and put them to work.

Let's say we have three versions of an antenna (Figure 2). The first version represents the antenna at rest, or as it appears before anything happens to it. The second version is bent to the right, while the third version is bent to the left, representing the extreme angles to which the antenna will vibrate. All three versions have the same point count and polygon order; in short, they are morphable.

If we use a repeating envelope (Figure 3) to set version 2 so it's morphing into version 3, we will get a vibrating antenna, right? Easy enough. But the antenna doesn't stop vibrating. In reality, the device would begin vibrating violently when struck (as the television set hits the ground), but the vibration would slow down and cease over time. So how do we achieve this? The answer lies in a layered morph.

If we use version 1 as our antenna (the one that's actually attached to the television set) and create a morph envelope (Figure 4), we can morph version 1, a static antenna, into version 2, a vibrating antenna (which is repeatedly morphing between the two bent antennas). When we envelope the morph from 0% to 100% in one or two frames, we'll make the antenna start vibrating as if a force has been applied to it. As we start decreasing the Metamorph Amount over time, the vibrations become less and less noticeable,

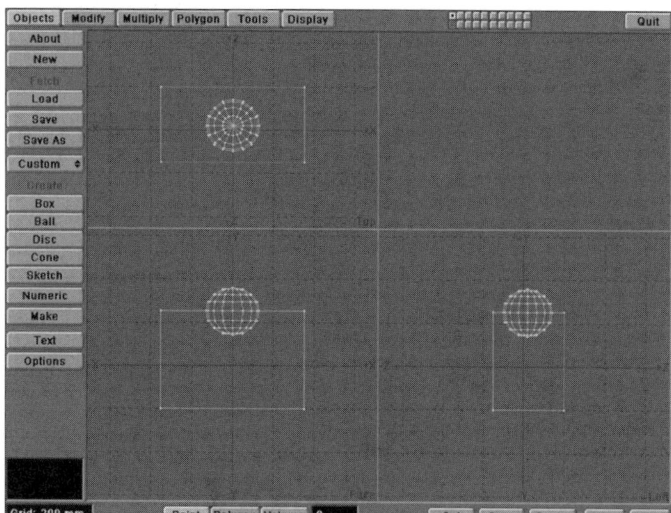

Figure 7: Dragging out a ball shape.

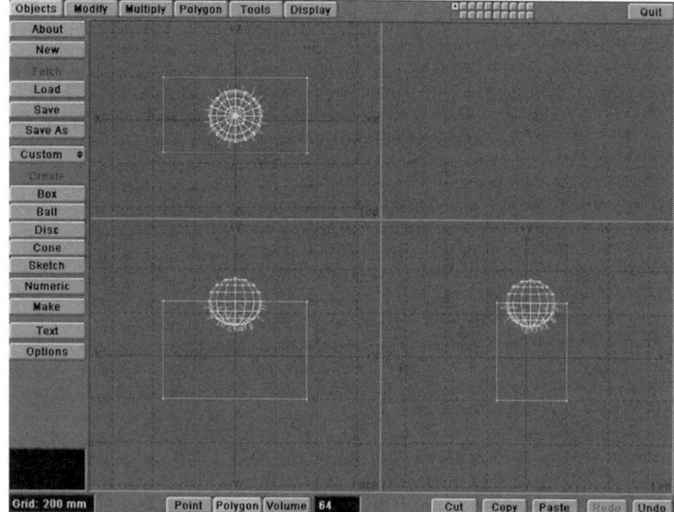

Figure 8: Trimming the ball into an antenna base.

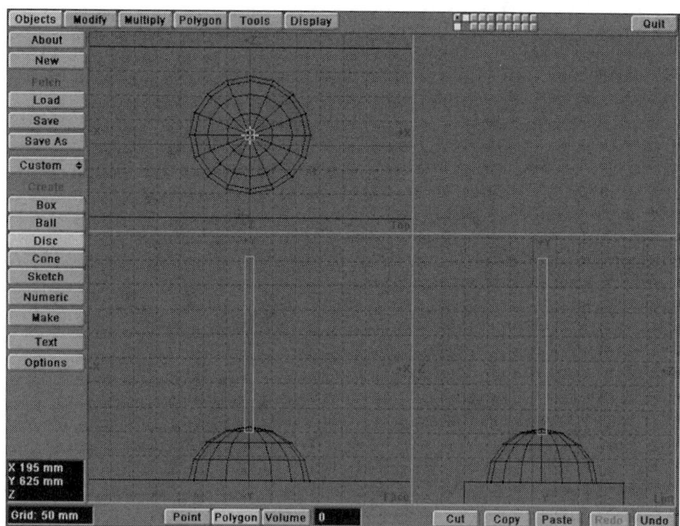

Figure 9: Modeling the antenna.

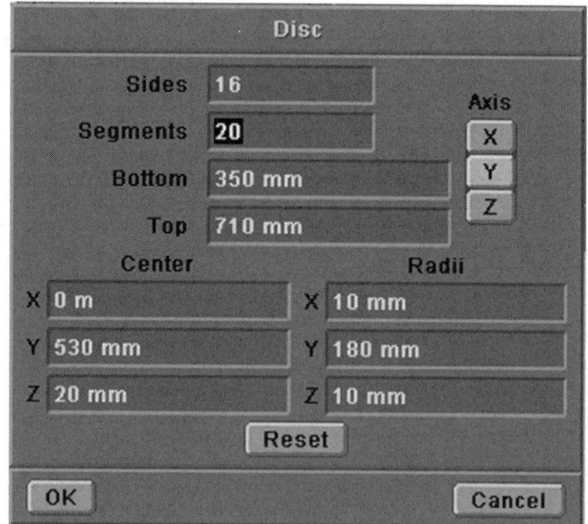

Figure 10: Numeric Options panel for Disc.

as if they are being reduced by physical forces such as air friction. Finally, when the Metamorph Amount has returned to 0%, the antenna has returned to its first, static position.

ACT I

- In Modeler, let's build a television object with antennas on top of it. We'll model an extremely simple TV such as the one in Figure 5. First, drag out a box for the television proper, and Make it (Figure 6). Next, drag out a ball for the base of the antenna at the top of the television set (Figure 7). Select the polygons making up the bottom half of the antenna and cut it off (Figure 8). You now have a simple television set object. Make sure you name your surfaces accordingly and save your TV object before continuing. (You may, of course, want to model a more sophisticated TV set.)
- Go to an empty foreground layer and place the TV box in a background layer. Using the Disc tool (Objects menu) drag out a really thin, upright antenna (Figure 9). Click on Numeric (n) to bring up the Numeric Options panel and enter 20 or so for the Number of Segments value (Figure 10). Click OK, then hit Make (return). This will give you a long, segmented antenna object.
- Since we're going to be bending and twisting our antenna, we will want to make sure that the bending process will not create non-planar polygons. Tripling our polygons beforehand will do the trick. Making sure that you are in Polygon Select mode and have nothing selected, go to the Polygon menu and click Triple (Shift–t) to triple every polygon (Figure 11). Save this object as "Antenna1.lwo".
- Select the Bend tool (Modify menu). In the top view, place your cursor in the middle of the disc. While holding down the Ctrl key (to restrict movements to one axis), click and drag the mouse so that the top of the antenna bends slightly to one side. Thirty degrees is a fairly decent amount by which to bend the antenna (Figure 12). Save this object as "Antenna2.lwo".
- Returning to the Modify menu, select the Bend tool again, and click Undo to return to the original upright antenna. Then click Numeric (n). In Bend's numeric panel, find the Angle requester (Figure 13) and make its value negative (e.g., if the value is 30, make it -30, and if the value is -30, make it 30). Do not modify any of the other parameters; they have already been set up from the last Bend operation (which created the Antenna2.lwo object), and we want to make an antenna that is exactly identical except that it bends the opposite way. Click OK to use these values, and save the object as "Antenna3.lwo".

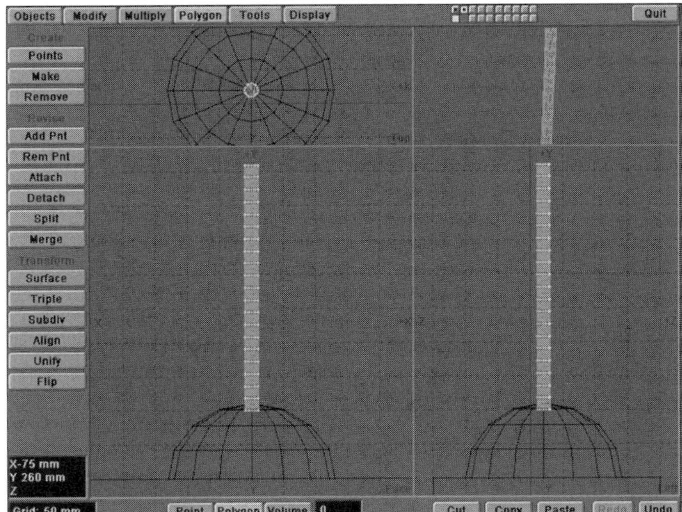

Figure 11: Tripling polygons in preparation for use as a morph target.

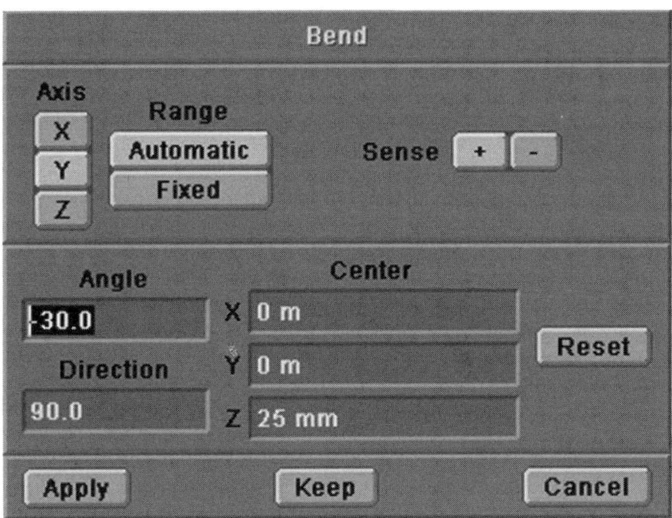

Figure 13: The Numeric requester for the Bend tool.

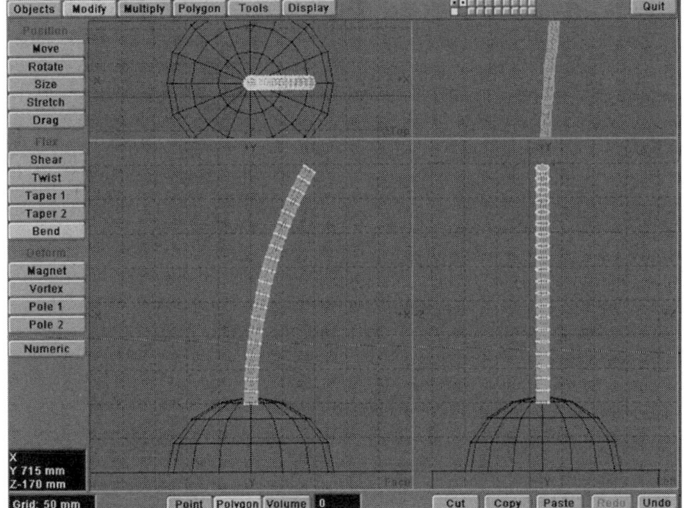

Figure 12: Bending the antenna object.

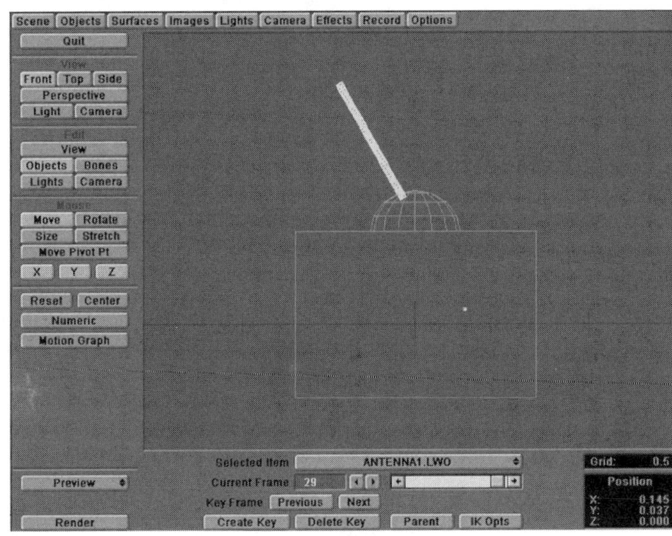

Figure 14: Positioning the antenna on the TV set.

ACT II

- Returning to Layout, Load all the objects we just created—the TV object and the three antennas. From the Objects panel, make both Antenna2.lwo and Antenna3.lwo 100% dissolved.
- With Antenna2.lwo as the current object, specify Antenna3.lwo as the Metamorph Target. Click the Envelope button (E) next to the Metamorph Amount requester to bring up the envelope graph. Set two more keyframes using the Create Key button (enter), at frame 4 and frame 8 (there will already be a keyframe at frame 0). For keyframe 4, enter a value (in the requester at the bottom of the envelope chart) of 100%. Open the Spline Controls panel (s) for all three frames and click on Linear for each of them. Finally, make sure that the envelope End Behavior is set to Repeat (default is Stop). You should have an envelope like the one in Figure 3. Click Use Envelope to keep these settings.

Our two antennas are now oscillating between each other. Of course, we can't see anything yet because we've made both of them 100% dissolved.

So let's continue:

- Select Antenna1.lwo as the current object and parent it to the TV set object. Once that's done, use the Front and Side views to move the antenna to its place on the antenna stand (Figure 14). Keyframe this, making sure, of course, that your current frame is 0.
- In the Objects panel, select Antenna1.lwo as the current object and Antenna2.lwo as its Metamorph Target, and then click on the Envelope button (E) by the Metamorph Amount requester.
- In the Envelope graph, create the following keyframes:

  Frame 30, Value 0%, Spline Tension 1.0
  Frame 32, Value 100%, Spline Tension 1.0
  Frame 100, Value 0%, Spline Tension 1.0

  Your envelope should look like the one in Figure 4. Click Use Envelope to accept these settings.
- You've just completed one antenna on the television set. To duplicate this process for the other antenna, simply clone Antenna1.lwo from the Objects panel, rotate its heading 180 degrees and move it into position on the other side of the antenna base. Don't forget to keyframe it (Figure 15). Note that this cloned object also has Antenna2.lwo as its Metamorph Target. This works just fine, and there is no need to clutter up your scene file with a different copy of a metamorph target object.
- From the Scene panel, adjust the Last Frame number of your scene to 110 or so. Keyframe a good viewing angle for your camera, save your scene file and make a wireframe preview.

Notice how the antennas start vibrating at around frame 30, looking like they've been hit, and then slowly stop vibrating? All you need to do is keyframe

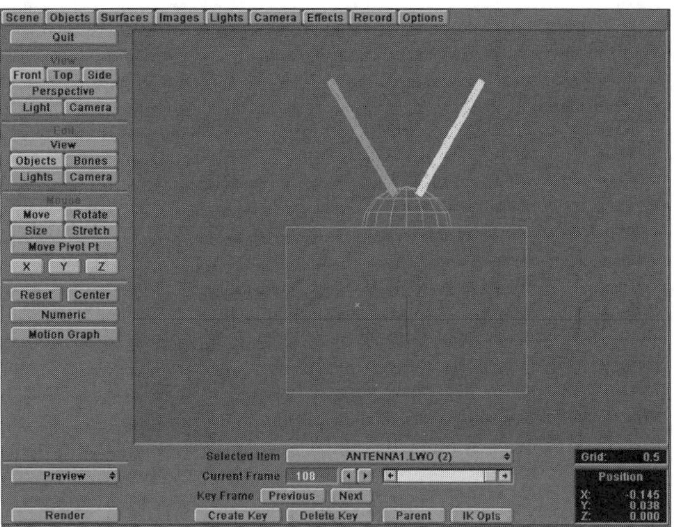

Figure 15: Cloning a second antenna object.

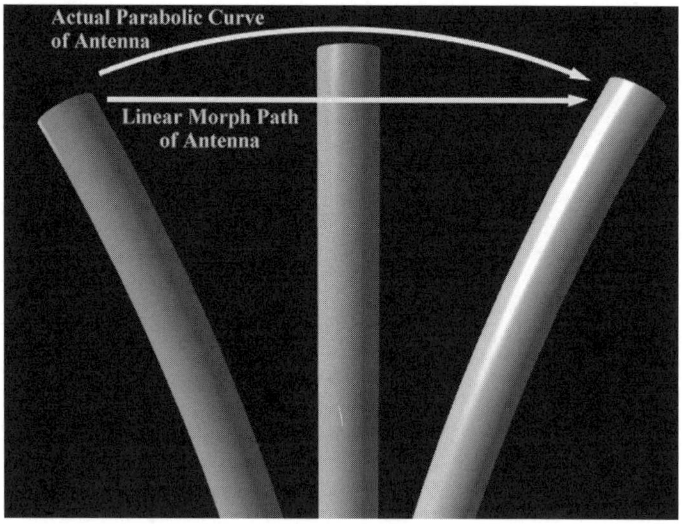

Figure 16: The problem with linear morphs.

the TV set so it falls and hits the ground (the motivation for the vibrating antennas) at frame 30.

ACT III

- Select your television object as the current object. Enter the following keyframes and values for it:

Keyframe 0:
X, Y, Z = 0, 2.687, 0
HPB = 0, 0, 9.7

Keyframe 30:
X, Y, Z = 0, 0, 0
HPB = 0, 0, 0
Spline Continuity = -1

Keyframe 35:
X, Y, Z = 0, 0.057, 0
HPB = -0.7, 0, -2.8

Keyframe 38:
X, Y, Z = 0, 0, 0
HPB = -1.1, 0, 0
Spline Continuity = -1

Keyframe 41:
X, Y, Z = 0, 0.018, 0
HPB = -1.6, 0, 0

Keyframe 45:
X, Y, Z = 0, 0, 0
HPB = 0, 0, 0

(Values may vary depending on the size of your TV object.)

- Make another wireframe preview. You will now see the television set fall and hit the (nonexistent) ground, which causes the antennas to vibrate.

EPILOGUE

You may have already noticed from doing this tutorial that if you bend the antennas too much while modeling them, your morph may not look too good. This is due to the fact that our morph is a linear morph. If you track a point on the top of an antenna through the morph, you'll see that it moves in a straight line toward its target. In reality, the same point on a real antenna would follow a parabolic path to the other side (Figure 16). In our example this error is small enough that it isn't noticeable, and the fact that it vibrates at a fairly high speed also helps to cover up the error.

If we bend it too far, however, the linear morph is pulled too far from the parabolic path and the antenna structure will begin to break down. In instances like these, you may place additional morph targets. Be aware, however, that each additional morph target means having to coordinate between morph envelopes, which can easily get out of hand as the number of morph targets grows.

This issue also brings up timing. In the last part of the tutorial, you blindly entered the keyframe values for the television. Where did these numbers come from? How were they derived? These, of course, are questions for another article.

Alan Chan is now a professional Ridge Racer and air combat veteran in between Boolean operations. His pit stop area is achan@ix.netcom.com.

MetaNURBS

A Handy Tool for Morphing

by Patrik Beck

I am predicting that LightWave 3D is about to become one of the most popular character animation software choices in the world. The reason for this is the powerful organic modeling features available with the new MetaNURBS function. MetaNURBS lets you create smooth flowing objects out of rough blocky approximations. More than that, it allows you to interactively mold and shape your model with a near real-time preview that looks embarrassingly close to the final object. Finally, all of us back-room freelancers can break out of the industrial video flowchart jungle and start working on that Saturday morning 3D cartoon show we've been planing to produce.

But wait! There is more to character animation then just building good-looking models; they also have to be animated! Not just animated, but have the ability to show expression, be squashed, stretched, and lip-synced. Unless you are a complete bones master, the most practical way to accomplish this is to use object morphing between various expressions and mouth shapes.

While it seems too good to be true, MetaNURBS makes it possible to create a crude object, alter and smooth it, then create a second object that is a proper morph target for the first object. By using multiple morph targets, objects can smoothly transform through several changes of expression. As usual with computer stuff, this is more complicated to explain than to actually do, but hang on. We will start by building a simple cartoon hand, make some morph targets, then apply what we have learned to more complicated objects.

Three Fingers and a Thumb

The first thing to do is to fire up LightWave Modeler. Go to the Options button in the objects menu. In the Polygons section, make sure the Quadrangles button is highlighted. This will ensure that all the polygons generated will be four-sided. This is important because MetaNURBS requires polygons to be four-sided in order to work properly. Later, when we freeze our MetaNURBS objects for rendering, we want to change this to triangles to reduce the possibilities of rendering errors that may happen if any of the quadrangles are non-planer.

Legend has it that most cartoon characters have three fingers because Walt Disney deemed that three fingers were plenty for a small mouse named Mickey. We can thank him for making our job 20 percent easier.

Let's start by modifying a box object.

- Create a box 1 meter square and 0.5 meters deep, with 3 segments on the X axis and 2 segments on the Y axis.
- Slightly round the edges by dragging the upper two corners down and the lower two corners up (Figure 1).
- Select the three top polygons. We will bevel these to make fingers. Hit the (b) key to bring up the bevel requester. We want to bevel without an inset, so set all values to 0 except for shift, which should be set at 0.5 m.
- Hit return and you have just created the first joint of the finger.

Because we lowered the top corners, the fingers are slightly separated. If the fingers are too spread for your taste, hit undo and tweak the angles to your lik-

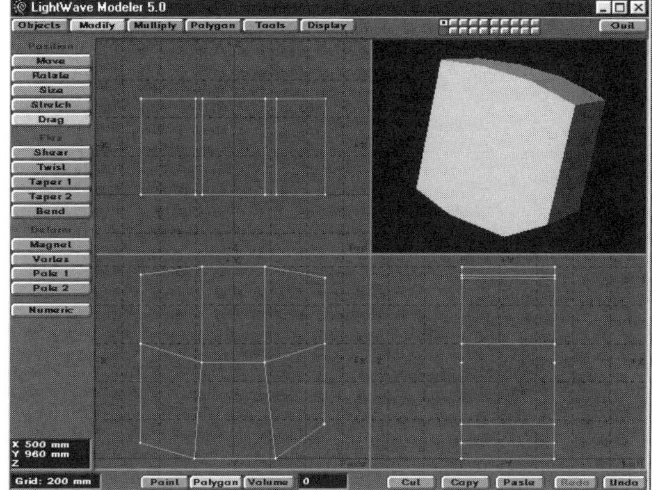

Figure 1: The basic starting block for the hand.

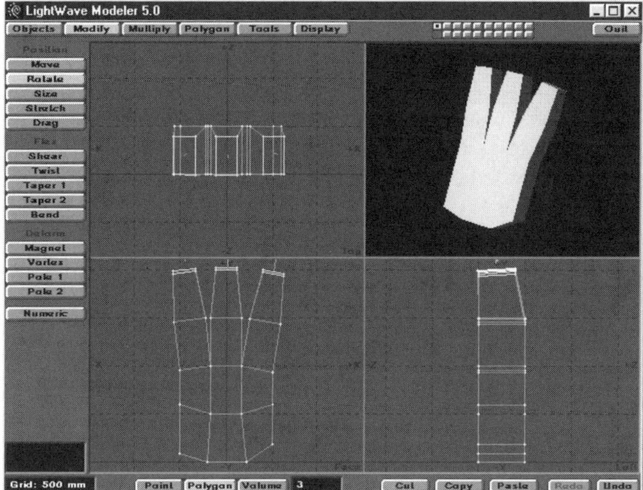

Figure 2: The block object with the finger joints extruded using the bevel command.

ing. To create the next joint of the fingers repeat the beveling procedure. With the second joint you may want to add a slight inset to give them a gradual taper.

This would be a good point to start previewing what our final object will look like.

- Activate the 'OpenGL Smooth Shaded' option in the display panel and with no polygon selected, hit Tab.
- Hitting the (a) key will center our viewing area on the object and there should be an OpenGL display of a chubby looking fork object. Resist the tempta-

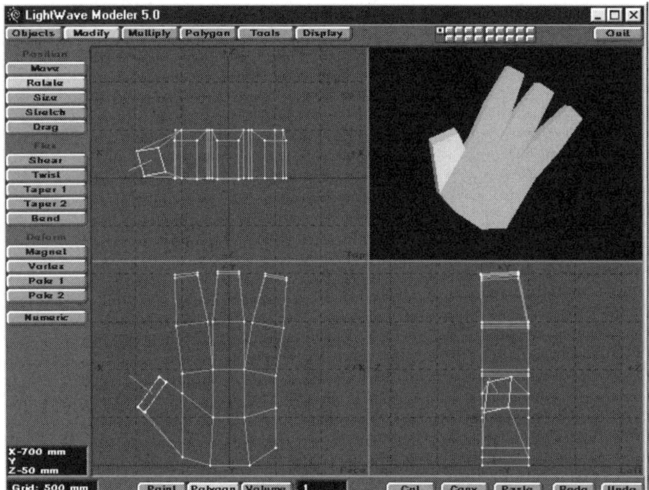

Figure 3: Extruding the thumb section.

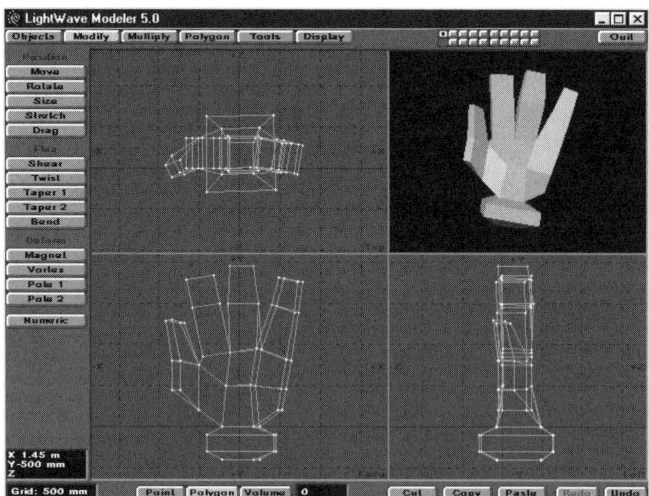

Figure 4: Hand object with all the fingers beveled out.

tion to modify the object until after we add a thumb (Figure 2).

•Hit Tab again to deactivate the MetaNURBS function. Select the lower left side polygon and again use Bevel with the shift value at 0.25 m and an inset at 0.075 m. After it's beveled, drag and rotate the still selected polygon into a position appropriate for the heel of a thumb.

•Now select the top of the just beveled thumb heel and bevel it again. Because we messed with the perfect geometry of our object, the last thumb bevel will probably need to be adjusted back to square before you bevel it again to make the next knuckle (Figure 3).

The final section is the wrist area.

•Select the bottom most polygon and bevel it with a negative inset of about -0.25 m and a shift of 0.1 m. Again, this does not produce a perfect extrusion so in the Modify menu select Stretch and modify the still-selected polygon until it is mostly square and about 1/3 less then the diameter of the full hand.

•Bevel the bottom-most polygon again with 0.0 inset and a 0.25 m shift, and then again with a 0.25 m inset and a 0.1 m shift to taper it back in (Figure.4).

Fun Starts Here

Hit Tab to reactivate MetaNURBS. You should be rewarded with a fairly good representation of a Mickey Mouse-like hand. It's like magic, isn't it? For making small adjustments to the object while in the MetaNURBS mode, I've found that the drag tool works best. For moving full fingers, select the areas just as you would regular polygons (Figure 5).

When you get your object close to what you want, save it because at some point you will get carried away with how far you can go with MetaNURBS smoothing—trust me, it happens. We want to have the hand and fingers in a neutral position to use as a base to start with and use as a morph source.

We need to convert our MetaNURBS object into a state that can be rendered in layout. This is easily done by entering the Tools panel and hitting the freeze button. In a few moments you will have a fully polygonal object. Save this as 'HandSource.lwo' (Figure 6).

Now that we have our source object, lets make some morph targets.

•Hit the undo button to bring back the original MetaNURBS form, or clear the scene and reload the object.

•Now we'll start altering the object.

•Manipulate the glove into different positions, such as pointing, a fist and thumbs up. When you come to a shape you like, freeze it and save it (Figure 7).

Remember, after you have done a freeze, created and saved the object that is your morph source, it is imperative that you do not add any more geometry to the object. If you add or remove any points or polygons, or even rearrange their sequence, the objects will morph together in interesting but totally useless ways.

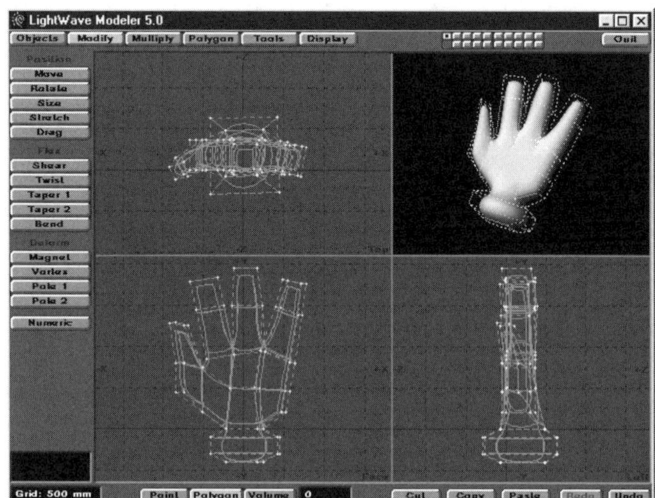

Figure 5: Hand object with fingers with the MetaNURB function turned on.

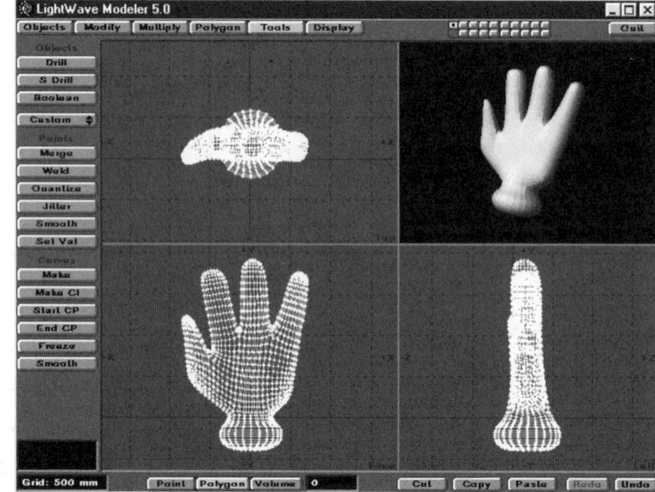

Figure 6: Hand object after Freeze function is employed to create an object that can be used in Layout.

Because the surface attributes of the morph targets are never seen, you can change the names of any polygon you wish. In this case we can name the different parts of the glove to make selecting the polygons easier for later on when quarters start getting cramped and it is difficult to sort out which polygon belongs to which finger.

Once you have a number of targets, we can jump into Layout and see if this really works

Stay on Target

Enter layout and set up a typical object morph.

•Load the source object and two target objects. In the objects panel have the current object be "HandSource.lwo," select MTSE for multiple morph targets (Multiple Target, Single Envelope), and put "HandTargetA.lwo" in the metamorph target box.

•Select "HandTargetA.lwo" as the current object and choose "HandTargetB.lwo" as the metamorph target.

•Go back to "HandSource.lwo" as the current object and click the (E) button to create an envelope. When the envelope is between 0% and 100%, the object will morph between the source object and the first target. When the envelope is between 100% and 200%, the object will morph from the first target to the second.

• Do a preview to make sure every thing is working right. To make a compliment of the left hand we have created, make a clone of the source object and under the stretch command numerically enter a value of -1 on the Z axis. This gives you a mirror image of the original.

This technique saves on geometry but because we're basically turning the object inside out, we have to turn on Double-sided in the surfaces panel to have it render properly. It will clone with the exact same morph envelope, so you probably want to alter that to loosen up the animation (Figure 8).

About Character?

The technique described above for gloves will work exactly the same for faces. Rather than walking you through the creation of a head and face, I suggest you refer to the LightWave User Guide and "Advanced Tutorial #7," which describes the creation of a cartoonish character object. By following the rules laid out above, you can easily create several morph targets of the object. It is amazing how easy it is to change an expression by simply dragging a point or two. Grabbing the right points at the edge of the mouth, for instance, quickly produces a groan-like expression. It is great fun to see how many expressions you can cycle through by hitting the undo and redo buttons.

MetaNURBS is so easy and intuitive, once you work through one tutorial, you will have learned enough to keep you busy for a long time.

LWP

Patrik Beck is a cool animator guy who can write. Reach him by e-mail at zippie@execpc.com.

Land Vehicle Movement
Spinning Your Wheels

by Joe Dox

One of the biggest challenges with animating land vehicles is wheel movement. This includes animating a car driving down a road at 10 mph and an aspirin tablet rolling across a 3D chart. To put it simply, the rotation of a particular object must be directly related to its velocity. Unlike a spaceship or a submarine, the wheels of a moving vehicle should have realistic rotating motion. Other issues with animating land vehicles involve body movement and track marks left behind by the rotating wheels.

The vehicle shown in Figure 1 is a military-style Hummer, otherwise known as a HUM-V. My goal was to create realistic movement of the wheels and body while it cruised across the desert. First, I'll describe how the Hummer's movement was set up. I will then discuss how to acquire rotational values for wheels moving at a particular speed, and how to create tracks left behind by the moving tires. Sorry, I won't be explaining how I modeled the Hummer—maybe in my next tutorial.

Figure 1: "Full Metal Hummer" uses simple geometric formulas to create realistic velocity and wheel rotation.

Setting Up a Vehicle Scene

When creating a scene with a moving vehicle, the objects must consist of at least the vehicle body and four wheels. One might say that the wheels should be parented to the car body. Well, they could be, but I recommend the following process:

- Load the vehicle body and the four wheels. The left and right wheels should be saved as individual objects from Modeler. Each wheel should have its pivot point in its exact center, so you'll have a smooth, even rotation. To do this, manually move the pivot point of each wheel from inside LightWave. I recommend loading (or importing) a wheel into Modeler, then selecting the **Macro** button (**Objects** menu) and executing the Center macro. The object will be placed in the exact center of the Modeler environment (Figure 2). Save (or export) the wheel and repeat this process for the others.
- Back in Layout, the next step involves creating a null object by hitting the **Add Null Object** button (**Objects** panel). Parent the car body and each wheel to this null object. After every object has been parented to the null object, you will need to position each wheel in relation to the car body. In other words, put the wheels where they belong (Figure 3). Don't forget to create a keyframe for frame 0 after each wheel has been put into position. The vehicle is now ready to be animated.

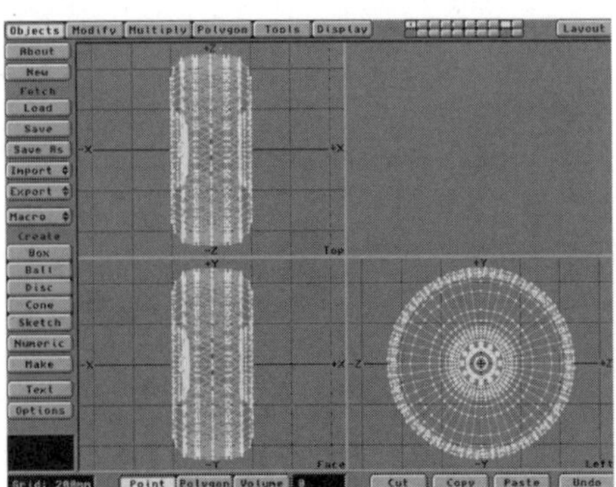

Figure 2: Wheels are centered in Modeler to make certain there are no "bumps" in their rotation.

The Hummer scene shown in Figure 1 was set up in this manner. I simply loaded the Hummer body and the four individual wheels. After parenting them all to a null object, I positioned each wheel under a wheel well (Figure 3). The advantage of parenting each object to a null object is that you can move the objects independently of each other. Effects like front-wheel braking lockup and body roll can be achieved by simply selecting the object and manipulating it in the desired manner.

Moving the Vehicle

OK, we have a vehicle. Let's say we want to move it at 30 mph for five seconds. There are two things we need to compute:

1. The distance the vehicle travels in 5 seconds at 30 mph.
2. The rotational value per second (degrees/30 frames) of each wheel at 30 mph.

First, we must establish the fact that, in this article, I will be measuring distance over time as miles per hour, not kilometers per hour. But fear not, road-warriors: The formulas that I will be using are completely interchangeable between miles per hour and kilometers per hour.

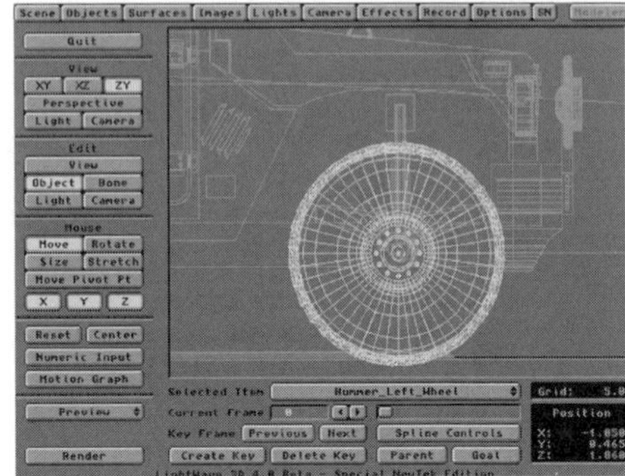

Figure 3: A wheel is positioned in one of Hummer's wheel wells.

Computing the Vehicle's Velocity

Let's begin. To get the value of No. 1 (above), we must compute meters/second (M) with a given value of 30 mph. The formula is as follows:

M = (((mph/60)x 5280)/60) x12)/39.37

For those of you who would rather work in the metric system, the formula is:

M = (((kph/60) x 1000)/60

To better understand this formula, let's chop it up. First, mph/60 x 5,280 will give you feet/minute, given that 5,280 feet = 1 mile. Next, divide that quantity by 60. This will give you feet/second. Multiplying this value by 12 provides inches/second. If 39.37 inches = 1 meter, divide inches/second by 39.37. This total is a value for meters/second, or in LightWave terms, meters/30 frames.

In our example, the vehicle is traveling at 30 mph. So our formula would look like:

M = ((((30/60) x 5280)/60) x 12)/39.37
M = [(2,640/60) x 12]/39.37
M = (44 x 12)/39.37
M = 528/39.37
M = 13.4112 meters/30 frames.

After you do the math for 30 mph, the vehicle will travel 13.411 meters in 30 frames. The next step is simple:

- Place the vehicle at its starting position and create keyframe 1. Move the vehicle (along the Z axis for this example) to a distance five times greater than the value we computed (5 seconds): 13.411 x 5 = 67.05 meters. Create keyframe 150. That's it! The vehicle is moving at 30 mph. Oh, don't set any spline controls. Acceleration and deceleration is something I'll discuss another time.

Computing Wheel Rotation

Now that we have the body moving at a "perfect" 30 mph, we need to rotate the wheels to match that speed. Guessing the rotational value of the wheels and rendering previews is something you could get away with, but slower speeds would be more difficult to match manually. I know—I've tried it. A quick glance at Figure 1 shows that the Hummer has huge tires with a well-defined tread pattern. It would be very easy for anyone to figure out that the wheels do not match the vehicle's speed.

We first need to compute the circumference of the wheel. The circumference of a circle is determined by a well-known formula:

C = 2 x π x radius

- To get the radius of your particular wheel, go into Modeler, import the wheel, select the **Measure** button (**Display** menu), then measure the distance from the center of the wheel to the edge. In the case of the Hummer scene, the radius of a wheel is 0.4712 meters. (I know, that's a pretty big wheel, but a Hummer is no Suzuki SideKick.) With a radius of 0.4712 meters, the circumference of the wheel is:

C = (2 x 3.14159) x 0.4712 = 2.9606

Remember, our goal is to acquire degrees of rotation for every 30 frames. With M = meters/seconds, and C = circumference of a wheel, the formula to get degrees of rotation/second (D) is:

D = (M/C) x 360
Thus,
D = (13.4112/2.9606) x 360
D = (4.5298 x 360)
D = 1630.76

Now that we have D, which equals the number of degrees the wheel rotates in one second, we must multiply that value by the number of seconds we have defined for the animation.

D = D x 5D = 8153.80

- We now have to set the keyframes for the wheels. Go to keyframe 0. (As described above, the wheels of the vehicle should be individual objects, each parented to the same null object that the vehicle body is parented to.) Select a wheel. The rotational value of each wheel at keyframe 0 is 0.00 degrees. Please note that we are *not* setting the starting position of the wheel at keyframe 1, because frame 1 must have a pitch value greater than 0. Now go to frame 150 (5 seconds later). Set the rotational pitch to 8153.80 (Figure 4). Set keyframe 150 with this value for each wheel. Done. The wheels will now travel at 30 mph for five seconds.

In the Hummer scene in Figure 1, I moved the Hummer at 15 mph for seven seconds. For those of you who have the *LWPRO* disk, load the scene and check it out. There's much more going on than just a Hummer driving across a desert. Also, for those of you who are interested, the scene rendered at an average of 1 hour, 45 minutes per frame on my Amiga 2000 with a 33 MHz GVP '040.

Figure 4: Set the pitch of each wheel to the value D = [(M/C x 360) x length]. Each wheel will then rotate this number of degrees throughout the animation.

Tracks in the Sand

I would now like to touch upon one interesting effect that I implemented in the Full Metal Hummer scene. Many people have commented on it. If you render this scene (or see it on our demo), you'll notice that the tires are leaving tracks in the sand. I've been asked many times to explain how this was done. Well, it's really quite easy.

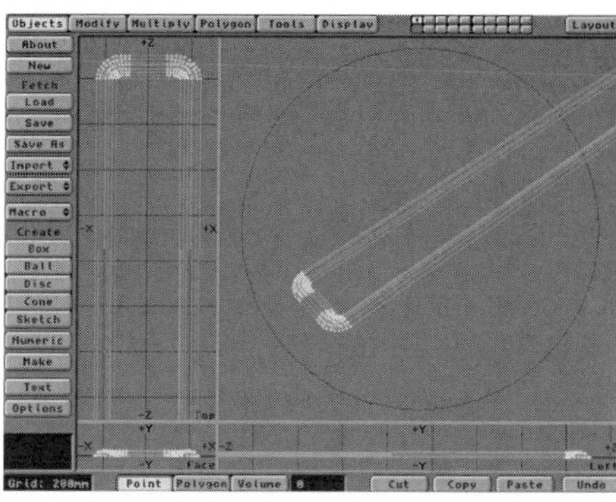

Figure 5: The tread-track object. The raised bump around the edges creates the effect of movement through soft sand.

The track objects are relatively simple. They consist of a surface polygon the tread pattern is mapped to and a raised "bump" that was extruded around the edges of the tread polygon (Figure 5). This was done to create the effect of the Hummer digging into the soft sand as it drove across the desert.

These track objects are parented to the null object, and positioned underneath and a little in front of the front tires. The raised edges have Fractal Noise diffusion and a bump map assigned to them. The tread tracks were created by applying a diffusion, transparency and bump map with a tread image I created in ToasterPaint.

- To create the effect that the Hummer's wheels are leaving tracks in the sand, simply set each texture map to world coordinates. As the track object moves with the Hummer, it will appear to be leaving tread marks in the sand.

Rotation and Distance Generator Macro

Scott Wheeler (my partner) and I developed a macro included on the *LWPRO* disk that easily computes distance and wheel rotation for a given velocity (Figure 6). This macro performs a variety of functions. It allows the user to save three individual motion files:

1. Wheel Rotation Motion File: This selection will cause the macro to save the rotation information computed from the user's input. Individual rotation files can be created for 5 mph, 10 mph, 27.8 mph, etc. Then the wheel can be parented to a vehicle moving at

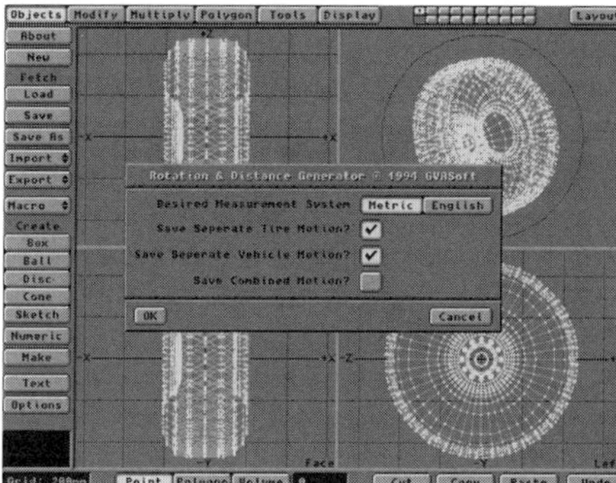

Figure 6: The Rotation and Distance Generator macro makes it easy to move and rotate a vehicle or wheel at any speed.

the same speed. Which brings us to:

2. Vehicle Movement Motion File: This selection will cause the macro to save vehicle movement along a particular axis. This can be used to create motion files for individual vehicle speeds (55 mph, 60 mph, 120 mph, etc.).

3. Combination Movement and Rotation Motion File: This selection will cause the macro to save a motion file containing both vehicle movement and wheel rotation information.

After the types of motion files, if any, have been defined, the user is prompted for wheel radius, speed and the number of frames in the animation. If there is an object in the current layer, the macro will attempt to compute the radius for you. It will then show you the results of the object motion, and prompt you to save the predefined motion files. We hope you find the macro useful.

About the Hummer Scene

I actually modeled the Hummer about two years ago. As a reference, I used a few pictures I saw in *Time* magazine. It was only recently that I went back to it and armed it to the teeth. I added the four barrel machine guns and the side missile launchers earlier this fall. Needless to say, it's one mean machine. But I seriously doubt that a vehicle with this much firepower actually exists, or can exist.

After I completed the movement of the Hummer, including the robotics of the guns and the missiles firing, Scott worked his magic on the desert environment. After that, it was just a matter of performing a Load Objects (Objects Panel) from the moving Hummer scene into the desert scene.

Beginner's Step-by-Step for Land Vehicle Movement:

1. Define vehicle's speed.
2. Define length of animation.
3. Compute vehicle's distance traveled with the formula:

$$M = \frac{\frac{\frac{(mph)}{60} \times 5{,}280 \times 12}{60}}{39.37} \times \text{length of animation in seconds}$$

4. Move vehicle M meters, then keyframe it as last keyframe.
5. Compute wheel circumference using the formula:
   $C = 2 \times \pi \times radius$
6. Compute pitch rotation of each wheel to match vehicle speed with the formula:
   $D = [(M / C) \times 360] \times (\text{length of animation in seconds})$
7. Set the pitch rotation of each wheel to D and keyframe as last frame.
8. Repeat for each wheel.

LWP

Joe Dox and Scott Wheeler operate a successful East Coast animation house called Galaxy Video & Animations. Together, this duo has created a very impressive demo tape. To contact them for suggestions or comments, or to obtain a copy of their demo, call GVA at (508) 535-8787; send e-mail to jdox@fastech.com (Joe), ord@dsn.com (Scott).

Spinning Your Wheels, Part II
Acceleration and Thrust

by Joe Dox

Greetings all! In my last article (*LWPRO*, Feb. 1995), I showed how a LightWave animator can create actual wheel rotation at any velocity. This technique can be used to depict a car cruising down a road at 30 mph or a medicine tablet slowly rolling across a desk.

But these examples are of objects moving at constant speeds. What about accelerating from zero velocity? Decelerating from warp 9.75? Or accelerating a car from 0 to 60 mph with the tires rotating accordingly? Well, you can either get a third-party utility to help you out with this problem, or you can follow the steps outlined below.

If possible, before continuing, read the tutorial referred to above about wheel rotation and velocity, as I will be referencing formulas and things that were mentioned there. However, reading it is not required. I'll do my best to explain what's going on as we move along.

Acceleration Curves

Everyone's probably thinking: "Great! I can accelerate my car or ship from 0 to 60 mph in four seconds!" Well, it's not that simple. Acceleration is tricky, especially accelerating a wheel on a flat surface when factors like gravity and mass do not take part in the equation. In fact, what I'm about to illustrate will not result in a 0-to-60-type scenario at all.

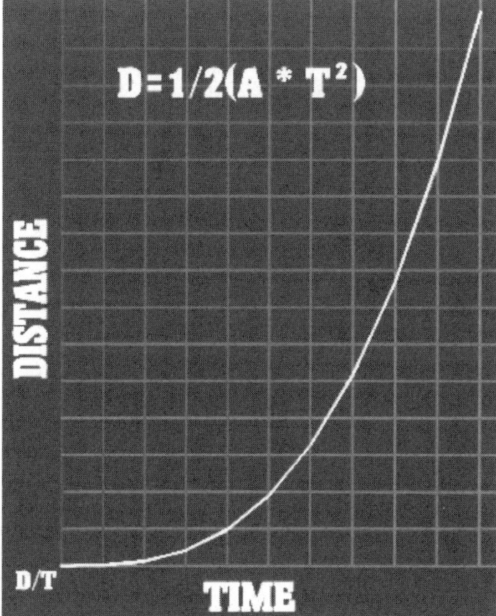

Figure 1: "Acceleration Curve" This curve was created by using the equation D = 1/2 x (A x (T x T)) to obtain an accurate change in velocity with respect to time.

What we need to do first is plot an acceleration curve (Figure 1). This curve depicts relative distance over time (velocity). Points are plotted at varying intervals from the results of an acceleration formula. Each point on the curve represents a particular distance traveled at a certain time interval. In other words, at each point we're traveling at a different speed, thus traveling a different distance (increasing for acceleration) at the end of each time interval.

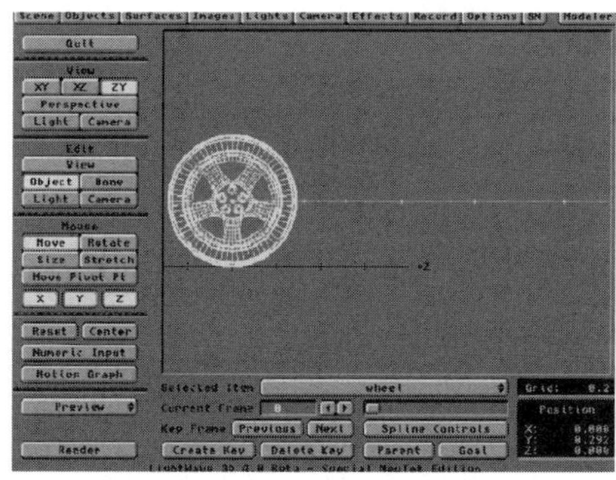

Figure 2: A wheel is applied to the acceleration curve. Note that distance and degrees of rotation are computed at each time interval.

To make a wheel accelerate on a flat surface, we simply need to compute the change-in-distance/change-in-time (delta-d/delta-t) and apply that velocity to the formula that, using the wheel's radius and circumference, computes wheel rotation at that specific velocity (see *LWPRO*, Feb. 1995). Simple, eh?

Constants and Variables

Let's begin. The example I'll be using is a wheel accelerating along the Z axis. We will be using the following equation:

D = 1/2 x (A x (T x T))

where D = distance

A = acceleration

T = time

other variables:

K = "granularity of key framing"

The K variable is equal to how often a new keyframe should be created. For constant velocity, only two keyframes are required, as there is no change in velocity. For acceleration, velocity is changing at relative distances, so we must define how "granular" our acceleration should be. Ultimately, you should define this level of granularity to 1, which creates a keyframe at every frame. (I know, that's a lot of keyframes, but the effect is more realistic than creating new keyframes every 15 or 30 frames. Trust me, you'll see a difference.)

For this example, we will be accelerating a wheel along the Z axis, and we will compute a new relative distance and velocity every three frames. So, for this case, K = 3.

Figure 3: The wheel has started accelerating. Distance = 0.324 meters.

In our acceleration formula above, we must also define T. That's simple, because we have already defined K (which is actually a factor of time). We are measuring relative changes in distance in seconds, or fractions of a second. So T would equal K/30 (T = K/30). For this example, T=3/30, or 1/10th of a second. This means we will be computing new distances (and degrees of rotation) every 1/10 of a second, or three frames. Of course we are assuming NTSC video rates of 30 frames per second here.

Next, we need to decide on an acceleration (A) factor. Think of this variable as how hard you step on the gas, or how much thrust your accelerating ship puts out. But also note that it is not a constant value throughout the time of acceleration. Instead, it increases by the value of A at each time interval. For example, at time-index 0, the starting value of A = 0.3; at time-index .1, A = A + 0.3; at time-index .2, A = A + 0.3; etc. It increases by the constant value of A. For our example, setting A = 0.30 will give us a nice acceleration curve.

Increasing this constant will accelerate your vehicle faster. As an animator, this variable is one of those you will be changing to meet the needs of your imagery.

The fact that we are accelerating a wheel means that we need some information about the wheel. If you're accelerating a spaceship or a jet, you obviously would not need to compute degrees of rotation at every time interval. For this example, we need to establish the size (radius and circumference) of the wheel we are going to accelerate. In our example, the wheel has a radius of 11.61 inches (approximately .295 meters). That would make the circumference C = 2 x π x .295. Thus, C = 1.8535 meters.

Acceleration Formula

We are now ready to start computing our acceleration curve. Explaining it in prose may be a little confusing, so I'll describe the process in computer code-type form:

```
A = 0.3
T = 0.1
K = 3
C = 1.8535 (Circumference of wheel)
A_FACTOR = A
T_FACTOR = T
frame = K
old_distance = 0

Begin loop:
total_distance = 1/2 x (A x (T x T))
total_distance = 1/2 x (.3 x (.1 x .1))
total_distance = 0.0015 meters

delta_distance = total_distance - old_distance
delta_distance = 0.0015
old_distance =  total_distance

velocity = delta_distance x (30 / K)
velocity = 0.0015 x (30 / 3)
velocity = 0.015

delta_rotation = (( velocity / C ) x 360 ) x T_FACTOR
delta_rotation = ( 2.913 x T_FACTOR )
delta_rotation = 0.2913 degrees
total_rotation = total_rotation + delta_rotation

Move object to distance : z = 0.0015 meters
   (total distance)
Rotate object # degrees : p = 0.2913 degrees
   (total rotation)
```

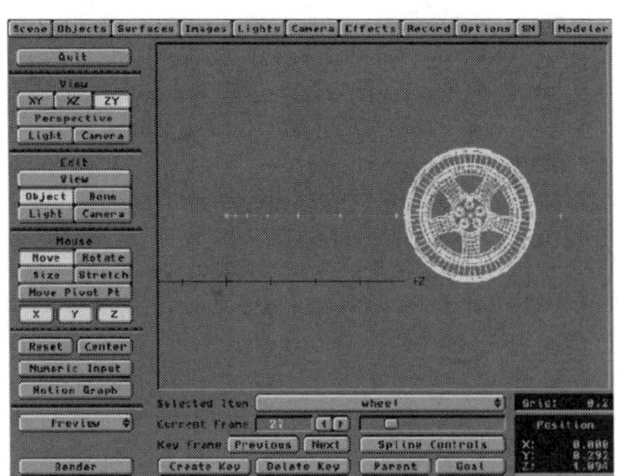

Figure 4: The wheel is gaining speed. Distance = 1.094 meters.

```
Create Key Frame #frame
A = A + A_FACTOR
T = T + T_FACTOR
frame = frame + K
End Loop
   <Repeat until you want to stop accelerating>
```

I hope this formula is not too confusing. And remember, if you aren't accelerating a wheel on a flat surface, you don't have to compute degrees of rotation and velocity. The only thing you are interested in is the change in distance for each keyframe. An example of this type of application would be a spaceship or a rocket launch.

Deceleration

Now that we have covered acceleration, let's talk about deceleration. With acceleration, the object essentially starts at zero velocity and works its way up the curve. Deceleration is the opposite. We start at a specific velocity (or time index) and work our way down to zero velocity.

Before we "hit the brakes," we must define the length of the animation. This will be the condition of the computational cycle. With acceleration, we can speed up infinitely, until our ears fall off. But with deceleration, we can only go down to zero velocity, so we must define how long it will take to decelerate our object.

The T_FACTOR constant can remain the same. This is simply a value that we will subtract from the T variable. So we'll leave T_FACTOR = 0.1, and our animation at 150 frames (five seconds). We will also leave the value of K, which is the keyframe "granularity," at 3. With these variables set, we know that the animation will have 50 keyframes, and a starting value of T = 5. What about A_FACTOR? The A_FACTOR variable will also remain the same, for it is a constant that never changes. But we do need to set the variable A to a new starting value. We know that there are 50 keyframes, and the A_FACTOR = 0.3, so A = 0.3 x 50 = 15.

Now that we have our new starting values, let's go through a deceleration formula:

```
K = 3
C = 1.8535 (Circumference of wheel)
A_FACTOR = 0.3
T_FACTOR = 0.1
frame = 0
max_frames = 150
key_frames = max_frames / K
old_distance = 0

A = key_frames x A_FACTOR = 15
T = max_frames / 30 = 5

Begin loop:
total_distance = 1/2 x (A x (T x T))
total_distance = 1/2 x (15 x (5 x 5))
total_distance = 187.5 meters

if (old_distance = 0 ) delta_distance =
   total_distance
else delta_distance = total_distance - old_distance
delta_distance = 187.5
old_distance  = total_distance

velocity = delta_distance x ( 30 / K )
velocity = 187.5 x ( 30 / 3 )
velocity = 1875

delta_rotation = (( velocity / C ) x 360 ) x
   T_FACTOR
delta_rotation = (364175.88 x T_FACTOR)
delta_rotation = 36417.588 degrees
if (total_rotation = 0 ) total_rotation =
   delta_rotation
else total_rotation = total_rotation -
   delta_rotation
Move object to distance : z = 187.5 meters
   (total distance)
Rotate object # degrees : p = 36417.588 degrees
   (total rotation)
Create Key Frame #frame

A = A - A_FACTOR
T = T - T_FACTOR
frame = frame + K

End Loop (Repeat while T >= 0)
```

Note that the formula above is similar to the acceleration formula, with a few exceptions. One difference is that we are starting with different values for A and T, and there is a max_frames variable needed to define T, which is also the loop conditional. We are subtracting from A and T because our velocity is decreasing down to zero. When rotation is computed, you'll see that the delta_rotation is subtracted from the total_rotation because the velocity and distance traveled is decreasing at each keyframe. Again, to create the effects to meet your needs, simply experiment with different values of A_FACTOR and T_FACTOR.

Acceleration and Deceleration Macro

What you need to do now is apply different values of A, K and T to make the motions you want. To simplify things, I've created a macro that generates acceleration motion files based upon the values of A and K entered by the user. Other variables, such as starting X,Y,Z offsets and total frames, are also entered by the user.

For those of you who want to accelerate your spaceships (no rotation needed) using the macro, simply leave the "Create acceleration with rotation" toggle off. I have also made a deceleration macro that helps "accelerate" the process of decelerating your objects. These macros are in Amiga ARexx format only.

This lesson has a number of applications. Missiles firing, drag races, jets taking off, ships entering warp, whatever! I hope this information proves useful to you all.

LWP

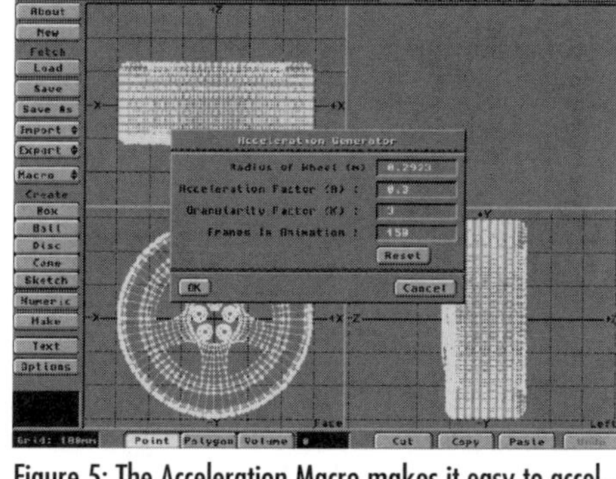

Figure 5: The Acceleration Macro makes it easy to accelerate or decelerate your objects.

Joe Dox operates Galaxy Imaging (formerly Galaxy Video & Animations) near Boston, Mass. He has been using LightWave since version 1.0, and is currently doing work for a Boston television station and other various companies in the region. To reach him for comments or suggestions, call (617) 334-6165, or e-mail jdox@galaxy.shore.net.

Creating Realistic Acceleration Curves

(1) Define how often to create a new keyframe (K).

(2) Define acceleration factor (A).

(3) Define time factor (T) equal to K/30.

(4) Define length of animation.

(5) Start counting up from starting frame.

- Compute D = 1/2 x (A x (T x T))
- If accelerating a wheel on a flat surface, compute the rotation of the wheel.

(6) Create keyframe for distance traveled and rotation.

(7) Increment A and T by their initial constant value. If decelerating, you must decrement A and T.

(8) Increment framecount by K.

(9) Repeat until you're done.

Makin' Tracks
Creating Working Tank Treads

by Joe Angell

For one of my personal projects, I needed a tracked anti-aircraft gun to menacingly roll over some terrain. The problem I had was figuring out how to get the tank's tracks to roll at all. After tinkering around for a few hours, I finally came up with a convincing way to make turning, rolling, terrain-hugging tank tracks.

Start Treading

The first step is to make the tracks themselves. I'm going to go ahead and assume you've already built the rest of the tank. *[Editor's note: Check out tomahawk.welch.hu.edu, an FTP Internet site containing various objects.—JG]* By that I mean you have the tank body that the guide wheels attach to and the guide wheels the tracks wrap around. You should also have a scene file set up with the guide wheels parented to the tank's hull and configured appropriately.

- To figure out how long to make the tracks, you'll have to Measure (Options panel) in Modeler around the wheels that the track will wrap around. Set up your tank in Modeler the way it would be in Layout, with the guide wheels in place on the body. Then measure around the wheels. I took four measurements around my wheels (top, bottom and sides) and added them up to get 7.1 meters. This measurement will be the length of the track.
- Select Box (Object panel) and hit (n) to bring up the Numeric options. Set the number of Segments on the Z-axis to 100. The Z-axis size should be set to the length of the track, which you got in the last step (in my case, 7.1 meters). The width should be slightly more than the width of your wheels, and the thickness just a centimeter or two.
- You may want to add some extra details to the tracks. I did a low Bevel (b) (Multiply panel) off of every other polygon from the Top view to get a tread effect. I also did another, lesser bevel on the bottom of the tracks for yet more detail.
- Save this object as "Track-Start". Move the track the length of two segments (polygons) on the +Z-axis. Save this again as "Track-Morph". An example of the slightly offset track is shown in Figure 1. What you've just made is a flat tank track and a copy of the track moved a slight bit on the +Z-axis. This will be used to move the track forward with a morph.

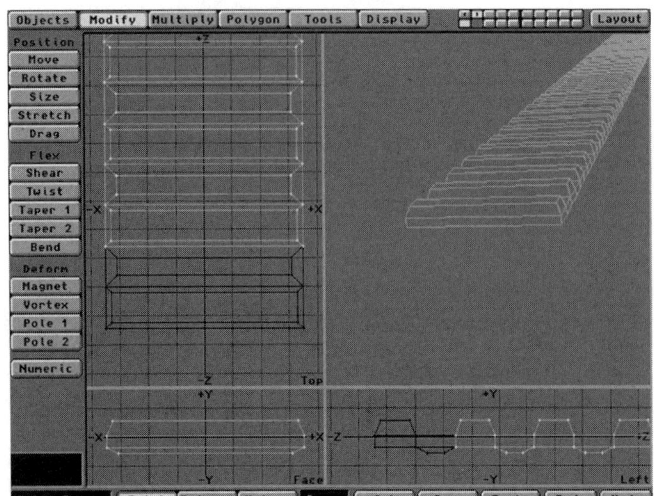

Figure 1: Track-Start (in Background Layer) and Track-Morph (in Foreground Layer) as an example of shifting the track two segments.

Moving By

- Go into Layout and load up a scene that has the tank and its wheels set up. Load both the Track-Start and Track-Morph objects. Parent the Track-Start object to your tank's hull, not the wheels, since you'll want them to spin separately from the track. Move Track-Start so it is resting over the wheels, with the "back" end about midway between the front and rear tank wheels.
- Go into the Objects panel and set the Object Dissolve for Track-Morph to 100%. Set the Track-Start's Metamorph Target to Track-Morph. Track-Morph is there only as a template to morph into, so it will never be seen. Now the whole morph is set up except for the envelope.
- By editing the Envelope (E) of the Metamorph Amount, the track will move forward or backward. It will only move two segments of track, but once we're finished, it will be a seamless transition. To make the track go forward, have the morph percentage start with 0% and go up to 100% over the number of frames you want. To go backward, start from 100% and end at 0%. You will want to set the envelope's End Behavior to Repeat. (This will all make more sense later on.)

A track that moves forward and jumps back to the beginning over and over again is useless unless it wraps around the wheels of the tank. That's where Bones come in.

Dem Bones

Bones are fairly painless in this case. All you need are a bunch of them. You don't even have to mess with any of the settings in the Bones panel. We're going to use bones to bend the track around the wheels.

The way this works is a bit strange. You will want to arrange your bones along the track in their rest position at Frame 0, and move your bones at frame 1. This way it'll be easier to add more bones for greater control later.

- Go into the Objects panel and select the Track-Start object, the object you'll be adding all the bones to. Select Object Skeleton and click Add Bone. Hit (p) to close the Bones panel and go back to the Layout screen. This first bone is going to be used to "hold down" the rear end of the track, so you'll want to position it there. Place the bone so the pivot is in the track and the other end is pointing upward. If you think of the bones as the control rods of a puppet, this setup will seem a little clearer. Those of you who are more technically minded can think of these as the control handles of a B-spline.
- Add two more bones by hitting the (+) key twice. Do not use Add Child Bone, as this will only complicate things. Position Bone 2 so it is over the

frontmost wheel. Bone 3 should go further beyond Bone 2 by an amount equal to a diameter and a half of the front wheel. Don't forget to hit (r) to set the Rest Position and activate each bone after setting its position and creating a key at frame 0.

- Now go to frame 1. Take Bone 3 and rotate it 180 degrees so it is pointing downward. Drag the bone down until it is under the front wheel. The track should now be more or less bent around the front wheel. Notice how this doesn't quite work. The track is a little bit off the front of the front wheel. Now you know why we are doing all of our setup on frame 0 and our final positioning on frame 1.
- Go back to frame 0 and hit (+) to add another bone. Position Bone 4 so it is between Bones 2 and 3. Create a key for it and hit (r) to set the Rest Position. Go to frame 1 and you'll notice that the track is warped severely. Rotate Bone 4 approximately 90 degrees and place it slightly ahead of the rear wheel. This extra bone is used to keep the track against the front wheel.

Enough With the Bones

We've covered the basics of setting up the tank track. To get it all working requires a fair number of bones—I used 18 for mine. For an idea of what the bones look like after they are all oriented correctly, Figure 2 shows frame 0 and Figure 3 shows frame 1. Pay attention to the front of the tank (on the right of the screen) to see how those first three bones are set up.

- If you need to adjust a bone (and you will), you'll want to move it at frame 0 and set the Rest Position again. If you move the bone at frame 1, the track warps as the bone stretches it. If you first change the positioning on frame 0 and reset the Rest Position, you can safely move it the same distance on frame 1 without any nasty warping effects.
- There are two other important bone placements. The bone at the rear end of the track on frame 0 should be moved on frame 1 so it exactly matches the first bone's position on frame 1. That way the entire track smoothly wraps around the wheels.
- The final trick is to put a last bone about two track segments (yes, we're back to that again) ahead of the frontmost bone, so it is actually off the end of the track. This should also be moved forward two segments past the last bone on frame 1. The reason for this bone will make sense in the next step, when we get this thing moving.

Did I say bones were painless? I lied.

Let's Make Tracks

Remember that morphing setup we did way back when? Now we're going to use it.

- Go to the Metamorph Amount envelope for TrackStart.
- For a test, set frame 0 to 0% morphed and frame 10 to 100% morphed. Make sure to set the End Behavior to Repeat.
- Now go ahead and make a wireframe preview.

When you play this back, the tank track should be smoothly turning around the tank's wheels. The reason for putting that last bone just forward of the front end of the track is to keep the track from warping as it morphs. Without that extra bone, the track starts bending upward, which ruins the illusion.

By now you've probably noticed a major limitation with this method: texture mapping. Since the track only moves two segment's worth, the texture map has to be two segments long and must be seamless, or else there will be a noticeable jump in the texture as the morph repeats. With a little work and some clever mapping, you can get around with a little work and a program like DeluxePaint.

I Failed Math

To control the speed of the tracks, you simply have to adjust the number of frames the morph occurs over. Add more frames and the tracks move slower. About five minutes of tinkering is all you need to synchronize the turning of the tracks to the turning of the tank's wheels. If you want to be scientific about it, try the following formula:

r = radius of guide wheel
l = length of track
d = distance to move track per full guide wheel rotation

$$\frac{\pi r^2}{l} = d$$

In other words, if you divide the circumference of the wheel by the length of the track, you get the distance the track should move for each full (360-degree) rotation. You will have to measure the distance of two segments worth of track in Modeler, and divide that by the distance to move the track. Then you will have the number of frames to morph the object over. As for an equation:

d = Distance to move Track per full Guide Wheel rotation
s = Distance of two segments of track

$$\frac{d}{s} = \text{Number of frames to morph over}$$

Remember to use meters for all of these distances! You can also use Joe Dox's acceleration and deceleration macros (from *LIGHTWAVEPRO* disk 10) to control the rotation of the wheels and to figure out the amount to morph the tank tread. If I ever learn ARexx, I'll have to write a script for this.

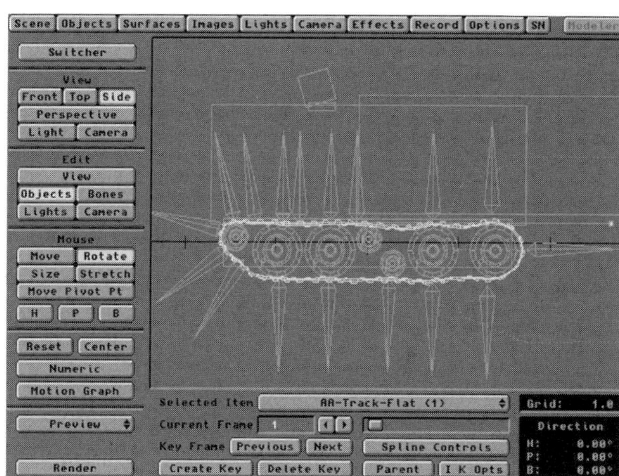

Figure 3: Frame 1 of the treads with the bones positioned.

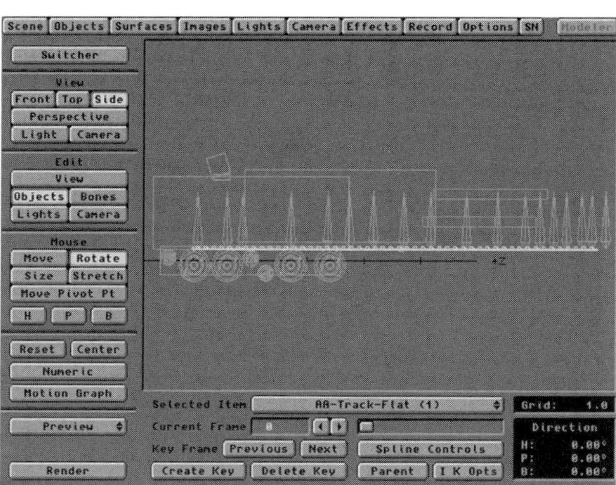

Figure 2: Frame 0 of the treads with the bones positioned.

Finishing Touches

One of the great things about using bones for this project is that you can have the tracks bend as the tank passes over different terrain. As it bumps over a rock, the track can compress against the wheel, and as the hull hangs in the air, the track can become more slack.

Making the track for the other side of the tank is easy. Just use Clone Object on the first track. The morphing information and bones are all kept during the clone, so all you need to do is move the track over to the other side of the tank.

This method of generating tank tracks gives you an incredible amount of control over making the track move and react to the terrain. Once you get everything set up, it's simple to control. Now all you need to do is build the terrain!

LWP

Joe Angell is a film/animation/video student at the Rhode Island School of Design. When he's not in class, he tries to actually get some CGI done. E-mail him at jangell@RISD.edu.

Tread On Me

Leave Your Mark With These Animated Tracks

by Adrian Onsen

A while back, I read Joe Angell's article "Making Tracks" (Nov. 1995 *LIGHTWAVEPRO)* on how to create moving tank treads. It was a great tutorial, but it left me wondering how I could make the actual impressions in the ground as the vehicle moves by. That's where this article comes in. You can use this effect for cars, tanks, or any other land vehicle that leaves impressions of its tires or tracks behind as it moves.

Creating the Objects

Let's start with creating the actual tire. First you'll need to know what a tire looks like in profile in order to create it. Figure 1 has my interpretation of a simple tire, but you can get more technical if you want. For now, draw something simple—the purpose of the tutorial is to make tracks, not tires!

•Go into Modeler and use the Sketch tool (Objects) to draw the outline of the tire in the Z-Y view. It should look something like an upside-down U shape (Figure 1). To get a nice large view, zoom in with the (.) key until your grid is 50 mm. Make sure the sketch is around 250 mm tall. Hit Enter when you're done sketching.

•Now you can more accurately arrange your points in order to create the look you want. (For this tutorial, try to stick to the values mentioned as closely as possible: Around 250 mm tall and 300 mm wide.) Once you're satisfied with the basic shape of the tire, you can position the outline into place.

•Position your shape in the X-Y view by pressing (t) and moving the outline around. I've placed mine 65 cm from the axis to the outermost point on the outline. If you've zoomed in, zoom out (,) until you can see the X axis. You need to have the outline exactly on the Y-axis . To do this, go to the Tools menu, and select Set Val. Click the X axis, and make sure you have 0 in for the Value. Select OK.

•Copy this shape and Paste it into Layer 2 (2), then go back to Layer 1 (1).

•Now you need to Lathe (Multiply) the outline about the Z axis with a center at 0, 0, 0. Access the panel by pressing (n). Increase the number of sides if you want a smoother looking surface, but this will increase the polygon count by quite a bit. For our purposes here, leave it at 16, and click OK. Then press Enter.

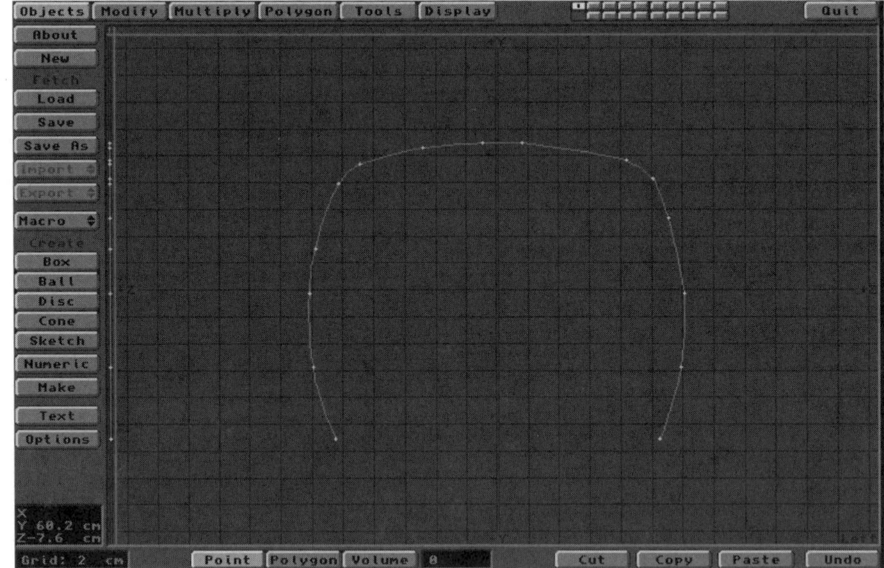

Figure 1: The outline of the tire.

•Hit (a) to Fill All, and you should now have a pretty nice looking tire on your screen (Figure 2). You now want to make sure that all the polygons are facing outward, so select a few polygons and see which way they are facing (which way the dotted line points). If they are pointing inward, unselect the selected polygons and hit (f) to Flip all polygons.

•It's time to assign a surface to the tire. Hit (q) to bring up the Surface requester in the Polygon menu and change the default to 'tire-surf'. Now save the object as 'tire.lwo'.

Our new tire is fine and dandy, but it won't leave the depression behind it just by rolling it around! Now we have to create the actual depression made by the wheel as it rotates over a surface, and have the depression appear behind the tire as it moves. The trick to this effect is knowing the path the wheel will take before you can create the depression.

Element Two: The Ground

•In Modeler, go to the 3rd Layer (3) and create a plane by clicking the Box button (Objects), then press (n) to bring up the numeric requester. Define the plane in meters with the following dimensions, then click OK followed by Enter:

Low
X= -7
Y= 0
Z= 3
High
X= 2
Y= 0
Z= 3
Segments
X= 1
Y= 1
Z= 1

•Hit (a) so you can see the entire plane on your screen.

•Now move the plane in the Y direction -60 cm by

hitting (t), then (n) For a Y value, enter -60 cm and leave zeros for X and Z, then click OK.

•Now you have a surface to work on, so gauge out the area that will be depressed by the tire as it moves. To do this, go to Layer 2 (2) where you copied the outline of the tire, and Rotate (Modify) it about the Z axis by 180 degrees. Enter 180 degrees about the Z-axis with a center at 0, 0, 0, and click OK. Copy it into Layer 4 (4).

•Now draw out the path you want the tire to travel. Keep it simple and just make it a straight line. Then go to Layer 5 (5) and in the Polygon menu, select Points and press (n). As a point, enter 0, 0, 0 and click OK. Then hit (enter) to place the point. Hit (n) again and add another point at -5m, 0m, 0m. Then click OK to place the second point.

•You should how have 2 points on the screen. Connect them by going to the Tools menu and clicking Make in the Curves section. This will make a single sided polygon between the two points. Use this as your path in order to Rail Extrude the shape of the tire.

•Go to Layer 4 (4). You should have the outline of the tire as a curve (not single sided polygons). In the Tools menu, hit Freeze. This will take the curve and make it into a polygon.

•In Layer 4 (4) where you have the tire polygon, put Layer 5 (Alt 5) in the background. Go to the Multiply menu and select Rail Ext, then click OK. This should create a 5 piece object in the center of your screen. Now find out which way the polygons are facing. You want them to face inward, so if they face the wrong way, unselect what you just selected and hit (f) to flip all polygons.

•Hit (q) to assign a surface to the new object, name it 'ground-groove' and click Apply.

•To actually cut this out of the plane, use the Boolean function. First have Laver 3 (3) in the foreground and Layer 4 (Alt 4) in the background. Select the Boolean tool in the Tools menu, then select Subtract and press OK.

•Next you need to flip all the polygons, so flip them up by pressing (f).

•Select only the ground plane polygon (not the actual polygons making the groove) and hit (q) to assign a surface name to the plane. Call it 'ground-plane'.

•Save the object in Layer 3 as 'ground-plane.lwo'

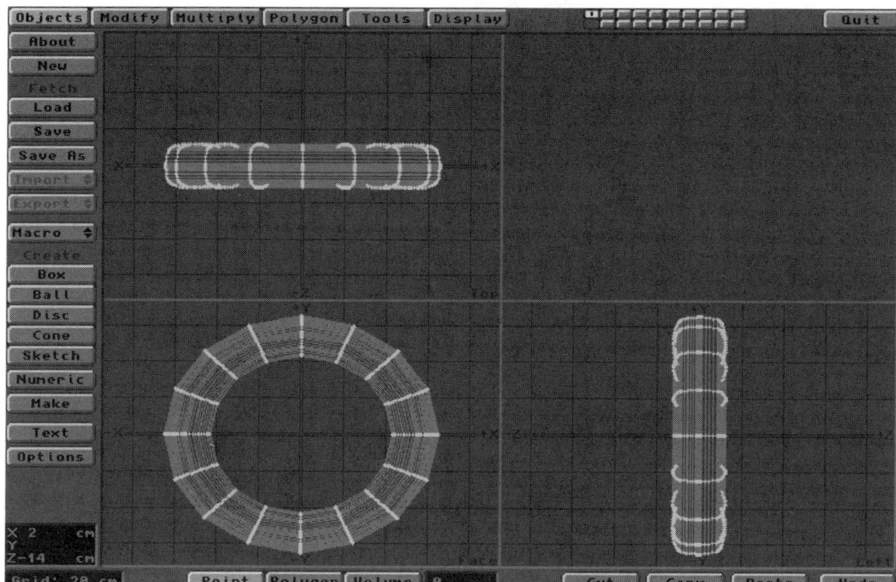

Figure 2: The result of the Lathe operation.

The only thing to do now is to create another plane to cover up the groove, which we'll make disappear gradually in Layout.

•Go to Layer 6 (6) with Layer 3 (Alt 3) in the background, and select the Box tool (Objects). Now draw another smaller plane, covering the part that we cut out of the ground plane. Make it the following dimensions, and click OK:

Low	
X=	-0.250 m
Y=	0
Z=	-0.3 m
High	
X=	5.25 m
Y=	0
Z=	0.3 m
Segments	
X=	1
Y=	1
Z=	1

•If .3 m isn't enough to cover the width of the tire groove, you might want to increase that to suit your situation.

•Now hit Enter to place the plane.

•Since this plane's polygon is facing downward, Flip (f) it upwards.

•Hit (q) to assign a surface name to the new object. You want to call the surface the same name as the ground plane, so click the box with the words "Default" and select the surface 'ground-cover', then click Apply.

•Save this object as 'ground-plane-cover.lwo'. Our work is done in Modeler, so let's go to Layout.

The way to pull this trick off is to uncover the groove you've made as the wheel moves, and create the illusion of the wheel actually making an indentation. You can accomplish this in two ways. By using a Clip Map, you can make an animated sequence where the screen starts off black, and with time gradually cover more and more of the screen with the color white, starting on the left side so the animation looks like a wipe from left to right. The other method is much simpler and works just as well. Just shrink the cover plane from one end over time, so it will appear as if it is vanishing. I mentioned the Clip Map method because the method of shrinking the plane won't work if you have a curved path to travel.

•In layout, load the objects you created in Modeler; 'tire.lwo', 'ground-plane.lwo' and 'ground-plane-cover.lwo'.

•Go to the Surface menu and select the 'tire-surf' surface and set the following:

Surface Color	40, 40, 40
Luminosity	20%
Diffuse Level	50%
Specular Level	10%
Glossiness	Low
Smoothing	On
Double Sided	On

This will make the tire look somewhat realistic. For added realism, you can add a few image maps to the tire.

•Surface the 'ground-plane':

Surface Color	60 100 0
Surface Texture	
Texture Type	Fractal Noise
Texture Size	1.5 (for X)
	1.0 (for Y and Z)
Texture Color	120 50 0
Frequency	3
Contrast	1.0
Luminosity	20%
Diffuse Level	50%

This is going to put patches of green and brown over your ground plane. Again, here's where you can get creative and put whatever texture you want over the ground plane. Use the same settings for the 'ground-cover' surface with one exception; In the Texture menu, select World Coordinates. You need to have World Coordinates turned on, because as the covering plane shrinks, you don't want the texture to shrink with the plane. This will prevent that.

•Finally, surface the 'ground-groove':

Surface Color	120 50 0
Luminosity	50%
Diffuse Level	50%
Smoothing	On

•Most of the objects are already set up in the scene. You only need to move a few things. Start with the 'ground-cover' object. Enter the following values for X, Y and Z: -5.25, -0.595, 0. If you remember back in Modeler, we offset the ground plane by 60 cm. Here, you're placing the covering only 5 mm above the ground, so you can't see the difference. If you place it on the same level with the ground plane, you're probably going to get rendering errors. Hit Create Key for all objects.

Figure 3: Position of the camera over the scene.

•Go to frame 30 and change the size in the X direction only of the 'ground-cover'. Stretch it on the X axis to 0.045 and leave the rest to 1.0. Click Create Key.

•Next Move the tire.lwo object -5.0 in the X direction, and 0 in the Y and Z directions. Click Rotate, then hit (n) and enter 440 degrees in the Bank requester so the tire will spin rather than drag along. Hit Create Key.

Well, that's it! You've done it! All you have to do now is render the 30 frames, and watch the wheel make an impression on the ground behind it. Like I said earlier, this can be used for more than just a car tire. For example, you can probably use this technique to create footsteps in snow with a few modifications, but that's a different tutorial!

Adrian Onsen is an Aerospace Engineering student at Ryerson Polytechnic University in Toronto. In his spare time he tries to make a buck animating with LightWave. Reach him at aonsen@ryerson.ca, or you can visit his home page at http://www.ryerson.ca/~aonsen. Hope to hear from you!

A Look at Displacement Mapping

By John Gross

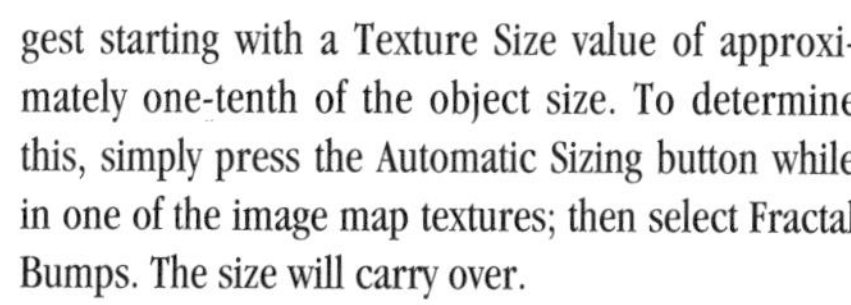

In previous versions of LightWave, I used bump maps for wavy or bumpy illusions. Unfortunately, the visual quality just wasn't good enough because the surface was never actually bumpy—it was shaded to appear bumpy. With the introduction of LightWave 3.0, a new tool called displacement mapping allows surfaces to actually change shape during an animation. Need to have waves ripple against the hull of a boat or a flag blow in the breeze? This is where a displacement map can help.

Displacement mapping is actually rather simple to use—you just need to know some basics. First of all, you cannot displace surfaces of an object by themselves; the object must be displaced as a whole. For this reason, the Displacement Map button is located in the Objects panel, not the Surfaces panel.

There are five different ways to displace an object. The first three are different types of image maps—planar, cylindrical and spherical. The other two methods are Ripples and Fractal Bumps. Sound familiar? These are the same options that you had for bump mapping a surface under LightWave 2.0; LW 3.0 has the exact same bump mapping options with the addition of a cubic image map.

For a displacement map to work properly, it's important to have a lot of polygons in your object; otherwise, your displacements will not be smooth. (How often have you seen waves that were pointy?) The best way to prepare an object for displacement mapping is to load it into Modeler and use the Subdivide option (located in the Polygon menu) to create more polygons. The polygons need to be tripled first. If your object is not a flat plane, you will almost always want to use the Smooth Subdivide option.

How much should you subdivide? It depends on how much you are going to displace the object and how close you want to get to it. Usually, some experimentation is required.

Once your object has been subdivided and brought back into Layout, it's time to start displacing. All of the different displacement textures have one thing in common: texture amplitude. This simply refers to how far, in meters, the surface of the object will displace.

After choosing an axis and size for your image, set the Texture Amplitude. For best results, start with low values. You can see the results of the value when the object redraws in the Layout screen. If your amplitude is set too high, instead of proper displacement, your object will look like a rat's nest.

Remember that when you use images for your displacement, the luminance (or brightness) values of the image determine the amplitude of the displacement. Solid white values in the image will displace the object the full amount of the Texture Amplitude value. Solid black values will not displace the objects at all; values in between white and black will displace accordingly. For example, 50 percent gray will displace 50 percent of the Texture Amplitude value.

Ripples and fractal bumps, the other two types of displacement maps, have a few additional values to input. Fractal bumps allow for a frequencies setting which determines how many "patterns" of bumps will be used. I recommend values between 3 and 16. The higher the value, the more "bumpy" your object, but the longer the render time. For fractal bumps, I also suggest starting with a Texture Size value of approximately one-tenth of the object size. To determine this, simply press the Automatic Sizing button while in one of the image map textures; then select Fractal Bumps. The size will carry over.

The Ripples texture has wave values that must be input. Wave Sources is simply the number of centers of waves (a value of 1 will have ripples emanating from one spot only). Wavelength determines the spacing between the waves, while Wave Speed determines how fast the waves move.

If you need to have looping waves moving for an animation, use this simple formula to determine the Wave Speed value: Take the Wavelength and divide it by the number of frames you wish the waves to loop in and enter that value for the Wave Speed. I generally use the object's size for the Texture Size when using Ripples.

History in the Making
How to Build a Virtual Prison

by Alan Chan

You know what they say: this wonderful thing called "virtual reality" will take you to places you've never been, worlds you've never imagined and fantasies you've always wanted to indulge in. Well, if you haven't realized it yet, that Layout screen that you keep staring at into the wee hours of the morning is in fact a virtual world! Yes! In addition to all those logos that clients keep paying you to do, you can also create your own virtual landscape!

Recently I had the opportunity to make approximately 80 seconds of animation doing just that: re-creating a world that no longer existed for a documentary on the subject. My job was to model and build a replica of the Civil War-era Andersonville Prison, located in Andersonville, Ga. During the Civil War, this prison housed an estimated 10,000 prisoners of war in such destitute conditions that half of them did not survive. Today the site is not much to look at. The stockade walls are all but collapsed, and only the occasional pine log here and there helps to suggest how things might have looked back in the 1830s. The producers of the documentary wanted some form of visual aid to help the viewers imagine the prison and how the geography of the land was part of the reason for its dismal failure—thus my involvement in the project.

Several months, countless bags of M&Ms and many late nights later, I hit the F10 button for the last time. Now, as the scenes are happily rendering their merry way along, I can take this writing break and share with you some of the cheats and tips I learned from this project. To explain the entire animation would probably take up too much space and rehash techniques already mentioned in this fine newsletter, so I'm just going to cover some of the techniques that haven't been discussed yet. If you've ever wanted to rewrite history, here's what you do.

Before Starting

First off, as with any other project, never jump straight into LightWave 3D or Modeler and start plotting points. Sit down and plan things out. I began by studying the maps of the area, trying to first visualize it in my head. Then I went over the narrative script, trying to select the best camera positions and movement, and to get an estimated time for the scene. Make notes of the detail that will be required in various objects (like cannons and such) according to their proximity to the camera. Make a list of the objects you'll need to build: the ground itself, the prison walls, the sentry posts, the cannons, etc. Once everything is laid out on paper, it's time to begin.

From the Ground Up

A good solid foundation is the key to success, or so they say. I've found that since everything relates to the ground (by way of this thing called gravity), it's good to have a ground plane built first. Because we are re-creating a real place, not an imaginary one, we will have to use real-world data. There are several ways of doing this.

DEMs: By far the most accurate way to model an elevation map, DEMs are the result of actual field surveys done by the U.S. Geological Society, and are available from various sources on and off the Internet. These maps can be converted into a LightWave object using conversion software such as Syndesis' Interchange Plus. Be aware, though, that object files generated from DEMs can get pretty large, so you may wish to reload objects into Modeler and crop them down to your area of interest only.

Displacement Mapping: A good method for creating elevation maps is to use displacement mapping on a polygon mesh. Understand that displacement mapping samples a pixel from your selected image and uses it to calculate physical placement for each point (vertex) on the object, so that lighter areas are displaced more than darker ones. For any given image, therefore, the brighter areas represent peaks and mountains, and the darker areas represent valleys. A good aerial map of a location can easily be converted for use as a displacement map, though some image processing will be necessary to ensure a proper range of elevation and to eliminate shadows.

On this project, however, I was severely limited. There were no DEMs available at the resolution needed, and I had no overhead map that I could process. The only map of the area that had any height information on it was a tattered old contour map. With a little bit of work, however, a contour map can be turned into a displacement map .

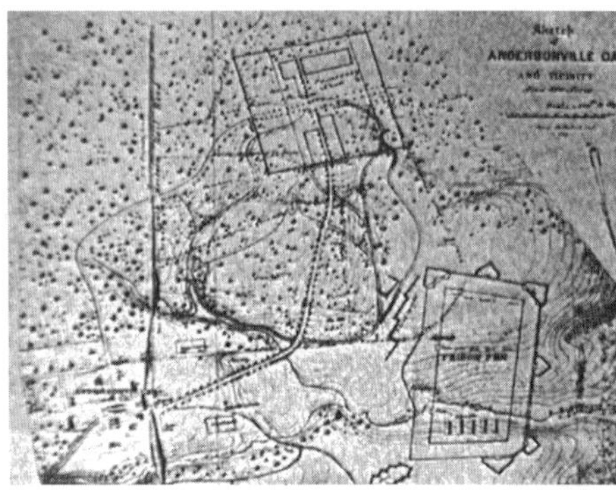

Figure 1: The framegrabbed image of the contour map.

Building a Displacement Map

The information for the displacement map was contained in the contour map. It was just a matter of reworking it into a usable format.

- After scanning the contour map into the system as a framestore (Figure 1), I selected it as a Modeler background image in the Y axis (**Display** menu), preparing to trace the contour shapes. Before beginning, however, remember to ensure that the aspect ratio of the image is accurate. The BG Image option always scales the image on a 1:1 ratio, while the framestore aspect ratio is 4:3, so we'll need to scale the image accordingly. Once the size and aspect ratio of your background image are finalized, write the settings down. There is nothing worse than coming back to a Modeler work-in-progress and not being able to resize the background image to its proper dimensions.
- The next step was to trace out the contour map. I used the **Sketch** tool (**Objects** menu) in Modeler, and beginning with the highest elevation, traced out the contour. Hitting Return or clicking on **Make** converts your line sketch into a curve that represents fairly closely the contour on the elevation map. I repeated this process with the rest of the contour lines, making sure that each line was at its proper elevation (Figure 2). Remembering that this will merely be a rough contour map, I set my **Curve Division** to **Coarse** (**Options** panel under

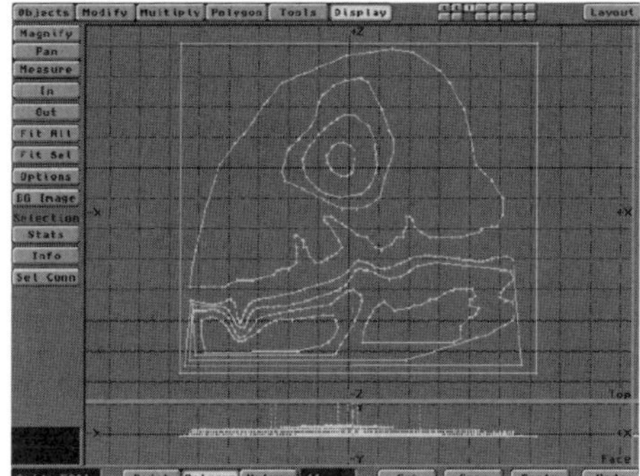

Figure 2: The traced contour lines in Modeler.

the **Objects** menu). Then I went to the **Tools** menu in Modeler and hit **Freeze** to convert the curves into polygons, after which I followed with the usual check to make sure all my polygons were facing in the right direction (in this case, the positive Y axis).

- I next assigned different surface names for each elevation, such as "Elev50ft," "Elev100ft," "Elev 150ft," etc., and **Export**ed the object to Layout.

Elev100ft	128,128,128
Elev50ft	64,64,64
Elev0ft	0,0,0

Luminosity settings for all of the surfaces would be 100% and Diffuse levels would be 0%.These numbers ensure that the colors will be exactly what I set.

- With the surface colors attached, I placed the camera directly on top of the map, at a pitch of 90 degrees so that it was looking straight down, and adjusted the camera position so that the map would fill as much of the frame as possible. I then rendered and saved an RGB frame (Figure 3).

OK, so what I had now was a nice, filled-in version of the contour map—no sloping hills and no gradients. I had to soften it and create gradients between the edges, which was done using ADPro. (Of course, your favorite image processing software should be able to do this easily.)

- Using the "Displace Pixels" operator I was able to spread out the pixels, sloping the gradient from white to black. (I used a Displacement probability of 100%, and have found that a Radius value of 5 to 10 pixels—about two percent of the image size—

100 for the Y axis, for an area of about 6000x6000 square feet. This meant that I would have about 60 feet from one point to the other on my map.

I then tripled and named the surfaces. Tripling the surfaces is important if you are going to be performing displacement mapping, to avoid rendering errors from multi-point polygons as they are bent out of their original shapes.

- Next, I exported the mesh object to Layout, where I proceeded to apply the image as a **Planar Image** displacement map (**Objects** menu) on the **Y Axis.** By hitting **Automatic Sizing**, you are assured that your image will fit the exact shape of your object.
- At this point your ground plane is ready, and you may either use **Save Transformed** to save the object as it has been displaced (thus doing away with your image map on subsequent uses of this object) or use the scene file as a basis for the rest of your work. Remember that your displacement map settings are stored in the scene file, *not* the object file, so if you do not use the **Save Transformed** function you will need to load the scene file in order to obtain the required displacement.

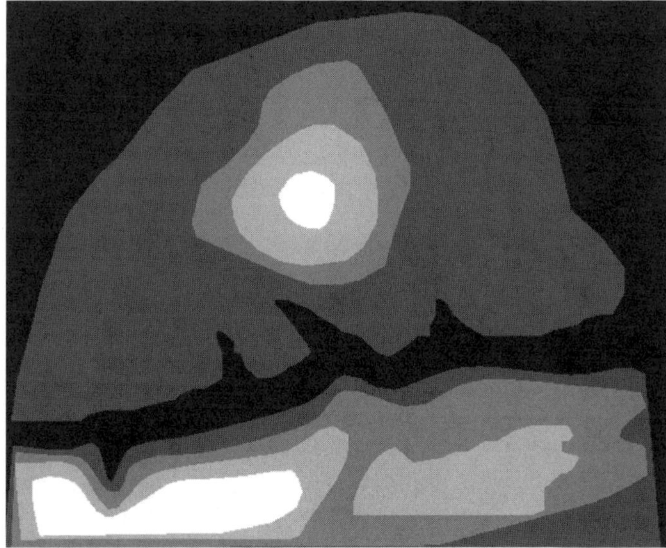

Figure 3: The rendered contour map.

Figure 4: The contour map with displaced pixels, blurred three times.

Now that I had my elevation represented by polygons at different levels, it was time to convert my work into an overhead image that I could use as a displacement map. What I needed was an image where the highest elevations were white and the valleys were black. Of course, this meant that anything in between would be a corresponding shade of gray. It was a simple matter of looking in the Surfaces list and figuring out how many shades of gray I needed for my rough map. For instance, if I had five surfaces (one being 0,0,0), I would divide 255 (the top color) by 4 and assign the following surface colors to them:

Surface Name	**Surface color (RGB)**
Elev200ft	255,255,255
Elev150ft	192,192,192

makes for an even displacement. These values, of course, will vary according to your needs.) This step gave me a graduated, although somewhat pixelish, map, which I then smoothed over using the "Blur" operator (Figure 4) with the following settings: Blur Center Weight 0, Threshold 0. You may wish to blur your map two or three times for a softer effect.

Once I was satisfied with the image map, I converted it to a grayscale to save on memory, then cropped and saved the image.

- Returning to Modeler, I used the **Box** function to build my polygon mesh. Hitting the **Numeric** option brings up a requester from which you can specify the number of segments for your polygon mesh. I entered a value of 100 segments for the X axis and

Keep in mind that this method does introduce some height discrepancies in your overhead map.

Displacing pixels on your image map works both ways off of the edge, and blurring the result provides a pixel value that is slightly lower than the original value. The discrepancies, however, are probably somewhat relative, and can be overlooked.

OK! So that gives you a nice overhead displacement map. By now, of course, some of you are asking, "How is it that you couldn't just have used your image processing program and *painted* the contour lines in?" Well, you can on simpler contour maps, and I would have preferred to do it that way, but there were a few too many contour lines in this map. So, in an effort to avoid confusion, I tried it this way.

There will be times, however, when painting in the contour lines will be more of a hassle, so it's up to you and your professional LightWave judgment to decide which method to use.

Virtual Walls

Another tip to stick in your LightWave arsenal is a Boolean trick I used in building the stockade. The narrative script went as such: "A ditch was dug to a depth of five feet. Into the ditches were dropped 22-foot pine logs. The earth was then packed around the logs." Therefore, the height of the stockade walls was 17 feet. The terrain on which the prison was built, however, was variable, and I had to match the height of the wall with the elevation. Rather than entering the points manually, I elected to use Booleans.

- Entering Modeler, I traced the outline of the stockade wall and made polygons from it, remembering to also give the walls a thickness. I then extruded the stockade in the Y axis and, using the elevation map object in a background layer, positioned the stockade outline in the proper position on the map.
- Next (this is the important part!) I went to the elevation map and copied to another layer the polygons representing the immediate area in and around the stockade wall (Figure 5). I raised it 17 feet, flipped the polygons and extruded in the positive Y axis (Figure 6). Flipping the polygons before extruding is important to ensure that the surface normals are facing the correct way, a critical consideration for Boolean operations. Reselecting my stockade wall as the current layer and placing the extruded map in the background layer, I simply did a Boolean Subtract, and the result (Figure 7) was a nice contour-hugging stockade wall raised 17 feet above the ground.

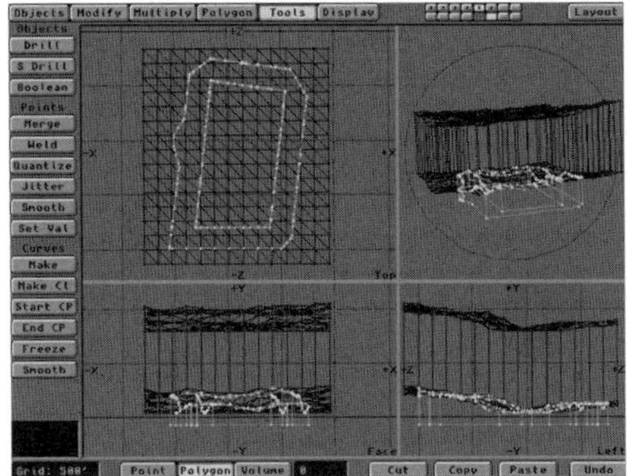

Figure 7: The result of a Boolean Subtract operation.

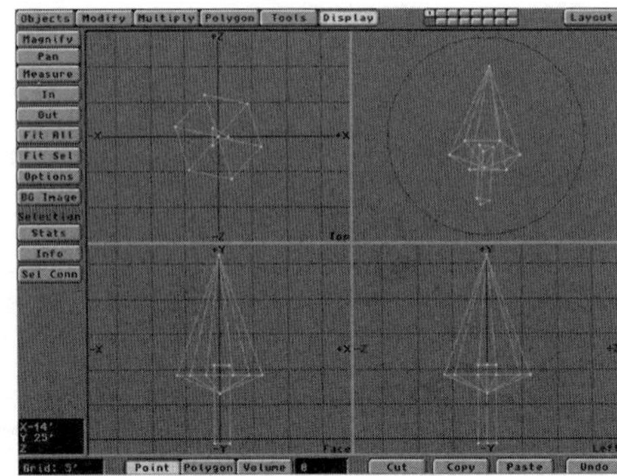

Figure 8: The simple tree object in Modeler.

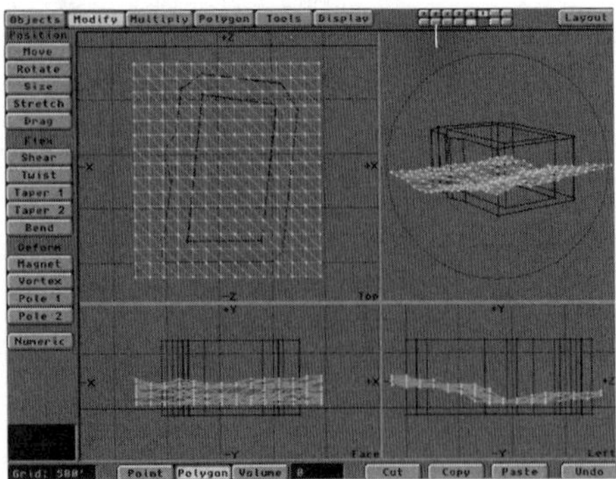

Figure 5: Preparing to do a Boolean operation.

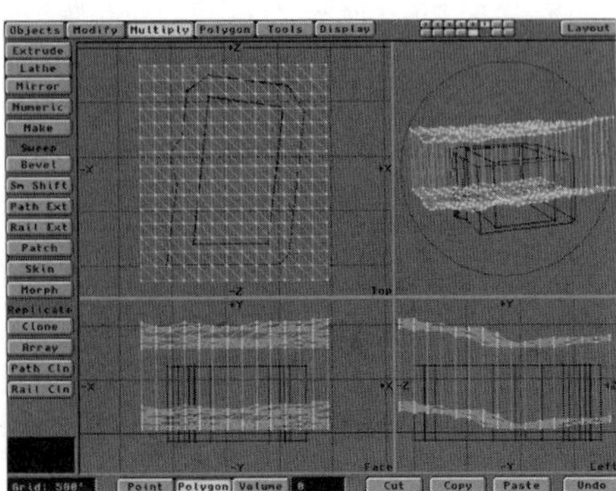

Figure 6: Extruding for depth.

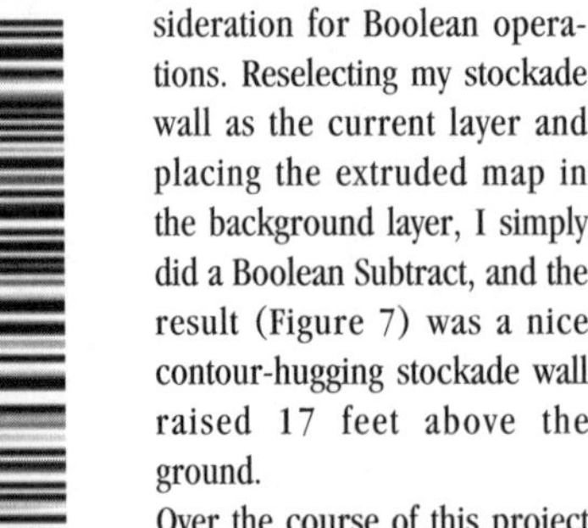

Figure 9: The image used for the tree transparency.

Over the course of this project I've found Boolean functions to be most useful. Besides just slicing polygons, it is also a good method for "dropping" points onto the surface of the elevation map. What good will that do? Well, let me explain further.

Johnny Appleseed

With the elevation map and the stockade walls finished, it was now time to add a bit of greenery to the whole thing. Archival photos showed that the predominant foliage in the area was pines, and a quick rough calculation showed that I would have a lot of trees. For the sake of conserving memory, I elected to keep the tree object as simple as possible, using transparency maps to try and add that leafy look. Figures 8 and 9 show the finished tree object, and the transparency map that was mapped in the Y axis onto the leaf surface. Note also that the tree trunk is in fact a three-sided cylinder, the simplest shape possible, to conserve memory.

Now, in order to take this object and replicate it to fill the area, I had to remember to "drop" the tree onto the ground surface. Otherwise, the trees would be floating in midair or buried in the ground.

- With that in mind, I went into Modeler and plotted a myriad of points, each one of them representing a tree, taking care to plot more points where the map indicated denser areas or a forest. Note that these points all have the same Y value (probably 0).
- Next, entering the macro list and executing the "Points->Polys" macro, I converted all the points into one-point polygons.
- With the elevation map as a background layer, I extruded these polygons in the Y axis, making sure that the top portion was above the highest point on the elevation map and the bottom portion was lower than the lowest point (Figure 10).
- If you've been following along in Modeler, at this point you will have a bunch of two-point polygons that, somewhere along the way, intersect with the ground plane. (Are things starting to make sense?) Performing a Boolean Intersect operation presents a bunch of points that are on the ground surface.

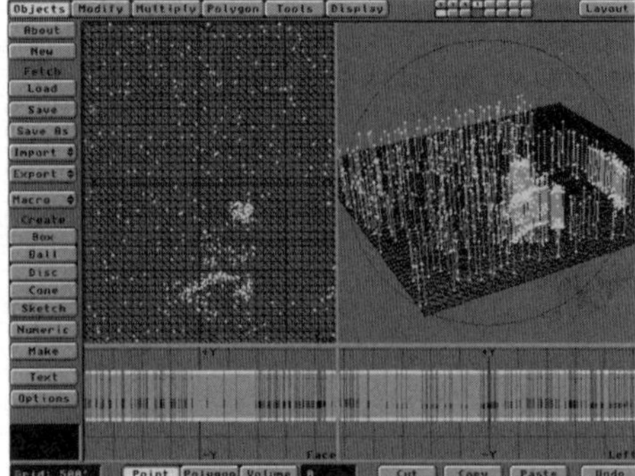

Figure 10: Two-point polygons through the ground plane.

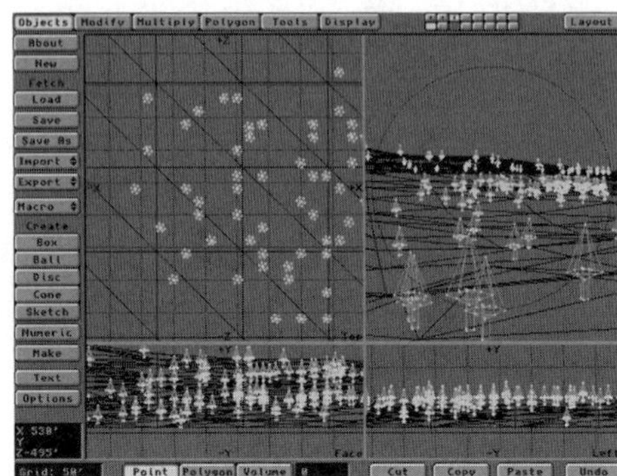

Figure 11: The result of a points clone function.

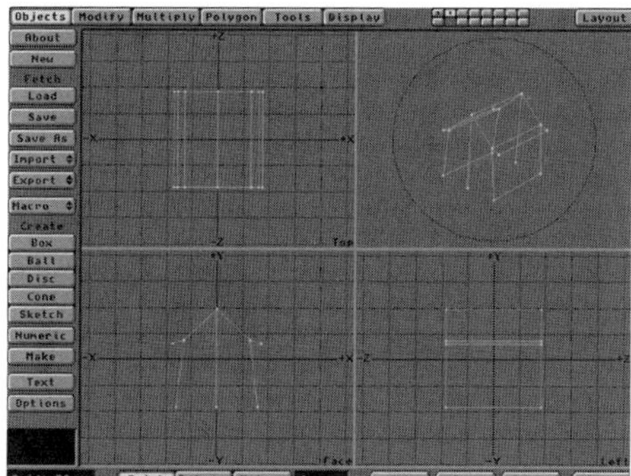

Figure 12: A simple tent object.

The final step is to cut these points out and place them into an empty layer.

- Now we plant our trees.. Selecting the tree object as the current layer (you *did* remember to build the tree at 0,0,0, didn't you?) and your tree points as the background layer, open up your macro list and select **Direct Command**. Then, when you are prompted for an ARexx script, select the pclone.lwm script and execute it. The Particle Clone macro is one of those included with LightWave, but is not in the defined macros list, so if you've never used it before it will probably not be configured with the pclone macro. (I've used it so much that I now have it on my macros lists for easy access.)

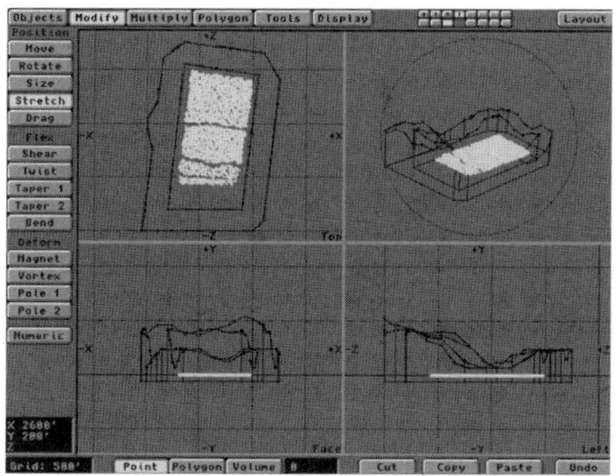

Figure 13: Tent points plotted and trimmed.

Voila! What happened? Modeler took the tree object and cloned it, placing a copy of the object at every one of the points specified in the background layer (Figure 11).

There are two things to note: One, the Particle Clone macro keeps the original tree object at 0,0,0, so you may need to delete that particular tree. Also, on the original tree object, the trunk extends a slight distance in the negative Y axis. This is a safety factor, in case a particular tree is sitting on a slope and the ground surface is not properly aligned.

To make things easier, LightWave also comes with a macro called Prick.lwm, which randomly generates points and automatically drops them onto the surface. If your project does not require specific placement of points, you may use this macro to generate your surface points instead of plotting each point by hand. Prick.lwm is not configured in your macro list, so you'll have to access it as a direct command or add it to your macro list.

It Gets Harder...

Now that the surroundings of the prison are modeled, it's time to take care of the interior. The history books report that Andersonville was so overcrowded that many prisoners of war died from unsanitary conditions and disease epidemics. The prisoners lived in tents, which were erected extremely close to each other due to a lack of space.

- To simulate these conditions I built a simple tent, again keeping the point count simple for memory considerations (Figure 12). I saved this object temporarily and went to an empty layer and called up the stockade wall object as a background layer. After plotting a point on the bottom left corner of the prison, I cloned it using the **Array** function (**Multiply** menu), using values to fit within the prison walls. I also used the Manual offset option, and because the length of the tent object measured 6 feet, entered an offset value of 9 feet for both axes. This gave me a dense points layer, which I then rotated and trimmed to fit the stockade walls (Figure 13). To "randomize" the points a little bit I applied a Jitter (Tools menu) of 1.5 feet to the X and Z axes.
- I then ran the points through the same macro routine as the trees to "drop" the points onto the surface. From here on things got a little more complicated.

Trees, by their very nature, grow straight up. Tents, however, should follow the lay of the land. Because of the fact that the topography of the prison interior was a gentle slope from the north and south sides to a valley stream in the middle, I decided to give the tents on the south side of the river a positive pitch (sloping north toward the river) and the tents on the north side a negative pitch (which would also slope them toward the river). Additionally, humans, being the fickle creatures they are, would probably never build tents in any one direction. I decided that roughly half of my tents should face north-south, and the rest face east-west.

This required me to break down the tent points into four sections:

(**1**) Tents on the north side, facing north-south
(**2**) Tents on the north side, facing east-west
(**3**) Tents on the south side, facing north-south
(**4**) Tents on the south side, facing east-west.

- To select which tents would face east-west and which would face north-south, I simply held down the left-mouse key and ran the cursor over the points as fast as I could, selecting points here and there, in an almost random pattern, until I had about half of them selected. These points were then cut and pasted into a separate layer.

Determining an average tilt angle for both the north side and the south side, I ran the Particle Clone macro through a separate pass for each of the four segments, with the tent object either rotated 90 degrees or not, and the proper angle for each segment. The result was a very big (almost 700K in size) and nicely complex object file.

Laying It All Out

While modeling my objects, I was also exporting them to Layout and surfacing each one as I completed it. I had previously set up a scene file so that as I exported each object and positioned it, I was also creating a "master scene" that I could later use as a template. In addition, a template scene file ensured that I was surfacing my objects under the same lighting conditions. An added safety margin is to parent all the objects to the ground object, which ensures that the objects are anchored to the ground, even if the ground object is accidentally moved or scaled.

- The surfacing itself proved to be no real feat. No fancy multiple surface morphs or transparency velocities, just plain old texture maps, fractal noise and lots of test render elbow grease. For what it's worth, here are some of the surface settings for several of these objects:

Stockade Walls:

Surface Color	154,109,65
Surface Texture	Fractal Noise
Texture Size	0.5,500,0.5
Texture Color	132,39,13
Frequencies	3
Contrast	8.0
Diffuse Level	80%
Smoothing	Off

Tree Trunk:

Surface Color	109,36,6
Diffuse Level	60%

Tree Foliage (Pine Tree):

Surface Color	26,82,0
Diffusion Map	Planar Image Map
Texture Image	treemap.trans (Figure 9)
Texture Axis	X axis
Texture Size	30000,6,30000
Specular Level	10%
Glossiness	Low
Edge Transparency	Transparent
Edge Threshold	0.7
Smoothing	On

Tent Fabric:

Surface Color	0,58,16
Surface Texture	Fractal Noise
Texture Size	0.01,0.01,0.01
Texture Color	0,35,0
Frequencies	3
Contrast	3.0
Diffuse Level	60%
Smoothing	On
Double-Sided	On

The Virtual Eye

With the modeling and the surfacing done, loading in the objects and flying the camera around them turned out to be the easy part. The script called for eight different shots, all of them highlighting a different part of the prison. With the exception of one shot, which required titles and such, I simply loaded up the master scene containing all the objects in their proper positions, set the camera path, and then saved it out as a separate scene file.

One thing to note about camera movements in simulations is that you are in fact trying to re-create the motions of a real-world camera. Note that in reality, the moves that a camera can make are broken up into two parts. One is the rotation of the camera head, which pivots on the tripod head and is handled by the camera operator. The other is the movement of the camera, which is handled by anything from dollies to cranes to camera trucks. Movement usually requires another operator such as a dolly grip (a person who pushes a camera dolly back and forth). It is the collaboration of these two people, the camera operator and the dolly grip, that combine to provide the fluid camera moves we are so accustomed to seeing these days.

For the same reason, complex camera moves in LightWave should also be broken down into their respective elements. This ensures that the spline controls used to affect camera rotation do not affect camera movement, and vice versa.

- First, create a null object and rename it by clicking on the **Save Object** button. I call mine "CameraXYZ Null" for easy reference. Then, upon returning to the Layout screen, I select **Camera** as my edit item and **Parent** it to the Null. To be safe, I also Reset the XYZ values for the camera and keyframe it at frame 0. This allows the camera to simply be concerned with the rotation aspect (as the camera operator should) and for the null object to perform the actual moves (as the dolly grip should). Remember, to only rotate the camera, not the null object, as things can get pretty frustrating otherwise.

Eight Scene Files Later

So here I am, sitting back writing as I watch my animation render. I must admit I've omitted some things, such as modeling the rest of the objects in the scene (the gates, the sentry boxes, cannons, etc.), but that's all just basic modeling techniques—nothing spectacular, although I am pretty proud of my cannon.

The files have been sent up, the check has been signed, and the client is happy. End of story? Well, for the moment. I've archived my files and copied them off for safe storage. Now I'll just sit and wait for the day when I can plug a VR headset into LightWave and walk around my own virtual prison.

Alan Chan is lost in cyberspace. Be nice and e-mail him at alan.chan@oubbs.telecom.uoknor.edu.

Beneath the Surface

by Greg Teegarden

The surface of the ocean is an ever-changing shape that lends itself well to the realm of the computer animator because of it's fluidity. LightWave has a number of tools that make the illusion of a body of water fairly simple to achieve. However, it's the amount of complexity and the factor of time spent rendering that will determine how successful and realistic your end results will be.

This month, I'm going to discuss how we at Amblin Imaging create the illusion of the underside of the ocean surface.

Come on In, the Water's Fine

There are basically two types of water surfacing employed to get the desired effect of an underwater environment. One is the actual creation of a water surface which is intended to be seen up close from its underside. The other is the caustic refraction of light traveling through the surface of the water and striking an underwater vehicle or creature. With the former, the latter is almost always employed, but usually not the other way around.

When I began working on *seaQuest*, it was determined that we would never see the underside of the ocean surface or even go above the surface. It was deemed too difficult and therefore unnecessary to even attempt it, but it was something I wanted to try nonetheless. One of the problems with attempting these types of tricks is that you will invariably create a situation that requires the use of raytracing, and this was often considered a bad word until fairly recently. With products on the market like the Raptor from DeskStation Technologies, raytracing becomes a practical possibility, especially within the constraints of a TV schedule and budget.

Usually the need for a certain look or situation is the catalyst for the discovery of a new technique, and realistic water was certainly one of them. The script for a *seaQuest* episode (titled "The Stinger")called for a "car race" underwater just below the surface of the ocean. Having posters on every wall showing what it looks like from six to 60 feet below the ocean surface, I had plenty of reference points.

The first thing I noticed was that the ocean surface resembled a crinkled piece of paper that had been unfolded. It is comprised mostly of smaller waves which I would consider calling wind "chop" riding on the backs of the larger waves. It is this "chop" that gives the ocean its unique look from its underside. This chop also creates all of the intricate caustic light patterns which seem to dance upon the surfaces of everything beneath it.

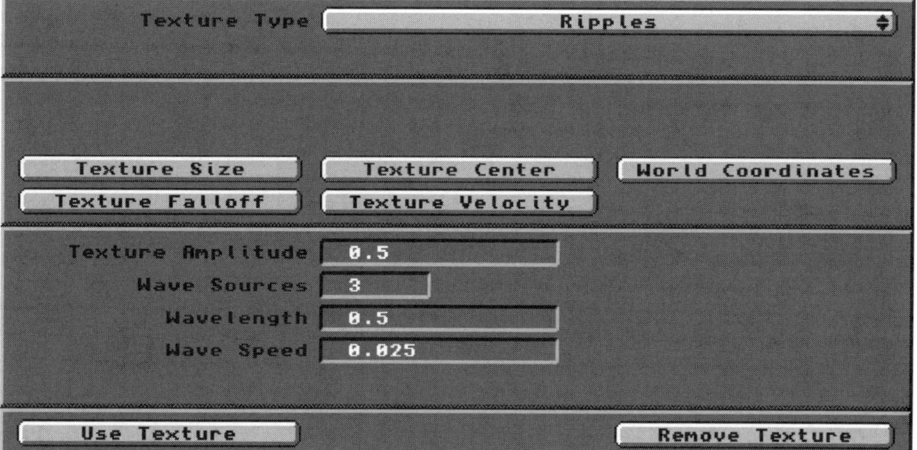

Figure 1

Dive In

In creating the water surface, the first thing I did was try and duplicate the larger waves which comprise the bulk of the movement across the ocean itself. This was done by creating a mesh of at least 20,000 polygons. This may sound like a lot, and it is, but to get something like a submarine underneath it and make it look believable requires at least a flat mesh of that size. I discovered that a mesh of around 24,000 suited my needs adequately. I should also note that the mesh is square in shape.

The next step was to create the larger or primary waves. Displacement mapping best suits this type of need, as it negates the need to morph, and LightWave has a good Ripple Displacement map. In the **Objects** panel you will find the Displacement Map area with the **T** button. Selecting this allows you to choose **Ripples** as your texture (Figure 1).

Since my mesh object was about 450 square meters , I played with the **Texture Size** values until I found one that gave me what I considered to be realistic looking waves, both in size and in separation from one another. I noticed that apart from the Texture Size button, a number of other options existed, including **Wave Sources**. The default value for this was three, but I found that the waves became more random as the value increased. With this in mind, I raised it to its maximum setting, which was 16.

Wavelength is another option that needed some adjustment. After a little experimentation, I found that a value of 16 seemed to work nicely here too.

Wave Speed is the distance, in meters per frame, that the wave travels across the mesh. I found that a setting of .025, the default, worked out nicely.

Finally, **Texture Amplitude** was set to .25, or that of a wave about 10 inches tall.

The Little Ones Get You

The next step was the creation of the secondary waves, which are most responsible for the caustic light refraction seen underwater. The best way to do this would have been to use another displacement map, however, you get only one per object in LightWave, and my object did not have enough complexity to support such a fine amount of actual displacement. The solution to this problem was to use a Bump Map. Bump maps work nicely because they actually bend raytraced light from an overhead source and concentrate it along the patterns on the map. Therefore, if you

Figure 2

have a semi-transparent object that has swirling patterns on it and trace shadows through it, those same patterns will cast down onto the receiving surface. This works well for water caustic because everything in the scene below the wave surface gets illuminated by this random pattern of swirling light.This is exactly what happens in reality.

The trick to make this work for an animation is to use sequentially numbered images as the Bump Map. I have discovered that Apex Software's Forge program contains a nice caustics algorithm which can be animated over time. If I had this tool at my disposal earlier, I would have used it, but at the time all I had was several pieces of crumpled paper which I had scanned on a flatbed scanner.

As mentioned previously, the paper looked like the underside of the ocean surface when crumpled, so I used about five sheets of this as source images. I then used Photoshop to generate the in-between images, which creating a type of morph from one page to another until I had about 50 distinct RGB files (Figure 2). These were loaded into LightWave and used as the Bump Maps for the secondary waves riding the backs of the larger, displacement mapped primary waves. No texture velocity is needed on these RGBs, as the transition of one image to another is sufficient to carry the illusion of moving water caustics. As far as the size of the maps involved, obviously the bigger you can fit into RAM the better. The ones I used were the default 752x480 Toaster size, reduced in color depth to 8-bits per pixel in grayscale. That seemed to work well enough, but remember that lower resolution maps can tend to show signs of aliasing in the map itself, which destroys the illusion.

Pouring it all Together

We now have the basic elements needed to produce realistic looking water surfaces from the caustics and wave movement point of view, but what about the other settings? Water in itself does not have a color, but because it tends to absorb light in the red end of the spectrum, blue is the color that we see. I've tried many different surface settings and found that it looks best and most believable if the color settings shift towards blue. This may seem obvious, but since transparency is used to a high degree in order to allow light to get through, and **Additive** could be used with blue Zenith and Sky colors in your background gradient, one could make the water surface red and it would make no difference. In the end I opted not to use Additive and instead make the surface a dark blue color, with a light Sky background color. Transparency was set to 85 percent, with **Color Filter** turned on. Due to the Color Filter setting, which causes any light cast through a transparent object to take into account the color settings of the object in question, Additive was not used on the water surface. I wanted the light cast through to be blue in hue, and the Color Filter option achieved that nicely. The color of the light itself was that of the sun, shifted towards the yellow end of the spectrum. This creates a little bit of green here and there which makes everything look right.

Speaking of light, which settings work and which don't? In order to get the caustic effects, you must raytrace. There is no other realistic option I can think of, both aesthetically and practically. I boosted my **Light Intensity** to 200 percent, made the color a little yellow, and pointed it almost straight down. A distant light was used to create even saturation throughout the scene.

In the Surfaces panel, I found that because all of the polygons needed to be tripled in order to get a good displacement, **Transparent Edges** should be used to prevent any polygons from revealing their edges during the run of the animation. **Smoothing** and **Double Sided** were also used.

One final setting that had to be worked out was the reflectivity of the water surface itself. Ideally, **Trace Reflections** (Camera panel) should be used, but in the interest of time I opted not to use this feature and instead used an image of a scanned piece of crinkled tin foil as a reflection map. It worked well, with the reflectivity cranked up to 100 percent. I also used a 100 percent **Specularity** setting, with **High** selected under glossiness.

This all took about two weeks to figure out and test until I felt it looked good enough to pass for believable water.

LWP

Greg Teegarden is an animator for Amblin Imaging. His work can be seen on seaQuest *and numerous commercials. He can be reached by e-mail on CompuServe at 71175,3025.*

The Depths of OCEANIC
How Long Can You Hold Your Breath?

by Tom Williamson

Every once and a while a project comes along that challenges us to think in a whole new way. A project that is so involved that we think we'll never finish it. One that, on the onset, seemed a whole lot simpler that it actually was. But, once it's finished, there's no more satisfying experience. Our work for Oceanic is the epitome of a truly challenging project.

The Concept

In mid-August 1994, Paula K. Productions approached Computer Café, the effects house I animate for, with what initially seemed like a pretty straightforward assignment. Oceanic, a leading scuba and dive equipment company, needed an opening for its corporate and promotional videos. The concept seemed simple enough: a 25-second spot with a dolphin morphing into a diver sporting Oceanic gear. The idea of using live-action footage was considered and quickly dismissed because of the logistics of finding two shots that met the strict criteria. The decision was made to create the entire environment with LightWave. After a few meetings the concept was locked: fade in with a slow camera move over underwater terrain. A dolphin morphs into a diver, who turns in front of the camera, exhaling as he passes. His bubbles clear to reveal a rippling Oceanic logo, which bursts into a school of fish that proceed to swim toward the camera and offscreen. Simple, right?

The Approach

One of the things that I think helps me the most in my animation work is my point of view. Coming from a traditional special-effects background, my way of thinking is rooted there, so most of the tools available to me in LightWave have "real-world" counterparts. When I start conceiving the approach I'll take on a project, I'm not thinking polygons. Generally, it's matte paintings, foreground miniatures and models. I don't know if it's a better approach, but it works for me. The Oceanic piece needed several elements and several programs. The plan was to render the background first, complete with all the small fish and residual animation. Then we'd render all the elements with alpha channels and composite them together. Before we were finished we had 12 layers of compositing.

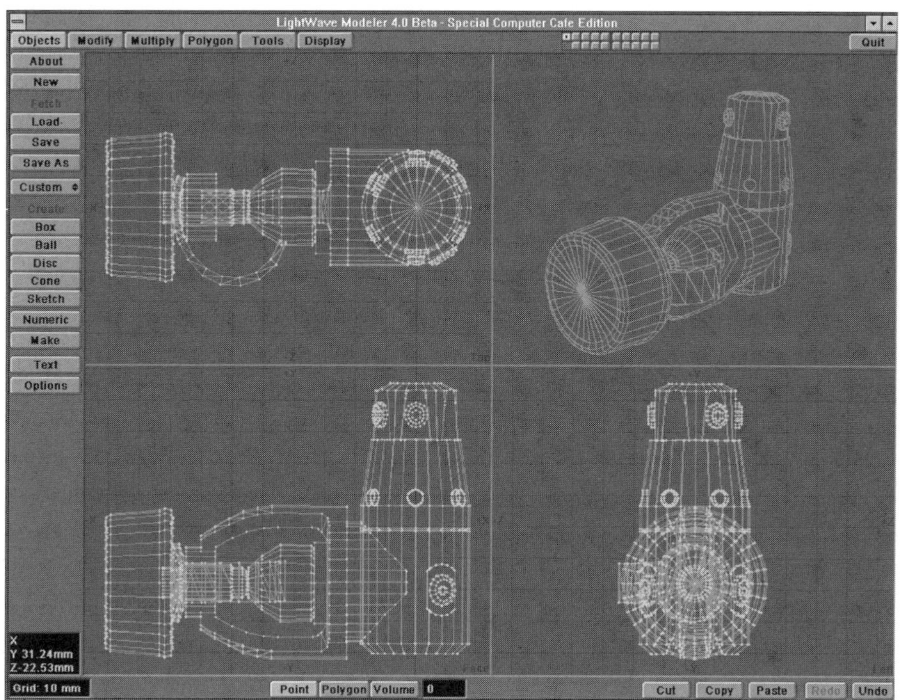

The 3D model of the first stage SCUBA regulator.

The Models

With the help of a stockpile of reference material, including actual dive equipment on loan from Oceanic, the modeling task began. While Dave Ebner started on the terrain, I began work on the diver. His equipment was first on my list. Using LightWave Modeler, I built everything to approximate scale. The diver was outfitted with a mask, regulator, BC vest, tank and fins. Using Tim Wilson's Humanoid as a base, we assembled the diver piece by piece. A null object was at the top of the hierarchy, allowing for gross repositioning without our worrying about any existing keyframes. The diver's hierarchy was the Humanoid default, with the equipment parented to the appropriate body parts. A portion of the diver that was particularly tricky was the air hose, which had to stay connected to both the first and second stages of the regulator. To do this we used a multi-segmented tube and parented it to the second stage (at the mouth). Then, using Bones, the tube was bent and carefully keyframed to stay connected to the first stage (at the tank). After all the pieces were in place, a scene was saved as "diver-master." Another cool piece was the Mako dive vehicle, which propels the diver through the scene. The model was built using splines. Starting with a cage generated by a macro, I refined the shape to make it pretty accurate. Once all the splines were finalized, I patched them, added some detail, and surfaced it. A propeller was also made and parented to the dive vehicle, then keyframed to spin. The dive vehicle proved to be a little tough to animate, since it was parented to the diver's right hand and the whole left arm had to track it. Having the actual dive vehicle for reference was invaluable. I can't imagine trying to model all those free-form curves with pictures. The spinner dolphin is a modified Viewpoint bottle-nosed dolphin object. (For more on stock objects, see Oct. 1995 *Video Toaster User*.) In addition to all these models there was a multitude of fish,

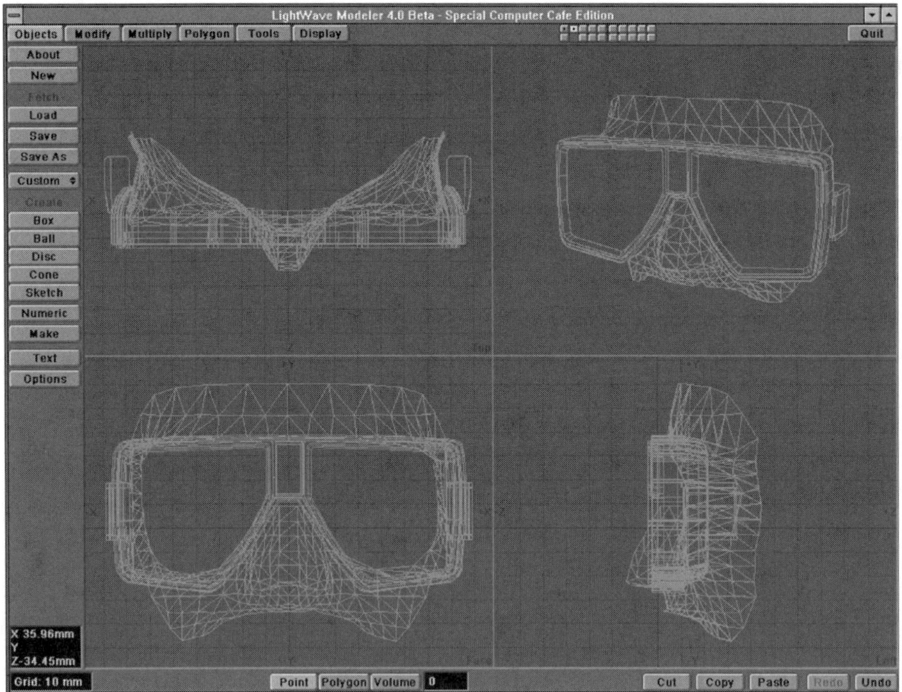

Having the Scuba mask model object saved time and made the job much easier.

coral, plant life and scenery generated by Dave and I. All of the models were surfaced as we went, using a lot of scans and maps painted in Opal Paint and rendering the images using Forge.

The Lighting

One aspect that improved the visual aesthetics and helped marry the composites was the lighting. To keep the lighting consistent, a base scene was made with the terrain and scenery and lit accordingly. Next, all the objects were removed but one null object, and the scene was saved again. After the animation was set for an element—the dolphin, for example—we simply loaded the "blank" scene (containing just the lights, fog and camera move), went to the Objects panel and loaded the dolphin from its scene. The caustics in the piece were done with LightWave's Underwater texture. After finding the right settings for the texture (following much experimentation), we applied those same settings to all objects. We used the texture in the luminosity setting of most of the surfaces with these values:

Texture type: Underwater
Texture size: 30.0, 30.0, 30.0
Texture center: 5.0, 0, 0
Texture fall-off: 0,0,0
Texture velocity: 0.005, -0.005, 0.005
World Coordinates: On
Texture value: 15% (slightly adjusted according to surface color)
Wave sources: 9
Wavelength: 0.75
Wave speed: 0.025
Band sharpness: 5.0

These settings were used on the separate elements as well, which helped unify the composites. The lights in the scene were minimal to keep it as realistic as we could (the client wanted everything bright and cheery, but realistic). The primary lights illuminating the scene were supposed to be the camera lights, so we had to parent the lights to the camera. To accomplish this we created a null object, called it "CamNull," parented both the camera and the lights to it, and animated the null object just like it was the camera. Other lights in the scene consisted of spotlights pointing up at the plane representing the water's surface, helping to simulate the sun high above, and a distant light for overall illumination.

The Morph

One of the hardest parts of this aquatic puzzle was the dolphin morphing into the diver, or the "dolpher," as it became known. It's also the piece I get the most questions about. Morphing in LightWave is usually pretty easy: just put two objects that meet the requirements (same point count and point ordering) in the scene, make a morph envelope, and voilà, morph city. However, what if you have a hierarchy and need to morph to a solid object? That's where you need 2D morph software. For our morph we began by animating the dolphin with Mark Miller's PowerMacro Snake and saved it in its own scene. Then we loaded our "blank" scene and loaded objects from the dolphin scene. Again, this gave us our lighting and camera move without all the scenery. Next, we rendered the dolphin, saving an alpha channel at the same time. At this point we moved on to the diver.

After loading the "blank" scene, we loaded objects from the "diver-master" scene. Using a background sequence of the dolphin frames, we carefully animated the diver, making sure to keep the morph in mind and the objects lined up. The diver was rendered and an alpha channel was saved at the same time. We then loaded the frames into Morph Plus and did the morph with that software. Once the first morph was completed on the frames, I built a custom morph project by copying the "dolpher" morph project, inserted a sequence of the alpha channel frames and rendered again. With the same vectors, the frames were identical and could be used just like a normal frame/alpha channel set.

The Animation

Along with the camera, dolphin and diver motion, there were a ton of other little things going on. The rays were animated using the PowerMacro "snake" again. This set of macros is great, and Mark was indispensable on this project. He must have made 10 custom revisions to his macros just for us.

A displacement map was used to make the rays swim. There was also the fish coming over the ridge. For these guys we used Jon Tindall's Sparks program and its "flock" option. The hard part was keeping the creatures on course up to the last second, and then having them scatter abruptly to avoid the "camera." After a few tests we locked it down. A lot of the more subtle animation was lost due to last-minute changes in the camera move, but there's still stuff all over the place, including waving plants, assorted little fish and a little crab. The crab was interesting. We were just going to use a little image of a crab with a clip map on a plane, and stick it in the background. As an experiment, I loaded the crab image into Morph Plus and did a still warp, trying to get his legs to move realistically. The results were better than anyone expected, so we put it in the foreground. Unfortunately, the client wanted us take it out, so we put it back in the background. It's still walking, but you can't see it!

The Bubbles

The bubbles turned out to be quite tedious as well. We used Sparks again for these. As anyone who has used Sparks will tell you, it's an incredibly powerful program, but it's not the most user-friendly application I've come across. To do the bubbles I tracked the regulator through the scene with a null object, and saved the motion file. Then, using Sparks, I created a scene using 600 points, five bubble objects, negative gravity (with no ground plane), random birthrate, recycling and a bunch of other parameters (I told you). The result was a scene file with 600 bubbles streaming out of an opening that wasn't there yet. Because the animation was random, we could just run it through three times, and we got three different layers of bubbles. We generated an additional scene with smaller bubbles, then image-processed it. This second scene was used for the gaseous cloud of tiny bubbles.

The School of Fish

After the bubbles clear, the rippling Oceanic logo is revealed. No tricks here, just some simple displacement. Then the logo bursts into a school of fish. A school of what? It seems so simple—just four words in the

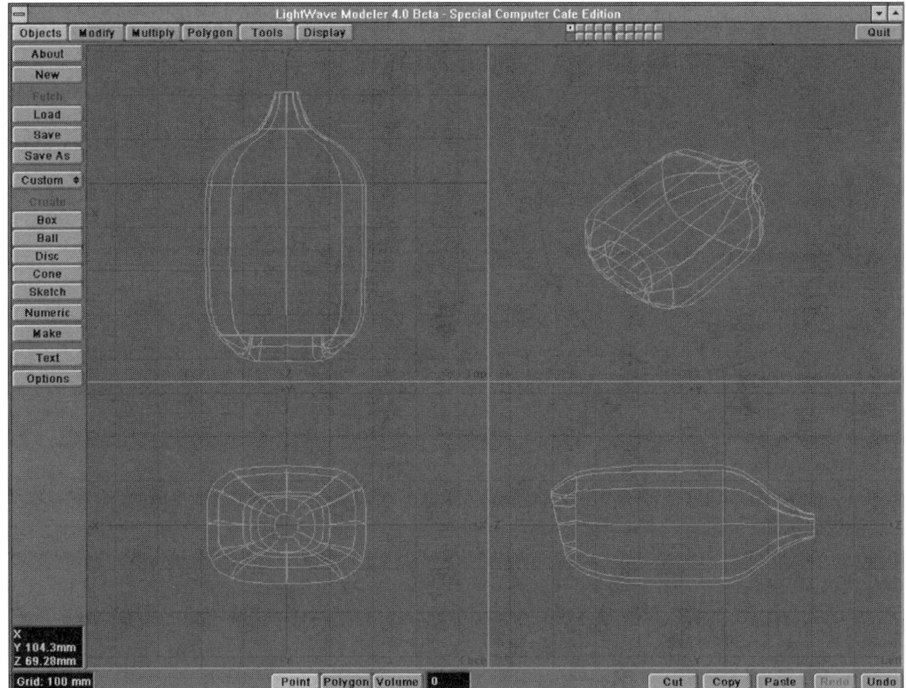

The spline cage used to generate the Mako dive vehicle.

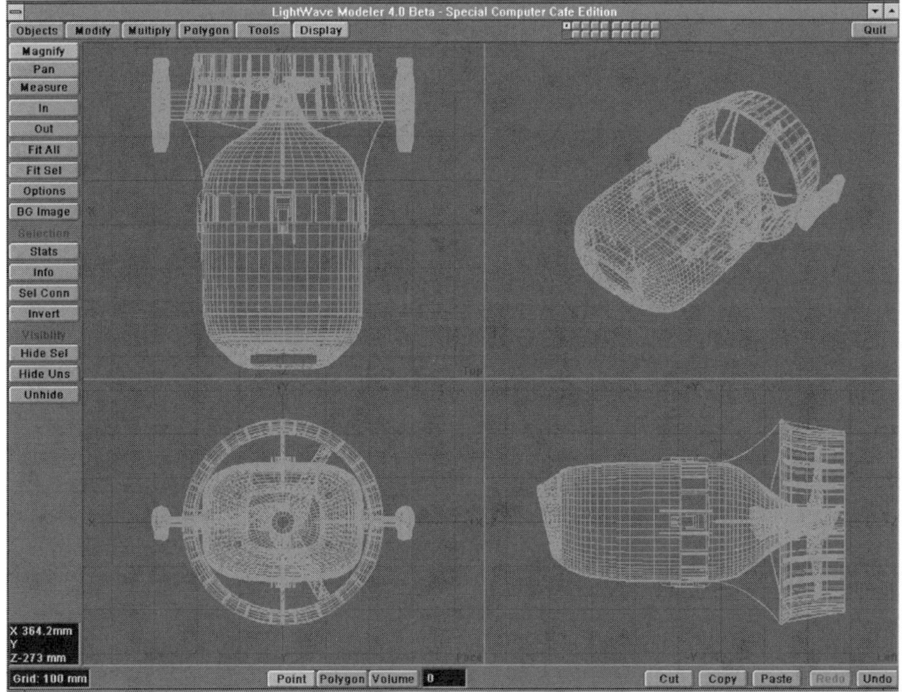

The finished Mako dive vehicle.

script—so why is it never as easy as it sounds? Well, we used the PowerMacros again for this one, namely "swarm." Mark came through for us on this effect again, modifying his macro to add the features we needed. We started with the logo, added 56 starter objects (outlining the logo) and oriented the starters the way we wanted the fish oriented. Next we added our attractors and one repulsor (the objects are drawn to attractors and repelled by repulsors). When we ran the macro, it created a scene with 56 fish facing the way we wanted. They started swimming on cue and went in the right direction. An animated wipe was used to reveal the fish, which began to swim as soon as they were visible.

The Compositing

After all the changes were made (and there were many) and rendering was complete, it was time to composite the over-3,200 frames. For the majority of the comps we used LightWave, loading the background sequence into the background and the elements with their corresponding alpha channels into the foreground. We composited the bubbles by transparency-mapping them on a plane in the foreground with the rendered sequence as a backdrop picture. By doing this, we were able to make small corrections to the color of the plane and its object dissolve, making it very easy to find the right balance.

Conclusion

Well, after three months, with a few other projects sprinkled in, we finished. After generating 75 scene files, over 200 objects and 120 brushmaps, filling up 2.5GB of disk space, and consuming two bottles of Tylenol, I was more than happy to see it end. But since then I've been able to step back and enjoy the piece. Being a perfectionist, I always see the little mistakes, but overall, it's a pretty cool spot I'm proud to have been a part of.

LWP

After a successful career in traditional special effects, Tom decided on a less toxic job and went to work for Santa Maria, Calif.–based Computer Café in mid-'93. His talents can be seen in over 20 films, including Speed, Hocus Pocus *and* Freaked. *He can be reached at (805) 922-9479, or by e-mail at tomcat@terminus.com.*

Displacement Envelopes

by Dan Ablan

One of the great things about LightWave 3D is, no matter how much or how often you use the program, there is always something else to discover. As soon as you think you've discovered all the tricks and techniques, surprisingly, another one pops up. With LightWave, you can always find new and exciting ways to create just about whatever you want.

The technique I'm going to talk about is no secret to many LightWave animators, but there are just as many who do not know about it. This undocumented method is great to know because of its many practical uses. Let's say you wanted to animate a leaf drifting onto a pond or pool of water. What would happen? The leaf would hit the water and a small ripple would start up, expand outward and then die down. How would you animate that? With a displacement map, of course. The problem is, how do you set an envelope to make that ripple start and then stop?

Huh?

Anywhere in LightWave where there's an envelope available, you see the ever-familiar **E** button. But, down near the **Displacement Map** section, under the **Objects** panel, there is only a **T** button, and no **E**. So what's up with that, you say? I've wondered myself.

Just below the **Displacement Map** section, there is the **Polygon Size** section. When a displacement map is set in conjunction with the polygon size button, you can set an envelope for any displacement map. The values in the polygon size window directly relate to the amplitude in a displacement map. This hidden feature of LightWave has been there since this program had the ability to displacement map.

So How Do You Do It?

The first step in this animation is to create the leaf. Probably the best way would be to get a leaf and scan it. Or grab a frame of one. If you are going to framegrab the leaf, place it under glass so it is nice and flat. Scanning in the leaf serves a dual purpose. The first is as an image map, and the second use is a template for building the leaf.

- Once you have the leaf captured, bring it into your favorite paint program for cleanup. I would recommend doing cleanup in Photoshop if you have access; otherwise, ToasterPaint will do the job. Black out the area outside of the leaf. Cut this out as a brush and then enter LightWave. If you use ToasterPaint, it is advisable to save the entire image, bring it into an image-processing program and crop it into the brush size you desire (ideally, right along the edges). This step is useful because of a problem with ToasterPaint brushes that manifests itself as black stripes along the edge of the brush in LightWave.
- Trace over the image in Modeler, first selecting **Load Image** in LightWave and then selecting your leaf image. From there, proceed to Modeler. Click on the **BG Image** button (**Display** menu). When the requester comes up, pull the top slider bar down and select your image. The image will show up here because it is loaded in LightWave. You can't directly load an image from Modeler.

Now you need to set your image up to trace over it.

- In the BG Image requester, click the **Z** axis, and in the size panels, choose 4 for X and 3 for Y.

The important thing is to keep the ratio set right. Before clicking OK, make note of the dark-to-light slider. You may need to adjust it, depending on how your image looks. Once you've clicked OK, the image will be in the Z view. Now all you need to do is place points around the leaf to create the polygon (Figure 1). Use the **Points** button in the **Polygon** menu.

- Once you've placed all the points around the leaf image, you can click **Make** (p) for a polygon, or hit **Ctrl-o** for a spline curve if your leaf image is curvy. When your points are in place with the spline curve, hit the **Freeze** button (**Tools** menu or Ctrl-d) to make it a polygon. It'll be a big leaf, so you should scale it down to about 100 mm.

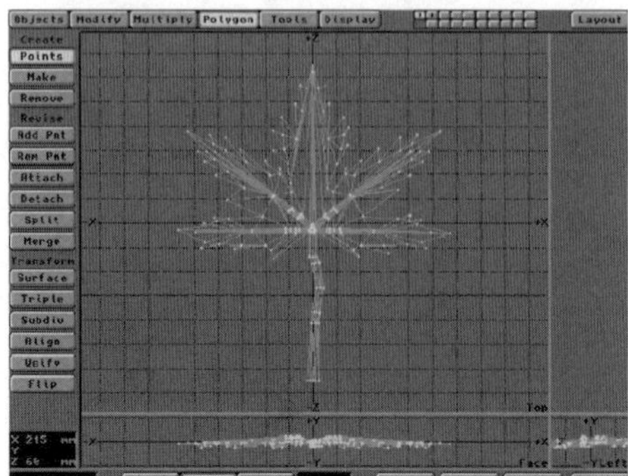

Figure 1

I was really short on time when putting this article together, so I cheated and used the Maple Leaf object from the LIGHT-ROM CD. Not to mention, it's winter in Chicago, and a good leaf is pretty hard to find this time of year. If you already have a leaf object, use that.

- Center the object by using the F1 key, the center macro that came with Modeler. You may want to slightly **Bend** (**Modify** menu) the object upward to give it a nice look when it's falling toward the water.
- Once you've built the leaf and like how it looks, give it a **Surface** name (q) and **Export** it to Layout.
- Go to LightWave, select a Surface Color texture (**T**) and select a planar image map using the leaf image on the **Z axis**. By clicking **Automatic Sizing**, you should have no trouble lining up the leaf image (assuming it was scanned or framegrabbed) with the polygon—if you built it precise enough. If you see dark edges or seams, simply adjust the size of the image map, and possibly move the **Texture Center** of the image.

Now you have a leaf. You should consider going back later, to create a bump map for the veins in the leaf. Also, subdivide your object so you can add Bones for a flowing look, or add a fractal bump displacement map with **World Coordinates** turned on. This would cause the leaf surface to fluctuate as it moved throughout the scene.

Bring Me Some Water

The next step is to make the liquid that the leaf will fall into.

- Back in Modeler, with your leaf object in a background layer, zoom out using the comma key to about four times the size of the leaf, or a 500 mm grid.
- Draw out a box in the top view, with 20 segments on the X and Z. Next, **triple** the flat box. You may want to **Subdivide** (**Polygon** menu) just once to get nice smooth ripples in LightWave.

•The water object should contain about 3,200 polygons (Figure 2). Your surface is likely facing down, and you'll need to have it facing up: use the (f) key to **Flip** any polygons that are not facing up. Then, give it a surface name of "water." **Export** this to LightWave.

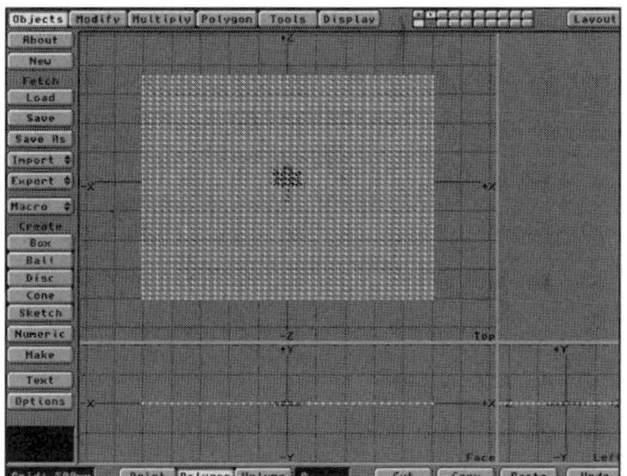

Figure 2

Surfacing the water is up to you. I chose to give it a dark, silky look rather than a shiny, sky-blue look. You can make it red if you want—it doesn't really matter for this tutorial.

To set up your animation, the first thing you should do is **Move** the camera to a point above the water from which there is a decent perspective.

The camera settings I came up with for position are 1.562, .860, -1.489. For rotation: -49.2, 40.6, 0.0.

You don't have to use these exact numbers. The idea is to have a good vantage point to see the leaf fall onto the water. Your camera position should look something like Figure 3.

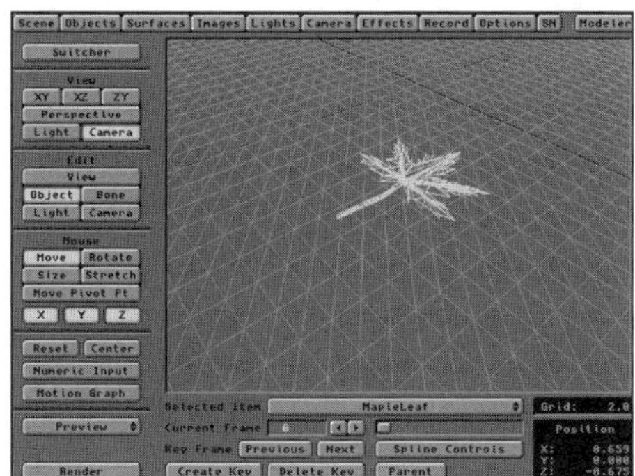

Figure 3

- **Move** your leaf to just outside of the camera view. Select **Create Key** and construct a key for it at frame 0. Now move it down on the Y until it's just above the water, actually sitting on it. Create a key at 90 or so, depending on how long you want it to fall. Then move the leaf toward the edge of the screen, on either the X or Z only, and create another key at 160. This means that the leaf falls and gently floats away.
- To really make this work, set a **Spline Control** at frame 90 when it lands, so it looks realistic. By setting a **Bias** of **-.5**, the motion path for the leaf will be soft and smooth. However, the motion of your leaf, when viewed from the side, curves under the water. At about frame 110, you can create a key, and move the leaf up so it's still sitting on the water.

If a leaf fell onto the water, it would create a gentle ripple that would swell up, then die down. In LightWave, you could use a bump map, but a displacement map will truly be 3D. The problem is making the ripple swell over time. As I mentioned, using polygon size with a displacement map creates an envelope for displacement maps. The polygon size value determines the amplitude of the displacement map. The first thing to set in this situation is the displacement map. Use these settings:

Texture Type	Ripples
Size	1.0, 1.0, 1.0
Texture Center	.646, .02, -0.75
Amplitude	.06
Wave Sources	1
Wave Length	.7
Wave Speed	.025

The texture center in my animation has been moved to these settings, because that's where I chose to have my leaf land, at frame 90. You can move your texture center to where you decide to have your leaf fall, or use the above texture center values as the position for your leaf at frame 90.

Now that you've set the displacement map, it's time to make it start up and then stop. The amplitude for the displacement map is .06. The **Polygon Size** value that equals that amplitude is 6%. If you set a polygon size of 10%, your amplitude would be .10.

- In the Polygon Size envelope window, create a key at 90, 110, 140 and 160. At 0, the polygon size value is 0%. At 90, it is also 0%, because the leaf is just landing on the water. Once it lands, the ripple begins, so at 100, set the polygon size value to 6%. A real-world ripple would stay for a second or two, so set a value of 6% at the keyframe 140. After 140, you want the ripple to die down, so at frame 160, your value should again be 0% (Figure 4). Remember, splines also work here, so a tension setting for the ripple beginning and ending may be a good idea.

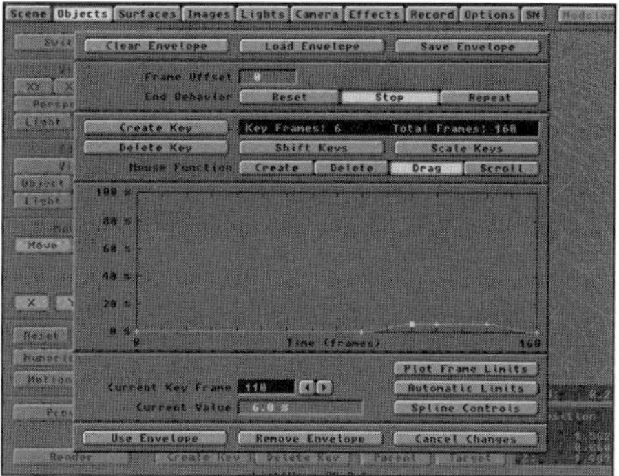

Figure 4

In the colored pages, Falling Leaves shows the leaf as it is about to hit the pool. Notice how the water is calm. The second image of the sequence shows frame 110 after the leaf has hit and the ripple has begun. The final picture shows frame 160, where the leaf has slid away and the ripple has died down. You should also consider morphing the leaf when it hits the water and travels over the ripples, so it "sticks" to the water.

Other Ideas

This is just one example of what you could do with this technique. Another idea is a pot of water on a stove that needs to boil, or a hot tub's bubble jets getting turned on or off. You may even be so daring as to apply this to a logo. It creates a really cool organic look when applied to objects that one wouldn't expect to ripple. And ripples aren't the only texture type you can use: fractal bumps work great, as would any image map. Displacement envelopes applied to different objects may just give the impression of a highly sophisticated morph.

LightWave is a fantastic program. There is always something else to learn about, experiment with and discover. By finding out more about what LightWave can do and using the different techniques and tricks together, you can create animations above and beyond what you thought you'd ever be able to do. Think big.

LWP

Dan Ablan animates full-time with LightWave for AGA, his Chicago-based company. Recent animations include work for Kraft Foods and Arthur Anderson Co. He can be reached at (312) 239-7957 or on the Internet at dma@mcs.com.

Simple Refraction

Creating a Realistic Magnifying Glass

by Dan Ablan

When people think of refraction, most don't consider it a part of everyday 3D jobs. But, if you look around you, many things refract. Incorporating this quality into your animations will bring you one step closer to achieving total realism.

Ever since I fell into 3D animation, I've been like a sponge. Everything having anything to do with 3D, whether high-end or low-end systems, intrigues me—especially when it comes to LightWave. There have been a few animations that, though relatively simple, had some ideas that were so effective, one would wonder how you could overlook such a great idea. With this tutorial, you'll create a magnifying glass, but you could use the following steps for eyeglasses, telescopes, binoculars, etc.

LightWave is great for many reasons, but one that I particularly admire is its ability to mimic real-world properties. This magnifying glass idea has always been in the back of my mind, and finally, one day, I decided to try it. In about five minutes, I had the look I was after. Later, I worked a little harder and longer on the idea, and thanks to LightWave, made a pretty convincing magnifying glass. As with just about anything in LightWave, by setting up objects, images and lights as you would in a real setting, you can pull off what the *Revolution* tape called "image miracles." Enough jabber, though—on with the tutorial.

For the magnifying glass, let's begin in Modeler.

Making The Glass

Whenever you model anything, it is always best to have that thing right in front of you, or at least a photograph of it. You may know exactly how something looks, but once you've modeled it, for some reason, it just doesn't look right. When you actually get a hold of that thing you modeled, you see the very subtleties that make that thing unique. It's the same for a magnifying glass. Yes, I know exactly how it should look, but, inevitably, it just doesn't look right if I build it from memory. By having a real magnifying glass in front of me, I can see the proportions, surfaces, and most importantly, how it reacts to its surroundings. Since I've built a magnifying glass already, you don't have to run out and get one for this tutorial.

- Clear out Modeler by clicking **New** (**Objects** menu or N). The first thing to do is build the glass. If you had that magnifying glass in front of you, you'd see that the glass portion is convex, like a contact lens. This is very important to model correctly because its shape, with refraction and the right surface properties, determines how realistic it will look when rendered. I wanted the glass to curve outward, so I chose to use the **Magnet** tool.
- First, create a disc in the Face view. Use the numeric requester and enter the following settings in **mm**:

Sides	40
Segments	1
Axis	Z
Center	0, 0, 0
Radii	1.5, 1.5, 0

Click **OK**, then the (a) key to fit all views.

- In another layer, create a box, using these settings with the numeric requester:

Low	-2.5, -2, 0
High	2.5, 2, 0
Segments	X = 20, Y = 20

The box will be used to create an even template to make the disc malleable.

- Go back to layer one and select layer two (the box layer) as your background. Pull out the face window view for a larger work area. **Extrude** the disc just 1 mm and then center it on the Z axis. (If you have not changed Modeler's config file, your F2 key should be center on one axis macro.)
- Choose **Boolean** (B) from the **Tools** menu and click **Intersect**. If you come up with extra points and your disc is not flat, delete the points that are off of 0, on the -Z axis.

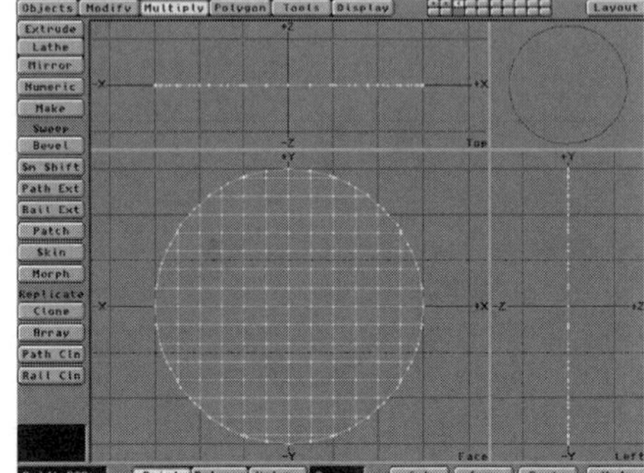

Figure 1

In a minute or so, you should have a disc that is made up of even polygons in the X and Y axes (Figure 1). The reason it's done this way that because by tripling and subdividing just a disc, you'd get a mess of uneven polygons, and it would be hard to use, and...well, it's a mess. Anyway, once the disc is made, save it as "disc flat." You won't need to use it like this in Layout; we're saving it just in case.

- Under the **Modify** menu, select the Magnet tool. With the left mouse button, drag out to cover the whole disc (Figure 2). Next, with the right mouse button, from the top view, drag out just a little, and you'll see the disc begin to curve outward. The larger the magnet area

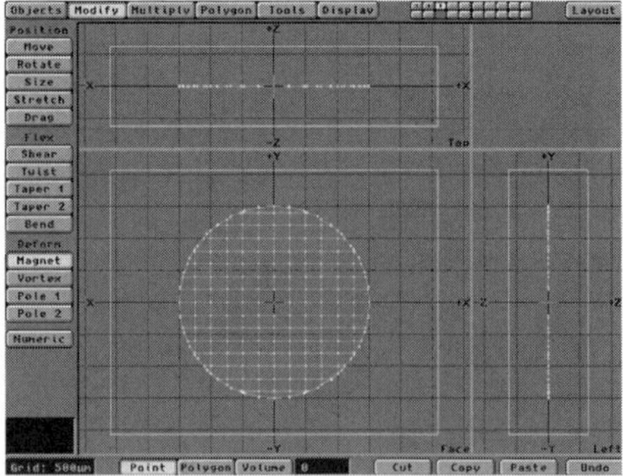

Figure 2

(left mouse), the larger the influence (right mouse) will be. You should end up with a disc that looks something like Figure 3. Save it as "disc magnet." Again, you won't need this particular piece in Layout, but if you screw up, or crash, it's much easier to reload this object, and later delete it, than to go through the steps again.

- Now, give the disc the surface name "glass." Then, using the **Mirror** tool under the **Multiply** menu, mirror the curved disc against itself so you have a two-sided curve (Figure 4). **Merge** points (m) to get rid of any duplicate points. **Save** this as "mag.glass."
- Now you need to build the edge of the magnifying glass that holds the lens in place. In a clean layer, make a disc using the numeric requester and these settings in **mm**:

Sides	40
Segments	1
Axis	Z
Center	0, 0, 0

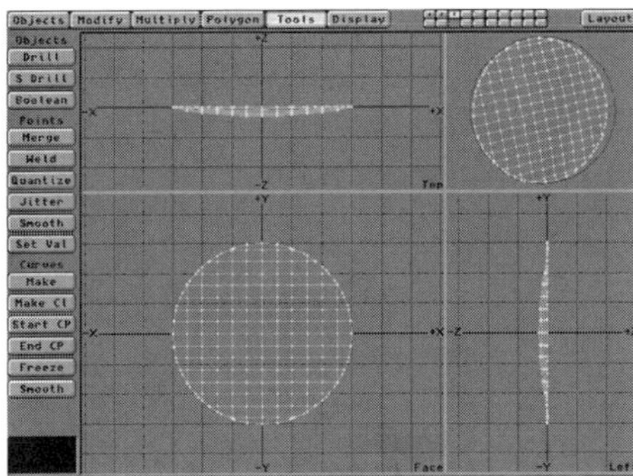

Figure 3

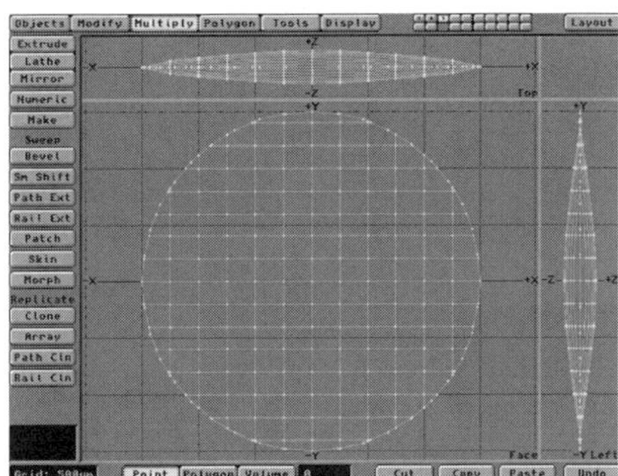

Figure 4

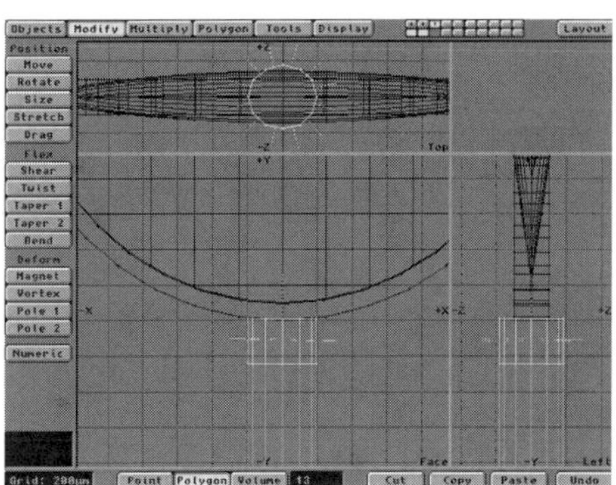

Figure 5

Figure 6: Using the proper refraction settings, a magnifying glass enlarges what's behind it.

Figure 7: As the magnifying glass gets closer to the object, it magnifies less, as would a real magnifying glass.

X	1.6
Y	.6
Z	0

- Copy this disc to another layer. Select **Size** (H) from the **Modify** menu and click **Numeric** (n). Enter **Factor** of 0.94 to scale it down just a bit. Next, **Extrude** (**Multiply** menu) it .2 mm on the Z axis. Finally, center it on the Z axis.
- Go back to the layer that has the larger disc and put the smaller extruded disc in the background layer. Select **Boolean** from the **Tools** menu (B) and hit **Subtract**. When the hole has been cut in the larger flat disc, **Extrude** it .2 mm on the Z axis. Center it on the Z axis, and give the hole a **Surface** name of edge. Finally, save it.

Now all that is left is the neck and handle. You can model these in the same step, by making one disc and surfacing two different areas. I made mine look like a fancy wood-type handle, but for now, just make a disc.

- Select **Disc**, and using the numeric requester, enter these settings in **mm**:

Sides	12
Segments	2
Bottom	-4.7
Top	-1.59
Axis	Y
Center	0,-3.145,0
Radii	0.195,1.555,0.18

- Using the right mouse button, select the center points with the lasso feature. Move these points to about -1.84 mm to create the neck area of the handle (Figure 5). Next, select just those polygons using the lasso tool again (right mouse button) and surface them as "neck." Surface the remainder of the handle as "handle." Save this, too.
- Now it's time to put it all together. The best way to join the pieces is through the Boolean operations. However, you can copy and paste all items to the same layer. Once you have all the pieces together, hit the (m) key to merge points. Export this object to layout, saving it as "MagnifyGlass."

Making It Work

Surfacing this thing is relatively simple. Place your favorite wood surface or image around the handle and use a silver/metal surface for the neck and edge. The glass is also easy. Use these settings:

Texture Color	172, 187, 200
Diffusion	95
Specularity	75
Glossiness	High
Reflective	5
Reflected Image	Fractal Reflections
Transparency	95
Refractive Index	1.55
Smoothing	On
Max Smoothing Angle	10

- Under the **Camera** menu, turn on **Trace Refraction**. Set the render resolution to Low for quick render tests. Refraction is the key here. As the magnifying glass is closer to the camera and farther away from another object, it will appear very magnified, as in the color image (Figure 6). I chose to just use a scan of a $5 bill as an object. You could use a scan of a page of words, a table with many objects spread across it, or a newspaper.
- As the magnifying glass gets closer to the object, it doesn't magnify as much (Figure 7). If you have a magnifying glass near you, look through it, and move it toward and away from a piece of paper on your desk. See how it reacts? It's the same in LightWave. The only difference is that you can't start a campfire in LightWave with a concentrated light source.

Refraction is interesting. To make it work properly in LightWave, you usually need more than one refraction index on the same object. Light enters one part of the object, refracts, travels through another part, and leaves through yet another. Realistically, you should have a refraction setting for each part, but this magnifying glass isn't quite thick enough to warrant that. If you were modeling a glass of water, however, you would set refraction for where the light enters, the water, and where the light leaves. [Ed itor's note: For a more detailed description of refraction properties, see Mark Thompson's "Understanding Refraction," *LWPRO*, January '95]

Other Ideas

I recently saw a great animation from a company in Europe. Called "Invisible Man," it was black and white and had a terrific idea. In one part of the piece, the invisible man pulls a pair of glasses out of a desk drawer and proceeds to put them on. You (the camera) are watching this move from the character's perspective. When he brings the glasses up to his face (camera view), you see the objects on the desk in front of him enlarge and slightly deform, just as if you were actually putting on a pair of glasses. The above steps could be used the same way for building a pair of glasses, or a telescope. Or how about a pair of binoculars? Even if you only do logos with LightWave, why not have a magnifying glass travel across the logo, instead of a typical glint of light?

With your eyes open, watching real-world properties, plus a basic understanding of LightWave, you can create those "image miracles." It's those little differences that will really make your animations stand out.

Dan Ablan is a LightWave animator for AGA, based in Chicago. He can be reached at (312) 239-7957 or via Internet at dma@mcs.com.

Faking Refraction
A Great Timesaver

by Dan Ablan

If you're like most animators, achieving great realism is a real challenge. One way to create that look you want is to use refraction. You've seen Allen Hastings' 2.0 Kiki Image, in which he used refraction for a glass of whiskey... so why not include refraction in your animations? LightWave certainly has the power, but do you have the time? Probably not. Here is a way that you can give the appearance of refraction without ever turning it on.

About eight months ago, while waiting for an animation to finish rendering, I began surfing through the cable channels. I came across an old episode of *Man From Atlantis*. I hadn't seen this show since the days of *That's Incredible!* and *The Incredible Hulk*. Also around that time, I had been paying close attention to the *seaQuest* animations. All of this gave me an idea to create an underwater city, or perhaps, rebuild the lost city of Atlantis.

After briefly storyboarding this animation short, I began working on the title. The idea was to have the title words floating up to the surface of the ocean, with the camera placed above the water. This was going to require using refraction in the animation. I had worked with refraction before, using settings primarily for glass. I knew the rendering time would increase with **Trace Refraction** turned on, but had no idea just how long it would take. Another major problem I ran into was the distortion involved. The water refraction index is 1.33, which adds great realism to a scene, but when you're trying to figure out what you're looking at through the refraction, it becomes difficult to read. Fortunately, I discovered a way to achieve the look I was after without using refraction. Not only was the rendering time significantly decreased, but the words did not break apart as they did using true refraction. When animated, the words appear to be under a flowing water surface.

Figure 1

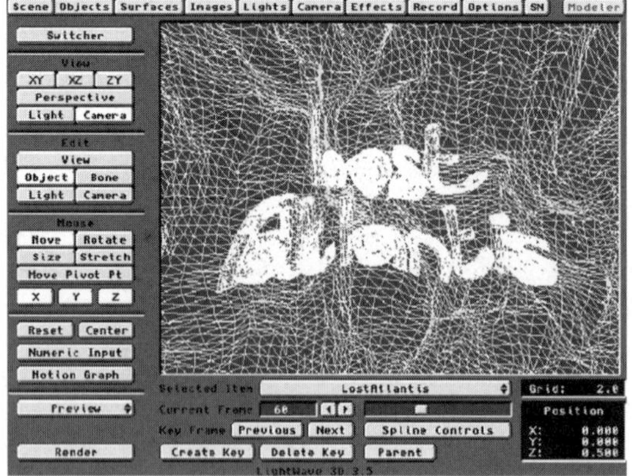

Figure 2

Making the Objects

The first thing to do is enter Modeler. Under the **Objects** menu, click on the **Text** button (W). Load the Acropolis font from The Font Bank A-C directory [Editor's note: If you own a LightWave without a Toaster, you will not have this font. Use a similar font].

Enter "Lost" in the Text field and select **OK**. In another layer, type "Atlantis". Then, select your first layer as the background layer. This allows you to position the Atlantis text, centered, under Lost, using the **Move** function (**Modify** menu). Once in position, copy Atlantis from its layer and paste it into the first layer. Now center the text object by using the Center macro.

Click on the **Multiply** menu and choose **Extrude**. Click **Numeric** (n) and enter Segment of 1, Extent 200; Axis Z; units are cm. Click **OK**. Select **Make** (Return key) to extrude the text. Select **Surface** from the **Polygon** menu and create a surface called "LA_sides" for all of the polygons.

The face needs to be given a different surface name, so click on the **Polygon** select button at the bottom of the screen. In the Left window, use the right mouse button to lasso just the front of the object (Figure 1). This will select the 14 front facing polygons. Now select from the **Surface** again, and create a surface called "LA_fronts". Save this object as "LostAtlantis_ORIG".

The above steps could be accomplished a bit more easily by loading the Acropolis font and then using the Text macro to create, center and extrude the text all in one operation. This also has the advantage of naming the side polygons differently from the front and back polygons.

The next step is to create the flat plane which will become the water. In a new layer, zoom out by using the , key so that you're working with a **1 Meter grid**. Select **Box** (Objects menu). Click on **Numeric** (n), and enter the following:

	X	Y	Z
Low	2.5	2	0
High	2.5	2	0

Segments should all be 1, and units should be set to meters. Hit **OK**, then Make or Return to create the plane.

Since we are going to use a displacement map to make the water flow, we'll need more polygons in our water. Under the **Polygon** menu, select **Triple** (T) button. Then, click on **Subdiv** (D), **Faceted** and **OK**. Now subdivide five more times so that you have 8,192 polygons, which will make the water very smooth, and prevent break ups when rendering. Name this surface "LA_water".

Now use the export feature under the objects menu, to save and put the object in layout. Save this as "LostAtlantis_water". If we were to render the Lost Atlantis logo with the water now, refraction would have to be used to make it appear bent. Since we don't want to use refraction, there's one more step. Go back to the layer that has the Lost Atlantis object. We want to Triple and Subdivide this object. Again, select **Triple**. Now **Subdiv**, but only once. This process takes a few minutes, but you're going to save a great deal of time rendering. [Editor's note: It will take a long time to triple and subdivide this object, but be patient; your machine has not crashed.) Once you've tripled and subdivided the Lost Atlantis logo, **Export** this to Layout, saving it as "LostAtlantis".

Setting It Up

Back in Layout, the first thing you'll need to do is position the camera, but before that, set your camera **Zoom Factor** (**Camera** panel) to 2.0. This helps with the desired effect by giving a slightly wider angle to the camera view. Make sure you are in the Camera view mode and select **Camera** as the edit item. Click on **Move**, and hit the **Numeric Input** button (n). Move the camera on the Z axis to -3.0 and create a key at frame 0.

Now select the Lost Atlantis object as the edit item. **Move** this to .8,.68,2. Now **Rotate** the object to 20,26.8,0. Create a key for this at frame 0. Set the Tension (**Spline Controls**) to 1.0.

Next, go to frame 60, move the object to 0,0,.5. Rotate it to 0,0,0 and create a key at frame 60. Set the Tension to 1.0. Now would be a good time to save this scene. But before you do, change the last frame to 160.

For the heart of this scene, we're going to make the water flow, as well as the object.-, as if you were looking at it through refracted water. In the **Objects** panel, make sure the Water object is selected as the current object. Click the **T** button next to Displacement Map and choose Fractal Bumps as the Texture Type. Then set the following:

Texture Size	.8,1.2,1
Texture Velocity	.01,.03,.02
Texture Amplitude	0.275
Frequency	3

All other values can be left at their defaults. When all the values are input, click on **Use Texture**.

Now select the Lost Atlantis object as your current object. Again, choose Displacement Map and Fractal Bumps. Use the exact same settings on the logo, as we did for the water and select **Use Texture**.

By using the same amount of bumps and the same movement for both objects, we've created the feeling that the rippling of the water is causing the logo to be distorted as it moves up to the surface (Figure 2). With proper surfacing, and identical movements, in the water and logo, we'll have the appearance of a logo under the surface. The advantage is no refraction and plenty of rendering time saved.

Figure 3 shows the text object before it was subdivided and rendered with refraction. On my A2000, '040 with 18MB of RAM, running LightWave 3.5, this frame took 33 minutes and 41 seconds. Figure 4 shows the subdivided object using the same surface settings and lighting. By using the subdivided object and turning off refraction, a similar look is achieved and is easier to read, yet this frame took only 10 minutes and 23 seconds to render. This means that our 160-frame animation will take only 27 hours to render, in medium resolution with low antialiasing, whereas the refracted animation would have taken 89 hours to render.

Figure 3

Figure 4

Final Thoughts

The last thing to be done is setting the surfaces. The only crucial part is the water. It needs to be transparent, obviously, so that the Lost Atlantis logo can be seen. Set the water surface to the following:

Color	200,200,200
Luminosity	0%
Diffusion	100%
Specularity	90%
Glossiness	High
Transparency	80%
Smoothing	On

In order to make the rest of the frame appear to be "sea-like," just set the **Solid Backdrop** colors to 30,170,205 (**Effects** panel). This will simply give a sea water color to the area behind the logo (see Faked Refraction in the color pages). For the surfaces on the logo, you may choose whatever you like. I added the underwater surface supplied with LightWave, with some color and size modifications, to simulate shadows of the water moving across the logo, as the water moves above. I gave my edges a slight bit of luminosity, about 50 percent, and some fractal noise to dirty it up. Also, you may run into trouble with shadow mapping in this scene. If so, turn off **Self Shadow** for the water-plane object, in the Objects panel.

When everything is surfaced to your liking, make sure to **Save All Objects** (**Objects** panel) and make a wireframe preview to see the movements. You may want to adjust your logo's movement. You may also consider slightly banking the camera, throughout the animation, to create more of a sea-like motion.

This is just one area of LightWave which offers the power to achieve greater realism. Hopefully, this article has provided some ideas to help work around major render times using refraction. By considering all of LightWave's features, you can save enormous amounts of time and energy while creating new and exciting animations.

After five years in the video production business, Dan Ablan now animates full time using LightWave. His company, AGA, was started in January 1993. He can be reached at (312) 239-7957.

Interactive Refraction

by Colin Cunningham

Computer-generated imagery has come a long way in the past few years, from the watery pseudopod in *The Abyss* to the Tex Avery-inspired nuttiness in *The Mask*.

The one element these films share is the seamless integration of computer graphics (CG) and live action. CG compositing is, in itself, an art form requiring a good eye and loads of patience.

With LightWave, animators have at their disposal an arsenal of tools to make this task less daunting. Shows like *seaQuest DSV* and *Babylon 5* have often made good use of LightWave's compositing tools to blend CG elements into a real environment, but generally remain in the 3D realm. On *RoboCop: The Series*, however, marrying LightWave elements with live action was a daily task involving 80 cans of Coca-Cola and a ton of raw meat (I won't go into details).

You've heard it all before, I'm sure: "Match-lighting, THIS..." and "Front projection mapping, THAT...". There are many articles available on CG compositing and you're probably all experts in the field by now, so before you think I've gone a bit screwy, read on.

The truth is, basic compositing is pretty much straightforward: use your video or film footage as a background image sequence and render your objects directly on top. Simple, right? Of course you'll probably have to match the lighting or cut a matte for your CG elements to move behind, but in the hands of a talented artist, there shouldn't be much to worry about aside from being time-consuming.

LightWave made it easy for the effects team at *RoboCop: The Series* to add 3D choppers and sometimes people into scenes convincingly; even my mom couldn't tell the difference (maybe she was just being nice). We did, however, run into problems trying to composite refractive elements over live action. Let me explain.

Know Your Physics

In episode No. 16, "Sisters in Crime," RoboCop battles evil and injustice within Delta City's corporate sector. More specifically, this episode called for Robo's holographic sidekick, Diana (played by Andrea Roth), to become engulfed in a syrupy, amber goop that would eventually harden into a crystalline tomb. Not only did the blob have to refract its surroundings, it also had to bulge and twist convincingly as Diana struggled to free herself from its sticky grasp.

Now some of you already know that refracting a background image/sequence is not as easy as it sounds, and I'll be the first to agree with you: it's not. For the other 90 percent who are probably scratching their heads right about now, here's a little experiment you may want to try when you have some free time on your hands.

Upon entering Layout, load your favorite framestore and select it as a background image through the Effects panel. Next, load a simple object like a sphere and position it centrally within the camera's view so we get a nice look at it. For our experiment, we'll need to give this object some refractive qualities; the following is a nice glass surface I've used from time to time:

GLASS	
Color	225,225,225
Specularity	95%
Glossiness	High
Reflectivity	15%
Transparency	98%
Color Filter	ON
Refractive Index	1.51

It would be a good idea to save this surface, as you'll need it later. The default lighting will do just fine for this scene, but turn on **Trace Refraction** (Camera panel) and hit **Render**. Notice anything interesting? You shouldn't have to look very closely to see that our glass sphere isn't refracting the background. The background may be tinted slightly through the sphere, but the image hasn't been distorted in any way.

The reason for this is that, simply put, the background doesn't exist. Sure, you can see it, but it isn't really there (now I've completely lost it, right?). No matter how many objects you place in your scene or how far you position them from the camera, they will always appear in front of the background image. This is because LightWave places the background layer at an infinite distance from the camera so that objects can simply be rendered on top in one step without having to composite.

The one thing I do remember from Mr. McSharry's physics class (aside from the fact that some things don't react well to open flame) is that calculations for refraction rely on the precise locations of objects, and since there is no measurable distance for our background image, LightWave does what it should and renders the sphere without any refractive qualities. It would appear as if we're in a bit of a rut, but then things are not always as they appear.

Building a Virtual Screen

In order to make the sphere refract our background, we must give the image physical qualities that LightWave can work with. The simplest way of doing this is to map the image onto a 3D object. Not any old polygon will do, mind you—we need a polygon perfectly sized to fit the camera's viewing area. This way, our rendered image will be indistinguishable from the original framestore.

- Enter Modeler and select the Box button in the Objects menu. Select Numeric.

The aspect ratio of a Toaster framestore is 1.346. This means the screen is 1.346 units wide by 1 unit high; the units aren't really important, only the ratio. Knowing this:

- Make a box that is 2.692 meters wide (1.346 x 2) by two meters high (it's important for this tutorial that we use meters) by entering the following values in the Box Numeric requester:

  Low
  X= -1.346
  Y= -1.0
  Z= 0.0

  High
  X= 1.346
  Y= 1.0
  Z= 0.0

Leave the number of segments set to 1 for X, Y and Z. Since we'll only be seeing this polygon from the front, it doesn't need depth, which is why there is 0 for the Z values.

- Press **OK** and then **Make** or return to make the box.
- With our "screen" hot off the assembly line, it

would be a good idea to name its surface to avoid confusion later on. To do this, hit q for **Surface** (**Polygon** menu) and enter "SCREEN". Press return to change the surface name.

- Save the object as "Screen.obj".

While we're in Modeler, create a simple cube using the Box tool again. Dimensions aren't important right now (we'll be re-sizing it later); just make sure to press f to flip the polygons so that they face inward. Next, change the surface name to "Box" as mentioned above and save the object. Don't worry if you're confused—I'll explain what this is all about later. Now go back to the Layout. Pretty simple so far, wouldn't you say?

STEP-BY-STEP

- Build the screen & Box
- Name the surfaces and save each one
- Position the screen in Layout
- Map background image onto screen
- Position objects and lights
- Position box around all objects
- Map image onto sides of box
- RENDER AWAY

Positioning our Screen

- Load the screen object just created.

This next step is crucial. If the screen is not positioned exactly right, our background image may appear slightly larger or smaller than it should be. It's doubtful that even those with a keen eye will ever notice that your background image is sized incorrectly, mainly because they don't have the original image for comparison. Because of this, you have some room for error, but for me, this wasn't an option, as I had to precisely rotoscope my blob to the actress' movements.

Positioning the screen can be done two ways: the hard way and the easy way. The hard way involves rendering your screen object with a framestore mapped onto it and comparing the render to the original framestore. By switching between the two very quickly, you'll notice any discrepancies and reposition your screen accordingly. Although somewhat accurate, this technique is nothing more than a time waster, and the last thing you have to waste in this industry is time.

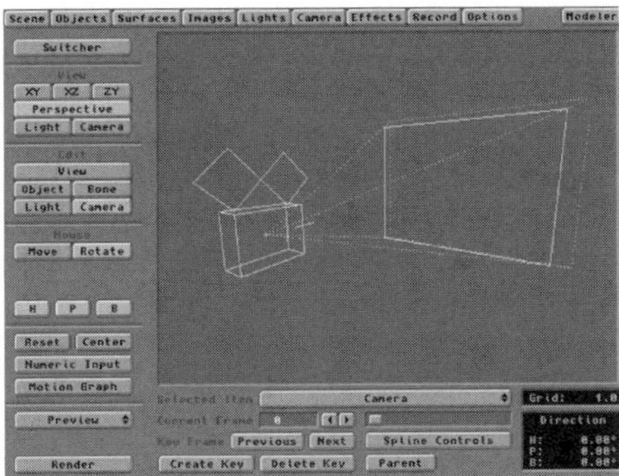

Figure 1: By following a few simple steps, the screen object can be positioned perfectly within the camera's view.

I bet you're just itching to know the easy way, so I won't keep you in suspense.

- Load the screen object into layout and position the camera at 0,0,0.
- Next, enter the **Camera** menu and note the camera **Zoom Factor** (the default is 3.2). Enter that value as the screen object's Z position and make a keyframe for the screen by hitting the return key twice. Presto! Our screen is now positioned so that it will precisely fit the boundaries of our camera view (Figure 1).

You can run the comparison test I mentioned above but I'll save you time and tell you not to bother, it's 100 percent accurate. It would be a really good idea to save this scene now so it can be used as a template for any future projects.

Now that the screen is in the right place, it's time to map something onto it (you wouldn't want to refract default gray, would you?).

- Load your favorite framestore and enter the **Surfaces** panel.
- Select the SCREEN surface that was named earlier and select the **T** button next to Surface Color.
- Use the **Planar Image Map** texture to map the framestore onto the screen along the **Z Axis**. Don't forget to click on **Automatic Sizing** before returning to the Surfaces panel.
- Set the Luminosity to 100 percent and the Diffuse Level value to 0 percent so it won't be affected by any lights in the scene.

Now let's retry our original experiment to make sure we've done things right.

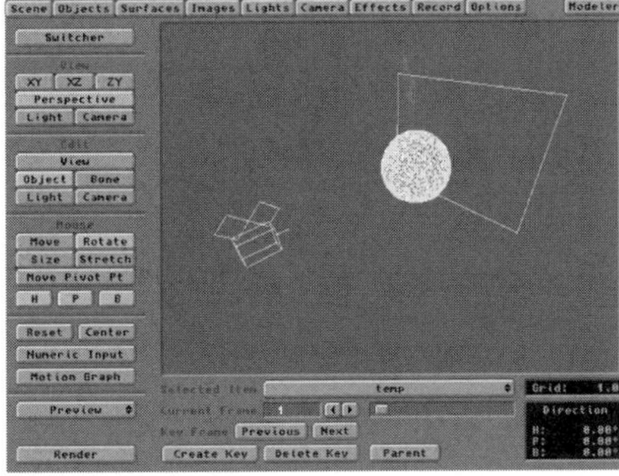

Figure 2: Because of the limited scene area, objects must be placed in front of the screen at all times.

Getting Interactive

Load another sphere and give it the glass surface we created earlier (you did remember to save it, didn't you?). We can't just position the sphere anywhere within the camera's view as we did before; we must keep in mind that there is now a screen object within our virtual soundstage.

- Select the ZY (side) view and make sure that all objects are positioned in front of the screen object and not overlapping or behind it (Figure 2).

Because you now have a limited "scene area" in which to move the objects around, you may have to fake distance by scaling your objects down if they have to move a great deal along the Z axis (Figure 3).

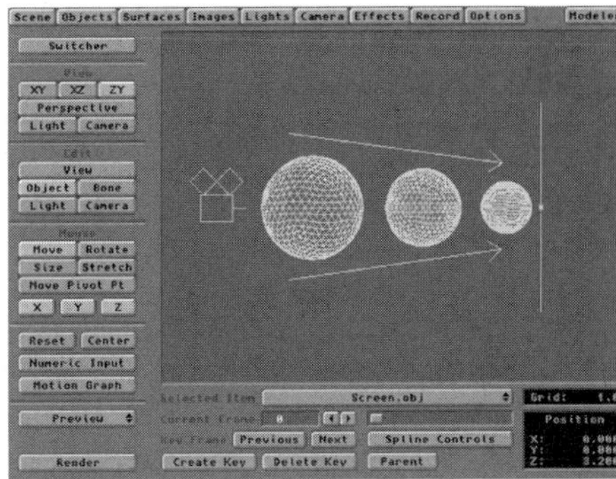

Figure 3: Scaling an object while moving it along the Z axis helps creates the illusion that it is moving a farther distance than it really is.

One more rule to remember when positioning refractive objects in relation to the screen: The closer the object is to the screen, the more discernible the background image will be. If you position your object closer to the camera, the background image will be distorted quite a bit; this may or may not be the effect you're after, so a judgment call is required.

With this in mind, place your refractive sphere within the scene area, make a key frame for it and hit **Render** once again (don't forget **Trace Refraction**).

If you've followed the steps correctly, you should now have a realistic glass sphere on your screen refracting the background image.

The Fine Art of Boxing

After fine-tuning this technique, sticking a refractive amber blob on our actress was a snap. We created a spline blob (this was pre-metaform) to match Diana's general form and bones were added to match the movements of her head and arms. As the bones twisted and stretched the blob, it looked as if Diana was really trying to escape from her CG prison; there were only a few minor things left to completely sell the effect.

Depending on how your refractive sphere was positioned in the last experiment, you may have noticed a black edge or black patches within the sphere. The same thing happened with our blob even though there were no black areas in our background footage. There is a simple explanation: the blob was bending light so much that it was beginning to refract the empty, black environment around it. This was a problem because the blob had to look like it was in a 3D environment, surrounded on all six sides by walls and furniture. We were simply faking 3D by placing a flat screen behind the blob; other than that, there was nothing else in the scene to refract except black. If you ever run across this problem in your refractive exploits, there is a simple but effective way around it.

Remember that box we made earlier?

- Load the box into your sphere scene and stretch it until it completely surrounds all the objects in your scene, including the camera and lights (Figure 4).
- Enter the **Surfaces** panel and find the BOX surface. Select T next to Surface Color and use a **Cubic**

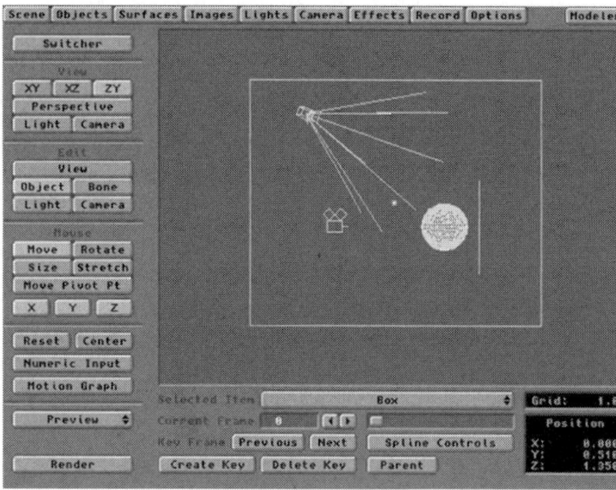

Figure 4: Stretch the box until it completely surrounds all the objects in your scene, including the camera and lights.

Image Map to map the current background framestore onto all six of its inward-facing sides (don't forget to select **Automatic Sizing**).

- Once again set the Luminosity to 100 percent and the Diffuse Level to 0 percent.

Re-render the scene and you'll see that the black areas are now gone. Because our blob now had something to refract from all six directions, it blended seamlessly with the background footage and didn't have a cartoony, black outline. For added realism, we made the blob 15 percent reflective using our background footage as a reflection map. This made the blob look like it was reflecting the surrounding room and completed the illusion.

Time for Coca-Cola

We managed to complete the effects on time and the sequence was a success. I eventually got some sleep, and a few caffeine-laden products later, I was up and running once more. (Of course, I missed the show when it aired, but my mom said it was good.)

LWP

Colin Cunningham served as an FX animator on RoboCop: The Series *and is currently enrolled in the Classical Animation program at Sheridan College, where he wreaks havoc on a daily basis. He likes Coca-Cola and is a MUCH bigger Elvis fan than Mojo (ah, thank yuh). He can be reached at (905) 338-8033.*

The Sunset Of My Life

by Alan Chan

Way back in my college days I wrote and directed a feature-length production in lieu of writing a senior paper. It was a small story, something I could manage on a very limited budget, about a young girl dying of cancer and the love that infuses her life. (Sad, I know. Sorry.) It was called *The Sunset Of My Life*, has nothing whatsoever to do with CGI or sunsets, and would be totally irrelevant here except for the fact that I thought it would be neat to see the title in print again.

Further on in the story of my life I did several projects that necessitated the re-creation of a summer scene—a wheat field dancing in the light of the setting sun. Then, in a cyber-plot twist straight out of a Gibson novel, I met a beautiful stranger, who is now my fiancée (but that's a different story). The upshot of all this is that I am now writing this article for you, dear LightWave users, detailing how to create a CGI sunset.

Sunshiny Skies

To begin with, I broke the project into its component objects and techniques as follows:

(1) The wheat field. It has to ripple gently in the wind.
(2) The clouds. They swim lazily by.
(3) The sky color, a wonderful gradient of reds and yellows.
(4) The stars, against the backdrop of night.
And for added effect, we include:
(5) The windmill, spinning in the distance, and
(6) A bird, swooping majestically past the camera.

We'll tackle each of these elements separately, then sew them together into a seamless scene. For reference, let's construct a timeline of events we want to have happen. Frame 0: Sky is a golden red-orange color, clouds in the sky blowing by, wheat field blowing in the wind. The windmill is spinning. Frames 25-85: A bird flies across the screen. Frames 50-200: The sky begins to darken. The clouds slowly become darker, turning into deep pools of grey. Frame 100 or so: The stars start becoming visible behind the wall of clouds. Frame 120: The clouds begins to dissipate, revealing the stars in all their glory.

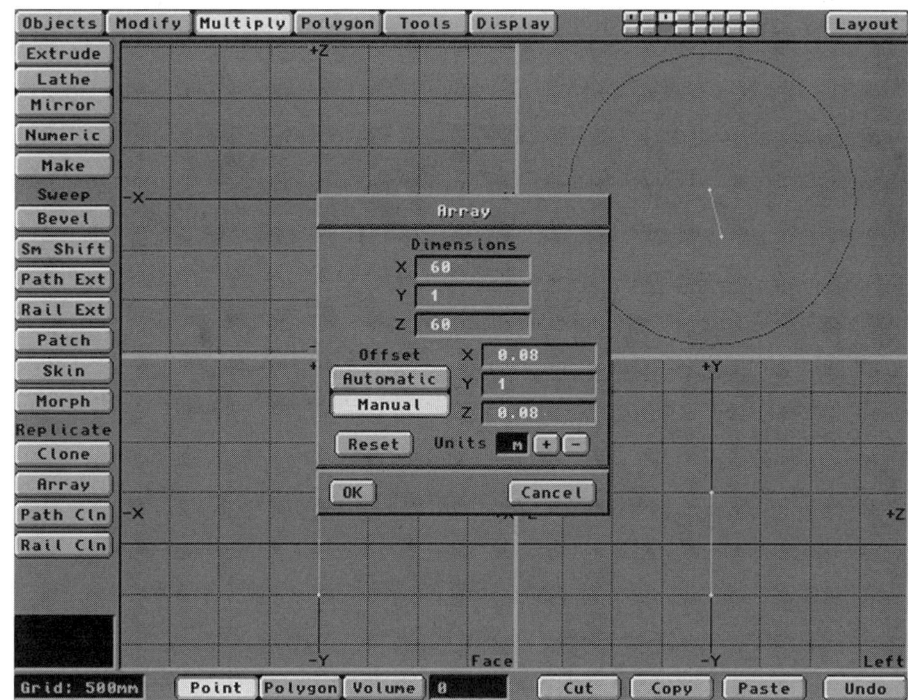

Figure 1: The Array requester panel

Wheat Is Good For You

Back in the premiere issue of *LIGHTWAVEPRO*, Mark Thompson demonstrated his method of creating a field of grass. This technique has since gone down in the LightWave Hall of Famous Tricks, and today we're going to use it to build our own wheat field. For the benefit of those who don't have that debut issue, here's a brief description:

In Modeler, we use the Make Points function to plot two points: one at 0,0,0 and another at 0,1,0 (measurements in meters). This will be our blade of wheat grass. Under the Multiply panel, hit Array and enter these values in the requester (Figure 1):

X = 60
Y = 1
Z = 60
Manual Offset
X Offset = 0.08
Y Offset = 1
Z Offset = 0.08

Hit Return, and in a moment you will have cloned one blade into an orderly array of wheat (Figure 2). Of course, nobody's ever seen wheat grow in such an orderly fashion, and it's unlikely anyone ever will, so we'll need to introduce a random offset to the wheat. From the Polygon menu, select Jitter, and enter these values into the requesters:

X = 0.05
Y = 0
Z = 0.05

This will randomly shift all the points by a given offset—in this case, 0.05—thereby making the blades look random. Additionally, I selected the points representing the tops of each blade of wheat grass and applied a jitter value of 0.01 on the Y axis, just to give the wheat field a less uniform topside (Figure 3). Once done, hit F1 to center the object, apply a surface to it, say "WheatGrass," and export it to Layout. In Layout, assign the following

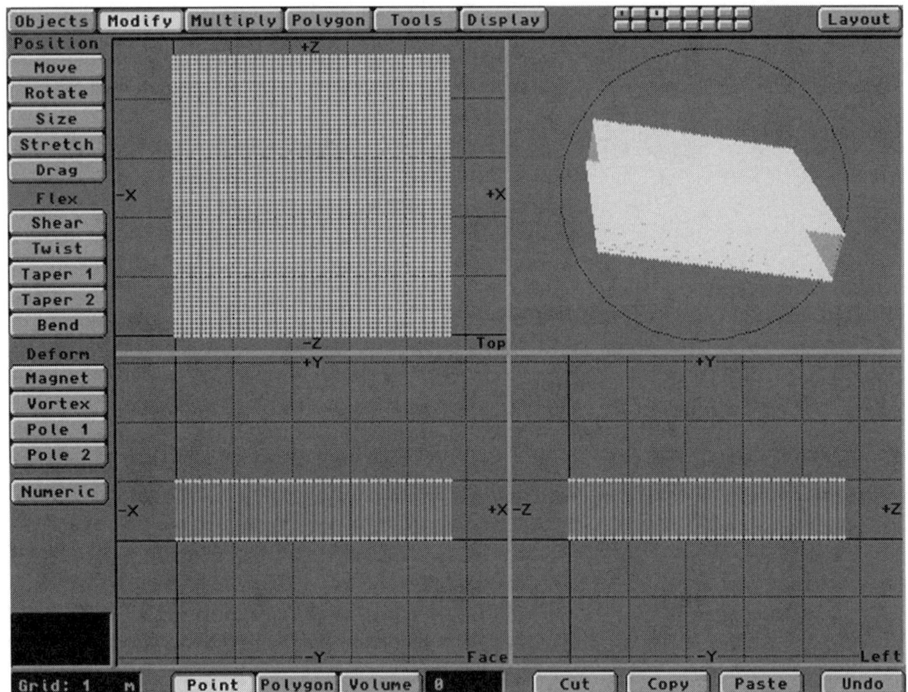

Figure 2: An array of wheat blades

surface settings to the WheatGrass surface:

Surface Name: WheatGrass
Surface Color: 2,0,0
Surface Texture: Grid

Texture Center:	0, 0.6, 0
Texture Falloff:	0, 250.0, 0
Texture Color:	0, 76, 0
Line Thickness:	1.0
Luminosity:	0%
Diffuse Level:	90%

This surface setting generates a color gradient along the top of the wheat patch ranging from green on top to black. When coupled with the sunset, the surface should provide a convincing suggestion of a thick patch of wheat, where the light is unable to penetrate to the ground. Finally, to add a soft breeze effect, we select our wheat field as the current object and enter the Displacement Map panel. Type these values into the requesters:

Displacement Texture Type: Ripples

Texture Size:	5.0, 0, 5.0
Texture Falloff:	0, 100, 0
Texture Center:	2.5, 0.5, 2.5
Texture Amplitude:	0.07
Wave Sources:	2
Wavelength:	0.25
Wave Length:	0.001

The result is a soft, slow ripple across the top of the wheat field (Y = 1), one that falls off to 0% at the bottom (Y = 0). Position your camera so that you see the top part of the wheat field. It looks like the wheat stretches out to infinity, rather than constituting a small patch in front of the camera (Figure 4).

The Virtual Environment

Now seems to be a good time to discuss our environment. Looking at our list of effects, we see that we will be using LightWave's often-neglected background gradient function to create our red-orange sunset sky. However, the background gradient functions don't use envelopes, so to fade from evening to night, we'll have to fake it by dissolving up a large black ball around the camera.

Don't forget the stars. To make the stars visible against the ball of a night sky, they'll have to be placed inside the ball, and dissolved up when appropriate. Add the clouds underneath all of that, and you'll end up with something that looks like Figure 5. First, let's go ahead and set up our background gradient colors. In the Effects menu, turn off the Solid Backdrop option and enter these values into the appropriate requesters:

Zenith Color:	0, 0, 34
Sky Color:	174, 101, 0
Ground Color:	174, 101, 0
Nadir Color:	0, 0, 0

Also, click on Gradient Squeeze and enter these values into the requester:

Sky Gradient Squeeze:	24.0
Ground Gradient Squeeze:	80.0

Note that the Sky Color and the Ground Color are the same values. Because our wheat field creates our horizon line for us, we don't want to add another artificial horizon, so we simply make these values identical to form a seamless crossover from sky to "ground."

Clouding the Issue

A good way to replicate clouds in LightWave is by the use of fractal noise mapped onto a plane or a dome. We'll use a dome in this case, so that if we need to move the camera we won't have to worry about moving the plane as well. Go into Modeler and, using the Cone command (Objects menu), make a cone with the default at 16 sides that is 10 km in height and approximately 200 km in diameter (Figure 6). Make sure that the base of the cone sits on the Y axis, then select the polygon forming the base of the cone and delete it. Hit F to flip the polygons inward, so they are

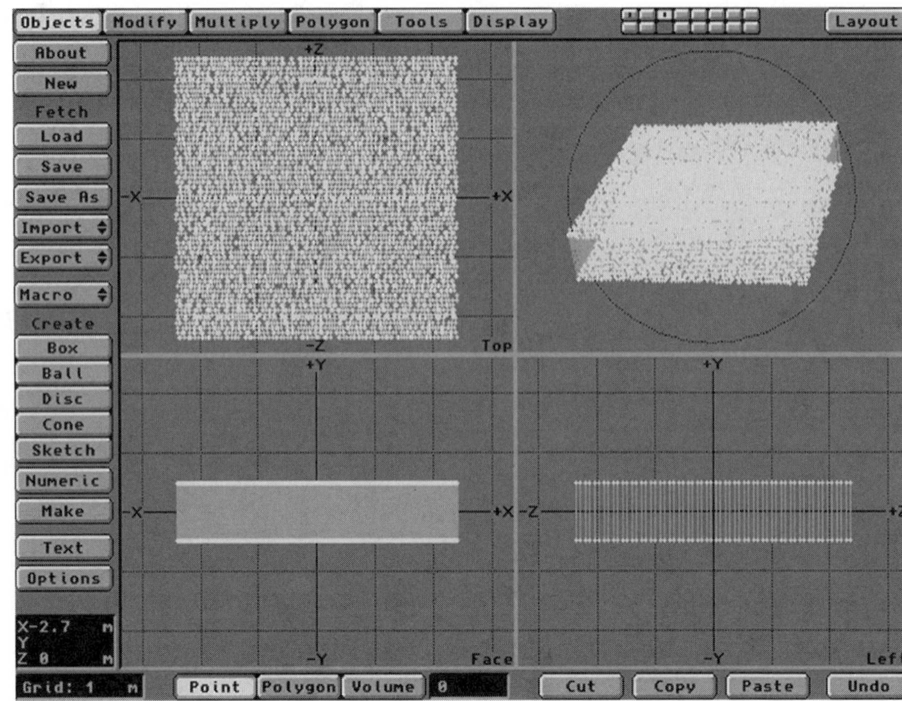

Figure 3: A more disorganized field of wheat

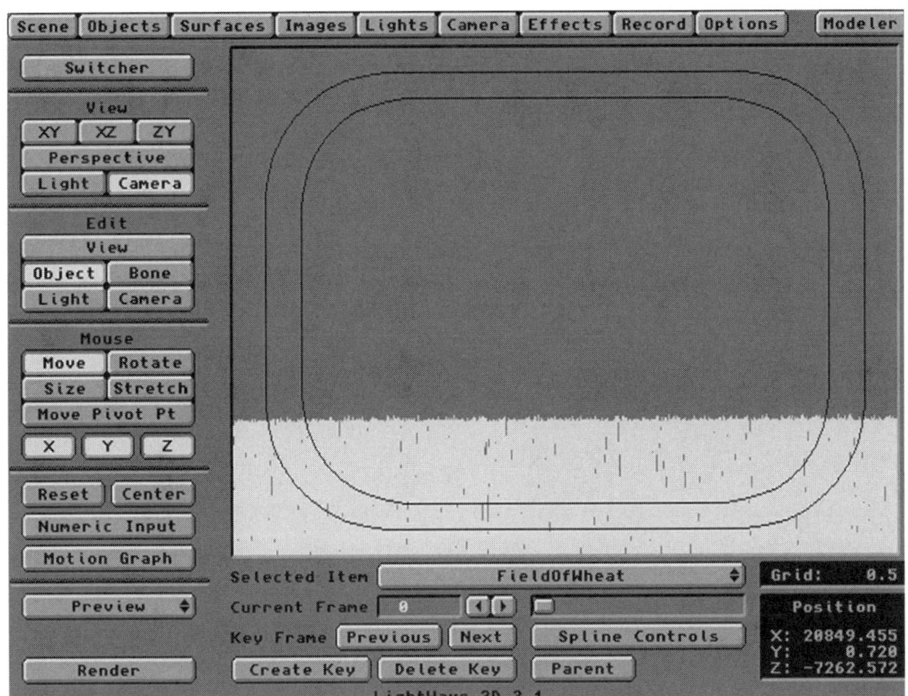

Figure 4: The wheat field positioned in front of the camera

visible from inside the cone (Figure 7). Give this cone a surface name of "Clouds" and export to Layout. In Layout, enter these values for the Clouds surface:

Surface Name: Clouds
Surface Color: 160, 150, 140
Luminosity: 20%
Diffuse Level: 100%
Diffuse Texture: Fractal Noise
Texture Size: 600, 600, 600
Texture Center: 0, 3000, 0
Texture Velocity: 35, 4, -45
Texture Value: 90%
Texture Frequency: 3
Texture Contrast: 1.0
Transparency Level: 100%
Texture Type: Fractal Noise
Texture Size: 6000, 6000, 6000
Texture Center: 0, 3000, 0
Texture Falloff: 0.0002, 0.015, 0.0002
Texture Velocity: 40, 5, -50
Texture Value: 15%
Frequencies: 6
Contrast: 2.0
Smoothing: On

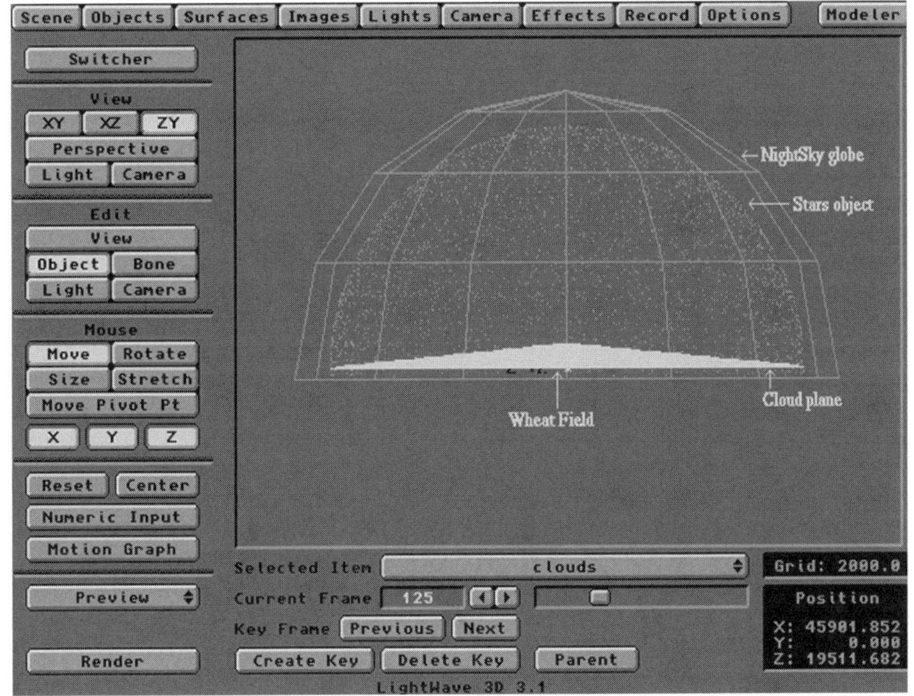

Figure 5: Order of items in our sunset scene

Note that one fractal noise pattern is used to affect the transparency of the cloud dome, making parts of it opaque (cloudy) and others transparent (clear sky), while another is used for diffusion, to add an extra texture layer to the dome. In addition, texture velocity is added to the transparency setting to generate slow-moving clouds, and a texture falloff causes the clouds to fade away into the distance. (Actually, the texture falloff is in the Y axis. But with the texture center at 0, 3000, 0, the falloff is complete at ground level at the base of the dome, which is in the distance.) Once you're done entering the surface settings, save the object, and we'll continue building our own little perfect world.

It's Full Of Stars!

Back in the days before LightWave 3.5 and Big-Medium-Small particles, I used the RandomStars object for my stars, resizing it and tweaking the surface settings as follows:

Surface Name: Twinkly Stars
Surface Color: 241, 221, 180
Luminosity: 80%
Diffuse Level: 0%
Transparency Texture Map: Fractal Noise
Texture Size: 4000, 4000, 4000
Texture Velocity: 50, 30, 0
Texture Value: 100%
Texture Frequency: 5
Texture Contrast: 3.0

To create stars of different apparent brightnesses, I used a fractal noise transparency texture. In addition, I attached a velocity to the texture so that the pattern would move through the stars, causing them to twinkle slowly. Of course, LightWave versions 3.5 and up allow for a variable particle size, so you may opt for that. If you've followed *LWPRO* diligently the past couple of months and dutifully read William Frawley's article on creating realistic starfields in the April 1995 issue, you may wish to try some of the techniques illustrated in that tutorial(Figure 8).

Next, we'll build our great black ball of night. Go into Modeler, select Ball (Objects menu) and build a sphere that is approximately 50km in diameter. Segments and Sides won't matter here because you won't be able to see the sphere anyway. Leave it as it is, however, and don't cut off the bottom to make a dome, because we want to ensure that everything is covered. Assign the surface name "NightSky," hit F to Flip the polygons so they face inward, and Export the object. In Layout, give this surface a color value of 0,0,9 (a slight blue tint, since we're not in space), a luminosity level of 100% and a diffuse value of 0%. Save the object, by the way.

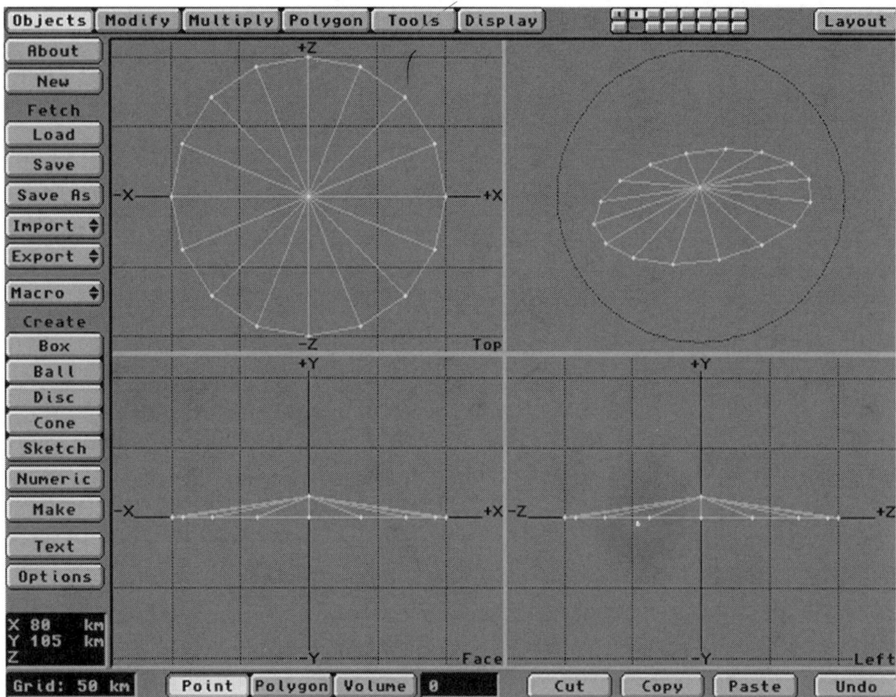

Figure 6: Our cloud cone

Piece by Piece

Other than the bird and the windmill, which are the icing on the cake, we now have all the elements we need to construct a sunset scene. Start by parenting the cloud dome, the stars and the black sphere to a null, just in case you decide to move it.

Note that if you did not keyframe your camera earlier, your camera position will jump outward to automatically frame the largest object (in this case the night sky dome). Once this happens, you will have lots of fun trying to reposition the camera by the wheatfield, so do keyframe before you load in big objects.

Also note that as as Grid Size gets bigger, Layout's screen begins to freak out. At a grid size of about 5,000 to 10,000, the left and right edges of your wheat field may disappear, though everything still renders fine. (This "undocumented feature" is still present as of LightWave PC 4.0's pre-release.) No problem. Simply bring your grid size back down and you should be fine (that is, if you keyframed earlier on).

Now just light the wheat and set our object dissolve envelopes to get everything to appear and disappear on cue! Enter these numbers into the dissolve envelope graph for the respective objects:

Object dissolve envelope for clouds:

Keyframe	Envelope value	Spline value
0	0.0	0.0
80	0.0	1.0
126	64.0	0.05
179	100.0	1.0

Object dissolve envelope for Stars:

Keyframe	Envelope value	Spline value
0	100.0	0.0
66	100.0	1.0
106	89.0	0.05
176	0.0	1.0

Object dissolve envelope for NightSky:

Keyframe	Envelope value	Spline value
0	100.0	0.0
53	100.0	1.0
96	87.0	0.05
160	0.0	1.0

What Light Through Yonder Wheatfield Breaks

Since the only objects we had to light were the clouds and the wheat field, I kept the lighting scheme simple and only used two lights in the scene. I placed the cloud light above the wheat field and gave it a wide cone angle to illuminate the clouds directly in front of the camera. I also made it a rich red-yellow color to accentuate the sunset.

These were the settings for the light:

Light:	Radiosity Red
Light Color:	255,32,0
Light Intensity:	650%
Light Type:	Spot
Falloff:	0%
Spotlight Cone Angle:	75 degrees
Soft Spot Edge Angle:	5 degrees

Last, I placed a key light for the wheat field slightly off-center from the camera, and set an envelope to turn the intensity down along with the night sky, so that it would appear to darken along with the evening. The settings for this light were as follows:

Light:	WheatFieldLight
Light Color:	237, 157, 56
Light Intensity:	envelope

Envelope settings:

Keyframe	Envelope value	Spline value
0	200.0	0.0
50	200.0	1.0
85	157.5	0.0
110	42.5	0.0

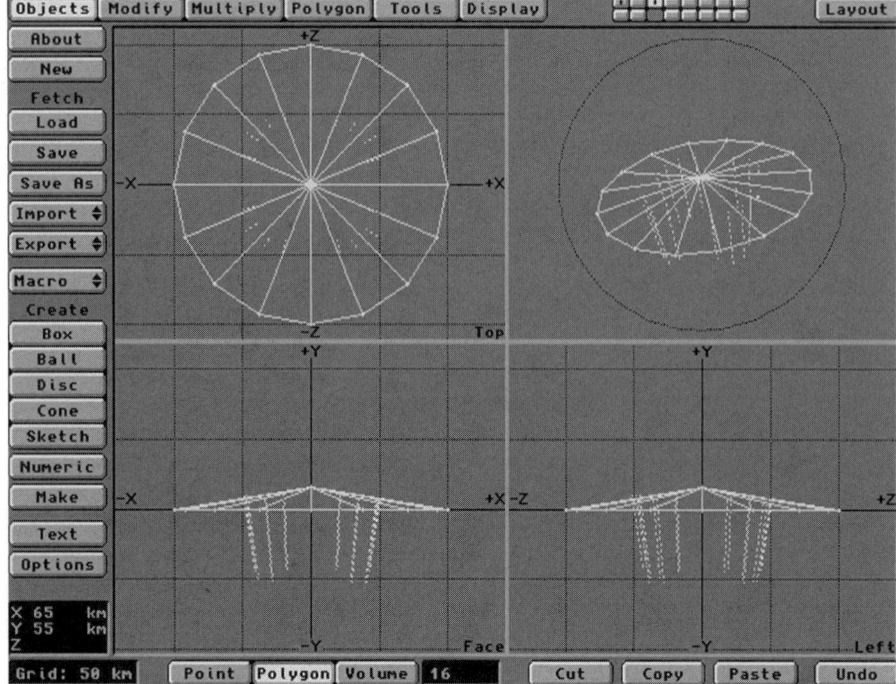

Figure 7: The polygons of the cloud cone flipped inward

Figure 8: A realistic starfield. Wish upon a star!

Light Type:	Spot
Falloff:	18%
Spotlight Cone Angle:	30 degrees
Soft Spot Edge Angle:	5 degrees

That was it! I added the windmill and the bird flying across the screen flapping its wings to help enhance the picture, but that is, of course, a small sampler course in morphing techniques. As it stands, this scene should give you a good little summery background setting. If you like, you might jazz it up by placing a lens flare sun early in the animation. In my work I found it most effective to simply do a slow move with the camera, tilting up imperceptibly to the night sky, whereupon a shooting star goes dancing across the heavens.

LWP

Alan Chan would like to sell you a used screenplay called The Sunset Of My Life. *If you buy it, he's also got some oceanfront property in Oklahoma for sale. To place your order, promptly e-mail alan.chan@oubbs.telecom.uoknor.edu.*

The Cumulus Effect

by Jim May

Obtaining photo-realistic effects in any 3D rendering package involves a large degree of complexity. Simulating lens flares, for instance, was a fairly elaborate procedure until LightWave 3.0 made it child's play. But this is not always the case. I'll show you how to render realistic, fluffy cumulus clouds in daylight, with only two polygons and no light sources.

This Isn't Kansas

Rendering authentic sky shots has always been a personal Holy Grail of mine. This fascination has been exacerbated by the fact that Vista Professional has shipped version 3.0 on the Amiga, and yet it still can't render decent clouds. Though VistaPro had Scenery Animator beat on many fronts, the latter does beautifully detailed clouds. World Construction Set doesn't even do clouds at all.

And none of them could do anything other than thin-wisp, flat, cirrus-type clouds. What about cumulus clouds? What could I do to simulate big, cumulonimbus thunderheads rolling across the sky (short of recording live cloud footage into a PAR)?

LightWave did not seem to be able to improve things, at first. Simulating clouds in LightWave consisted primarily of transparency-mapping a white polygon layer. Not only was this a flat, wispy solution, much like the others, but the resulting clouds had a 50 percent coverage limitation—no more, no less.

So I was stuck with using still images of actual sky to achieve particular weather. Then I pondered what would happen if I stacked not one, but two cloud layers, one on top of the other, with the top one white and the bottom one darker. The initial results were startling, and I wound up working into the wee hours of the night exploring the possibilities.

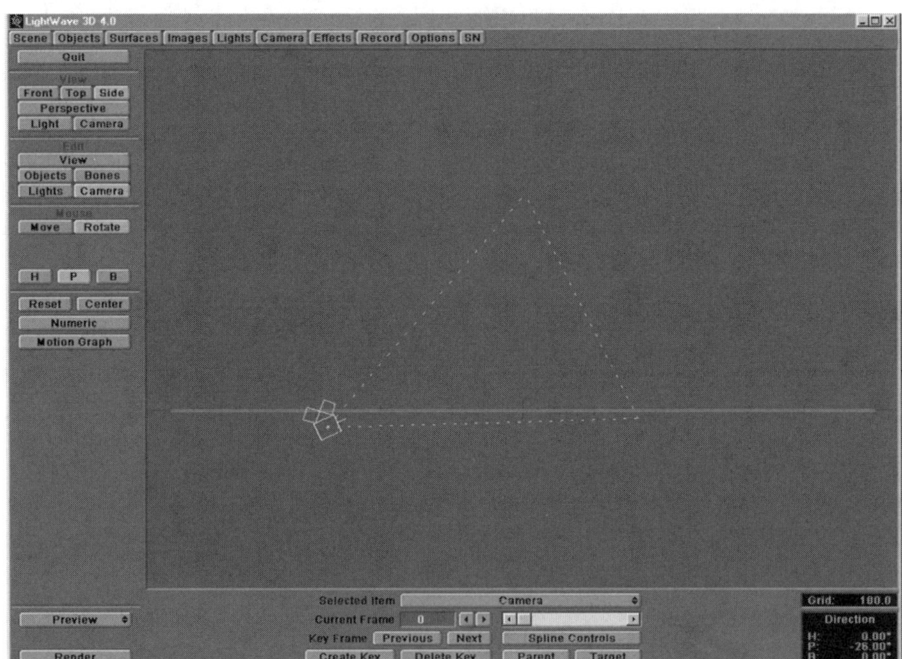

A side view of our scene shows the camera pitched up at two closely placed cloud planes. Fog is used here to fade the distant clouds into the sky colors. See the color pages for the rendered image from this scene.

The Calm Before the Storm

- The first, essential step for this effect is to create two large, flat surfaces—in this example, two simple squares. Either single-sided polygons with double-sided surfaces or straight double-sided polygons will do. One will form the upper cloud layer (surface name Highclouds) and the other will form the underbelly of the cloud cover (Lowclouds).
- Make these two layers using the Box command (Objects panel) in Modeler with the Top view. Do not build actual boxes! Instead, we need two large single polygons. Be sure to make them very large, so that you can use them in scale with other objects. Our examples are one kilometer square.
- Assign surfaces (if necessary) using Surface (Polygon panel or (q)), and then Export or Save (Objects panel) each polygon as a separate object into Layout. We are keeping the polygons separate to retain control over the effect, as we'll see later. In our example, the final objects are named High and Low.
- Once in Layout, set the Grid Size under Options to a number at least 25 times smaller than the original object size; we want the polygons to extend far to the horizon from the camera's point of view. Now, switch to Side (ZY) or Front (XY) under View. In this example, the cloud polygons are one kilometer per side. With that scale, set the High cloud layer to 25 meters or so above the camera; set the Low clouds to be between 23 and 24 meters up. With different sizes, the numbers are different, but the distance between the cloud layers must be around 12 to 25 times smaller than the distance to the camera. Now, aim your camera up a bit, and create a key for all items at frame 0. It would also help to make the effect clear if you set the camera lens wide. (In the Camera panel, use 2.2 or so for Zoom Factor; in 35 mm SLR terms, you want between 17 mm and 24 mm.) It also helps to set LightWave to use Gradient Backdrop (Effects panel) to see your clouds against a blue sky.
- Now, go to the Surfaces panel. For the upper cloud layer (Highclouds), set the following:

  Surface color 255, 255, 255

Luminosity 100%
Diffuse Level 0
Transparency 0%
Transparency Texture
Texture Type Fractal Noise
Texture Size 15.0 (X, Y and Z)
Texture Value 100%
Frequency 15 or higher (for detail)
Contrast 3.0 or higher

(Bigger Contrast values yield more cumuluslike, solid clouds with thin fringes and big areas of clear sky. Lower values will result in thinner, wispier, hazier clouds.)

All other settings are OK with defaults.

- For the Lowclouds surface, use the same values except for the following: Surface color of dark gray (96, 96, 96). Otherwise, Luminosity and Diffuse Levels are the same as for the Highclouds surface. Most crucial is the Fractal Noise texture map to be applied to Transparency; it must have identical values to that applied to the Highclouds transparency.
- From the Objects panel, select Save All Objects.
- Once everything is shipshape, go to the Camera panel and set your desired resolution, and then render the image. If you want to put my initial claim to the test, go to the Lights control panel and turn the only Light down to 0% intensity. If you really want to cover every escape hatch, don't forget to also set Ambient Intensity to 0.0.

Stormy Weather

LightWave's Fractal Noise texture uses a seed value in its random number generator. My cloud technique takes advantage of the fact that the seed value is the same each time out. As a result, the pattern on each cloud layer is exactly matched to the other, so long as your Texture Center, Texture Size, Contrast and Frequencies values are the same!

Now try the following:

- Alter the distance between the layers—try bigger distances. Try using a very wide angle on your camera to take in more (down to about 1.8). Then try slightly modifying the Texture Center values for the transparency map of only one of the layers, or simply move the cloud layers from side to side by small increments.

You will find that increasing the distance between the layers exaggerates the directionality of the apparent "sunlight," whereas moving the layers off XZ center from one another alters the direction of the "sun." In both cases, the effect ranges from "flat" at the apparent center of "sunlight" (whose direction actually corresponds to the line linking the cloud objects' axes) to fluffy, directional lighting as you look further away from center. Beyond a certain point, however, the effect breaks down as the two layers become distinct. There is a definite "comfort zone" ringing the center, in which the effect works. Its size (radius) is directly proportional to the separation of the cloud layers in relation to the distance to the camera.

In mathematical terms, the effect becomes more pronounced as the angular distance (as viewed by the camera) between two corresponding points on the surface of each cloud layer increases. When that angle exceeds a certain value, however, the two layers become distinct and the effect is lost.

The central cloud areas, in this example, are solid, featureless gray areas, suggesting flat-bottomed cumulonimbus clouds. You can mitigate this by taking advantage of Fractal Noise's static random seed. Simply assign another Fractal Noise texture to the Surface Color attribute of Lowclouds, again using the same values as the others. This adds detail to the solid areas of the lower layer. Use Contrast values below 2.0, and give the texture a color lighter than the original surface. This will give the effect of the cloud being lit from all sides, as the light/dark areas of the texture will align precisely with the clear/solid areas of cloud. Using a color that is darker than the original surface will make the clouds look as though they are being lit from below and above (useful for clouds over a city being lit by the moon).

Lighter cloud bottoms give the impression of light clouds, while darker colors suggest thick, lumpy cumulonimbus thunderheads. Making the texture X values greater than the Z values can yield a wind-streaked, jet stream stratus appearance.

You can also try adding light sources now, to have the upper layer cast shadows onto the lower, and you can now alter the Luminosity and Diffuse Level values to your taste. The goal I most often shoot for is to try to lighten up the fringes as much as possible to enhance the effect of bright sunlight filtering through the edges.

Time-Lapse Photography

After discovering this technique, I decided to simulate the effect of sunlight flashing through the clouds. By animating the Fractal Noise textures making up the clouds, I aimed to re-create some realistic and inspirational imagery.

- Starting with the scene assembled above, turn the light back on and set it above the clouds. Turn on Lens Flare (Lights panel), with Lens Reflections, Random Streaks and Fade Behind Objects activated, and use Texture Velocity to move the clouds. Take care to keep the upper and lower layers aligned and matched.

Using this technique, I got acceptable results with the flare set to a bright value (greater than 150%) and solid clouds (Contrast at 3.5). The effect of the sun bursting out was remarkable! However, there was no anticipation of its appearance, since the flare was completely dark until it was clearing the clouds. In reality, there is a skyglow surrounding the sun, and you know that it is about to come out as this glow brightens the blue sky beyond.

- To simulate this skyglow, add a second light behind the first, with a large, diffuse glow and Glow Behind Objects turned on. (Intensity high, but mitigated with a Flare Dissolve setting of 30%. Different Dissolve and Intensity settings for this flare will simulate different haze levels.) Make sure that this flare is a long way from the camera, or else it will "curve around" and pop through the cloud cover, especially with wide-angle camera settings.
- Here comes the best part. If you give a Y value to the clouds' velocity, you will see the clouds "boil"! Now, with the rolling, boiling clouds and the sun drifting across the sky, you can simulate time-lapse sequences with amazing realism. Your storm clouds can now have that tornado-suggestive turbulence, enhanced by the cumulus effect.

Using this effect, you can now simulate nearly any meteorological condition. For example, if you give the cloud textures large X and Z sizes, you will have a sky dominated by one or two large cloud masses with expansive, clear areas in between. Once you have this, you can position them by either moving the cloud objects or adjusting the Texture Center such that the sky is mostly clear, and then animating a huge, dark cloud mass to roll across the scene, blocking the sun. By hiding a light source between the layers, you can simulate lightning! (You can vary the appearance of this effect by setting the default Transparency value of the lower layer to 10% or so. This adjustment will preserve the cloud bottom effect, but will permit the lightning flash to show more clearly.)

Those skilled at simulating volumetric lighting can have sunbeams bursting through cracks in the cloud cover.

The Aftermath

One thing I haven't tried yet (due to its probable long rendering time) is placing a few buildings with reflective windows around a vertically facing camera, with the clouds high above. With Trace Shadows on (shadow maps, which render solid shadows, won't work for this effect), the clouds will cast shadows over the towers while their windows reflect the turbulent sky overhead. (You only need one of your cloud layers to cast the shadow. The other shouldn't cast any.)

Another application of this technique was used to simulate a twilight sky for use in Vivid's (the company I work for) up-and-coming VR simulation, Turbo Kourier. By reversing the color scheme and making the lower layer a light orange with a dark purple upper layer, I simulated a twilight sky with clouds lit from underneath by a setting sun—all behind the lights of a huge, bustling, 21st century city.

I will be using this technique to simulate clouds over a full moon in an upcoming animation based on the legend of the Internet CancelMoose, in which our hero will fight to clear the world of Spam. I look forward to seeing applications of this idea elsewhere, and hope you can make use of it yourself!

LWP

Jim May is the primary LightWave dude at The Vivid Group in Toronto, Canada. His specialty is the application of real-world photographic techniques and camera work to the realm of computer imaging. May can be reached at vivid@gpu.utcc.utoronto.ca.

Let It Pour!

Simulating Pouring Water With LightWave

by David Warner

One of the best things about asking questions regarding a particular animation challenge on the LightWave newsgroup or LightWave mailing list is that you will typically end up with numerous responses that will provide you with many different options.

Recently, someone asked what the best way would be to animate pouring water in LightWave. Though there were a few very good replies, none of them were really all that detailed. So I took it upon myself to sit down and actually try to simulate water pouring from one glass into another.

To get an idea of what is involved here, pour some water from one glass to another. It's a simple thing that we do many times a day, but there are a lot a steps we need to take to simulate this effect realistically in the 3D environment. It would be much easier to create the illusion if we used non-transparent water container objects, but I think the animation looks much better when you can actually see the liquid leave one container and flow into another.

This animation will require a total of eight objects: two containers (one to pour water out of, one to pour water into); two water objects that will stay within each of these containers; three morph targets for our first water object; and another water object that will actually "pour" from the first container into the second container.

Modeling the Objects

Our first step is to model a container to pour the water from. Run Modeler and, using the comma (,) key, zoom in until the grid size equals 50 mm.

- Start by creating a polygon that looks like the one in Figure 1. Copy the polygon to a new layer and **Lathe** it 360 degrees around the Y axis (center at 0, 0, 0) with 32 sides. Then, use the **Magnet** tool (**Modify** panel) to pull out the lip of the container to form a pour spout that points toward the +Z axis.
- Select a new layer and use the **Sketch** tool (**Objects** panel) to draw a curve where the handle should be.
- After selecting a new layer, choose the background layer with the curve that you just sketched. Position a **Disc** (**Objects** panel) at the beginning of the curve. Make sure it is aligned to the curve so the plane of the disc is "perpendicular" to the start of the curve. Click on the **Rail Ext** button (**Multiply** panel) and highlight the **Uniform Lengths** button. Click **OK**. The water container should now have a handle.
- Use the **Surface** button (**Polygon** panel or q) to name the polygons of your water container and the handle. I used the names "WaterContainer" and "WaterContainerHandle". Hold down the shift key and select the two layers that contain these objects. **Save** or **Export** (**Objects** panel) these two layers as "Contnr1.lwo", the object that water will be poured out of. **Save** or **Export** another copy of these two layers as "Contnr2.lwo" so that we will have an object for the water to pour into. Our completed water containers should look like the object shown in Figure 2.

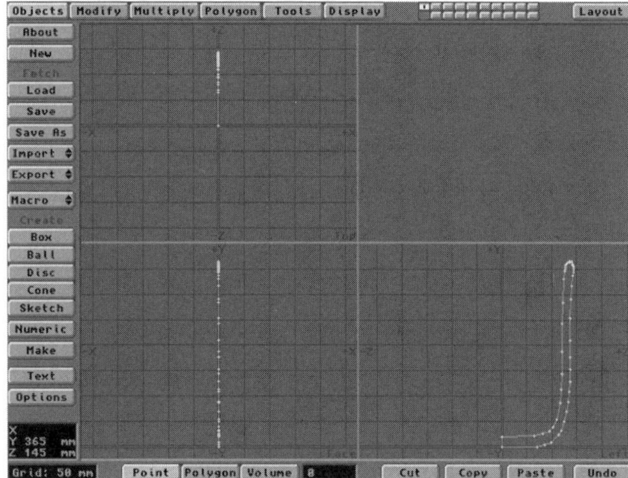

Figure 1: The initial polygon shape for the water container object.

Now we need to model our water objects. There will be three different objects, two of them with multiple morph targets. We'll start with the water that will pour out of the container.

- With the water container object in a background layer, use the **Points** tool (**Polygon** panel) to create a polygon that matches the shape of the water container bottom (Figure 3). Use the **Lathe** tool (**Multiply** panel) with 32 sides and alignment set to the Y axis to form the basic shape of our water object. (If you want to be exact, you can select the points that form an inside edge of the container and lathe it to obtain a perfect fit.)
- Press the (w) key and select all of the polygons in

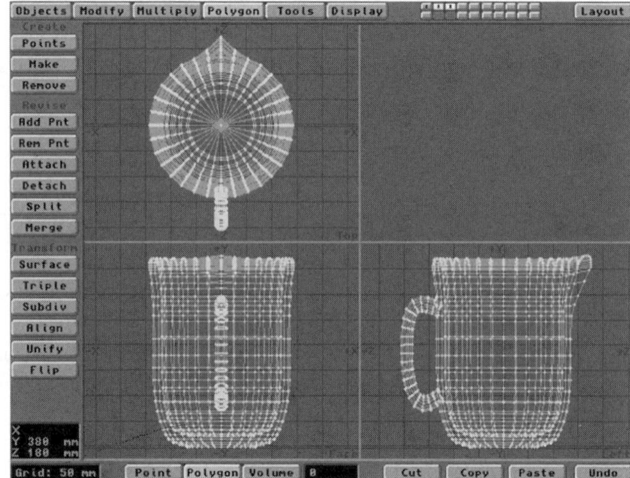

Figure 2: The completed water container object.

this object to make sure that they are pointing outward. If they're not, click on the **Flip** button (**Polygon** panel or f) to align all of the polygons correctly. Now click on the **Triple** button (**Polygon** panel or T) to make all of this object's polygons triangular (because we will be morphing its shape), and then use the **Surface** function (**Polygon** panel or q) to name the polygons in this object "Water".

- **Save** or **Export** this object as "Water1.lwo". It will be used as the morph source object for the water that will pour out of "Contnr1.lwo". **Save** or **Export** another copy of this object as "WaterB1.lwo", which will be used for the water that is poured into "Contnr2.lwo".
- Select the **Stretch** tool (**Modify** panel or h), and with the center of the tool positioned at the bottom of your water object, double the height of the water object along its Y axis. Select the **Taper2** tool (**Modify** panel), and with the center of the tool positioned at the bottom of the water object in the Face (XY) view, taper the shape of the object down to .1 on the Y axis only. Next, select the **Stretch** tool again and resize the tapered water object by .9 along the Z axis to make the object fit better into the bottom of the water container. Your values may differ slightly depending on the shape of your object.
- To save some memory, click on the **Remove** button (**Polygon** panel or k) to eliminate all of the polygons from this object in order (morph targets only need to contain points if you are using **Surface Morph**). You should end up with an object that looks like the one in Figure 4.

You may have noticed that the tapered water object is facing the "wrong" direction. Don't worry—we will correctly orient the water objects in Layout.

- **Save** or **Export** this object as "Water2.lwo". It will be the first morph target for our water object.
- For our second water morph target, select the **Pole2** tool (**Modify** panel), click on the **Numeric** button (n), highlight the X button and type in the following values:

Radius:	0, 330, 380
Center:	0, 45, 200
Factors:	1.0, 1.0, 0.5
Center:	0, 40 , -150

- Click **Apply** to make the change and then select (n) again and apply them once more to reshape the water object even further.
- Select the **Taper1** tool (**Modify** panel). With the center of the tool over the bottommost edge of the object, as seen from the Top (XZ) view, **Taper** it by a factor of .5. You will have to **Move** (t), **Rotate** (y) and **Stretch** (h) (**Modify** panel) the object a little so that it fits correctly within the water container, but you should end up with the shape displayed in Figure 5. **Save** or **Export** this object as "Water3.lwo".
- To make the final morph target for our water object, all we need to do is select the Size tool (**Modify** panel or H) and center it over the highest point in our object, as seen from the Left (YZ) view. Resize the object by a factor of 0 so that the only thing visible is a single point. **Save** or **Export** this object as "Water4.lwo".

Once the morph envelopes have been set up correctly, these three morph targets will make our water object "pour" out of the water container until it is empty. We still need to model objects to show where the water is going as it pours out and where it all ends up once it is done flowing.

Now we'll model the water object that will actually pour out of the first glass and into the second.

- Select the **Disc** tool (**Objects** panel) and draw out a shape that is aligned to the Z axis with one centered end at 0, 0, 0 and the other end extending to 0, 0, 1. Select numeric or press (n) and set the number of segments to 10 along the Z axis. Click on the **Make** button (return).

You should now have a 1-meter-long tube that is aligned to the Z axis and has segments at every .1 meters.

- Highlight the two polygons on each end of the tube and select the **Bevel** tool (**Multiply** panel or b) in preparation for making three bevels to round off each end of the tube.
- For the first bevel operation, enter 1 for **Inset** and 3 for **Shift**. For the second bevel operation, enter 3 for **Inset** and 2 for **Shift**. And for the final bevel operation, enter 5 for **Inset** and 1 for **Shift**. Now select all of the polygons, name the **Surface** (q) "WaterPour", and **Triple** and **Subdivide** (**Polygon** panel) all of these polygons twice. **Save** or **Export** this object as "WaterPour.lwo".

We are now finished modeling the objects necessary for this tutorial, so let's return to Layout.

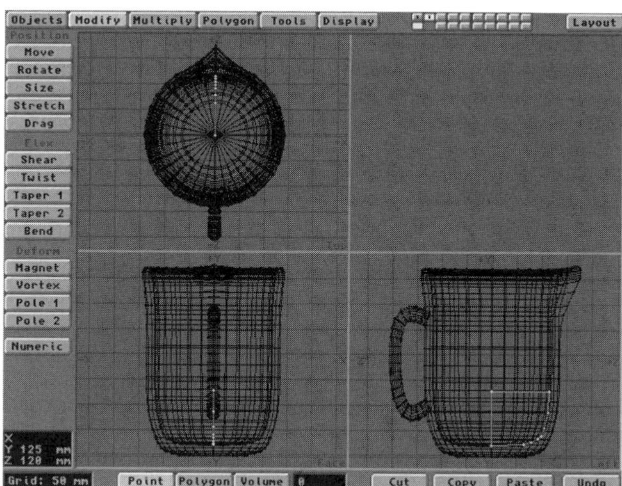

Figure 3: The initial polygon shape for the water object.

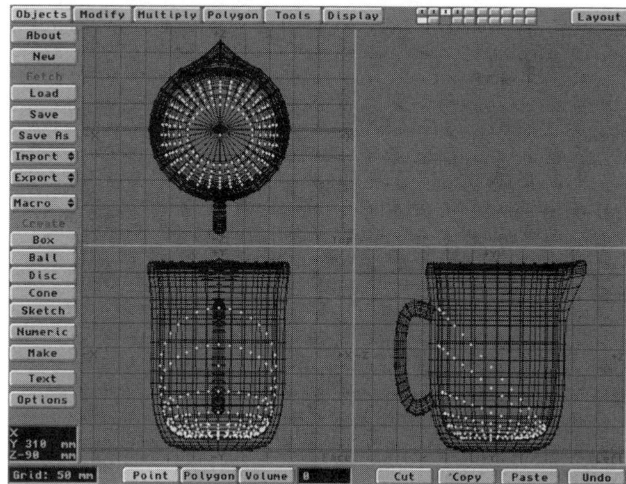

Figure 4: The first water morph target, minus polygons.

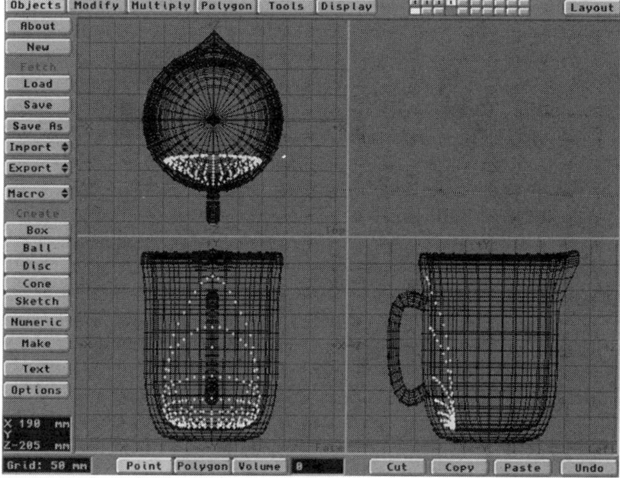

Figure 5: The second water morph target.

Setting Up the Scene

We will be making a scene that is approximately 12 seconds long, so in the **Scene** panel set the **Last Frame** to 360. If you haven't been exporting your objects to Layout during the modeling part of this tutorial, use **Load Object** (**Object** panel) to import all of the objects that were just modeled.

Now, let's set up the initial positions for all of our objects.

- Go to the Layout screen. Select the "Contnr1.lwo" object, highlight **Move Pivot Point**, click on the **Numeric** Input button and enter 0.0, 0.265, 0.135 for X, Y and Z. This will change how the object rotates as we pour the water from it.
- Select **Move** and change its position to .5 on the Y axis and 0.1 on the Z axis. Make a keyframe at frame 0.
- Now, select the "Water1.lwo" object, **Parent** it to the "Contnr1.lwo" object, **Rotate** it 180 degrees around the **Heading**, and make a keyframe at frame 0.
- Choose **Move** for the "Contnr2.lwo" object, change its position to -0.025 on the Y axis and 0.135 on the Z axis, **Rotate** it 180 degrees around its **Heading**, and make a keyframe at frame 0.
- Select the "WaterB1.lwo" object and **Parent** it to the "Contnr2.lwo" object.

Let's set up all of the dissolve envelopes now.

- Go back to the **Objects** panel and set **Object Dissolve** to 100% for the "Water2.lwo", "Water3.lwo" and "Water4.lwo" objects.
- Open up the **Object Dissolve** Envelope panel (E) for the "Water1.lwo" object and make one keyframe at frame 270 with 0% dissolve and another keyframe at frame 280 with 100%. Tap **Use Envelope**.
- Open the **Object Dissolve** envelope panel for "WtrPour.lwo" and change frame 0 to 100%. Make a keyframe at frame 170 with 100%, a keyframe at frame 180 with 0%, a keyframe at frame 340 with 0%, and a keyframe at frame 350 with 100%. Click **Use Envelope**.
- Open the **Object Dissolve** envelope panel for "WaterB1.lwo" and change frame 0 to 100%. Make a keyframe at frame 240 with 100%, make another at frame 245 with 0%, and then hit **Use Envelope**.

Next, we'll set up all of the morphs.

- From the **Objects** panel, choose the "Water1.lwo" object, set its **Metamorph Target** to "Water2.lwo", and open up the **Metamorph Amount** envelope panel (E). Create a keyframe at frame 30 with 0%, click the **Spline Controls** button(s), highlight **Linear** and click **OK**. Make another keyframe at frame 120 with 100%, and then click **Use Envelope**.
- Select the "Water2.lwo" object, set its **Metamorph Target** to "Water3.lwo", and open up the **Metamorph Amount** envelope panel. Create a keyframe at frame 120 with 0%, click the **Spline Controls** button, highlight **Linear**, and click **OK**. Make another keyframe at frame 210 with 100%, and then click **Use Envelope**. (Yes, this is a bit repetitive, but it's very necessary.)
- Choose the "Water3.lwo" object, set its **Metamorph Target** to "Water4.lwo", and open up the **Metamorph Amount** envelope panel. Create a keyframe at frame 210 with 0%, hit the **Spline Controls** button, highlight **Linear** and click **OK**. Make another keyframe at frame 270 with 100%, and then click **Use Envelope**.

Now that all of the morphs are set up properly, save your scene file.

It's time to set up the water object that will actually "pour" out of the first water container and into the second.

- Select the "WtrPour.lwo" object in the **Objects** panel, click the **Displacement Map** texture button (T) and select **Fractal Bumps** for the **Texture Type**. Click the **Texture Size** button and enter 0.01, 0.01, 0.03. Hit the **Texture Velocity** button and enter 0.005 for Z. Set the **Texture Amplitude** to 0.005 and keep the number of **Frequencies** at 3. Click **Use Texture**.
- Open up the **Object Skeleton** panel for this object, and click the **Add Bone** (not **Add Child Bone**) button 10 times. Change the **Bone Rest Length** to 0.1 for all 10 of these Bones. Finally, click **Continue** and return to Layout.
- Parent the "WtrPour.lwo" object to the "Contnr1.lwo" and take a look at the scene from the Top or XZ view. You should see the "WtrPour.lwo" object highlighted and sticking straight out along the Z axis with one end centered at the middle of the "Contnr1.lwo" object.
- Select **Bone** (B) from the **Edit** section. Beginning with Bone (2), move each Bone .1 meters along the Z axis, away from the Bone preceding it, and make keyframes at frame 0 for each Bone after you move them. So Bone (1) will be positioned at 0, 0, 0, Bone (2) will be positioned at 0, 0, 0.1, Bone (3) will be positioned at 0, 0, 0.3, etc. Once you have all the Bones keyframed and lined up properly along the "WtrPour.lwo" object's Z axis, press the (r) key to set each Bone's rest position and make it active.
- **Move** the "WtrPour.lwo" object to 0.0, 0.285, 0.115 and **Rotate** it 70 degrees around its **Pitch** axis so that the object is just inside the pour spout of the "Contnr1.lwo" object. Make a keyframe for the "WtrPour.lwo" object in this position at frame 0. Compare the Side (ZY) view of your Layout screen with the one in Figure 6 to make sure all of your objects' initial positions are correct.

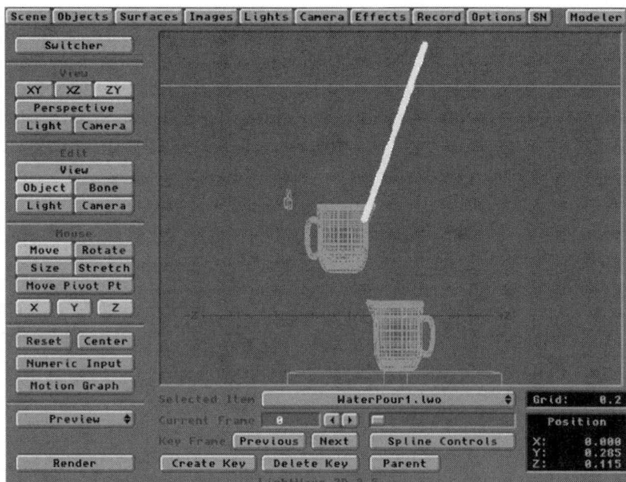

Figure 6: All objects are positioned and ready for animating.

Figure 7: The Bones will need some tweaking so they all follow the same path.

Our next step is to set up new keyframes for the "Contnr1.lwo" object.

- Select the "Contnr1.lwo" object and, at frame 30, make a keyframe. This keyframe will be a copy of the one at frame 0 except that **Linear** in the **Spline Controls** panel is turned on (at frame 30).
- Go to frame 120, **Rotate** the object to 45 degrees around its **Pitch** axis and make a keyframe. Next, go to frame 275, **Rotate** the object to 95 degrees around its **Pitch** axis, make a keyframe, and then open up the **Spline Controls** panel and change the **Tension** to 1.0. *[Editor's note—You can also interactively adjust the spline controls at a keyframe by holding down (t), (c) or (b) while moving the mouse right or left. The Coordinates window will give you numeric feedback. —JG]*

Next, the keyframes for the Bones of the "WtrPour.lwo" object need to be set up so that they move downward into the "Contnr2.lwo" object with a smooth, sloping motion.

- Select the "WtrPour.lwo" object and highlight the **Bone** button. Starting with Bone (10), select **Move** and then **Reset** its position back to 0, 0, 0. Then select Size, click the **Numeric** button and enter 1.0, 0.1, 0.1. Now make a keyframe for Bone (10) in this position for frames 0 and 180.
- Go to the keyframe at 180, open up the **Spline Controls** panel and highlight **Linear**.
- Go to frame 190, **Move** the bone to 0.0, -0.01, 0.095, **Rotate** the Bone to 25 degrees on its **Pitch** axis, change the Bone's **Size** to 1.0, 0.1, 0.5, and make a keyframe.
- Go to frame 200, **Move** the Bone to 0.0, -0.07, 0.15, **Rotate** the Bone to 67 degrees on its **Pitch** axis, and make a keyframe.
- Proceed to frame 210, **Move** the Bone to 0.0, -0.16, 0.185, **Rotate** the Bone to 77 degrees **Pitch,** and change its Size to 1.0, .5, 1.0. Create a keyframe.
- Go to frame 220, **Move** the Bone to the position 0.0, -0.31, 0.235, and **Rotate** the bone to 75 degrees **Pitch**. Create a keyframe.
- Go to frame 230, **Move** the bone to 0.0, -0.45, 0.3, **Rotate** it to 73 degrees **Pitch**, and make a keyframe.
- Advance to frame 240, **Move** the Bone to 0.0, -0.575, 0.375, **Rotate** it to 71 degrees **Pitch** and make a keyframe.
- Finally, go to frame 250, **Move** the Bone to 0.0, -0.645, 0.43, change its **Size** to 5.0, 5.0, 0.1 and create a keyframe.

Whew! If you don't want to go through all of that again (in case of an accident), now would be a good time to resave your scene file.

Next, we need to save the motion path for this Bone and apply it to the other nine Bones in this object, but with an offset of 10 frames for each Bone.

- Make sure that Bone (10) is selected and click on the **Motion Graph** button (m). Select **Save Motion**, type in any file name to save this motion path, and then click on the **Use Motion** button.
- Select Bone (9) from the Layout screen and select **Motion Graph**. Load in the same motion path file that you just saved. Click on the **Shift Keys** button, enter 10 for the **Shift Frames By** value, hit the **OK** button, and then tap the **Use Motion** button.
- Repeat this process for all of the Bones, shifting Bone (8) by 20 frames, Bone (7) by 30 frames, Bone (6) by 40 frames, and so on.

When you're done setting up motion paths for all of the Bones, you will need to tweak them with the **Move** and **Rotate** functions to make each Bone's motion path look exactly the same as the motion path we set up for Bone (10). These tweaks are essential because the "WtrPour.lwo" object is changing position while the "Contnr1.lwo" object rotates. It may be helpful if you add a few nullobjects and use them as reference points to mark the path your Bones should follow, as seen in Figure 7.

Finally, we need to make a few keyframes for the "WaterB1.lwo" object.

- Select this object, go to frame 350 and make a keyframe. Change the **Tension** to 1.
- Go back to frame 0, **Move** the object to 0.025 on the Y axis, change its **Size** to 0.0 on all three axes, make a keyframe at frame 0 and make another keyframe at frame 240. Select **Linear** (**Spline Controls**) at frame 240.
- Advance to frame 255, **Move** the object to 0.02 on the Y axis, change its **Size** to 0.85 on the X and Z axes and 0.2 on the Y axis, and make a keyframe.
- Finally, go to frame 275, **Move** the object to 0.14 on the Y axis, change its **Size** to 0.9 on the X and Z axes and 0.4 on the Y axis, and make one final keyframe.

Finishing Touches

You may also want to add some background objects (a table, some walls, etc.) to complement the scene, but it isn't mandatory. All we really have to do now is change our surfaces:

- Select the **Surfaces** panel. The "WaterContainer" and "WaterContainerHandle" surfaces should both have a very high **Specular Level** (150%) with **Glossiness** set to **High**. **Reflectivity** should be low (5%) with a very subtle reflected Image. **Transparency** should also be very high (95%) with a slight change to the **Refractive Index** (1.03), and **Opaque** edges with an **Edge Threshold** of about 0.65. You'll also want to turn on the **Smoothing** and **Double Sided** functions.
- The "Water" and "WaterPour" surfaces should have very similar settings, except they should be a light blue color, the **Refractive Index** should be set to 1.33, and the **Edge Threshold** should be somewhere around 0.25.
- Finally, position your camera and set up some basic lighting conditions (Key, Back and Fill with little or no **Ambient Intensity**).

Save all of your work, render the scene out and admire the results of your newfound skill. Feeling thirsty yet?

Despite the length of this tutorial, I could suggest a few additional things to make this animation look even better. Try adding an enveloped **Displacement Map** to the "WaterB1.lwo" object so that the water bubbles and roils as it is being poured into the second container. Also, the first container could have a few water droplets falling off of it after the water is done pouring.

The techniques used in this tutorial can be applied in many other ways. For instance, the "WtrPour.lwo" object, with stationary Bones and a moving displacement map, would make a nice waterfall effect. Or, if you changed the surface attributes for the water container objects to solid black and the "WtrPour.lwo" object's surface attributes to a glowing red, you would be pouring molten steel instead of water.

LWP

David Warner runs the LightWave and Video Toaster mailing lists on the Internet and can be reached through e-mail at dwarner@albany.net. He also happens to be legally blind and yearns for the day when LightWave will allow users to change the interface colors.

Explosion Shockwaves

by Lloyd B. Eldred

It's a peaceful day in deep space. Suddenly, an incredibly intense flash appears, accompanied by a very deep thud. Soon, an expanding, burning shockwave begins racing away from the source of the explosion.

Science-fiction movie fans may recall the spectacular explosion of Praxis in *Star Trek VI*. Or perhaps the explosion of the pyramid ship in *Stargate*. A similar effect also appeared in the *X-Men* animated series. This two-dimensional burning shockwave effect is quickly becoming a science-fiction staple.

The physics of such a wave are dubious at best, but the effect is still stunning enough to add to your repertoire. This article will cover the details of the basic effect and hopefully give you lots of ideas for using and improving on it.

Strips and Rings

The construction of the wave is rather similar to the Saturn's Rings tutorial in the LightWave manual (pages 23-25). On the off chance that you, like me, didn't get it to work on your first few tries, I'll run through it and attempt to clarify surfacing and morphs at the same time.

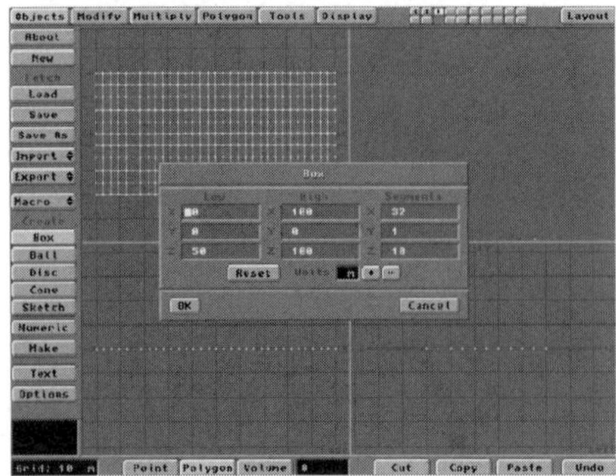

Figure 1: Setting up the wave strip

The first step is to create a rectangular strip. Use the **Box** button (**Objects** panel) and the **Numeric** options shown in Figure 1 to create a subdivided strip.

The number of segments in the X direction determines how round the ring will appear. The number of segments in the Z direction control how smooth a gradient our textures will have from the leading edge, or outside, of the wave to the trailing edge, or inside. The polygons will be facing downward, but that's OK.

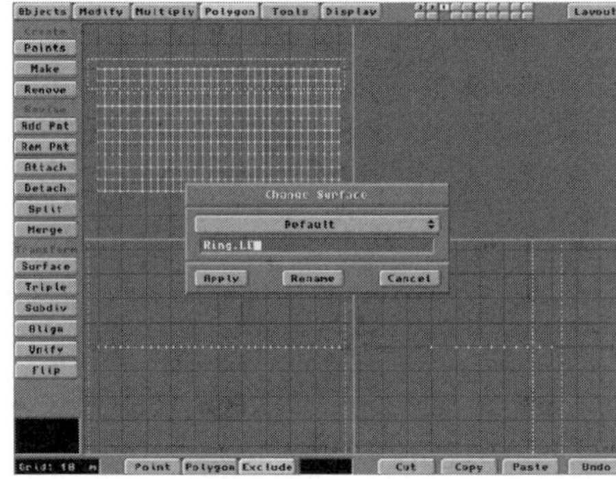

Figure 2: Surfacing the strip

The next step is to assign surface names to the strip. Use the volume selection tool to individually select each of the 10 horizontal rows one at a time. Assign each a different surface name using the **Surface** button (**Polygon** panel). Figure 2 shows the topmost row selected, to which I assigned the name "Ring.LE." I chose the name "Ring.LE-1" for the next row in, "Ring.LE-2" for the third row, etc. The bottommost row (trailing edge) will be called "Ring.LE-9."

Once you're finished, choose the polygon selection tool, then hit the **Stats** button (**Display** panel or w). Select the surface name pop-up menu that (probably) reads "Default." Verify that there are 32 polygons with each of the 10 "Ring.LExx" names. If there are missing polygons, pull down to the problem name, then hit the (+) beside the "**with Surface:**" option. That will select and highlight the polygons with that name. Identify and fix any problems before proceeding.

Because we only have 10 different surfaces, there will be fairly visible lines between each section on the finished frames. I decided to break up these lines somewhat by jittering the internal faces. If you choose to do this, use the Volume selection tool to select everything except points in the leading edge (+ Z side) and the sides (including the trailing edge is fine). Use the **Jitter** button (**Tools** panel) to move the inner points around some. I used the Gaussian option with the radii set to X = 2 m, Y = 0 m, Z = 2 m. Figure 3 shows the result of this operation. Save the completed strip object. I named my strip "WaveStrip.lwo."

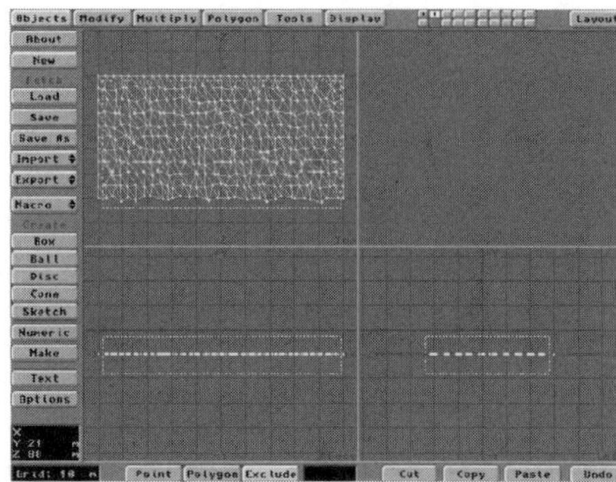

Figure 3: Jittering the internal points

The time has come to make our ring-shaped morph target. Copy the strip to another layer using the copy and paste tools. Hit the **Bend** button (**Modify** panel). Press the **Numeric** input button (n), and configure the settings to match those shown in Figure 4.

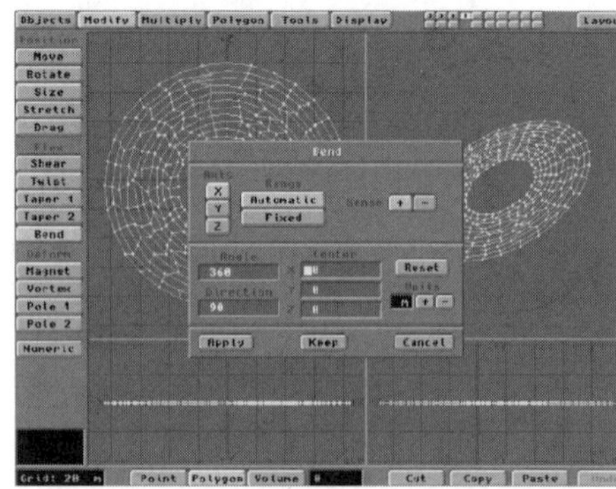

Figure 4: Bending the strip into a ring

The result should be a nice ring. Using the Center macro command, center this object, then save it as "WaveRing.lwo." [Editor's note: Modeler versions before 3.5 do not keep the point order of an object intact when you copy and paste in another layer. For those with pre-3.5 Modeler, perform the Bend operation in the same layer on the original object (after saving, of course).]

Now, switch over to Layout, and load the two objects from within the **Objects** panel. Adjust the camera to a position above the objects with both visible, so you can watch what's going on (remember to set a keyframe for the camera position). For the wave strip object, set the **Metamorph Level** to 100% (**Objects** panel) and the **Metamorph** Target to "WaveRing.lwo" (make sure **Object Dissolve** is 0%). If you will be setting up a scene using ray-traced or cast shadows, you can select the shadow options you want for this object to save rendering time. For the wave ring object simply set the **Object Dissolve** to 100%.

At this point, you should see just one copy of the ring, which is actually the strip morphed into the ring shape.

Burning Surface Questions

The main trick to this special effect is proper surface settings. The leading edge is bright and luminescent. As we move to the trailing edge, the surface gets slightly darker and dissolves further and further out, using fractal noise for transparency.

The most important thing to remember is to set the Fractal Noise textures to use **World Coordinates**. This setting allows each section of the rings to closely match its neighbors. Plus, when the ring is animated, the features of the texture will flow smoothly from one section to the next.

For the Ring.LE surface, I used the following settings:

Color: 46, 20, 255
Luminosity: 80%
Diffuse Level: 10%
Specular Level: 0% (Texture Mapped)
Glossiness: Medium
Reflectivity: 0%
Transparency: 0% (Texture Mapped)

Set the two texture-mapped channels to the same values:

Texture Size: 10, 10, 10
Texture Center: 0,0,0
World Coordinates: On
Texture Falloff: 0,0,0
Texture Velocity 0,1,0
Texture Value 10%
Frequencies: 3
Contrast: 1.0

Save these surface settings as "Wave.surface." Load it into the other nine surfaces. We'll be using it as a basis.

The explosive wave object that appears in the color pages varies smoothly in color down to 0,0,165. The **Luminosity** decreases by eight on each surface, until it reaches a value of eight at the trailing edge (Ring.LE-9). I decided to use a little extra transparency on the inside region, so Ring.LE-6 has a **Transparency** setting of 20%, Ring.LE-7 has 30%, Ring.LE-8 has 40%, and Ring.LE-9 has 50%.

The most important surface setting for this effect is the **Fractal Noise** Texture Value for the **Transparency** Map. Though it's not well documented, many of LightWave's settings can be set as high as 400 percent. The wave makes good use of this feature to vary smoothly from a solid wavefront to a trailing edge that has just a few wisps of smoke. Moving from Ring.LE to Ring.LE-9, my settings for the Texture Value were 10, 60, 100, 140, 180, 220, 260, 300, 340 and 380.

Now would be a good time to save your two objects. Hit F9 to do a quick test render of the current frame. If you don't see anything, your camera is on the wrong side of the wave. Move to the other side and re-render.

Animation Extras

It sure is pretty, isn't it? But there are still a number of things missing.

You certainly need a nice starfield for a background. LightWave comes with two that will fit the bill. In the Objects/Space directory, you'll find the ActualStars and the RandomStars objects. Select one and load it.

That helps. Now, what is it that's exploding? A spaceship? A planet? A star? A whole galaxy? Design something, or load one of the spaceships included with LightWave. Parent your wave ring object to your victim. Next, use the **Size** feature to reduce the scale on the wave strip object to 0,0,0. Point the camera at the victim and set up a few moments of animation of just your victim object: the calm before the storm. Why does the victim explode? You may want to add a laser beam or some other weapon striking it just prior to the explosion. Or, your poor ship may just suffer a spontaneous core breach. It's up to you.

The time is here. Our victim must go, in the most spectacular way possible. One important addition is a brief but very bright flash of light. LightWave's lens flares are the thing to use. Add a new light (**Lights** panel). Rename it "explosion." Set the intensity to 0, unless you have some other objects in the scene that you want the explosion to light up, in which case it should be a point light with an intensity envelope like that described for the lens flare.

Hit the **Lens Flare** button and select **Flare Options**. For starters, use the default settings, except for the **Flare Intensity**. Set up an envelope (**E** button) that keeps the flare invisible (0 intensity) until the explosion occurs. Set a key for the frame, also with a 0 value, immediately before you want the explosion. Make a key to start the explosion with a large value. Something like 300 percent will turn the screen nearly completely white. Quickly ramp the flare back down with a few more keys. You may want to leave it flickering around a value of 10% to indicate a small burning ember. Examine your envelope and adjust the tension, or set the Linear option (**Spline Controls**) to fix any odd features in the curve.

Exit the **Flare**, then **Lights** panels. Parent the explosion light to your victim. Go into the **Objects** panel and set up an **Object Dissolve** envelope for the victim that takes it from 0% dissolved just before the explosion to 100% dissolved as the explosion starts. Finally, set up some keyframes for the size of the explosion wave. Take it from 0,0,0 as the explosion starts to something that fills your shot and moves past the camera over the course of a few seconds. The exact values to use depend on your camera settings and the size of your victim object. Save your scene, then experiment away!

I recommend doing several test runs in low resolution with Antialiasing off. This allows you to quickly experiment with all of the various surface and timing issues without waiting too long. My stock Amiga 4000/040 takes about eight minutes to render a Medium Resolution, Low Antialiasing frame of the wave. When you're ready, open all the stops. Turn on Antialiasing and Motion Blur. Depth of Field might also make a good addition. Depending on how your camera is moving, particle blur may also be appropriate. Hit the Render button, check that you have all the options set the way you want (including Automatic Frame Advance), then head off to bed. Don't worry—there won't be anything to see for hours.

Explosive Possibilities

The finished product looks pretty amazing. Before I leave, I thought I'd share a couple of ideas to get you started on spiffing it up even more.

The Texture Velocity setting is worthy of experimentation. The X velocity causes some spiraling of the flames. The Z velocity setting controls radial movement of the texture. The Y velocity setting causes the flames to evolve or boil over time. Don't go overboard. A little movement goes a long way. Remember the dimensions of our object and that the velocity is the distance the texture moves for each frame. If you're animating at 30 frames per second, it doesn't take much velocity to be noticeable.

The breaks between each band of the wave are somewhat distracting if you get too close to the wave. This problem could easily be lessened by adding more rows of polygons in the original objects and thereby having more variations in the surface changes. Perhaps an easier route is to create the original objects with only one surface name and use a combination of **Texture Falloff** and **Fractal Noise** applied to **Luminosity** and **Transparency** to create the wave effect.

Burning debris flying from the explosion past the camera could be a nice addition. Secondary waves were used in the *Star Trek* shot, as well as a very rapidly expanding 3D sphere. This wave shot also had some thickness to its leading edge.

Add in other space animation suggestions that have appeared here in *LIGHTWAVEPRO*. Mojo's tips for improved starfields, easy laser beams and burning starships would all make wonderful additions to this shot.

Above all, remember that this tutorial is designed as a jumping board for experimentation. Be creative!

LWP

Rocket scientist Lloyd Eldred is head of an amateur film group, Galtham Films, in his spare time. Its current project, Space Rogues, T.S.E., *may be finished by the turn of the millennia. Eldred can be reached at galtham@universe. digex.net.*

Have Starfield, Will Travel

by William Frawley

Anybody out there still relying on the "Random Stars" object for their space scenes? If so, you need help. Dr. Starfield to the rescue! I mean, really, we've all seen them—shining examples of rich, cinematic starfields in movies such as *Star Wars*, *Star Trek* (all seven), and more. Heck, even the Universal logo background looks pretty impressive! In the vacuum of space, there's not much standing in the way of you and the glorious bounty of millions of visible stars. Here then, let the Doctor fill the required prescription for respectable starfields: caffeine, LightWave, good tunes and...more caffeine.

What Are Particles Again?

Just in case you've recently been revived from a successful cryogenics experiment, the basis of starfields in LightWave involves the use of particles, or more specifically, single-point polygons. This special type of polygon has the characteristic of being completely dimensionless, which causes it to uniformly render at the same screen size regardless of its distance from the camera. Created by converting a point into a polygon, particles possess all the surfacing capabilities of polygons, but because of the dimensionless nature of points, contain none of the spatial properties of polygons. Incidentally, two-point polygons, or lines, behave similarly as particles, except lines have a second dimension. Since version 3.5 of LightWave, users have been able to control the rendered screen size of both particles and lines: small, medium or large. This means that each particle renders as one pixel, a 3x3 pixel array or a 5x5 pixel array, respectively (similarly, lines are drawn as one, three or five pixels thick). This ability to control the size of rendered particles will play an important role later on in our endeavor for enhanced realism.

A Starfield of Dreams

OK, so now you're ready to get serious. You're in Modeler and you're wondering how many licks does it take to reach the center of a TootsiePop—uhh, I mean, how many particles does it take to make a convincing starfield? Well, since we'll be constructing a fully functional, spherical starfield to be used in scenes where camera movement is quite dynamic (a lot of panning, tilting and warping), I've found that approximately 57,000 is the minimum for a nice plenteous look. (A dense starfield is one thing; we'll see later that a resplendent starfield takes multiple objects and surfaces.) However, you must consider your memory situation. On an 18MB T2000, this many particles uses about 75 percent of the available space, leaving only enough room for about another 20,000 polygons for a successful render. You can reduce the amount of particles needed if you're camera doesn't pan much by slicing the starfield in half and discarding all the particles behind the camera. Or parent those remaining particles to a Null and use the camera's motion file for the Null's motion file. Consider this option as well: If you do have enough RAM, you can again slice the field in half, but this time take those particles and add them to the remaining particles (rotate 180 degrees) in front of the camera, thereby increasing the starfield's density twofold.

With an idea of how many particles you can comfortably get away with on your machine, there's just one more thing to consider before we create the starfield: its size. Again, consider what the camera's motion will be. If it's warping through space, you might want to size the starfield as large as possible to reduce the apparent motion of the more distant stars. Otherwise, if the starfield is too small, all stars will show motion, destroying the illusion of the galaxy's expansiveness, and in no time you'll be at the Outer Rim with no stars in sight (we'll cover special star columns for warping a little later). On the other hand, if the camera merely needs to pan or remain static, pivoting motion won't divulge the stars' actual distance from the viewer. Therefore, keep these points in mind when using the appropriate particle-creating macro. [At press time, I'm still working on "Starfield.lwm," a starfield/particle macro that is much faster and more appropriate for our purpose than the "Point Distributions" macro. Look for it on a future *LIGHTWAVEPRO* disk.]

- For now, enter Modeler, select **New** (N, **Objects** menu) and use the "Point Distributions" macro to create 10,000 particles. Set Falloff Towards to "Center" and Density Distribution to "Constant," leaving everything else at their defaults. This process could take about 10 minutes, but once it's done, these particles will serve as "seeds" for building most of our starfield. Enter Polygon selection mode (space bar) and rename the **Surface** (q, **Polygon** menu) to "Stars 1" or something similar. Export this first object to Layout, saving it with some name like "Stars1.10K" where the 10K signifies that this object is made up of 10,000 particles.
- Now **Copy** (c) these particles, enter layer 2 (2) and **Paste** (v). Next we need to randomly shift the positions of the particles so they don't overlap with those in layer 1. Because the radius is only 1 m (suitable for our purpose), **Jitter** (J, **Tools** menu) the points of the object by .1 m (5-10 percent of the radius) on all axes (Figure 1). Rename the surface (q) for these particles "Stars 2" and again **Export** to Layout with a name of "Stars2.10K."

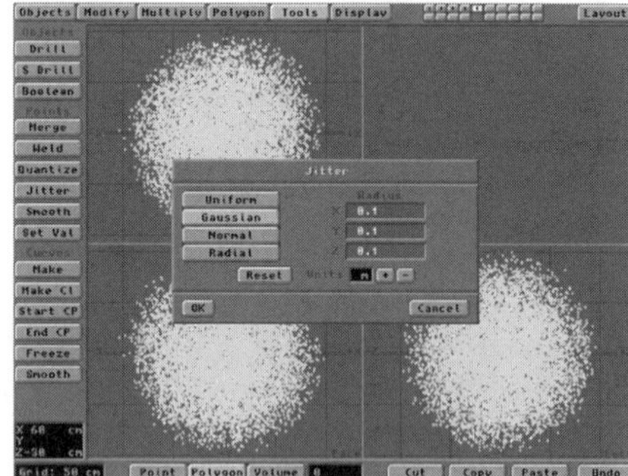

Figure 1: To avoid having to create any more particles than necessary with the "Point Distributions" macro, construct a percentage of the total number, then copy this object to other layers. Use the Jitter tool to randomize the locations of the cloned particles.

- Repeat this procedure three more times so that there are 10,000 particles in each of the first five layers, each with distinctive surface names and saved as separate objects.
- Now enter layer 6, and again use the "Point Distributions" macro to create 5,000 more particles (same parameters as before). Rename this surface "Stars 6" and Export/Save as "Stars6.5K."

- For the last step, enter layer 7 and create 1,000 particles, rename the surface "Stars 7" and Export/Save as "Stars7.1K."
- Enter Layout, shut down Modeler and **Reset** the camera to the origin. **Create** a keyframe (Return) for the camera in its new position. Since we constructed multiple star objects earlier, we can now assign each group of particles a different particle size to give the starfield the appearance of depth. Without this feature, each star looks as though it was at the same distance as its neighbor. Pretty boring, eh? Therefore, make the Particle/Line Size (**Objects** panel) of Star objects 1 to 4 "small," that of Star objects 5 and 6 "medium," and that of Star object 7 "large." Since each particle won't be affected by a light source, you can save some rendering time by turning off each star object's "Self Shadow," "Cast Shadow" and "Receive Shadow" options.
- In the **Surfaces** panel, set each object's surface **Luminosity** to 100% and **Diffuse Level** to 0%. Change the color of each surface to include some yellow, blue and red varieties. By varying the Surface Color and Luminosity of each surface, you can fine-tune the subtleties of the starfield to suit your particular taste.
- Next, turn **Ambient Intensity** (**Lights** panel) and **Light Intensity** to 0% and make sure to set the **Antialiasing** (**Camera** panel) to at least **Low**. Before you do the test render, do a **Save All Objects** (**Objects** panel) to record the surface settings and then **Save Scene** (**Scene** panel).

From now on you can load this starfield into any of your space projects by doing a very handy Load From Scene (**Objects** panel). With that business out of the way, try a test render and compare it with the Actual Stars object (Figure 2).

To increase the richness of the field even more, try further subdividing each object into multiple surfaces back in Modeler. I'm sure you can figure out how to do this simple task. You'd then have multiple particle sizes with multiple surface attributes. The Milky Way never looked so good.

Figure 2: With a little effort, you can overcome the "girlie-starfield" syndrome. On the left is the Actual Stars object (≈1500 particles); on the right could be your own 56K (memory permitting) award-winning starfield.

Yes, My Sun

A good starfield wouldn't be worth its weight in hydrogen if it didn't have some local stars asserting their presence in your scene. This is where lens flares really shine (pun intended). Depending on how you want a local star to look, you'll want to use at least two flares for the actual star and another for any associated glare or lens spikes (star filter). For example, Figure 3 shows the settings I used for each of the Seven Sisters shown in the color image "Pleiades."

For each nearby sun, I used three flares. One was used as a faint blue flare and to produce lens spiking using the Star Filter option (**Flare Options** panel). The other two flares were colored white and used to produce the actual star. By combining two or more flares with similar attributes, the edges of the central hotspot will be more pronounced and the overall glare surrounding the lens flare will be reduced. Next, in order to vary the apparent size of each star, I used the Fade With Distance option so I wouldn't have to concern myself with each flares intensity. Simply set a Nominal Distance, parent all the flares for each star to a null object, and move the null to the desired distance. For a really cool effect, if you happen to be animating the scene (I do a lot of still images), use Grant Boucher's "Random Envelope Generator" macro to create an envelope for each flare's intensity channel. This will give each local star its own pulsating look (Hint: Keep the envelope peaks fairly moderate).

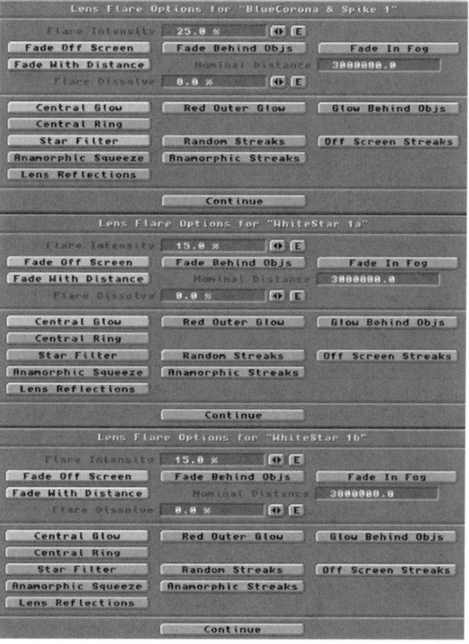

Figure 3: Three lens flares were used for each of the Pleiades suns in the related color photo. Shown are the settings used for one blue lens flare acting as the flare and lens spike element. The other two identical white flares were used as the basis for the sharply defined star element.

In "Pleiades" I added a little extra eye candy in the form of dust clouds surrounding various members of the open cluster. Using OpalPaint (or any good 24-bit paint application), I simply painted a series of images using a combination of airbrush and watercolor tools to blend the blue into the black background and vice versa. After saving the color version of each image, I converted each one into a grayscale negative, making sure to boost the blue channel considerably more than the red or green in order to heighten the contrast between the dust and the background. This step ensures that, when applied as a Transparency texture map, the blue region (now represented by black in the negative) will be fairly opaque; hence, more visible (Figure 4).

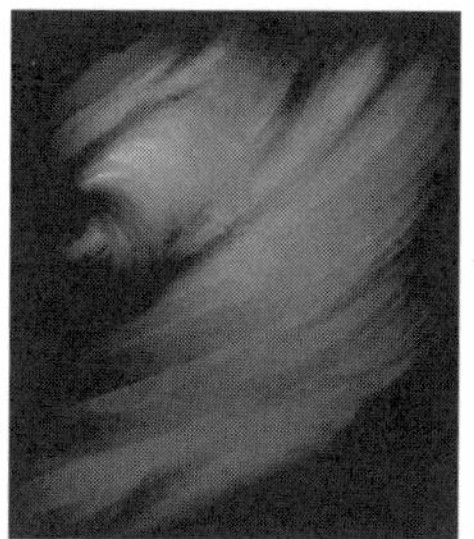

Figure 4: A good 24-bit paint program makes adding subtle details to your scene easy. In this case, the color (shown in black and white) image on the left was texture-mapped to a plane for the dust cloud's color, and then converted to a grayscale negative for the transparency texture map (right).

Ahead, Warp Factor 9

So now you want to warp, do ya? "I'm givin' it all she's got Captain! I can't give any morrrrrrrre!" Well, if you plan on testing the limits of your inertial dampening system, a different kind of starfield—a kinder, gentler starfield—is required. For straight-ahead warping through space, it's best to construct a columnar-shaped starfield; a tunnel full of stars, more or less. To preclude excessive redundancy on creating a warp column, I refer you to Mojo's excellent treatment of this subject in his article "Simple Space Stuff: Part I" (*LIGHTWAVEPRO*, August 1994).

Once you understand this concept for creating a nice warp column (don't forget to use Particle Blur, in the **Camera** panel), let me take it one step further by

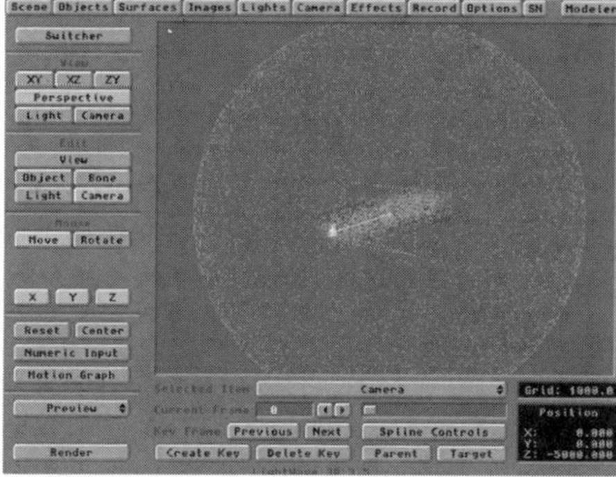

Figure 5: To get that DS9-end-credit look, more accurately reflecting the principle of parallax, the camera travels through an elongated star column, which is in turn surrounded by a much larger spherical shell of particles. (The Spherize macro was used on a Point Distributions-created starfield.) This gives the illusion of extremely distant stars in the background as the closer ones warp by.

offering this additional tip. As seen in the end credits for *Deep Space Nine*, the principle of parallax provides a more accurate representation of what warping through space might look like. This means that as we are traveling forward (or any direction, for that matter), the closest stars will appear to move the greatest, causing the longest blurs, and the most distant stars might not appear to move at all. Two possible solutions exist to mimic this phenomenon. Either build a completely realistic, physically accurate spherical starfield, as we did earlier (scaled extremely large), to act as a mock galaxy, or create a "shell" of particles surrounding the warp column to act as a static background wall of stars (Figure 5). In both cases, make sure to set a Distance Dissolve (**Objects** panel) for the star objects you'll be warping through. Aren't space scenes fun?!

Docking Bay

Here are some astronomical constants that might be useful:

1 astronomical unit = 1.5 x 1011 m
1 light year = 9.4605 x 1015 m
1 parsec = 206,265 A.U. or 3.262 light years
Milky Way radius = ≈55,000 light years
Number of stars in the Milky Way = >200 billion

Send questions, comments or frozen pizzas to Blue-Line Imaging, c/o William Frawley, 315 W. Fifth Street, Muscataine, IA 52761.

Missile Contrails Made Easy

by Mojo and John Teska

One of the more action-packed episodes of *Babylon 5* last season was the two-parter "Voice in the Wilderness," in which we discover that the planet the station orbits isn't as lifeless as everyone had believed.

Upon conducting a routine survey mission in the planet's upper atmosphere, a shuttle awakens an ancient defense system, which fires a series of missiles. The rockets streak past the camera, narrowly missing our heroes, who manage to safely return to *Babylon 5*.

Many people have commented on how good the missile smoke trails looked in this sequence and have often asked how it was accomplished. John Teska, Foundation Imaging's godlike animator, was responsible for coming up with the effect and should be given sole credit for it. I, being simply a humble writer, had absolutely nothing to do with it and am only chronicling the details of its creation. Anyway, he asked me to make that clear. Now, on with the details you've all been waiting for!

Love Missile F1-11

Before you can have a smoke trail behind your missile, you need to make a missile. It's best to build your missile (or whatever) along the Z axis and not the Y, as you might anticipate. This assumes you want to use the **Align to Path** feature in Layout's motion graphs, which will easily allow your object to face in the direction it's flying.

The sequence in question from *Babylon 5* had the missiles flying in a crazy zig-zag pattern, so this feature came in handy. However, LightWave 3D assumes that objects using **Align to Path** are facing the positive Z axis (as all good vehicles should) and enforces this as a default. If your objects don't face this direction, LightWave will disorient them when you try to align them to a path. So, in short, this means that all references to height in this tutorial will be made along the Z axis and not the Y, as would normally be the case.

- Make sure the bottom (exhaust) of the missile is located at 0,0,0 in Modeler, since this would be the axis of rotation for an object propelled from the base.
- The smoke object is a simple, subdivided tube that should have the same circumference as the missile's base. Make it considerably long (maybe 10 times the height of the missile) and subdivide it to approximately 4,000 polygons. You'll be adding a displacement map to this object, so make sure you triple it as well in order to avoid polygon errors. The top of the smoke cone should be located at 0,0,0, right at the base of the missile (although saved as a separate object). Only one surface name is needed.

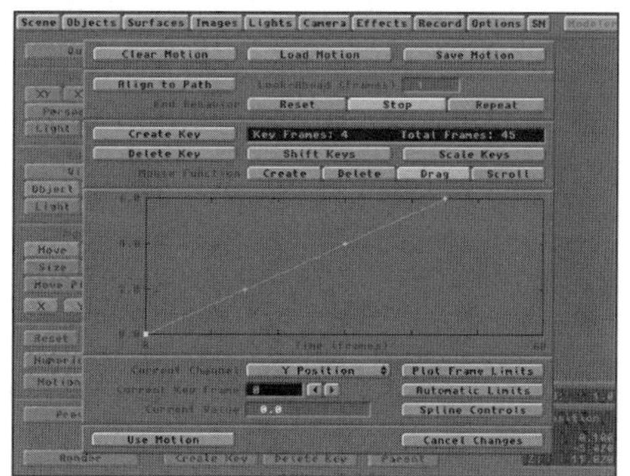

Figure 1: The motion path of the missile and the top Bone. Copy it to the middle Bone and shift all keys by 15 frames.

Blowing Smoke

- In LightWave, load your missile and smoke trail. Create a motion path for the missile to your liking, perhaps start by simply moving it straight up (the zig-zagging is a bit more difficult and will be explained later). Keep in mind that this effect was designed to be photographed from a bird's eye view, with the rockets winding their way up into the camera. If you're going to take my advice and save the zig-zagging for later, move the camera off to the side and have the missile fire upward and to the right (or left), since a move straight up into the camera will obviously hide the smoke trail.
- Don't parent the smoke trail to the missile. Instead, select it and add three Bones to it (**Object Skeleton**). Yikes! Bones! I know, I know, Bones are the thorn in any animator's side. Trust me, this scenario makes them almost completely painless. You'll see.

Name the Bones something along the lines of Top, Middle and Bottom.

- Save the motion from the missile and load it into each Bone's motion graph by hitting (m) from the keyboard to bring up any items's motion graph. The Bones will now be on top of each other (with the exact same keyframes), so position each of them within the missile according to their names and set a new first keyframe for each. Go to the last keyframe and move the Bones back into their proper positions, then remake this last keyframe. Set the Bones' **Rest Lengths** (r) and your smoke trail should now follow behind your missile, wherever it may go.
- As the missile flies upward, the smoke trail needs to taper out at the bottom and expand. This is where the middle and bottom Bones come into play. Simply increase the size of the middle Bone during the animation, and roughly double that size for the bottom Bone. This will spread out the contrail evenly from the middle to the bottom while the top Bone will keep the upper portion of the smoke locked to the shape of the missile's exhaust.

Hey, guess what? That does it for the Bones! I bet you never imagined they could be so useful and simple.

Billowing Made Easy

The key to making that silly cone actually look like rippling, spewing, ozone-depleting smoke is to use a displacement map. An easy one. Your favorite one. Yes, I'm talking about Fractal Bumps!

- Load that puppy up into the cone's displacement map (**Objects** panel) and set the **Texture Center** at the bottom of your object. (Load it into Modeler and put the cursor there to be certain of the exact coordinates— it'll be something like 0,0,-100 if you're doing this right). Set the **Texture Falloff** to dissipate near the top of your smoke trail, so the billowing will grow more pronounced toward the lower portion of the smoke (as happens in the real world). Try to avoid too much displacement at the top of the cone, or else you may see it separate from the missile exhaust. Having it fall off to zero at the top would be best.

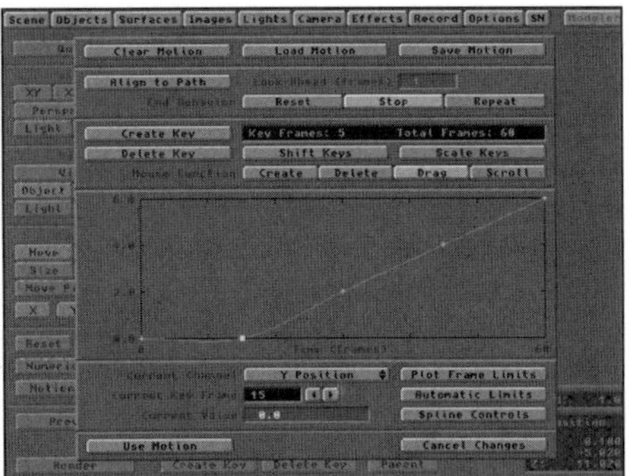

Figure 2: A new frame has been created at 15. However, it shares the same location as 0, which means the middle Bone will stay locked in the same position for half a second. This is bad.

Make sure you give it a nice velocity along the negative Z axis (downward/backward), with a slight velocity on the X and Y (maybe a tenth of the Z) to liven things up a little.

- You might also consider putting an envelope on the amplitude that increases over time, since the smoke should only billow slightly at launch but increase heavily as the seconds go by. But wait! Look! There's no envelope button next to the amplitude box! Gee wilikers, you're right! By gum, I know there's got to be a way. Aha! I've got it! A trick that's so crazy only Allen Hastings could have come up with it.

Whenever an object has been given a displacement map, the polygon size requester automatically becomes the envelope for that object's displacement amplitude. Talk about counterintuitive! Just make sure you don't simply type a number into the polygon size and expect it to change the amplitude—it *must* be an envelope. LightWave will detect that it is and automatically apply the envelope to the displacement map. Yes, this does mean that you cannot change the polygon size of an object that has a displacement map. Why not just put an envelope on the amplitude itself? Good question! I've been asking Allen that for over two years now...

[Editor's note: Check out "Displacement Envelopes" in this issue for more information on this procedure.]

Just a Little More...

At this point, you should be able to make a wireframe preview to see if your smoke trail is looking good. If it isn't, keep working at it. If it is, then it's time to set some surfaces and render this thing!

- The color of the smoke trail should be bright white (or maybe even a yellowish tinge), falling off to gray somewhere toward the middle or bottom (whatever you like). Set this by making the base color gray, but add a brighter fractal noise in the texture panel for **Surface Color** (**T**). The **Texture Center** should be at the top (0,0,0) and fall off to whatever point on the object you want your smoke to become gray. Make sure you add a **Texture Velocity** to the noise, similar to the settings for the displacement map but not exactly the same (different velocities on all your noise channels help break things up and look more chaotic).
- Similar settings for **Luminosity** help make the plume seem as if it is white-hot at the base of the missile. However, the majority of the cloud should not appear to be glowing, so give this fractal noise pattern a much sharper falloff. Again, apply a similar yet different velocity.
- Give the **Diffuse Level** some fast-moving noise, but this time, don't add any falloff—the entire cloud should have this texture moving through it. Play with the amount of the noise's diffusion until you get it as dark (or as light) as you prefer.
- Last but not least is **Transparency**. The main requester should be set for 0%, but inside the texture panel give it some fractal noise that's 100% transparent. Like the displacement map, this **Texture Center** should start at the bottom and fall off toward the top. This will ensure that the smoke trail is solid at the top but becomes transparent at the bottom, where the smoke would naturally begin to dissipate. Of course, add some velocity so this requester doesn't feel left out.
- **Edge Transparency** is also important, so your smoke doesn't have any hard edges. This value varies greatly, depending on what angle your smoke trail is at in relation to the camera. Try different numbers until you get a nice balance between edges that are too hard and smoke that begins to completely disappear.
- Make sure you turn **Smoothing** on and increase the **Max Smoothing Angle** to at least 120 degrees. Displacement maps bend and distort your polygons in all sorts of nasty ways, almost certainly creating shapes that render hard-edged unless you tell LightWave to smooth at a higher angle.

Look! The bottom of the surfaces panel! By Jove, that must mean you're finished! Go ahead and render a test.

(Wait until render is done before reading this.) Ha! Fooled you. Does it look like crap? Of course it does. This is a complicated procedure and thus will never work on the first try. However, this effect has been proven to work and has been seen on TV, no less.

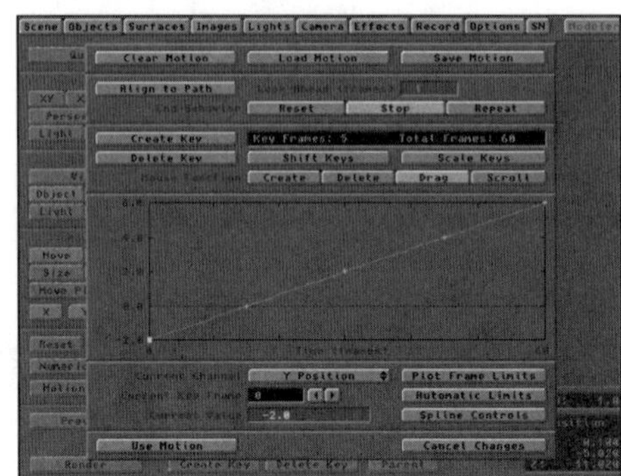

Figure 3: Frame 0 is dragged down to smooth out the path and start the middle Bone at a position under the top Bone. This motion will follow the original with a 15-frame delay. Perfection at last!

Therefore, you can bet your bottom dollar that with a little persistence and some creative tweaking, you can have missiles flying off your screen in no time.

Advanced Lessons for Smart Alecks

OK, so it's not such an advanced idea, but adding a lens flare to the base of the missile will make it look much cooler. Since it will be moving an extreme distance in relation to the camera, it's probably worth your time to figure out the proper **Fade With Distance** settings for the flare. If you're feeling really game, add a nice flickering dissolve and size envelope to make the exhaust look that much more realistic.

The true advanced lesson is in how to make the smoke trail snake properly behind a zig-zagging missile, as it did in the episode of *B5*. The first step is to make a decent motion path for your missile, which takes it weaving in and out like a drunk behind the wheel of the space shuttle.

- As before, copy this motion path to all your Bones, but use **Shift Keys** to shift each successive path by 15 frames. This forces the smoke trail to follow in the path of the missile at a slight delay in three separate sections, creating the illusion of the contrail "staying" in place while new smoke pours out of the exhaust.

Copying and shifting the motion paths can be a little tricky, so pay close attention.

- After copying the missile's path to the three Bones, you'll end up with all the Bones on top of each other, as you did before. The top Bone can be left alone, since you want it to follow the missile exactly. To shift and lower the middle Bone, call up its motion graph (Figures 1 to 3) and shift all frames by 15. Assuming you have a key every 15 frames, you will now have a gap between 0 and 30. Create a new keyframe at 15. This places your Bone in the same location from frames 0 to 15. You want it to start lower than the top Bone, so, from the motion graph's Y position, simply drag frame 0 down until the path is smooth.

That's it! The middle Bone will now follow the path of the missile and the top Bone with a 15-frame lag. Now simply copy the motion from the middle Bone to the bottom Bone and follow the same 15-frame shift procedure. After a little tweaking of the paths by eye, you should now be able to exactly duplicate the contrail effect from *Babylon 5*.

LWP

Mojo can't think of anything else to write about and is facing the grim possibility of not getting any extra money for contributing to LIGHTWAVEPRO. *Please send in your topic ideas, no matter how ridiculous, so he can continue to fund his pig farm.*

LightWave & PhotoCD

by Dan Ablan

Just about every serious LightWave animator I know uses image maps in his 3D world. Many, like myself, get images from real-world textures, usually via camcorder, videotape or prepackaged disk sets. Some also use textures from CD-ROMs. But another area that many animators overlook is PhotoCD technology.

Kodak introduced the PhotoCD a number of years ago, and those who have attended any of the yearly Consumer Electronic Shows have seen the demonstrations. It was a great idea: take any film, from any camera, and transfer it to a compact disc, and have your images preserved forever. You can even take existing photographs and have them put on a disc. No photo albums to buy, no sifting through shoeboxes of photographs—just one simple compact disc. Sounds great, right? Well, it seems that the price for a PhotoCD unit was just too much for the average consumer (anywhere from $600-$800), so there wasn't the hype that Kodak had hoped for.

The Technology

It's been said that one person's misfortune (in this case, one corporation's misfortune) is another's fortune. The PhotoCD never made it big in the home consumer market. Sometime last year, the prices on consumer PhotoCD players dropped dramatically, and I was able to take home a brand-new, top-of-the-line Kodak PhotoCD player for $179. Big deal, you say? To me it was. Before I moved into animation and before broadcast, I was studying to be a photojournalist. Even though I had found my niche in 3D, including photography into my animations was always a great interest. Plus, I knew the advantages of using image maps in LightWave. By using a PhotoCD from the Kodak PhotoCD player, I was able to use the video out directly into input number one on my Toaster, without a TBC, and I didn't have to deal with shuttling through video tape, frame-grabbing, then stabilizing my images. The PhotoCD unit lets me crop, enlarge or scale my images before I grab, which is just one less step to go through in the computer. Any roll of film that you take pictures on can be developed onto a PhotoCD. Your local drugstore or photo shop can develop the CD for you. It's not very expensive, and although prices vary, you can expect to pay around $15 for a roll of 24 exposures. Don't feel that you need to go to the best camera shop in town to have your film developed: every store sends your film out for processing to PhotoCDs, so shop around. WalMart usually does a pretty nice job, and turnaround time is about seven to 10 days. You can also take existing negatives or prints and have them transferred to a PhotoCD. Each disc holds up to 100 images.

What About My CD-ROM?

Most of today's CD-ROMs, whether internal or external, will read a PhotoCD. With the right CD-ROM software, such as ASIM CDFS (a PhotoCD manager that makes your CD-ROM readable) you can grab images. This is a great way to go, especially if you are using the standalone LightWave version. The standalone LightWave, obviously, has no Toaster, which means no frame-grabbing capabilities. Using ASIM CDFS, you can have a "contact sheet" of the images on your PhotoCD. From there, you select the particular image you want to load and tell the computer where to save it. This process works just fine; however, I've found that if you have frame-grabbing capabilities, you're better off.

Through the CD-ROM, loading an image takes a few minutes, and saving it adds more time, because the image is uncompressed, sometimes consuming nearly 5MBs of disk space. Then, you need to crop, scale and resave the image before using it in LightWave. ASIM does let you flip or rotate the image, but cropping needs to be done in a paint program, or more likely, through Art Department Professional or ImageFX.

When you use the Kodak PhotoCD player and frame grab the image, the whole process takes less than one minute, and as you may know, the more time you can save, the better. Also, the PhotoCD unit lets you crop and zoom into any area of the image you desire. A remote control is provided, with directional keys that allow the user to position a rectangular box anywhere on the image. Once you've selected the area you want to enlarge, just hit the button, and you'll see the blown-up image right on your monitor. If you want to scale an image down for use as a diffusion map or an image in the distance, you can hit the full-view button on the PhotoCD player and get an image that is scaled down 50 percent but maintains the proper aspect ratio.

Image Quality

Either way you choose, frame-grabbed or CD-ROM, there are bigger advantages to using PhotoCDs in your work. Making scenes appear realistic in LightWave is always a challenge, and the proper lighting and surfacing are keys to creating that perfect look. I use image maps in just about every animation, for simple reflections, image maps, bump maps, etc.

By taking just an hour or two, using a 35mm camera and a good roll of film, you can have a supply of texture maps better than anything you could buy, and these images will make your work more original and unique. For example, in the warehouse image in the color pages, I used a PhotoCD image of my windowsill as a diffusion map for the walls, wood beams and floor. By taking a single PhotoCD image and manipulating it a bit—cutting it up, darkening certain areas through ToasterPaint or some other paint package—I now have different-looking PhotoCD images. I used a PhotoCD image of some rocks for the bumps in the tank. That particular rock texture has been used countless times for roughing up a surface, bump maps, specularity maps and helping add realism to my scenes. Figure 1 shows the actual image of the rocks that I grabbed from my PhotoCD.

Probably the single best advantage of using PhotoCD technology in your animations is the quality. The image resolution of film looks so good that if you

Figure 1: This image of rocks started as a photograph and was grabbed into the Toaster through a Kodak PhotoCD unit.

begin using CD images on a regular basis, you'll have a difficult time when taking your images from video or pre-packaged sets. Also, with the image quality being so crisp, you can scale down the image, saving memory in LightWave, without much degradation to the final output.

For example, if you were building a front hallway and wanted the camera to fly across the room, ending up on a closeup of a picture on a bookshelf or wall, and you grabbed that particular image from video, you would have to either (a) use a large image taking up too much memory, or (b) not travel in so close. By using PhotoCD image quality, you can have an image that takes up only 200K and still be able to travel up close to it.

Figure 2 shows a front hallway. Total image memory used is 1.13MB. The floor is a variation of the rock image (Figure 1), and each photograph and texture is from PhotoCD, taken with 200 speed film and developed at a small camera shop around the corner. The closeup image in the color pages shows pictures on the wall that still look clear and sharp when the camera travels by, though each one is only about 200K.

One thing to think about with PhotoCDs is putting your own pictures into your scenes. Carry your camera around with you and take pictures of whatever catches your eye. Take a picture of your blue jeans and use it for a nice background for text. Or how about the bricks or concrete on that building you always walk past? Wouldn't that be a nice texture to use in LightWave?

Figure 2: This image of a front hallway uses a total image memory of only 1.13MB. The floor is a variation of the rock image and each photograph and texture is from PhotoCD.

An interesting thing will happen when you begin using image technology like this. You'll develop your eye even more, paying closer attention to textures, surfaces and light in the real world. And you know that creating a 3D computer-generated world that looks like the real world is the ultimate goal.

Results

Experiment with textures as often as you can, for image maps, bump maps, clip maps, etc. Perhaps you could mimic a $50,000 ADO (digital video effects unit) and use PhotoCD images mapped onto flat polygons slowly moving across the screen. If you've seen the TV series *Viper*, you've observed LightWave's powerful Front Projection Image Mapping (FPIM)capabilities in scenes such as those of the vehicle launching a probe out of its back end. Think about using a PhotoCD for your next FPIM project. Take a photo of the street you live on. Get the PhotoCD image of it and bring it into LightWave. Now use front projection image mapping to make a dinosaur or spaceship fly out from behind a car or building.

The more you play with all of LightWave's buttons, the more familiar you'll be with what they do, and you'll open the doors to creativity, thinking of new and exciting ways to achieve that look you want. LightWave is a very powerful 3D program and is constantly improving. By adding elements from the real world through a process such as PhotoCD technology, your animations can become even better.

LWP

Dan Ablan is the president of AGA graphics in Chicago.

LightWave Tech

by Phillip Hice

This new column actually starts at the next paragraph. Because John Gross runs the *LWPRO* editorial department like a dictator, I was ordered to include a brief introduction, so here it is:

Hi. You are probably aware that John Gross, Grant Boucher and John Parenteau (among others) not only write *LWPRO* articles, but are also animators at Amblin Imaging. I also work for Amblin Imaging, except, rather than animate, I handle all of the technical aspects of 3D work. These areas include, but are not limited to, building file servers and disk array sub-systems, network administration and design, and on-site workstation service.Anytime John has a technical question, he comes to me. With my joining the LWPRPO writing staff, you now have the same opportunity. It is my intention, with this column, to evaluate new hardware, inform users of potential bugs and how to avoid them, and to assist with anything that has to do with your system in general.

Well, as you know, LightWave for the PC is just about here, and, as with every type of change, both good and bad come from it. On the good side of this change we have faster rendering times, inverse kinematics, HIIP (host independent image protocol), distributed network rendering, and more colors available for the interface, just to name a few. Now for the bad side. I am sure that many of you, even the ones who can't currently afford a new system, have been looking into pricing on various PC- type systems to run LightWave, such as 486s, Pentiums, MIPS and DEC Alphas.

Although each of these systems runs a different processor, they all have certain things in common. Some of these items—like floppy drives, hard drives, mice and keyboards—are obvious similarities, but there are more important, not so obvious similarities that you need to be aware of. Of these, not-so-obvious similarities, two of them, bus architecture and video display, stand out as areas that require immediate understanding in order to make the best purchase decision.

Bus Architecture

Bus architecture refers to the style of adapter card slots your motherboard contains. In the Amiga, you had your Zorro slot, your video slot, a few Amiga slots, and even several PC-style slots. In the world of PCs, however, you normally have two main bus types on the motherboard. The first type of bus, which happens to be the very first PC-type bus, is the ISA slot. ISA stands for Industry Standard Architecture, and includes both XT and AT bus types. The ISA-type slot is the same PC slot found in your old Amiga. The XT slot refers to the small 8-bit slot not normally found on new systems. The AT slot refers to the larger, 16-bit slot, which is an XT slot with an additional 8-bits of data path included. As stated earlier, the ISA bus type is found on all PC systems, because it was the first design and has, as its name implies, become the industry standard for all systems. Because of this broad-base support, the ISA bus has the largest selection of peripherals to choose from. For certain items, the ISA bus is just fine, and sometimes recommended. Such is the case with I/O devices. The design of serial and parallel communications cards was done back when there were only eight bits to use, and thus they have only 8-bit memory addresses. If the cards only use an 8-bit memory address, there is no reason to use a 16-Bit card/slot to handle the communications. Also, the ISA slots timing is based on a fraction of the clock speed, usually somewhere around 8 to 12 MHz depending on the overall system speed.

The next step in bus design is the **EISA** type. EISA stands for Enhanced Industry Standard Architecture, and once again, as the name states, this design is an enhancement of the ISA type. Like the ISA bus, the EISA bus utilizes a fractional method for determining clock speed, also somewhere in the 8 to 12 MHz range. Where the enhancement comes in is that the EISA bus breaks the 16-bit ISA barrier with a full 32-bits of data path, effectively doubling the data transfer capabilities. But that's not all. Along with 32-bit data transfers, the EISA bus brings in another feature to further enhance its abilities—Bus Mastering. Bus mastering is a system function that allows multiple cards to utilize the same physical hardware settings without causing a conflict within the system. This is highly desirable in file servers, as it allows for multiple network cards to share settings that normally could only be used by one card. Another performance enhancement over the ISA bus is in improved DMA (direct memory access) transfers, as they are done at 32-bit wide request rather than 16- or 8-bit.

The bus structure that won wide approval after the introduction of the EISA bus was the **VESA-Local Bus** (VLB). VESA stands for Video Equipment Standards Association. This group which determines the standards computer video devices should be built to meet, such as the pin-out configuration for an SVGA monitor or the standard refresh rates for specific resolutions. The reason the VLB bus came about was that with the introduction of Windows and other graphical software, something was needed to allow for performance gains in the video display area of PC computers. Thus VESA stepped in with the Local Bus standard. Like the EISA bus, the VLB is based on the original ISA bus, with additional connections to allow for 32-bit data transfers. The significant performance increases come from a combination of two things. First, the local part of Local Bus refers to the electronically close proximity to the CPU, which allows for quicker data exchange. Secondly, in order for the VLB to communicate directly with the processor, it runs not at a fraction of the system speed, but at the true system speed at a maximum of 33MHz. This combination of 32 bits and 33MHz allows for data transfer rates that are approximately 3 to 4 times that of EISA. The only drawback from VLB is that it doesn't allow for the Bus Mastering capabilities of the EISA bus, making it not as functional as an EISA machine designed for file server usage.

The fourth, and currently the final, bus structure to discuss is called **PCI**, or PCI Local Bus. PCI stands for Peripheral Component Interconnect, and was developed by Intel, the company we all know is the world's largest manufacturer of PC processors, which helped convince the industry to accept PCI. Currently, the PCI bus design is the bus of choice for PC users, for both obvious, and not so obvious reasons. First the obvious: the PCI bus is basically all of the best things from the VLB and EISA bus types in that it has 32-bit data paths, can communicate at 33MHz clock speeds, has improved DMA performance, and Bus Mastering features. All of these make the PCI bus the best choice for performance in both workstation and file server applications.

Well, now that we've spoken about the obvious reasons for going with the PCI bus, I would like to mention a couple of other primary reasons for its acceptance. First is the fact that the current PCI conventions have provisions not only for a 32-bit data path, but it also calls out specifications for a 64-bit version of the bus, which with no other changes will give double the performance of the original 32-bit version. Although the specs for the 64-bit version exist, I have only seen one system with a 64-bit slot, the Carrera EV5 tested in last month's benchmark article. Currently manufacturers have devoted manufacturing of both motherboards and peripherals to the 32-bit version. But, that leads us to our second, not so obvious reason for choosing PCI, expansion. The 64-bit slots are merely enhancements to the 32-Bit slot, and will handle 32-bit cards without any problems (as a matter of fact I ran the 32-bit video and SCSI cards for the EV5 in 64-bit slots without fail). Another aspect of expansion comes from cross-platform expansion. This is to say that not only is the PCI bus the primary performance bus for x86 and Pentium systems, but is also the case in RISC machines as well. As an example, my personal Cobra 275 machine from Carrera utilizes my old Matrox PCI video card that I previously had in my 486DX2-66, as well as my SCSI card. This cross platform usage allows for significantly less expensive upgrades, as you can utilize some of your existing hardware, thus keeping down the costs.

Video Display Cards

Now that we have decided that the PCI bus is the best way to go, let's talk about another confusing area of the PC world, video cards.(Although I am specifically discussing PCI cards, the information discussed concerning video cards can apply to all different bus types.) Unlike the Amiga, PCs and similar machines have no inherent video capabilities. All systems require a display card to interpret the digital data and convert it into visual data. Back in the early days of computers, a black screen with a single or 'monochorme' display color was more than sufficient for the tasks of the day. Now that we have Windows, Windows NT, OS/2, and various other graphical type operating systems, we require the ability to display millions of colors at resolutions that even five years ago were merely dreams. It is this color/resolution ratio that needs to be understood in order to select the proper video card for your application.

As you are now aware, the current standard for the PCI bus is 32-Bits wide. This means that the CPU/system can send data to the card 32-bits at a time (VLB and EISA also send 32-Bits at a time, while ISA only sends 16-Bits at a time.) This is where the confusion starts for some people. Someone might ask, "If a true color image is only a 24-bit image, then a 32-bit bus is overkill." WRONG! The 24-bits that are talked about in regards to an actual digital image such as an IFF file is bits-per-pixel of resolution. Which means that for every pixel of on screen data, you have 24-Bits of information in memory to determine its color. On the other hand, the 32-bits referred to by the PCI bus is the number of information bits that can be sent to the video card, from memory, at any one time. So, if a 32-bit PCI display card is sent 24-bit per pixel color information, the card is capable of receiving approximately 1.5 pixels worth of information at a time (1 pixel =24 bits of data, 1.5 pixels = 36 bits of data).

If you understood the last paragraphs explanation of the difference in image data, and video display data then you should be ready to tackle the next question, "What is a 128Bit PCI video card?" Well as we have touched on several times, only 32-bit PCI cards are available, so what is a 64-bit card then? What this means is that the PCI card communicates with the CPU/system in 32-Bit blocks. Then once the video card has those blocks, it puts them together and processes them in 64-Bit wide chunks. The way that this is done is by VRAM, which is short for Video-RAM, is a type of fast memory used in video display cards. What the card does is load the data from the system through the 32-bit bus as fast as it can into VRAM, then the video processor, the chip on the video card that converts the pixel information into displayable color information, retrieves the data from VRAM and processes it out to the monitor in 64-Bit blocks. What this does is allow for faster screen updates as the card can process more data to the screen in the same amount of time. Currently, the graphics accelerator cards are available in 64-Bit, and 128-bit versions. What these allow for is two to four times the display processing power of a standard 32-bit display processor connecting to the system through a PCI bus.

Understandably there are many other decisions to be made during the purchase of a system. Most of these decisions are easy to make with little or no help. I'll be here to help you with the tough ones.

LWP

Phillip Hice, Amblin Imaging's technical director, has been involved with this aspect of computers for longer than he cares to remember.

LightWave Tech

Making the Move

by Phillip J. Hice

I have had a large number of requests from Amiga users who now find it necessary to get all of those old Amiga animations and files, over to their new systems.

As stated last month, in this column I plan to address the ever-increasing need for converts from the Amiga to the world of PCs to transfer data from one system to the other. For those of you who have managed to figure this out on your own, never mind As for the rest, I feel that the suggested solutions are easy to understand and implement.

Software Utilities

In looking at software as a possible solution, several options arise. The first, and probably the one that most people who think that they have this figured out are using, is the old Amiga favorite CrossDOS (built into 2.05 and higher or available commercially). This utility enables the Amiga operating system to read, write, delete and perform all standard Amiga DOS functions on a PC-formatted disk via the Amiga floppy drive. With this utility you simply copy the data from your Amiga to the PC floppy disk, then transfer the diskette to the PC system and copy them to the local hard drive and you're done. One thing that you will need to remember in using this method, and a few I will discuss later is that PC DOS has the ridiculous limitation of only eight characters per filename, and a maximum of a three character extension. Because of this, any file on the Amiga that does not meet the PC DOS filename conventions will be truncated to match. That means, for example, that if you have files named "FrontLeftSideObject.02" and "FrontLeft TopObject.02," copying them over to the PC disk will truncate or rename them something like "FrontLe~.1" and "FrontLe~.2."

As you can see, if you have a large number of files with even slightly similar names, transferring them without first renaming them and creating a listing of what they were originally named can cause a world of headaches. Many of you may wonder why the eight-character filename is needed since Windows NT can handle larger filenames. While NT can write long file names to floppies, CrossDOS can't.

Another solution that is software-based uses a utility that most Amiga users who have transferred files via a modem will probably have: LH Arc. LHA is a software-only, data compression utility that lets Amiga users decrease the size of a file or multiple files for either modem transfer or archival purposes (to save hard drive space). The LHA utility for the Amiga is only one-third of the solution. The second part is a new version of the LHA utility that was designed specifically for Windows NT: LHANT. Unlike other PC DOS versions of LHA, LHANT utilizes the NTFS ability to handle long filenames, even if the file being de-compressed was compressed on an Amiga system. This will allow you to take a file named "LeftRearWing.part.02.a," and compress it on the Amiga, and when it is decompressed on the NT machine the filename will be completely intact. The third and final part to this solution is the inclusion of the first solution; you will need CrossDOS to transfer the compressed files. Once again, you should conform to the xxxxxxxx.xxx convention for the name of the compressed file, although it will not harm the compressed file in any way as far as data integrity. Naming the compressed file something larger than the eight-character limitation will result in CrossDOS truncating the filename when it is copied to the floppy. One other thing to keep in mind when using the LHA utility is that when you name your compressed files, it is not only good practice, but somewhat of a standard, to use the .LHA extension. This will enable you to immediately identify compressed files. It may not sound like a big deal, but it will be when you think that your data file is corrupted when no application on the planet can open it.

Hardware Solutions

The title "Hardware Solutions" is true only with the understanding that software will be required to run the hardware. There are several hardware-type options currently available, some of which require very little hardware or software knowledge. Others may not require any more initial understanding, but an ability to comprehend networking techniques.

The first hardware solution is both the least expensive and the easiest to install and operate. This solution requires the purchase of two things: a telecommunications software package for both of your computer systems (preferably one(s) that have the ZModem protocol, as it is currently the most efficient) and a null modem cable. When communicating via a modem, the connection between the modem and the computer is called a serial connection. In a serial connection, each device—in this case the host computer and the modem—has what are known in the industry as RS-232C serial ports. These ports are designed with the ability to both send and receive data on separate physical connections. So while one "pin"on the serial connector receives data, a different one is used to send data. This basic principle of the design allows for the use of what is known as a null-modem cable. This cable connects two computer serial ports in a crossover-type configuration in which the data out pin from one system connects to the data in pin on the other. By doing this the computers are able to establish, via telecommunications software, the same type of link that they would had they connected via modems/phone lines, and they can upload or download files to and from each other.

Which leads me to the next hardware solution: modems. Although it is more expensive, you can usually get better transfer rates by directly connecting the two systems via modems and a phone cable. This is due to the fact that most modern modems have built-in hardware that compresses the data before transmitting it. Another reason why modems are preferable to the null-modem cable approach is that a null modem cable will only work if both systems have their serial ports set to transfer at the exact same speed, whereas with modems, each system can be configured to optimize the serial port for its best possible connection with the modem.

Networking

The final hardware solution I am going to discuss is networking. As most of you are aware, networking is currently the most effective means of transferring data between two systems, especially if these two systems are running different operating systems. Networking is also the most costly. These costs are increased by the number and types of machines that you have, as different operating systems will require different software to communicate over the network, and each system will require a NIC (Network Interface Card).

When I state that networking is the most expensive means of transfer, remember that network card prices start at around $100, so even though this process is more expensive, it doesn't have to break the bank. Because it is beyond the scope of this article to fully explain all networking aspects for Amigas and PCs, I am only going to discuss the most readily available means of networking for LightWave users—ScreamerNet.

As most of you know, ScreamerNet was added to LightWave for the purpose of connecting to external rendering engines, the first of which was the Screamer. Although ScreamerNet is part of LightWave, it was based on one of the oldest networking protocols TCP/IP. The TCP/IP protocol is extremely easy to implement, as you basically have numeric or IP addresses for each system on the network. These numbers are stored in an ASCII text file that the TCP/IP software uses for reference when trying to establish a remote connection, or when a remote connection is trying to be established with the host system. Although ScreamerNet takes all of its commands in the background from LightWave, all of the standard shell accessibility is still there. In order for the TCP/IP setup to work, you need only follow these steps:

(1) Install ScreamerNet onto your Amiga, if you don't already have it.

(2) Install the TCP/IP & FTP Networking Services on the NT machine.

(3) Update the TCP/IP reference text files with ScreamerNet address information.

(4) Set the Computer Name and Computer Address on the NT machine.

(5) Use the FTP protocol to establish connection, and transfer files.

The first item, installing ScreamerNet onto your Amiga, should be easy, as NewTek has created basic install disks to fully set up your Amiga system fully. Once this is done it is time to set up TCP/IP on your NT machine. In order to install the TCP/IP protocol you will need your original NT install disks or CD ready to go, as NT will need to load and install the proper drivers. (I am assuming that NT networking has already been activated. If this isn't the case, refer to your NT users manual for help in installing the network.)

In the Main group double-click on the Control Panel icon. Once the control panel window has opened, double-click on the Network icon. At this point NT will bring up a window that shows all of the network hardware and software installed. The first thing to do is select the button Add Software. This will bring up a window with a pulldown-style menu that will have a large list of all of the "built-in" networking software that NT can install. Scroll down the list until you reach the selection "TCP/IP Protocol and related components." Upon selecting this item, yet another window is opened that allows you to select from the various TCP/IP and related services. In addition to the connectivity utilities that NT pre-selects for you, you should also select the FTP Server service and the Simple TCP/IP Services.

After you have selected these, proceed by clicking on the continue button. NT will begin installing the needed drivers either from CD-ROM or from the floppies that it will prompt you for. During the driver install process a window will appear that warns you that FTP Server Service is not the most security-oriented application and ask you if you wish to proceed? Yes, you do. Failing to install the FTP Server Service will prohibit you from transferring files.

After the FTP drivers have been installed, yet another window will appear and prompt you for FTP information. You should leave all of these settings as they are except for the home directory setting. When a remote system, such as your Amiga, connects to your NT machine, this home directory is the path on the NT hard drive where the initial connection is made. I recommend setting this to a specific drive and directory that has the most free space available to store the received files. If you haven't set up this directory yet, you can multi-task out to file manager and create one, then go back and set the path. Once the path is set select the appropriate button to continue.

After all drivers are installed you will want to change the name of the machine to SCREAMER001 by simply clicking on the change button next to the machine name. After this is done, in the installed software window, select the TCP/IP services item and hit the configure button. This will bring up a window for you to install the TCP/IP address for this machine. The address for the machine named SCREAMER001 should be 200.000.000.001, and the default mask should be 255.255.255.255. Now you will be back at the main network settings window again. Click on OK or Close. Windows NT will display a horizontal bar graph showing the progress of rebuilding the network to include the changes you just made, then request that you restart your system for the changes to take effect. *Don't restart yet.*

Now for the last part of the software config. Run the notepad program located in the accessories group. Under the FILE menu option choose open. Under the D:\WINNT35\drivers\etc you will want to open a file named "hosts." In this file you will want to add the following lines as the last lines in the file:

```
200.0.0.200     amiga amiga ami
200.0.0.1       screamer001 d1
```

Once you have added these lines, resave the file with the same filename, and from the same location open the file titled "networks." In this file you will simply need to add the following line as the last line that reads:

```
AmigaNet        200.0.0
```

Then, as before, resave the file with the same name. Close the notepad program. Now you will want to shutdown and restart your NT machine so that all the changes you've made can take effect.

Now that you have the software installed, let's discuss how to use it to do the transfer. I prefer to establish the connection from the NT machine to the Amiga machine, the reason for which I will get into shortly. In order to make the connection the Amiga needs to have the ScreamerNet software running, which is done by simply double-clicking on the "Start Screaming" icon created by the ScreamerNet install disks. Starting this will cause a window to appear and state that the software has detected a second network card, but is ignoring it. Disregard this message, as it has nothing to do with what you are doing. After this is done, go back to your NT machine and open up the command prompt window by double-clicking on its icon in the Main group window. Here's where you really need to pay attention, and maybe even take notes.

From the shell window you should CD to the drive and directory that you selected as the home directory during the FTP setup. The reason for this is once the connection has been established you won't be able to change directories or drives on the local machine. You will, however, be able to move about the remote machines drives freely, which I will explain in just a moment. After changing to the home directory location at the prompt type FTP amiga, and hit enter. A message will appear asking for the user name to connect under. Type: screamer001 and hit enter. This will return another message requesting the password for the user screamer001. Type: toaster and hit enter. You should now receive a message that you are connected to amiga as screamer001 and receive the FTP> prompt. The first thing that you should do now is type binary and hit enter. This tells the system that you want to transfer binary information, not simply text, and you should receive a response of Type set to I, and then receive the FTP> prompt. At the prompt type DIR and hit enter. This will give you the listing of the Amiga's RAM drive, as that is the standard home directory on the Amiga for ScreamerNet. If you copy the files you want to transfer to the RAM disk, you will see them. If not, you can use the CD (change directory) command, with AmigaDOS paths to move to any other location on the Amiga's hard drives, including external Bernoulli drives and the like. Once you have moved, and found the files you wish to move, just implement one of two commands: GET or MGET.

GET and MGET are both FTP commands for transferring files from the remote system to the local systems home directory. The main difference between them is that MGET is for "getting" multiple files, while GET is for a single file. Another difference is that you can use the * wildcard with MGET, while GET wants to find the actual filename entered. Most of the time you will want to move more than just one file, and thus be using the MGET command. However, there is a slight problem with MGET, in that you must verify every file selected for transfer. That is, if you have 100 files named Image001, Image002, Image003, and so on, and you use MGET with the wildcard filename of Image*, the FTP window will prompt you MGET Image001?. Hitting enter without entering anything will accept, hitting no, or N will cancel that files transfer and then prompt for the next file that meets the wildcard specs. Even though this seems like a real pain in the #$!, it is somewhat less of a problem due to the fact that computer systems contain keyboard buffers that hold the last keystrokes made until the system is ready to process them. That means that, though you do have to hit the enter key for every file, you can load up the buffer with a number of return keystrokes so that as soon as the system prompts for the next file, the enter key to accept it is already waiting in the buffer, which actually speeds up the process a little. Then, once some of the files have begun transferring, just load up the keyboard buffer with a few more returns.

Although this sounds like a lot of work, it really isn't once you've done it once and see just how easy it really is. Besides, if you want a less complicated connection, it will require quite a bit more money and time to set up, which really isn't worth it if you only have a few frames, or a few hundred for that matter.

So, what solution is best for you? If you are abandoning your Amiga in favor of a newer machine, you'll only need the "one-time" transfer of your files. If you are going to be using your Amiga along with your new machines, you need to figure out how much transfer you are going to do. If it's just a few files at a time, the floppy based system works just fine, If you need more powerful networking solutions, you may want to take a look at making your Amiga a permanent part of your home network.

LWP

Phillip Hice is the head of Amblin Imaging's technical department and is responsible for (among other things) keeping 33 Alpha workstations and the last of Amblin's Amiga rendering farm on-line.

LightWave Tech

by Phillip Hice

I would like to start out by thanking Joe Straitiff (via the Internet) for pointing out a few inaccuracies in the ftp/ScreamerNet section of my last article. The errors are related to ftp commands. I stated that you couldn't change directories on the local machine during a connect, which was wrong. In my haste to put together a simple networking solution article, I did an injustice to my readers in that, rather than carefully re-reading my article for technical accuracy, I performed more of a quick scan to check for major errors in grammar and spelling. I apologize, and will do everything I can to keep mistakes from reoccurring. In an effort to compensate, you'll find included at the end of this article a listing of the ftp commands, their syntax, and a brief explanation as to what they are used for. I hope this helps, even if just slightly more than the information I have already given.

This month I am going to touch on a few problems that seem to be popping up more and more often for new non-Amiga LightWave users. First, I want to address the topic of PC clone systems. Over the last several weeks I have been bombarded with questions about PC motherboards having problems with Windows NT. The problem is that the board(s) seem to run inconsistently. In other words, you can't even install NT; you can install NT, but it won't run; or you can install and run it, but it crashes with irregularity.

I have received several comments on the problem, with several different opinions as to what it is. Some believe it's a bug in NT, and that rather than address it, Microsoft has decided to label boards that have this problem non-compatibles. I have also heard that it was a problem with Pentium chips or specific chipsets from Intel. In an effort to try to pinpoint the problem, I have acquired several different manufacturers' PCs. These systems are of various configurations—anywhere from 386s with ISA or VLB buses to Pentiums with PCI. In working with this diverse selection of machines, I felt that I should be able to come to some conclusion. Yeah, right!

Of the seven machines tested (all clones, no name brands), three of them ran without a hitch, right out of the gate. These three include a 386, a 486 and a 586 (Pentium) processor. The motherboards had nothing in common other than that the processors were all genuine Intel x86. The Chipsets and peripherals varied.

As for the other four systems, I encountered some unusual results. On all of these systems I ran into one or more problems needing either minor or drastic action for NT to run (if at all). Two of the systems, which were Pentium 100s, required that both the internal and external cache be disabled during the install processes. Once installed, with caches enabled, the systems worked fine. If you are having difficulties with your system, I suggest you try this solution first; it's worked for several of my friends who do nothing but build systems for resale. On the other hand, the next machine I tested required that the caches be left off during the install process, and wouldn't boot NT unless they remained disabled. The last machine I tested just wouldn't get through the setup procedure completely until I clocked it down to run at 90 MHz rather than 100 MHz.

If you seem to be having a problem with the installation of NT, try disabling cache(s) and/or clocking down your system. To reduce the clock speed of your system, you will need the motherboard documentation to help you identify which jumpers on the board are for setting clock speed, and what the proper setting is for the desired speed. As for disabling cache(s), every PC that I've seen uses a setting in the BIOS (Built-In Operating System) setup utility. Most of you have probably seen the message onscreen during bootup that says "Hit <del> to enter setup," or something similar. This is where you will change the BIOS settings. In order to get to the BIOS setup, you must reboot. Then, during bootup, when you see the message prompting you to press a key to enter setup, do so.

Since there are several different BIOS manufacturers on the market, the procedures will be different from system to system, but generally speaking, all you need to do is locate the setting for Internal Cache and External Cache, and then press the proper key to change the settings to disable them.

Once you have finished your install, boot up NT once more to verify that it runs out of setup mode. Once you have done this, select Shutdown and Restart from the Program Manager's File menu. Once the system restarts, re-enter the bios setup utility and re-enable the caches one at a time, starting with the internal. After saving changes, reboot NT. If it runs correctly, go back through the same process and enable the external cache and try it all over. If these suggestions do nothing to help NT install and run, there isn't much else you can do.

As you can see, just about every possible combination may be needed to get a system to install and run NT if you are experiencing these problems. As for my testing, I started out with everything enabled, then, step by step, disabled and re-enabled cache settings to get the machines to function as closely to normal and with the greatest performance possible.

After all of my testing, I have come to the following conclusions regarding PCs and the Windows NT operating system:

(1) **Make every attempt to purchase a system that is listed on the Windows NT hardware compatibility list.** Not only is this the only way to be sure that Microsoft has tested and qualified the product for use with Windows NT, but if you have a problem and call Microsoft tech support, they may actually be able to help. If your system isn't on the list, chances are you won't get very far, since tech support has no way of knowing if your system is able to run NT. It's much easier for them to blame problems on non-compatibility than a software issue.

(2) **Purchase only from reputable companies.** This recommendation, along with the above, should always be followed, whether purchasing a PC or anything else for your system. Only a reputable company determined to provide quality product and service will be willing to help you through your problems, even if it means returning the system for a refund.

(3) **Document your purchase.** With thousands of computer dealers nationwide, finding a reputable one is possible, but not always easy to do by just walking in. So you should fully document your

purchase. That is, when you plan on purchasing a system, submit a formal list of your desired configuration, including (preferably in large, boldface type) an explanation that you intend to run Windows NT. By doing this, in the event that your system fails, and the company you got it from is less than honest or willing to help, you will have documented proof of your intention to run Windows NT. You'll be in a better position to demand a refund from the seller based on the fact that he/she failed to sell you a system capable of doing the work for which it was purchased.

As for the official explanation of the problem, I am still waiting for a response from Microsoft, but let's speculate. One of the possible reasons that I've come up with, based on what I've seen, it's most likely a hardware issue. As with the last system I tested, I have had several people with problems clock their systems down to 90 MHz, and these machines have run fine.

I feel that this could be true based on the following information: When 60 to 75 MHz Pentiums were introduced, they ran at +5 volts. With speed increases came increased heat, so one way to reduce the heat was to reduce the power required to run the chip. Thus the introduction of the 90 MHz Pentiums powered with +3 volts. Due to the change in power requirements, totally new board designs were needed, so PC manufacturers went back to the drawing table and designed a board that could run the 90 MHz chips. Then, several months later, the 100 MHz chips came on the market. These chips used the same pinout and +3-volt power that the 90 MHz chips did, so systems manufacturers simply designed in the ability to change clock frequencies on the motherboard, allowing jumper changes between 90 and 100 MHz clock speeds. This is fine except for the one area that I feel is the problem: the board was made to run with a 90 MHz chip, and, as a result, performs better with a slower processor. Adding a 100 MHz processor only puts a greater strain on all of the motherboard components, which were also designed around the 90 MHz Pentium. If this is true, the recent release of the 120 MHz and greater processors will force the clone manufacturers to once again redesign their boards for these faster processors, thus fixing the problem for the slower (100 MHz) processors as well. Once again, I'm just speculating, and only time will tell if the release of new, faster Pentium motherboards brings an end to this problem.

Along with the motherboard problem, I have received several requests for tips regarding PC video cards for use with LightWave and Windows/NT. The first thing you must decide before buying a video card is the maximum color depth (256, 32000, 65000, 16.7M-True Color) and resolution you wish to run, because the color depth/resolution ratio is directly related to the amount of RAM you have on board. That is, if you intend to run with True Color (24-bit) at a resolution of 1024x768, you will need:

(1024x768) x 24 bits = 18,874,368 bits = 2,359,296 bytes = approximately 2.3MB of RAM needed on the video card

As you can see, if you reduce either the color depth or resolution, you can increase the other. Since most video cards come with a default of 2MB of RAM, you will be able to have relatively high resolution and color depth settings without the purchase of additional RAM.

As for which video cards, I have used the ATI mach 64, Matrox Impression +, Diamond Stealth and the #9 Imagine 128, to name a few. All of them performed with great results. A 128-bit card will always perform better than a 64-bit card on the same task due, obviously, to the increased processing bandwidth. The one thing that you do need to look out for is what type of system you have. If you are running standard x86/Pentium-type systems, all of these cards will function fine, but if you plan on getting an Alpha system, be cautious—not all systems have drivers for all of the cards. Ask your vendor which cards they have drivers for, or better yet, stick with cards on the NT compatibility list, since there will be drivers for these on the NT CD-ROM.

LWP

Phillip Hice is the head of Amblin Imaging's technical department.

Cleaning House

Performance-Increasing Tips for Windows NT and LightWave

by Glyn Williams

Picture this: There are just seven weeks till the deadline. In that time, you have about 20 shots to storyboard, models to produce and texture, and scenes to build, animate and render. Losing sleep? Working long, long hours? Is this your life?

If so, you may have opted to save time and run LightWave on a more powerful system—and that probably means an Intel- or an Alpha-based platform. (The term "Intel platform" is a nice way of saying "PC-compatible." PC seems to send a shiver down many a spine.)

LightWave for Intel is nice enough to allow you the choice of Windows 3.1, Windows 95 or Windows NT. While Windows 3.1 is inexpensive and Windows 95 offers a bunch of new features, NT is by far the best choice for LightWave users because it is simply much faster at throwing around the vast lumps of memory that LightWave requires.

If you are using an Alpha-based machine, NT 3.51 is your only option. NT is not a version of Windows, but a completely new, 32-bit operating system produced by Microsoft to capture the workstation market. NT is designed with features like true preemptive multitasking and broad, uncluttered access to a real 32-bit memory space. And yes, while AmigaDOS did this happily on a 512K Amiga, NT finds it a bit of a squeeze on a 16 MB Pentium. To provide backward compatibility on top of the NT kernel, the programmers added a look-alike GUI and a facility to run old 16-bit Windows applications.

It's time for a simile, I think. If AmigaDOS was a rodent—fast, agile and light on its feet—then NT would be a huge, rumbling battle tank: massive, complex, unstoppable and pretty heavy on fuel. Because NT is so complex, you'll want to squeeze a little extra performance out of it using a range of methods. That added boost can be a real boon—a three-minute-per-frame speed-up over 1,000 frames can make the difference between meeting a deadline and missing it. Here's a collection of tips for improving the performance of LightWave under Windows NT.

Find the Bottleneck

There's always one somewhere. With a program like LightWave, the bottleneck is either going to be the processor or memory. Examining your system while running a rendering task is helpful. If the disk light is always on, the hard disk is thrashing, the system monitor says there are hundreds of page faults per second and the free-memory indicator says there is less than 3 MB of free RAM in the system, then chances are the bottleneck is memory.

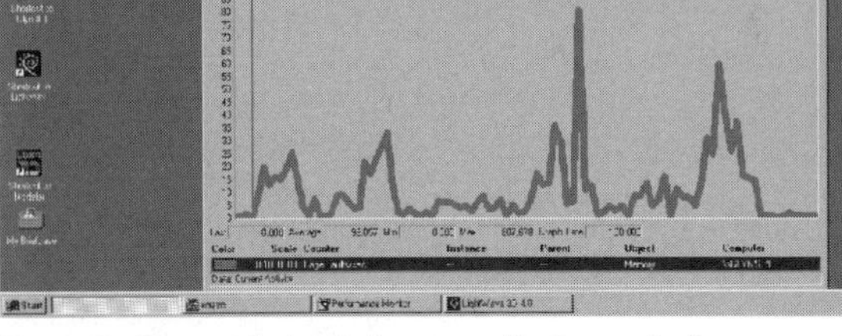

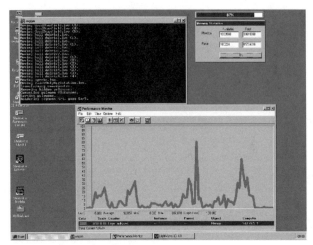

Figure 1: Here, with the Performance Monitor tool, the memory/page-faults-per-second index shows a rendering session very low on memory.

When NT runs out of real memory, it starts to use virtual memory (a swapfile on the hard disk). Though a little paging to disk is acceptable, if more memory is required, the system will start to thrash, the machine will access the hard disk constantly and performance will plummet. Remember, a silent PC is a happy PC. Or, if you prefer, the drive light on the front of the PC is a reminder to get in your car and drive to the computer store and buy some more RAM chips.

If the bottleneck is not RAM, the only way to improve performance is to get a faster processor. LightWave is written in 32-bit code and makes heavy use of the math coprocessor, meaning it really benefits from the architecture of the Pentium processor. A P90 will run LightWave about four times faster than a 486 DX2-66. Better still, a DEC Alpha 21164-based machine may achieve six times the performance of a P90!

The overhead for NT itself is a modest 12 MB. If you are running LightWave on a 16 MB system, only the tiniest of models can be accommodated before the system has to start using virtual memory extensively. For most professional work, 32 MB is really the required minimum.

Reduce LightWave's Memory Usage

LightWave and similar programs eat RAM for breakfast. The software itself uses amazingly little memory, but loaded objects and images consume a great deal. The good news is that you can reduce the memory consumption of a scene by taking the following steps:

Reducing the Segment Memory Setting

- LightWave uses a big chunk of memory to buffer the image being rendered. For large images, this can be a significant amount of RAM. The **Segment Memory** setting (**Camera** panel) allows you to specify how much RAM LightWave allocates to this buffer. A typical NTSC video image requires a Segment Memory setting of approximately 8.7 MB to hold the entire image. By reducing this setting to 4.5 MB, LightWave will render the image in two half-screen segments—a little slower than usual, but now you'll have an extra 4.5 MB of RAM at your disposal. If the system was desperately out of RAM, this extra 4.5 MB would boost performance. With a bit of experimentation, you should be able to balance these conflicting requirements. *[Editor's note: To determine the size of the image buffer needed (in bytes), multiply your output width by output height by 24.—JG]*

Cutting Out Unwanted Geometry

- Objects that are never seen still use precious RAM, so cut 'em out or cut 'em down. Consider hidden or obscured features—objects behind the camera—or complex objects in the far distance, where a simpler object would do.

Reducing Image Memory Usage

- Image files use a lot of memory. LightWave 4.0 shipped with HIIP image converters, allowing the program to load JPEGs and other file formats. Unfortunately, HIIP loaders pad out images to 24-bit, regardless of the number of bitplanes they contain. I suggest you avoid using these loaders completely. To do this, rename the IFF.EXE and TGA.EXE files to OldIFF.EXE and OldTGA.EXE. (LightWave's internal loaders will then take over, which won't pad out the images to 24-bit for smaller bitplanes.) LightWave has internal loaders for IFF and 24-bit TGA files. *[Editor's note: NewTek is aware of various HIIP problems and is working on a patch to resolve them.—JG]*
- Use 8-bit IFF images wherever possible. Whenever you are using an image map solely for a surface value other than Surface Color, you can use an 8-bit image because only the luminance value is taken into account. This can save megabytes for modest-size maps. And don't use a 2K-pixel-by-2K-pixel map when a 1K-pixel-by-1K-pixel map will do. Make a habit of browsing the image list and looking at memory usage. You may be surprised. If using a clip map, you can get by with two-color—black-and-white—images, as only two values are used for clip maps.

Maximizing NT's Available Memory

There are a number of tricks you can try:

- Close down any programs not in use—don't have Photoshop running in the background. Don't use wallpaper, NT's OpenGL 3D screensavers, or any screensavers for that matter. (Even NT's clever circular clock is a waste of perfectly good RAM.)
- Disable unwanted services. For example, if you don't have a printer attached to your machine, disable the spooler service from the control panel, which will save more than half a MB of real memory. You'll need to log on as an administrator to do this.
- I've heard rumors of other ways to reduce NT's voracious RAM requirements: Stop the automatic loading of the WOW subsystem (which involves altering the registry), allowing NT to run old 16-bit Windows apps. Or rename OS2.EXE, which apparently allows character mode programs for the OS/2 operating system to operate. (I cannot say whether there are any real benefits to these procedures.)
- Disable BIOS shadowing features. NT would rather have the RAM. (I suspect this will only liberate a few K.)

I'm not going to go into depth about how to perform these procedures. If you are interested, there are a number of ways of finding out how, including NT manuals, Internet newsgroups and Microsoft.

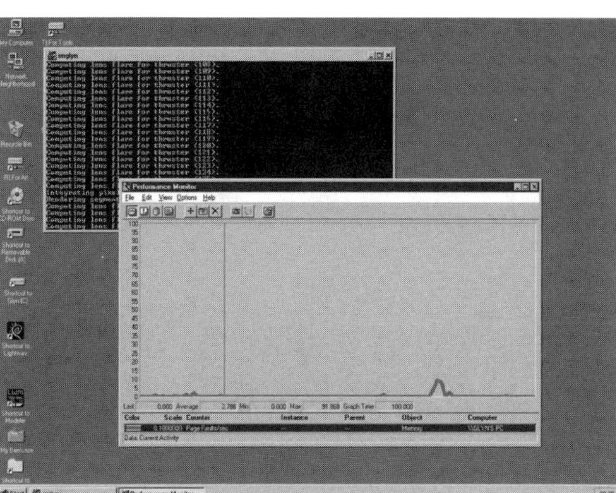

Figure 2: In this rendering session, memory consumption has been reduced, resulting in less paging and faster rendering times.

Improving Virtual Memory Performance

NT uses virtual memory, to some extent, all the time. When RAM is used up, the system swaps pages of real memory to disk into a swapfile called PAGEFILE.SYS. In a memory-bound application, improving NT's usage of virtual memory can make quite a difference.

- Using the Control panel/system, set the minimum amount of swapfile so it's at least your actual amount of RAM+12 MB. You'll need to be logged on as an administrator to do this. Having to grow the swapfile amount past its initial setting slows down NT a lot and you won't need to do this if you have increased the amount of RAM in your system since installing NT.
- If you have multiple disk drives, place swapfiles on each of them. (Note: Never have a swapfile on a compressed area.)
- If you are using NTFS and are feeling adventurous, use striped volumes and put your swapfile on them. Striped volumes share data across more than one disk, so if each of two disk drives works at 4 MB per second, you can read and write data to a striped volume at 8 MB per second. Be smart about backing up if you are choosing this method: If you lose one disk, you'll lose all the data!
- Don't fragment swapfiles all over the disk. If you can make a contiguous swapfile, you'll be helping yourself out. If you are using a FAT disk and have access to Windows 95, use this method: (1)Boot up Windows 95. (2) Delete Pagefile.sys (95 doesn't use it). (3) Run Defrag. Ignore what it says about fragmentation and get it to unify free space. (Don't use a DOS de-fragger—you'll lose your nice long filenames.) (4) Reboot NT. NT will remake a large, contiguous swapfile onto unused disk space.

Avoiding the Memory Leak

LightWave and NT allocate and free memory differently. When LightWave loads a big scene file, it uses vast tracts of memory (virtual and otherwise). When you press Clear Scene, this RAM is not recovered until you either exit LightWave or load another scene.

When doing a large rendering operation, even on a single machine, use LightWave in ScreamerNet mode. This renders significantly faster than using Layout itself to do the rendering. If you work like we do, the last thing you do at night is set up ScreamerNet with a nighttime batch of rendering work. If the machine running the ScreamerNet control panel is also going to be used for rendering, press Clear Scene and close down LightWave completely to free up the RAM. Run the ScreamerNet node (LWSN.EXE) and then run LightWave once more to get the ScreamerNet control panel. *[Editor's note: A bug in the Microsoft compiler used with LightWave and Modeler causes memory to be "tagged" as freed rather than actually freed. This situation can cause problems when loading images sequences and loading and clearing large scenes. The same patch that NewTek is working on for the HIIP problems will contain a workaround for these Microsoft problems.—JG]*

Finally, here are some cool features of NT you may not have heard about:

- The NewShell for NT is a replacement GUI for NT that is almost identical to Windows 95. This much-improved interface has several benefits for LightWave users, but beware: it does require more memory. You can download it from many on-line services or at ftp.microsoft.com.
- If you are using an NTFS volume, you can elect to employ file compression. NT will apply a fast, reliable and transparent compression to any directories you wish, which is particularly useful for volumes containing 24-bit movie sequences and large texture maps.
- If you do manage to get home, why stop working? With NT's remote-access server (RAS), you can log onto your office server machine exactly as if you were in the office, albeit with a pretty sluggish network link.

After a career of designing and programming games, Glyn Williams is now co-owner and director of Particle Systems, a startup games development house based in Sheffield, England. The company is making heavy use of LightWave in the production of its current title, due for release in 1996.

LightWave 3D 5.0 for Power Macintosh

by Chris Tome

With the addition of LightWave 3D for the Power Macintosh, NewTek can finally claim a product that is a fully cross-platform-compatible application. LightWave now runs on the PC, Sun, Silicon Graphics, DEC Alpha, Amiga, and PowerMac, and allows for easy file translation of standard scene files over multiple platforms.

The only current drawback to cross-platform compatibility at this time are scenes that require external plug-ins, as not all plug-in manufacturers port to every platform. NewTek, however, is working to solve this problem, and the PowerMac version will include plug-ins currently available on other platforms, most notably the Wintel-based version. One company that has committed to porting its plug-ins is Dynamic Realities, which makes two of the most widely used and popular enhancements for LightWave: Impact! and Particle Storm.

LightWave 3D is a popular application and has a wide following on many levels of the computer graphics industry, from film and television to large and small gaming and production houses.

A closeup in QuickDraw 3D of the dartboard scene that comes with LightWave free of charge. This is only one of many free scenes provided on the CD.

One remarkable thing about LightWave, from a programming standpoint, is that the code is highly optimized and the programs take up only a couple of megabytes. The talent of the two main programmers, Allen Hastings (Layout) and Stuart Ferguson (Modeler), is the reason. The code is compact and efficient because for years it was available only on the Amiga, and the relatively slow Amigas (by today's standards) made it necessary to optimize in every way possible. Thanks to its somewhat humble beginnings as part of the Video Toaster system, we all benefit from an efficient and solid 3D program, with a wide variety of information available from tens of thousands of rabid users.

QuickDraw Apples and OpenGL Oranges

The major difference in running LightWave 3D on the PowerMac is its use of QuickDraw 3D (as opposed to OpenGL) for real-time shaded previews of objects and scene files. While it is rumored that OpenGL will soon be supported by Apple, QuickDraw 3D is Apple Computer's answer to OpenGL and has unique features that are absent from the OpenGL file format. Older versions of QuickDraw 3D may cause problems, but the new versions seem to work fine. However, OpenGL is a more stable format, although the differences between the two formats would not be obvious to most users.

One of the first things any current LightWave user will notice (and most likely be slightly annoyed by), is that the OK and Cancel buttons have been reversed, making it possible for your worst nightmare—losing an unsaved scene—to occur by a simple left-click of your mouse. Apart from these small variations on the theme, LightWave 3D for PowerMac is essentially identical to its cousins on other platforms.

Seeing the Light: Power Features for Power Users

Of the many powerful features unique to LightWave, one of the most important is MetaNURBS, an extremely intuitive modeling tool. What makes MetaNURBS different is in its mimicry of NURBS (non uniform rational B-splines) and its organic modeling attributes, while it maintains polygonal geometry underneath. You work with MetaNURBS much as you would a piece of clay, pushing and pulling geometry in a smooth, organic fashion. When you are ready to use the model in a scene, you can either "freeze" the model to get a nicely smoothed polygonal mesh, or you can hit the <Tab> key to bring you back to the polygonal geometry and use the Subdivide-Metaform tool to smooth the geometry to the Level Of Detail (LOD) you desire. Game designers especially appreciate this function, which allows the creation of multiple versions of the same object in low, medium, and high polygon counts.

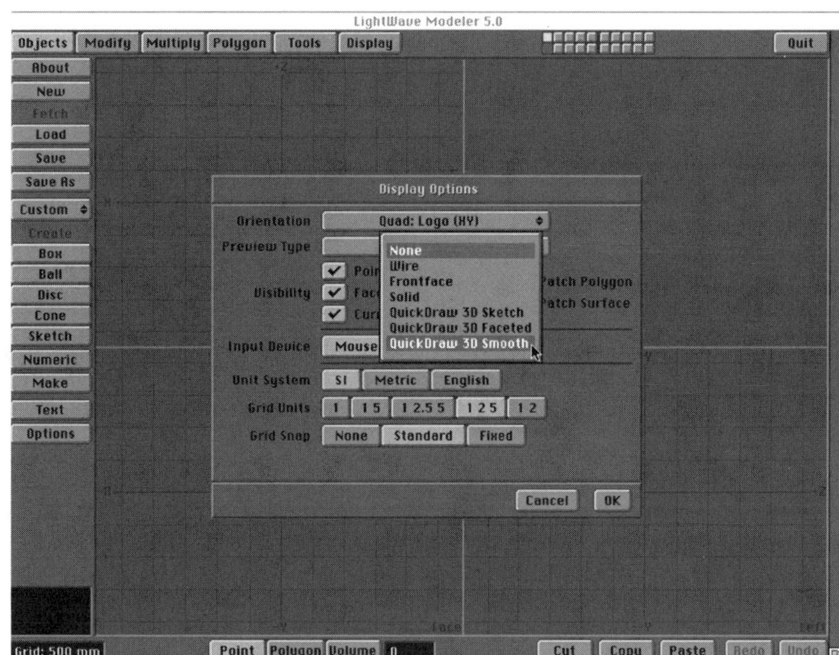

A screen shot of the Display panel, where you can choose to turn on QuickDraw or use wireframe mode for previews.

Some other modeling tools that LightWave provides are splines, polygonal primitives, and the ability to import and export DXF, 3D Studio, and Wavefront .obj files. Most mid- to large-sized 3D houses will use many different programs, and sometimes even platforms, to create their art, and standard 3D file formats must be supported. With these formats, LightWave is not a stunning file importer, but it definitely gets the job done.

Another interesting feature in LightWave is its ability to generate single-point polygons. These objects are useful in creating elements as diverse as starfields, fireworks, and even explosion particles. The great thing about one point polys is that they render quickly. This speed allows you to create pseudo-particle and real-world particle animation while allowing your machine some room to breathe.

LightWave could really use a facelift on its Bones system. LightWave's Bones is convoluted and confusing, and needs an overhaul if it wants to become the character animation program it could be. The real problem with the Bones system in LightWave is that the bones cannot be linked to specific areas or vertices of parts of an object. Also, the areas of influence some bones have over others can be difficult to control. However, on the positive side, with a lot of practice and time, the Bones system in LightWave can be effective in creating stunning character animation.

Inverse Kinematics, on the other hand, is a dream. It's easy to set up a complex model with linked hierarchies and to constrain their rotation parameters so that you can easily organize and manipulate a complex IK chain. If the Bones system were a little better, LightWave could challenge almost any other character animation software package.

Apple Issues and Other Maladies

Although the Macintosh has its advantages, the one area in which it doesn't excel is memory management. The Mac likes to allocate RAM to a program during startup and wants more than is really needed to run a program effectively. Beyond that, NewTek claims that a comparable PowerMac renders faster than a Pentium Pro. Also, there have been issues with a few of the tested QuickDraw 3D accelerator cards.

One thing Mac users will have to get used to is the interface. Although intuitive and well laid out, LightWave makes any computer look as if you switched to an Amiga. It's not a big deal, and the interface is easy to navigate, but the hardest thing for Mac users will be learning new hot keys. While you'd need to learn these for any Mac 3D application, the lack of standard Mac hot-key assignments might be frustrating at first.

Of all the 3D applications available for the Macintosh, LightWave needs the least amount of RAM to run efficiently. This is not to say that a 150,000-polygon-count scene with raytracing and print resolution turned on will render, but you can work with the program.

Sometimes animators like to start rendering a scene and then go into Modeler to continue working. Unfortunately, this option is not possible on the Macintosh

Another provided scene file using QuickDraw 3D in Layout. Notice the yellow lines, indicating the direction in which a spotlight casts light on the scene.

because the OS can't multitask. If all goes well with the integration of the NeXT OS on the Mac, that problem may change. The NeXT Operating System is highly efficient and is an excellent multitasker, so Mac users shouldn't have to wait too long for true multitasking.

Porting Is No Party

One of the largest issues surrounding pure cross-platform compatibility for NewTek has been its third-party vendors, who make a wide variety of useful and innovative plug-ins for LightWave 3D. These companies are usually smaller, with very few employees, and their choice to port to a given platform is made on the basis of the number of copies they plan to sell. This wise business move is a good decision, but can cause major headaches to any person or company running LightWave on more than one platform.

Plug-ins are a necessary part of any animator's toolbox, and the lack of a plug-in on one platform that exists on another means it's not possible to do network rendering and use both machines to increase rendering speed.

In this scenario, it should be NewTek's responsibility to help its third-party vendors to port their code to all platforms, which could be achieved by providing a more

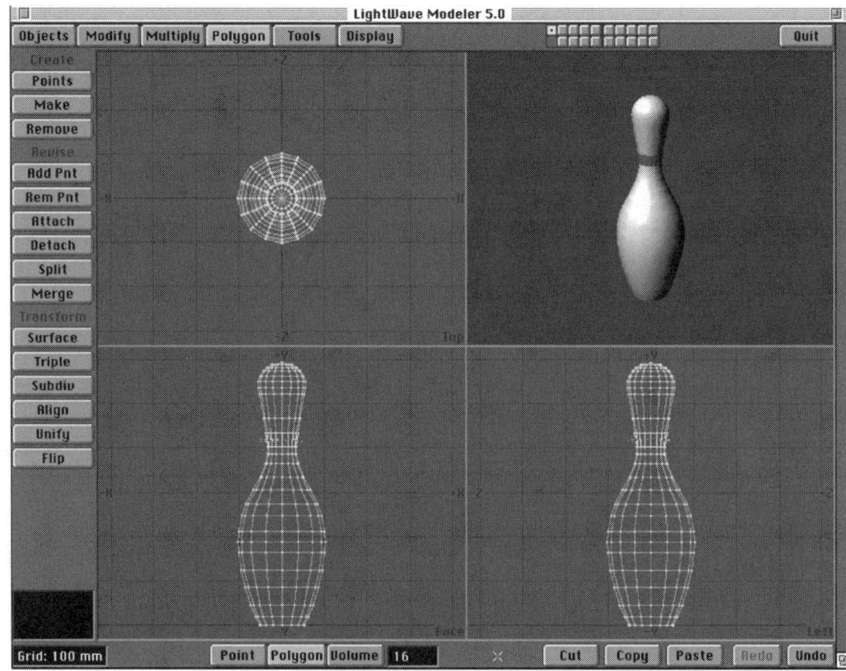

A bowling pin, with standard Modeler settings, and QuickDraw 3D preview.

An expanded view of the QD3D window in Modeler.

robust Software Development Kit (SDK), "loaning" out programmers to help with the ports, or simply paying the third parties to port. Any of these choices would ensure LightWave's already strong hold on the 3D industry, and make it the 100 percent cross-platform application it should be.

Novice to Pro: Something for All

Bottom line: LightWave is one heck of a program. Just ask the more than 40,000 users worldwide who use it to create everything from flying logos to film effects, and even video games. With a straightforward working style, tutorial, help resources too vast to name, and a beautiful rendering engine on a level with workstation class software (which LightWave is as well—it's available on SGI and soon will be on Sun), it's a fine choice for anyone from beginners all the way up to seasoned pros. If you want affordable 3D on the Mac, it might be time to see the light, namely LightWave 3D.

Chris Tome is the technical editor for 3D Design.

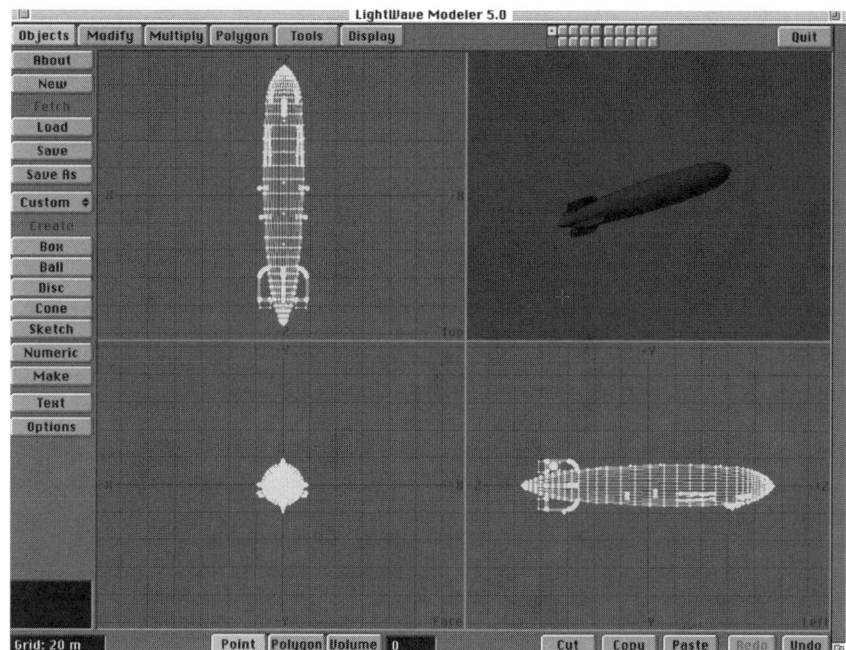

Another Modeler shot, with a Zeppelin model loaded.

Rendering Algorithms
Part 1: The Theory of Z-buffers

by William Frawley

While many types of rendering algorithms exist, those explained in this two-part series are some of the more popular ones. Each of the different methods described has advantages and disadvantages, which I assume might explain why LightWave programmers Allen Hastings and Stuart Ferguson incorporated aspects of both Z-buffer and ray tracing techniques. And one is still hard-pressed to find much, if any, commercially available 3D software incorporating radiosity techniques.

This study of rendering algorithms won't necessarily be dealing with the specifics of LightWave's implementation, but some of the rendering techniques incorporated by this and most other 3D software may prove of interest to those who are curious about what's happening after they hit Render. I know I was—hence this study. But before we begin to look at the mechanics of Z-buffers this issue, and ray tracing and radiosity next month, a brief exposition on the geometries of 3D space and frame buffers is definitely in order.

The 3D Universe

Common to most image synthesis software, objects exist relative to an origin in three-dimensional object space represented by some coordinate system, usually Cartesian (XYZ). Much like a camera taking a photograph, the rendering of these 3D objects projects them toward the eye or **camera view** onto the two-dimensional **screen space**, where the total area covered by the view is dependent on the **view angle** (see color image 3D Object Space). In order to reduce the chaos, not to mention time, of rendering an infinite amount of space, **object space** is bound on its sides by **boundary walls** and near and far planes called **hither and yon planes**, respectively. These **clipping planes**, as they are called, constitute the boundaries for the **viewing volume**. Any object inside this volume potentially makes it into the final image, and any object or part of an object outside this volume gets "clipped," hence the term clipping planes. Usually, the **viewscreen** (where the final image is drawn) serves as the hither clippingplane as well. Finally, for rendering purposes it is common to have the Z-axis oriented perpendicular to the viewscreen and pointing away from the camera into the object space—similar to LightWave's implementation. As we shall soon see, the significance of this orientation method becomes apparent when dealing with Z-buffer rendering algorithms. However, understanding the nature of Z-buffers requires a brief explanation of frame buffers.

Frame Buffers

Simply put, a **frame buffer** is a specialized piece of memory storage hardware whose memory locations are arranged in a gridlike pattern. A frame buffer's main objective is to "buffer" one "frame" of video, each memory location roughly corresponding to one pixel on screen. Therefore, for a full-color frame buffer, each memory slot would contain one or more numbers representing a certain color value for that pixel. Alternatively, the number could be an index or pointer to a reduced bitplane **color map** or look-up table. (Unfortunately, space does not permit an in-depth discussion of color maps.) Suffice it to say that a typical frame buffer represents a full-screen image. However, this memory array concept may also be creatively used to store numbers representing something completely different.

Z-buffer Rendering

The basic concept of Z-buffer rendering is quite simple. Two buffers are used for this technique. One is a frame buffer that will eventually contain the final rendered image, while the other buffer used contains the **z-depths** or distance of the nearest visible surface along the Z-axis as seen from the corresponding pixel of the viewscreen. This is why the axis orientation is transformed with the Z-axis pointing away from the screen. It would be helpful for understanding the entire process if we break down the algorithm itself into a series of simple steps.

First, once the three-dimensional model is constructed, including the final positioning of the camera and lights, the computer starts with the first screen pixel and decides if anything should be drawn there. It selects an object and mathematically determines if that object is visible from the current pixel center. If it is visible, the next step is to ascertain whether it is the closest object thus far encountered at those XY coordinates. It does this by checking the Z-buffer, which, in addition to the image buffer, had been previously cleared to some default value prior to rendering. For the image buffer, that value would have been the background color, and for the Z-buffer, the initial value in each memory location would have been set to the z-distance of the yon clipping plane, the farthest possible point in object space. If the current visible object's surface distance is closer to the eye than the current value in the Z-buffer for that point, that object's surface distance or z-value replaces the one currently in the Z-buffer, signifying that this new object is the closest one visible in the camera view thus far. Finally, the color shading of the closest visible point on the surface of this object at this point on the screen is determined from the object's surface properties and light source characteristics and entered into the image buffer. This completes the process for one pixel or point making up the screen. The next pixel in line repeats this entire sequence of steps for the current object. Once the entire screen is completed for this

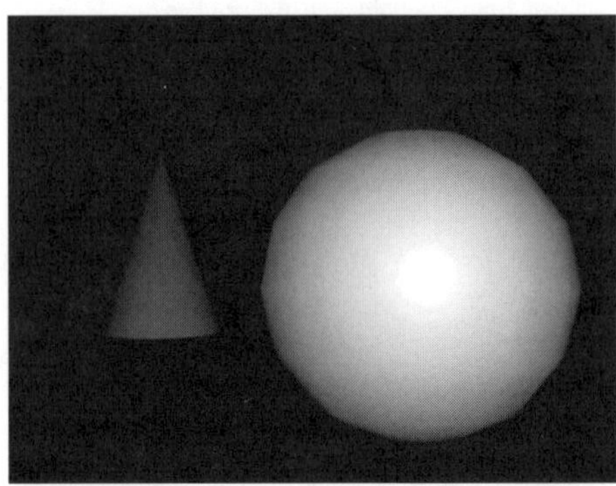

Figure 1: If translated to a luminance map, a typical Z-buffer might look like this. The lighter values represent z-values closest to the camera view. See color image "Z-buffer" for the scene layout from another view.

object, the next object in the scene is considered, and, as before, checked pixel by pixel via the Z-buffer for visibility. Wow, try doing this by hand!

If you watch LightWave's rendering screen, you'll notice the image generally being built up one object at a time. The accuracy of the image is constantly changing as closer objects eventually replace more distant objects in the frame buffer. Hence, the erasability of the buffers proves invaluable to this algorithm's method. In other words, it is inconsequential as to what order surfaces (or points of a surface) are chosen to be processed. In the end, after all surfaces have been processed, it is the closest object seen at each pixel that will remain in the Z-buffer, ready to be shaded for the final image (see color image Z-buffer).

Interestingly, although the Z-buffer is not intended to represent any kind of an image—only z-values—because of its implicit nature, if translated to a color map it will probably exhibit a certain likeness to the final image nonetheless (Figure 1).

Z-buffer Shadows

At the expense of time and memory, the Z-buffer algorithm technique can produce rudimentary shadows. However, the process does not take into account transparent/translucent objects and requires extra memory storage for each light's shadow buffer in addition to the normal image and Z-buffers. Another requirement relates to the type of light source that can be used to produce shadows. As you've probably seen in LightWave's Lights menu, only directional Spotlights work with shadow mapping, because each light must render its own Z-buffer, called the **shadow** or **illumination buffer**, for the scene. Considering the nature of the geometry involved, Directional and Point lights will not work for this method.

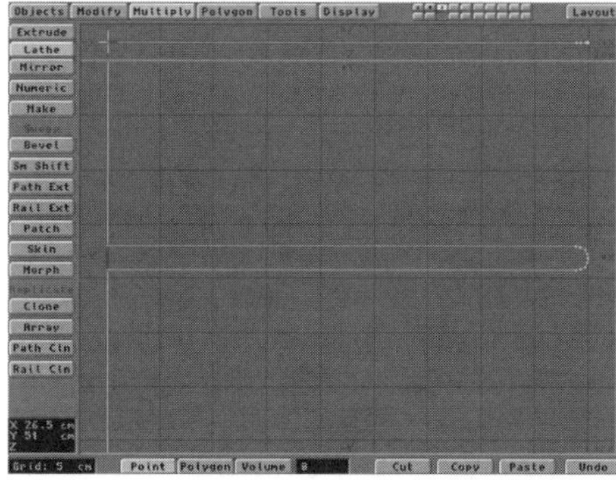

Figure 2: For Z-buffer shadows, all surfaces and objects not directly seen by the light source, such as the sphere and back surfaces of the box and cone, would be excluded from the light source's shadow buffer. Only the z-distances of the nearest visible surfaces would be included.

Shadow buffers enter into the proverbial equation at the shading stage for each visible object's surface point. Before the normal image is rendered, the scene (or frame for animations) is rendered from the point of view of each light, creating its own Z-buffer of any visible objects. Therefore, if an object's surface makes it into the light's shadow buffer, it can be considered to be illuminated by that light source. If not, that object must not be illuminated by the light, or is obscured by some other object, and thus in shadow (Figure 2). Once the shadow buffers for each light source are rendered and saved in memory, normal rendering begins for the camera view image.

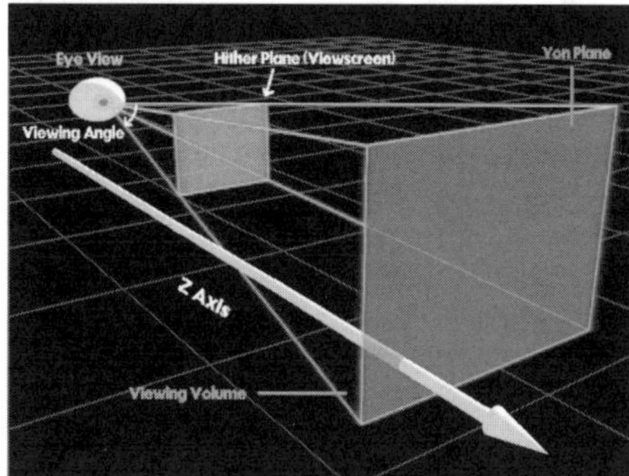

Figure 3: An overview of 3D object space. All objects within the viewing volume would be potentially visible from the viewpoint of the camera; all others outside would be clipped.

When a visible point on a surface is encountered, the shading procedure begins. From the view of each light source, the pixel containing the surface point in question is computed. Then the z-distance from that pixel of the light's view to the object's surface point is calculated. If that z-value equals the value in that light's shadow buffer, the surface point must be receiving illumination from that light source, and is added into the shading of that surface point in the final image buffer. If the distance is greater than the value in the shadow buffer, it must be farther than the nearest object, and is thus in shadow. Therefore, no shading for this light is added into the final image. The algorithm then proceeds to the next light source (if any) for computation of any additional shading information for that point in the image, repeating the entire procedure as before. As you may have guessed, the extra time and memory required to store shadow buffers are directly proportional to the number of shadow-casting lights in the scene.

Z-buffer Pros and Cons

When all you require of your images is simplicity, Z-buffers can be quite fast. And if available memory is a concern, pure Z-buffer algorithms allow a nearly un- limited number of objects within your scene, because each pass through the Z-buffer calculation requires only one object in memory at a time. This is contrary to other algorithms such as ray tracing, which requires all objects within the scene to be held in memory simultaneously. Another advantage owing to the singular object algorithm includes the ability to add independent plug-in modules or subroutines to handle the rendering of different types of modeled objects, such as polygons, curved-surfaces or fractal objects. Once the information from one object is written to the picture and Z-buffer, each new pass can be handled by a new program catering to a new kind of primitive. Theoretically, a whole library of plug-ins could be used for multiple object types.

On the other hand, Z-buffers have problems or are extremely inefficient in dealing with transparency and reflections. With the transparency subroutines, the sorting loops needed become too slow to be efficient. Similarly, pure reflections become impossible, except with time-consuming subroutines using mirrored textures. Other possible problems with Z-buffers include aliasing, motion-blur and good shadows, but, as we witnessed, these can be overcome with some crafty programming workarounds.

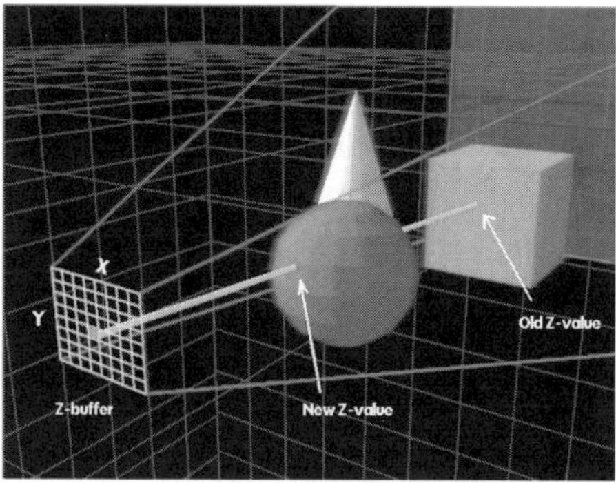

Figure 4: Each time through the loop, a new object's distance from the screen is checked against the value in the Z-buffer. If it is closer than the one currently there, it replaces the old value. This is the heart of the z-buffer algorithm.

LWP

William Frawley is president of Ecliptic Arts, a developing 3D animation and special effects production house. To ensure he has no free time whatsoever, he is also currently the author of a monthly graphics column for an Amiga-related publication called Amazing Computing, *a part-time sales jockey for a local wine and beer establishment, and an enthusiastic philosopher and mystic with a hankering for good pizza. Send questions or comments to Ecliptic Arts, c/o William Frawley, 315 W. Fifth Street, Muscatine, IA 52761.*

Popular 3D Algorithms

Part II: Ray Tracing and Radiosity

by William Frawley

If you tuned in last month, you'll recall my explication into the nature of the Z-buffer rendering algorithm. If it's a bit hazy or you're just joining us this month, don't worry, we'll trip the light fantastic with a short review to get us primed for the way-cool exploration of the wowities of ray tracing and radiosity techniques. (Sorry 'bout the '60s-like vernacular, dudes, but I never did like introductions. Hang tight, you stiffers, we'll get back to "professionalism" in the next paragraph.) Trust me, if you make it through this algorithm article, you'll never look at that Render button in the same light again.

The Review

As you recall, all objects exist within 3D object space, bound on all sides by clipping planes. Any object or part of an object lying outside of a clipping plane does not enter into the final image. For the most part, the side clipping planes are determined by the viewing angle, and the hither (near) plane usually coincides with the viewscreen. The yon (far) clipping plane may be some arbitrary distance determined by the programmer or may be a virtual backdrop image like that available in LightWave's **Effects** panel. When 3D objects are finally rendered, they are "projected" onto a 2D screen called the viewscreen. This, incidentally, is the final image that is seen.

As we saw last month, the essential ingredient in the Z-buffer rendering technique is the use of frame buffers, not only as the buffer to store the final image, but also as a repository for the distances of the nearest surfaces to the viewscreen. With the help of this additional buffer, the algorithm constructs a virtual picture of the closest object surfaces within the scene, which is then used as a guide in the final shading stage of those surface points visible from the camera view. This shading information is then written to the image buffer. Recall that with this rendering technique, in its purest form anyway, each object is processed individually, negating the necessity of storing all objects in memory simultaneously. Unlike ray tracing, which we'll look at next, this is a great advantage for low-memory systems. Z-buffer rendering is fast and simple, but for more realism in dealing with more complex objects, ray tracing is usually considered.

Ray Tracing

Due to its procedural parallel to light's behavior in the physical world, this is probably the oldest and most popular algorithm responsible for producing some of the most realistic images ever seen. First popularized in the Amiga community with such groundbreaking software for the personal computer as Impulse's Turbo Silver and then Imagine, ray tracing achieves its marvelous realism by mimicking the physics of light rays—including the laws of reflection and refraction—with prisms, lenses, mirrors and other objects. By its very nature, ray tracing also handles optical effects such as shadows, antialiasing and motion blur well.

Unlike the Z-buffer algorithm, ray tracing can be thought of as a random-sampling rendering technique because each pixel can be computed independently. However, all objects within the scene need to be present simultaneously for the procedure.

The general idea for ray tracing is as follows: Each light source emits rays of illumination. These rays travel through space striking and bouncing off of objects, eventually reaching the viewer's eye. Of course, the odds of the algorithm tracing just the right rays that will reach the viewer are enormous, considering the infinite number of rays emanating from each source. Therefore, ray tracing approaches matters from the opposite direction. Here, a singular ray is traced from eye to pixel out into object space, until it encounters an object (if any). From that surface point, which is now the shading point, the light ray is either absorbed or traced back to its many possible component origins via its reflection and transmission to other objects or its direct illumination from other light sources. The resultant shading for the surface point then is a summation of all these possible sources for the original eye ray. This is much more efficient than starting a ray from a light source and hoping it finally reaches the viewscreen. Interestingly, although an object may not be seen directly within the viewing volume, it may be seen as a reflection in another object. Since a ray may then originate outside the clipping planes, it is necessary to construct a **bounding** sphere initialized to some background color so the ray isn't traced forever (Figure 1).

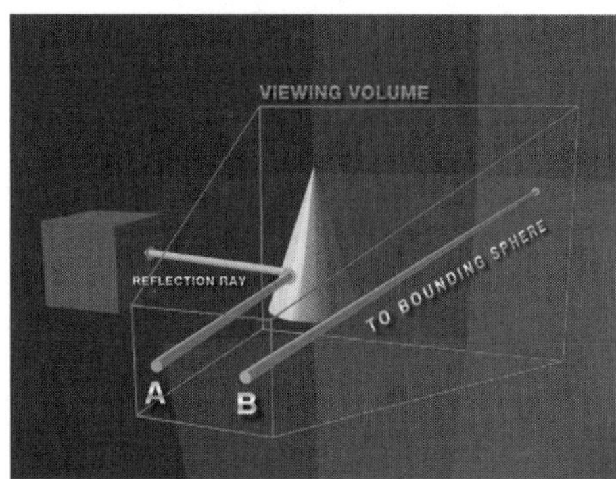

Figure 1: Just because an object lies outside the viewing volume doesn't mean it won't enter into the final image. In ray tracing, an object may contribute light rays via reflection or transmission even though it resides outside of the clipping planes (A). However, if a ray never strikes an object, a virtual bounding sphere ensures that some background color shades the pixel (B).

Basically, ray tracing can be considered a two-step process. First, for each ray passing from your eye through each pixel out into the viewing pyramid, a tree diagramming the interactions of the ray with all the other objects and lights within the scene is constructed. The ray in this case is simply the path the light will take from objects and lights back to the camera. Second, the tree is processed. This is where the shading is computed. The color value of each pixel is determined at this final stage—neglecting any antialiasing and motion blur effects for the moment.

In the construction phase of the ray tree, what happens when a ray strikes an object is determined from the surface properties and the complexity of the scene. If, for example, there is only one opaque, diffusely reflecting object and one light source, a ray traced from the eye striking the surface may follow a path leading directly to that light source. This is called a direct illumination path. It is helpful when tracing a ray to construct an abstract tree diagramming its interactions within the scene (Figure 2). It is these interactions of the ray's path with other objects and lights that will eventually construct the final picture.

Imagine now a more complex scene containing multiple objects with both transparent and reflective surfaces and multiple light sources. The ray strikes the first object, which might be a prism, for example. Because of the prism's surface properties, reflective and transparent, the ray splits into two component rays upon striking the surface: a transmitted ray (because of the transparent property of glass) and a reflected ray (because of the reflective property of glass). Continuing to follow the path of each of these rays might lead to more objects being encountered and subsequently split, depending on the surface properties of these new objects and the angles of the rays leaving the first object. Combine these two types of component rays (reflection and transmission) with the direct illumination rays from each light source and you might get a very complex, multi-level ray tree, depending on the number of lights and objects in the scene (Figure 2). As you might guess, as the tree gets deeper, more calculations are required, and therefore more computer rendering time is needed. It's up to the programmer to determine how extensive the ray tree becomes, but there must be some limit to the ray's path, or rendering of the image might outlast your lifetime.

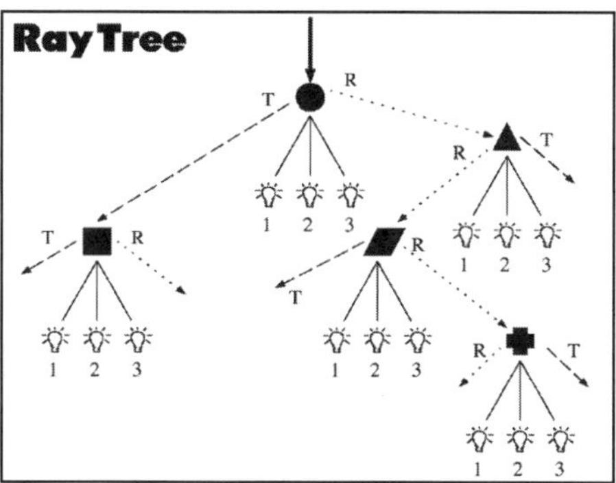

Figure 2: A ray tree diagramming a scene with four objects and three light sources. The construction of a tree helps determine all the possible interactions of a light ray as it travels within the scene. For each pixel, a ray is typically shot from the eye outward until it strikes an object (if any). From there, the surface material deems whether the ray splits into reflection or transmission paths. The direct illumination paths are also calculated.

To process the ray tree, consider all the possible incoming sources of light rays striking the surface point in question. Then sum the entire illumination contributed by these sources, be it direct, reflected or transmitted rays, to find the outgoing light to the appropriate pixel. Therefore, an important part of the calculation for the shading of a point takes into account the object's surface properties and the interaction of these properties with the summation of all the incoming colors and intensities of the various illumination rays. It is important to note that the reflected and transmitted rays that we are dealing with here are specular in nature, not diffuse. Remember that specular reflection is such that the path of light obeys the angle of incidence/reflectance law — one unique path for the ray relative to its origin. We'll explore diffusion effects when we discuss the radiosity preprocessing technique shortly.

Finally, to determine if a shadow contributes to the shading information, each light source is considered for its potential illumination of the surface point. By tracing a ray from each light source to the object, you determine if any other object blocks the illumination ray's path. If so, the point must be in shadow. If not, the total illumination is added into the shading. Because of the mathematics of this algorithm, however, it is possible to include penumbra effects, or partial shadowing, by calculating the proportional light intensities reaching the surface point of partially blocked objects.

Because each pixel can be thought of as a separate entity for processing, all objects must reside in memory at once when building the ray tree. This approach differs from the Z-buffer technique, which deals with one object at a time for each Z-buffer pass. But this is again due to the mathematical nature of ray tracing, which does have the benefit of locating hidden surfaces and knowing immediately which object is the first to be hit by a ray.

Other limitations with basic ray tracing (although each programmer may fine-tune various aspects) include realistic shadows and **caustics**, extremely focused spots of light. There are many ways around this problem, however, such as creative reflection mapping (*LWPRO*, Vol. 1, No. 9, "Beneath the Surface"). Finally, the biggest hurdle for obtaining extremely realistic images lies with the phenomenon of diffuse inter-reflections.

Diffuse Inter-reflections

Diffusion, or the scattering of light based upon a surface's material properties, is a concept you may already be familiar with if you've dealt with surfacing in LightWave. Recall that a more diffuse material scatters light in all directions, whereas a less diffuse surface tends to focus or absorb incoming light rays. Diffuse inter-reflection then is the reflection and transmission of scattered light between different surfaces (no surprise). Unlike specular reflection and transmission, which depend also on the glossiness of the surface, this phenomenon is usually witnessed regardless of the viewing angle.

For instance, imagine the corner of a normally lit room. One wall is red, the other is white. What you would probably notice is that the junction between the walls is a little darker than the flat surface of the walls, and the corner of the room even darker yet. This gradual decrease in light reaching the corner is the result of a falloff of light reflecting and scattering from surface to surface. In fact, at the junction of both the red and white wall, you would notice that the white wall is tinted slightly red and the red wall is a little brighter due to the scattering of light of the white wall. Consequently, the total light reaching each surface is the sum total of both the light source and the diffuse inter-reflections. If the walls are glossy, throw in some specular reflection as well.

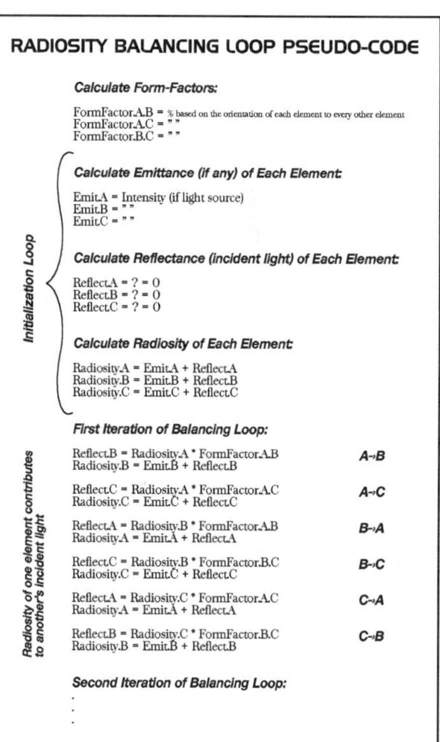

RADIOSITY BALANCING LOOP PSEUDO-CODE

```
Calculate Form-Factors:

FormFactor.A.B = % based on the orientation of each element to every other element
FormFactor.A.C = " "
FormFactor.B.C = " "

Initialization Loop
  Calculate Emittance (if any) of Each Element:

  Emit.A = Intensity (if light source)
  Emit.B = " "
  Emit.C = " "

  Calculate Reflectance (incident light) of Each Element:

  Reflect.A = ? = 0
  Reflect.B = ? = 0
  Reflect.C = ? = 0

  Calculate Radiosity of Each Element:

  Radiosity.A = Emit.A + Reflect.A
  Radiosity.B = Emit.B + Reflect.B
  Radiosity.C = Emit.C + Reflect.C

First Iteration of Balancing Loop:
(Radiosity of one element contributes to another's incident light)

Reflect.B = Radiosity.A * FormFactor.A.B        A→B
Radiosity.B = Emit.B + Reflect.B

Reflect.C = Radiosity.A * FormFactor.A.C        A→C
Radiosity.C = Emit.C + Reflect.C

Reflect.A = Radiosity.B * FormFactor.A.B        B→A
Radiosity.A = Emit.A + Reflect.A

Reflect.C = Radiosity.B * FormFactor.B.C        B→C
Radiosity.C = Emit.C + Reflect.C

Reflect.A = Radiosity.C * FormFactor.A.C        C→A
Radiosity.A = Emit.A + Reflect.A

Reflect.B = Radiosity.C * FormFactor.B.C        C→B
Radiosity.B = Emit.B + Reflect.B

Second Iteration of Balancing Loop:
.
.
.
```

Figure 3: A pseudo-code example to help show how radiosity is calculated. For simplicity, only three elements (polygons) are considered here.

Diffuse inter-reflections cannot be solved with ray tracing alone. Ray tracing handles the shading of surfaces strictly by calculating the rather straightforward geometries of specular reflection and transmission, taking into account the surface properties of other objects and the color and intensity of lights striking such surfaces. Since diffuse light can originate from an infinite number of paths, it would be time-prohibitive to shoot a large number of rays in all directions just to determine if light is being diffusely reflected from some other objects to the surface point in question. What is needed is a different method to handle this problem.

Radiosity

More of a pre-processing technique, radiosity deals with diffuse inter-reflections based on the physics of **energy** transfer. By breaking down the objects within a scene into a sufficient number of **elements** (polygons), you can calculate the amount of light that is being diffusely reflected by every polygon to every other polygon, thereby simulating the realism of diffuse inter-reflections. **Radiosity** simply refers to the overall amount of light leaving each element or polygon.

One of the factors necessary for achieving an accurate calculation of radiosity lies in effectively subdividing the objects into the proper number of elements. Too few may cause insufficient detail and too many may unnecessarily increase rendering time. Once the subdivision factor is determined, the algorithm proceeds in two major steps.

First, some idea of how much each element is visible from every other element is calculated mathematically. These **form-factors**, as they are called, are basically a percentage, or value between 0 and 1, determining how much of each element can be seen by another element. In other words, the form-factor expresses numerically the geometrical orientation of angles and distances between each and every element as a basis for accurately assessing the resultant energy (light) transfer.

For example, if two elements (read: polygons) are parallel and proximate to each other, the form-factor associated with this pair will be nearly 1. If, however, they are perpendicular to each other, the form-factor might be closer to 0, since very little of each element's surface can be seen by the other. Any other orientation of the two elements begets a form-factor somewhere between 0 and 1. Additionally, the form-factor is inversely proportional to the distance between elements. Once the form-factors for all elements is calculated, the second stage of the radiosity process can begin.

The algorithm then proceeds with a **balancing** loop to find the total radiosity (light energy) emanating from each element. This radiosity consists of both emitted (if a light source) and diffusely reflected light. By using the form-factors calculated earlier, this procedure eventually reaches equilibrium, whereby the energy absorbed and radiated by each element becomes balanced and further energy transfer between elements ceases. Perhaps this balancing process would best be understood by examining the mock pseudo-code illustrated in Figure 3. In this very simplistic example, assume that there are only three elements and that one of these elements happens to be a light source. It might be helpful to imagine the walls and ceiling in the color image "Room Corner" as representing the variables in the pseudo-code, with the ceiling acting as a light source.

As the code shows, first the form-factors are calculated. Then the separate components of an element's total radiosity, the emittance and reflectance, are calculated. Only those elements that are actually light sources emit any energy, so that intensity is found for A, but the emittance of elements B and C are always zero. Secondly, the reflectance of each element, the light that is absorbed from other elements and redirected, depends upon the radiosity of the other elements modified by the form-factor, the physical orientation between the two elements. Since this is the initial phase of the loop, the radiosities of all the elements have yet to be calculated, so we approximate the reflectances with zero. Now the first estimates of the elements' radiosities are calculated — the summation of the emittance and reflectance variables. Finally, the code repeats this process of adjusting the reflectances based on the new radiosities as many times as necessary until an element's incident light equals its reflected light.

When the system has **converged**, the radiosities are then used in the final shading calculations to add some valuable extra color produced by the diffuse inter-reflections within the scene. Furthermore, besides the diffuse, specular and direct illumination now accounted for, shadow effects like penumbras and umbras are automatically handled by the form-factors. Not only are the direct shadows from light sources incurred, but shadows from other objects are inherently natural as a result of the form-factor calculations. At the cost of rendering time, the realism of an image can be greatly enhanced with the use of these subtle effects. It will be a great day when desktop processors become fast and inexpensive enough to feasibly handle these awesome rendering features.

C-Ya...Bye

I certainly hope this material has increased your appreciation of the nature of current and future 3D software. I'd hate to think of all you successful animators out there who have no idea of how your tools actually work underneath those fancy GUI veneers. It'd be kind of like a painter not knowing the subtleties of how one pigment might react with another when mixed together. Well, maybe not that extreme, but I think you get the rendering. LWP

William is president of Ecliptic Arts, a developing 3D animation production house, and is also currently authoring a monthly graphics column for an Amiga-related publication called Amazing Computing. *He is considering changing his name to simply "Bilfro," as this might procure much-sought-after membership in the elite-status-one-nickname clique inhabited by such greats as "Sting," "Cher" and "Mojo." Send questions, comments or frozen pizzas to Ecliptic Arts c/o William Frawley, 315 W. Fifth Street, Muscatine, IA 52761.*

Cross-Platform Images

The Heartbreak of Non-Square Pixels

by Ernie Wright

When moving images across computer platforms or rendering for media other than video, how do you determine the pixel dimensions, and avoid the squashing and stretching that can occur?

I once caught a friend who has a Master of Science in structural engineering holding a ruler against the glass face of his computer monitor to measure some circles his program had drawn. The problem was that his circles weren't circular, and he wanted to know how much to correct them. (Many of you will remember the first time you drew a "circle" in DeluxePaint on the Amiga.)

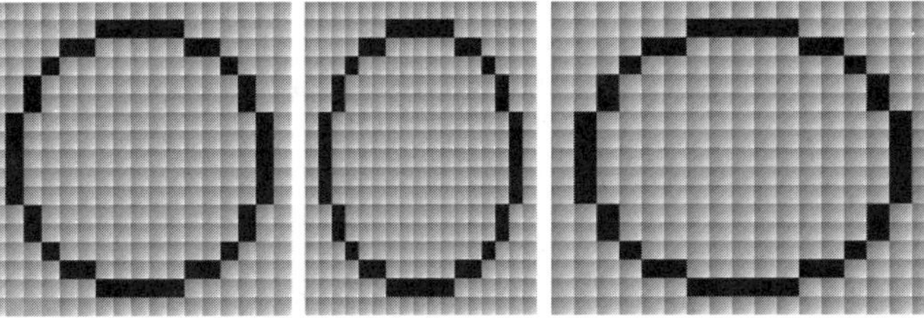

Figure 1: The same image displayed with different pixel aspect ratios.

Being an engineer, and therefore an empiricist by definition, my friend regarded his measurements rather seriously, as if they had a reality that was independent of the hardware and the methods he happened to be using. But his program was going to be used by other people on other machines. What if he'd used a different size monitor or a different screen mode, or a tape measure that conformed to the curvature of the screen? What if he'd measured near the edge of the screen rather than the center, or early in the morning, before the components of his monitor had reached thermal equilibrium? What if a friend of his was about to sneak up behind him and mess up his monitor adjustments?

Unless you've done some graphics programming, the arcana of pixel and image aspect ratios and the transformations required to map an abstract image to a particular output device are probably unfamiliar. Even if you're a graphics programmer (or an engineer), you most likely learned about non-square pixels on the street, because no textbook author wants to acknowledge their existence, much less try to explain them. (The references I normally reach for first—Foley, van Dam et al., Watt, the Graphics Gems books—have nothing to say on this subject, while the lower-tier, $30 paperbacks get almost everything wrong.)

This article won't entirely fill the void, but I'll try to give you enough background and practical advice to make you comfortable with the subject and ready to ask the right questions.

Aspect Ratio

Aspect ratio is the ratio of a rectangle's width to its height. Maybe you've always heard this term applied specifically to images, pixels and screens, but it's meaningful for any rectangle. It was used 90 years ago to refer to the shape of an airplane's wings (and is still used for that purpose, although the definition has been modified to account for the fact that, by and large, airplanes no longer have rectangular wings). The aspect ratio of U.S. letter-size paper is 8.5/11 = 0.773; for many front doors, it's 36/80 = 0.45; and for the shelves in my Swedish bookcases, it's 65/26 = 2.5.

You'll often see an aspect ratio written only as an explicit ratio of two numbers—"4/3," for example, or even "4:3," with a colon in the middle. Don't be misled by this. Aspect ratio is a single value, the result of dividing the first number by the second one. Every square has an aspect ratio of 1.0. Conversely, every rectangle with the same aspect ratio has the same shape.

We'll be dealing with two different aspect ratios in the discussion that follows. Image (or frame) aspect is the shape of the entire image. Pixel aspect is the shape of each pixel in an image. It's important not to confuse the two.

A Frequently Asked Question

"How do I convert a 752x480 LightWave image so that it displays correctly on a PC (or on almost any computer display other than the Amiga's)?"

Most computer displays use square pixels while NTSC/D2 does not, so you need to correct for the pixel aspect. You have a couple of options.

If the frames haven't been rendered yet, you can use LightWave to set the Pixel Aspect Ratio (on the Camera panel) to Square Pixels. By default, this option sets the resolution to 640x480, which gives you an image aspect ratio of 4/3 = 1.333, very nearly the same as the 1.346 image aspect for 752x480 with NTSC/D2 pixels. (In versions of LightWave prior to 4.0, the pixel aspect setting is ignored when a Custom Size is being used. I'll have more to say about this a little later.)

If you use LightWave 4.0 primarily to generate images for display on PCs, you can edit the LightWave configuration file so that Square Pixels is your default pixel aspect. The LightWave configuration file is called LW-config on the Amiga, LW.CFG on platforms running Microsoft Windows and .lwrc on SGI machines. Find the line containing "DefaultPixelAspect" and change the value to 2. (The value is the position of the option in the Pixel Aspect Ratio pop-up list, counting from 0.) If you're using an earlier version of LightWave, you might want to create a scene file named "default" (or whatever you like) in which to store default settings that, like this one, can't be added to the config file.

If the frames have already been rendered, you'll need to scale them in an image-processing program. You can either reduce the width to 640 or increase the height to 564. Reducing the width is preferred because it's less likely to introduce scaling artifacts—from an image-quality point of view, it's better to slightly reduce the amount of information in an image than it is to try to add information that doesn't really exist.

It usually isn't necessary, but if you want, you can account for the slight difference in image aspect, either by cropping before scaling or by scaling to slightly different dimensions. The crop should remove seven pixel columns, divided any way you like between the left and right sides of the image, so that the new width is 745. You can also scale to either 646x480 or 752x559, though you may find that these "unusual"

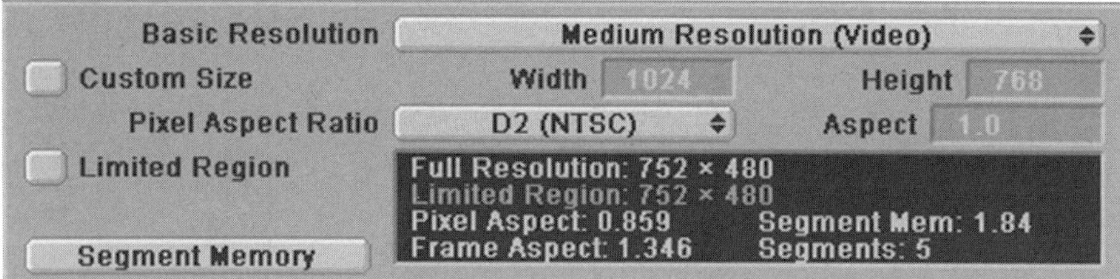

Figure 2: The Camera panel's resolution controls.

sizes aren't as convenient to use in other applications.

What about PAL/D2?

Pretty much the same deal. You won't go terribly wrong by scaling to 640x480, but to preserve more of the image information, you can also scale to 752x565 (height reduction) or 766x576 (width enlargement). Or you can decide not to mess with the images at all. LightWave gives PAL/D2 pixels an aspect of 1.019, which is well within the range of variation for most devices claiming to use square pixels.

Magic Formulas

At this point, you might be wondering where all of these numbers are coming from. Well, there are formulas. They can be a little confusing—there are three aspect ratios and four pixel dimensions involved—so don't expect all of this to be instantly clear. In practice, you'll probably find yourself using just one or two of the formulas all the time, and if you need them often enough, the calculations will become second nature.

Let's define some shorthand references to the values:

w1, h1—the width and height of the source image

w2, h2 — the width and height of the target image

p1 — the pixel aspect of the source image

p2—the pixel aspect of the target device

i— the image aspect (the shape of the image)

The aspect ratio of an image can be found with either of the following:

$i = (w1 * p1)/h1$

$i = w1/(h1/p1)$

When the pixels are square, $p1 = 1.0$ and both formulas reduce to the definition of aspect ratio, $i = w/h$.

To correct an image for distortion-free output on a different device (no change in image aspect), use one of the following:

$w2 = p1 * w1/p2$

$h2 = p2 * h1/p1$

Don't use both! You'll be applying the same correction twice. I recommend using the formula that results in a reduction of one of the pixel dimensions whenever possible. If $p1 < p2$, then use the first one (reduce the width). If $p1 > p2$, use the second one (reduce the height). One of the pixel aspects (either p1 or p2) will often be 1.0, which can simplify the calculation. (And if $p1 = p2$, the formulas collapse to $w2 = w1$ and $h2 = h1$, of course.)

When you know both the image aspect and pixel aspect and you have one of the pixel dimensions in mind, you can find the other one with this formula:

$w1 = h1 * (i/p1)$

$h1 = w1/(i/p1)$

You have to know one of the two pixel dimensions before you can calculate the other one; this is how you determine the scale of the image.

Finally, to calculate a pixel aspect for an image with a known image aspect and dimensions, use the following:

$p1 = (h1 * i) / w1$

For displays that use square pixels, $w1 = h1 * i$ and $p1 = 1.0$.

Custom Size

If you'd like to apply these formulas to custom-size images and you're using LightWave 4.0, hakuna matata. Turn on the Custom Size checkbox, select Custom from the Pixel Aspect Ratio pop-up list, and enter values for Width, Height and (pixel) Aspect. LightWave displays the frame (image) aspect, i, in the information box next to the resolution controls. Typically, the pixel aspect will be known, and you'll have some idea of what the image aspect and one of the two dimensions should be. You'd use these in the formula for w1 or h1.

If you're using Custom Size in an earlier version of LightWave, you'll have to do the pixel aspect correction outside LightWave, in an image-processing program. When rendering custom-size images, versions 3.5 and earlier of LightWave ignore the Pixel Aspect Ratio setting and instead always use NTSC/D2 pixels, with an aspect of 0.859. (This is a holdover from LightWave's origin as an application for the Video Toaster. The resolution and pixel aspect controls in LightWave 3.5, the first version not tied directly to the Toaster, hadn't yet made a complete transition to device-independent rendering.) The approach when using pre-4.0 LightWave is to set the Width and Height so that the image aspect is correct for pixels with NTSC/D2 aspect, then scale the rendered image to account for the intended pixel aspect.

Suppose you want to use LightWave 3.5 to render a 300x300 image for display on a device that uses square pixels. Since the need for Custom Size with square pixels is common, it's worth stating a rule of thumb here: Divide the desired width by 0.859, render, then scale to the desired width. So for a 300x300 square-pixel image, set the Width to 300/0.859 = 349 and the Height to 300, render, then scale the rendered image back to 300x300.

In general, you first need to convert from the desired pixel dimensions to the NTSC/D2 dimensions. Use the formula for w2 or h2, whichever makes the pixel dimension larger. Set w1, h1 and p1 to the desired width, height and pixel aspect, and set $p2 = 0.859$. Render at the new pixel dimensions (w2xh1 or w1xh2), then reduce the rendered image to w1xh1.

Hopefully I've shed some light on the oft-confusing aspect ratio question. Learning these values and applying them when needed will give you the image you're looking for!

LWP

For the past five years, Ernie Wright has been a programmer doing scientific visualization for several defense-related agencies. His code can also be found in LightWave (the HAM routines in 3.5 and wireframe previews in 4.0 for Windows). Ernie works from his home in Maryland while watching his 2-year-old daughter, whose little brother is due in January 1996.

Getting to Know Networks

A Two-Part Primer on Linking LightWave Machines

by John Crookshank

Thanks to the inclusion of ScreamerNet with LightWave 4.0 and higher, you may use a single copy of LightWave to render your work on multiple computer systems, greatly speeding up rendering times. And, if you have several computers around, ScreamerNet will allow you to use Modeler on one system while the others are busy rendering. ScreamerNet is even flexible enough to allow distributed rendering on different computer platforms, provided LightWave is running on each platform that you intend to use. Finally, even with only one computer, ScreamerNet can automatically batch render several scenes without intervention. This is quite handy if you have some smaller scenes and want to render them overnight.

Before you can start "Screaming," you have to have a network up and running. Is it worth the time, effort and expense? If you have multiple computers and use LightWave to make a living, the answer is a *resounding* yes. Although this article is aimed at LightWave owners with both Amigas and Windows systems, most of it also will apply to SGIs and Macs.

A Network Guide

This article will guide you through the process of setting up a simple network linking an Amiga and a PC using either Windows 95 or Windows NT. The NT instructions also apply to other Windows NT platforms such as Alpha and MIPS systems. Note that the emphasis here is simplicity. The information is intended for small guys who just need to move a bunch of pictures around a lot. A larger shop with many computers will have networking needs much more complex than the simple setup discussed here. If you already have an existing network, please consult with the person who maintains your network before trying any of this.

The basic requirements to network your systems together are:

- An Intel system running either Windows 95 or Windows NT (or an Alpha or MIPS system running NT).
- An Ethernet card for the PC.
- NFS Server and/or NFS Client software for the PC.
- An Amiga running AmigaOS version 2.1 or higher.
- An Amiga Ethernet card.
- INET-225 TCP and INET-NFSd software or AmiTCP and Samba software.
- Ethernet cables and connectors.
- Pad of paper for notes.
- Patience…

The most common types of network hardware are 10-Base-T, 10-Base-2, and 100-Base-T.

The 100-Base-T Ethernet cards are faster and more expensive, but are incompatible with Amiga Ethernet cards. The 10-Base-T card is the most popular network card in the PC world. However, it requires the extra expense of a 10-Base-T Hub and is supported by only two Amiga networking cards.

The 10-Base-2 Ethernet, which uses coaxial cable, is not quite as popular in the PC marketplace. However, PC Ethernet cards that support 10-Base-2 are readily available. Many manufacturers have "combo" cards that have both 10-Base-2 and 10-Base-T connectors on them. You can then purchase any Amiga Ethernet card and be assured that it will be compatible. Using the coax 10-Base-2 cabling is by far the easiest and cheapest network to set up, and there are no performance advantages to using one over the other on a small and simple network.

A warning on PC Ethernet cards: Do not buy the cheapest card you can find. If you purchase an Ethernet card with 32-bit drivers for Windows 95 or Windows NT, and get a PCI card if you have an available PCI slot, you will probably be OK.

Almost any Amiga Ethernet card will work fine. However, I have heard from NewTek that the ASDG Lan Rover (EB920) cards do not work with AmiTCP, so you should probably avoid that brand. Unfortunately, Amiga Ethernet cards cost more than three times as much as a PC Ethernet card.

Windows Does Networks

Windows 95 and Windows NT (all platforms) come with the software required to share files with other Windows systems. Unfortunately, the software included with Windows will not directly allow file sharing with any other types of computers.

When talking about networking software, you will hear the terms Client and Server. If you have Server software installed on your system, other computers on the network running Client software can "see" your computer. They can connect to your drives, but you can't connect to their's unless you install Client software on your system. When all the systems on a network run both Client and Server software, it's called a peer-to-peer network because all systems have equal access.

This is a very cool arrangement, since you can get at any graphics file that is on any computer you have, including PAR, PVR and Flyer drives. Yes, you can have a remote computer directly use Perception or Flyer video clips as image sequences without having to break them up into frames first. And you can send rendered frames from your networked computers to a Perception or Flyer for playback. This feature alone makes the expense and work of setting up a network worthwhile.

ScreamerNet requires a network where all your systems can connect to a common drive that contains the scene file and all it's elements, as well as a common drive to store all the rendered frames. ScreamerNet does not require a full peer-to-peer network system, but you get the most flexibility in sharing your graphics files between computers and applications if you set up a full peer-to-peer network.

Going Peer-to-Peer

For a full peer-to-peer network, you will need the basic networking software, plus network file-sharing Client and Server software for each system. Windows 95 and Windows NT (any platform) already include the basic networking software. You have to add NFS Server and NFS Client software to a Windows system to be able to share files with any other type of system.

On the Amiga, you will need the basic networking (TCP/IP) software, plus a Server package. Both available Amiga TCP/IP packages come standard with NFS Client software, so you will only have to add a Server package to complete the two-way connection desired.

Interworks, maker of the basic INET-225 TCP/IP software for the Amiga, also makes an NFS Server package to mount your Amiga drives on your PC system. It requires adding an NFS client package on the PC to complete the connection. The Interworks NFSd package is very easy to set up, and is a standard NFS Server package, so it can be used with virtually any system on the market that has an NFS Client package available for it. Interworks has a U.S. office for telephone support, which is a real plus if you have problems with your setup.

The other TCP/IP package for the Amiga is AmiTCP. Although it does not offer a NFS Server package, there is a shareware add-on for AmiTCP called Samba. Samba is a Server application used in place of a NFS Server package. Samba only allows connections from Windows systems. Samba is very cryptic to set up and is very slow, but it works OK once it's running. Samba also does not require NFS client software on the PC. It works with the standard Microsoft networking software that is included with Windows 95 and Windows NT. AmiTCP is produced in Finland, and has virtually no US support at all, a "feature" that must be considered carefully.

Getting Started

Before you start doing anything, you need to plan a little bit. You will need to make a list of your systems and usernames, etc. and write these down before you begin. You will need a list of the following:

- A name for each computer.
- An IP address for each computer.
- A login name for the user who will use each computer.
- The drive names that you need to make available to the other systems.

Keep your names short and simple, and do not use spaces or punctuation in the names. When you are done, you'll have a list something like this:

Computer (Host) name:	pc1
IP Address:	200.0.0.1
Username:	john
Password:	Lightwave
Workgroup:	workgroup

Computer name: amiga1	
IP Address:	200.0.0.2
Username:	john
Password:	Lightwave
Workgroup:	workgroup

If you have additional computers, continue adding them to this list. Use the IP numbers that I have here. Don't make up your own IP numbers, unless you have an existing network and your network administrator tells you to do so. The only thing that will change from system to system is the computer name and IP address. The rest of the data will stay the same on all the systems. Notice that I used the same username, password, and workgroup name on each system, and that I used only lowercase when typing the names, but upper and lower case on the password. The AmiTCP software requires passwords to be in mixed case, but the rest of the settings can be however you want. Be sure and write these down, as you will need this information again later.

Windows 95

We'll start off with installing networking for Windows 95 since it's so popular. Windows 95 will most likely automatically detect the presence of your new Ethernet card when you turn the system on, and automatically install the driver software for you or prompt you to insert the driver diskette. If not, load up the Control Panel and select 'Add New Hardware'. Windows 95 will again try to figure out by itself what you have, but if it does not, you can select 'Network Adapters' and then select the "Have Disk' option to have the driver installed from the disk that came with the Ethernet card.

After the driver for the card has been installed, you'll need your Windows 95 CD to install the networking software. Make sure that you select "Client for Microsoft networks," NetBEUI, and TCP/IP to be installed. You can select Add -> Protocol -> Microsoft -> TCP/IP and NetBEUI to put these items in the list. When you are finished, the list of networking items should show the following:

- Client for Microsoft Networks.
- Your Ethernet adapter.
- NetBEUI.
- TCP/IP.
- File and Printer sharing for Microsoft Networks.

You will also be prompted to enter your computer name, workgroup name and user name once the networking installation process is started. In the Network panel, select the entry that shows TCP/IP -> Ethernet adapter and click the "Property" button to set up the TCP/IP software. Click the IP address tab and click Specify an Address. Enter the number 200.0.0.1 in the IP Address box, and enter 255.255.255.0 in the Subnet Mask box.

Click the File and Print Sharing button and make sure that "I want to be able to give others access to my files" is selected. If you also select Windows Logon in the Primary Network Logon box, you won't have to enter a password every time you start up your system. Select OK, and the information will be saved, and your system will reboot.

For the NFS Server software on Intel Windows 95 and Windows NT, I use TropicNFS Server. If you have a DEC Alpha system, Intergraph sells several NFS Client and Server packages that you could use instead. Install the NFS Server software on the PC in a directory of your choosing. In the NFS Server directory, you only have to create a file called exports to tell the NFS Server software which drives to make available (export) to the Amiga. Use Notepad to type in the lines below and then save the file as 'exports' in the NFS Server directory. My exports file looks like this:

```
# Export root directory of disk D: and E: to amiga1
d:/ 200.0.0.2
e:/ 200.0.0.2
```

The line starting with the (#) character is a comment, and is not required. In this example I am exporting my drive D:\ and E:\, and the IP address is the IP address of the computer(s) that will be allowed to connect to the drive. Note that I used a forward slash, not the typical back-slash after the drive name. Add extra lines for extra drives that you wish to make available to the Amiga. If you have more than one Amiga, list all the IP addresses one after the other, such as:

```
d:/ 200.0.0.2  200.0.0.3  200.0.0.4
```

This would allow these three systems to connect to your drive D:\. Save the exports file, and you're done on the PC side for now.

Windows NT

After installing your Ethernet card, Windows NT may automatically detect it and prompt you to install the software for it. If not, enter the Control Panel and select Network. You will be prompted for the Windows NT CD-ROM , then follow the prompts to select the card driver and software components that you want installed. Make sure that you have the following items selected in the list when you are finished:

- NetBEUI.
- NetBIOS Interface.
- Server.
- TCP/IP Protocol and related components.

To configure the TCP/IP software, select TCP/IP Protocol in the list and click Configure. At the TCP/IP configuration panel, enter 200.0.0.1 in the IP Address box, and 255.255.255.0 in Subnet Mask. Click OK to save and reboot.

The setup of TropicNFS software is identical under Windows NT, so it won't be repeated here. At the time of this article, only a Windows 95 version of TropicNFS was available, but it installed and ran with no problems whatsoever under Windows NT on an Intel system. They should have a NT version soon. An Alpha NT version of TropicNFS is not planned. Intergraph has several NFS Server and Client packages available for the Alpha NT, and their setup will be fairly similar.

Amiga Setup

Your Amiga Ethernet card will come with a driver disk. The disk should have an Install program to install the driver for you. If not, find your SYS:Devs directory, create a new directory there called Networks, and copy the driver into the SYS:Devs/Networks directory. The designation SYS: refers to the drive that you boot Workbench from, so you could substitute DH0:Devs/Networks if your boot drive is DH0. If you use the SYS: designation, the Amiga will know you want your Workbench boot partition.

INET-225/NFSd

When you run the Installer program included with INET-225, you will be asked for a user name, host name (computer name) and IP number, plus a few other questions, like the name of your Ethernet driver, which must already be installed. The driver will be in the SYS:Devs/Networks directory, and have a name like hydra.device or ariadne.device if you are using either a Hydra Ethernet card or Ariadne Ethernet card, respectively. INET-225 supports a variety of TCP/IP connections, including modem and Internet, so be sure you select the Ethernet option, and use the file requester to point to your Ethernet card driver file in SYS:Devs/Networking. INET-225 picks a home directory for you; just accept the defaults. Answer the rest of the prompts as they come up. One of the question panels asks if you want to use DNS servers, and it is on by default. Turn this off before continuing. When the install is finished, you will have an icon called StartInet in your INET:C directory. Edit the tooltypes of this icon to remove the parentheses around the (NFSD) option. Drag this icon to your SYS:WBStartup drawer so it starts up every time you start your Amiga.

Install the INET NSFd software, and when you are finished, you will need to edit the file INET:rexx/startnfsd.rexx. Scroll down until you find the line that refers to your exports. It should look like this:

```
* The exports variable declares the partitions
you wish to export.
*/
exports = 'dh1:/ dh2:/ VideoB:/jonesproject/'
```

Change the drive names to match whatever drives you intend to make available to your PC. Note the colons and slashes after the drive names. A word here on performance: If you export the entire drive as I have in my example, the access to this drive will be slower than if you just export a single directory, since the PC will have to build a directory table of all the files and directories that it finds when it connects to that drive. Limiting access is both faster and safer. When you are done with the entries here, save this file.

Reboot your Amiga, and the INET software and NFSd Server software will be started automatically.

The only thing left to do is to test the NFS connection to the PC. On the PC, start up the NFS Server software. Back on the Amiga, open a shell and type:

```
nfsmgr mount pc1:/d N
```

You should see an icon appear on your Workbench in a couple of seconds with the name N. If you get an error message, either the NFS Servers exports file on the PC has not been set up properly or your INET:rexx/startnfsd.rexx file is incorrect, and you'll need to check to see if you have your exported drives listed properly, and that you have the proper IP address entered there for your Amiga. Double-click the N icon, and it should open up to an empty window. Select the menu item Window/Show/All Files, and you should see all the folders on your PC's drive D:\. Start up your favorite file utility program like Directory Opus, and list the drive N:. It should appear and behave just as any other Amiga hard drive partition, except that loading or saving files to/from it will be slower than a regular hard disk.

Repeat the nfsmgr command for each PC drive that you set up for exporting. Note that pc1:/d refers to computer pc1 and drive D:, change these to match your system. Be careful to use the colon and slash exactly as shown in the example. The last part, N, is the name that will show up on your Workbench when it gets mounted. This could be anything that you like, and you can rename it from Workbench at any time, just like you can rename any other disk. Stay with N for now, it will be used later in the Screamernet examples. If you want to automate the mounting of your PC drives, you can type the mount commands with a text editor and then save that file and attach an icon to it so you can just mount your PC drives whenever you want by clicking the icon. If you want the drives automatically mounted every time that you start your Amiga, drag that icon into your SYS:WBStartup drawer after the StartInet icon.

All of the PC NFS Client software that I looked at worked through Windows itself, so to mount the Amiga drives there, you only have to open up the Network Neighborhood and use the Map Network Drive option to mount and open your Amiga drives. If you are using Windows NT, use the File Manager and use the Connect Network Drive option in the disk menu. You must assign a drive letter to your Amiga drive. Give the Amiga drive that has your LightWave or Toaster software on it the letter V. If you want these drives to always get mounted every time that you start your system, check the option Reconnect at logon before you click OK to mount this drive.

AmiTCP/Samba

The AmiTCP installation is similar, just make sure you select an Ethernet connection and select the proper Ethernet card. AmiTCP will ask for your computer name in two parts, which is technically correct for proper Internet use, but confusing within the context of our simple setup. When asked for the host name, enter amiga1, and when asked for the domain, enter system. You will then be allowed to enter an alias, enter amiga1 to this question. When it asks you for the location of your home directory, enter AmiTCP:. Note the colon after the word, don't forget that. You will be asked for domain names to search, leave this section blank and just click continue to skip this section. You will also be asked if you want to have servers started when AmiTCP starts, be sure and answer yes to this question. The installer will also ask if you want to make alterations to your user-startup, answer yes to these as well. During the install process, AmiTCP will open a shell for you and prompt you for your first-time password. Enter it, and you're basically done with AmiTCP after this.

Samba Installation

Installing Samba is fairly cryptic, and involves studious use of the installation instructions and a text editor. There are two versions of Samba, written by different authors. I prefer the newest version, listed in Aminet archives under the name Samba-1.9.15p8.lh. It starts as a deamon automatically when AmiTCP starts, is more robust, and survives a system reboot (either the Amiga or PC) without having to restart the other system. You will also need a file called ixemul-040fpu.lha or ixemul-020fpu.lha, depending on whether you have an '040 or '020/'030 CPU in your Amiga. The ixemul files are located in dev/gcc/ on Aminet sites. When this file is unpacked, you have the files ixemul040fpu.library and ixnet040fpu.library. Rename them to ixemul.library and ixnet.library, and then copy them to your LIBS: directory.

Create a Samba directory in your AmiTCP: directory, and unarchive the Samba files there. Load up and print out the Amiga Installation Notes file for instructions on how to perform the file editing and joining. Basically, you have to edit two of the files. The first file is Amitcp:Samba/lib/smb.conf. To add the definitions of the drives that you want exported to your PC. Scroll down until you see the section that looks like this:

```
[SYS]
 comment = System boot volume
 valid users = pcguest
 path = /SYS/
 read only = yes
 public = yes
```

Change this to match the drive(s) on your system that you want exported. If you want to export DH1: and a Flyer VideoB: drive to the PC, change the above entry and use cut and paste to create a second drive entry so it looks like this:

```
[DH1]
  comment = amiga1 DH1: drive
  valid users = pcguest
  path = /DH1/
  read only = no
  public = yes

[VideoB]
  comment = amiga1 Flyer VideoB: drive
  valid users = pcguest
  path = /VideoB/jonesproject/
  read only = no
  public = yes
```

The line that starts with comment= will show up in File Manager next to the drive name when you select the Connect Network Drive option. Be careful of how you specify drive names here. Note that the standard colon after the drive name in the path line is assumed. Do not actually type a colon in the path to your exported drives. In the second example, I also only exported the "jonesproject" directory on my Flyer VideoB drive instead of the entire drive. I also changed the read only = definition to no, so that the PC can write to these drives. Do not change the valid users line, leave it set to "pcguest." Save this file when you are finished entering your Amiga drives for exporting.

Next, edit the file Amitcp:Samba/inetd.conf.addon. It will look like this:

```
# This is for Samba
# You should modify the arguments for nmbd to suit your setup and network.
netbios-ssn stream tcp nowait root AmiTCP:samba/bin/smbd smbd
netbios-ns dgram udp wait root AmiTCP:samba/bin/nmbd nmbd -n k4315 -G Kampsax -C "Amiga 4000/030 på værelse 4315 (rask@kampsax.dtu.dk)"
```

At the end of the second line, change k4315 to amiga1, which is your computers (host) name. Change Kampsax to workgroup, which is your workgroup name. Change what is inside of the quotes to a description of your system. When you are finished, it should look like this:

```
# This is for Samba
# You should modify the arguments for nmbd to suit your setup and network.
netbios-ssn stream tcp nowait root AmiTCP:samba/bin/smbd smbd
netbios-ns dgram udp wait root AmiTCP:samba/bin/nmbd nmbd -n amiga1 -G workgroup -C "Amiga Flyer"
```

Save this file, and follow the directions in the "Amiga Installation Notes" file that pertain to joining the various files together. You can use cut and paste in the Amiga "Ed" text editor to do this if you have never used the join command before.

Next, load up the file Amitcp:db/ch_nfstab. Cursor down to the very bottom of this file, and enter the next two lines:

```
pc1:/d N:
pc1:/e M:
```

The first part of each line, pc1:/d, refers to computer pc1 and drive D or drive E. Pay attention to how the colons and slashes are placed. The last part, N and M, refer to the names that your PC drives will show up as on the Amiga Workbench. These names can be anything that you like, but keep them short and do not use spaces in the names. Again, stick with N: and M: now, the ScreamerNet examples will expect this. When you are finished, save this file.

And last, load up the file S:User-Startup. Cursor down until you see the section where the command AmiTCP:bin/startnet is located, and cursor up a line or two above that command, and hit Enter a couple of times to open a blank line or two, and add the following lines to the file. Make sure that you add them before the AmiTCP:bin/startnet command line.

```
assign etc: amitcp:db
assign tmp: t:
assign proc: nil: path
```

Save this file when you are finished, and this completes the AmiTCP/Samba setup. Whew! Isn't shareware software just loads of fun? Reboot your Amiga, and AmiTCP and Samba should start up automatically when your system boots up.

To test things out, go to the PC and start up the NFS Server software. Go back to the Amiga and open up a shell and type the following:

```
ch_nfsmount N:
```

If you get an error message, either your AmiTCP ch_nfstab file has an incorrect definition, or your PC NFS Server software exports file has an error. You should see a disk icon with the name N show up on your Workbench within a few seconds of entering this command. Double-click on this icon, select the Workbench menu option Window/Show/All Files, and you should see all the folders on your PC drive D. Repeat this command for M:, and that drive will show up, too. If you want these drives to be automatically mounted every time you start up your Amiga, edit your S:User-Startup file, and put the ch_nfsmount commands at the very end of the User-Startup file.

Samba works through Windows itself, so to mount the drives there, you only have to open up the 'Network Neighborhood' and use the Map Network Drive option to mount and open your Amiga drives. You must assign a drive letter to your Amiga drive. Give the Amiga drive that has your Lightwave or Toaster software on it the letter V. If you are using Windows NT, use the File Manager and use the Connect Network Drive option in the disk menu. If you want these drives to always get mounted every time that you start your system, check the option 'Reconnect at logon' before you click OK to mount this drive.

We'll get to ScreamerNet in Part Two of this primer.

John Crookshank is president of MicroTech Solutions, Inc., a Chicago-based video and graphics systems dealer, and one of NewTek's appointed "Top Ten Dealer" group members. MicroTech can be reached at 630-495-4069, and their World Wide Web address is http://www.mt-inc.com/.

Software Resources:

INET-225, INET-NSFd, AmiTCP v4.x

Available at Amiga software dealers. (Commercial software). Also see the Interworks site at http://www.iworks.com.

Amiga Samba Server

Aminet Internet archive sites, /pub/aminet/comm/net/samba-1.9.15p8.lha.

Ixemul software required for Samba

Aminet Internet archive sites, /pub/aminet/dev/gcc/ixemul-040fpu.lha, or /pub/aminet/dev/gcc/ixemul-020fpu.lha, depending on your CPU.

Internet Sites

A web-browsable access to Aminet can be found at: http://www.germany.animet.org/aninet/.

Sample Aminet Internet FTP archive site: ftp.netnet.net.

All of the non-commercial Amiga software mentioned here as well as the TropicNFS software is also available at ftp.mt-inc.com, /pub/amiga/ and /pub/windows/ as well as on the World Wide Web at http://www.mt-inc.com/amiganet.htm.

Setting Up ScreamerNet

Part Two of a LightWave Networking Primer

by John Crookshank

Having gone through the rigors of setting up networks for both PCs and Amigas, we're now ready to tackle ScreamerNet. But before we discuss what Screamernet can do, a word about what it can't.

ScreamerNet won't speed up rendering of single images, such as when you hit F9 in LightWave. It won't help with Modeler at all. And it will not render directly to a Flyer clip, AVI file or other animation format, only to single images.

In addition, when you use ScreamerNet with multiple computers, you can no longer render directly to a video drive like the Flyer, Perception or PAR. Even with absolutely identical systems, the frames will arrive at the disk recorder out of sequence. To prevent this, you will have to render to a system drive first, and when all the frames are finished, move them onto the Flyer, PVR or PAR drive afterward.

Third-party add-ons for LightWave are being created that promise to deal with this issue, but most are not available yet. If you have a Flyer system, there is an ARexx program, WaitClip.rexx, which will take all the output frames from a ScreamerNet network and record them to a Flyer clip in the proper order, regardless of the number of systems that you have rendering. We've used WaitClip.rexx with our Flyer ever since NewTek ported LightWave to Windows and we added a Raptor 3 to handle all our rendering.

What's *Not* in the Manual

ScreamerNet is documented quite well in the LightWave 5.0 User Guide, pages 185-193, so I'll just explain what is NOT in the manual but should be. From the message traffic on the LightWave sections of the Internet, it is obvious that 90 percent of the trouble people have with ScreamerNet is understanding drive paths, especially the relative drive paths as they are used in LightWave 4.0 onwards. The Options panel in LightWave lets you set the Content Directory, and this helps to overcome most of the problems you run into when you move a scene file from one computer to another, or share scene files over a network. Understanding how this works and using relative paths is the real key to ScreamerNet. We have just made ScreamerNet even more complicated by connecting computer systems with totally different operating systems to the same network.

If you sit back and look at both your PC screen and Amiga screen now that you have all your drives mounted to each other, the problem that you will have to solve should be obvious to you. Well, maybe not. After all, I said this was the part that causes trouble for most people.

On your PC, you have a drive V:\, which is really your Amiga drive with LightWave on it. On your Amiga Workbench screen, you have a drive icon named N, which is the PC drive with LightWave on it. Even if all you have are PC's on your network, you'll probably have the same problem. The 'host' computer with LightWave on it will have LightWave on drive D:\ perhaps, but the other systems can't use that drive letter because it's already in use by their own internal drive D:\, so they might end up with this drive mapped as drive E:\, for example.

It is absolutely imperative that all systems can see the same drives and that the exact same path and drive letters are used to access the files from all the systems on the network, or ScreamerNet won't work properly.

In addition to this problem, several letters are permanently used by the Amiga operating system, and cannot be used at all if there is an Amiga on the network without screwing up the Amiga operating system. The letters that cannot be used if you have an Amiga on the network are C:, S:, L:, and T:. Fortunately, there is an easy way to get around this dilemma.

With Windows, you can share your drives so others can mount them. Other Windows systems should be set to map your D:\ drive as their drive N:\. The problem here is that the other systems will expect to load LightWave files from their Drive N:\, but your 'host' computer expects to find LightWave on Drive D:\. You need to fool your 'host' system into expecting LightWave to be on Drive N:\ also. If you have Windows NT, you can do this by selecting your own Drive D:\ in the File Manager, and using the "Connect Network Drive" option to map your own Drive D:\ as Drive N:\. If you open either drive, you will see that it is the same drive. You have just fooled Windows into thinking that you really have a Drive N:\. You cannot 'Map Network Drive' to yourself with Windows 95, but you can achieve the same effect by using the subst command. Open the MS-DOS Prompt program, and enter the command subst N: D:\ and hit Enter. When you open the Explorer, you'll see that you now have a drive N: listed with your other drives, and it's identical to drive D:\. You've just fooled Windows 95 in the same way.

If you set your Content Directory in LightWave to N:\NewTek\, all of your systems will now look for (and find) LightWave and all the Scene and Object files on the same PC drive, regardless of where they are on the network. If you edit your lw.cfg file and change all the occurrences of D:\ to N:\ where your plug-ins are defined, all your Windows machines will be able to find your plug-ins, too. If you make your SN\Command directory in N:\, and use drive N:\ instead of drive S:\ as the example is written in the LightWave manual, everything will work properly. The example in the LightWave manual is correct, it just doesn't go into enough detail on how to make all your systems *see* the same path to all of the LightWave files. However, the example in the manual is not recommended if you are running ScreamerNet on an Amiga, because S: is a reserved directory for the Amiga operating system. This is why I had you use drive N:\ instead.

If you set the Content Directory to N:Newtek in your Amiga LightWave, the Amiga will use the exact same scene files and image data that your Windows system(s) do, located on your D:\ drive. Be careful if you edit your Amiga lw.cfg file, though. You *must* leave the definitions on where to find the plug-ins to point to your Amiga drive, and *not* the N:\ drive. Change the paths for your Amiga plug-ins to the *full* Amiga path of DH1:NewTek/Plugins/Layout/etc if they are not already listed that way. If you change the plug-in paths to N:, your Amiga will try to load the Intel plug-ins from your PC, and they won't work. Any time that you have mixed computer systems on a ScreamerNet network, you have to be very careful with the path definitions to your plug-ins to be sure that they are loading the proper plug-ins.

You want all your systems to use the same Content directory, but only systems of the same CPU type can share their plug-ins. If you have a plug-in for Intel LightWave, you must also purchase the same plug-in for Alpha and Amiga, if you also have those platforms involved in a ScreamerNet render session.

Another "feature" of LightWave rears its head here, and must be addressed. When you set your 'Save RGB Images' option to a certain file type, such as JPEG, LightWave does not save the instructions to save your files as JPEG in the scene file. It uses a number to refer to the filetype. The actual command that you will see at the end of the scene file will say "RGBImageFormat 8" if you have your scene set to save JPEG images. The number 8 refers to the position that JPEG occupies in the drop-down list when you click the RGB Image Format button in the Record panel. LightWave actually doesn't know that you selected JPEG, it will just use the 9th HIIP saver that is defined in your lw.cfg file. (The first item in the list is 0, so an item number of 8 is the 9th item listed). You must be extremely careful that all of your systems have the saver modules defined in the same order, or you will get what I got when I first used a HIIP saver during a ScreamerNet session: Our PC rendered to JPEG, our Raptor3 rendered to JPEG, and the Amiga rendered to BMP. They were all rendering to "'RGBImageFormat 8." Unfortunately for us, on the Amiga, #8 was BMP, not JPEG.

Workarounds

If all you have are Windows systems, you're ready to start up and use ScreamerNet. Unfortunately, a couple of bugs in Amiga LightWave ScreamerNet 4.0 will give you some grief when it's used in a ScreamerNet network where the other systems are LightWave for Windows. LightWave automatically translates the forward and backward slashes in pathnames if you take a scene file created on a PC and load it into Amiga LightWave or vice versa. The Content Directory on your PC's is N:\NewTek\ and your objects will load from N:\NewTek\Objects. On the Amiga, the Content Directory is N:NewTek/ and your objects will load from N:NewTek/Objects. Notice that the PC uses backwards slashes (\), and the Amiga uses forward slashes (/) in the pathnames. LightWave and ScreamerNet will automatically translate a \ to / and vice versa as required. If you tell ScreamerNet to save your rendered images in N:\jonesproject\, the Amiga version of ScreamerNet will translate this to N:/jonesproject/, and it won't work. The slash immediately following the colon is invalid in AmigaDOS, whether it is a forwards or backwards slash. The Amiga will happily render the frames, but will not save anything. There is, as usual, a workaround for this.

When you have a multi-platform ScreamerNet network, always render to your Content Directory, and things will work OK, because you aren't using any drive letters at all in the "save to" path. If you make the directory for your rendered frames inside of the Content Directory, all your systems will find that directory with no problems. This is because they are all using a relative path instead of a fully-defined path, and there aren't any drive letters being used. For example, you would make a directory called "jonesproject" inside your N:\NewTek directory. Load the scene and set it to save the output images to jonesproject/framename.xxx. Since there is no drive name, only the directory path is used in your scene file, and both the Amiga and PC will handle this with no troubles.

You also won't be able to use any of the HIIP saver modules when you have multi-platform ScreamerNet, due to another bug involving the HIIP savers. The scene file is a text file, and the Amiga saves scene files with only a linefeed character at the end to indicate the end of each line. PCs use a carriage return character followed by a linefeed character. LightWave translates this automatically when you cross-platform load scene files, but the HIIP savers do not. If you save the scene file from Amiga LightWave set to save frames as JPEG for example, the Intel and Alpha HIIP savers will crash ScreamerNet with a Windows GPF failure when they go to save the very first frame.

If you save the scene file from Windows LightWave set to use a HIIP saver, the Amiga ScreamerNet will again happily render the frames, but will not save anything. This only affects ScreamerNet and the HIIP savers, not LightWave itself. If you use only the first two image options of either .iff or .tga, LightWave and ScreamerNet will use their own internal image saver modules, and will have no problems in this regard. If you manually edit the scene file and add or remove the offending carriage returns as required and keep the Content Directory separate between platforms, each platform will be able load a working version of the scene file. This will also work, but require you to copy all of your content on the other systems, and your chances of missing a crucial object or texture file when setting this up skyrocket. If you are using ScreamerNet multi-platform, stick to the built-in image saving functions of either IFF or TGA.

Give It a Try!

OK, ready to give this all a try? Here's the last final steps to start up a successful ScreamerNet session.

•Make a directory of N:\SN\Command on your PC. Make a directory of N:\Newtek\Frames on your PC.

•Start LightWave on your PC and make sure that the Content Directory is set to N:\NewTek and that the ScreamerNet Command Directory is set to N:\SN\Command. Exit and shut down LightWave to save the lw.cfg file and then restart LightWave again.

•Load the intended scene file. It MUST load up with no errors or drive searching directly from your Content Directory. Set your Save RGB Images to Frames\outname, which can be any name for your frames that you wish, but cannot use spaces in the filename or directory name. ScreamerNet does not like spaces in any of its filenames or directory names. Set the type of images to save as either IFF or TGA. Save this scene file.

•Load up LightWave on the Amiga and also make sure that the Content Directory is set to N:NewTek and that the ScreamerNet Command Directory is set to N:SN/Command. Load the scene file that you just saved on the PC to make sure that your Amiga can find all the scene elements. Shut down LightWave on the Amiga to save the lw.cfg file.

•On the Amiga we will assume that your LightWave or Toaster software is located on drive DH1: Open a shell on the Amiga and type:

```
CD DH1:Newtek/Programs
lwsn.fp      -2      N:SN/Command/job1
N:SN/Command/ack1
```

•Wait a second or two, and you should see a message of "Can't open N:SN/Command/job1". This is normal, and the message will repeat itself every few seconds.

•On the PC, open the MS-DOS Prompt program and type:

```
N:\
CD \NewTek\Programs
lwsn.exe     -2      N:\SN\Command\job2
N:\SN\Command\ack2
```

•If you have more computer systems than just these two, repeat the above, but make the next system use job3 and ack3, the next after that job4 and ack4, etc. But keep the rest of the command structure the same.

•Wait a second or two, and you will see the same "Can't open N:\SN\Command\job2" message. This is also normal.

•Flip back to the LightWave screen and open the ScreamerNet panel. Set the Maximum CPU option to 2, and click the Screamer Init button. After a brief delay, it should tell you that it found 2 ScreamerNet CPUs. Click Add Scene to List, select your scene file, and then select æScreamer Render," and they should both start rendering. Look at the open shells where you typed your commands, and you should see a stream of status messages telling you what each system is currently doing. Check with a disk utility to make sure they are all actually saving something.

•If something goes wrong, go back to the LightWave ScreamerNet control panel, click the screen to make sure it has the focus, and hit the escape key to stop the ScreamerNet process. Go to the computer that is having the problem, bring the command shell to the front and type a CTRL/C to stop that particular ScreamerNet node. Check to see that you have the proper paths set in your command line and try again.

•Once you get this all working, automate the process a bit by typing the ScreamerNet commands for that system in a text editor and save it on each system. To avoid confusion, I recommend saving with a different name each time that includes the ScreamerNet node number, such as "StartScreamer1.bat", "StartScreamer2.bat", etc. Both Windows and AmigaDOS allow attaching an icon to this file, so that the next time you want to run ScreamerNet, you can start it all up just by clicking it's icon.

You can use ScreamerNet to batch render multiple scene files by just clicking the Add Scene to List button multiple times. This is great if you have a couple of smaller scene files that would render overnight or maybe some longer ones to render over the weekend while you're away. This sure beats coming back to the office in six hours just to load up the next scene to render. One limitation of this is that all of the scenes to be rendered must be within the same Content Directory path. The LightWave manual says that you can tell ScreamerNet to batch render up to 16 scene files at a time, but the scene counter in the ScreamerNet control panel goes up to 100. Go figure. Maybe that's coming in LightWave 6.0.

There you have it, networking and ScreamerNet in a nutshell, albeit rather lengthy. In addition to being able to double, triple, quadruple or more to your rendering speeds by simply adding more systems on your network, you will also save a ton of time the next time that you want to use a video clip sequence in LightWave from your Flyer or Perception, and won't even have to leave your comfy chair to go and fetch all those frames. LWP

John Crookshank is President of MicroTech Solutions, Inc., a Chicago-based video and graphics systems dealer, and is one of NewTek's appointed "Top Ten Dealer" group members. MicroTech can be reached at 630-495-4069, and their World Wide Web address is http://www.mt-inc.com/.

Software Sources:

INET-225, INET-NSFd, and AmiTCP v4.x: Available at Amiga software dealers. (Commercial software).

Also see the Interworks site at http://www.iworks.com.

Amiga Samba Server: Aminet Internet archive sites, /pub/aminet/comm/net/samba-1.9.15p8.lha.

Ixemul software required for Samba: Aminet Internet archive sites, /pub/aminet/dev/gcc/ixemul-040fpu.lha, or /pub/aminet/dev/gcc/ixemul-020fpu.lha, depending on your CPU.

A web-browsable access to Aminet can be found at: http://www.germany.animet.org/aninet/.

Sample Aminet Internet FTP archive site: ftp.net-net.net.

All of the non-commercial Amiga software mentioned here as well as the TropicNFS software is also available at ftp.mt-inc.com, /pub/amiga/ and /pub/windows/ as well as on the WWW at http://www.mt-inc.com/amiganet.htm.

TropicNFS: http://www.webcit.com/br/tropic/. (Win95 and WinNT Intel-only NFS Server).

Intergraph: http://www.intergraph.com/nfs/. (Win95 Client, WinNT Server and Client, versions for Intel and Alpha).

Painless ScreamerNetting

by John Gross

With the release of LightWave 4.0 comes a new version of ScreamerNet. For those of you unfamiliar with ScreamerNet, here's an introduction. The Screamer was a product that NewTek announced a few years ago. The idea behind it was to provide a faster, easier way of rendering than using the large, Amiga-based rendering farms. The original Screamer was designed to have four MIPS R4000 (or was it 4400?) processors and was controlled by an Amiga computer that would send the Screamers the files needed to render scenes.

A major limitation to the way the Screamer would render frames was that the Amiga had to send it the scene, object and image files necessary to render. After the frames were rendered, the Screamer would have to send the final rendered image back to the Amiga where it would then be saved out by LightWave. Needless to say, the transfer time was enough to make you almost not want to use a Screamer. If you wanted to render frames in film resolutions, you could forget it. The time for transfer was too long.

For various reasons, the Screamer never really got off the ground, but Raptors did. Soon, people were using ScreamerNet and Amigas to render frames faster (although somewhat painfully).

Let's jump forward to the release of LightWave 4.0. Now, LightWave has the original ScreamerNet plus a new and improved ScreamerNet II. ScreamerNet II has the much needed benefit of allowing individual machines on the network (up to 1,000) to render and save images to a network location. There is no longer a need for the control machine to act as the gateway between files. ScreamerNet II tells machines to render frames, and the machines deal with everything else.

I will show you how to set up and maintain a ScreamerNetwork for rendering your LightWave scenes. This article is geared to Windows users, but the same concepts apply for Amiga and SGI users.

Because the original ScreamerNet rendering method is somewhat outdated, those still using it will find little changes in the controls for this method (with the major exception that you can control up to 1,000 CPUs as opposed to only eight). This article also explains the new ScreamerNet II rendering method.

Here's what's needed in order for ScreamerNet II to work correctly:

- A copy of LightWave 4.0 and a dongle (for the control machine).
- A number of CPUs connected to a network. All of these "render nodes" must have access to common directories for loading scenes, objects and images, and saving out RGB files.

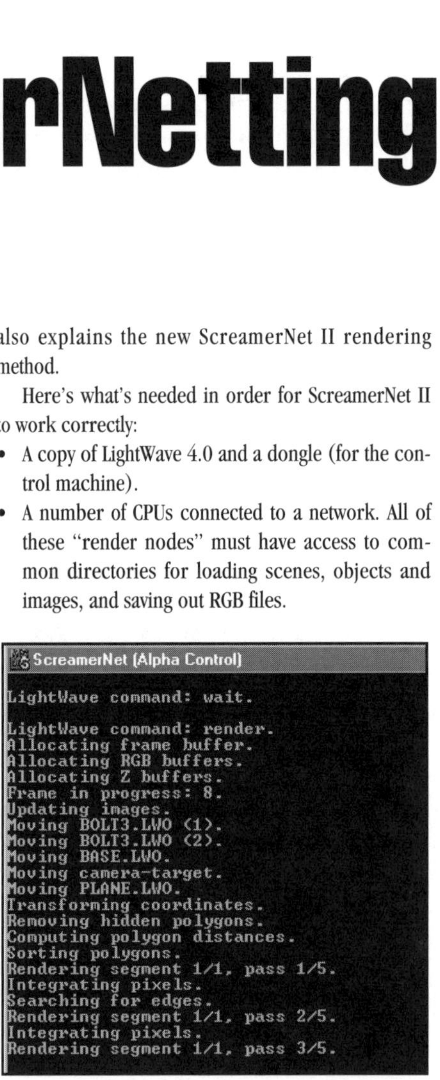

```
ScreamerNet (Alpha Control)
LightWave command: wait.

LightWave command: render.
Allocating frame buffer.
Allocating RGB buffers.
Allocating Z buffers.
Frame in progress: 8.
Updating images.
Moving BOLT3.LWO (1).
Moving BOLT3.LWO (2).
Moving BASE.LWO.
Moving camera-target.
Moving PLANE.LWO.
Transforming coordinates.
Removing hidden polygons.
Computing polygon distances.
Sorting polygons.
Rendering segment 1/1, pass 1/5.
Integrating pixels.
Searching for edges.
Rendering segment 1/1, pass 2/5.
Integrating pixels.
Rendering segment 1/1, pass 3/5.
```

Figure 1: The ScreamerNet Node Feedback window.

- The LWSN (LightWave ScreamerNet) program appropriate for the type of CPUs on the network. This program will come with the version of LightWave that you purchase. If you buy MIPS LightWave, you get a MIPS LWSN program.

It is possible for a single control machine (using a Pentium processor, for instance) to control Intel, Alpha and MIPS CPUs on the network at the same time if the proper LWSN programs are running on each type of machine. This configuration isn't usually recommended as you may be using a shader or image filter plug-in available for one type of CPU, but not another. In this case, some images would render using the plug-in and others wouldn't. It's a good idea to use the same type of CPU for rendering.

Remember, ScreamerNet doesn't actually need a network to work. You can use it on a single machine to batch render up to 16 scene files. We'll go over the three cases of ScreamerNet use: single machine, two machines and more than two machines.

Setting Up a ScreamerNet Rendering Node

Setting up a node machine to render is the first thing to do. LWSN is a command line program, meaning that it has no real interface. You simply assign it a number and a place to look for job files, and the control machine will do the rest. If you don't follow the correct steps, however, you will have problems. In order to set up a ScreamerNet node, you must perform the following steps:

1. Make the program called "LWSN.EXE" (the name may be slightly different depending upon your CPU type) available to all machines that you wish to be render nodes. This can be done by copying this file to each machine, or placing it in a directory that is accessible to all CPUs. The latter is the easiest method and one I recommend.

2. Make sure there is a directory the control machine and all ScreamerNet nodes can see that will act as a common Command Directory. This location is where the control machine will send jobs to and the ScreamerNet nodes will send acknowledgment files to.

3. Open the SN panel and select the Command Directory button. When the requester opens, find and select the network accessible directory that is going to be used as the Command Directory. When you are asked if you would like to "Initialize Now?", choose No.

4. Quit LightWave, then copy the LW.cfg file (.lwrc on SGI machines and LW-Config on Amigas) to the place where you will be running LWSN.EXE from. (If this is the same directory that LightWave is run from, LW.cfg is already there).

Performing step 4. above assures that both the control machine and any machines running the ScreamerNet render module will be looking in the same place for commands. If you change your command directory on the control machine, you must also edit the LW.cfg file in the location of the

LWSN.EXE program to reflect the change of command directories. Also, if you make any major changes to the configuration file (such as the addition of plug-ins), you must also change the remote LW.cfg files (if any) as well.

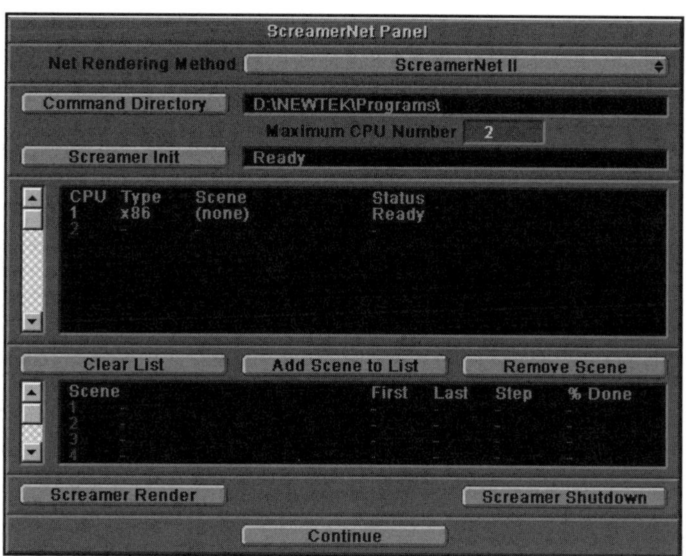

Figure 2: LightWave's ScreamerNet Control panel.

ScreamerNet on One Machine

So, let's start out with our most basic setup: a single machine that will use ScreamerNet to batch render scene files. If you followed the normal LightWave install setup, you have the LWSN.EXE program located in your drive name: \NewTek\Programs directory. For the purposes of this example, let's say that your hard drive containing the NewTek directory is labeled as D:. There's no need to worry about common directories because you're only using one machine.

The process for rendering would be for you to start the LWSN program, then go into LightWave's SN panel and initialize the CPU so LightWave can find the render node. After this is done, list the scene files that you wish to render and hit the Screamer Render button. After all of the scene files have rendered, the programs (LW and LWSN) are sitting idle, waiting for more input.

There are two ways of starting the LWSN program. You can either type it in with all of its arguments into a command line, or you can create an icon that will launch it with all of its arguments. The second method is easiest and I will cover that in more detail, but to start LWSN from a command line, perform the following step:

1. From a DOS shell on the node machine, CD to the directory containing the LWSN program and type (all on the same line):

LWSN.EXE -2 D:\NewTek\Programs\job1 D:\NewTek\Programs\ack1

That's all there is to it. Let's break it down: LWSN.EXE is the command name. Make sure to replace it with the name of your ScreamerNet module if it's different. The -2 argument tells LWSN to use the ScreamerNet II rendering mode. If you were to use a -1 as this argument, LWSN would use the Original ScreamerNet method.

The second argument tells this node the full path name of the job file that will be reserved for this node. Notice that this is the full path of the command directory. Using a "job1" as the file name labels this node as CPU #1. If you used "job954", you would label this CPU as #954. It's important to not lead any CPU numbers with a 0. For instance, job1 is allright, but job01 is not correct.

The third and final argument is the complete path name of the acknowledgment file that LightWave uses to know what a render node is doing. This ack file must be numbered the same as the job file number.

Once the command and arguments are entered properly, a window will open that lists feedback for the render node. If this window opens briefly and closes, you did not type in the argument correctly. Note that this is true for NT machines, but if you are trying to run ScreamerNet on a Windows for Workgroups 3.11 machine (running WIN32s), I have heard that's exactly what happens. However, ScreamerNet is still active—you just don't have a feedback window.

To create an icon for the ScreamerNet render module that you can click on to start LWSN, perform the following steps (this assumes a Windows operating system):

1. Create an icon for LWSN by selecting a Program Group and then selecting New from the File menu. Choose Program Item, and then choose OK in the requester that appears.

2. In the Description: field, type "ScreamerNet Render" or something similar. This will be the name that appears with the icon.

3. In the Command Line: field, type the full path of LWSN.EXE, followed by the arguments listed above. In the case of our one-machine setup, it would be "D:\NewTek\Programs\LWSN.EXE -2 D:\NewTek\Programs\job1 D:\ NewTek\Programs\ack1".

4. For the Working Directory: field, type the path of where the LWSN program is located. In our example, it would be input as "D:\NewTek\Programs".

5. Select OK. You now have an icon that will run the ScreamerNet render module for that machine when it is double-clicked.

Using the ScreamerNet Panel

Now that you can get LWSN running on your machine, how do you control it? Let's talk about the different functions.

- Selecting the Command Directory button allows you to change this directory to another location. Again, the Command Directory is the shared directory where nodes will look for jobs and send acknowledgment files. The control machine will write job files here and look for acknowledgments from the nodes in this location. In our one-machine setup, the Command Directory is simply the NewTek\Programs directory. If you wanted to use another, you would need to select it here.
- It's important to note that when you change the Command Directory and then exit LightWave, LightWave will write the new location to the configuration file, LW.cfg. If your node machines do not have access to this file (i.e., LWSN is not run from the same directory or uses the same working directory), the machines may not look to the same command location. You'll know there's a problem if you initialize CPUs and they don't all show up.
- By changing the value in the Maximum CPU Number field, you can tell the control machine how many nodes it should check for. You can input a number up to 1,000, but I suggest keeping the value set to the number of available nodes to save time.
- After starting LWSN on the individual ScreamerNet nodes, you must select Screamer Init on the control machine to initialize all the nodes and prepare them to accept commands. After initialization is completed, you will receive a message stating how many ScreamerNet CPUs were found. Also, the available CPUs will be listed by node number and will give a status of "Ready".
- Once you see all of your available CPUs, click Add Scene to List and it will present a requester allowing you to select a scene that you wish to render over the ScreamerNet. You can add up to 16 scenes at any one time.
- Selecting Screamer Render will start rendering the scenes in order from the first added. At this point, the control machine is tied up controlling the machines and you cannot use LightWave. (You could minimize this version and start another LightWave process if you have enough RAM.)
- As the list is being rendered, each ScreamerNet CPU will list the scene and frame it is working on. In the Scene list, you can see what percentage of the scene is rendered.
- At this point, if you go and look at the individual ScreamerNet nodes, you will see a line-by-line status of what they are doing as they render away.

- The ScreamerNet panel also has commands for removing a scene in the list (the one currently at the top of the list) and clearing the entire list.
- Finally, if you want to abort a session in progress, hit the Escape key while the ScreamerNet info field reads "Waiting for CPUs to finish rendering." There may be a long pause before all of the ScreamerNet nodes are ready again—while they finish up their current task—and make the ScreamerNet panel available for more input.
- When all CPUs are finished rendering, selecting the Screamer Shutdown button will close all windows on all ScreamerNet nodes. To start a new session, you must restart ScreamerNet on each CPU and perform a Screamer Init from the control machine.

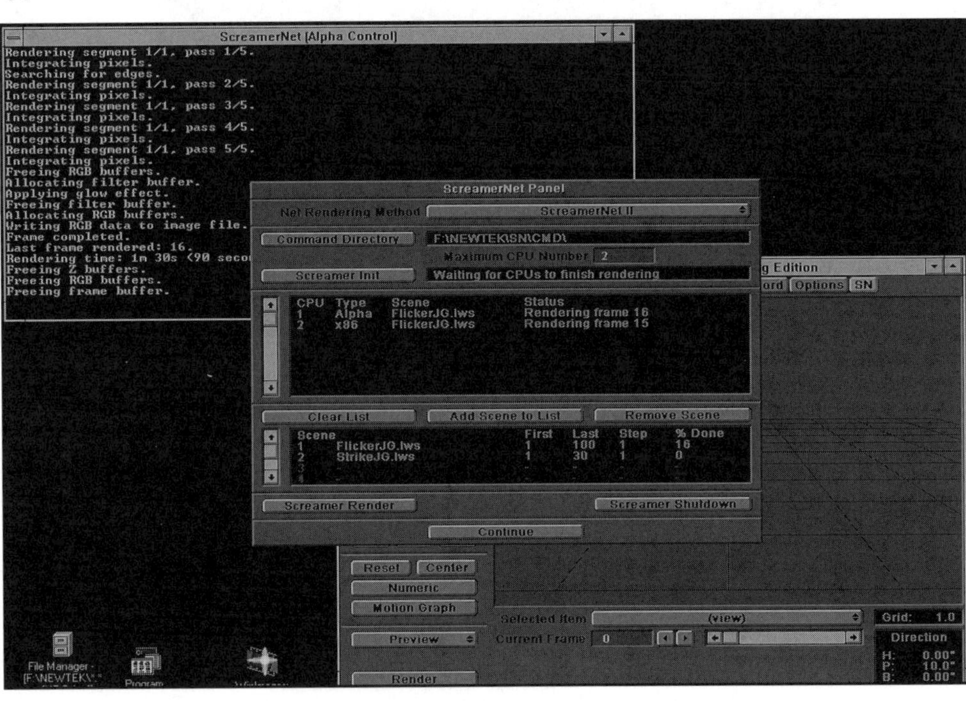

Figure 3: A typical one-machine ScreamerNet session.

ScreamerNet on Two Machines

Using ScreamerNet on more than one machine can get a bit more involved, but it's still pretty easy. Here's what you have to look out for:

If you read the config file for LightWave, you will see that the Command Directory is set to D:\NewTek\Programs (in our example above). Let's say that you have another machine networked to the first and you wish to use it for rendering. If you follow the directions above for setting up another node, you may end up with an icon that reads "D:\NewTek\ Programs\LWSN.EXE -2 D:\NewTek\ Programs\job2 D:\NewTek\Programs\ack2".

Notice that we changed the job and ack files to "2". If not, they would have interfered with the other machine.

There is still a potential problem here. You are telling the second machine to look for LWSN on the D: drive in the NewTek\Programs directory. This location may not even exist on the second machine! To get around that, you will need to connect to the first machine's D: drive using another drive letter (assuming that a D drive already exists for the current machine). Let's say you need to map the first machine's D drive as F: on this machine. Your icon Command Line: settings would now read "F:\NewTek\ Programs\LWSN.EXE -2 F:\NewTek\ Programs\job2 F:\NewTek\Programs\ack2" and the Working Directory: line would read "F:\NewTek\ Programs".

This will get the node up and running, but there is a major potential problem—the Content Directory and plug-in location descriptions are found in the LW.cfg file.

Because the Working Directory is set to F:\NewTek\Programs, LWSN will look for a LW.cfg file in that location so it knows where to find out the location of the Content Directory (the location where the scene/object and image files exist).

The problem with the above setup is that this second node will see a LW.cfg file (in F:\NewTek\Programs) that contains lines such as this:

ContentDirectory D:\NewTek

Plugin ImageSaver Alias(.als) D:\NEWTEK\Plugins\ LAYOUT\HIIPSAVE.P Alias (.als)

Plugin ImageSaver BMP(.bmp)D:\NEWTEK\ Plugins\LAYOUT\HIIPSAVE.P BMP (.bmp)

Plugin ImageSaver Cineon(.cin) D:\NEWTEK\ Plugins\ LAYOUT\HIIPSAVE.P Cineon (.cin)

Plugin ImageSaver IFF(.iff) D:\NEWTEK\ Plugins\LAYOUT\HIIPSAVE.P IFF (.iff)

Plugin ImageSaver JPEG(.jpg) D:\NEWTEK\ Plugins\LAYOUT\HIIPSAVE.P JPEG (.jpg)

The problem here is that the Content Directory and plug-in locations are all relative to the original machine (the one with LightWave installed). When another node sees lines like this and does not have this setup on its own D: drive, you can imagine its confusion. One way around this is to make a copy of the config file and change it so all the D: references read F:, and then place this copy in a different location and change the Working Directory: field in LWSN's icon to point to the place where the copy of the config file resides.

This, of course, can be confusing, especially when you add new plug-ins or change the Content Directory. This would require that you remember to make changes to the extra LW.cfg file located in the other location.

Perhaps a better way around this problem is to plan for it in the beginning. For instance, if you know you are going to have two machines, one with the full LightWave and one with a LWSN node, you may want to label your drives (when first setting up your machines) differently. For instance, let's say we have two PCs: one with LightWave running and one with just LWSN. One of the machines could be set up so that LightWave is located on a drive named F: (you can change drive letters in Disk Administrator). On the other PC, there may be two drives, C and D, and you would have it connected to a network drive called F: (which is the same drive as the other PC's F: drive). When you start a LWSN node on the non-LightWave PC, you should have its Command Line and Working Directories set to the F:\NewTek\Programs directory so it sees the same config file that the other machine sees. You can even run the same LWSN program found in the F: directory on both machines—just change the arguments so they use different CPU numbers.

This way ensures that both nodes would see the same Content Directory of F:\Newtek so they could both find the correct files. You would also most likely want to save to the F: drive as well, since that would be the "shared" drive that both nodes saw as F:.

ScreamerNet on More Than Two Machines

Finally, we come to our final setup, which after getting a good grasp on the two-machine setup, is easy to follow. When using ScreamerNet with more than two machines, you generally have one machine that is your server. This server is the machine (or location on the net) that contains all of your LightWave content files. In order for the greater-than-two setup to work most effectively, all render nodes need to be mapped to this common location using the same drive letter. If the config file that a LWSN node reads says that the Content Directory is located at S:\Clients\Voyager, all render nodes must see this location the same way or you will have bad or missing frames in the final output. Remember, LWSN will look for the LW.cfg file in the location it is launched from or where the Working Directory: field is pointing to if the config file is launched from an icon.

Setting up a system this way would allow you to have an LWSN program located somewhere on the net, and every machine could start the program from there, using a different number for the job and ack files it will read/write. Also, you could have a common location for a config file that all nodes will see when launched. Remember, any plug-ins that you may be using to render with need to be found in a common location that the config file all the nodes read can see. If this isn't the case, you may get bad results when using plug-ins (including the HIIP savers).

Hopefully, this has gotten you up and running with a minimum of fuzz with ScreamerNet. Now, there shouldn't be any reason for your machine(s) to sit around every night doing nothing!

ScreamerNet Tips

- ScreamerNet will always save images to the paths found in the scene file. These paths are written anytime you save an RGB or Alpha image while setting up a scene. Remember that if you save an Alpha image once, the path will be written in the scene file and an LWSN node will attempt to save an alpha image to this location. If you don't want any alphas saved (or an RGB) delete the lines near the end of the scene file that make reference to the saving location and name.
- ScreamerNet will render the scene based on the First Frame/Last Frame values saved in the scene file. If you need to interrupt a ScreamerNet session and want to finish rendering later, you will need to edit the scene file's First/Last Frame values to reflect the new changes or ScreamerNet will re-render rendered frames when started again.
- If a scene was set up using a different Content Directory (Options panel) than currently listed for the ScreamerNet CPU's, you must change the Content Directory listing in the LW.cfg file located where the LWSN program is launched from. When a ScreamerNet CPU is first started, the window that appears tells you what the current Content Directory is.
- Only scenes sharing the same Content Directory can be batch rendered in the same ScreamerNet session.
- Even though LightWave contains a SN panel allowing you to control ScreamerNet CPU's, ScreamerNet control software is open to third party support, so expect to see other ScreamerNet control packages available.

Troubleshooting ScreamerNet

Occasionally, ScreamerNet may not perform as you may expect. Under these conditions, check for the following:

Problem: ScreamerNet node not being recognized by a Screamer Init command.

Solutions:

1. Manually shut down all ScreamerNet CPUs and delete all job and ack files from the command directory. Then, restart all CPUs and reperform a Screamer Init.

2. Make sure that the Maximum CPU Number value is equal to or greater than the highest numbered ScreamerNet node, then perform a Screamer Init.

3. Make sure that the command line arguments for an individual nodes are correct as outlined above.

4. Make sure that a LW.cfg file is located in the working directory of the LWSN program (usually the directory where LWSN is executed from) and the CommandDirectory line in this file matches that of the control machine.

Problem: After performing a Screamer Init, LightWave states that there is one more CPU available than the actual number and stays in a "busy loop."

Solution:

1. There was an extra ack file found in the command directory. You will need to end the LightWave task (Ctrl + Esc); delete all of the job and ack files in the Command Directory; stop all of the ScreamerNet CPUs and restart them. Finally, start LightWave again on the control machine and perform a Screamer Init.

Problem: ScreamerNet CPUs can't find object or image files it needs.

Solutions:

1. Make sure that the ContentDirectory setting in the LW.cfg file found in the Working Directory of the LWSN program is set to the same path LightWave used when the scene was created.

Tip: When you first start a ScreamerNet node, a message stating the "Current Directory" will appear. This is the directory that the ScreamerNet node is seeing as the Content Directory.

2. Make sure that all ScreamerNet nodes have the same access to the directories containing object/image files and that the location of these files is mapped the same for all nodes.

Problem: ScreamerNet nodes render, but no images are saved.

Solutions:

1. Make certain that you have save paths set up in the scene file. In order for this to happen, you must select Save RGB Images or Save Alpha Images (or both) in the Record panel and select a path and name for the saved images before you save the scene file. Make certain that the path can be found by all ScreamerNet CPUs.

2. The ScreamerNet node does not have the ability to write to the save directory or can not see it.

3. The ScreamerNet node does not have access to the HIIP loader/savers and you are attempting to save a HIIP format image.

Problem: ScreamerNet nodes render alpha images, but I didn't want to save them.

Solution:

1. At one point, before saving the scene file, you had selected a path and name for Save Alpha Images. Even if you turn this button off later, the path and name is still contained in the scene file. If you edit the scene file, and delete the line that starts with SaveAlphaImagesPrefix near the end of the scene file, you will tell LightWave not to save Alpha images when you load this scene and render with ScreamerNet.

Problem: ScreamerNet nodes do not save computer-animation files.

Solution:

1. Currently, ScreamerNet only saves single images —RGB and/or Alpha. You could render the images, then later compile them into the desired animation formats.

Problem: Plug-in shader, image filters, etc. are not being rendered on the ScreamerNet nodes.

Solutions:

1. ScreamerNet pulls its plug-in information from the configuration file found in its launch directory. If the plug-in information found here was not updated to reflect that of the original LW.cfg file, plug-ins will not be found and, therefore, not rendered.

2. The plug-ins themselves are not located on a shared drive. In order for all of the ScreamerNet CPUs to access a plug-in, it must be located in a place where the nodes can see it, and the LW.cfg file for the ScreamerNet CPUs must state this location properly.

3. Your scene was set up on a different CPU type than you are trying to render it upon, and the plug-ins do not exist for the type of CPU you are using.

Problem: No HIIP images are being saved from ScreamerNet nodes.

Solutions:

1. In order for the HIIP savers to function properly, they must be located in a HIIP directory that is found on the same directory level as the directory containing the LWSN program. For instance, by default, LWSN is run from the Programs directory and the HIIP Loaders/Savers are found in the HIIP directory that is located, along with the Programs directory, within the NewTek directory. If you were running LWSN from a directory called SN located in S:\LW, you would also want to copy the HIIP directory from NewTek to S:\LW. You will get an error message when the LWSN program tries to save a file if it can't find the HIIP stuff.

2. The HIIP DLLs need to be found in the path where LWSN is launched from (or the Working Directory). These include ERBUFIO.DLL, ERCORE.DLL, ERUTILS.DLL, HIIP.DLL and HIIPUNV.DLL, which by default, are found in the NewTek\Programs directory.

LWP

John Gross is the editor of LIGHTWAVEPRO.

Catch the Internet Wave

LightWave 3D Meets VRML

by Arnie Cachelin

The Internet is big and it's getting bigger every day. Much of the current excitement over the Internet stems from the seemingly infectious spread of the World Wide Web. Although it sounds like something from a conspiracy theory, the Web is just a bunch of files on Internet-connected computers around the world. All these files have in common is their adherence to the HTML (Hierarchical Text Markup Language) standard. HTML files contain text and images to be attractively laid out by a viewer or browser software. Most importantly, HTML files contain links to other files, such as other HTML Web pages, anywhere on the Internet. When people create HTML pages to communicate their information (or lack thereof) to the world, they include links not only to their own information, but also to other sites they have found. These links, in turn contain their own hierarchy of links, and so on. From this dynamic set of HTML files and their haphazard links to one another, the WWW has emerged.

Text-only and now text and 2D-graphics interfaces on the Internet have spawned an incredibly complex community of virtual individuals and places. Yet they are a far cry from *my* expectations of Cyberspace. Even the coolest HTML Web page doesn't match the disembodied data spaces of William Gibson's *Neuromancer* not to mention the mall of quirky avatars in Stephenson's *Snow Crash*. Adding 3D scenes to the Web is an essential step toward immersive virtual reality.

Figure 1: The panel for the VRML scene export plug-in.

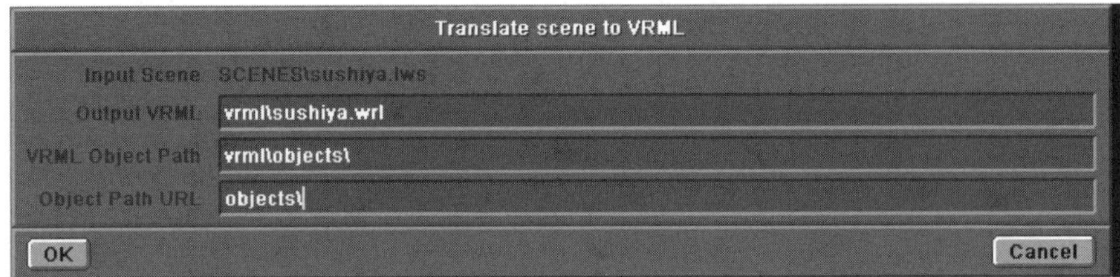

Figure 2: The panel for the VRML export model plug-in.

Putting the Space in CyberSpace

VRML stands for Virtual Reality Modeling Language. It is a standard for describing 3D objects and scenes via the Internet. Like HTML pages, VRML 'worlds' can contain links to remote files. Rather than using images or text for links, VRML uses 3D objects, thus the Web browser for VRML resembles a 3D animation program more closely than a DTP program. VRML worlds can be embedded in HTML pages and vice versa, and the browsers are generally closely connected. While the current v1.0 incarnation of the VRML standard limits you to pretty much static scenes floating in space, version 2.0, due to be released at SIGGRAPH '96, will add support for scripted, animated objects, collision and proximity sensing, and niceties like backdrops, fog, and 3D sound effects. Combine this with the explosive growth of the Web, and the increasing availability of low-cost 3D accelerator hardware, and it seems reasonable to believe that the 3D Web is also on the verge of explosive growth. LightWave 3D animators have the tools and skills to catch this wave

VRML models are based either on primitives-like spheres, cubes and cones, or more likely, on sets of points and polygons. Since this is basically the approach used by LightWave's polygonal models, it isn't hard to build objects with Modeler that look pretty good when translated to VRML. More often, the problem lies in making models that don't look too good for VRML. Although the format is capable of describing complex scenes, current 3D browsers are limited by the real-time rendering capabilities of their underlying computers. Thus exquisitely crafted models with painstaking detail—suitable for those print-res closeups—will fail painfully when they enter the realm of VRML renderers (You can actually get a decent approximation of a LightWave object's VRML appearance and rendering speed from the OpenGL preview on the Windows and SGI versions of Layout or Modeler.)

To avoid the twin perils of long download times and slow rendering, remember: The first key to VRML success is efficient, low-polygon count models. Similarly, elaborate layers of diffuse, specular and luminosity textures, whether images or algorithmic, will not survive any conversion to VRML. Don't even ask about bump maps, displacement maps, or shaders. Love it or leave it, VRML supports a single image map for a color texture, as well as having diffuse color, specular and transparency values. Since that image may very well have to fly through a modem someday, you'll probably want to keep it small too.

LightWave Meets VRML

The VRML files produced by LightWave are text files that follow LightWave's style of separate object and scene files. This is not a requirement of VRML, but a powerful feature that allows a VRML scene to include objects in different files, even from some remote library. These "In-line" objects in the scene file consist of a file URL, a bounding box, and a set of position, rotation and scaling transformations.

The URL, or Universal Resource Locator, specifies a file stored in a computer somewhere in the world. It is a critical element in the formation of the World Wide Web. The bounding box information is generally used by browsers to render stand-ins while the objects are loaded.

VRML scenes also include multiple point lights, directional lights, and spotlights with adjustable cones. Although LightWave scenes currently only have one, there may be several cameras that browsers can use to jump between points of views. VRML objects created by LightWave include a set of standard viewpoints for the object.

In LightWave, VRML object output is organized along the same lines as LightWave object creation. A list of X, Y, Z coordinates describe the vertices in the object, and a list of surface names and characteristics are defined. Since these items are the easiest to modify by hand, they appear at the top of the object file.

For each surface, there is also an "IndexedFaceSet," which has the polygons with that surface. They are described as groups of numbers, referring to a vertex in the main list of point coordinates. If the original LightWave object had a color texture map image, there will be an image file name and a set of texture coordinates. Texture coordinates, also known as U, V coordinates, are 2D pixel positions in an image. They describe how the image lies on the 3D surface, by pinning certain pixels to each polygon's vertices. These values are calculated from LightWave's mapping and texture size settings. In the case of planar mapping, U and V are simply X and Y, (for Z-Axis Planar).

Spherical mapping yields U, V coordinates somewhat analogous to longitude and latitude, with the Us all bunching up at the poles. Cylindrical mapping uses Us from the spherical case, then the Vs are the coordinate lying along the texture axis.

The entire object is embedded in a VRML "anchor," which makes it an active link in the Web. If you supply a URL for the object when you create it, then any time that object appears in a scene, it will act as a clickable link to some other page. This should be used sparingly: Think about how annoying it can be to keep jumping around the Web when all you really want to do is just inspect an object.

A recent addition to LightWave's VRML-saving software will embed multiple URLs in an object, tied to surfaces named such as "URL:http://www.whatever." The uses for URLs in your objects can range from billboards or ads for your favorite Website, to inventory data for some widget. A very nice example is the VRML origami site, where each step in the folding of a paper menagerie has a simple model with a link to the next stage.

This is similar to the VRML level-of-detail mode, where multiple models are grouped together and the viewer's distance determines which model, if any, is actually rendered.

Of GIFs, JPEGs and the Web

Web browsers can support a multitude of media types, either directly or through plug-ins. Despite this, two image formats are dominant on the Web: JPEG, a standard formulated by the "Joint Photographic Experts Group," and GIF, Compuserve's "Graphics Interchange Format." JPEG format (.jpg) is useful because it offers tremendous compression of 24-bit color images. The price is that the compression changes the image, throwing away some information, which can never be recovered. The amount of loss can be controlled, and many JPEG images actually throw away no data. The compression is still very good.

GIF images use a fixed palette of 2 to 256 colors, which by itself is a massively lossy form of compression. They are particularly suited for logos, graphic adornments, and buttons on Web pages because they have a transparent color, where the Web page below shows through. GIF images can also be saved in an "interlaced" format, which allows partially transmitted images to appear at full size, in lower resolution, and fill in progressively as the rest of the image is received.

Thomas Boutell and the Quest Center at Cold Spring Harbor Labs (http://www.boutell.com/gd/) has created a freely distributable software library for creating GIF images. I made it into a freely distributable image saver plug-in for LightWave 3D. Download the file gif.p from: http://www.newtek.com/cool/staff/arnie/lwgifsaver.html. Currently, only Windows Intel and Alpha versions are available.

Gif.p adds two entries to the Image Format list, Gif and Gif_NoBkg, both save 256-color interlaced images. Gif_NoBkg uses the rendered alpha channel to fill the image background with a transparent color. Because GIF uses a single color for transparency, there may be some newly visible jagged edges around your objects, which were previously smoothed over by LightWave's anti-aliasing. There are a few things you can do to minimize this problem.

When LightWave anti-aliases an object which is placed over only the background, it blends the object colors with the background colors just along the edge. Since LightWave output GIF images use LightWave's alpha channel for determining the transparent parts of an image, none of the background will show up in the image, it will be replaced with whatever background the browser of display program specifies. If you know in advance what color this is, you can make sure the visible edge pixels are blended with an appropriate color by simply setting the LightWave background to match the Web page.

Making Worlds

To create a VRML object, load some suitable object into Modeler. If it is a complex model, you might want to eliminate some polygons by removing unseen faces or poly-laden details like the steering wheel of a truck. When your model is ready, select the SaveVRML plug-in from Modeler's Objects/Custom pop-up. Select a VRML .wrl file name to save to, then modify the fields in the SaveVRML control panel as you like. The Object Name field specifies the internal VRML object name and is pretty much irrelevant. The link URL is the Web link for that object. Although this is filled in initially for (in?)convenience, you should consider making that field empty. Finally a comment is embedded in the object, if you specify one. This may be where you take credit for the model, put a less obtrusive URL, or just say No Comment. Click OK, and your .wrl is done.

If your model has a texture map image associated with it, there are a few tricks that can minimize the nuisance of hand-editing your VRML models. Because some browsers will have to load the image named in the object, it's critical to save that image name in the LightWave object. It pays to use LightWave's content directory system, so that the image path will be relative to that content directory (i.e. images\wood.jpg). It may even pay to move the image to the content dir (or vice versa) so the name in the object will have no path, and browsers will seek the image in the same directory as the object. In any event, wherever the VRML object finally resides, you will want a matching directory hierarchy in which the browser will find the image. Or you can just edit the VRML file.

Another image issue is that of image format. JPEG and GIF images are almost universally supported on the Web. Although LightWave only loads and saves JPEG images, there is a free plug-in to save Web-friendly GIF images available (See sidebar). JPEG images are nice and small. While their high-powered yet lossy compression causes visible artifacts, they should be virtually invisible at Web/VRML resolutions. If you have nice high-quality texture images for your rendering work, and want VRML versions, make smaller, JPEG versions of the images for the Web. A happy legacy of LightWave's (and HIIP's) non-PC origins is that file name extensions don't really matter. So, although it may cause some confusion, you can rename your texture.tga to texture.jpg, and use that on your model. When you install the VRML model, just use the smaller JPEG image. Or you can just edit the VRML file.

Make the Scene

Making a scene is not much harder than making an object. Because VRML scenes need their objects' bounding boxes, the Scene2VRML plug-in runs in Modeler (where it can load each object in the scene) quickly get its measurements and moves on. As a result, it can also determine whether the VRML version of the object exists yet, and run SaveVRML for you *automagically*. If the VRML object exists already, Scene2VRML plays it safe and leaves it undisturbed.

Once you have a LightWave scene to make into VRML, select Scene2VRML from Modeler's Objects/Custom pop-up. Select the scene in the file requester, then set the fields in the Scene2VRML control panel. Output VRML is the VRML scene to save, by default, the same as the LightWave scene with a .wrl extension. The VRML Object Path field should have the directory path where the VRML versions of your objects are stored. This is where Scene2VRML will look for the objects, and will create them if they don't already exist.

This is half the confusing part. The other half is that the Object Path URL should be the same directory, but formatted as an URL, for the benefit of the browser loading the VRML scene. So on your machine, the .wrl object files may reside in "C:\webpage\vrml\objects\", while the URL for it might be "FILE:///C|/webpage/vrml/objects." If the scene lived in "C:\webpage\vrml\," then you could get away with specifying just objects/ for the URL. Similarly, if the scenes and objects are in the same place, the URL could be empty. Because the browser finds the object through a full-blown URL, rather than just a filename (as images currently do), scenes all over the Internet could refer to the same object. So if you want to use a remote object, or are eventually setting the VRML scene up on a different computer, specify the correct URL. It doesn't alter Scene2VRML's behavior. Or you can just edit the VRML file.

The Future and VRML

Version 2.0 of VRML will significantly extend the capabilities of VRML worlds not only by making the worlds prettier (or at least, closer to your LightWave scene), but by adding powerful interactivity, animation and scripting. Even now, NewTek's VRML team is working to bring these new features to you. Things that are natural for LightWave, like non-linear fog and a backdrop image will translate to VRML 2.0 scenes. In fact, VRML 2.0 supports six backdrop images for front, back, top, bottom, left and right views. Objects will have keyframed motions, so lights and even colors can be enveloped. And there also will be ways of doing things that LightWave 3D does not directly support. These will likely include collision detection, visibility/proximity/touch sensing, and level-of-detail objects.

VRML2.0 has some nice texturing improvements, including a 2D transformation on an image or movie(!) texture map, and a list of URLs in place of an image file name. If you need more info, check out www.vag.org (the site for the VRML Architecture Group).

VRML is maturing into a comprehensive standard for creating and sharing virtual realities that will broaden the appeal and extent of 3D cyberspace. There's infinite room for virtual models, so why not populate this brave new world with some of your own creatures? LWP

Moj-O-Rama
A Collection of Tips and Tricks

by Mojo

Not everything I've learned about LightWave is worthy of an entire article in *LWPRO*. Sure, I might be able to stretch out a topic like making a lightbeam into two or three pages, but why bother when a simple paragraph or two will suffice? So, for the next few pages, I've compiled several Really Useful™ tips and tricks I've learned over the years in the hope that some readers may find them helpful.

Modeler

Project Saving

By holding down the ALT key while selecting **Save As**, Modeler will save all objects in all selected layers in project form. This cannot be loaded into Layout, but when this file is reloaded into Modeler, all the objects are placed back into their respective layers. Make sure to select each layer as either a foreground or a background layer in order to have it saved as part of your project.

Amazing!

Multiple Foreground

There are a few benefits to shift-selecting several foreground layers at once. In many cases, Modeler will place newly created polygons in the highest-selected layer only. This is quite useful, especially during spline patching, when having to constantly separate polygon faces from your spline cages can be a real nuisance.

Simply place your cage in (for example) layer two. Shift-select the first layer *before* selecting your splines, then create a patch in the usual fashion. Presto! Your new polygons have been created in the first layer, leaving your splines in the second uncluttered and ready for the next patch.

Constant cutting and pasting can be avoided by shift-selecting all occupied layers, cutting and then pasting. All objects from all previously selected multiple layers will now be placed into the first single layer.

Incredible!

Figure 1A

Figure 1B

Object Signing

Have you ever spent long, arduous hours making the best object of your career and wondered, "Gee, what if this got into the wrong hands and someone sold it before I could? How could I ever prove that it was mine?" Well, now you can.

Simply create a "signature" (just your name and date will do) using a PostScript font and shrink it down to the size of a point. Place it wherever you like in the object and give it the same surface name as adjoining polygons. It is now a needle in a haystack. Since it looks like every other vertice in the object (remember, *really* shrink it down), it will be impossible to detect and you can rest knowing that every illegal copy of your work bears your hidden ID. Even if someone knew it was there, hunting it down would be nearly impossible. Of course, since you know its exact location, you can find it in an instant and show the jury.

Lawyeriffic!

ToasterPaint

Dirt Streaks

On *Babylon 5*, just about all our texture maps have "dirt" added to them in ToasterPaint. This gives the objects a weathered look and helps a great deal in achieving realism. Set the Transparency controls as you see in Figures 1A and 1B and use the Filled Box tool in Darken mode. The streaks will start out dark at the top and taper off toward the bottom. Try varying the box size and layer streaks on top of each other.

Layout

Saving Memory

Image maps are the biggest memory hog in LightWave. Each full-size 24-bit image takes over one MB of render space and just a few of these will quickly kill your RAM. Fortunately, full 24-bit color depth is actually needed in very few cases. Most of the time the images in memory are texture maps for objects. Unless your object is going to be brightly lit and fill the frame, most maps can be reduced to at least 256 colors in Art Department Professional (ADPro), ImageF/X or any other image processing program.

Grayscale maps can contain as little as 16 colors and work just as well (on *Babylon 5*, 90 percent of all our object maps are reduced to 32 colors, exceptions being the smoothly graduated nebula and planets).

Alpha images can be reduced to 16 colors without causing rendering flaws and clip maps need only be two colors.

When images need to be 24-bit, try halving the map in ADPro and doubling the texture sizes in LightWave. So keep tabs on those maps, and you'll have double the RAM you're used to in no time.

RAM-azing!

Shadow Maps

Shadow maps take a lot of time and memory to render. Just a few 512K Z-buffers and you'll find that render times go up and RAM sinks faster than the Titanic. If the light from a shadow-mapped source isn't on screen all the time (such as a traveling spotlight), envelope the light intensity to zero while it is off screen. This will prevent LightWave from calculating shadow maps, which saves time and RAM!

In addition, I sometimes shadow map a spotlight, not to get shadows, but to prevent the light from traveling through objects. These maps can be as low as 64K and cause no rendering flaws, again saving valuable resources. Of course, when using shadows of any type, do not forget to select only the object shadow options (**Objects** panel) you need (cast, receive and self-shadow). This saves a lot of render time.

Shadown't-stop-me!

Lens Flares

Fade Behind?

Sometimes you want flares to fade behind certain objects (like spaceships) and not others (the base of light beams). The **Cast Shadow** button (**Objects** panel) acts like a toggle for "fade behind" lens flares on a per-object basis, allowing you to pick and choose which objects will obscure lens flares and which won't.

Flare-icious!

Testing Lens Flare Envelopes

When creating explosions, timing is everything. A great deal of work is put into the speed at which a lens flare expands and contracts, often requiring delicate balancing of an envelope's spline controls. Unfortunately, the only way to test your flare envelopes is to render a time-consuming test. Or is it?

Transfer your envelope temporarily to the light's intensity channel and give it a falloff. The three orthographic views in Layout will now display the light's falloff circle. Create a preview with the light visible and you'll see the circle expand and contract according to the envelope. Tweak it as necessary and reapply it to the lens flare channel.

Flare-tastic!

Object Distance

The toughest part of setting up a rack-focus animation is the math necessary to determine an object's distance from the camera. A simple way to ballpark this is to play with the fog radius until you see the fog circle touch the object from the top view.

Fog-tabulous!

Underwater Electricity

Here's a quick and easy way to simulate electricity around an object using the Underwater texture.

Make a slightly larger version of the object you want to wrap with electricity and give it a single surface name. Change the **Surface Color** to black and select the Underwater texture in the color channel (T), adding a bluish tinge (or whatever suits you) to the **Texture Color**.

Input the following values for the rest of the Underwater texture (example is for an object with a 100-meter radius):

Size: 50,000 for X,Y and Z
Center: 100 on XYZ
Wavesources: 10
Wavelength: 30
(Adjust only this and the wavespeed to accommodate larger or smaller objects.)
Wavespeed: 1
Band Sharpness: 10

Make sure the object is **Additive** and give it whatever Luminosity setting you like (**Transparent** Edge Transparency also helps). The additive nature of the surface will make the object transparent wherever it is black and visible where there is color present (the texture). Parent this larger, textured object to the original version, and presto! It will now appear to be surrounded by a moving electrical field (see the Underwater Electricity image in the color section).

Static-ocious!

Faking Luminosity

Before there was luminosity mapping, I needed a way to map bright little windows onto spaceships. Diffusion and color mapping wouldn't work, so I figured out how to use a reflection map to simulate luminosity (take a look at the Space Destroyer object included with the Toaster for an example).

To make a black-and-white reflection map of windows, the same way you would a luminosity map, make the surface 100 percent reflective and use a small, single-color brush (off-yellow works well) as the reflected image. No matter what angle the object is viewed from, the reflective areas will always display a bright, uniform color (the brush). And the luminosity channel is still available for your use.

Windo-licious!

LWP

Mojo likes sausage and onion on his pizza, maybe a little garlic, too.

Moj-O-Rama II

by Mojo

So many people responded positively to the first "Moj-O-Rama" (October 1994 *LWPRO*) that I knew a sequel was inevitable.

After almost a year, I have finally amassed enough new helpful LightWave hints to put together a few new pages of tips and tricks. Though no one did the first time, I again encourage readers to send in their own little secrets so they can be included in a future installment. The reward? The satisfying knowledge that fellow animators have been aided in their quest to make life a little easier.

Easy Debris

We all know what a pain it is to Boolean an object into a billion bits for an explosion scene. Perhaps a trick using the **Sketch** and **Drill** tools may help quicken the pace. Let's say we want to slice a section of the wing from the popular DC-10 object. With the wing section in a secondary layer, use the **Sketch** tool to draw a curve in a rough shape over the section of wing you want to slice off

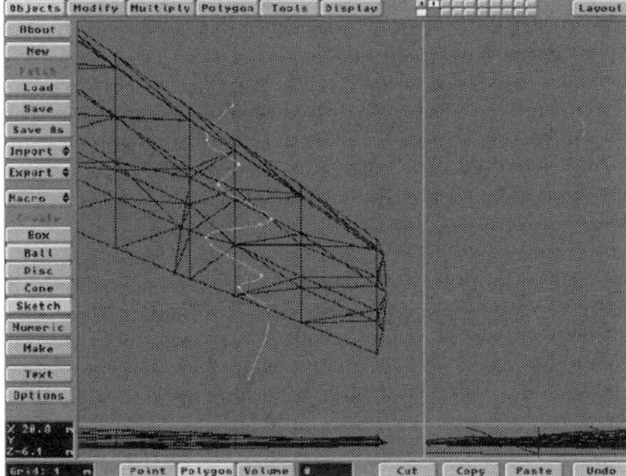

Figure 1

(Figure 1). Switch layers as you would to Boolean, but instead use the Template Drill **(Drill)** feature's **Slice** command. Presto! The wing now has a section with a squiggly slice through it. You can easily select and cut these polygons, saving it as a piece of debris (Figure 2). In addition, unlike with **Boolean,** the rest of the object remains, ready for you to chop off the next piece.

Better still, you can easily draw a new curve for each cut, making the edges of each chunk more random. Keep in mind, however, that this technique will not create polygons along the cut edges as Boolean does. If you're going to be close to your cut sections, their absence may be noticeable and Boolean should be used where necessary. As always, consult a physician first.

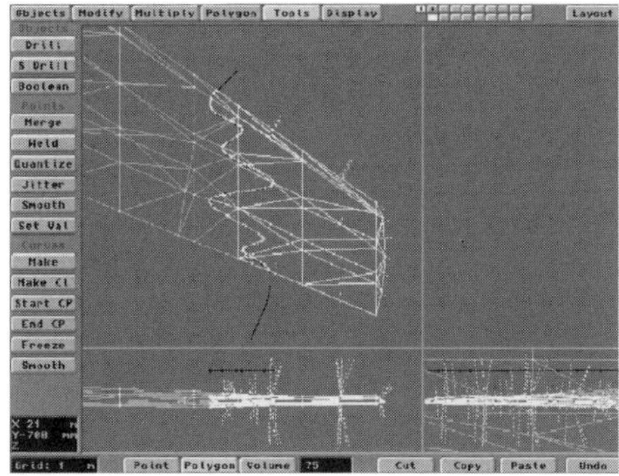

Figure 2

Better Debris

While we're on the subject of debris, any good animator knows that the job doesn't end once the piece is cut. Oh no. If we're talking about an explosion, the debris that is strewn forth from an object needs to look as burnt and damaged as possible. One problem I've seen in many explosions is too much clean debris. Of course, you could Boolean little holes in the debris itself to make it look really good, but this process would take forever. You don't have forever!

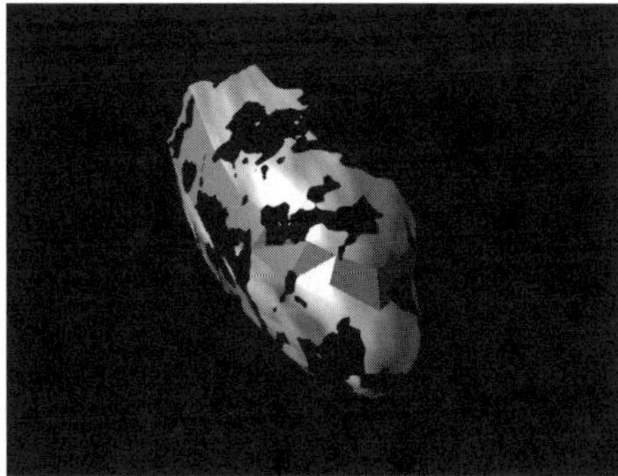

Figure 3

So use a **Clip Map** of **Fractal Noise** on your debris sections. Figure 3 shows this on the sliced nose section of the jet. The clip map makes the object look like metallic swiss cheese—kind of how wreckage would look! As with Drill, the clip map shows no inside faces, so it is best used on smaller pieces that tumble away quickly. For added nastiness, those using the latest version of LightWave may want to consider adding the new **Crumple** procedural in the **Bump Map** channel. If used subtlety, it can really help debris look badly damaged. Try this especially on the edges created with Booleaned pieces.

Flare on a Polygon

Glow behind lens flares *hates* transparent objects when there is a solid object behind both of them. Since the flare doesn't know an object is transparent (only if it's there or not), it won't shine properly through them and often creates black edges along them. On *Babylon 5*, we encounter this problem particularly during explosion scenes, when the glow behind flares used for the nebulas turns spark particles black.

To fix this, we simply rendered a full-screen lens flare against a black background and transparency- mapped it onto a polygon. The polygon was then positioned way in the background, occupying the same space the flare would have. Problem fixed! The polygon can easily be sized to change the flare intensity and dissolved to match the look of any flare.

In addition, if you map the flare image into the polygon surface's **Luminosity** channel, the color channel is open for tweaking. By turning off the texture **Antialiasing** (unnecessary for such a soft image), the lens flare polygon will also render faster than an actual flare. So, even when it's not causing a problem, sticking a flare on a polygon can be advantageous compared to the "real thing."

Wide-Angle Tricks

How often do you adjust the **Zoom Factor** on LightWave's camera? Most people almost never do. However, this feature does mimic real lenses by compressing or elongating space, depending on the length of the lens. By typing in a very low setting, weird distortion effects can be achieved as they are with wide-angle camera lenses. Figure 4 shows what the director's chair object looks like with a 4mm lens. As the camera pans and tilts, the object appears to smear across the screen like a bad acid trip. While these effects aren't very useful for everyday work, they can spice up a logo animation by stretching and bending text in impossible ways. Remember that the zoom can be enveloped, allowing you control when the distortion effects take place. Experiment by making a wireframe preview with any object. Try this feature with particles! At the very least, I guarantee you'll find it interesting.

Faster Wireframes

No matter what you do, even with stand-in objects, wireframes can sometimes take forever. To cut the time in half, create your preview "on twos." Simply make it with a frame step of 2 and play it back at 15 frames per second (fps). It won't be as smooth as 30 fps, but it will be more than good enough to preview your action and save a lot of time!

Speedy Modeler Redraw

Turn off the polygon **Normals** display option in Modeler (d). Selected polygons will still turn yellow (or white) when selected but will redraw almost twice as fast. I find that the majority of the time I simply don't need to know what direction my polygons are facing, and the Align feature easily fixes errors that may occur.

Quicker Tedious Input

You know the story. You've just LightSwarmed 100 lens flares to a spaceship so they all have the same settings. Now you must assign a **Fade With Distance** number to each and every one individually. Or you have to change the diffuse value for 50 surfaces. No matter how you look at it, you're going to spend a lot of time pointing, clicking and entering numeric values. Want an easy way around this? Ha! Wouldn't we all! However, there is a way to do this that can save you some time. I find that moving the mouse and clicking in the requester box repeatedly takes the most time. How many of you remember that simultaneously pressing the left ALT and Amiga keys simulates a left mouse button click? By placing the pointer directly on top of the requester and pressing these keys, you'll see the cursor appear, ready for input.

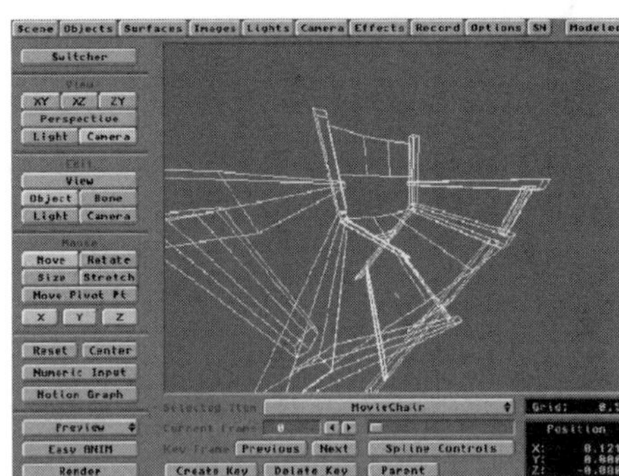

Figure 4

Input your number, hit the down arrow to advance to the next light (or surface or object or whatever), *make sure you don't move the mouse* and click those two keys again. Presto! The cursor appears, ready for input.

Now all you need to do is keep hitting the arrow, (left ALT+ Amiga) and the numeric value. It may seem close to the same amount of work, but trust me, by avoiding the mouse, you can get those values entered much more quickly—no more than a second each, if you're good!

Mirror Object in Layout

Yes, you heard me. Imagine being able to mirror a mapped object! Let's say you're building a left airplane wing and it has 25 surfaces. To make the right side, you can mirror it in Modeler, but then you need to map 50 surfaces. Instead, load the finished, mapped wing into Layout and scale it to -1 on the X axis. This will literally turn your object inside out and create a mirror image, maps and all! Be careful to make your surfaces **Double Sided** (remember, you'll be flipping all the polygons inside out as well) and keep in mind that any maps with text or numbers will be reversed. In addition, entire objects can be inverted to suit your tastes. If you had an asymmetrical object and decided you liked it better with the features reversed, this would save you the trouble of having to rework it in Modeler.

Motion Removal

Did you know that if you size a light or camera to zero, they cannot move? Well, you can't size a light or camera, but you can parent them to a null object that's been sized to zero. We once had a long, (two-minute) shot at Foundation Imaging that involved the camera flying smoothly through a valley. Everything was fine, but a moment later the camera had to begin shaking and vibrating for the rest of the animation. Making the camera shake for 90 seconds is easy—simply create a two-second-long repeating envelope. But to keep it steady for 30 seconds and then make it shake? Envelopes don't let you repeat a limited range, so it would mean handmaking a shake envelope over 2,700 frames! Not very appealing.

To remedy this, the camera was given a short, repeating shake envelope as first suggested. It was then parented to a null object, which provided the motion path through the canyon. However, for the first 30 seconds of the move, the null was sized to .0001, and scaled up to 1 afterward (you can't size the null all the way to zero or else the camera becomes inverted). While the null had a size of nearly zero, the camera shake was imperceptible. However, as the null sized up, the shake became more obvious until the null reached 1 (when the shake was normal).

Remember that this technique applies to motion only, not rotation. The shake could not have been done with tilts and pans. You may never find yourself in a similar situation, but isn't it neat to know that problems like these have such bizarre solutions?

That's all for now!

Mojo works as an animator/technical director for Foundation Imaging.

Reader Speak

Subscribers' Questions and Comments

by John Gross

This section of *LightWavePRO* will be a continuing column devoted to printing questions, tips, feedback and complaints from readers.

This month's question comes from Lynn Weiski of Los Angeles, who writes:

Could you please show some examples of using LightWave Modeler's Extrude to Path function? Whenever I try it, I get unpredictable results, and the manual is not very clear on the subject.

Technically, extrusion along a path in Modeler is called **Path Extrude**, while extrusion along a Modeler spline, or rail, is called **Rail Extrude**. When most people refer to extrusion along a path, they are referring to Rail Extrude, but I will cover both functions.

For either function to work correctly, you should start with a single, flat polygon (see closeup in Figure 1).

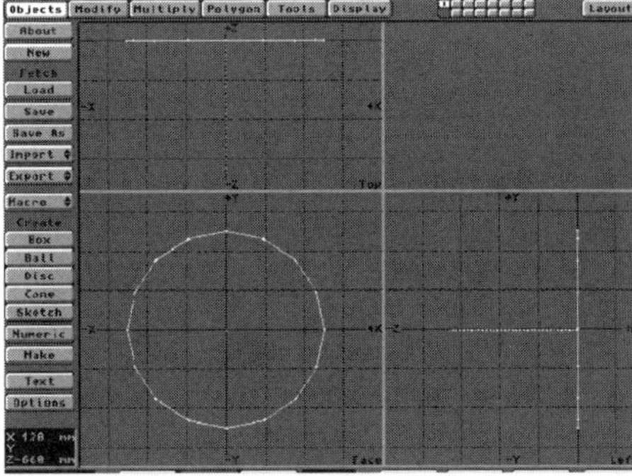

Figure 1: A single, flat polygon

Path Extrusion

Now that you have your flat polygon, you need to have a path or a rail to extrude along. If you decide to use a path, you will be using a motion file from LightWave.

Enter Layout and create a quick, 60-frame path for the camera. Create the path from the Overhead (XZ) view. Make sure to rotate the camera at the keyframes, so it aligns to the path (don't use the **Align to Path** function in the Motion graph). Also, be sure to view your path from the front and side views, and change the Y position of some of the keys so the path is not located in the same plane (make sure to change the Pitch angles to follow the path).

After the path is created, enter the Motion graph for the camera by clicking on the **Motion Graph** button (**m**), and adjust any keys to smooth the motions (except velocity) for each channel, if needed. Once you like the motion, save it to the Motions directory. Figure 2 shows the same motion path from the top (left) and side (right) views.

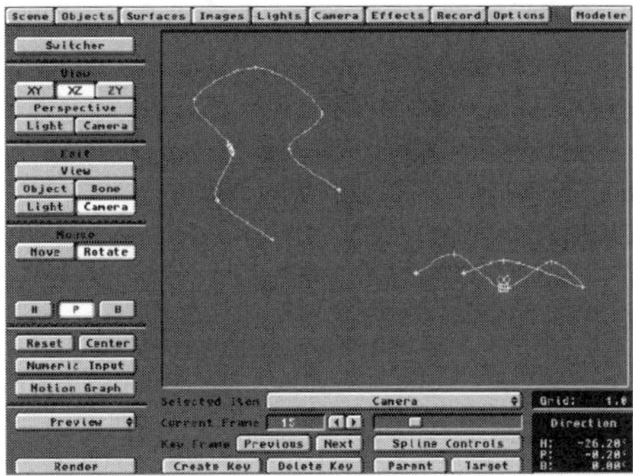

Figure 2: A motion path from top (left) and side views

With your path saved, return to Modeler and go to the **Multiply** menu. Make sure the flat polygon is in the foreground layer and click on the **Path Ext** button (**shift-p**). You are presented with a file requester asking for the motion. Choose the saved motion and click **OK**. Another requester asks for the **First** and **Last** frame of the path you wish to use as the start and end points for the extrusion. The third value to enter is the **Step**, which refers to the number of "cross sections" you will have along the path.

For this example, enter 1 for **First**, 60 for **Last** and 1 for **Step**. This extrudes your polygon along the path just as it appeared in Layout. The amount of rotation in the path determines how the polygon "rounds" corners. If you use a higher value for step (i.e., 10), you would end up with six (60 divided by 10) cross sections in the object. If you use .5 for the step, there will be 120 cross sections in your object.

If the path is too small for your object, select **Undo**, then decrease the size of the flat polygon and try again.

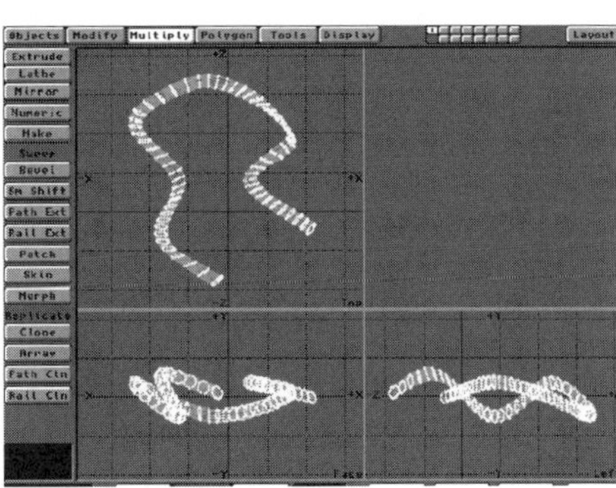

Figure 3: The completed object

Figure 3 shows the completed object. Notice how the shape in the top and side views match the path's shape in Figure 2.

One important note: To get good results, be sure the flat polygon starts centered at the origin (0,0,0), because that is the center point of the extrusion process. An off-center polygon gives unexpected results.

Rail Extrusion—Single Rail

Rail extrusion is a similar process to path extrusion, except that the path is drawn in Modeler. Start with an original polygon in Layer 1 and then make Layer 2 active. With Layer 1 in the background, use the **Sketch** tool (Objects) and draw out a path. Hit the **Return** key to turn the path into a spline, then use the **Drag** tool (Modify) to move the points around in the other views to create an acceptable path (Figure 4).

Once the rail is complete, switch layers so the polygon is in the foreground and the rail is in the background. You can achieve the best results if you rotate and move the polygon so it is located perpendicular to the start of the path (as if you were going to shove a needle straight through a piece of plastic). It helps to use the **Static Display** mode to view your work. Once the polygon is positioned properly (Figure 5), click on the **Rail Ext** (**Ctrl-r**) button (Multiply).

You are now presented with a requester with a few options (Figure 6). First of all, choose the type of seg-

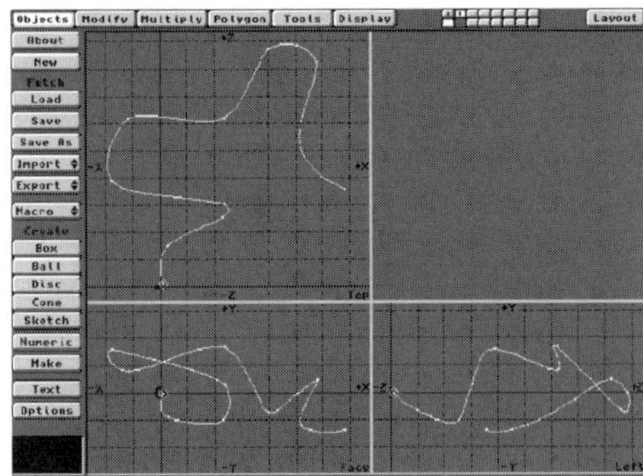

Figure 4: Use the Drag tool to move points.

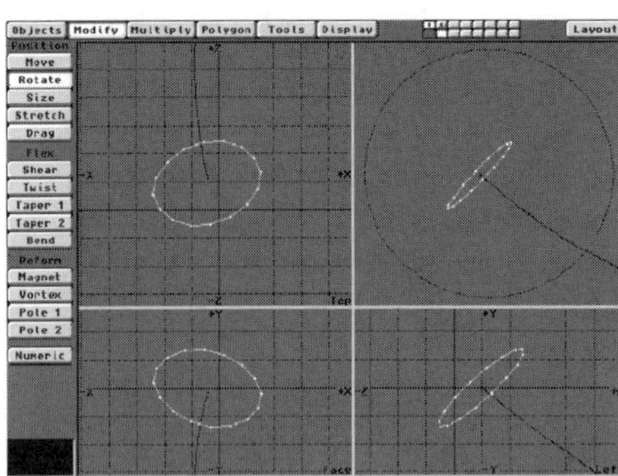

Figure 5: Once positioned, click on Rail Ext.

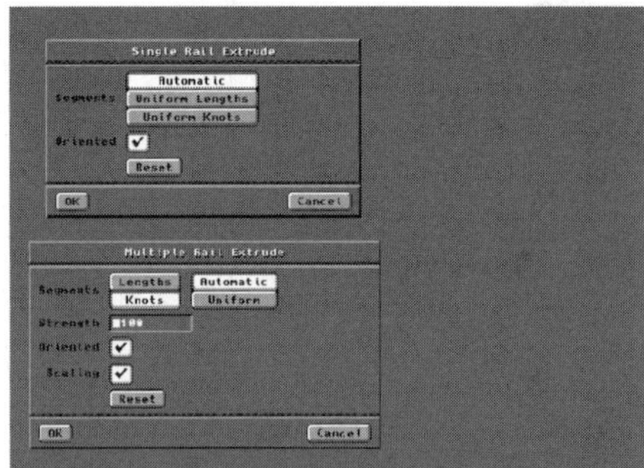

Figure 6: The Multiple Rail Extrude requester

ments to make up the object. For most cases, Automatic works fine and allows Modeler to decide what's best. One hint: The **Curve Division** parameter in the **Options** section (Objects) determines the amount of segments in an Automatic extrusion.

Uniform Lengths and **Uniform Knots** are similar in that they extrude along the rail in a number of user-defined segments. The difference is that Uniform Lengths makes equal-length segments along the rail, while Uniform Knots creates segments of different length while creating an equal number of them between knots or points on the rail. For instance, there may always be two and a half segments between knots, although the segments will be different lengths.

Finally, the **Oriented** check box aligns a polygon to the spline as it is extruded. Deselecting this keeps the polygon in the same orientation throughout the extrude.

Rail Extrusion—Multiple Rails

If there's more than one rail in the background layer, the Multiple Rail Extrude requester appears when you click the **Rail Ext** button (Figure 6). When using multiple rails, place your polygon so that the rails' lines start at its edges. Think of the rails as guides to slide your polygon along.

The Multiple Rail Extrude requester has basically the same functions as the single rail extrude, with a few additions. **Strength** refers to the amount of influence the rails have on the extrusion. The higher the values, the more the polygon conforms to the rails when Scaling (see below) is deselected.

The other new function in this requester is a **Scaling** check box. With Scaling selected, your extrusion scales larger or smaller as your rails spread farther apart or closer together. If your rails travel apart from each other, the effect is a flaring, like the end of a trumpet.

With Scaling deselected, the extrusion either remains a constant thickness with two rails, or tries to run along multiple rails, depending on how high the Strength value is.

Some Extra Tips

It's important to start a polygon extrusion at the beginning of the rails. If you get unexpected results, you can use the **Flip** (f) command to change the starting points of the rails (look for the little diamonds when selected).

If extruding a polygon along a closed spline, be sure to align the polygon at the starting point of the curve and make it perpendicular to the curve for best results.

LWP

John Gross is Editor of LightWavePRO. *He is also a* Video Toaster User *columnist and frequent contributor of tutorials and product reviews.*

Reader Speak

Subscribers' Questions and Comments

This month's Reader Speak answers two questions from Craig Sneiderman of Florence, Ky., who writes:

I want to thank you and the entire staff at *LWPRO* for your efforts. I enjoy every issue and have learned a lot already.

Now that I have sufficiently buttered you up, could you explain what antialiasing is all about? I know that it makes images look better, but I'm not entirely sure how it works. And what exactly does Adaptive Sampling do?

Plus, I have had a problem with clip maps—sometimes they work and sometimes not. Is there a bug in LightWave or am I doing something wrong?

Good questions. Let's explain antialiasing first.

LightWave's antialiasing controls, found in the middle of the Camera panel, include three levels (Low, Medium and High), plus the Adaptive Sampling toggle and a Sampling Threshold level (see figure). There is also a button to enable a Soft Filter method of rendering.

First, let's define the term aliasing. Aliasing refers to the jagged edges found on computer-generated images. The edges are not perfectly horizontal or vertical and appear because computers use square pixels. You can never actually have a line that is not jagged if it is not entirely horizontal or vertical.

The trick is to give the appearance of smooth lines by using a method called antialiasing, which looks at two neighboring "stair steps" and places another pixel of a differing color on the "stair" between them. The color of the pixel depends upon the neighboring colors. If the steps are black and the background white, the pixel placed would be a gray color. In this manner, the hard edges are smoothed away.

LightWave's three levels of antialiasing refer to the number of antialias passes to be performed. With

LightWave's antialiasing controls

Antialiasing set to Low, Medium or High, the image (or segment) is rendered once and then a number of passes are performed to antialias. Each pass adds more colors to smooth lines. Low antialiasing adds four additional passes, Medium adds eight and High adds 16.

During the rendering process, notice the display that reads, for instance, "Rendering Segment 1, pass 3 of 9." This means the first segment of an image is rendering with Medium-level antialiasing. There are nine segments because the original pass plus the Medium setting's eight levels of antialiasing add up to a total of nine passes.

LightWave's three levels of antialiasing refer to the number of antialias passes to be performed.

How does LightWave know what to antialias? It depends on whether Adaptive Sampling is turned on or off.

If it is off, LightWave looks at everything (including background images) and attempts to antialias it. If you enable Adaptive Sampling, LightWave performs edge detection and only antialias edges that stand out. LightWave determines which edges stand out by using the Sampling Threshold that you input.

LightWave's threshold level ranges between zero and 256. The default threshold level is eight. This means that LightWave looks at two neighboring pixels and checks to see if the green component of the RGB value is more or less than eight from its neighbor. If it is eight or less, LightWave will not antialias at that point. If it is more than eight, LightWave will antialias. You can tell if LightWave is antialiasing by watching the render screen and looking for the white edging that appears as the process works (only if Adaptive Sampling is on).

If you drop the level to zero, LightWave operates as if Adaptive Sampling was not turned on and antialias everything. You'll see a lot of white as the antialiasing takes place. If you raise the level to 256, no antialiasing occurs. Render times can definitely improve by using higher values. Try testing your particular image to determine the proper level; however, a setting between eight and 32 seems to be a good starting point.

Now, what happens if the green component is the same between the two neighboring pixels, but the red or blue component is different? Don't worry, LightWave will still antialias. Whenever it attempts to antialias, LightWave checks for these factors: 1) a green component higher than the threshold; 2) a red component higher than twice the threshold; and 3) a blue component higher than four times the threshold. If any of these factors are present, LightWave will antialias.

If the pixels are so close in color that antialiasing doesn't take place, and with low threshold levels you cannot notice the difference. Another option is to turn Adaptive Sampling off (or down to zero), and you get antialiasing automatically.

The only other function in the antialiasing section of the Camera panel is Soft Filter. When enabled, Soft Filter gives your final image a bit of a soft edge that looks a little more like film.

Here's some antialiasing tips:

1. For most video work, using Medium resolution plus Low antialiasing is acceptable.
2. If you are using antialiasing and your texture image maps look a bit too blurry, try turning off the Antialiasing button in the Texture panel to avoid antialiasing twice.

3. Try rendering in Low resolution with High antialiasing to get a more blurred, film-like look.
4. If objects contain a lot of intricate detail, you may have to render in High resolution in order for good visibility.
5. Sometimes High resolution with no antialiasing renders faster than Medium resolution with Low antialiasing and looks as good or better. Try it and see which works best for your project.

On to your second question regarding unreliable clip maps.

Chances are, you are using an image as a clip map. You can get strange results (even within the same animation) if Antialiasing is enabled in the Clip Map texture panel. Antialiasing should never be used with clip mapping. There may be times when an antialiased image gives strange results to a clip-mapped object, causing it to render strangely or disappear completely. This is because of the way antialiasing is performed in LightWave.

Unfortunately, Antialiasing is selected by default, so remember to turn it off when you are clip mapping. I generally turn off Pixel Blending as well, since there isn't a need to blur pixels in a clip map. Chances are that in a future version, LightWave programmer Allen Hastings will remove these buttons so they do not interfere.

LWP

Reader Speak

Subscribers' Questions and Comments

by John Gross

Well, the "reviews" are in and it doesn't look like everybody enjoyed issue No. 6. Here's some of the mail I've received.

Hi John,

I am a subscriber to both *Video Toaster User* and *LWPRO*. I enjoy *VTU* and find it highly insightful with its variety of columns and timely reviews. I paid for the *LWPRO* subscription because I am trying to achieve my dream of making a living from the activity I most enjoy: 3D Graphics. I anticipate the arrival of each month's *LWPRO* to hear the latest batch of tips, tricks, secrets and constructive suggestions from those artists whose work I have come to admire.

At $48 a subscription for 19 pages (including the cover and four pages of color photos), *LWPRO*'s info comes at a premium. As important as I found the reviews in April's *LWPRO* to be, I would much prefer to see these articles in *VTU*. I would not, however, object to an article about how to achieve a specific effect with Sparks or a tutorial on how to most efficiently combine several Power Macros with "X" to achieve some special effect.

Angel Freire
via Internet

Hi John,

I wanted to send you a short note about the current issue of *LIGHTWAVEPRO* (No. 6). I have been very pleased with all of the previous issues of *LWPRO* and I have found that it was well worth the subscription. However, I didn't feel that this issue quite lived up to that standard.

As a subscriber to *LWPRO*, I anxiously wait for each issue, expecting to learn new, important things about LightWave. An issue devoted to third-party software was a little disappointing. I expect that I will see that kind of information in *AmigaWorld* or *VTU* or even on the Internet or CIS.

Matt Mower
via CompuServe

Dear John,

I have been completely happy with *LIGHTWAVEPRO* since issue No. 1, regardless of the high introductory subscription fee. However, I am not satisfied with my new issue devoted entirely to product reviews. Are you running out of LightWave ideas?

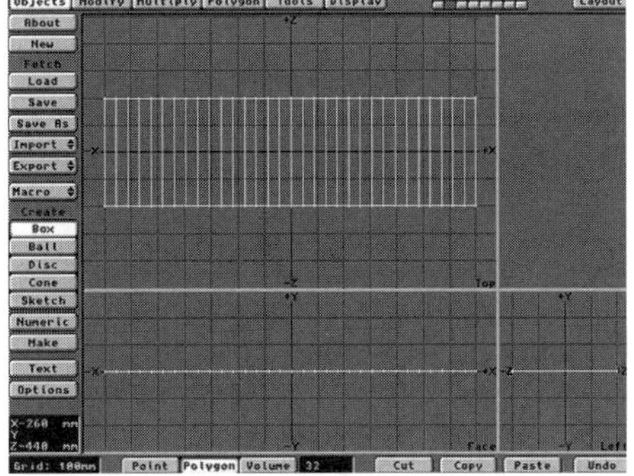

Figure 1

Please continue to provide issues filled with LightWave info. I wouldn't mind if reviews were included in regular issues. Tutorials for third-party products would also be acceptable. Please don't make this "review only" thing a habit.

Dan Kosmal
Albany, CA

In Response

It was entirely my idea to have an entire issue devoted to third-party products. I feel it is an important part of the information a competent LW artist needs in his/her arsenal. The reason the entire issue contained reviews is that I wanted to 'catch up' on the products that had been out for a little while.

Chances are, in future issues, there will not be a need to devote an entire issue to product reviews. However, I will continue to include reviews of products that are designed to work with LightWave in order to keep you up to date on what is out there and what can be beneficial or detrimental to your animation projects. Expect these reviews to be 'scattered' throughout the issues and not lumped all together.

I feel that, because *LWPRO* is a newsletter, the reviews can be a bit more beneficial than those seen in magazines. Not just because our turnaround time is not as lengthy (3-4 months for many magazines), but also because the reviews in *LWPRO* are conducted by LightWave professionals who provide the kind of information you need to make an informed decision about products you are considering buying (and not products you have already bought).

As a side note: I've been told by a few people that they feel the subscription price of *LWPRO* is too high. I'm not going to defend the price by saying that it can easily pay for itself with a few tips that speed up a project (Oops, I just did). Or that you could write it off on your taxes (Oops, there I go again).

You may not realize this, but in many cases, subscribers do not pay for most of the costs involved in producing a magazine, but rather the advertisers do. As a newsletter, however, *LWPRO* relies on its subscribers' loyalty to survive.

Regardless, I know cost is a relative thing in this case, but think about this: I subscribe to some newsletters that are well over $100 per year.

Before I get any complaints about wasting a column, let me answer several LightWave questions I received last month.

Dear John,

I sometimes get a message while trying to lathe an object in Modeler that says "Source contour contained no edges. Only points were generated." Is this a bug or am I doing something wrong?

Denny Stone
Downer's Grove, IL

In order for an object to be lathed, it must be an open contour in order to work. This means it must be composed of curves and/or open polygons arranged into a shape which is not closed on itself. For instance, a flat disc created with the disc tool will work, but a 3D disc will not.

Theoretically, the same should hold true for extruding as well, but I have noticed that with version 3.1 of Modeler, if you try to extrude a primitive built from the Objects panel, you will get the same message, but it will generate a duplicate of the object with all of its polygons facing in the opposite direction from the originals.

Dear John,

I have had a hard time getting ray-traced refractions to work properly. I am trying to re-create my dining room table (which is made out of glass), but when I render it with refractions on, it does not seem to refract light the same way the real table does. I saw a post on a local board that referred to a possible problem with refractions in LW. Is this an error in LightWave, and can it be corrected?

Francisco Négron

Tallahassee, FL

First of all, there was a bug in LightWave 3.0 with refraction. When many of the rendering calculations were changed to use floating point, one of the variables in refraction was not properly changed, which could lead to rendering errors. However, this bug was fixed in version 3.1.

It is possible that your dining table object wasn't constructed properly for ray tracing. Each surface that a ray passes through changes the index of refraction. To be perfectly accurate, the outward-facing polygons should have a surface with the refractive index of glass, and each of these polygons should be paired with an inward-facing polygon whose surface has the refractive index of air (or whatever material the ray would then be entering). This is quite simple to create in Modeler. Suppose you have a glass table with the surfaces named "table top" facing outwards. Simply copy this object into another layer, change the surface name to "table inner" (or something appropriate) and then press the **f** key or select the **Flip** button in the Polygon menu. This will flip all of the polygons inward.

Now copy this object back into the original layer. You can then merge points to get rid of the duplicates. Save this object out and reload it into Layout. In the Surfaces panel, set your refractive indices for the appropriate surface names. With fully defined transitions, you should get accurate results.

You could also be experiencing one other problem. Version 3.1 has another bug in the refraction calculations which prevents rays from bending when exiting glass (in other words, when they pass through the inward-facing polygons that have a refractive index of 1.0). There is a simple method to avoid this, however, by giving the inward-facing polygons a refractive index slightly greater than 1.0.

Figure 2

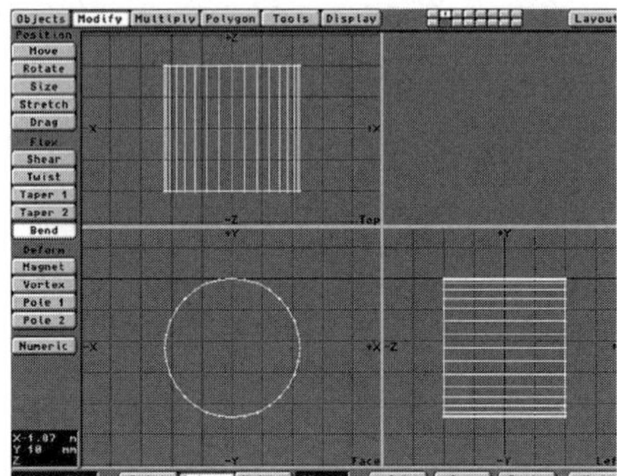

Figure 3

Dear John,

I've read and re-read Grant Boucher's Lightning Ball article, but I don't understand this paragraph:

"If you build a lightning image box that has a lot of segments on the X direction (say 32 or 64), you can then morph that object into one that has been bent around the Z axis into a disc in LightWave's Object menu. The sticky texture can..."

I don't understand this entire paragraph or what Grant is getting at. What is a segment? What is a sticky texture? Also, do you know what happened to the LightWave mailing list? It just stopped all of a sudden. Do you have any other suggestions on how I can get LightWave questions answered?

Doug (dnakakihara@BIX.com)

via Internet

A segment is simply a polygonal "cross section" of an object. For instance, Figure 1 shows a flat plane composed of 32 segments along the X direction. You can create such an object by using the **Numeric Box** tool and inputting a value greater than 1 for the **Segments** field (Figure 2). You can change the number of segments in any of Modeler's primitive objects by using the Numeric requester before you make the object. If you need to bend, twist or modify objects, they must be composed of many segments to do the bending or twisting along.

Grant was referring to creating such an object, saving it, and then using the **Bend** tool (Modify menu) to bend it back onto itself to create a rolled up section of polygons (Figure 3). This new object can then be saved as a morph target for the original flat object. This is where the "sticky texture" comes into play.

What Grant meant by this is to simply apply an image map to the flat plane of polygons (the morph source) and then morph that object into the rolled up object. There is no need to use an envelope. A value of 100 percent will be just fine. When an object is morphed, any texture applied to it "goes along for the ride" as if it is sticking to the surface. This is a great way to get image maps to appear properly wrapped on odd shaped objects.

Tip No. 1: When bending an object, first use the mouse to get the bend in the approximate position then **Undo** it. Next, select **Numeric** to bring up the Bend requester and look at the values. These values are those that you just performed with the mouse. Chances are they aren't going to be nice round numbers, so just change them so they are. For instance, if the **Angle** value is 179.432, change it to 180. If the **Direction** reads -87, change it to -90. When you select **Apply**, the modification will be perfect.

Tip No. 2: When creating a morph target, do not cut and paste the original object into another layer to modify it. Doing so changes the point order of the object and will cause a morph to take on the qualities of a rat's nest.

Instead, create the source object in one layer and save it, then modify it directly in that layer and save it out as your target object. You can place a copy of the original in another layer if you wish to use it as a background template for you modifications.

Tip No. 3: Your target object does not need to have any polygons. Since LightWave is only concerned with the point order when performing a morph, it doesn't care if there are polygons or not. Removing the polygons (**k**) before saving a morph target will help save memory, and you won't have to make your target invisible since points do not render in LightWave.

Finally, the Internet LightWave mail list that you are referring to was canceled because the sysop (Bob Lindabury) lost his Internet connection. A new list has been started and chances are you have been automatically subscribed. For those of you interested in signing on to the LightWave mail list, you can subscribe by sending e-mail to listserv@netcom.com and state in the body of the letter: subscribe lightwave-l *yourname*. You will begin receiving mail from users all over the world that is geared towards LightWave and Modeler. Posts by Allen Hastings and Stuart Ferguson and other LightWave professionals are not uncommon.

LWP

Reader Speak

Subscribers' Questions and Comments

by John Gross

This month's Reader Speak column addresses questions I've been asked regarding LightWave 3.5.

I've heard people mention loading and saving wireframe previews. I don't know how to access this feature. All I see is Make, Play and Free Preview in the Preview requester. Where do I load and save previews?

Martin Lind
Los Angeles, CA

The Load and Save Preview features are only available if you have a Toaster and run LightWave 3.5 from the Switcher. The original wireframe preview code was written by an ex-NewTek employee in assembly language. Allen Hastings had to rewrite the preview code in C when he was developing the standalone version and unfortunately there was not enough time to get the loading and saving features in before shipping time.

If you run LightWave from the Switcher, the assembly language calls will be made and the load and Save Preview features will work. Rest assured, this will be functional in future versions.

I can't figure out what purpose the Preview Layout background serves. Can you tell me?

Sandy Coffey
Kaneohe, HI

Preview Layout Background (Options panel) only serves a useful purpose when you have the ability to load and save previews (see above). If you have ever used an image sequence as a background and selected Show BG Image, you will understand why this feature was added. LightWave must load a new image from your sequence whenever you go to a different frame (while in the Camera view). This can be a time-consuming process, and it's usually more trouble than it's worth.

Preview Background comes in handy while performing composite shots, and was actually requested for this very purpose. We had a *seaQuest* shot where a WSKR had to follow a whale. The live footage of the whale we received had a 'hand held' camera feel that

Figure 1: The Options panel showing the three different Layout Background options.

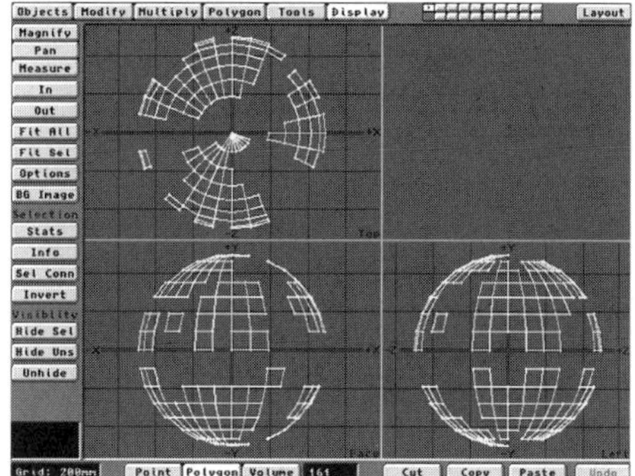

Figure 2: This is a complete object with some of its polygons hidden.

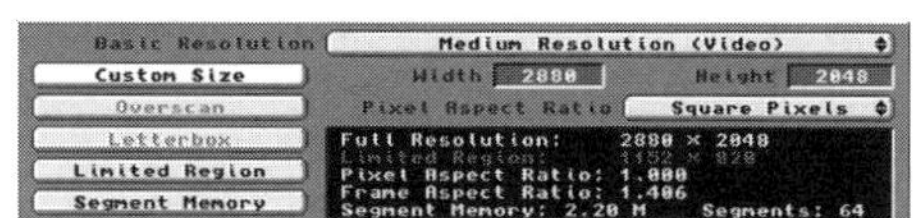

Figure 3: This section of the Camera panel shows how many segments will be used for a selected resolution.

was very jerky. Matching LightWave's camera to this proved almost impossible because it would take too long to update the background with the required image from the whale sequence.

Greg Teegarden, the artist working on the shot, requested the background preview feature to make work like this easier. The way it is used for a shot like this is simple: Simply load the sequence as a background (with nothing else in the scene) and select BG Image for the Layout Background (it helps to turn off the grid as well). Generate a preview and then save it. After your preview has generated, you can select Preview as your Layout Background and it will show up as the background image sequence, but will be accessed much faster when you go to a different frame. Of course, since you saved it, you can load it up as the background in any shot.

Keep in mind that you can only have one preview in memory at a time.

If you render a frame or enter Modeler, LightWave will automatically free the preview. However, as you are working in LightWave, you may wish to free up memory. Selecting the Free Preview (Preview pop-up) option will do this for you.

If you wish to generate a new preview utilizing the background preview plus any objects you have added to the scene, you need to load the sequence back in, select BG Image as your Layout Background and regenerate the preview. A wireframe preview will not appear in the 'background' of another preview.

Also, make sure that you are in the Camera view when you use these previews as they will not show up in other views.

I think I found a bug. I can't render Print Resolution images anymore! Is this a bug with 3.5 or is it a new "undocumented" feature?

Jonathan McNoo
New York, N.Y.

It is a new feature—sort of. The way LightWave handles the framebuffer memory (its own, not the Toaster buffer) was changed to help implement plug-in post processing effects for future versions. LightWave used to 'segment' the frame-buffer memory so you could render any size image you wish. Since a non-segmented buffer is necessary for future plug- ins, it was implemented at this time.

There is a simple formula to determine the amount of RAM required to render an image. Take the width of your desired output resolution and multiply it by the height. Multiply the product by four to give you the amount of RAM (in bytes) needed to render the image. For example, a square pixel Print Resolution image would require 19,660,800 bytes (about 19MB) of free RAM in order to render.

Just because you have 19MB free doesn't necessarily mean you can render this image, however. You also need to account for the number of images used in the scene (image filtering takes memory) and the amount of RAM you have set aside for Segment Memory (see below).

Now that you know what is happening, how do you get around it? Possibly by the time you read this, Allen Hastings may have implemented a fix which will most likely be some type of virtual memory scheme. In the meantime, keep your old version of LightWave around for rendering large images.

I can run LightWave on my Picasso II card in 800x600, but when I go to Modeler, everything seems fine until I try modifying something I have created. Then the object is not redrawn properly, but if I select points or polygons, they will show up. I have talked to others that this has happened to, so I know it is not my setup. What's going on?

Stoney Runion
Prairie View, Kan.
via Internet

The latest versions of the ChangeScreen program included with the Picasso board does not promote Modeler correctly. At the moment, it is unsure what the problem is, but earlier versions of ChangeScreen worked correctly with Modeler. We'll have to wait and see what happens with this one.

I had a little dot show up in one of my layer buttons in Modeler. I did an 'a' to fit the view, but there was nothing in the layer. The weird thing is, when I loaded the object that I was working on a few days later, it had another object 'stuck' to it. What did I do wrong?

Greg Vanacyk
Downers Grove, Ill.

You should have paid more attention to that dot. It was telling you that you had something in that layer. The reason you couldn't see it is because it was hidden using the hide tools in the Display menu. You may have accidentally clicked on one of the keyboard shortcuts to either hide the selected items or hide the unselected items (- or =).

Items hidden are not affected by any modifications to the layer unless, of course, you happen to move points shared by visible and hidden polygons. They are always a part of the object, though, and your saving of the visible object also saved the hidden object.

I almost always use the hide tools instead of copying and pasting to another layer. It took a little getting used to, but the keyboard commands make it simple. The hide tools are quite useful when you wish to work on certain areas of a detailed object.

Could you explain what the Segment Memory button's exact function is?

David Holtenbrau
via CompuServe

Remember the button labeled Use Fewer Segments in 3.1? That was a 'preset' segment memory. Basically, Segment Memory allows the user to decide how much RAM will be devoted to the rendering of segments of an image. The number of segments that a given resolution output will require is shown in the Camera panel. Selecting Segment Memory will allow you to devote a higher amount of RAM to rendering so fewer segments are used. This can be a great time saver when rendering with Motion Blur selected as there will be less time devoted to the moving of objects. Ideally, you would have enough RAM to get the amount of segments down to one.

By the way, do not confuse this Segment Memory with the segmented frame buffer discussed above.

LWP

John Gross is the editor of LWPRO and a supervising animator at Amblin Imaging. In his 'non-writing time,' he is writing the LightWave 4.0 user's guide. Contact him via e-mail at jgross@netcom.com.

Reader Speak
Subscribers' Questions and Comments

by John Gross

This month's Reader Speak takes a look at some of the LightWave questions in the queue...

Q: I've been finding your newsletter to be extremely useful. You've answered a lot of questions for me. I especially appreciated the articles on macros, but really, every issue has been full of terrific information.

One thing I wish I could learn more about is the use of fog. I've never been able to get it to work. When I use it, it blocks out the whole scene, except for some lights that are aimed into the camera (with Intensity set high enough).

A question you might also deal with is how fast different systems are at rendering the same scene. I have a 2000 with an 030 (33MHz) and 12MB of RAM. A scene with a few objects, three or four lights, bump maps, smoothing on and some surface mapping takes about 40 minutes to render per frame. If I add Motion Blur or go to Low antialias instead of none, it might take an hour and 20 minutes. If we did exactly the same thing on a 4000 with an 040 or a "Warp Engine," how much time would I save per frame? Lastly, why is it that when you create an envelope for a light that has Lens Flare on, it will never go off? I've tried many times to place a light inside or behind an object, and if Lens Flare is on, no matter how opaque the surface it is behind, no matter if it's set to absolute zero intensity or even negative values (both Intensity and Ambient Intensity), it still shows when rendered (the central glow at least). Can you help with this?

Pete Wagner
MinneHA! HA! Studios
Minneapolis, MN

A: Hi Pete. It's good to hear from a fellow Minnesotan again.

To start with, let me discuss the system speed tests you mention. In this issue, Grant Boucher runs some tests on some of the ScreamerNet CPUs that are available (or will be soon). We have not run any official tests on the Warp Engine yet, nor on 030 systems. We are including a scene that Grant used for his "nasty" benchmark tests on this issue's disk. Perhaps some readers with these systems will perform the tests and report back. Also expect more coverage of speed tests in upcoming issues as more options are available.

The other two questions I believe I can help with.

Let's talk about fog first. The Fog options (found in the **Effects** panel, Figure 1) have been greatly modified since earlier versions. LightWave 3.5 now includes two types of nonlinear fog and **Minimum** and **Maximum Fog Amounts** (a *seaQuest* lifesaver).

It's important to realize what's happening when you enable fog. First and foremost, turning fog on does not automatically create a foggy haze around your objects. It works a little bit differently than that.

When you enable fog, you are instructing LightWave to "tint" an object the color of the fog, depending upon certain parameters that you input in the fog options. Fog color can consist of either a single solid color selected with the **Fog Color** requester, or **Backdrop Fog**, which will use whatever values the background is, whether it is a **Background Image**, a **Solid Backdrop** color or a gradient color spread (between the **Zenith, Sky, Ground** and Nadir colors).

LightWave will systematically replace the object's color with the fog color depending upon how "deep" the object is in fog. This is where the minimum and maximum distances as well as the minimum and maximum amounts come into play. For all of these distances, it is important to remember that the measurements are always measured in units from the camera.

For our example, let's take three urns located at an increasing distance from the camera. The first urn is approximately .7 meters from the camera. The second is located 1 meter away and the third is 1.3 meters away.

Think of fog as a sphere surrounding the camera. If we had a Maximum Fog Distance of 1.5 meters, any object past this measurement would take on 100 percent of the fog color. Therefore, if you had a light blue background and a fog color of yellow, any objects located farther than 1.5 meters from the camera would be yellow, regardless of their previous colors. However, the real power of fog works when you select **Backdrop Fog** as the color. With Backdrop Fog, the object will seem to disappear the further it is in fog until it is past the **Maximum Fog Distance**, where it will become "invisible." Selecting a maximum distance of 1.5 meters would place the fog just behind the urn farthest from the camera. If you choose **Show Fog Radius** in the **Options** panel, you will see a circle representing the Maximum Fog Distance sphere in the three orthographic views (Figure 2).

Now, whenever you move the camera closer to the urns or the urns closer to the camera, they will appear to "come out of the fog." Likewise, an object moving farther from the camera will recede into fog. Now you get the idea of how underwater scenes are effectively created.

The **Minimum Fog Distance** tells where (in relation to the camera) the fog effect begins. Usually this is left at 0, which means it begins right at the camera. For certain special effects, you may want the fog to begin at a distance from the camera. Any object between the camera and the Minimum Fog Distance setting will take on no fog values.

The **Maximum Fog Distance** instructs LightWave where to create a total fog effect. As stated above, any objects located past the Max setting will take on the total fog colors. Of course, any objects in between the two settings will have some value of the fog color added to their surfaces, depending upon their distance from the camera.

The amount of fog effect at the minimum and maximum distances was always calculated at 0 percent and 100 percent, respectively, until LightWave 3.1 added the ability to determine how much of the fog effect would be calculated at each distance value. The **Minimum Fog Amount** refers to the percentage of the fog effect at the Minimum Fog Distance. Before this ability, it was a common practice for *seaQuest* animators to use a negative Minimum Fog Distance in order to create some "fog" right at the camera. Now, inputting a value for Minimum Amount assures that you can be close to objects yet have the objects partially obscured in fog (you know, like a nice smoggy day in Los Angeles).

This image demonstrates a Nonlinear 1 fog with the maximum distance placed just behind the farthest urn.

Figure 1

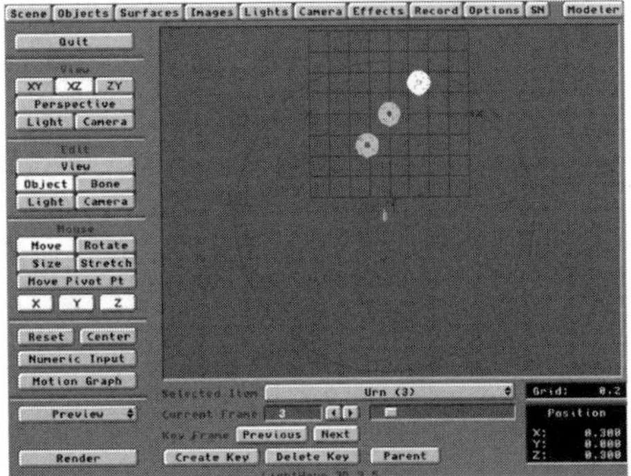

Figure 2

Of course, you can adjust the maximum amount of fog to assure that objects will never be completely obscured by the fog color as well. The fog graph shows the amount of the fog effect dynamically change as you adjust the Minimum and Maximum Fog Amount values (try using the mini-sliders). By creatively adjusting these values, you can achieve a fog that grows thicker the closer you are to the camera and gets less and less thick as you move away from the camera (Figure 3) for interesting effects.

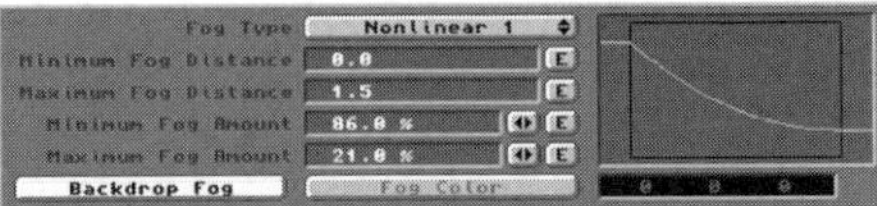

Figure 3

Figure 4

The fog graph also shows you how the different types of fog affect the way the fog is applied. **Linear** fog is evenly ramped up as you get further away. **Nonlinear** 1 is a bit more realistic look using an uneven ramp of fog that is "thicker" closer to the camera than Linear. **Nonlinear 2** is even thicker near the camera. Figure 4 shows side-by-side comparisons of the different fog types. Also note that all of the fog values can be enveloped for interesting effects (such as fog rolling into town).

Now that you know how fog works, I bet you can figure out what is happening when you are using it. Chances are you are leaving the default values of fog in place, which will give you a **Maximum Fog Distance** of 1 meter and a Fog Color of black (0,0,0). Even if you are using **Backdrop Fog**, a 1-meter maximum distance is probably a bit small for many scenes. This would cause anything past this distance from the camera to take on the fog colors, whatever they may be (assuming, of course, that you have left your Fog Amount values at their defaults).

So, why aren't your lights showing through the fog? Well, first of all, in order to even be able to see the light source, you must have **Lens Flare** selected for the lights. The Lens Flare panel has defaults of its own (Figure 5), the least of which is a little button called **Fade In Fog** being deselected. With this button in the default state, any lens flare using these settings will not fade in fog, and therefore pokes right through.

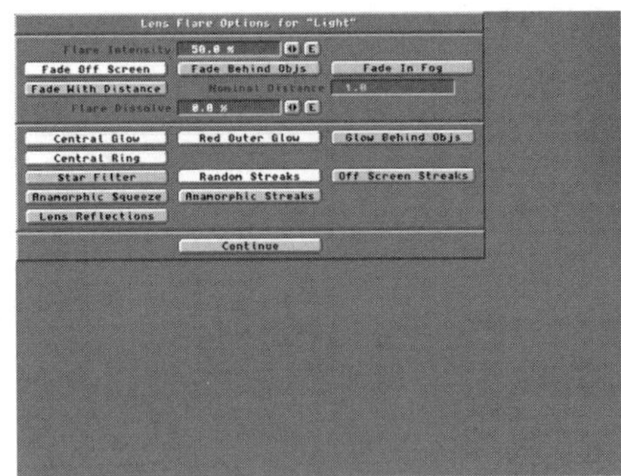

Figure 5

Along the same lines is the answer to your last question. It sounds to me as if you are mistakenly creating an envelope for Light Intensity, when what you really desire is an envelope for the light's Flare Intensity (Lens Flare panel). These are two different things. The Light Intensity determines the amount of light that is cast onto other objects, while the Flare Intensity determines the brightness of the flare (if any). Either can be used without the other.

If all you wish is to have a flare dim down and disappear as it goes behind an object, simply select **Fade Behind Objects** and LightWave will automatically calculate this for you. When using Fade Behind Objects, the object in front of the flare must have Cast Shadows (Objects panel) enabled in order to calculate when the flare needs to be hidden.

John Gross is the editor of LWPRO *and a supervising animator for Amblin Imaging.*

Reader Speak
Explaining Configuration Files

by John Gross

It's been awhile since we've been able to include a Reader Speak column and the mail has been building, so let's respond to some of it this month.

Q: I know there are ways to customize LightWave and Modeler. Could you talk about the config files and how to go about changing them?
Paul Ortega
Lubbock, TX

A: Indeed, you can customize some features in both LightWave and Modeler by modifying some ASCII configuration files. Configuration files for LightWave and Modeler are found in the Toaster/3D directory and are called LW-config (LightWave) and MOD-config (Modeler). Two full sample config files are listed below and then reprinted with explanations and tips.

LightWave Config File

LWCO
0
FileReqPreset1 DF0 DF0:
FileReqPreset2 BOX BH0:
FileReqPreset3 WORK DH1:Toaster/3D
FileReqPreset4 EXTRA DH2:Toaster/3D
ScenesDirectory DH1:Toaster/3D/Scenes
ObjectsDirectory DH1:Toaster/3D/Objects
HierarchiesDirectory DH1:Toaster/3D/Scenes
SurfacesDirectory DH1:Toaster/3D/Surfaces
ImagesDirectory DH1:Toaster/3D/Images
OutputDirectory DH1:Toaster/3D/Images
FramestoresDirectory DH1:Toaster/3D/Images
MotionsDirectory DH1:Toaster/3D/Motions
EnvelopesDirectory DH1:Toaster/3D/Envelopes
PreviewsDirectory DH2:Toaster/3D/Previews
StatusFilename (none)
DefaultTension 0.000000
DefaultSegmentMemory 2200000
DefaultZoomFactor 3.200000
DefaultOverlay 0
FrameEndBeep 1
RenderDisplayDevice 4
RecordSetup1 (none)
RecordSetup2 (none)
RecordCommand (none)
RecordDelay 0.000000
FirstFrameDelay 0.000000
DefaultLayoutGrid 8
AutoKeyAdjust 0
ExpertMode 0

Modeler Config File

MDOP
0
FlatnessLimit 0.500000
QuadTriMode 1
TwoSided 0
CurveDivision 1
UnitSystem 0
FontsDirectory /ToasterFonts
MotionsDirectory Motions
MacrosDirectory DH2:LWM
MacroListsDirectory DH2:Toaster/3D
MacroList DH2:Toaster/3D/JGMacros
StartupMacro
KeyMacroF1 DH2:LWM/Text.lwm
KeyMacroF2 DH2:LWM/Router.lwm
KeyMacroF3 DH2:LWM/PointSpread.lwm
KeyMacroF4 DH2:LWM/LightSwarm.lwm
KeyMacroF5 DH2:LWM/CutFaces.lwm
KeyMacroF6 DH2:LWM/NextEmpty.lwm
KeyMacroF7 DH2:LWM/NearBG.lwm
KeyMacroF8 DH2:LWM/PointCenter.lwm
KeyMacroF9 DH2:LWM/Center1D.lwm
KeyMacroF10 DH2:LWM/Center.lwm
ColorInterface 1
ScreenModeID 0

Both config files have several things in common. Some defaults are automatically written whenever you exit the program, like most of the Modeler options, and some you need to type in yourself using any word processor or text editor, such as most of the LightWave options. Both files list an option, all as one word, then a space, and then the default (whether user-defined or written by the program). By the way, both of these files are for the shipping (3.5) version of LightWave and may be different from those for your version.

Let's break them down. All explanations and comments will appear in italics.

LW-config

LWCO
0
These first two lines are file identifiers and should not be modified.
FileReqPreset1 DF0 DF0:
FileReqPreset2 BOX BH0:
FileReqPreset3 WORK DH1:Toaster/3D
FileReqPreset4 EXTRA DH2:Toaster/3D
The FileReqPresets allow you to change the four drive buttons listed at the top of all LightWave requesters. The first word after the space is the name you wish to appear on the button, while the second word (or group of words) is the full path you wish to appear when you click on the button. These four are not written by LightWave. You must assign them or LightWave will use its defaults.
ScenesDirectory DH1:Toaster/3D/Scenes
This is the directory you wish LightWave to look at when you click on Load Scene. It and the following default directories are not written by LightWave, but instead must be entered by the user if you wish to use directories other than the programs defaults.
ObjectsDirectory DH1:Toaster/3D/Objects
This is the directory you wish LightWave to look at when loading Objects.
HierarchiesDirectory DH1:Toaster/3D/Scenes
This is the directory LightWave looks for when using Load From Scene.
SurfacesDirectory DH1:Toaster/3D/Surfaces
The directory LightWave first looks to when you choose to load or save a surface.
Images Directory DH1:Toaster/3D/Images
This is the directory LightWave looks at when you choose Load Image or Load Sequence.
OutputDirectory DH1:Toaster/3D/Images
*This is the default directory that LightWave looks for when you choose **Save RGB** or **Save Alpha.***
FramestoresDirectory DH1:Toaster/3D/Images

The default directory for loading or saving framestores.

MotionsDirectory DH1:Toaster/3D/Motions

The default directory for loading or saving motions while in the motion graph panels.

EnvelopesDirectory DH1:Toaster/3D/Envelopes

This is the default directory for loading or saving envelopes while in an envelope panel.

PreviewsDirectory DH2:Toaster/ 3D/Previews

Finally, this is the default directory you will see when you choose to load or save a wireframe preview.

StatusFilename (none)

This was an option that was used for certain render farm software and has become fairly obsolete with the advent of ScreamerNet.

DefaultTension 0.000000

By changing this value, you can cause any keyframe generated to automatically have a tension value set to this number (between -1 and 1). This can be handy if you do a lot of logos, as logos generally have tension at their start and end frames.

DefaultSegmentMemory 2200000

*This value is used to determine the amount of **Segment Memory** (Camera panel) LightWave will use when rendering images. If you have enough RAM, you may want to set it higher than this default. This value will cause four segments to be generated for a Medium Res image. If you want to be really anal, a value of 8663040 will give you one segment at Medium Res. Whenever you start a new scene, LightWave will use this number.*

DefaultZoomFactor 3.200000

This value is used to determine the equivalent lens setting of LightWave's camera whenever a new scene is started. This default creates a 24mm lens (assuming you are using a Film Size of 35mm).

DefaultOverlay 0

This value (0 or 1) will determine if LightWave's Data Overlay option will be on (1) or off (0) by default whenever you begin a new scene. If Data Overlay is on, whenever you save a scene, you will be asked if you want the scene name inserted into the Data Overlay label. (Data Overlay started life as a seaQuest *feature and has been a lifesaver ever since.)*

FrameEndBeep 1

Like Data Overlay, a 0 will default Frame End Beep (Scene panel) off whenever you start LightWave and a 1 will default it on. The state of this option is written whenever you exit LightWave. If you exit with it on, it will be on the next time you start, and vice versa.

RenderDisplayDevice 4

This option is written by LightWave each time you exit using your current setting. This determines what the Render Display will be set to the next time you run LightWave. The current options are None (0), Toaster (1), 6-bit HAM (2), 8-bit HAM (3) and Picasso II (4).

RecordSetup1 (none)
RecordSetup2 (none)
RecordCommand (none)
RecordDelay 0.000000
FirstFrameDelay 0.000000

*The five lines above are written by LightWave upon exit. They refer to the text strings entered for **Record Setup 1, Record Setup 2** and **Record Command**, as well as the **Frame Record Delay** and **Extra First Delay** items found in the Record panel. These are used if you single-frame record direct from LightWave to a video device.*

DefaultLayoutGrid 8

*This option is not written by LightWave, but I think it is supposed to be. This determines the default settings for your **Layout Grid** (Options panel). They range from Off (0) to 16x16 (8).*

AutoKeyAdjust 0

*This line is written by LightWave depending on the state of **Auto Key Adjust** (Options panel). A 0 means the button is off, a 1 means it is turned on. Watch out for this. It is great for composing stills, as it will automatically create a new key whenever you modify an item on a keyframe. It can be devastating if you want to just "try out" a new position. Try using it while showing motion graphs for some fun!*

ExpertMode 0

This feature is no longer implemented, but when it was turned off (0), you were warned that whenever you selected a raytracing button (Camera panel), it would take a long time to render.

MOD-config

MDOP 0

This is the file identifier and shouldn't be changed.

FlatnessLimit 0.500000

*This value and all of the remaining values, with the exception of the last two, are written by Modeler each time you exit the program. Flatness limit is taken from the value you enter in the New Data Options (**Options** under the Objects panel) requester. This is the flatness percentage that Modeler will use when determining if a polygon is non-planar or not.*

QuadTriMode 1

*This value—0, 1 or 2—will determine if **Triangles** (0), **Quadrangles** (1) or **Automatic** polygon generation takes place when you create new objects. If set to Automatic, Modeler will generate triangles whenever it is going to create polygons outside of the flatness limit. Otherwise, it will generate quads. These selections are also found in the Options panel.*

TwoSided 0

*A value of 0 will generate one-sided polygons while a value of 1 will generate two-sided polygons. These correspond to the **One Side** or **Two Sides** buttons in the Options panel.*

CurveDivision 1

*The Options selections of **Coarse** (0), **Medium** (1) or **Fine** (2) will be used to determine how smoothly curves should be calculated when performing operations involving curves (such as lathing a curve or generating PostScript fonts).*

UnitSystem 0

*This option is written from the Display **Options** (Display menu). It will determine what unit of measurement is used the next time Modeler is started: **SI** (0), **Metric** (1) or **English** (2). By the way, SI stands for the International System of Units (from the French "Le Système International d'Unties").*

FontsDirectory /ToasterFonts

This is the directory Modeler will look to when loading PostScript fonts. If you find fonts in a different directory from what appeared, Modeler will use that directory next time.

MotionsDirectory Motions

*The default directory for finding motion files for **Path Extrude** or **Path Clone** (Multiply).*

MacrosDirectory DH2:LWM

This is the default directory for finding macros.

MacroListsDirectory DH2:Toaster/3D

This is the default path for finding macro lists used in the << CONFIGURE LIST >> option in the Macro pop-up menu.

MacroList DH2:Toaster/3D/JGMacros

This is the last used Macro list.

StartupMacro

This is the macro that was last selected to be executed when Modeler was started (<< CONFIGURE LIST >>):

KeyMacroF1 DH2:LWM/Text.lwm
KeyMacroF2 DH2:LWM/Router.lwm
KeyMacroF3 DH2:LWM/PointSpread.lwm
KeyMacroF4 DH2:LWM/LightSwarm.lwm
KeyMacroF5 DH2:LWM/CutFaces.lwm
KeyMacroF6 DH2:LWM/NextEmpty.lwm
KeyMacroF7 DH2:LWM/NearBG.lwm
KeyMacroF8 DH2:LWM/PointCenter.lwm
KeyMacroF9 DH2:LWM/Center1D.lwm
KeyMacroF10 DH2:LWM/Center.lwm

The above 10 options are written into the config file if you selected any keyboard macro shortcuts with the << CONFIGURE KEYS >> option in the Macro pop-up menu.

ColorInterface 1

This option is for the standalone Modeler and determines if Modeler will be started with a four-color interface (0) or an eight-color interface (1) when run by itself. Otherwise it takes on the interface that LightWave is using. This option and the next one are the only two not written by Modeler when you exit the program.

ScreenModeID 0

This number is determined by the ChangeMode program that comes with the standalone version of LightWave and is used to determine the screen resolution of Modeler when it is run by itself.

Reader Speak

by John Gross

It's been quite awhile since we've had a "Reader Speak" column in *LIGHTWAVEPRO*. The fact that I have been very busy these past few months is mostly to blame, but I felt that this month we needed to address some of the questions that have been coming in.

Q: A while back, I received LightWave version 3.5 for the Amiga. I loaded it onto my Amiga 4000 and proceeded to be amazed by the sheer excellence of this superb rendering package.

Unfortunately, I have a great deal of learning to do. Layout isn't much of a problem, but Modeler is. There is much to learn, and very few guides to assist me. I'd rather not rely on videotapes and can only hope that a LightWave tutorial book is released soon. As it turns out, *LIGHTWAVEPRO* is one of the only good LightWave information sources available.

I really enjoy *LWPRO*, and I realize that, as the name suggests, it is a magazine that outlines professional techniques. Despite this, I am still requesting that more time be spent on basic tutorials showing how to effectively and efficiently use Modeler and Layout. Hopefully, a number of extra pages could be added to the magazine in order to cover this material. After all, this is likely the most expensive computer magazine in the world (per page).

Your instructional format is quite good, yet it isn't the clearest. The best format I have ever seen in any magazine is the one that Amiga Format (Future Publishing) used in order to give instruction for the Image rendering package. You can find these articles in issues 53-57, the first of which is dated December 1993. Please adopt this format.

And now, one last request:

I am trying to duplicate the type of Cray-rendered images that appeared in the motion picture *Tron*. My first project was supposed to be simple: build a recognizer. This object is quite simple in form. The problem lies in rendering the object with a solid dark tone and a thin, luminescent/glowing red outline of light around it. I can't seem to get LightWave to do this. The same effect is used on the *Tron* city, and a more advanced effect is to place a "trace" pattern over all of the city objects near the end of the film.

How do you create this outlined polygon effect, exactly the same as the original Cray renders?

Thank you for your time. By the way, keep *LWPRO* going. This is an absolutely fantastic magazine. Also, to Mojo, keep those excellent articles coming. You're a demigod!

W. Jared Brookes
Calgary, Alberta, Canada

A: Your letter brings up some interesting topics. One of the things that we at Avid Media Group have been discussing lately relates to the direction of *LWPRO*, especially with many new LightWave users coming on board. From fairly early on, we realized that the majority of *LWPRO* readers may not be "high-end" users, and we have tried to balance the content of the newsletter to reach everyone. At times we've succeeded; other times we've failed. With the advent of many "newbie" users, we would like to have informative content geared toward all users without compromising the goal of making eventual LightWave pros out of everyone.

In regards to this, *LWPRO* will be undergoing some changes soon. How it changes partially depends on the readers. We welcome feedback of all kinds. If you have e-mail access, we can be reached at jgross@netcom.com and avid@cup.portal.com.

In regards to your *Tron* question, there are a couple of ways to achieve a similar effect. If you happen to be running LightWave 4.0, the best way is to simply assign a glow effect to the surface of the objects of your recognizer, and then select **Enable Glow Effect** in the **Effects** panel. You can then input a **Glow Intensity** and **Glow Radius** (in pixels) that you wish the glow to contain. Remember that because Glow Radius is measured in pixels, if you are rendering tests in **Low Res** and then bumping up to **Medium Res** or higher for your final image, you need to increase the Glow Radius to achieve similar results, since the pixels become smaller as you increase your **Basic Resolution**.

If you are not running 4.0, you could parent a second, slightly larger recognizer object (with different surface names) to the original. Make sure the surfaces of the parented object are mostly transparent and you are using **Transparent** for **Edge Transparency.** While this approach isn't as effective as 4.0's glow effect, it can look pretty good.

I won't tell Mojo about the demigod part, as I'm sure it will just go to his (omnipotent) head.

Q: I just read your Editor's Message in April's *LWPRO,* and though this publication is immensely helpful and I love my subscription, I have to respond to some things said about the pre-release version of LightWave. You said that it is close to the actual commercial version that is coming out in a couple of weeks, but have you actually seen it? I own the pre-release version and I certainly hope that the commercial version packs substantially more than this one. This so-called "upgrade" not only lacks the ability to view the rendered image, but you cannot render to useful IBM formats besides Targas. Who uses IFFs on PCs?! Where are the macros in Modeler that we have grown fond of and even dependent on? Why can't the image file requester recognize or load standard IBM format files such as GIFs, JPEGs and BMPs? Why, when you click (in the Record panel) on the Save Anim button, does it say "only available on Amiga version"? I know that Anim format is an Amiga format, but, in that case, why is it there taking up space? Shouldn't it have been changed to some kind of Flic format saver?

I want to take time to thank you for advice you've given me, and I don't want to sound ungrateful (just frustrated and disappointed), but when you praise the new LightWave for its great beta version that you have access to, all I can say is, try the pre-release. You pay nothing for being a beta-site, but we users paid $150 for a sizable downgrade!

I'm not one of the people claiming to have lost business for depending on the new product. I switched from my Amiga because I had a golden opportunity fall into my lap when someone who needed an Amiga offered to buy mine for $700 more than dealers were normally selling them at, because Amiga dealers had dried up. I thought, great time to move to a Pentium. LightWave is coming out soon on PC, so I won't wait too long. To be honest, the wait wasn't long—I just wish it had been worth it. I have a great opportunity to submit some animations to a well-known expanding game company in Cambridge called LookingGlass, which used to work with Origin Systems. Maybe you've heard of them—they made SystemShock, a best-seller. They are interested in me and want to see more. I wish I had my Amiga. The pre-release, with all its shortcomings, also crashes often! Tech support has no answers, either.

(Sigh) I guess I'll have to switch to the mega-expensive 3D Studio until LightWave becomes the incredible, versatile, pleasure-to-use tool that it once was.

Tearing my hair out in Amherst,
David Bryant
Amherst, MA

A: When I wrote April's Editor's Message, I mostly meant that the *tools and functions* that shipped with the pre-release were pretty much finished, and the only things that needed adding were plug-ins and a few extra little things. Re-reading that column, it's apparent to me that I wasn't very clear. It's also apparent that I wasn't very correct.

At the time I wrote it I was using the pre-release version. Now that I look back (with the additional hindsight that new beta releases provide), I can safely say that most, if not all, of your concerns have been, or are being, addressed.

Full-sized rendered images are now viewable. Elastic Reality's HIIP architecture will allow for multiple save and load image formats. Modeler plug-ins will support the important macros that you've gotten used to (it's amazing how much I took Center for granted). To top it all off, Bones and Inverse Kinematics have been greatly improved and some other new features (such as distributed rendering) have been added.

It's important to remember that the pre-release of LightWave was just that, and that you will be getting a free upgrade to the final shipping version (plus manuals, etc.) when it is released. Hopefully, when you receive it, you'll have renewed faith.

LWP

John Gross is a supervising animator for Amblin Imaging and the editor of LIGHTWAVEPRO. *Questions and comments can be sent to* LWPRO, *Avid Media Group, 273 N. Mathilda Ave, Sunnyvale, CA 94086-4830. Send e-mail to jgross@netcom.com or avid@cup.portal.com.*

INDEX

What's on the CD-ROM?

Did you say CD-ROM?!

The free LIGHTWAVE 3D compilation CD-ROM is packed with over 600 MBs of cool objects, effective scenes, professional images, useful utilities and superb information!

How to Use: There are two basic ways to use the included CD-ROM depending on the computer platform you are using and the version of NewTek's LightWave 3D you have. If you are using version 4.0 or greater, you can access the content by simply setting your content directory to your CD-ROM drive name. The Objects, Images, and Scene files can then be loaded directly by LightWave. If you are using version 3.5 or earlier on the Amiga platform, you'll need to assign your CD-ROM drive to "LWPRO:". The CD's contents are then located in a directory called LW3_5 with the same content as found in the main Scene/Images/Objects directories, but set up so early Amiga versions of LightWave can easily read the Scene/Object files. Besides the Objects, Images and Scenes, there are a few other directories on the CD:

DEMOS: Includes new work by some of the most innovative 3D animators.

DOCS: the DOCS directory contains Readme files that pertain to certain Scenes, Objects and directories. It's a good idea to run through these.

LW3_5: This directory contains a copy of all of the Scenes/Objects/Images files configured to load in LightWave 3.5 and earlier.

OTHER: Includes a demo of LIGHT-ROM textures, images and objects by Graphic Detail, Inc.

PLUGINS: Includes the PowerView Plug-ins for the Amiga and PC versions of LightWave 3D.

PROGRAMS: This directory contains some Amiga and PC programs that can be quite useful. For programs that are not outlined in articles, text files can be found in the appropriate places within the PROGRAMS directory.

SETUPS: This directory contains setup files for Enrique Munoz's "Sparks" tutorial.

Enjoy and happy rendering.